A Catalogue of Paintings in
the Folger Shakespeare Library

POET.

The Poets eye, in a fine frenzy rowling,
Doth glance from heav'n to earth, from earth to heav'n.
And as imagination bodies forth
The forms of things unknown the Poets pen
Turns them to shape, and gives to airy nothing
A local habitation and a name.

Published May 20 1775 by J. MORTIMER, Norfolk Street, STRAND.

Midsummer Nights dream. Act V. Scene 1.

A Catalogue of Paintings in the Folger Shakespeare Library

"As Imagination Bodies Forth"

WILLIAM L. PRESSLY

6/26/12

To Charley,

Thank you for your friendship and support! I very much hope to see you in Atlanta.

Until then,

Warmest wishes,

Bill

Published with the assistance of the Getty Grant Program
and the National Endowment for the Arts

Yale University Press   New Haven and London

Designed by Sonia L. Scanlon.

Set in Trump type by The Composing Room of Michigan, Inc., Grand Rapids, Michigan.

Printed in the United States of America by Arcata Graphics Halliday, West Hanover, Massachusetts.

Library of Congress Cataloging-in-Publication Data

Pressly, William L., 1944–

    A catalogue of paintings in the Folger Shakespeare Library : "as imagination bodies forth" / William L. Pressly.

      p. cm.

    Includes bibliographical references and index.

    ISBN 0-300-05214-6

    1. Shakespeare, William, 1564–1616—Portraits—Catalogs.

    2. Shakespeare, William, 1564–1616—Illustrations—Catalogs.

    3. Painting, English—Washington (D.C.)—Catalogs.   4. Painting—Washington (D.C.)—Catalogs.   5. Folger Shakespeare Library—Catalogs.   I. Folger Shakespeare Library.   II. Title.

PR2933.F64P7   1992

704.9'4982233—dc20   91-46630

                    CIP

A catalogue record for this book is available from the British Library.

The paper in this book meets the guidelines for permanence and durability of the Committee on Production Guidelines for Book Longevity of the Council on Library Resources.

10 9 8 7 6 5 4 3 2 1

Frontispiece. John Hamilton Mortimer, *The Poet*. Etching, 15¾ × 12¾ in., 20 May 1775.

Contents

Foreword

Few, even among the Folger Shakespeare Library's readers, are aware of the full extent of its holdings in the fine arts. Notable works of sculpture, ceramics, tapestry, stained glass, and furniture complement approximately fifty thousand prints, watercolors, drawings, and photographs. Many of these works are uncatalogued, and the total does not include the graphic contents of thousands of illustrated books. Better known than any of these aspects of the collections, the Library's two hundred oil paintings also pose the most intriguing questions and challenges for the scholar.

In this book, Prof. William L. Pressly rises to those challenges and resolves almost all of those questions. Starting with the fragmentary and often erroneous data assembled by the Folgers when they bought the pictures, Mr. Pressly has examined every visual and documentary aspect of the Folger's paintings, many of which have in the process undergone revealing campaigns of conservation.

The results are extraordinary. Nearly half of the pictures have been reattributed. In many instances, subject matter has also been newly identified. Extensive evidence relating to the Folgers as collectors and their trade relations with important dealers has been recovered and evaluated. The history and provenance of each painting have been carefully reconstructed.

The Library and its trustees are grateful to Mr. Pressly for his painstaking and imaginative scholarship. As a result of his catalogue raisonné, and his historical and interpretive essays, which make for absorbing reading, the remarkable collection of paintings which hangs in the Folger will now be newly and completely accessible to scholars and Shakespeare enthusiasts everywhere. The author has described the collection, in terms of Shakespearean painting, as "the finest of its kind," surpassing even those of the Royal Shakespeare Company and the Garrick Club in London. To assemble a collection of such independent interest and distinction was clearly never the goal of the Library's founders, but we are pleased that their cautious and temperate efforts in this area yielded such significant results.

It is also a pleasure to acknowledge the generosity of the many individuals and institutions in the scholarly and philanthropic communities who contributed to the progress of this ambitious project. All are mentioned in Mr. Pressly's acknowledgments. I add my thanks, as well as the gratitude of the Library's trustees, to all of them.

Werner Gundersheimer
Director
The Folger Shakespeare Library

Acknowledgments

In writing this book I have incurred many debts, not the least of which is to Henry Clay Folger and Emily Jordan Folger, whose passion for Shakespeare lay the foundation for this remarkable collection. At every turn, I have received the most generous support from the staff of the Folger Shakespeare Library. Jean Miller was an invaluable guide to the Library's many resources. I also profited from the assistance of Laura Cofield, Jean Dunnington, Rachel Doggett, Rosalind Larry, Joan Morrison, Elizabeth Niemyer, Henry Raine, and Betsy Walsh. Laetita Yeandle was of great help in uncovering documents and in the ciphering of faint inscriptions. Whenever an object required close scrutiny, Frank Mowery and his conservation staff always graciously assisted with their expertise. Julie Ainsworth undertook a heroic labor in supplying photographs of all the pictures, many of which are reproduced here for the first time. She also photographed related materials that appear as figure illustrations. Those reproductions not otherwise specified are from the Library's collections. I am indebted as well to Lilly Lievsay, who supervised the project in its early stages before her retirement, and to Philip Knachel, the Library's associate director, who took over this responsibility. Finally, I am most grateful to the Library's director, Werner Gundersheimer, for his unfailing support and encouragement.

Funding for this project came from two sources: the Getty Grant Program and the National Endowment for the Arts. I am most grateful for their support both in sponsoring the research on the catalogue and for subventions for its publication. I would particularly like to thank Deborah Marrow, director of the Getty Grant Program, and Lynne Fitzhugh, the deputy director of development at the Folger, for having made this process run so smoothly.

Many institutions outside the Folger also assisted me in my research, and I would like to single out for particular thanks the staffs of the following: Corcoran Gallery of Art, Washington, D.C.; Guildhall Art Gallery, London; Library Company of Philadelphia; Mead Art Museum, Amherst College; National Gallery of Art Library, Washington; National Portrait Gallery Archive, London; the Paul Mellon Centre for Studies in British Art, London; Pennsylvania Academy of the Fine Arts, Philadelphia; Rosenbach Museum and Library, Philadelphia; the Royal Shakespeare Company Collection, Stratford-upon-Avon; the Shakespeare Birthplace Trust, Stratford-upon-Avon; the Witt Library, London; and the Yale Center for British Art, New Haven.

Several individuals are mentioned in the entries to which they contributed, but I would also like to thank numerous others who gave assistance, in particular Brian Allen, the late Geoffrey Ashton, David Bidman, Martin Butlin, Ellen Chirelstein, Yvonne Dixon, Elizabeth

Einberg, Jill Finsten, James Fowler, Catherine Gordon, Martha Hamilton-Phillips, Robin Hamlyn, Joseph Leach, Douglas Lewis, Ellen Miles, Joe Mitchenson, John Murdoch, Patrick Noon, Edward Nygren, Malcolm Rogers, the late Gert Schiff, Robert Stewart, Sir Roy Strong, John Sunderland, Andrew Wilton, Sarah Wimbush, and Christopher Wood. Their comments have proved of great value.

The faculty and students at the University of Maryland have been extremely supportive. Douglas Farquhar, chair of the Department of Art History and Archaeology, generously provided me with time and assistance. I would also like to thank those graduate students who helped as research assistants (Martha Bari, Julie Dabbs, Kim Donley, Jennifer Jones, and Richard Raymond) and those who, while participating in my courses, wrote papers on paintings in the collection: Beryl Bland (no. 54), Lorna Carmel (no. 23), Beth Garnier (nos. 16–17), Kim Jones (no. 27), Susan Libby (no. 21), Pam Potter-Hennessey (no. 45), Richard Raymond (no. 82), Debbie Rindge (no. 176), and Lee Vedder (no. 123).

Mrs. Francis T. P. Plimpton deserves special thanks for her permission to include George Gower's portrait of Queen Elizabeth I, a magnificent work that greatly enhances the section devoted to images of Shakespeare's contemporaries.

For their helpful readings of the manuscript, I am most grateful to Nati Krivatsy and Jean Miller and to David Weinglass for his reading of the Fuseli entries. Catherine Johnson deserves special praise for her careful reading, undertaken while she was involved in her own projects at the Harvard Theatre Collection. As always, I owe a great deal to my wife, Nancy, who enthusiastically supported me in this project from the beginning and was of enormous help in revising the final draft. I have been extremely fortunate in my editors at Yale University Press. Judy Metro and Harry Haskell provided numerous excellent suggestions and made the final stages of the project move with surprising ease. Last, I would like to express my deep appreciation to my parents for their encouragement and for having introduced me to Shakespeare in the first place.

Henry C. Folger as a Collector of Paintings

Henry Clay Folger is deservedly remembered as a collector of books, more specifically, books by or about William Shakespeare. In his *American Book Collectors and Collecting,* Carl Cannon praises him for his vision, calling the Folger Shakespeare Library "one of the most carefully planned and brilliantly executed enterprises in the field of American book collecting."[1] The story of Folger as a collector of paintings is much less well known. The art—paintings, sculpture, prints, drawings, and watercolors—was acquired in a far more haphazard fashion and often from the same sources as the books: the auction houses and book dealers. Folger consistently maintained he was not an art collector. Even allowing for the fact that his disclaimers were often made in the context of negotiating for a reduced price for a picture, there is a modicum of truth to his assertions. His offhand purchasing of pictures never came close to competing with his central passion—his library. Yet, despite his diffidence, he ended up assembling the world's greatest collection of Shakespearean paintings. There are collections such as the Garrick Club's in London which surpass it in the broader category of theatrical paintings, but not even the gallery at Stratford-upon-Avon surpasses it in Shakespeare holdings.

Folger, the son of a wholesale milliner, was born in New York City on 18 June 1857. He went to college at Amherst, graduating in 1879. In his senior year, inspired by a lecture given by Ralph Waldo Emerson, he read Emerson's essay on Shakespeare, which ignited a life-long interest in the Bard. After graduation he studied law at Columbia University and then joined Charles Pratt & Company, an oil company owned by one of his college friends that formed a part of John D. Rockefeller's Standard Oil Trust. Folger eventually became president in 1911 and board chairman in 1923, retiring five years later. On 6 October 1885 he married Emily C. Jordan, a graduate of Vassar College who went on to receive a Master of Arts in 1896. The two shared the same passion for Shakespeare, and, as is often recounted, the seed for the library was planted when, soon after his marriage, Folger bought a copy of the Halliwell-Phillipps "reduced" facsimile edition of the First Folio for $1.25. Discrepancies between this text and contemporary editions of the plays led Folger to take an interest in textual research and consequently in book collecting. He acquired his first rare book in 1889, when he bought the Fourth Folio of 1685 at Bangs auction house in New York for $107.50, which he paid in four installments over a thirty-day period. Although his income later became considerable, he never enjoyed the seemingly unlimited resources of his millionaire rivals.

Folger is often grouped in a triumvirate of great American book collectors alongside John Pierpont Morgan (1837–1913) and Henry Edwards Huntington (1850–1927). All three men at approximately the same time assembled important libraries that became distinguished public institutions. The differences among them, however, are even more instructive. With a great deal more money at their disposal, Morgan and Huntington also collected art on a grand scale. Morgan spent $100 million on art, books, and the palatial library he built on 36th Street in New York. He collected on such a lavish scale that his home could never have begun to contain all his pictures, most of which were bought with the Metropolitan Museum of Art in mind. Huntington, too, poured millions into both his book and art collections. Under the influence of his uncle's widow, Arabella Huntington, he began to collect paintings in earnest around 1907, and even before he and Arabella married in 1913, they were working together on a joint collection. Soon the Huntingtons decided to specialize in British portraits of the Georgian period. Folger was chiefly collecting paintings of the same period and country, but unlike the Huntingtons' masterpieces, most of the works he bought were considered so marginal that they did not even pass through the hands of art dealers. In 1921 Huntington bought Gainsborough's *The Blue Boy* for $850,000 from the most powerful of the art dealers, Joseph Duveen. In contrast, both of Folger's Gainsboroughs have turned out to be copies. One, a painting after Gainsborough's portrait of Garrick, was purchased for $1,000 from Michelmore, a London bookseller, five years after Huntington acquired *The Blue Boy*. The two men obviously were operating on very different levels of the art market, and despite Duveen's inflated prices, in this instance Huntington easily got the better bargain.

Folger spent more than $2,000 for a painting only seven times, and only once did he pay a princely sum: £10,500 (about $51,000) for Romney's *Infant Shakespeare* in 1927. The second most expensive painting in the collection, *The Felton Portrait of Shakespeare*, cost £1522.10.0 (approximately $7,500) in 1922. Even at his most extravagant, Folger did not come close to challenging those of his contemporaries who wished to assemble impressive collections of the Old Masters. When it came to buying books, however, he did not hesitate to spend $100,000 on a single volume.

That Folger did not spend more on paintings is perhaps as much a reflection of his circumstances as of his interests. Given his limited financial resources—that is, compared to those of a Morgan or a Huntington—he could not afford to deviate too far from his primary goal of forming a literary collection of Shakespeareana. In pursuit of this goal, he and his wife lived relatively modestly. Their marriage proving childless, most of their energy and their money went into the book collection. They were in their seventies before they even built a modest home for themselves in Glen Cove, Long Island, and for much of his career Folger's expenditures exceeded his available income. Obviously the acquisition of books, the Folgers' first love, left little money for any other diversions.

For want of a place to house their collections, most of their books and artworks went into storage as soon as they were bought. The case numbers from these warehouses are in many instances the pictures' only accession numbers. Collecting books and paintings require different sets of criteria. Book collectors must be wary of dealers who reconstitute books that are missing a few pages, but paintings require a higher degree of sophistication in determining a work's condition and in sorting out copies from the original and originals from fakes. Folger never pretended to be a connoisseur of pictures: he accepted on faith what dealers told him. Moreover, he had little opportunity to improve his eye, since most of his paintings were put into storage as soon as they were purchased, and the few works that apparently hung in his house were not among the most distinguished. The Library's copy after Gainsborough's *Sarah Siddons* is listed as "from Mrs. Folger's house," and one presumes the couple had never doubted its authenticity. The painting of Shakespeare's coat of arms, a work more valuable for its associations than for its artistic quality, carries the same designation, as does the *Apotheosis of Shakespeare*.

It should also be remembered that the area in which Folger was collecting had limited appeal for his contemporaries, and the state of knowledge about British art was such that, apart from the major masters, even the dealers had little idea of who painted what. Like most collectors, Folger disliked purchasing a picture unless he knew the artist's name. One suspects that the dealers he patronized often attributed a painting to a certain artist on the basis of little more than an uninformed guess. Almost half of the attributed pictures he acquired have been reattributed. Folger's instincts were those of an antiquarian, and both he and his wife considered the portraits of Shakespeare the heart of their collection. The normal standards of quality often do not apply in this area; nor did these paintings necessarily have an artist's name attached. The entire Library is on one level an effort to recover Shakespeare the man, and even the crudest portraits helped conjure up for the Folgers some aspect of the Bard's presence.

In 1897 Folger purchased the Warwick Castle collection of Shakespeare literature and relics. The excellence of his library was firmly established in 1908, when he acquired additional material from Marsden J. Perry of Providence, Rhode Island, the leading American collector of Shakespeareana. The painting collection, however, was much longer in forming. Folger acquired his first painting on 19 March 1900, when he purchased at auction *The Cosway Portrait of Shakespeare*. Then in successive years he bought at Sotheby's two other portraits (nos. 183 and 149) and in 1903 the miniature of the Bard's contemporary William Herbert, third Earl of Pembroke. In 1905 the collection grew in numbers and in scope: in addition to another Shakespeare portrait (no. 163), Folger bought five portraits of actors in Shakespearean roles (nos. 128, 130, 131, D12, D60) and two depictions of scenes from the plays, including his first picture by Fuseli (nos. 14 and 26). All of these works again came from auctions, but in the following year one dealer, who early on perceived that Folger was broadening his interests, approached him with offers of pictures. John Anderson, Jr., sold two paintings to him in July 1906: Hall's *Sir Toby Belch* and *The Dexter Portrait of Shakespeare*. Up to this time the highest recorded price that Folger had paid for a picture was the $110 he spent at Christie's on 16 December 1905 for his painting of Garrick as Hamlet, said to be by Zoffany, one of three works purchased at the sale of Sir Henry Irving. For the Dexter Portrait Folger paid $1,500, indicating a significant jump in the seriousness of his commitment to paintings.

Folger bought Nast's *Immortal Light of Genius* at auction in New York in 1908, and in the next two years he acquired Felix Darley's *Touchstone and Audrey* and three indifferent portraits of the Bard (nos. 158, 162, and D66). In 1911 he purchased the first Boydell Shakespeare Gallery painting—William Hamilton's *The Carousing of Sir Toby Belch and Sir Andrew Aguecheek*—followed within

a month by Hamilton's *Olivia's Proposal* from the Hoe sale, an auction far more famous for its books than for its pictures.

Augustin Daly (1838–99), a playwright and influential producer, owned a succession of New York theaters, the last of which contained an expansive foyer decorated with theatrical paintings, many of which were copies. Folger had already bought books at the sale of Daly's literary effects, and in 1912 he purchased six paintings at the Daly sale of pictures, including the highest price paid at the auction—$1,000 for a heavily overpainted portrait of Garrick said to be by Reynolds (no. 135).

The next year Folger acquired an important picture by Thomas Stothard, misidentified as *The Seven Ages of Man*, but no paintings are listed as having been bought in 1914 and 1915. After this, however, no year passed without purchases.

Of all the dealers Folger encountered, John Anderson, Jr., was by far the strangest. The man was a modern-day alchemist who could transform base matter into gold, buying inferior art that he could with the aid of signatures turn into minor masterpieces. The truth was simply not in him, and perhaps the person he most frequently deceived was himself. He opened an auction house in 1900 and sold it eight years later to strike out on his own as an art dealer. Folger was one of the clients he assiduously cultivated, beginning with the sale of the Dexter Portrait, an expensive fake (see no. 153). On 6 April 1916, having rented the Grand Ballroom of the Plaza Hotel, he held a sale through the American Art Galleries entitled "Old and Modern Paintings by the Great Masters Forming the Important Collection of Mr. John Anderson, Jr." For the most part, it was an assemblage of decidedly unimportant pictures with important attributions packaged in a handsome catalogue. Folger bought three works, two of which (nos. 33 and 100) had false signatures, although one is an authentic Boydell painting, and the third (no. 51) a supposed signature that still escapes detection. He sold a number of such works to Folger over the years, mostly in the area of drawings. Often even Folger could not find the signatures that Anderson said were there, and when he inquired for further details, the dealer never backed down from his original assertion, supplying even more specific instructions as to their location. In the case of the drawing Folger bought as Sir Joshua Reynolds's preparatory study for Garrick in the painting *Garrick between Comedy and Trag-*

edy, not only is there no signature, despite Anderson's repeated claims to the contrary,[2] but the work is not even a drawing. Rather, it is a retouched photograph.

Anderson specialized in "rediscovering" art by Turner. He amassed a collection of more than ten thousand of his works, none of which had previously been attributed to the artist. In 1926 he published a book on his "finds" entitled *The Unknown Turner: Revelations concerning the Life and Art of J. M. W. Turner with an account of the discovery of his hidden signatures and dates and the publication of the only known original manuscript of any of his sketching tours.* In this work of fiction (which was privately printed), Anderson claimed that every one of the artist's drawings and sketches "bears Turner's full signature and its date, affixed by him in a hidden place and manner."[3] In addition to several watercolors, Folger bought one of Anderson's Turner paintings, a work now identified as after Henry Liverseege (no. 47). Anderson claimed that Turner's signature appeared on the upper portion of the sword scabbard, but he is the only person ever recorded to have seen it. Anderson was careful to establish a personal relationship with both the Folgers, who never could bring themselves to admit that the emperor wore no clothes.

In 1918 Folger bought a picture from the important New York book dealer Gabriel Wells, paying $2,100 for what was described as Kneller's portrait of Shakespeare (no. 154). From the same dealer he acquired the Lumley Portrait (no. 156) in 1922, and later he paid relatively substantial prices for two more portraits, one said to be of Garrick (no. 137), the other of Shakespeare (no. 159).In the late twenties Wells sold him three extremely important pictures: Sully's *Portia and Shylock* and Romney's *Infant Shakespeare* and *Titania, Puck and the Changeling.*

Another important bookseller, A. S. W. Rosenbach of Philadelphia and New York, also sold art to Folger in addition to books and manuscripts. At the important sale of the Burdett-Coutts Collection held at Christie's in May 1922, he acquired three Fuselis and *The Felton Portrait of Shakespeare* on Folger's behalf. Rosenbach assisted in the purchase of other paintings, the most important of which are Sully's *Macbeth in the Witches' Cave* and Zuccarelli's *Macbeth Meeting the Witches.* Folger paid $1,388,990 to Rosenbach for his purchases over the years, but only a tiny fraction of the total was spent on art.

More and more booksellers were learning of Folger's interest in pictures. He purchased the bulk of his art collection between 1922 and his death in 1930. During these years, the London dealers replaced the auction houses as his principal source, and he acquired nearly one hundred paintings from three firms: Michelmore, Maggs Brothers, and Edwin Parsons. Some dross was mixed in, but a number of important works were also included.

Michelmore clearly had access to Boydell paintings. The three Smirkes, two Westalls, and two Wheatleys, one of which was later deaccessioned, all came from him. Folger could be a tough bargainer. On 12 December 1921 Michelmore offered the first of his Boydell pictures, Smirke's *Awakening of King Lear* and Westall's *Shylock Rebuffing Antonio.* He asked £700 for the two, to which Folger cabled the laconic response, "Paintings much too high." Michelmore countered with an offer of £500, to which Folger replied, "Price still much too high." The dealer continued to lower his figure, and Folger, who had been spoiled by the prices he had paid earlier for Boydell pictures, eventually acquired the two works for £250. Obviously, there was little competition for this type of painting.

From Maggs Brothers, Folger acquired Fuseli's superb *Macbeth Consulting the Vision of the Armed Head* for £50, an absurdly low figure even then but one that was in line with what he had previously paid for the Fuselis at the Burdett-Coutts sale. Most of the remaining pictures from this source tended to be on a more modest scale, including the dozen tiny Smirkes, Frith's small canvas, Stone's sketch, and Stothard's pair featuring Falstaff.

From Parsons, Folger acquired Fuseli's *Romeo Stabbing Paris before Juliet's Bier,* Peters's magnificent *The Death of Juliet,* Stothard's *Marina Singing before Pericles,* and a virtual monopoly on pictures by John Cawse. Soon Parsons stopped advertising his firm as Fine Art Book and Print Sellers and Picture Dealers and changed it to the simpler Fine Art Dealer—a shift for which Folger may have been responsible. As a tribute to his best customer, Parsons wrote on 26 June 1930: "I had a great admiration for his business methods, one very rarely meets in these days clients like the late Mr Folger, he knew exactly what he wanted, accepted or rejected and paid cash, the average client of today does not know

A8. Frank O. Salisbury, *Henry Clay Folger* (see Appendix II).

A7. Frank O. Salisbury, *Emily Jordan Folger* (see Appendix II).

what he wants and the question of payment, well the subject is better left alone."[4]

Folger of course continued to buy works at auctions and from other dealers. Three of his more important acquisitions were Pine's portrait of Garrick, which he bought at auction at the American Art Galleries in 1925; Hamilton's *Isabella Appealing to Angelo,* which he acquired at a sale at the Walpole Galleries that same year; and the Dance portrait of Garrick, which he bought from Walters the following year. One reason he began to buy in quantity was availability: works were increasingly being brought to him as the dealers found a willing client. Yet one suspects that an equally important consideration was Folger's formulation of a plan for the future disposition of his library. On 22 June 1922 he wrote thanking Frank Keeble for his letter about the Lumley Portrait: "It will be placed on file with the other papers about this portrait for future reference and use when a catalogue is prepared including this item." Unfortunately, not until now has each painting been given a file, but clearly in 1922 Folger was already starting to think in terms of a

collection of paintings deserving a systematic survey. The next year, his mind was definitely on the future when he wrote Rosenbach, "Just now I am studying with the lawyers a change in my Will to protect the Shakespeare collection."[5] When in 1927 he was negotiating through Wells for the purchase of Romney's *Infant Shakespeare,* he wrote the dealer, "If bought, the Painting will go into the Shakespeare Library we are founding in the American Capital, at Washington, for public service for everyone."[6]

Also in 1927, the Folgers for the first and only time acted as patrons rather than collectors of painting. In March they received their portraits (nos. A7 and A8) from the fashionable London painter Frank O. Salisbury (1874–1962). They paid $7,596 for the pair, making each portrait more expensive than all but four of the paintings in the collection. The portraits were part of their public personae, intended from the start for the Library. The Folgers are shown in their academic gowns, grandly imposing and austerely looking out at the viewer. Mrs. Folger holds a fan, still in the Library's collections, that is decorated with what appears to be the scene in *Cymbeline* where Imogen and Posthumus pledge their love by exchanging a ring and bracelet. Mr. Folger holds a small, thick book inscribed on its cover "EDWRD+GWYNN." Edward Gwynn was a collector of the first half of the seventeenth century, and the book Folger holds, acquired from Rosenbach in 1919, is Gwynn's assemblage of no less than nine Shakespeare quartos and the portion of a tenth. The inside cover of the actual book is inscribed, "The first attempt at a collection of the works of William Shakespeare." This first attempt appropriately announces Folger's unparalleled collection, the last attempt that can be made of its kind. The reference in the painting is a discrete one, available only to the initiated familiar with the Library's treasures. Even when presenting themselves and their collections to the public, the Folgers do not invite intimacy.

Alexander B. Trowbridge, one of the architects of the planned building, inquired of Folger about pictures to decorate the proposed Library, and in his reply of 19 October 1928 even Folger seemed surprised by the extent of his holdings: "We have never tried to buy paintings or other Shakespeare illustrations, concentrating on the literary side of the subject; but when paintings were offered, not too costly and they seemed worth while, we have taken them and put them away in storage. They are more in number than I had supposed, and I know some of them are not very decorative: But many of them are, and a number are well worth while displaying."[7] The collection was even more remarkable then than now, a number of works having been deaccessioned, particularly from the late Victorian period. Despite these losses, it remains one of the outstanding collections of Shakespearean painting.

Folger died on 11 June 1930, just two weeks after the cornerstone to the Library had been laid. Mrs. Folger was to live another six years, but she added few paintings to the collection. Mr. Folger passed up a chance to buy *The Ashbourne Portrait of Shakespeare* in 1928, finding it too expensive, but Mrs. Folger bought it for the Library in March 1931 for $3,500—more than had been asked three years before. In 1932 she acquired another important work, *The Janssen Portrait of Shakespeare.* According to an article in the *Washington Star*, this acquisition was in accordance with the donor's will, where "he provided that the quest for the best por-

traits of Shakespeare might proceed."[8] In June 1934 Mrs. Folger presented *The Vroom Portrait of Shakespeare*, a purchase that proved embarrassing to her. The dealer who sold it to Mrs. Folger for $5,000 had it on consignment from a gallery that had been unable to find a buyer at the asking price of $450. (Presumably Shakespeare was not then identified as the sitter.) When the dealer tried to cheat the gallery out of its share of the windfall profit, the case ended up in the courts and the newspapers. Mrs. Folger did not again venture into the art market.

Besides the Janssen Portrait, the Library added a few minor purchases to the collection in the 1930s and 1940s. It also received gifts, the most important of which was a group of paintings and miniatures from a descendant of the Cushman family. In recent years it has again benefited from generous donations, including a version of Phillips's painting of the Stratford Bust, the Shakespeare Signboard, the portraits of the third earl of Southampton and the countess of Southampton, Umberto Romano's portrait of Shakespeare, and Hilliard's miniature of Lettice Knollys.

Folger made more than his share of mistakes in his acquisition of pictures, but he deserves to be judged by his successes rather than his failures. These successes were remarkable, for the same reason that accounts for his success as a book collector. The collection's strength lies in its strong focus on Shakespeare, his plays, and the actors who performed them. The sum of the minor pictures is greater than the parts because they all bear on these central themes, and anchoring the whole collection is a large number of distinguished pictures whose importance is only now coming to be fully appreciated.

1. Carl L. Cannon, *American Book Collectors and Collecting from Colonial Times to the Present,* New York, 1941, p. 341.
2. Anderson to Folger, 28 March and 7 April 1921, Folger Shakespeare Library (hereafter FSL) files.
3. John Anderson, Jr., *The Unknown Turner,* New York, 1926, p. 38.
4. Edwin Parsons to A. G. Welsh, 26 June 1930, Bills and Receipts, Folger Archives, FSL.
5. Folger to Dr. A. S. W. Rosenbach, 22 June 1923, Rosenbach Museum and Library, Philadelphia.
6. Folger to Gabriel Wells, 14 August 1927, FSL files.
7. Folger to Alexander Trowbridge, 19 October 1928, Folger Archives, box 57, FSL.
8. A clipping of this article is in the Folger file for the painting. The will, dated 10 March 1927 and probated on 25 June 1930, is actually less specific, calling for "additions to the collection in keeping with its original character" (p. 4).

Introduction

The catalogue is divided into five major sections: "Literary Illustrations," "Theatrical Portraiture," "Portraits of Shakespeare," "Portraits of Shakespeare's Contemporaries," and "Shakespeareana." Within all but one of the sections, the paintings are listed alphabetically by artist, with the anonymous works placed last. The exception is "Portraits of Shakespeare," where the works are organized by type, the earliest types coming first. In the subsection "Memorial Portraits," the paintings are arranged in chronological order. In the first two sections, when there is more than one work by an artist, the paintings are listed alphabetically by play rather than by title, with non-Shakespearean scenes placed last. Miniatures are grouped together at the end of the appropriate portrait sections.

The divisions into act and scene and all quotations from Shakespeare's plays are from the 1942 edition of the plays by William Allan Neilson and Charles Jarvis Hill. When a painting is clearly derived from an earlier edition of the text with a different division of the scenes, this information is given in the discussion.

Measurements are given in both inches and centimeters, height (the left-hand edge) before width (the bottom edge).

"Inscribed" refers to an inscription other than a signature written by the artist, "annotated" to one by another hand.

In 1932 most of the paintings donated by Mr. Folger were relined and/or cleaned and their frames repainted and gilded or newly furnished by two members of the conservation staff of the Museum of Fine Arts, Boston: John A. Finlayson and H. E. Thompson. This work was done in Washington with equipment from the Freer Gallery; as Finlayson seems to have had the primary responsibility, only his name is mentioned in the Condition sections of the commentary. Over the years a number of other conservators have worked on the collection, and in these later instances documentation of the paintings' condition and treatment are on file. In addition, in 1985 Charles H. Olin wrote examination reports for most of the pictures, helping to complete the information about the collection's state of preservation.

Only works acquired by the Library after Folger's death were given accession numbers. Most of the earlier paintings have case numbers, which refer to the cases in which Folger had them stored. These numbers are given when known.

Folger did not bid on items at auction in person. He was represented by dealers who acted as his agents. Their names are given when known. The standard 10 percent dealer's fee presumably applied to all such purchases, but it is recorded only when it is given in the records.

I Literary Illustrations

For the artist, as for the general audience, there are two approaches to William Shakespeare's plays: the experience of reading the plays in private and the experience of seeing them performed on stage. The paintings in this chapter generally fall into the first category, those in chapter 2, "Theatrical Portraiture," into the second. Yet the two approaches are not mutually exclusive: paintings that are primarily the product of a communion of the artist with the text may also be influenced by the memory of an actor's interpretation. For example, William Hamilton's painting *Isabella Appealing to Angelo* (no. 32), first exhibited in 1793, was executed independently of any performance, yet one cannot help but suspect that it was conceived in response to Sarah Siddons's interpretation of this role. Any painting, on the other hand, which sets out to depict a particular performance is filtered through the artist's own sensibilities; even *ad vivum* records cannot be taken purely at face value. It is also important to remember that the various editions of the plays differ, and that during the time many of the artists represented in the Folger collection were active, some of the plays were never performed, and none were performed exactly as Shakespeare wrote them.

In 1642 the theater that Shakespeare knew came to an end with the disruption caused by civil war and the puritan government's ordinance banning theatrical productions. By the time performances resumed in London after the accession of Charles II in 1660, attitudes had changed. Even the architecture of the theater itself, which helped determine the relationship of the actors to their audience, reflected a different approach: fan-shaped auditoriums, with deep stages permitting perspective scenes, replaced the old circular structures with their densely packed crowds. Some of Shakespeare's plays still proved popular, but they often needed to be "improved" to accommodate changes in taste. From the perspective of the late seventeenth and eighteenth centuries, Shakespeare was an untutored genius who violated the classical canon: his plots ignored the unities, not being confined to one place nor transpiring in one day; low comedy was mixed with tragedy; and the wicked were not always punished, nor the virtuous rewarded.

Nahum Tate's 1681 version of *King Lear* is the most egregious example of how Shakespeare's "flaws" were corrected. Tate entirely excised the Fool with his indecent humor; he provided a subplot featuring Edgar and Cordelia as lovers; and he ensured that poetic justice was not violated by supplying a happy ending in which Lear and Cordelia triumph to live happily ever after. In the eighteenth century, David Garrick and George Colman created their own versions of the play. Although they restored parts of the original text, it remained

Fig. 1. Pieter van Bleeck, *Mrs. Cibber as Cordelia*, 1755. Oil on canvas, 84 × 82 in. Yale Center for British Art, Paul Mellon Collection.

true throughout the eighteenth century that *Lear* as read and *Lear* as performed were decidedly different works.

This dichotomy can be seen in comparing a painting of 1755 by Pieter van Bleeck of Mrs. Cibber as Cordelia (fig. 1) with James Barry's *Lear and Cordelia* (fig. 2), exhibited at the Royal Academy in 1774. The first shows Mrs. Cibber as Cordelia being rescued by Edgar from two ruffians sent by Edmund, who now wants Cordelia for himself—a scene that is entirely the creation of Nahum Tate. The second painting shows a moment in the play that Barry and his contemporaries never could have seen performed. It is the distressing final scene with Lear, his heart bursting, holding his dead daughter in his arms, uttering the anguished cry

Howl, howl, howl! O, you are men of stones!
Had I your tongues and eyes, I'd use them so
That heaven's vault should crack. She's gone for
    ever!

Not until 1838 did William Macready's production allow theatergoers to see this ending as Shakespeare wrote it. Yet although the nineteenth century showed greater respect for Shakespeare's words, actor-managers still did not hesitate to edit the plays to suit their sense of what was appropriate to the theater. Of course, this type of editing, in greater and lesser degrees, continues today.

In addition to the texts and performances, artists drew their material from the traditions of painting itself. They looked to other artists for ways to depict the Bard. Many literary critics, finding similarities between works of art, raise the charge of plagiarism. In fact, the theory of imitation as taught by the art academies encouraged artists to build on the works of past masters. It is a virtue rather than a vice that Barry's painting, for example, makes a visual equation between Lear and Cordelia and images of the Pietà. Barry deliberately drew on the art of Annibale Carracci in constructing his design, associating the pathos and drama of religious paint-

Fig. 2. James Barry, *King Lear and Cordelia*. Barry's print ca. 1790 after his Royal Academy picture of 1774. By courtesy of the Trustees of the British Museum, London.

ing with the suffering of an ancient British king. In making such a connection, Barry offered a critique of how Shakespeare should be interpreted, one that ran counter to those of his contemporaries. A reviewer of the exhibition of 1774 remarked, "Had Shakespeare's Ideas been as demoniac and extravagant as Mr. Barry's, we should never have enjoyed those artless Scenes which compose his inimitable Lear. The Artist certainly meant it as a Burlesque: Cordelia represented by a Fat Billingsgate Fishwoman overpowered with Gin, and Lear personated by an old Cloaths-man, or Jew Rabbi picking her pocket. Even this can carry no Idea of the Extravagance of this Production."[1] The "extravagance" to which this critic so vehemently objected seems far from inappropriate today.

In the final analysis, the artists offer their own interpretations of Shakespeare. The best of their work is an act of criticism on a par with that of the literary critic and the actor.

In looking at paintings illustrating Shakespeare's plays, one also has to be aware of the artistic conventions observed by each painter. Obviously, van Bleeck's picture is rooted in traditions of portraiture and the theater, while Barry's work is based on a different set of premises. Eighteenth-century audiences would not have considered these two approaches equal. In publicizing the prints after his Shakespeare paintings, Robert Edge Pine wanted to make sure that his audience knew which camp his works belonged in: "It may be proper to observe, that the pictures proposed, are not meant to be representations of stage scenes; but will be treated with the more unconfined liberty of painting, in order to bring those images to the eye, which the writer has given to the mind; and which, in some instances, is not within the power of the Theatre."[2]

From its beginnings in the Italian Renaissance, academic instruction had stressed the close relationship of painting to poetry, one that was conveniently summed up in Horace's phrase *ut pictura poesis* ("as is painting, so is poetry"). Yet, literary illustration was itself divided into various categories. At the top of the hierarchy was history painting. Concerned with man not as he is but as he should be, it explored a realm of heroic action in a suitably idealized style. A lesser category such as genre painting was more concerned with the everyday and commonplace. Shakespeare's work offered a broad range of situations and emotions: an artist might choose subject matter conveying high-mindedness and grand passion, on the one hand, or broad, low humor, on the other. Fuseli's *Romeo Stabs Paris at the Bier of Juliet* (no. 27) and Peters's *The Death of Juliet* (no. 49) both belong to the realm of history painting, depicting in an idealizing vocabulary moments of high seriousness. John Masey Wright's *Mercutio Bidding Farewell to Juliet's Nurse* (no. 91) relies on the distorted features of the nurse for its humor, her comical expression hardly exemplifying human behavior at its finest. Although still a work of elegant sophistication, this last painting makes no pretense of attempting the grand style.

A scene drawn from one of Shakespeare's history plays is not by definition a history painting. Prince Hal is a historical figure, but when Cawse depicts him with Falstaff (no. 5), he is drawing on the conventions of Dutch genre painting to create a humorous setting. Smirke also juxtaposes Prince Hal and Falstaff (no. 57), but it is a moment of pathos rather than humor, and the artist accordingly attempts a higher, more ennobling presentation.

Shakespeare's preeminence is in part a product of his ascendancy to the role of National Poet. The theater played its part in keeping his work before the public by continually performing his plays, and the Shakespeare Jubilee, which Garrick organized in 1769 in Stratford-upon-Avon and then adapted to the London stage, went far to boost the poet's reputation (as well as Garrick's). Throughout the eighteenth century, climaxing in the work of Edmond Malone, critics offered insights into the life and work, and editions of the plays appeared with great frequency. Yet artists who chose Shakespearean scenes for subject matter were not simply following the lead of their contemporaries. England had produced no painters in the highest realm of art, no Raphaels or Michelangelos, Rubenses or Poussins. Artists embraced Shakespeare as a native genius. If greatness could be achieved by an Englishman in

this arena, then why not in painting as well? In exalting Shakespeare, they were also promoting a sense of their own worth.

In 1775, John Hamilton Mortimer exhibited a drawing entitled *Poet*, one of a series of Shakespearean heads that he etched (frontispiece), in this case illustrating lines from *A Midsummer Night's Dream*:

> The poet's eye, in a fine frenzy rolling,
> Doth glance from heaven to earth, from earth to
> heaven;
> And as imagination bodies forth
> The forms of things unknown, the poet's pen
> Turns them to shapes and gives to airy nothing
> A local habitation and a name.

The lines are spoken by Theseus, but Mortimer clearly intends them as representative of Shakespeare. In the drawing the poet wears an earring in his left ear (the right ear in the reversed image of Mortimer's etching), as he does in *The Chandos Portrait of Shakespeare* (see fig. 110), and he is shown as a youthful Bard with a full head of hair. This moment of inspiration is filled with a demonic power. It is the poet as a rival creator to God himself, one whose originality is stressed above all. Mortimer also sees himself in this role: the painter too is called upon to body forth the forms of things unknown.

William Marshall Craig's early nineteenth-century watercolor *Shakespeare and His Creations* (fig. 3) is a more benign image of the Bard, but one that also stresses his originality. In a gesture commonly used for God creating Eve, Shakespeare conjures up some of his characters. On the left is Hamlet with Yorick's skull, the castle at Elsinore looming in the background. At the right are Othello, Hamlet's father's Ghost, Ariel, and Caliban. Caliban is the most prominent, as Shakespeare is in the very act of calling him forth; again the emphasis is on Shakespeare's ability to create shapes from his imagination that have never existed in nature. The reassuring message for artists is that English genius can compete with any nationality in terms of its fertile power.

Scenes from Shakespeare soon dominated English literary illustration, but its beginnings were decidedly humble. To a degree its fortunes were tied to the development of British painting. As the native school of art developed, Shakespearean illus-

Fig. 3. William Marshall Craig, *Shakespeare and His Creations*. Watercolor, 10½ × 8¼ in.

Fig. 4. After François Boitard, frontispiece to *Henry V*. Engraving by Elisha Kirkall, 1709.

tration prospered from, and contributed to, that development. The first images devoted to Shakespeare's plays appeared in the form of book illustrations. In the seventeenth century the plays were issued in the four Folios, illustrated only by a portrait of Shakespeare on the title page. In 1709 Jacob Tonson published a multivolume edition by Nicholas Rowe. Each play had an engraved frontispiece, and although none of the images are signed, there seems to be little doubt that the artist was the Frenchman François Boitard.[3] In some cases, as with the frontispiece to *Henry V* (fig. 4), one can see the influence of the stage: the combatants fight on a shallow foreground with a scene of the battle behind rendered as a painted backdrop; the figures are even cropped at the bottom where the backdrop ends. In the case of an image such as *Coriolanus* (fig. 5), Boitard relies entirely on an engraving after Poussin's painting for his conception.[4] The resulting illustration has more to do with Plutarch than with Shakespeare, but it became part of the Shakespeare iconography: there is evidence that it determined how the play was later staged, the image

proving stronger than either the text or the performance tradition it altered.

In 1714 Tonson brought out a new, smaller edition of the plays with designs by Louis Du Guernier that revised and even replaced some of Boitard's earlier conceptions. These works were then re-engraved for Pope's 1736 edition. But it was Hubert François Gravelot's set of decorative rococo frontispieces to Theobald's 1740 edition of Shakespeare that established a higher standard for Shakespeare book illustration. This publication was closely followed by Hanmer's even more luxurious edition of 1744, most of its large, impressive illustrations being provided by Francis Hayman.

William Hogarth was the first to execute paintings based on Shakespeare's plays; most are closely tied to the theater. *Falstaff Examining His Recruits,* signed and dated 1730, is based on a sketch that was probably taken from an actual performance in late 1727 or 1728.[5] This sketch is also related to Hogarth's drawing of a scene from *The Beggar's Opera* (see fig. 65 for an example of Hogarth's paintings of this subject), which is indisputably based on a performance of this play by John Gay.

Francis Hayman also executed scenes from Shakespeare's plays, some of the most important of which were executed for Jonathan Tyers's Vauxhall Gardens. Tyers opened Vauxhall, a refurbished Spring Gardens, in 1732. A pleasurable retreat on the south bank of the Thames, the gardens were filled with entertainment catering to the aristocracy and the middle class. Tyers, apparently

Fig. 5. After François Boitard, frontispiece to *Coriolanus.* Engraving by Elisha Kirkall, 1709.

prompted by his friend Hogarth, commissioned more than fifty paintings to decorate the supper boxes (small alcoves opening on the tree-lined walks). These paintings, the majority of which were by Hayman, focused on games and other amusements, but a few illustrated scenes from the theater and literature, including *Falstaff in the Buckbasket* and *Falstaff's Cowardice Detected* (see no. 38). Art was seldom publicly displayed in the first half of the eighteenth century, and such exposure was important for both the artist and his audience.

The most prestigious structure in Vauxhall Gardens was the Prince of Wales's Pavilion, for which Hayman executed four paintings, all illustrating Shakespeare. At least three of these paintings were in place by 1745, and the choice of subject matter may have been determined by the contemporary political situation (see no. 36). The scenes from Shakespeare did not just offer homage to the National Poet: they were a living presence in dialogue with the prince, who, as the rallying point for the opposition, was at the center of national life.

In 1760 artists for the first time organized to promote an exhibition of their work at the Society of Arts. The more important artists associated with this exhibition went on to exhibit annually at the Society of Artists, while a splinter group remained at the Society of Arts, exhibiting as the Free Society of Artists. In 1768 the Royal Academy was founded, and the first of its annual exhibitions was held the following year. From the beginning Shakespearean subjects were to be represented in these various exhibitions.[6] The most popular play of the first years was *Macbeth,* its scenes of witchcraft exerting a strong appeal. Zuccarelli's painting *Macbeth and the Witches* (no. 95) appears to be dated 1760, and, though not exhibited, is one of the earliest paintings from this play.[7] Zuccarelli's painting belongs to a different tradition than the narrative pictures of Hogarth and Hayman. It is a remarkable example of epic or historical landscape, a genre originating with the Franco-Italian artists Poussin and Claude Lorraine. Zuccarelli's painting was purchased, and probably commissioned, by Lord Grosvenor, a sophisticated collector and patron who had traveled extensively in Italy. The painting is a reflection of aristocratic Italianate tastes, in contrast to the popular culture embodied in the Vauxhall Gardens pictures.

Fig. 6. Nathaniel Dance, *Timon of Athens.* Oil on canvas, 48 × 54 in. Copyright reserved to Her Majesty Queen Elizabeth II.

Most of the early Shakespeare paintings belong to the more informal type of subject pictures executed by Hogarth and Hayman. Hayman's *Falstaff Reviewing His Recruits* (no. 37), though a relatively large canvas, is still characteristic of this native style. The first painting of a Shakespearean scene that fully deserves to be described as a history painting is Nathaniel Dance's *Timon of Athens* (fig. 6), which was exhibited at the Society of Artists in 1767. Dance had studied for a number of years in Rome, and it is not surprising that he chose a subject from one of Shakespeare's plays with a classical setting as suitable for treatment in the grand style. The composition is derived from that of his teacher, Hayman, who executed a design of the same scene for Hanmer's 1744 edition (fig. 7). Yet the differences are telling. Hayman's drawing, executed in a rococo style, emphasizes elegant, twisting figures and active, shimmering surfaces, while Dance's oil shows large Raphaelesque figures handled with a sober palette. As more and more artists had the experience of studying abroad, history paintings of Shakespearean subjects appeared with increasing frequency. Continental masters had long explored

such "universal" texts as the Bible or classical history and mythology, but in treating Shakespeare in the exalted mode of history painting, English artists were breaking new ground.

The greatest single act of patronage for painters in eighteenth-century England revolved completely around Shakespeare. On 4 May 1789, Alderman John Boydell, a successful print publisher, opened his Shakespeare Gallery with thirty-four pictures by a number of the most distinguished artists of the British school. Boydell's plan was ambitious: he hoped eventually to commission a hundred large paintings illustrating Shakespeare's plays along with a hundred smaller ones, all of which would be on permanent exhibition in the gallery he had built for this purpose in Pall Mall. Although Boydell charged admission to the gallery, most of his profits came from subscription sales of the prints after the paintings. In 1802 he published a two-volume folio edition of engravings after the large paintings, and three years later his firm brought out a nine-volume edition of the plays, edited by George Steevens, with engravings after the small pictures. Each year more paintings were added to the original thirty-four, but the project collapsed before all two hundred could be commissioned. The wars with France having closed the Continental markets, Boydell, who paid the participating artists handsomely, could not sustain the expense of his gallery. However, he was able to persuade Parliament to allow him to dispose of the paintings and the remaining stock of prints through a lottery. The winner of the lottery, held on 28 January 1805, was William Tassie, the nephew of the designer of medallions; he disposed of his winnings at Christie's in a sale that ran from 17 to 19 May of that same year.

Boydell's Shakespeare Gallery may have been a financial failure, but it did provide British artists with an opportunity that had not been previously afforded by the church, the state, or the country's nobility, institutions that had done so much to promote painting on the Continent. Boydell obviously hoped to make a profit on his venture, but his altruistic claim that he wished to advance the art of painting in his own country is warranted. In his

Fig. 7. After Francis Hayman, *Timon of Athens*. Engraving by Hubert Gravelot, 1744.

first catalogue he pointed out the difficulties that his undertaking would encounter "in a country where Historical Painting is still but in its infancy" and concluded, "To advance that art towards maturity, and establish an *English School of Historical Painting,* was the great object of the present design." It is no coincidence that the National Poet should be the vehicle by which the nation's art was to be elevated.

Of course, not all of the paintings executed for Boydell's Shakespeare Gallery can lay claim to the category of history painting. The pictures are as diverse as the plays themselves: some show sublime scenes drawn from the revered past, others scenes of fantasy; some depict pastoral interludes, others comic situations. The Folger Library's collection encompasses a wide range. Within the work of a single artist such as Hamilton, one encounters the high-minded seriousness of *The Duke of York Discovering His Son Aumerle's Treachery* (no. 33), the comic playfulness of *The Carousing of Sir Toby Belch and Sir Andrew Aguecheek* (no. 34), and the charming sentimentality of *Olivia's Proposal* (no. 35). Smirke's paintings show a similar variety, although he is far more successful in his comic rendition of *Stephano Confronting the Monster* (no. 59) than in his more austere attempt at history painting in *The Awakening of King Lear* (no. 58). Nine of the ten paintings executed for Boydell in the Folger collection are from the small series. The tenth, Romney's *Infant Shakespeare* (no. 176), which is on the same scale as the large series, is the only picture exhibited in the Shakespeare Gallery that did not illustrate a scene from one of the plays. One presumes that the impetus for this impressive allegorical composition came from the artist rather than from the alderman, but the work, completed soon after the gallery opened, makes a fitting introduction to Boydell's collection as a whole.

Boydell's enterprise, which had been conceived as early as 1786, quickly prompted imitators. Thomas Macklin, a print and picture dealer, issued a prospectus in 1787 for his Poets' Gallery, which he hoped would eventually consist of one hundred paintings. His first catalogue appeared the following year. Only twenty-four engravings were issued and, although all the poets were British, only one Shakespearean scene was included—de Loutherbourg's *Shipwreck* from *The Tempest.*[8] The Folger Library—fittingly, in light of its large Boydell holdings—also has a painting related to this rival venture: a sketch of Rigaud's illustration to Chaucer (no. 52) that was bought as Angelica Kauffmann's *Lear and Cordelia*.

Macklin went on to sponsor a lavishly illustrated Bible, and his and Boydell's galleries were joined by that of yet another entrepreneur, Robert Bowyer. In 1792 Bowyer announced plans to commission paintings to be engraved for an illustrated edition of David Hume's *History of England*, the first volume of which had been published in 1754.[9] Even more ambitious, in that the artist was forced to embark on his venture alone, was Henry Fuseli's gallery of pictures devoted to the work of John Milton. Fuseli's Milton Gallery first opened in May 1799, and one of the works he exhibited was *Faery Mab* from *L'Allegro*. Believing it to be *Queen Mab* from *Romeo and Juliet*, Folger purchased the latest of three versions of this subject (no. 29), the most complex and sophisticated of the interpretations. Thus, by accident rather than design, the Folger collection reflects a broad spectrum of some of the most innovative attempts at patronage in late eighteenth-century England.

Boydell's Shakespeare Gallery spawned an even more direct imitation. James Woodmason, an English businessman based in Dublin who acted as the stationer to the king in Ireland, created the Irish Shakespeare Gallery, which opened in Dublin in May 1793.[10] Finding little enthusiasm, he moved the collection to London the following year. As the New Shakespeare Gallery, it competed for a short time across the street from Boydell's pictures. Woodmason planned to commission two paintings from each of thirty-six plays, engravings of which would illustrate an edition of the plays. Unlike Boydell, he insisted on a standardized size and a vertical format suitable for book illustration. Only twenty-seven paintings were executed, three of which are in the Folger collection, presently the only collection to contain more than one. One of these, Fuseli's *Macbeth Consulting the Vision of the Armed Head* (no. 24), was acclaimed by a contemporary critic as perhaps the artist's best picture. The Rev. Matthew William Peters also rose to the challenge, creating in his *The Death of Juliet* (no. 49) the most powerful of all his compositions. The third picture owned by the Folger Library, Hamilton's *Isabella Appealing to Angelo* (no. 32), must also be numbered among the artist's finest compositions in the grand style.

As already seen in some of the portraits of Shakespeare, one aspect of the poet's character that was particularly admired was his strong imagination. As Addison wrote in the *Spectator* as early as 1712,

> There is a kind of Writing, wherein the Poet quite loses sight of Nature, and entertains his Reader's Imagination with the Characters and Actions of such Persons as have many of them no Existence, but what he bestows on them. Such are Fairies, Witches, Magicians, Demons, and departed Spirits. . . . Among the *English, Shakespear* has incomparably excelled all others. That noble Extravagance of Fancy, which he had in so great Perfection, thoroughly qualified him to touch this weak superstitious Part of his Reader's Imagination; and made him capable of Succeeding, where he had nothing to support him besides the Strength of his own Genius.[11]

This supernatural world proved popular with artists, who could more easily conjure up its denizens than could any stagecraft, no matter how sophisticated. *A Midsummer Night's Dream* and *The Tempest* offered a range of subjects extending from sylvan romance to grotesque comedy, and in the case of a painting such as *Titania Caressing the Drowsy Bottom* (no. 103), the viewer is given both. The horrific subject matter of *Hamlet* and *Macbeth*, with their ghosts, witches, and apparitions, also appealed to artists and their public. Herrick's exhibited picture of 1857 of the chamber scene from *Hamlet* (no. 39) provides a dramatic rendering of the Ghost's appearance to his son that could not have been shown on any stage. Two scenes from *Macbeth*, Macbeth's meeting the witches on the heath and his visit to the witches' cave, were repeatedly depicted by artists, as in the cases of Zuccarelli (no. 95), Romney (nos. 53 and 124), Abbott (no. 1), Barker of Bath (no. 3), and Sully (no. 81).

No artist was better qualified to explore this world of fantasy than the Swiss painter Henry Fuseli. Inspired by his own vision of Michelangelo's *terribilità*, Fuseli was especially attuned to the violence and sexual energy underlying Shakespeare's text. The sublime in art, for him, was more than the depiction of lofty sentiments and exalted ideas. His interpretation of Shakespeare's imagination owes a debt to Edmund Burke, for whom the sublime was the product of mankind's strongest passions and had as its basis feelings of terror. Fuseli responded to Shakespeare with heroic, visionary forms dramatically emerging from dark obscurity.

His *Macbeth Consulting the Vision of the Armed Head* (no. 24) relies on extravagant distortion, hypnotic repetition of gesture, a low point of view, and the lack of spatial stability to help convey the horrific nature of the subject matter. In *The Two Murderers of the Duke of Clarence* (no. 26), one is forced to confront the killers in a psychologically intense close-up view. One head emerging from the gloom offers a study in maniacal blood-lust, while the other, attempting to recede, exhibits a reluctant, melancholy power. The mischievous Puck (no. 25), who in Reynolds's interpretation for Boydell's Shakespeare Gallery is an impish child seated on a toadstool, is for Fuseli a figure of titanic energies who straddles the entire globe. Even the lyric grace of Ariel (no. 28) is conveyed through extravagant gesture and a heroic rendering of youthful adolescence. Fuseli's intense personal vision of the Bard is of epic proportions.

Judging from the Folger collection, the scenes that appealed most were comedic ones, and no figure was more popular than Falstaff. Of the 118 paintings that show scenes or characters from the plays, no fewer than 28—almost one-fourth of the total—feature the fat knight, beginning with Hayman's early images of the 1740s and ending with Alfred Dever's painting from 130 years later. The vast majority of these pictures draw on the two parts of *Henry IV*. Falstaff is one of the few Shakespearean characters whose costume changes very little over the years. He appears as early as 1662 in a frontispiece (fig. 8) to the book *The Wits*, and the main accoutrements seen there—a round hat (usually with a feather), a lace ruff, protruding jerkin, and high boots turned down below the knees—carry on well into the nineteenth century. Falstaff's uninterrupted popularity on the stage accounts for this continuity. The color of his outfit, though, does change. In the early paintings—Hogarth's *Falstaff Examining His Recruits* of 1730, Hayman's painting of the same subject (no. 37), Marcellus Laroon's *Falstaff and Bardolph* of 1746 (Yale Center for British Art), and the McArdell painting of about 1750 (no. 118), Falstaff is invariably shown in a gray or silver jerkin with a red coat or cloak. However, yellow soon becomes dominant. Yellow was the traditional color for the buffoon and perhaps is meant to suggest as well Falstaff's seemingly cowardly conduct, but more likely it became closely associated with him because of allusions in the plays to his butter-

like appearance. The Carrier's terse description of one of the robbers in *I Henry IV* is particularly memorable:

> *Sheriff.* One of them is well known, my gracious lord,
>   A gross fat man.
> *Carrier.* As fat as butter.[12]

By the middle of the nineteenth century, the traditional costume is less rigidly maintained. Both Weekes (no. 83) and Dever (no. 18) present more idiosyncratic interpretations of the fat knight in terms of both the color and design of his attire.

The artists' interpretation of Falstaff's character also changed over time. Hogarth's and Hayman's Falstaff, a figure of debased appetites, conveys a sense of moral corruption. Beginning in the middle of the eighteenth century, critics began to treat him in more favorable terms. In 1777 Maurice Morgann staunchly defended his personality in his *Essay on the Dramatic Character of Sir John Falstaff*. The vast majority of nineteenth-century artists were content with a benign image of the amiable humorist, a man embodying a love of laughter, a charming frankness, and a generous spirit. This sanitized Falstaff was a fitter companion for a prince, one who would not be out of place on the walls of a Victorian home. Writing in 1857 in the *Athenaeum*, a critic nostalgically described his vanished type, calling him "an Epicurean gentleman, shrewd, careless, witty, suspicious of too much virtue, and a moral cosmopolite, sociable from his birth,—a character grown impossible since taverns have become extinct."[13] This approach to Sir John as a witty, cultured, and worldly companion is in evidence in almost all the nineteenth-century interpretations in the Folger collection, but perhaps none is more finely executed than Stothard's *Falstaff and Doll Tearsheet* (no. 76), where the figure embracing a prostitute appears more like a genial, courtly uncle than a debauched reprobate.

Shakespeare's heroines are also well represented in the collection. A feminine cast of characters begins to emerge in the late eighteenth century sharing the stage with the earlier Falstaffs, Hamlets, and Macbeths. Wheatley's painting from *All's Well That Ends Well* (no. 87) has a charming Helena as its main protagonist, while Hamilton's *Olivia's Proposal* (no. 35) focuses on an attractive, fashionable heroine with a small, high waist above the

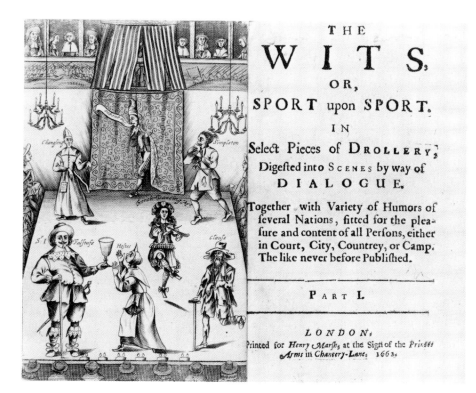

Fig. 8. Anonymous, frontispiece to *The Wits*. Engraving, 1662.

elongated sweep of a full figure. Yet, some paintings go beyond the depiction of enchanting types of female beauty. Two of the most impressive pictures, both commissioned for Woodmason's Irish Shakespeare Gallery, are Hamilton's *Isabella Appealing to Angelo* (no. 32) and Peters's *The Death of Juliet* (no. 49). Each is a work of high drama in which the women, one imposingly dignified, the other tenderly beseeching, play out grand passions on a grand scale. Smirke's *Awakening of King Lear* (no. 58) and West's *King Lear and Cordelia* (no. 84) also provide an interesting comparison; painted within about a year of one another, both depict the same scene. Smirke sees the subject as revolving around the slow awakening of the befuddled king, with his attentive daughter very much a secondary figure, her face seen only in a lost profile. West, on the contrary, views the moment as Cordelia's rather than Lear's. Her fluttering hair, veil, and robes animate her impressively large form, as her dominating classical profile establishes the picture's central focus.

The nineteenth-century heroines are generally far less heroic than the two women executed for Woodmason. The conventionally pretty, such as Stothard's Mariana (no. 77), or the appealingly pathetic, such as Ophelia or Desdemona, replace the stoically heroic. Even the quick-witted, intelligent Portia, who is able to best men on their own terms, appears in Sully's painting (no. 82) as a figure of melting beauty whose golden locks, limpid eyes, and small, full lips would seem to doom her masquerade as a young man.

Shakespeare's heroines played an important role in Victorian culture as examples of womanhood at its finest. The canonization of Shakespeare's female characters required certain distortions in the interpretation of the plays, and critics reinvented these roles for an eager public. Anna Jameson's *Shakespeare's Heroines—characteristics of Women, Moral, Poetical and Historical*, first published in 1832, went through numerous editions and was soon joined by Mary Cowden Clarke's *The Girlhood of Shakespeare's Heroines* (1850–52), a work more of imaginative fiction than of criticism. Many Victorian artists were only too happy to cater to the accompanying demands for idealized types of feminine virtue as seen through the lens of Victorian morality. In 1836–37 Charles Heath issued a series of prints entitled *The Shakespeare Gallery: Containing the Principal Female Characters in the Plays of the Great Poet*, which was composed of more than forty images of sentimentalized women by a number of artists. In scope and intent, this book of keepsake pictures differed markedly from Boydell's Shakespeare Gallery, whose goal had been to elevate the arts in Great Britain. Other such series were to follow, including Heath's own reworking of his first idea, published as *The Heroines of Shakespeare* in 1848. Altick colorfully characterizes the proliferation of such images, which the print market did so much to promote:

> The "Keepsake beauty," indeed . . . was, by common agreement among all persons professionally interested in art except those who profited from her popularity, an offense against all judicious taste. Her cloyingly malign influence persisted from the late Regency almost to the end of the Victorian era; her person, as represented by countless paintings and drawings and the engravings that disseminated those images, was the quintessence of the age's notorious sentimentality, in which the preceding century's *sensibilité*, a prized affectation of the elite, was coarsened for, and by, the middle classes. It would not be too daring to suggest that pictures of her were icons secularized for Protestant homes, hung and reproduced in places where, in Roman Catholic societies, images of the Madonna and female saints could be found. They were the most familiar visual manifestation of the Victorian cult of woman worship.[14]

Thomas Francis Dicksee built an entire career around the production of attractive literary heroines, and his painting of Anne Page (no. 20) is the quintessential Keepsake Beauty; *The Merry Wives of Windsor* is little more than an excuse for depicting a winsome female in an attractive setting of comfortable abundance. Without the painting's title one could not even be sure Anne Page is intended, as the image is so generalized. The costume itself hovers somewhere between Elizabethan and Victorian fashion, archaic enough to evoke Merry Olde England but at the same time still appealing to contemporary tastes. Yet, the portrayal of Anne Page does not necessarily require the profundity associated with other Shakespeare heroines, and, despite the howls of the critics as to the superficial nature of the Keepsake Beauty, it is impossible not to be captivated by Dicksee's ideal portrait.

The Folger collection has several mid-nineteenth-century pictures set in Venice or its colony, Cyprus, which were shown in the London exhibitions. (See nos. 40, 42, 55, and 74, which was preparatory to the exhibited picture.) These scenes are from *The Merchant of Venice*, the fourth most popular play in the nineteenth century in terms of pictures shown at exhibition, and from *Othello*, the eighth most popular. The two pictures from *Othello*, James Clarke Hook's *Othello's Description of Desdemona*, exhibited at the Royal Academy in 1852, and William Salter's *Othello's Lamentation*, exhibited at the Society of British Artists in 1857, are among the latest of the collection's exhibited pictures, and they demonstrate the marked difference in quality between works shown at the Royal Academy and those shown at the Society of British Artists. Salter, who studied for five years with the Royal Academician James Northcote and for an even longer time in Italy, seems never to have fully mastered the fundamentals of painting, as his large canvas is often clumsy in execution. Hook also spent years in Italy, but unlike Salter he took full advantage of the exotic setting. Just as theater managers were looking back to paintings of the Venetian Renaissance to inspire their stage designs, Hook was also strongly influenced by the Old Masters. His work is a mid-nineteenth-century interpretation of the theme of love and music making as seen in the works of Giorgione and Titian and their followers. The subject is derived from images of the Garden of Love, and it is fitting that Hook should have employed his version of the Venetian Renaissance as a setting for a scene conjured up in a play written around the very end of the reign of Queen Elizabeth I. While reflecting the theater's concern for historical accuracy, the painting is unquestionably the product of the communion of the artist with the text. It in fact depicts a moment of tranquility recalled by Othello rather than one that is actually enacted on stage. For Hook, in a way that escaped Salter, Shakespeare's tragic lovers inspired a personal vision of intense poetry. The fact that the scene was not performed on stage liberated the artist to imagine his own Venetian reverie, a powerful Victorian conflation of Shakespeare and Titian.

1. *Public Advertiser*, 3 May 1774, signed "Dilettante."
2. Quoted in Altick 1985, p. 256.
3. For the attribution of the designs to Boitard and of the execution of the engravings to Elisha Kirkall, see H. A. Hammelmann, "Shakespeare's First Illustrators," *Apollo* 88 (August 1968), Supplement, pp. 1–4.
4. Merchant provides an informative chapter on this connection: "A 'Coriolanus' after Poussin, 1709." An engraving after Poussin's painting is reproduced as plate 66.
5. The painting is reproduced in color in the exhibition catalogue *Manners and Morals: Hogarth and British Painting, 1700–1760*, Tate Gallery, London, 1988, pl. 82.
6. A helpful list of the Shakespearean subjects can be found in Dotson 1973, Appendix B, "Subjects from Shakespeare in the Exhibition of the Artists' Societies from their Inception [in 1760] through 1830."

    Altick has computed that "pictures from Shakespeare accounted for about one-fifth—some 2,300—of the total number of literary paintings recorded between 1760 and 1900" (1985, p. 255). For the second half of the eighteenth century, he ranks in descending order the most popular plays for representation as *Macbeth, King Lear, As You Like It, Romeo and Juliet*, and the two parts of *Henry IV*, a ranking that has little correlation with a list of the plays most frequently preformed during this period. He goes on to give a breakdown of the plays from which paintings were derived in the nineteenth century: "The most popular plays (in a descending range of 170–100 each) were *Romeo and Juliet, The Tempest, Hamlet, The Merchant of Venice, As You Like It*, and *A Midsummer Night's Dream*. In the middle category (100–150 paintings ["100–50" is meant]) fell *Macbeth, Othello, Henry IV, Twelfth Night, The Taming of the Shrew, Cymbeline, The Merry Wives of Windsor*, and *King Lear*. In the range of 50–25 paintings were *Much Ado about Nothing, Henry VIII, The Winter's Tale, The Two Gentlemen of Verona*, and *Antony and Cleopatra*. Each of the remaining plays in the Shakespeare canon was the source of fewer than 25 pictures" (pp. 259–60).

    Geoffrey Ashton offers some interesting statistics for Shakespearean paintings exhibited just at the Royal Academy, a total of nearly 1,400 works from 1769 to 1900: "There was an annual average of five Shakespearean subjects for the first twenty years of Royal Academy exhibitions until 1789 when the Boydell *Shakespeare Gallery* boosted the average for a few years. The excitement quietened down in the mid-1790s and there was an average of five to ten works each year until about 1830 when the average increased to fifteen. The 1840s and 1850s were the bumper years for Shakespearean subjects and the average increased to about twenty works a year. The average decreased to fifteen during the 1860s, 1870s and 1880s and there was a final reduction to about ten per year in the 1890s." Ashton provides corresponding details on illustrated editions: "A similar trend is evident in illustrated editions of Shakespeare although the spurt of the 1840s and 1850s lasted a little longer. In the first ten years of the nineteenth century about twenty illustrated editions of Shakespeare were published; the average rose to about fifty in the 1850s and went down again to twenty in the 1890s" (Buxton Museum and Art Gallery, *Shakespeare's Heroines in the Nineteenth Century*, 1980, p. ix).
7. William Dawes exhibited *Macbeth at the Cauldron* at the Society of Arts in 1760. It vies with Zuccarelli's work as the earliest painting from *Macbeth*.
8. A fragment of the painting is in the Royal Shakespeare Theatre Collection, Stratford-upon-Avon.
9. Bowyer's multivolume edition, illustrated with well over 100 engravings, appeared in 1806. All of these rival galleries to Boydell's project are discussed in T. S. R. Boase's article "Macklin and Bowyer," *Journal of the Warburg and Courtauld Institutes* 26 (1963), pp. 148–77.
10. An excellent discussion of Woodmason's gallery can be found in Robin Hamlyn's "An Irish Shakespeare Gallery," *Burlington Magazine* 120 (August 1978), pp. 515–29.
11. Addison, *The Spectator* 419 (1 July 1712), pp. 213 and 215.
12. *I Henry IV* II, 4, 559–60. (This and subsequent references are to act, scene, and line number.) For other references to Falstaff as butter, see *I Henry IV* II, 4, 134, and IV, 2, 67, and *The Merry Wives of Windsor* III, 5, 118.
13. *The Athenaeum*, 23 May 1857, p. 667.
14. Altick 1985, pp. 86–87.

John White Abbott (nos. 1–2)

Abbott, a talented amateur landscape painter, was born in Exeter in 1763. He worked as an apothecary and surgeon, studying art in his spare time under the landscape painter Francis Towne. Abbott exhibited annually at the Royal Academy from 1793 until 1805 as an honorary exhibitor, and again in 1810 and 1822. Eventually he became a country gentleman, presumably living off an inheritance from his wealthy maternal uncle, James White. In 1831 he became deputy lieutenant for the county of Devon, and he died at Exeter on 9 May 1851.

1

MACBETH RECOILING FROM THE APPARITION OF THE CROWNED CHILD
Macbeth IV, 1
1829
Oil on panel, 7³⁄₄ × 9³⁄₈ in. (19.7 × 23.7 cm.)

Initialed and dated at lower right: "JWA / 1829." (This inscription is difficult to see and is more easily read from a photograph taken when the work was being restored in 1988.)

Provenance: Since Abbott is said never to have sold a picture, these works may have descended to one of his four surviving children. Bought by Folger from Barnard, January 1918, £3.3.0 (for pair).

Condition: There are vertical cracks and wide separation cracks in the paint surface, and the wrinkling of the surface indicates excess oxidation of the oil. Overall there is solvent abrasion from past cleanings. The wood is radially cut and the edges are beveled on the back. The panel is severely warped in a convex curve from left to right.

1

2

2

PROSPERO COMMANDING ARIEL
The Tempest I, 2
1829
Oil on panel, 7³/₄ × 9³/₈ in. (19.7 × 23.7 cm.)

Initialed and dated at lower left: "JWA / 1829"

Provenance: As above

Exhibitions: Amherst, *The Tempest*, 1951

Condition: The paint surface, like that of its pendant, suffers from cracks and wrinkling due to oxidation. It also shows evidence of solvent abrasion. The panel is similarly cut and beveled, but the convex curve from left to right is not so severe as that of its companion.

Identical in size and date (1829), the two Folger panels were obviously meant to be seen together and may possibly form part of a larger Shakespearean series. Both scenes show an interest in magic: black magic in *Macbeth* and white in *Prospero*. These two works are atypical of Abbott's usual repertoire of pastoral and elegiac landscapes, and as figural compositions are unique among his known paintings. Without the initials on the panels, it would not have been a likely first attribu-

tion, although the indistinct quality of the execution, as if the works were seen through a haze, is characteristic of many of Abbott's paintings. In an undated draft of a letter from the artist Ozias Humphry to Abbott written sometime before Humphry's death in 1810, the academician chastises the amateur: "The pictures are faint, and appear in comparison with works of the greatest Masters as if they were mildewed. They want depth and distinctness. The trees in your picture at Fordland [Abbott's home] are not inferior in drawing, taste and grouping to any of the greatest Masters, but in their scale and effect they are altogether too faint and foggy."[1]

The "foggy" technique works well in evoking supernatural horror in the scene from *Macbeth*, where Macbeth is shown reacting to the third apparition conjured up by the witches. The crowned child rises in a bluish smoke from the cauldron, holding in his left hand a branch, as he prophesies, "Macbeth shall never vanquish'd be until / Great Birnam wood to high Dunsinane hill / Shall come against him." The three witches are crowded along the left-hand side, the bottom one holding a serpent in her right hand while pointing to the child with her left. Another serpent hisses at the foot of the cauldron to the right. The provision of the witch with a crutch is derived from nineteenth-century stage tradition rather than from the text.[2] Hecate, holding a wand, can be seen between Macbeth and the apparition. A bat flies between her and Macbeth, while at the bottom right lies a skull and perched beside it what appears to be an owl, another creature associated with night and sorcery. Elements of these creatures also appear as part of the witches' brew, which includes "wool of bat," "adder's fork [tongue]," and "howlet's [small owl's] wing." The sternly challenging figure of the crowned Macbeth is contrasted with the gentle figure of the crowned child. Macbeth first recognizes the baby as "like the issue of a king," and while the child's words initially soothe him, the apparition's suggestion of the birthing of a new line of kings leads to his demand to know if Banquo's issue shall ever reign in the kingdom, the answer to which will bring torment rather than relief.

The second panel shows an early scene from *The Tempest*. After relating the story to his daughter Miranda of how they came to be marooned on their island, the magician Prospero, the former duke of Milan, induces in her a deep sleep. He then summons and commands Ariel, an airy spirit he had, on first arriving on the island, rescued from the tormenting spell of the witch Sycorax. Abbott depicts Ariel, dressed in white with light, butterfly wings, as he makes his departure, obediently pointing in the same direction as his master while looking back at him. Miranda is shown at the right asleep at the entrance to their cave. In the next moment, Prospero will awaken her and summon Caliban, the bestial son of the deceased Sycorax. Caliban can be seen lurking just beneath the departing Ariel, his dark, contracted form associated with the earth, while Ariel's graceful, expansive figure is linked with the bright sky. Their juxtaposition suggests the two poles of human nature, the one bestial and the other angelic. Prospero, a dignified, patriarchal figure, is wrapped in his magic mantle and, like the sorceress Hecate in *Macbeth*, holds a staff or magic wand. Abbott's composition is indebted to John Thurston's 1812 print of this scene (fig. 9), a conception that ultimately goes back to William Hamilton's more dramatic rendering for the Boydell Shakespeare Gallery, the engraving for which was published on 23 April 1798. Abbott adapts the composition to a horizontal format and molds Ariel's

Thurston del.   Rhodes sculp.

TEMPEST.

HAST THOU, SPIRIT,

PERFORM'D TO POINT THE TEMPEST THAT I BAD THEE

Act 1. Scene 2.

London, Published by Thomas Tegg, N°111 Cheapside April 1, 1811.

Fig. 9. After John Thurston, *Prospero Summoning Ariel.* Engraving by Rhodes, 1 April 1812.

body to Prospero's gesture, thereby transforming Ariel into an extension of the old man's thoughts.

1. Quoted in A. P. Oppé, "John White Abbott of Exeter," *Journal of the Walpole Society* 13 (1924–25), p. 74. The letter is in the Library of the Royal Academy.
2. See Sprague 1944, p. 228.

Thomas Barker of Bath

Barker was the most distinguished member of a family that produced three generations of artists, beginning with his father and including his brothers and his sons. Born in 1767, Thomas moved with his family in 1783 to Bath, where his father, Benjamin, struggled as a stable hand and as an indifferent painter of horses and carriage doors. Largely self-taught as an artist and showing early promise, Thomas was soon befriended by Charles Spackman, a wealthy coach builder and property developer who paid for his schooling and supervised his art instruction, which consisted primarily of copying the Dutch and Flemish old masters in his personal collection. Thomas Gainsborough's canvases also had a strong impact on the youthful painter. By 1790 Spackman, who by agreement with the family owned whatever pictures Barker produced, held a well-received public exhibition of his work. In that same year he sent Barker to Italy for a three-year sojourn. On his return, Barker embarked on his own in London, but, unable to duplicate his earlier success, he returned permanently to Bath by 1800. He immediately began plans to build an impressive home called Doric House containing his own picture gallery, which he opened in 1805. He exhibited sporadically at the Royal Academy from 1791 until 1829, and more frequently at the British Institution from 1807 to 1847. Along with his brothers, he also participated in exhibitions in Bath and other provincial centers. Barker's work is varied, but he is best known for his landscapes, scenes of peasant life, and fancy pictures. In 1826 he even unveiled an ambitious fresco, 12 by 36 feet, executed on one of the walls of his picture gallery, showing the massacre of the Sciotes by the Turks, a subject that had also fascinated Delacroix. Surviving until the age of eighty and having outlived his popularity, he died on 11 December 1847.

3

MACBETH AND THE WITCHES
Macbeth IV, 1
ca. 1830
Oil on canvas, 46¼ × 37¹⁄₁₆ in. (117.5 × 94.3 cm.)

Case no. 1524

Provenance: John Hugh Smyth Pigott sale, English & Son, 8 (10) October–7 November 1849, lot 26, as "Its companion—The Incantation Scene," £7.0.0 (the preceding lot 25 is entitled "Macbeth's interview with the Witches" and sold for £6.15.0); bought from Meagher, May 1926, $300, as showing Macready in the character of Macbeth. In a letter to

Folger of 26 April 1926, Meagher supplied the following provenance: "The owner an artist himself, and an Englishman wishes to go to Florida and could use the money to good advantage If I could sell the painting for him. I have known of its existence here for about six years and he always claimed that he intended to take it back to England with him, but that is all changed now."

Condition: The canvas has a number of tears, and it was glue-lined onto a commercially prepared canvas by Finlayson in 1932. A 2½-inch section has been added along the bottom by the artist. Olin gives the evidence for a section having been cut off on the left: "Two vertical paint cracks on the right appear to have been caused by two past stretchers. There is only one on the left and it is close to the frame. The witch on the right is 3" from edge, the one on the left is ½"; the proportion of space seems off." Yet, as it stands now, Macbeth is in the center of the canvas. If a strip has been cut off on the left, it may have been by the artist in order to center Macbeth. The measurements in the 1849 sale catalogue (49 × 37 in.) demonstrate that the width is the same as when the painting was in the original owner's collection. If anything has been lost, it is in the vertical dimension. Markings on the upper corners of the canvas indicate that the picture was at one time in a frame with an arched top. Pentimenti of the witch's head at the right reveal that she was originally seen in three-quarter view rather than in profile.

This painting is one of a pair of scenes from *Macbeth*, both of which sold in 1849 at the sale of one of Barker's principal patrons.[1] The first painting of the two, now missing, showed the meeting of Macbeth and Banquo with the witches on the heath in act I, scene 3, while the Folger picture shows Macbeth at the witches' cave from act IV, scene 1. Despite their popularity as subjects, both having been frequently painted by artists,[2] the two scenes were not often paired, although there was the highly successful precedent of Fuseli's choice of these subjects for Woodmason's Gallery (no. 24). The Folger picture, however, owes more to Reynolds's interpretation of this scene (fig. 10), executed for Boydell's Shakespeare Gallery, than to Fuseli's. Reynolds compiles a catalogue of all the scene's apparitions, while Barker concentrates only on the final revelation with the procession of the eight kings, the last

Fig. 10. After Sir Joshua
Reynolds, *Macbeth and the
Witches.* Engraving by Robert
Thew, 1 December 1802.

holding a mirror showing many more. These kings
are the descendants of the murdered Banquo, whose
line prospers whereas Macbeth will beget no dynasty. Barker, though, omits Banquo himself, who,
in Reynolds's picture, points to the mirrored image.
The three witches, carefully individualized, encircle Macbeth as one stirs the cauldron, its unusually
small size perhaps also inspired by Reynolds's depiction. The cauldron is circumscribed by a magic
circle with bones scattered along its perimeter.

The picture is executed with the bold strokes
characteristic of Barker's late style. The draperies
swirl about the figures, and even the bare back of
the one witch is handled with the same broad free-
dom. Red sparks fly upwards from the fire of the
cauldron, and the figures are tinged with red reflections. The flames also turn Macbeth's sword red
near its point, a reminder of the blood he has shed
and will continue to shed. Macbeth's face is rendered in the same sickly green tones employed for
the witches, further binding him to them.

Despite the scene's macabre elements, Macbeth is
shown in deep meditation, oblivious to the nightmare world he inhabits as if he were at the quiet
center of a raging storm. Barker's conception of
a composed Macbeth suggests that these supernatural occurrences are the product of the hero's
own imagination, a playing out of the evil thoughts
that haunt him.

1. J. H. S. Pigott of Brockley Hall near Clevedon was an avid collector of Barker's work. He first bought one of the pictures Barker
   sent back from Rome in the early 1790s and eventually spent
   more than £7,000 on his paintings (this figure is quoted in Mary
   Holbrook, "Painters in Bath in the Eighteenth Century," *Apollo*
   98 [November 1973], p. 381).
2. Dotson 1973 lists in her appendix sixteen images of the first
   subject and twenty of the second. The next subjects in order of
   popularity are Macbeth and Lady Macbeth after the murder of
   Duncan and Lady Macbeth sleepwalking, which tie at fourteen.

Friedrich Brockmann

A relatively obscure German painter, Brockmann
receives only a brief mention in Thième-Becker. He
was born on 20 January 1809 in Güstrow in Meck-
lenburg. Around 1830 he studied at the Düsseldorf
Academy and throughout this decade occasionally
contributed works to the exhibitions of the Berlin
Academy. His career was somewhat peripatetic. He
worked in Rostock, just north of his hometown,
around 1838, in Dresden around 1844, and had settled in Hamburg at least by 1854. In 1849, when he
executed the Folger painting, he may have already
been living in this last city, a seaport with ties to
England.

4 (Plate 16)

PORTIA AND NERISSA

The Merchant of Venice I, 2

1849

Oil on canvas, 41½ × 35¾ in. (109.4 × 90.9 cm.)

Case no. 1101

Signed and dated along the edge of the table at lower right: "F Brockmann 1849"

Provenance: Presented by a Mr. J. A. H. Bell to the Museum of the Brooklyn Institute of Arts and Sciences (now the Brooklyn Museum) on 28 June 1898; deaccessioned for $22 sometime between 1900, when it appeared in a publication of the museum's holdings, and 1906, when it was absent from the next published catalogue (the museum's file card is marked "unfit for Exhibition"); bought by Folger from Rosenbach, December 1922, $577.50.

References: Museum of the Brooklyn Institute of Arts and Sciences, *Catalogue of Paintings,* 1900, no. 27, as "Portia and Narissa [sic]"

Condition: The canvas is a tabby weave; the tacking edges have been removed; and the canvas has been glue-lined onto a commercially prepared canvas with a ground.

This picture entered the Folger collection as portraits of the two American actresses Charlotte and Susan Cushman in the roles of Portia and Nerissa. In 1849, when the painting was executed, the two sisters, who were thirty-three and twenty-seven years old, respectively, had already enjoyed a triumphant reception in England. (They had made their debuts as Romeo and Juliet in London on 30 December 1845.) Susan's career, however, was extremely brief, as she retired from the stage after her marriage in March 1848. Yet when the painting entered the collection of the Brooklyn Institute of Arts and Sciences in 1898, it had no association with the Cushmans, nor do the generalized figures resemble them. Rather than in the traditions of the theater and theatrical portraiture, the painting's pedigree is to be found in works such as Friedrich Overbeck's *Italia and Germania,* completed in 1828 (Neue Pinakothek, Munich), which pairs two idealized women.

Portia is depicted pensively reflecting on her predicament, her father before his death having sworn her to marry only the suitor who could pick the correct casket from three choices. Each bears a cryptic inscription engraved on its top and each contains a scroll and an object inside assessing the suitor's choice. Portia holds in her right hand the piece of paper found in the gold casket; the silver casket appears beside the open gold one on the table; and Nerissa holds the correct choice, the lead casket. The moment illustrated is presumably when Nerissa voices her support of Portia's father's injunction: "Your father was ever virtuous, and holy men at their death have good inspirations; therefore the lott'ry that he hath devised in these three chests of gold, silver, and lead, whereof who chooses his meaning chooses you, will, no doubt, never be chosen by any rightly but one who you shall rightly love."

Brockmann's style is one of simple contours and smooth surfaces. The women, with their large hands and bulky Venetian costumes, exhibit a somewhat ponderous beauty, a nineteenth-century interpretation of works by such Renaissance artists as Sebastiano del Piombo and Palma Vecchio. Nerissa is subordinated to Portia in both her position and dress. She has blond hair, while Portia's is dark, this last a surprising detail in light of Bassanio's rapturous description of her picture contained in the lead casket: "Here in her hairs / The painter plays the spider, and hath woven / A golden mesh t'entrap the hearts of men / Faster than gnats in cobwebs" (III, 2). The two women stand in a lavish interior with marble table, doorway, and columns. The space, however, is not entirely coherent: three walls are shown but none of them seem to join at a right angle. Outside the window can be glimpsed a corner of the Doge's Palace on the Grand Canal.

Brockmann clearly embraced the subject as a suitable example of *Schwesterschaft,* but he seems to have had little understanding of the play itself. He conveys Portia's melancholy mood with which the scene opens but suggests none of her lively wit. The women at this point in the story are also not privy to the caskets' contents, as each chest is opened only after it is selected by a suitor. Shakespeare also takes pains to differentiate Belmont, Portia's home, from the world of Venice. Belmont is a serene haven away from the cares of the masculine, mercantile city, and Brockmann's juxtaposition of the two worlds, with his placement of a glimpse of Venice outside the window, violates the spirit as well as the letter of the text.

John Cawse (nos. 5–13)

Born around 1779 in London, Cawse started out as a political cartoonist. *The State of the Bowels*, his earliest known caricature, is dated 4 November 1794, but the majority date between the fall of 1799 and the spring of the following year. In 1801 he began to exhibit at the Royal Academy; his early work consisted primarily of portraits and genre pieces. In 1814 and 1815, he exhibited only paintings of horses, most, if not all, commissioned by a single patron, J. P. Kellerman. After 1816, he did not appear again at the Royal Academy until 1830, exhibiting portraits and literary subjects every year but one until 1834 and making one last appearance ten years later. He exhibited sporadically at the British Institution from 1807 until 1845 and at the Society of British Artists from 1827 to 1845. The addresses given in these various exhibition catalogues show that Cawse moved frequently, perhaps because of difficulties with creditors. He supplemented his income by teaching painting and published two books offering practical rather than theoretical advice: *Introduction to the Art of Painting in Oil Colours*, 1822 (second edition, 1829), and *The Art of Painting Portraits, Landscapes, Animals, Draperies, Saints, &c. in Oil Colours*, 1840. At the end of the latter

book he included an advertisement for pupils at "Half-a-Guinea for a lesson of two hours, at the residence of the pupil." Cawse often repeated subjects, obviously happy to turn out additional versions of successful compositions. He was particularly attracted to the common, often comic characters in Shakespeare's history plays *I Henry IV*, *II Henry IV*, *Henry V*, and *II Henry VI*. His favorite characters—not surprisingly, given his background as a cartoonist—were Falstaff and the figures who surround him. The artist died on 19 January 1862.

5

FALSTAFF BOASTING TO PRINCE HAL AND POINS
I Henry IV II, 4
ca. 1820s
Oil on canvas, 13¹¹/₁₆ × 17⁷/₁₆ in. (34.9 × 44.3 cm.)

Case no. 2061

Inscriptions: The piece of paper tacked to the wall above Falstaff appears to read, "Bill of Fare."

Provenance: Parsons, May 1930

Condition: There are severe drying cracks in the background and the paint appears to have been

5

burnt during a previous lining (probably by Finlayson in 1932), particularly on the left side. There is some abrasion to the paint from a heavy-handed cleaning in the past. A lining fabric was attached to the reverse in a restoration of 1988.

Versions: A larger version of this subject (27 × 32½ in.) is in the collection of Mr. and Mrs. E. Hal Dickson, Mr. and Mrs. James R. Duncan, and Mr. and Mrs. Frank W. Rose, San Angelo, Tex. It is reproduced in Montgomery, 1985–86, no. 10, and in color in Ashton 1990, pp. 80–81.

6

FALSTAFF MOCKING BARDOLPH'S NOSE

I Henry IV III, 3
ca. 1820s
Oil on canvas, 13¼ × 16⅞ in. (33.6 × 42.8 cm.)

Case no. 2061

Provenance: Parsons, May 1930, £18. (The subject is incorrectly identified in an old photograph of the painting by A. C. Cooper [ART File S528kla, no. 79], which Parsons presumably sent to Folger, as "Merry W. of W.")

Condition: The paint surface is scarred by deep drying cracks and wrinkled paint, as Cawse seems to have used bitumen, soft resins, and fast-drying glazes over slower-drying underpaint. The picture has in the past been extensively repainted to compensate for the faulty technique. A linen fabric was attached to the reverse in a 1988 restoration.

Similar in size, nos. 5 and 6 are surely intended as pendants. Both focus on moments when Falstaff's

imaginative wit is seen at its best. The floorboards in the first painting slant to the right, those in the second to the left, helping to bond the two images together. Except for Falstaff's butter-yellow doublet, the colors of the costumes vary slightly from one painting to the other.

Both scenes enjoyed great popularity with artists. In the first scene, Falstaff, holding his buckler and sword, describes to the Prince and Poins, who attempt to refrain from laughing, how he valiantly fought with a hundred men. Falstaff, accompanied by Bardolph, Gadshill, and Peto, had robbed travelers of their money, only to have a disguised Prince and Poins set upon them and easily seize the money, though outnumbered. Only one of the henchmen appears with Falstaff, and it is surely Bardolph who is depicted behind him making a contemptuous gesture for the telling of a lie. Behind Bardolph is Mistress Quickly, the hostess of the inn.

In the second picture, Bardolph points to Falstaff's stomach, joking about its large dimensions, while Sir John, retaliating, launches into a peroration on Bardolph's flaming red nose. Falstaff holds center stage, Bardolph being relegated to the role of a foil for his humor. Despite his ample girth, Falstaff, still holding the buckler from his previous scene, looks almost heroic next to the ungainly, crouching Bardolph, whose fanciful costume adds to the ridiculousness of his appearance.

7

FALSTAFF, PRINCE HAL, AND MISTRESS QUICKLY

I Henry IV III, 3
ca. 1820s
Oil on canvas, 25 × 30¼ in. (63.6 × 76.9 cm.)

Case no. 1827

Provenance: Parsons & Sons, September 1928, £45

Condition: When Finlayson's lining of 1932 was removed and replaced in 1988, some remnants of an old inscription were found. Those parts that could be read gave the artist's name, "J. Cawse," and the play, "Henry II, Part 2nd." There is a thin, off-white gesso ground. The oil-paint film appears to have been applied at two times. The original paint layer is of medium thickness with some light impasto, and there is a less hard design layer over it. Even this top layer shows the result of changes: Mistress

6

7

Quickly's gown has undergone alterations and the window at one time extended further to the right.

Despite the writing on the canvas's verso citing the play as "Henry II, Part 2nd" (by which is presumably meant "Henry IV, Part 2nd"), the scene appears to be the confrontation between Falstaff and Mistress Quickly over his accusation that she had picked his pockets, which takes place in *I Henry IV.* Prince Hal is drawn into the argument as Mistress Quickly seeks his support. Cawse chooses to leave out Peto, whose role is minimal, and depicts Bardolph coming around the arras rather than already part of the company. Presumably this is the same arras behind which Falstaff had earlier been sleeping when his pockets were searched. Cawse depicts Falstaff mischievously enjoying Mistress Quickly's distressed anger, while an aloof and somewhat foppish Prince listens to her ranting with benign amusement. Even though the Prince takes Mistress Quickly's side of the argument, he too is enjoying her discomfort over Falstaff's witty rejoinders. Cawse conveys this visually by having Mistress Quickly stand alone, while the Prince and Falstaff are side by side.

It is perhaps the king's portrait that hangs above the arras, as the figure appears to wear a crown. The subject of the tapestry on the rear wall is difficult to discern, but it may also show a king, surrounded by soldiers and courtiers. Prince Hal stands directly beneath this figure, a foreshadowing of his transformation from a dissolute youth into a dignified monarch.

8

FALSTAFF CHOOSING HIS RECRUITS
II Henry IV III, 2
1818
Oil on canvas, 25⅛ × 30 in. (63.8 × 76.1 cm.)

Case no. 2022

Signed and dated at lower left at bottom of carpet: "J. Cawse 1818"

Provenance: Parsons, January 1930, £31.10.0, as a scene from *The Merry Wives of Windsor.* (This misidentification may have been deliberate, since Parsons had already sold a painting by Cawse of this subject to Folger. An old photograph with this identification can be found in ART File S528klb, no. 57.)

Exhibitions: A painting of this subject was exhibited at Amherst in 1959. Since there were then four paintings with the same title in the collection (see nos. 9, 10, and D13), it is impossible to know which one was exhibited.

8

Condition: Finlayson's 1932 lining was replaced in 1988. There is the remnant of an inscription under the lining fabric: "In Examination of the Recruits by / Justice and Shallow in Interior / by Sir John Falstaff / 2 Part of King Henry 4th / Carente[?] J. Cawse 1818." The ground consists of a thin, coarse off-white gesso. Preliminary drawing on the gesso ground is visible in the floor and back wall. The underdrawing is in blue, and the lines often do not correspond to the stonework as completed. The paint layer has been thinly applied, and there is considerable abrasion, particularly at the top and bottom. The paint film was prepared with an excess of oil, leading to shrinkage and the appearance of nondirectional, linked rifts in the dark colors. There is old damage located just behind Francis Feeble's left hand. The other versions make clear that he was holding a scissors, although the handles of the scissors, falling in the damaged area, are now lost.

Versions: See no. 9 and figs. 11 and 12. In 1818 Cawse exhibited this same scene at the Society of Painters in Water Colours (no. 134). The catalogue entry reads, "Sir John Falstaff examining his Recruits / *Falstaff.* What trade art thou? *Feeble.* A

Woman's tailor, Sir. / *Second Part of King Henry the Fourth.*" Another version, closest to the Yale version (B1975.5.22), was sold at Sotheby, London, 16 May 1984, lot 212, repr., incorrectly identified as "Pistol announcing to Sir John Falstaff the Death of King Henry IV." It was signed and dated 1819 and measured 24 by 29½ inches.

Falstaff has come to his old friend Justice Shallow in order to select recruits for his company. They are accompanied by Shallow's cousin Silence, who records the selections with his quill pen. Even the dog at the fat knight's feet seems to be skeptical about the motley group gathered at the right.

Cawse condenses two moments in this picture. The first is when the tailor Francis Feeble, identified by the pair of scissors he holds, steps forward unafraid to be picked for service. The second is a later moment when Peter Bullcalf, whose example is soon followed by Ralph Mouldy, bribes Bardolph into letting him remain behind. As arranged by Cawse, Feeble would seem to be followed by Thomas Wart, who is described as ragged in appearance. Next to him is presumably Ralph Mouldy, his knock-kneed pose suggesting moldy inactivity and his finer clothes the ability to afford a bribe. Then

Fig. 11. John Cawse, *Falstaff Choosing His Recruits.* Lithograph, 13½ × 17¾ in. (image).

Fig. 12. John Cawse, *Falstaff and the Recruits.* Oil on canvas, 25¼ × 35¼ in. Yale Center for British Art, Paul Mellon Fund.

comes the thin-faced Simon Shadow, who "presents no mark to the enemy." At the right, Bardolph accepts the bribe from Bullcalf, while the last figure is an old bearded man, his hands clasped together in supplication. The stage directions mention servants and a soldier who enters with Bardolph, but this last figure is probably intended as an unnamed recruit who helps fill out the ranks of those called for inspection. The scale of the figures is slightly awry, with those on the right too large in relationship to the seated figures on the left.

This is the only dated version of this scene, and it may well be the earliest. Cawse also executed a lithograph in 1824 or later (fig. 11),[1] which offers a close-up view of the scene excluding Shallow at the left and Bardolph and the two other figures at the right. In addition to a phallic hat and scissors, Francis Feeble holds a corset beneath his left arm, and the concentration on the figures' comic expressions is even more pronounced.

Another version (fig. 12) at the Yale Center for British Art was once owned by Folger. It is more closely related to this work than to no. 9, although the rendering of the interior is simpler. Whereas the 1818 painting has a carved coat of arms over the doorway, and its device is surely comic (it is used again in no. 10), hanging on the wall in the Yale version is a shield with a rabbit painted on it, a reference to the cowardly nature of the majority of the recruits and of the men selecting them.

1. Previously the lithograph has been identified as by Bunbury, but it is signed within the image at lower left, "J. Cawse." The watermark dates the paper to 1824. Only the tops of the numbers are visible, the rest having been cropped when the paper was cut, but comparison with other dates by J. Whatman, the firm that made this paper, confirm these numbers. The image is 13 1/2 × 17 3/4 in.

9

FALSTAFF CHOOSING HIS RECRUITS
II Henry IV III, 2
ca. 1820s
Oil on canvas, 21 × 28 in. (53.5 × 71.2 cm.)

Case no. 1404

Written in black ink at upper left on the back of the canvas used in relining the original (presumably repeats earlier inscription that was covered over): "Sir John Falstaff. / Chosing his Recruits / Henry the 4th / -Shakespeare-."

Provenance: Maggs, March 1925, $235, as by Thomas Stothard

Condition: Lined by Finlayson in 1932.

Versions: See the entry for no. 8.

This version lacks the detailed, precise execution of the 1818 painting, and most likely is a more rapidly executed later work. Particularly noticeable is Cawse's scaling down of the room and his abandonment of the rigid grid pattern formed by the small squares of the pavement and the ruled lines of the coursing on the stone wall. The positioning and the cast of characters remain virtually the same, but the figure at the far right in the earlier version has now been dropped. In addition, at the left Shallow now pricks the names on the list, while Silence looks on holding a red book. The size of the figures has not altered, but the compressed format brings the viewer closer to the scene, and the two groups of figures at left and right are better integrated.

As with the lithograph (fig. 11) and the Yale version (fig. 12), no. 9 has military paraphernalia in the foreground, in this case a drum with a spear that directs the viewer's attention back toward Silence.

10

BARDOLPH AND FALSTAFF PUTTING WART THROUGH THE DRILL
II Henry IV III, 2
1827?
Oil on canvas, 23 9/16 × 33 1/8 in. (59.8 × 84.1 cm.)

Case no. 2052

Provenance: Bought by Wills at Hodgson & Co. sale, 28 November (year not given), no. 264, £25, according to note in file; Kelly, March 1930, $300

Exhibitions: Cawse exhibited a painting of this subject at the Society of British Artists in 1827. The catalogue entry reads, "376 Sir John Falstaff at Justice Shallow's in Gloucestershire, selecting his Recruits / Bardolph—'Hold, Wart traverse thus, thus, thus.'" It is possible that this was the Folger picture.

Condition: The canvas is separating from its lining and is starting to buckle. The surface of the paint is solvent-abraded, and the ground is visible in the bottom right corner where the paint has flaked.

9

10

The moment depicted occurs soon after Falstaff has made his final pick of his recruits. To prove the suitability of his choices, he instructs his corporal, "Put me a caliver [light musket] into Wart's hand, Bardolph." Bardolph, who holds a halberd, then orders the recruit, "Hold, Wart, traverse [quick march]; thus, thus, thus." And Falstaff encouragingly adds, "Come, manage me your caliver. So: very well; go to; very good, exceeding good. O, give me always a little, lean, old, chapt, bald shot. Well said, i' faith, Wart; thou'rt a good scab." The luckless Wart is put through the drill, while Francis Feeble, still clutching his scissors, looks on. The knock-kneed figure is presumably still Ralph

Mouldy, with Simon Shadow, as befits his name, barely visible between him and Peter Bullcalf. At the left Falstaff, now in a more expansive mood, shows off his recruits to an astonished Justice Silence and Justice Shallow, who have exchanged the hats given them in the picture of an earlier moment in this same scene (no. 8).

The figures are handled with a dramatic flair and animation that at times eluded the artist. Folger must have been unusually fond of the painting, as he had it hung in his office at 26 Broadway. Unfortunately, he was not able to enjoy it for long, dying soon after it was acquired.

11

PISTOL ANNOUNCING TO FALSTAFF
THE DEATH OF THE KING
II Henry IV V, 3
ca. 1820
Oil on canvas, 20½ × 30⅝ in. (52.2 × 78 cm.)

Case no. 1719

Provenance: Parsons, August 1927, £45

Condition: Lined by Finlayson in 1932.

Versions: See no. 12. Cawse exhibited a version of this subject at the British Institution in 1820 entitled *Pistol Announcing to Sir John Falstaff the*

Death of King Henry IV (no. 294) with the line, "Sir John, thy tender lambkin now is king." In 1819 he had exhibited this subject at the Society of Painters in Water Colours (no. 47). A version was also sold at Sotheby, London, 16 May 1984, lot 213, repr., incorrectly identified as "The Quarrel between Sir John Falstaff, Doll and Pistol" (*II Henry IV* I, 4). It was signed and dated 1820. Though its proportions (24 × 29½ in.) and background are closer to those of no. 12, in its arrangement of the figures it more closely resembles no. 11.

The scene is set behind Justice Shallow's home, where the party partakes of his hospitality. At the far left sit the Page and Bardolph. A boisterous Silence, dressed in blue with red stockings, sings with empty glass and bottle held high. Falstaff listens attentively to Pistol, who, after bantering with an anxious Shallow, finally blurts out, "Sir John, thy tender lambkin now is king." To the right stands Davy, Shallow's servant.

The decorated frame of the large doorway contains carvings of sardonic figures: a lion at the upper left and a cloven-hoofed devil at the right. The shield over the door has the same design that appears in the escutcheon in the 1818 *Falstaff* (no. 8). The painting's long rectangular shape suggests that it may have been intended to hang over a mantelpiece or a door.

11

12

12

**PISTOL ANNOUNCING TO FALSTAFF
THE DEATH OF THE KING**
II Henry IV V, 3
ca. 1820s
Oil on canvas, 24⁷⁄₈ × 30¹⁄₈ in. (63.2 × 76.5 cm.)

Case no. 1443

Provenance: Maggs, July 1925, £52.10.0 (purchased as by Thomas Stothard, and as a pendant of no. 9, but given their different dimensions, there is no reason to see these works as pendants).

Exhibitions: The measurements for the British Institution picture of 1820 (no. 294) were listed as 39 by 42 inches. Since this includes the frame, it is not impossible that the Folger picture is the exhibited work.

Condition: The painting was last conserved in 1988, when it was relined. Distracting drying cracks and some minor abrasions were also retouched at this time.

Versions: See the entry for no. 11.

More broadly painted than no. 11, no. 12 is also more compact in composition, permitting a stronger focus on the figures. Silence, who under the influence of drink is anything but quiet, is dressed all in red, his thin, elongated form now more noticeably contrasted with Falstaff's pumpkin-like rotundity. Shallow is still between the two principals, but his sober attire makes him less obtrusive, and Pistol, with a full head of hair, now appears a more dashing figure. Bardolph and Davy at the right have identical expressions, the only difference being that Bardolph has the required red nose.

13

AUTOLYCUS SELLING HIS WARES
The Winter's Tale IV, 4
ca. 1830[1]
Oil on canvas, 25¹⁄₈ × 30¹⁄₈ in. (63.8 × 76.5 cm.)

Case no. 2061

Signed beneath railing of stairway at the far right in black paint: "[Ca]wse"

Provenance: Parsons, May 1930, £44

13

Condition: The original canvas is a tabby weave, commercially prepared, with a ground. The bottom tacking edge is an original tacking edge, which has not been painted. The left, top, and right tacking edges have been cut off, and the painted canvas has been folded around to provide the present tacking edges. There is a second tacking edge along the bottom, further indicating that the canvas has been on a larger stretcher and that the earliest conception of the painting was larger than what we see now. The window at the left continues on into the tacking edge. The strip of wall or post at the left (cropped in the reproduction) was added to close the composition visually when it was reduced to this smaller format. The dark strip continues down over the chair, creating an awkward perspective. On the far right, pentimenti reveal changes in the staircase. While repaint is extensive throughout the painting, it is particularly noticeable in the bottom portion of the figure of Autolycus and on the clown's red suit. This repaint covers both the extensive cracking and solvent abrasion of the paint surface.

Traditionally, this scene is set out of doors on a green in front of the shepherd's cottage, a pastoral landscape suitable for dancing. Cawse, however, sets his figures within the cottage, where the roguish peddler Autolycus has been invited in during a celebration so that the company might examine his wares. Standing at the left with a patch on his cloak, he selects a ballad from his overflowing box. In the center stand the two shepherdesses Dorcas and Mopsa. Mopsa, holding a blue ribbon, turns to her suitor, the clown, who had promised to buy her a present. The clown, dressed in a striking costume of red and black, appears less of a simpleton than is customary.

The spears and buckler with the long center spike are familiar props in Cawse's paintings, and the spiral staircase at the right appears more decorative than functional. In what is very much a staged performance, the posing of the figures is somewhat stilted, Cawse offering another reincarnation of a simpler, more idyllic time. The figure style has changed from his earlier paintings, as he now relies more on bright colors and broader modeling.

1. The picture can be dated to around 1830 based on a penned inscription in the lower right quadrant of the back of the canvas: "Autolycus Mopsa Dorcas / vide Winters Tale / Painted by Cawse / No 9 Henrietta St. / Covt Garden / London." In 1828, Cawse was living at 6 Great George Street, Euston Square, but in 1830 he is listed as living at 9 Henrietta Street, Covent Garden, where he resided until 1832.

14

Alexander Christie

Born in Edinburgh in 1807, Christie trained at the Trustees Academy beginning in 1833 and then worked and studied for a short time in London. Beginning in 1837 he exhibited almost annually at the Royal Scottish Academy, becoming an associate member in 1848. A good many of his early exhibition pieces were taken from Shakespeare, including subjects drawn from the comedies, history plays, and tragedies. He died on 5 May 1860.

14

HAMLET FINDING THE KING AT PRAYER
Hamlet III, 3
1842
Oil sketch on canvas, 28½ × 36 in. (72.4 × 91.5 cm.)

Signed and dated at lower left: "A Christie 1842" (the "C" is superimposed over the "A"). Lettering in Gothic style beneath crucifix at right: "Deus Ultionum."

Provenance: Collection of Sir Henry Irving; his sale, Christie's, 16 December 1905, lot 90

Exhibitions: Edinburgh, Royal Scottish Academy, 1842, no. 472, as "Drawing: Hamlet finding the King at Prayer"; Washington, 1976–77, no. 1

Condition: The oil is thinly applied as a wash over penciled lines, some of which have been drawn with a ruler.

The central scene depicts the kneeling Claudius praying before a crucifix as he asks God for forgiveness for his crime against his brother, whom he had secretly killed in order to obtain his wife and his throne. At the same time, he realizes that true repentance requires restitution and that this he is not willing to do. His crown beneath the crucifix is a reminder of his worldly ambition. Hamlet, gray against a blue background, comes around the curtain prepared to kill his uncle, but pauses as he resolves to wait for a more opportune moment.

This scene is placed within a simulated frame with elaborate strapwork across its top. In the center is an image of the Ghost, a gem sparkling on his chest. He and the drapery beneath are painted in the same gray color, almost as if it were an extension of his body. He and Hamlet are both rendered on the same small scale in order to focus attention on Claudius's meditation. But the Ghost's centrality and looming presence are appropriate reminders of his importance in instigating the play's action. He hovers over his brother at the same time as he compels his son to seek vengeance for his murder. A bust of Queen Gertrude is on the left and one of Ophelia on the right. Gertrude is supported by a bat-like wing, while Ophelia is endowed with an angelic one.

The framed central image is superimposed on a red stage-like curtain with an elaborately embroidered bottom. The curtain curls over on itself at both ends. Christie perhaps intended *Hamlet Finding the King at Prayer* as a virtuoso display of his abilities in handling complex ornamental patterns on several levels of reality. At any rate, the Trustees' School was impressed enough with his talents to employ him the following year as an assistant in its ornamental department and two years after that as its director.

George Clint

George Clint, a painter of portraits and genre and literary subjects, is best known for his theatrical portraits, to which he turned in mid-career. Born in London on 12 April 1770, he struggled in his early years, working first for a fishmonger, then in an attorney's office, and later as a housepainter. After marrying, he took the risk of attempting to become an artist, finding employment as a miniature painter, an engraver, and even a sign painter. He exhibited his first work, a portrait, at the Royal Academy in 1802. He was introduced to theatrical circles while executing his mezzotint, published in 1819, after George Henry Harlow's painting *The Court Scene for the Trial of Queen Katharine* (see fig. 92). He submitted his first theatrical portrait to the Royal Academy that same year, a picture of three actors in a scene from the eighteenth-century play *The Clandestine Marriage*. In 1820 he exhibited his celebrated picture of Edmund Kean as Sir Giles Overreach (see fig. 97). The next year he was elected an associate of the Royal Academy, but, disillusioned when he failed to advance to full membership, he resigned in 1835. He exhibited numerous theatrical portraits until 1832, when he turned to scenes from plays that were not based on specific productions. He last exhibited at the Royal Academy in 1845 and at the Society of British Artists in 1847. He died on 10 May 1854.

15

FALSTAFF RELATING HIS VALIANT EXPLOITS
I Henry IV II, 4
ca. mid-1830s
Oil on canvas, 34³⁄₄ × 47 in. (88.3 × 119.5 cm.)

Case no. 1648

Provenance: Robson, March 1927, 60 guineas (£63), as "Falstaff at the Boar's Head Tavern" by Robert Smirke

Exhibitions: Amherst, 1959, as by Smirke

Condition: The original canvas is a twill weave. Its tacking edges have been removed, and it has been glue-lined to a commercially prepared canvas with a ground, probably in 1932. The paint is thickly applied with impasto in some areas, but the surface has suffered from solvent abrasion in an earlier restoration, from extensive repainting in the separation cracks and areas of paint loss, and from having been flattened when it was lined.

Falstaff, dressed in a yellow jerkin and red pants, is describing to Prince Hal and Poins his invented tale of having fought with a hundred men who had taken from him the money he had just stolen from travelers. His two amused listeners were, of course, the "hundred" men who, unaided and wearing disguises, had routed Falstaff and his gang. At the left are Sir John's three cohorts, Gadshill, Peto, and Bardolph, while at the right Francis brings in refreshments.

When Folger acquired this painting from Robson & Co. in 1927, it was ascribed to Robert Smirke and said to have been painted about 1800. The date is too early for the style of the picture, and it is given here to George Clint. The skillful grouping of the figures, the scene's dry humor, and bravura passages such as the treatment of Francis's costume are typical of Clint's style. The characterization of the figures closely resembles a painting by Clint of this same scene depicting an 1832 performance at Drury Lane in which William Dowton played Falstaff,

15

John Cooper played Prince Hal, and John Balls played Poins.[1] The heads, though, in the Folger picture do not appear to be portraits, removing this work from the realm of theatrical portraiture.

In 1833, Clint exhibited at the Royal Academy another version of this same scene, a work executed for Lord Egremont and still at Petworth House.[2] The entry in the Royal Academy catalogue reads, "Falstaff relating his valiant exploits at the Boar's Head, Eastcheap," and the line quoted is, "I tell thee what, Hal, etc." Falstaff takes a defensive position at the left, holding his buckler in his left hand and his sword in his right. He faces a smirking Prince Hal and Poins, who are seated at a table at the right. In this work and the Folger painting, the prince and his friend appear as identical twins with a slight overbite, an eccentricity that helps to confirm the attribution of the Folger painting to Clint. The artist also exhibited this subject at the Society of British Artists in 1836 (no. 103) with the title *Falstaff at the Boar's Head* and Falstaff's line, "I made no more ado, but took all their seven points in my target, thus." It is possible that this was the Folger painting, although from the line quoted one would expect to see Falstaff holding his buckler.

The Folger picture, which is considerably larger than the Petworth painting (18½ × 28 in.), is ulti-mately a more heroic interpretation. The costumes are elaborate and the figures somewhat decorous participants in a comic scene treated on a grand scale.

1. Reproduced in Raymond Mander and Joe Mitchenson, *A Picture History of the British Theatre*, London, 1957, fig. 240. At that time it was in the Child's Gallery, Boston.
2. Reproduced in Altick 1985, pl. 104.

Richard Cook (nos. 16–17)

Although Cook was a Royal Academician, surprisingly little is known about his career, in part because his output was limited and the whereabouts of few of his paintings are now known. Born in London in 1784, Cook entered the Royal Academy schools in 1800. His exhibited pieces have often been confused with works by other artists apparently bearing the same name, one of whom was a portrait painter, another a landscapist.[1] Cook first exhibited at the British Institution in 1807, submitting two biblical subjects, and the following year he submitted two more works, one scriptural and the other from Homer's *Iliad*. In 1809 and 1810 he also exhibited classical subjects at the British Institution. He was first represented at the Royal Academy in 1809, submitting a work from English history with, for him, an unusual emphasis on portraiture, *The Bill of Rights Presented by the Lords and Commons of England to the Prince and Princess of Orange.* During this time he was also active as a book illustrator, executing a number of works published by W. Suttaby as well as illustrating editions of two Scottish poets, Scott's *The Lady of the Lake* and Campbell's *Gertrude of Wyoming.* In 1814 Cook exhibited a scene from Ovid at the Royal Academy and in 1816 four of his subjects from *The Lady of the Lake.* In the latter year he was elected an associate member and in 1822 was made an academician. His diploma picture *Ceres, Disconsolate for the Loss of Proserpine, Rejects the Solicitation of Iris, Sent to Her by Jupiter,* from Homer's *Hymn to Ceres,* also exhibited in 1816, forms part of the Royal Academy's permanent collection and is the only other painting by Cook whose present whereabouts is known. In 1819, the last year his work appeared in public, he exhibited one more subject from *The Lady of the Lake.* From this time he seems to have abandoned painting. Marrying a wealthy lady, he was able to live comfortably in his London home at Cumberland Place, Hyde Park, until his death on 11 March 1857.

1. The addresses given in the catalogues make clear that more than one "R. Cook" was at work during these years. While Algernon Graves has scrambled them together in his list of works exhibited at the Royal Academy and at the British Institution, it is possible, using the addresses, to separate the academician's work from that of his similarly named contemporaries. Redgrave's entry in his *A Dictionary of Artists of the English School* and the entry in the *Dictionary of National Biography* also confuse Richard Cook, R.A., with these other artists.

16

HELEN AND PRIAM AT THE SCÆAN GATE
Homer, *Iliad*, book III
1808
Oil on canvas, 11½ × 9½ in. (29.3 × 24 cm.)

Case no. 1916

Provenance: See no. 17.

Engravings: F. Engleheart, published by W. Suttaby, London, 31 August 1809, 3 × 2⁷/₁₆ in. (image). This engraving appeared in Suttaby's Edition of Poetical Translations according to Hamilton 1831; engraved by Normand, *fils,* for Hamilton 1831.

16

17

HECTOR REPROVING PARIS
Homer, *Iliad*, book VI
1808 (written at top of relined canvas in pencil, presumably what had been on the original canvas: "April 1808")
Oil on canvas, 11⁹/₁₆ × 9½ in. (29.4 × 24.1 cm.)

Case no. 1916

Provenance: A number of oil sketches of *Hector Reproving Paris* sold at the artist's posthumous sale held at Christie's on 1 June 1857 (lots 246, 276, 290, and 315). If the Folger paintings were in the sale and were sold together, then the likely lots are narrowed to 246 ("Hector and Paris, &c.—in oils" [five works in all]) and 264 ("Two, from the Iliad; and two, from the Odyssey"); Parsons, June 1929, £11 less 10 percent (information on back of Parson's photograph of each painting), both works sold as by Thomas Stothard, no. 16 as a scene from *Pericles,* no. 17 as a scene from *Antony and Cleopatra.*

Exhibitions: Washington, 1976–77, no. 21, as Stothard's *Anthony and Cleopatra*

Condition: Both paintings were lined by Finlayson in 1932, and both linings are still in good condition. Each painting suffers from some solvent abrasion, and no. 16 has a hole filled in 6 inches from the right and 9 inches from the bottom.

Bought as by Stothard and as depicting scenes from Shakespeare's *Antony and Cleopatra* and *Pericles*, the paintings are illustrations by Richard Cook to Alexander Pope's translation of Homer's *Iliad*. The first scene shows Helen on the Scæan Gate, having just entered with her two attendants Clymène and Æthra. A seated Priam greets her with two Trojan chiefs behind him.

> They [the chiefs] cry'd, No wonder such
>   Celestial Charms
> For nine long Years have set the World in Arms;
> What winning Graces! what majestick Mien!
> She moves a Goddess, and she looks a Queen!
> Yet hence Oh Heav'n! convey that fatal Face,
> And from Destruction save the *Trojan* Race.
> The good old *Priam* welcom'd her, and cry'd,
> Approach my Child, and grace thy Father's Side.
>
> (Book III, lines 205–12)

17

The moment is prior to the duel between Paris, Helen's Trojan husband, and Menelaus, her former Greek husband. It was Helen's departure with Paris that had led to the war, and in this painting she appropriately appears as a demure vision of classical beauty who is subdued by the consequences of her earlier defection. In the distance one sees Paris riding out in his chariot to meet his challenger. Soldiers are lined up awaiting the outcome of the combat, and beyond them can be seen the tents and ships of the Greeks.

The second scene shows Hector, the leader of the Trojan army, chastising his brother Paris for lingering at home rather than continuing to fight. Both Paris and Helen are shamed by his rebuke, and Paris is about to lay aside the lyre in favor of the weapons at his feet.

> A Spear the Hero [Hector] bore of wondrous
>   Strength,
> Of full ten Cubits was the Lance's Length,
> The steely Point with golden Ringlets join'd,
> Before him brandish'd, at each Motion shin'd.
> Thus entring in the glitt'ring Rooms, he found
> His Brother-Chief, whose useless Arms lay
>   round,
> His Eyes delighting with their splendid Show,
> Bright'ning the Shield, and polishing the Bow.
> Beside him, *Helen* with her Virgins stands,
> Guides their rich Labours, and instructs their
>   Hands.
>
> (Book VI, lines 394–403)

Cook departs from the text, influenced by two earlier paintings depicting a different moment from the *Iliad*. In book III Paris was soon bested by Menelaus in their combat, only to be rescued from certain death by Venus, who, returning him to his palace, reunites him with Helen before their bridal bed. David had made this moment famous in his painting *Paris and Helen* (Louvre, Paris), which he exhibited at the Salon of 1789.[1] Richard Westall also exhibited his *The Reconciliation of Helen and Paris, after His Defeat by Menelaus* (Tate Gallery, London) at the Royal Academy in 1805. Cook shows Paris in apparel resembling that of Westall's hero, including the panther's speckled hide mentioned by Homer, and, again like Westall, he shows the pair of lovers flanked by a torchère on the left and weapons on the right.[2] Cook, however, was even more strongly influenced by David's work in that he shows Paris holding a lyre, although he is careful to depict it accurately as silver rather than gold, and in that he deploys as a backdrop a curtained screen beyond which are glimpsed caryatids. He ignored the text in favor of these earlier images in order to stress the contrast between the soft, luxurious effeminacy of Paris's self-indulgent life with Helen and the stern world of martial arts to which his brother, relying on his sense of honor, summons him.

Hector Reproving Paris is dated on its back "April 1808" and is thus almost certainly related to the larger, now missing painting of this same scene (41 × 36 in., including the frame) that Cook exhibited at the British Institution in the spring of that year. *Helen and Priam at the Scæan Gate*, on the other hand, was published in an engraving of 31 August 1809. Despite the compositions' different histories, the two Folger paintings were obviously executed as a pair. Given their small size, they may have both been intended for book illustration. Cook's posthumous sale reveals that he executed a number of subjects from the *Iliad* and the *Odyssey*, including *Achilles Drawing the Dead Body of Hector behind His Chariot* and *Ulysses and Mentor*. The two Folger works may indeed be part of an even larger series.

1. In the early nineteenth century David's painting was on view at Versailles, but it had also been engraved twice by the time Cook executed his work, in 1790 and 1802. See the exhibition catalogue *David*, Editions de la Réunion des Musées Nationaux, Paris, 1989, no. 79.
2. One would like to know if there is also a relationship between no. 16 and Westall's now missing *Helen on the Scæan Gate, Come to View the Combat between Paris and Menelaus*, which he exhibited at the Royal Academy in 1805.

Alfred Dever

Dever exhibited frequently at the Royal Academy from 1859 to 1876, and occasionally at the Society of British Artists. Judging from the titles, his subject matter could be cloyingly sentimental. He lived in London, one of a number of minor Victorian painters competing for the middle-class market. He exhibited only one Shakespearean subject, a work listed in the 1862 Royal Academy catalogue as "M. Fechter as Hamlet; a sketch." If this picture was an oil sketch rather than a drawing, then *Sir John Falstaff and Mistress Quickly* might also fit this description in terms of its lack of finish.

18

SIR JOHN FALSTAFF AND
MISTRESS QUICKLY
II Henry IV II, 1
ca. 1870 (date on Folger file card)
Oil on canvas, 23⅝ × 19¹¹/₁₆ in. (60 × 50 cm.)

Case no. 1383

Monogram on stool at lower right: large "A" over small "D" (obviously intended to resemble the monogram of Albrecht Dürer)

Provenance: Maggs, February 1925, $90

Condition: The support is a fine canvas glue-lined, presumably by Finlayson in 1932, onto a pale green commercially grounded canvas. The picture was again restored in 1988.

Mistress Quickly admonishes Sir John Falstaff before the Chief Justice, "And didst thou not kiss me and bid me fetch thee thirty shillings? I put thee now to thy book-oath. Deny it, if thou canst."[1] Dever shows the moment she is describing, one that is not enacted on the stage. Mistress Quickly dips into her purse as Falstaff successfully cajoles her into giving him the money. The setting is the Boar's Head Tavern in Eastcheap. Later in the scene Mistress Quickly laments that she will have to pawn her plate and the tapestry on the wall in the dining room if Falstaff does not pay. Dever includes these details along with Falstaff's buckler and sword, since he has just returned from battle. Two onlookers peek around the tapestry to laugh at his cunning in convincing Mistress Quickly to advance him money. The two principal figures, however, are sympathetically portrayed, Dever obviously delighting in the opportunity of depicting period dress.

The paint is thinly applied, particularly in the background passages. Artists such as Sir William Orchardson had already popularized this combination of fully developed figures against a sketchy background.

1. These lines are penned on a label glued to the top center of the stretcher.

George James De Wilde, attributed to

The painting is clearly signed "DeWilde," but the initial before the name is difficult to read. Although a curving line, it does not appear to be an "S," and

18

the picture is in any case too primitive to attribute to Samuel De Wilde (1748–1832), the prolific practitioner of theatrical portraiture between the careers of Zoffany and Clint. The initial appears most like a "J," raising the intriguing possibility that the painting is the work of George James De Wilde, Samuel's son. He was born in London on 19 January 1804 and was trained as an artist from an early age by his father. His talents, however, ultimately lay elsewhere. He took a post at the Colonial Office when he was about twenty-one, working under Sir James Stephen. It was Stephen's connections that secured him an appointment on the *Northampton Mercury* newspaper around 1830. De Wilde enjoyed

a distinguished career in Northampton, dying in his home at the *Mercury* offices on 16 September 1871. A skilled writer, he also continued to sketch throughout his life. If the inscription on the Folger picture can be trusted, it could well be an early work painted when he was around nineteen years old. The naive quality of the execution makes such an attribution at least plausible, and the design's patterned simplicity is in fact only a crude exaggeration of Samuel's style. The painting is also a self-conscious attempt at imitating Dutch painting of the seventeenth century, and, given the De Wilde family's Dutch origins, such homage is perhaps not surprising. The painting's program is complex and suggests a creator with a strong literary bent. If it is the work of George James De Wilde, it is his most ambitious painting to survive.[1] As a subject for painting the Seven Ages of Man had already proved popular,[2] but his father, Samuel, may have been the first to execute a painting in which all the characters are combined in a single canvas. One would like to know how the Folger picture relates to the missing work that Samuel exhibited at the Royal Academy in 1815 (no. 188); it seems likely that the son had a great deal of help from his father in composing his interpretation.

1. The exhibition catalogue *The De Wildes* (Northampton Central Art Gallery, 1971) reproduces only a few of his sketches, paintings by him apparently being extremely rare.
2. J. C. Gear published a print on 5 November 1792 entitled *Shakespear's Beautiful Idea on the Seven Ages of Man*, consisting of seven oval vignettes around a portrait of Shakespeare in the center. On 1 January 1796 Sarah Ashton published seven vignettes suitable for mounting on a fan. Thomas Stothard designed seven scenes for a set of prints published on 24 January 1799, and the most famous set of all was Smirke's for Boydell's Shakespeare Gallery, prints of which were issued in June 1801. Smirke had also exhibited *The Seven Ages of Man* at the Royal Academy in 1798 (no. 88), and one suspects that, though presented under one catalogue number, the entry consisted of seven separate paintings framed together. Earlier in 1796 George Francis Joseph had exhibited *The Lover* at the Royal Academy (no. 344), a painting that featured only the third stage of Shakespeare's Seven Ages.

19

THE SEVEN AGES OF MAN
As You Like It II, 7
1823
Oil on canvas, 23⅛ × 33¼ in. (58.7 × 84.5 cm.)

Case no. 1831

Signed and dated at lower left: "J [difficult to cipher with certainty] DeWilde 1823 [or possibly 1825]"

Inscribed on the title page of the book to the left of the monkey: "VORTIGERN / AND / ROWENA" (a reference to Henry Ireland's forgery, first performed in April 1796 and published in 1799). To the right of the monkey the Shakespeare Folio is opened so that one sees indications of Ben Jonson's dedication at the left and the Droeshout engraving at the right, beneath which is inscribed: "MR WM. SHAKSPEARE / 1623." Title page of book right of center: "THE / SILENT WOMAN / by / B. JONSON / A / TALE OF A TUB."

Provenance: Collection of T. L. Collins, Ramsbury (this information accompanies an old reproduction of the painting in the photographic file of the Witt Library, London; presumably the painting was published when it was for sale at the time Rosenbach bought it; it is listed as "'All the World's a Stage'" by De Wilde and dated 1823; its measurements are given as 29 by 39½ inches, which presumably includes the frame); Rosenbach, October 1928, $175.

Condition: Finlayson glue-lined the canvas on to one with a commercially prepared ground. The sky seen through the center arch is curiously divided in tone between a brighter right-hand side and a darker left.

Jaques, a companion of the banished Duke in the Forest of Arden, discourses with a jaundiced eye on the progress of an individual's life, using as his model the traditional structure of the Seven Ages of Man. The painting, with its complex arrangement of chambers and openings off a central staged space, takes literally Jaques's metaphor that all the world is a stage with exits and entrances. The birth chamber at the far left offers a happier scene of domestic contentment than is warranted by Jaques's sour description, and above the doorway a verdant landscape with a sunrise also helps strike an optimistic note. In the next of the ages the reluctant schoolboy is graced with a painting of the allegorical figure of Hope above him. The viewer is then led into the painting's deepest recess where the sighing lover, his face appropriately heavily shadowed, looks on his as-yet-unattainable love. The fourth and fifth ages are combined into one central scene, the soldier being brought before the justice. De Wilde continues the theme of the lover, suggesting that the hot-headed soldier, his glove thrown down in a challenge, now stands accused of wronging the weeping maid behind the scowling justice. The figure leaning over the scribe appears to hold a gold ring, evidence of the soldier's broken vow. De Wilde's overall conception of this central scene is indebted to Smirke's painting of the fifth age for Boydell, where the justice adjudicates a case of a wronged maid with amused servants peering through a door. At the schoolboy's feet are the games he must give up in going to school, while the soldier is associated with such vice-filled pastimes as card playing and dice (the dice are ominously showing "snake-eyes"). Over this central scene is a canvas depicting the Judgment of Solomon, a fitting choice for the judicial drama being enacted below.

Flanking this picture are two works that appear to allude to two of Christ's parables—the Good Samaritan and the Return of the Prodigal Son—stories of charity and love that point out the type of conduct that is sorely lacking in the life unfolding below. Next comes the sixth age as the old man totters toward death, the child next to him alluding to his entering a second childhood. Appropriately, above him is a figure of Father Time. The final scene is the death chamber, the old man being fed with a spoon as one would feed a child. Above hangs a desolate sunset, and the black draperies are like stage curtains ready to be drawn across this closing act.

The division of the life of man into seven ages goes back to the Ptolemaic formulation that an individual's life is governed by the seven planets. De Wilde alludes fleetingly to this scheme in his inclusion of Father Time, or Saturn, in the painting on the wall.[1] Other divisions of the ages were also popular, the most usual in terms of the traditions of painting being Aristotle's Three Ages of Man, and the Folger painting incorporates this scheme as well. The old man outside the death chamber at the right represents the sixth age in the one scheme, but when seen with the two flanking male figures he forms part of a triumvirate representing childhood, vigorous manhood, and old age. De Wilde

also pairs off his main protagonists. The two chambers at either side bring together life's beginning and end, both figures being dressed in white. The stance of the schoolboy deliberately echoes that of his counterpart, the old man, and both are dressed in brown. The schoolboy is paralleled by the young boy in the group of the Three Ages, the lover dressed in green by the gallant gentleman also dressed in green who completes the Three Ages at the right. Finally, the soldier and justice are coupled in the central scene. Life's ascent is mirrored by its decline.

1. For a discussion of the various schemes involving the ages of man, see J. A. Burrow's *The Ages of Man: A Study in Medieval Writing and Thought*, Oxford, 1986. Shakespeare's lines are specifically discussed in the context of the planet-gods on pp. 50–54.

Thomas Francis Dicksee

Born in London on 13 December 1819, Dicksee, who showed an aptitude for painting at an early age, began to study at nineteen with the Royal Academician H. P. Briggs, copying works by his mentor and by Reynolds and Van Dyck. He first found employment as a portrait painter but soon concentrated on fancy pictures of children and idealized portraits of fictional characters, especially Shakespeare's hero-

19

ines. While his repertoire was limited, he achieved excellence within his specialization and was content to paint for the market rather than for the critics, who too readily dismissed his work as pretty confections. Dicksee exhibited regularly at the Royal Academy from 1841 until 1895, the year of his death. For two decades beginning in the mid-1840s, he was also a frequent exhibitor at the Society of British Artists and the British Institution. A daughter and two sons, the most prominent of whom, Sir Frank Dicksee, was to become president of the Royal Academy, followed him in his choice of profession.

20 (Plate 19)

ANNE PAGE
The Merry Wives of Windsor I, 1
1862
Oil on canvas, 14 × 10⅞ in. (35.4 × 27.7 cm.)

Case no. 1571

Monogram and date in red at lower right: "18 TFD 62" (the three letters are superimposed on one another)

Provenance: Maggs, September 1926, £36. (Folger was offered this painting along with Dicksee's *Juliet and the Friar* [D23] by Maggs in September 1925 at £40 and £60, respectively. He must have declined, as they appear in a Maggs catalogue of 1926 [no. 251], and he acquired them in September of that year at a 10 percent discount.)

Condition: The painting has been stretched twice on smaller stretchers of different sizes. It is now on a stretcher of the original size, and the earlier tack holes have been filled and repainted.

The Folger picture is closely related to a painting of Anne Page that Dicksee exhibited at the British Institution in 1862, a wood engraving of which was published ten years later (fig. 13).[1] This last painting was one of two Dicksee placed in the 1862 exhibition, and the critic for the *Times* praised it at the expense of the other: "Mr. Dicksee, besides a rather wooden 'Hetty' (from *Adam Bede*), sends a charming little 'Anne Page,' who will have almost as many admirers as Mr. Wyburd's voluptuous Nadira."[2] The *Art Journal* bothered only to mention *Anne Page*, remarking on the "pretty girl carry-

Drawn by W. J. Allen.]   ANNE PAGE.   *[Engraved by J. D. Cooper.*

Fig. 13. After Thomas Francis Dicksee, *Anne Page.* Wood engraving drawn by W. F. Allen and engraved by F. D. Cooper in the *Art Journal* 1872, p. 5. Photograph: Library of Congress.

ing a tray," having earlier set the stage for a work of this type with the generalization, "light reading in pictures, as well as in literature, is much the most popular, and therefore the most profitable department to which an artist can now devote himself."[3] The Folger picture, dated 1862, was presumably painted in response to the success of the exhibited picture. It is a variation on the theme of the pretty heroine who offers a visual feast as well as a gustatory one in the idealized setting of Merry Olde England. In its sale catalogue Maggs identified the scene as the moment when Anne Page invites Slender into dinner: "The dinner attends you, sir." In fact, it is an earlier moment in the play, when Anne, at her father's bidding, carries the wine back inside, following on the heels of the moment depicted in the British Institution picture.

In the Folger work, Dicksee chooses a coquettish back view, Anne looking over her shoulder, her blue eyes sparkling with white highlights and her cheeks and lips a rosy red. A delicate gold net covers her wavy brown hair, and her dress is a magical, pink satin. In this, her first appearance in the play, Anne does not speak, and neither in the Folger painting nor in the exhibited picture does she make eye contact with her audience. She is there for the viewer's admiration, delicately not returning the admiring gaze. The Folger picture poses her against the wall of her substantial home, whose large, sun-filled windows and verdant plantings offer a sense of charmed contentment.

1. The wood engraving, drawn by W. J. Allen and engraved by F. D. Cooper, appears in the *Art Journal*, 1872, p. 5. The article describes the work as Anne Page "carrying wine and fruits to Sir John Falstaff and the rest of her father's jovial customers of the Windsor hostelry; the figure is extremely elegant, the face modestly sweet and charming" (pp. 6–7). It adds, "The picture was painted for the late Mr. Herbert, of Clapham Common, and was exhibited at the British Institution in 1862." Surprisingly, the British Institution catalogue lists the painting at 50 guineas, although the article states that it was a commissioned piece.
2. *The Times*, 10 February 1862, p. 10.
3. *The Art Journal*, 24 March 1862, pp. 70 and 69.

Monogrammist T. E.

Although the painting, bought in Rome, bears a monogram, the artist has yet to be identified. One assumes that the letters are "T. E." although "E. T." is not impossible. Even the artist's nationality is open to debate. On the basis of the picture's style, one suspects it may be by a Continental artist and dates to around 1880.

21

OPHELIA
Hamlet IV, 7
Late nineteenth century
Oil on canvas, oval, 26¾ × 21¹⁵⁄₁₆ in. (67.9 × 55.7 cm.)

Monogram in red at lower left (now covered by mat): "TE" (the "T" and "E" share the same vertical stem and the upper right portion of the crossbar)

Provenance: Purchased by Gen. Lew Wallace in Rome; given by him to Prof. Arthur B. Milford (Wabash College, 1893–1913); by descent to his son, Mr. Morton Milford; gift of Mrs. Morton Milford, May 1934.

Exhibitions: Amherst, *Shakespeare*, 1951; Washington, 1976–77, no. 28

Condition: The canvas is commercially prepared with a gray ground. At some point it was unevenly mounted on an oval stretcher. It is now cut vertically and horizontally to the present dimensions and has been glue-lined to a layered paper board. There is some paint loss at the upper left.

Depictions of Ophelia did not become popular until the late eighteenth century, beginning with the Boydell Shakespeare Gallery. Early eighteenth-century critics were uncomfortable with her irrationality and her role as innocent victim, yet it was these very characteristics that appealed to later audiences. Indeed, in the nineteenth century Ophelia was the single most popular literary subject for artists, with more than fifty portrayals recorded in exhibition catalogues.[1] These audiences perceived her as gentle, innocent, exquisitely delicate, and pure.[2] Once she was driven mad by her disappointed love for Hamlet, they felt it was these same virtues that led her into hysteria, insanity, and possible suicide.

The Folger painting depicts the episode most frequently chosen by artists (for another example, see D21), the moment just before Ophelia plunges to a watery death. Her demise is not played out on stage but is reported instead by Gertrude to her husband and Laertes, Ophelia's brother.

> *Queen.* There is a willow grows aslant a brook,
> That shows his hoar leaves in the glassy stream.
> There with fantastic garlands did she come
> Of crow-flowers, nettles, daisies, and long
>   purples
> That liberal shepherds give a grosser name,
> But our cold maids do dead men's fingers call
>   them;
> There, on the pendent boughs her coronet weeds
> Clamb'ring to hang, an envious sliver broke,
> When down the weedy trophies and herself
> Fell in the weeping brook.

Ophelia is typically shown adorned with flowers, a symbol of her feminine purity and transient beauty. She bears a garland on each side and the "coronet weeds" are in her hair, whose loose tresses are also typical of Ophelia iconography. At the very bottom edge, one glimpses the brook toward which she purposefully advances.

Ophelia wears a white satin dress enlivened with blue sleeves, with a yellow lining and with gold trim on its bodice. The theater historian George

21

Odell mentions that white satin, in contrast to black velvet, is the usual dress for gentle, less tragic heroines, such as Juliet, and for mad ladies.[3] In choosing this material, the artist is again following convention.

Ophelia is dramatically highlighted as if painted in direct sunlight, while the densely executed background is dark and subdued. Instead of being portrayed as manic or sweetly sad, she is shown with an intense, abstracted expression, her left hand clenched, her eyes shrouded in melancholy shadows. One blue slipper peeps out from beneath her gown, suggesting her inexorable progress toward the beckoning brook with its promise of welcoming oblivion.

1. See Altick 1985, p. 299.
2. These are all adjectives used by Anna Jameson in her book *Characteristics of Women*, first published in 1832.
3. Odell 1920, vol. 1, p. 448.

Henry Joseph Fradelle

Fradelle, a French artist, was born at L'Isle around 1778 but early in his career made his home in London. He exhibited frequently at the British Institution beginning in 1817 and was partial to literary and historical subjects in medieval and Renaissance settings. At the Royal Academy, where he exhibited from 1817 until 1855, he was more inclined to display his talents as a portraitist. Redgrave offered the less than enthusiastic critique that "his art was not of a high class, but was popular."[1] Fradelle died on 14 March 1865.

1. Redgrave 1878, p. 160.

22

OTHELLO AND DESDEMONA
Othello III, 4
ca. 1827
Oil on panel, 12 × 9⅞ in. (30.5 × 25.1 cm.)

Case no. 1565

Provenance: Michelmore, 1926, as Kean and Ellen Tree in act III, scene 3 of *Othello* by John William Wright (see Michelmore catalogue *Shakespeareana Illustrated* [1923?], no. 46, pp. 111–12, repr. in color); asking price in catalogue £125, but Folger apparently paid £60, as the file card lists it at $300.

Condition: The edges of the rectangular panel appear to have been filled in later, so in its original state the work provided a close model for the vignette, which has rounded, uneven corners. The edges of the back of the panel are beveled. The maker's name is incised into the center of the back: "R. DAVY / 83 NEWMAN ST."

Engravings: Vignette engraving by Charles Pye, published by Hurst, Robinson & Co., 1827, 4⅛ × 3½ in. (image, irregular) (ART File S52801, no. 32)

This work entered the Folger collection as by John William Wright (1802–48) and was identified as Desdemona appealing to Othello on behalf of Cassio in act III, scene 3. It was said to depict Edmund Kean in his final performance as Othello on 25 March 1833 at Covent Garden Theatre, with Ellen Tree as Desdemona. The Folger painting, a grisaille sketch, is, however, a modello for a print by Charles Pye of 1827, and the print makes clear that the artist is Henry Joseph Fradelle, the moment depicted is from act III, scene 4, and no specific actors are intended.

The picture depicts Othello framed by an exotic

arch of the castle on Cyprus as he angrily responds to Desdemona's overture on Cassio's behalf. Poisoned by Iago's manipulations, he suspects his wife of having an affair with his lieutenant and keeps demanding to see the handkerchief, a gift from his mother that he had given to Desdemona. Its loss becomes an important link in the chain of evidence that convicts Desdemona in the Moor's mind.

> *Oth.* Fetch me the handkerchief; my mind misgives.
> *Des.* Come, come;
> You'll never meet a more sufficient man.
> *Oth.* The handkerchief!
> *Des.* I pray, talk me of Cassio.
> *Oth.* The handkerchief!
> *Des.* A man that all his time
> Hath founded his good fortunes on your love,
> Shar'd dangers with you,—
> *Oth.* The handkerchief!
> *Des.* In sooth, you are to blame.
> *Oth.* 'Zounds! [Othello exits]

The modello's sketchy style differs from Fradelle's more finished exhibition pieces, such as *Othello Relating the Story of His Life to Brabantio and Desdemona* (fig. 14), shown at the Royal Academy

22

Fig. 14. Henry Fradelle, *Othello Relating the Story of His Life to Brabantio and Desdemona,* RA 1824. Oil on canvas, 20½ × 25½ in. From the RSC Collection, with the permission of the Governors of the Royal Shakespeare Theatre ©.

in 1824 and at the British Institution in the following year. It is executed in gray and white with only touches of brown in Othello's skin tones, and its edges appear to have been filled in later, so that in its original state it followed closely the format of the vignette with its rounded, uneven edges.

Othello's costume closely resembles his attire in the earlier exhibition picture, though it of course lacks the colorful decorative detailing of the larger canvas. Othello's dramatically posed left hand, with the fingers expressively parted, is also a feature carried over from the earlier work. As before, Desdemona strains toward the man she loves, but now it is as an uncomprehending victim.

William Powell Frith

Born in 1819 near Ripon, Yorkshire, Frith aspired as a young man to become an auctioneer. At his father's insistence, however, he enrolled at age sixteen in Sass's School of Art in London. Soon thereafter he entered the Royal Academy schools, where he became a member of "The Clique," a group of young artists interested in literary illustration. He first exhibited at the British Institution in

1838 and at the Royal Academy two years later. He was elected an associate of the Royal Academy in 1845 and a full member in 1852. He was attracted to historical and literary subjects and to scenes from contemporary life. In 1854 he exhibited *Life at the Seaside (Ramsgate Sands)* at the Royal Academy, a large composition conceived while on holiday at Ramsgate in 1851. It was an immediate success, purchased by no less an admirer than Queen Victoria. Other large paintings from modern life followed, including *Derby Day* of 1858 and *The Railway Station* of 1862. Frith also proved a prolific writer, publishing his three-volume *My Autobiography and Reminiscences* in 1887 and 1888. He outlived his popularity, dying in 1909.

23 (Plate 20)
OLIVIA UNVEILING
Twelfth Night I, 5
1874
Oil on canvas, 12⅜ × 10⅜ in. (31.5 × 26.2 cm.)

Signed and dated at lower right: "W. P. Frith / 1874"

Case no. 1388

Provenance: Maggs, January 1925, £42, as "Romeo and Juliet"

Exhibitions: Washington, 1976–77, no. 4, as "Romeo and Juliet"

Condition: The canvas has been lined in the past, and, despite an early restoration, solvent abrasion is minimal.

Frith was an inveterate theatergoer who held Shakespeare and Shakespearean actors such as Macready in high regard. With gentlemanly self-deprecation, he wrote of his involvement with the Bard, "Shakespeare inspired me with terror as well as admiration. . . . I have never meddled with Shakespeare without regretting my temerity, for though I have painted several pictures from different plays, I cannot recall one that will add to my reputation."[1]

The Folger painting is, in terms of its size, one of Frith's less ambitious illustrations. Folger acquired the painting as a scene from *Romeo and Juliet,* showing the meeting of the two lovers in act I, scene 5. The setting, however, is not grand enough for a hall in Capulet's house, and the so-called figure of Romeo with fair skin, red lips, long, wavy hair, hint of a bosom, and wide hips suggests a most feminine hero. The scene clearly illustrates *Twelfth Night,* where Viola, disguised as Cesario, approaches Olivia. Viola has entreated, "Good madam, let me see your face," and Olivia replies, "Have you any commission from your lord to negotiate with my face? You are now out of your text, but we will draw the curtain and show you the picture. Look you, sir, such a one I was—this present. Is't not well done?"

The painting is one of several by Frith illustrating *Twelfth Night.* He exhibited *Malvolio before the Countess Olivia* at the Royal Academy in 1840 and three years later the Duel Scene at the British Institution. He depicted Olivia for *Shakespeare's Heroines,* the print being engraved in 1846. In 1855 he exhibited *Maria Tricks Malvolio* at the Royal Academy and in 1869 *Malvolio Married to the Countess in Imagination.* The Folger picture is dated 1874 and may be one of the "small matters" the artist mentions having executed before the Royal Academy exhibition of that year.[2] He exhibited another picture of Olivia unveiling at the Royal Academy in 1898. Frith obviously found the play's coupling

Fig. 15. William Powell Frith, *The Artist and His Model,* 1860. Oil on panel, 13 × 10¼ in. Photograph: A. C. Cooper.

of comic situations with feminine beauty, often spiced with cross-dressing, an ideal mixture for his talents.

The scene of Viola's interview with Olivia had long appealed to artists. It appeared in book illustration as early as 1744, when Hayman used it as a frontispiece for *Twelfth Night* in Hanmer's edition of Shakespeare; William Hamilton's late eighteenth-century painting for Boydell is the first painting of this moment. Yet the scene was not exhibited at the Royal Academy until 1825, when it appeared in paintings by both Fradelle and Henry Singleton. Part of its attraction lay in Olivia's comparison of herself to a painting, accompanied by her appeal, "Is't not well done?" Frith emphasizes the scene's erotic and comic potential: the lifting of the veil is akin to the bride's offering herself to her husband. The comedy is conveyed in Viola's awkward confusion, but the erotic tension underlying Frith's interpretation is paramount, a tension that led Maggs to identify the subject as Romeo and Juliet.

The scene is closely related to one of Frith's favorite subjects, the theme of the artist and his model. In one of these paintings (fig. 15), dated to 1860 and

Fig. 16. Charles Robert Leslie, *Viola and Olivia*, 1859. Oil on thin card, mounted on linen, 9⁵⁄₁₆ × 12¼ in. Tate Gallery, London/Art Resource, New York.

identical in size to the Folger picture, he shows the newly arrived model lifting the veil of her hat much as Olivia lifts her veil. A variation on this theme, *The New Model* in the collection of Lord Beaverbrook, depicts the woman unbuttoning a cuff while the nude figure seen in the painting on the artist's easel makes clear that the model's unveiling does not always stop with her hat. Frith's images of artists and models celebrate the artist's power over women, the models demurely revealing themselves to him. Olivia's response, however, is a joyous act of abandonment, and the fact that the recipient is also female only adds spice to the offering.

Charles Robert Leslie's sketch of 1859 (fig. 16), said to be his last painting, offers a different interpretation of this same scene. It shows Olivia dressed in mourning as she poignantly lifts her veil, suggesting a figure of wisdom revealing secrets from the other side of the grave. Where Leslie saw Thanatos, Frith saw Eros, but the two responses are hardly antithetical.

1. W. P. Frith, *My Autobiography and Reminiscences*, New York, 1888, p. 109.
2. Ibid., p. 306.

Henry Fuseli (nos. 24–29)

Born on 6 February 1741, Fuseli, one of the most learned of eighteenth-century painters, grew up in the stimulating intellectual atmosphere of Zurich. His father was an artist, town clerk, and a writer on art, and he was the student of the progressive teacher Johann Jakob Bodmer, who introduced him to the then unfashionable authors Homer, Dante, Shakespeare, and Milton, and to the German *Niebelungenlied* epic. Fuseli was ordained a Zwinglian minister in 1761, and the following year he and his friend Johann Kaspar Lavater found it prudent to leave town after writing a pamphlet critical of Zurich's chief magistrate. After travels in Germany, Fuseli arrived in London in 1764, where he was again active in literary circles and published two books, an English translation of Winckelmann's *Reflections on the Painting and Sculpture of the Greeks* and *Remarks on the Writings and Conduct of J. J. Rousseau*. With the encouragement of Sir Joshua Reynolds, he decided to become a professional painter and from 1770 to 1778 studied in Rome, where he was greatly influenced by Michelangelo and classical art and to a lesser degree by mannerist art. After a stay in Zurich, he returned to London, gaining fame with his painting *The Nightmare*, which he exhibited at the Royal Academy in 1782. Drawn to unusual literary sources, Fuseli delighted in the dramatic possibilities offered by supernatural subject matter evoking sublime terror. An active participant in Boydell's Shakespeare Gallery, he went on to create singlehandedly his Milton Gallery, which, opening on 20 May 1799, proved to be a critical success but a financial failure. Having been made a full academician in 1790, he became Professor of Painting at the Royal Academy in 1799, a post he held until 1805 and again from 1810 until his death. In the last decades of his life, he continued to write on art and, after his death on 16 April 1825, was awarded the honor of burial next to Reynolds in St. Paul's Cathedral.

24 (Plate 6)

MACBETH CONSULTING THE VISION OF THE ARMED HEAD

Macbeth IV, 1
1793
Oil on canvas, 66 × 52⁷⁄₈ in. (167.7 × 134.3 cm.)

Case no. 1111

Provenance: Commissioned by James Woodmason for his Irish Shakespeare Gallery, which opened on 1 May 1793; bought by John Knowles before the artist's death in 1825; Knowles sale, Christie's, 22 April 1842, lot 87; presented to Sir Herbert Tree by Weedon Grossmith (information contained in letter of 3 November 1922 from Parsons to Folger; Parsons offered the painting for sale less than two weeks after Maggs); Sir Herbert Beerbohm Tree sale, Phillips, Son & Neale, 13 September 1921, lot 167; Maggs, December 1922, £50

Exhibitions: Dublin, 1793, no. XII; London, 1794–95, no. XII; this or another version of this subject, Royal Academy, 1811, no. 12; Amherst, *Shakespeare*, 1951; Washington, 1976–77, no. 8; San Francisco, 1979–82, repr. in color p. 170

References: Knowles 1831, vol. 1, pp. 189–90; Schiff 1973, vol. 1, pp. 107, 163, 187, 514 (no. 881); Hamlyn 1978, pp. 521, 526, 527, and 529, repr. pl. 33; Altick 1985, pp. 313–14; Schiff and Weinglass (forthcoming)

Versions: Der bewaffnete Kopf erscheint vor Macbeth, oil painting, 1774–79, Schiff 1973, no. 363; two drawings for above, Schiff 1973, nos. 457 and 457a; also see lost works, nos. 27 and 83 (no. 27 refers to the drawing, which is presumably preparatory to the Folger painting, that Fuseli exhibited at the Royal Academy in 1793 as "Macbeth, the cauldron sinking, the witches vanishing; a sketch for a large picture" [no. 110]; no. 83 is the work exhibited at the Royal Academy in 1811, which in fact may be the Folger picture).

Engravings: According to Knowles, William Sharpe was in the process of engraving the painting when Woodmason abandoned his project. Sharp's squared working drawing is in the British Museum Print Room (1853–12–10–482)

Condition: A large slash has been repaired between Macbeth's legs. It runs horizontally to the right beginning at the witch's big toe. A puncture has been repaired in Macbeth's left calf. There are repairs as well to the center of the painting and to the left of Macbeth's lower back. The paint surface is dry and brittle, and the figure of Macbeth is abraded. The old lining was removed and replaced in 1979. The cauldron ends in claw feet, and the leg at the right, as revealed by the pentimento, was originally shown as almost straight.

Fuseli had been introduced to Shakespeare's works as a young man studying with Bodmer. His favorite play was *Macbeth*, which he translated into German before leaving Zurich. He exhibited more compositions from this play at the Royal Academy than he did from any other literary source. While in Rome, he did over a dozen drawings illustrating the play and in 1777 sent back to London for exhibition a work entitled simply *A Scene in Macbeth*. Gert Schiff believes that the painting *The Armed Head Appearing before Macbeth*, now with Fabrizio Apolloni in Rome, may be this work.[1] It is one of the artist's earliest oils and, as it depicts the same scene as the Folger picture, shows him involved with this subject matter, considered in the eighteenth century to be among the most sublime, from the beginning of his career.

The Folger painting was executed for Woodmason's Irish Shakespeare Gallery, which opened in Dublin in 1793. It was one of five works Fuseli painted for the gallery and one of two illustrating *Macbeth*, its pendant being *Macbeth and the*

Fig. 17. Henry Fuseli, *Macbeth and the Witches*. Oil on canvas, 66 × 53 in. Petworth House, The National Trust. Photograph: Courtauld Institute of Art.

Witches (fig. 17) from act I, scene 3.[2] Woodmason imposed a standardized size on the works he commissioned, and John Knowles, a friend of Fuseli and his biographer, recorded the artist's unhappiness at the restriction: "Fuseli always complained of not being able to effect all he wished in these pictures, in consequence of being limited to shape and size, as it was stipulated by Woodmason, that those painted for his gallery should be 5 feet 6 inches high, by 4 feet 6 inches broad." The prints after the paintings were to be bound in a book, and the vertical format was best suited for such a project. While in the case of *Macbeth and the Witches* one can sympathize with the artist's predicament, the format enhances the interpretation of *Macbeth Consulting the Vision of the Armed Head*, where the emphasis on rising and sinking, movement on a vertical axis, plays an important role in the composition.

Macbeth is shown precariously straddling the edge of a dark abyss gazing downward on the rising apparition of the armed head. The three witches on his left point downward as well. The composition is compressed into a narrow space, dramatizing the

confrontation between Macbeth looking down and the head with its luminescent eyes looking up. Fuseli deliberately built the composition around a series of triangles, the triangle being for him, as reported by Knowles, a mystical figure.

As in the pendant, Macbeth is seen from below, his towering figure occupying almost the entire left-hand side. His abbreviated, skin-tight orange clothing, reminiscent of mannerist painting, is not identifiable with any one period; only the red and green tartan lying at the lower left indicates that the action takes place in Scotland. Macbeth is presented as a heroic, muscular warrior, but the exaggerated, vertebra-like scales along his arched back suggest a brutal and monstrous character.

There is a striking resemblance between Macbeth and the armed head, the intention of which is explained in the artist's remarks about his two paintings of Macbeth for Woodmason:

When Macbeth meets with the witches on the heath [act I, scene 3], it is terrible, because he did not expect the supernatural visitation; but when he goes to the cave to ascertain his fate [act IV, scene 1], it is no longer a subject of terror: hence I have endeavoured to supply what is deficient in the poetry. . . . I have endeavoured to shew a colossal head rising out of the abyss, and that head Macbeth's likeness. What, I would ask, would be a greater object of terror to you, if, some night on going home, you were to find yourself sitting at your own table, either writing, reading, or otherwise employed? would not this make a powerful impression on your mind?[3]

The idea of the apparition as a doppelganger introduces an imaginative dimension to the encounter.[4] Fuseli adds yet another level of association: the helmet that the head wears is identical to the helmet worn by Banquo in the painting's pendant. Thus, the armed head also evokes the terror and remorse Macbeth feels over the murder of his old friend. Macbeth holds a finger to his lips, a gesture of anxious meditation that Fuseli had employed in his earlier Roman version, but by having each witch also hold up a finger to her mouth, he now bonds Macbeth more closely to them.[5] Gert Schiff has observed that the faces of the witches resemble Bodmer's, as can be seen, for example, in Fuseli's painting of himself with his old mentor (fig. 18). It is not strange to see the witches depicted in masculine terms (Banquo describes them as having

Fig. 18. Henry Fuseli, *Self-Portrait with Bodmer*, 1778–81. Oil on canvas, 64 × 59 in. Kunsthaus, Zurich.

beards, and in the theater men often played these roles), but it is initially astonishing to see Bodmer cast as the model. In the earlier picture of Fuseli with Bodmer, the poses of the two men are reminiscent of the main protagonists in Michelangelo's *The Creation of Adam* on the Sistine Chapel ceiling. Bodmer is the active force who reaches out toward the passive Fuseli-Adam. In *Macbeth Consulting the Vision of the Armed Head*, Bodmer is again present in the triple role of the witches and is again revealing profound truths to his listener, who in this instance is perhaps also intended as a spiritual self-portrait of the artist.

Fuseli considered the Folger picture one of his best poetical conceptions.[6] One critic was so impressed on seeing it exhibited in 1794 in London at the New Shakespeare Gallery that he wrote that it was "perhaps the very best picture he has ever painted."[7] In it imagination literally bodies forth the forms of things unknown to the conscious self, and the message from the abyss is truly an unsettling one.

1. Schiff 1973, no. 363.
2. The other three pictures Fuseli painted for Woodmason were *Oberon and Titania* and *Titania Embracing Bottom* from *A Midsummer Night's Dream*, and *Gertrude, Hamlet and the Ghost of His Father*.
3. Quoted in Knowles 1831, vol. 1, pp. 189–90.

4. Fuseli was not the first to propose that the head symbolized Macbeth's own. Writing in 1746, John Upton had described the armed head as symbolizing Macbeth's severed head being presented to Malcolm by Macduff at the end of the play (*Critical Observations on Shakespeare*, p. 53, n. 16). The relevance of Upton's remarks to Fuseli was first pointed out by Robin Hamlyn in his article "An Irish Shakespeare Gallery" (Hamlyn 1978, see p. 521).
5. This gesture is characteristic of the witches, as Banquo had earlier replied on their first encounter, "You seem to understand me, / By each at once her choppy finger laying / Upon her skinny lips." Fuseli had already used this motif in earlier paintings focusing solely on the witches.
6. After Knowles purchased *Macbeth Consulting the Vision of the Armed Head*, Fuseli remarked to him, "You have another of my best poetical conceptions."
7. *St. James's Chronicle*, 28–30 January 1794, p. 4.

25

PUCK

A Midsummer Night's Dream II, 1
ca. 1810–20
Oil on canvas, 36¼ × 28⅛ in. (92 × 71.5 cm.)

Provenance: Burdett-Coutts sale, Christie's, 4 May 1922, no. 25, 25 guineas (£26.5.0), Rosenbach acting as agent

Exhibitions: Amherst, *Shakespeare*, 1951; Amherst, 1952; Washington, 1976–77, no. 9; San Francisco, 1979–82, repr. in color p. 155; Montgomery, 1985–86, no. 25

References: Schiff 1973, vol. 1, p. 495 (no. 751), dated ca. 1785–90; Schiff and Viotto 1977, no. 77, dated ca. 1785–90; Schiff and Weinglass (forthcoming), dated ca. 1810–20

Condition: The painting was sent to Boston to be relined and cleaned when it was on loan for the exhibition at Amherst in 1951. It was conserved again in 1959 and 1979. It was during this last restoration that the sketch on the verso was noted for the first time when the secondary support was removed. According to the condition report, the painting of the woman on the couch on the recto was probably uncovered during a previous restoration. The restorer also noted that two figures are visible in the background if the right side of the painting is at the bottom. In inpainting losses and abrasions an attempt was made to minimize the confusion resulting from the multiple images.

Versions: The Boydell painting, its location now unknown, is reproduced in Schiff 1973, vol. 2, pl. 750.

25 (verso)

25 (Verso)

A GROUP OF COURTESANS
ca. 1790–1800

References: Schiff and Weinglass (forthcoming) as
*Group of Courtesans Perhaps Engaged in Child
Mutilation or Similar Activity,* dated ca. 1790–1800

Condition: The image can be seen only dimly
through the lining applied over it in 1979. The figures appear to be executed in grisaille, but the figure of the child is colored a blood red.

Versions: Fuseli executed a number of works of
courtesans; one image that resembles the right-
hand group in the Folger sketch is reproduced in
Schiff 1973, vol. 2, pl. 924.

While Fuseli frequently reused old canvases, the
Folger picture is unusual in having been made to do
triple duty. The scene of Puck is painted over a
clearly visible pentimento of a woman reclining on
a sofa (oriented on the horizontal axis); a sketch for
a group of courtesans with elaborate hairdos and
pointed feet appears on the verso.

The image of Puck is a reworking of an earlier design that Fuseli had executed for Boydell's small series of paintings which was engraved and published
on 29 September 1799 (fig. 19). In this earlier work,
Fuseli depicts Puck's or Robin Goodfellow's response to Oberon's instructions to fetch a flower
pierced by Cupid's arrow: "I'll put a girdle round
about the earth / In forty minutes." An impish
Puck is shown trailing astral bodies as he races
through the air on bat-like wings. At lower left the
fairy who greets Puck in the beginning of the scene
dashes on her way. Before her are two fantastic creatures, one playing his trumpet-like nose, the other a
hobgoblin with a lantern, who, like Puck, misleads
night-wanderers. The rearing horse is another reminder of Puck's mischievous pranks: "I jest to
Oberon and make him smile / When I a fat and
bean-fed horse beguile, / Neighing in likeness of a
filly foal."

The Folger interpretation departs significantly
from this earlier scene. A plumper Puck with his
right leg raised in a more dynamic stride is shown
holding in his hands the ends of the cord with
which he girdles the earth, the arc of which can be
glimpsed beneath him. He now more closely resembles Fuseli's conception of the related Friar Tuck
drawn from Milton's *L'Allegro* (fig. 20), which is

Fig. 19. After Henry Fuseli, *Puck.* Engraving by J. Parker, 29 September 1799.

Fig. 20. After Henry Fuseli, *Friar Tuck.* Engraving by Moses Haughton, 23 December 1806. By courtesy of the Board of Trustees of the Victoria and Albert Museum, London.

in its turn related to the puckish hobgoblin with lantern in the Boydell picture. The details of the earlier picture are banished from this simplified composition. Only one figure appears with Puck, the fairy poised on the moth at the right, and this figure must again refer to the fairy with whom he banters at the scene's opening. She resembles the delicate creatures who appear in *Faery Mab* (no. 29), and also recalls in pose and size the fairy riding the moth in Fuseli's *Titania Awakening* (Kunstmuseum, Winterthur, Switzerland), also painted for Boydell. The source of the pale, silvery light would appear to be the moon, which must be positioned behind Puck.

Puck in the Boydell version looks out at the spectator. In the Folger painting he looks back, with a gaze more lecherous and diabolical than impish, toward the fairy, who demurely looks away. The sex-

ual tension is palpable, and it is fair to say that the erotically charged depictions of the nude reclining woman over which Puck has been painted and the courtesans on the verso have permeated the artist's interpretation.

26

THE TWO MURDERERS OF THE DUKE OF CLARENCE
Richard III I, 4
ca. 1780–82
Oil on canvas, 27 × 21 in. (68.6 × 53.3 cm.)

Provenance: Fuseli sale, Christie's, 28 May 1827, lot 6, as "A subject from Richard III. (two heads)," bought by Rev. J. Ludkin, £6.6.0; Anderson Auction Company, 27 April 1905, lot 13, as the head of Richard III and an attendant, $14

Exhibitions: Amherst, *Shakespeare,* 1951, as "Two Warriors from *Richard III*"; Washington, 1976–77, no. 10, as "Two Warriors from *Richard III*"; Washington, 1985, as "Dighton and Forrest, the Murderers of the Princes"

References: Schiff 1973, vol. 1, p. 491 (no. 728), as *Dighton and Forrest: The Murderers of the Princes;* Schiff and Weinglass (forthcoming) as *The Two Murderers of the Duke of Clarence*

Condition: The canvas was last conserved in 1985, when thick accumulations of dirt, old varnish, and discolored inpainting were removed. Small paint losses in the wall were then newly inpainted.

Related works: A drawing, preparatory to the painting, is listed in Schiff 1973, no. 814. Now in the collection of the Jan Krugier Gallery, New York and Geneva, it measures 51.5 by 46 centimeters, and the composition cuts off the balustrade at the bottom.

At first glance this work appears to be a fragment of a larger picture, but the preparatory drawing confirms that it has not been cut down. Obviously influenced by the physiognomic theories of his close friend Johann Kaspar Lavater, Fuseli chose to focus on heads showing the intense reactions of two contrasted characters, the one excitedly leaning forward, the other holding back with a grim reserve.

When the painting was sold in 1905, it was described as showing the terrified Richard III awakening from his dream and peering into the darkness with an undisturbed attendant beside him. Yet, in this scene (V, 3), Richard is alone in his tent, and it seems unlikely that he would have been wearing a helmet or have brought a balustrade along on his campaign. By 1951, when it was exhibited at Amherst, the painting bore the title "Two Warriors from *Richard III*," and in 1973 Gert Schiff identified it as *Dighton and Forrest, the Murderers of the Princes.* This is the moment drawn from Sir James Tyrrel's soliloquy in act IV, scene 3, in *Richard III.* Tyrrel, who has been instructed by the king to kill the two princes, the sons of the recently deceased Edward IV, agonizes over what Dighton and Forrest, the men he hired to carry out this deed, have told him. These two hardened villains had wept when relating their story of how they had been struck by the innocent beauty of the two sleeping children. Yet, though they almost turned back, they did carry out their mission. When James Northcote painted

this scene for Boydell (fig. 21), he obviously recalled Fuseli's heads of the two executioners.

Fuseli's painting, however, surely depicts an earlier moment in the play, one that occurs on stage. Richard, then the Duke of Gloucester, had sent two murderers to kill his brother George, Duke of Clarence, who had been imprisoned in the Tower after Richard had turned their elder brother, Edward IV, against George. Though they remain unnamed, Shakespeare characterizes these two men in far greater detail than he did Dighton and Forrest. The first murderer is far more ruthless than the second, whose conscience troubles him and who in fact eventually refuses to participate. These are the two men Fuseli depicts: the one with a deathly pallor, bulging eyes, arched eyebrows, and gaping mouth is eager to press forward; the other with rigid, grim mouth, knitted brow, and head recoiling slightly backwards only glances out of the corners of his eyes. The men, positioned behind a balustrade whose heavy forms stabilize the bottom of the composition, have presumably entered the room at

Fig. 21. After James Northcote, *The Royal Children and Dighton and Forrest, the Murderers.* Engraving by F. Legat, 4 June 1790, 22³⁄₈ × 16¹⁄₈ in.

the top of a stairway and are looking down on their victim. The rail and balusters are thinly painted in brown, and Fuseli has apparently used the handle end of his brush to scrape in dynamic lines in the murderers' armor. Light plays a dramatic role. The reluctant murderer wishes to recede into the shadows of the dark, sinister background, and only his nose is caught by the light. The other murderer aggressively projects out into the light, which fully illumines his diabolical nature.

27 (Plate 12)

ROMEO STABS PARIS
AT THE BIER OF JULIET

Romeo and Juliet V, 3
ca. 1809
Oil on canvas, 28 × 36¼ in. (71.2 × 92 cm.)

Case no. 1506

Provenance: Parsons & Sons, February 1926, 50 guineas (£52.10.0)

Exhibitions: London, Royal Academy, 1809, no. 149, as "The Encounter of Romeo and Paris in the monument of the Capulets. 'Romeo. Wilt thou provoke me? etc.'"; Amherst, 1950, no. 41, dated 1789; Amherst, *Shakespeare,* 1951; Washington, 1976–77, no. 6; San Francisco, 1979–82, repr. in color p. 151

References: The Morning Chronicle, 29 April 1809 ("Mr. Fuseli has two pictures from *Romeo and Juliet* in his usual style."); Knowles 1831, vol. 1, p. 415; Schiff 1973, vol. 1, p. 322 (no. 1206); Schiff and Viotto 1977, no. 231; Kestner 1986, p. 14, repr. in color p. 11; Schiff and Weinglass (forthcoming)

Condition: Patterns from a design underneath the paint can be seen in certain areas, in particular above and to the right of Romeo's right hand and in front of his face. These suggest another painting is beneath this one which X rays might be able to reveal.

Fuseli depicts the scene in which Juliet, having taken drugs whose effect counterfeits death, lies on her bier in the family tomb. Paris arrives at night to mourn her loss, followed by Romeo, who has come to die by her side. On their unexpected encounter, Paris provokes Romeo to a duel. Fuseli has chosen a moment at the end of the fight with Romeo lunging forward to stab Paris in the chest, Paris's body arching back in erotic surrender as he receives the fatal

thrust. Soon Romeo will kill himself by taking poison, only to be joined by Juliet when she awakens to find her lover dead at her side. Romeo's tunic is dark gray-green trimmed in red, the same red also being used for his shoes, while his cloak is a muted violet. His skin-tight garments accentuate the clean, taut lines of his body. Pentimenti show that Fuseli tried two earlier upright positions for Romeo's left arm before stretching it out behind him. Juliet is a spectral white, a black ribbon in her hair and black trim on her bodice and sleeve. Her flowing hair merges with the cloth on which she rests. Although difficult to see, there appears to be a ring on the first finger of her left hand, an allusion to Romeo having earlier told his servant, Balthasar, that his chief reason for visiting Juliet's tomb was to take "a precious ring," their wedding ring.

Like so many other Shakespeare plays, *Romeo and Juliet* was often performed in a variety of adaptations. The earliest of these, Thomas Otway's *The History and Fall of Caius Marius,* even took the liberty of transferring the setting and the characters to classical Rome. Theophilus Cibber's adaptation of 1744 at least restored the play to Verona, giving back the characters their original names, and it was replaced in its turn four years later by Garrick's version. Later in the century, John Philip Kemble was to restore even more of Shakespeare's text, but it was not until the season of 1845–46 that the unaltered play was performed by Charlotte and Susan Cushman. These reformulations of the play did not harm its popularity, indeed they may have helped it, as it was the most frequently performed Shakespeare play of the second half of the eighteenth century. For artists it also proved popular, in the nineteenth century ranking as the third most frequently painted of Shakespeare's works. Yet Fuseli was the first to paint the duel between Romeo and Paris, the only earlier rendition of this subject being Robert Smirke's book illustration of 1787 (fig. 22). Smirke concentrates on Romeo's remorse after having slain Paris, while Fuseli chose the more dramatic moment of the fatal stabbing. Both Smirke and Fuseli depart from the text and from stage tradition by condensing the action to show the two antagonists in front of Juliet's body. In the original text and in the many performed versions, the fight takes place outside of the tomb, with the dying Paris asking Romeo to carry his body into the crypt.[1] Garrick and many of his imitators per-

Fig. 22. After Robert Smirke, *Paris Slain by Romeo*. Engraving by Isaac Taylor, 1 August 1787, 9½ × 7¼ in.

matic opposition, the one depicting a violent scene of lightning combat, the other a frozen moment of eternal adoration.[5] Both, however, use the dramatic contrast of light and shadow to underscore a duality seen in the two lovers from the play's beginning. Juliet, who "doth teach the torches to burn bright" (I, S5, 46) and who indeed is the sun itself ("But, soft! what light through yonder window breaks? / It is the east, and Juliet is the sun." [II, 2, 2–3]) is contrasted with Romeo, who is "bescreen'd in night" and hides in "night's cloak" (II, 2, 52 and 75). In the final scene as rendered by Fuseli, Romeo is again a powerful dark force who effectively contrasts with Juliet's radiant light. While he appears to be the living figure and Juliet the dead one, the reality is just the reverse. It is Romeo who brings death into the tomb, killing Paris, then himself, and thereby ultimately extinguishing even Juliet's light.

1. Perhaps the reason Smirke chose to show the aftermath of the fight was to leave open the suggestion of this possibility.
2. See Sprague 1944, pp. 315–16.
3. Quoted in ibid., p. 315.
4. See Schiff 1973, vol. 1, no. 1207.
5. Ibid., p. 322.

28 (Plate 11)

ARIEL
The Tempest V, 1
ca. 1800–1810
Oil on canvas, 36½ × 28¼ in. (92.7 × 71.5 cm.)

Case no. 1086

Provenance: Burdett-Coutts sale, Christie's, 4 May 1922, lot 24, 28 guineas (£29.8.0), Rosenbach acting as agent

Exhibitions: Amherst, *Shakespeare,* 1951; Amherst, *The Tempest,* 1951; Washington, 1976–77, no. 5; San Francisco, 1979–82, repr. in color p. 189

References: Schiff 1973, vol. 1, pp. 563–64 (no. 1208); Schiff and Viotto 1977, no. 234; Schiff and Weinglass (forthcoming), as *Ariel Riding on the Bat, below Ferdinand and Miranda*

Condition: The canvas was lined for the first time in 1979. With the exception of Ariel himself, the canvas is thinly painted. It has suffered from abrasion and overpainting, particularly in the bat's wings.

Versions: A drawing in the Öffentliche Kunstsammlung, Basel, of Fair Margaret and Sweet William

formed the duel with Romeo wielding the crowbar he used to break open the doors of the tomb instead of his sword, a substitution that was often maintained well into the nineteenth century.[2] Critics, however, frequently complained about this innovation, and John Hill, for one, as early as 1755 noted his disapproval of this stage business: "The weapon of a gentleman is his sword, he naturally has recourse to it, and to no other."[3]

The Folger painting was exhibited at the Royal Academy in 1809, along with another canvas depicting a slightly later moment from this same scene, *Romeo Contemplating Juliet in the Monument* (R.A. no. 58).[4] This painting, a vertical composition, shows Romeo gazing on Juliet one last time before taking the poison. As Gert Schiff observed, the two canvases, while similar in their Caravaggiesque technique, are ultimately in dra-

from an old English ballad repeats the painting's lower group of Ferdinand and Miranda (see Schiff 1973, no. 1555).

Ariel, soon to be freed by Prospero, impulsively erupts into song:

> Where the bee sucks, there suck I.
> In a cowslip's bell I lie;
> There I couch when owls do cry.
> On the bat's back I do fly
> After summer merrily.
> Merrily, merrily shall I live now
> Under the blossom that hangs on the bough.

Fuseli picks up on the imagery in the song, showing Ariel merrily balancing on the back of a bat. Directly beneath his left foot appears a crescent shape perhaps intended to associate him with the moon and night's magical powers. The sky behind forms a dramatic backdrop: blue around the sprite, it becomes darker in the upper corners, while one last burst of the sun can be seen at lower right.

Ariel's body, with its straight left leg and raised left arm, forms an elongated vertical axis that inclines to the viewer's right. In counterbalance to this tilt, his right leg extends out from his body, its position echoed by the pink drapery's graceful arc. The pentimenti of both legs reveal that Fuseli had originally tilted the figure at an even more precarious angle. Ariel holds aloft a slender branch, a reference to the song's last line, "Under the blossom that hangs on the bough," while his right arm crosses over his torso. Tied to his extended limp finger hangs an astral leash connected to the bat. Elegantly adorned with a coronet of flowers, an armband, and a cameo on an ankle bracelet, Ariel glides on the bat's back, his sprightly, adolescent grace and complicated contrapposto reminiscent of such mannerist sculptures as Giovanni da Bologna's statues of Mercury.

The play's two lovers, Ferdinand and Miranda, are locked in an embrace at the bottom. As is often the case with Fuseli, the male is dominated by the female, who in this instance also wears a dress of a passionate purple. The dark ground slopes away from the couple as if they were perched on top of the globe itself in a world of their own. In contrast to their reclining poses and mutual interdependence, Ariel appears even more exuberant, a spirit free from earthly entanglements.

29 (Plate 13)

FAERY MAB

John Milton, *L'Allegro*
ca. 1815–20
Oil on canvas, 27½ × 35⅞ in. (70 × 90.8 cm.)

Provenance: Fuseli sale, Christie's, 28 May 1827, lot 8, this or another version as "Queen Mab, from Milton's Allegro," £23.14.6; Burdett-Coutts sale, Christie's, 4 May 1922, lot 26, as "Queen Mab from *Romeo and Juliet*," 56 guineas (£58.16.0), Rosenbach acting as agent

Exhibitions: International Exhibition, 1862? (this is the puzzling citation in the 1922 Christie's sale catalogue); Amherst, 1950, no. 42, as "Queen Mab from *Romeo and Juliet*"; Amherst, *Shakespeare*, 1951; Amherst, 1952; Washington, 1976–77, no. 7, as *Faery Mab*

References: Knowles 1831, vol. 1, p. 416; Gert Schiff, *Johann Heinrich Füsslis Milton-Galerie*, Zurich and Stuttgart, 1963, p. 94, pl. 50; Schiff 1973, vol. 1, p. 603 (no. 1498); Schiff and Viotto, 1977 no. 303; Schiff and Weinglass (forthcoming)

Condition: The ground is red, and it is thinly and evenly applied. In earlier restorations, the paint layer had been overcleaned and greatly overpainted. One of the more egregious additions was a black lump faintly resembling a bird at the far right. This curious form consisted only of repaint with no original basis underneath and in 1988 was removed. Presumably an earlier restorer wished to "improve" the composition by more firmly anchoring the right-hand side.

Versions: Fuseli executed his first painting of *Faery Mab* in 1793 (see Schiff 1973, vol. 1, no. 909). This work was executed for his Milton Gallery, which first opened in 1799. He executed the same subject in a vertical format in 1795–97 (see Schiff 1973, no. 910).

Engravings: The 1793 version was engraved by W. Raddon in 1834.

When sold at auction in 1922, this painting was listed as "Queen Mab from *Romeo and Juliet*," one of the pictures Fuseli had exhibited at the Royal Academy in 1814.[1] It has subsequently been reidentified as an illustration to Milton's *L'Allegro*, one of three episodes from this poem that the artist executed for his Milton Gallery, a project inspired by

Boydell's Shakespeare Gallery. All three images are drawn from the short passage describing fairies:

> With stories told of many a feat,
> How Faery Mab the junkets eat,
> She was pincht, and pull'd she sed,
> And he by Friars Lanthorn led
> Tells how the drudging Goblin swet,
> To ern his Cream-bowle duly set,
> When in one night, ere glimps of morn,
> His shadowy Flale hath thresh'd the Corn
> That ten day-labourers could not end,
> Then lies him down the Lubbar Fend,
> And stretch'd out all the Chimney's length,
> Basks at the fire his hairy strength;
> And crop-full out of dores he flings,
> Ere the first Cock his Mattin rings.

The Folger painting illustrates the line "How Faery Mab the junkets eat," an allusion to the custom of country people of placing junket out at night for fairies. The other two scenes depict Friar Tuck (see fig. 20) as an impish youth in a monk's habit in the guise of a will-o'-the-wisp or jack-o'-lantern and as a sleeping Lubbar Fiend or Puck stretched out in front of a hearth (fig. 23). *Faery Mab* is more closely related in format to this last work. Fuseli painted versions of both *Faery Mab* and *Puck* for his friend William Roscoe, and in a letter of 29 October 1795 he discussed them as pendants: "I have [in *Puck*] endeavoured to express an Ideal nature of Child and Man at once in a posture perhaps one of the most difficult that Can be Composed, and to add glow of Colour with freshness and force of chiaroscuro without heaviness . . . . The Companion which I wished to Send with it, but have not yet been able to finish is *"How Fairie Mab the Junkets eats"* from the Same Poem. And in that I have attempted to express the Same Ideas with respect to female Nature."[2] Thus, in *Faery Mab* the artist wished to convey the playfully mischievous nature of the child-woman.

The Folger painting is the last of three versions Fuseli executed of this subject, and it contains more detail than its predecessors. The earlier versions consist only of the platform at the left set with basket, jars, and pitcher and at the right a brownie, a common type of fairy, shown with his hands crossed over his chest rather than drinking from a bowl as in the Folger version.[3] The Folger canvas contains five small additional fairies, and

these figures make this version more sexually explicit than the earlier ones. The female at the far left holds a bowl over her lap and next to it a phallic spoon. A male rides the back of a dragonfly, whose long tongue is about to probe the slender neck of the elegant pitcher. Even more telling is the male who slips out from under the bowl with quill pen in hand, beneath which is a letter. Letters appear twice earlier in Fuseli's art, both times as a billet-doux that signals the beginning of a young maiden's seduction.[4]

The Folger *Faery Mab* conjures up a world of sensuous abandon. Food here is seen as a metaphor for lovemaking. There is a wanton excess in this debauchery as one fairy buries her face in a cream bowl, while the apparently inebriated brownie raises his bowl to imbibe some more, his lecherous smile slyly echoing that of Faery Mab. This is the erotic world of a young girl on the threshold of sexual experience. The subject's pendant (fig. 23) depicts Puck stretched out after having emptied his cream bowl, which lies at his right hand. The irony is of course that Mab, who is here the child-woman, overflows with provocative charm, while Puck, the child-man, lies exhausted after having eaten his fill. Throughout Fuseli's art males have difficulty in keeping up with the sexual appetites of women, and surely there is no figure more brazenly bewitching than his Faery Mab.

1. Fuseli's painting of Queen Mab has since been identified (see Schiff 1973, no. 1496).
2. David H. Weinglass, ed., *The Collected English Letters of Henry Fuseli*, Millwood, N.Y., 1982, pp. 141–42.
3. Gert Schiff was the first to identify this figure as a brownie. One author describes them as small men "raggedly dressed in brown clothes, with brown faces and shaggy heads, who come out at night and do the work that has been left undone by the servants" (Katherine Briggs, *An Encyclopedia of Faeries*, New York, 1976, p. 45). Patricia Milne Henderson, in a note of November 1959 in the Folger file, has offered a different interpretation. She identifies the grinning figure as a large, broad-faced country girl who is the narrator of Milton's tale of Faery Mab eating the junkets. The girl spins this tale in order to cover up the fact that it is her own gluttony that has depleted the stock of food.
4. In *Belinda in the Cave of Spleen* (Schiff 1973, no. 1751, as *Belinda Awakening* [new title is that of forthcoming edition]), an illustration to Alexander Pope's *The Rape of the Lock*, the heroine is shown next to her toilet composed of jars and vases set on a table not unlike the platform in the Folger painting, on which there also rests the letter which begins her journey from innocence to experience. The other painting with a billet-doux is Fuseli's *Girl at a Spinet with an Elf* (Schiff 1973, no. 746). The girl is Shakespeare's Perdita from *The Winter's Tale*, and Peter Tomory has shown how a girl playing the spinet represents "the

Fig. 23. After Henry Fuseli, *The Lubbar Fiend.* Engraving probably by Moses Haughton, 11½ × 11¹¹/₁₆ in. By courtesy of the Trustees of the British Museum, London.

transition between virginity and the breaking of the hymeneal chord" (*The Life and Art of Henry Fuseli,* London, 1972, p. 169). The letter brought by the elf can be no other than a love letter marking the beginning of this denouement.

George Henry Hall (nos. 30–31)

Born on 21 September 1825 in New Hampshire, Hall grew up in Boston, where he turned to painting at an early age. In 1849 he traveled to Düsseldorf to study at the Academy and later visited Paris and Rome. On his return to the United States, he settled in New York City around 1852. In these early years he was best known for his still lifes and scenes from Shakespeare. Between 1860 and 1895, he made a number of lengthy trips abroad, particularly to Spain, Italy, and Egypt, sojourns that helped to inspire his many pictures of Mediterranean peasant life. He had been made an associate member of the National Academy of Design in 1853 and a full academician in 1868, and he exhibited there almost continuously until 1908. He died in New York on 17 February 1913.

30

SIR TOBY BELCH
Twelfth Night II, 3
1854
Oil on canvas, 23³/₄ × 19¹³/₁₆ in. (60.5 × 50.4 cm.)

Signed and dated at lower left in red, the letters slanting at the same angle as the floor: "G. H. Hall / N.Y. '54." In brown ink on the back of the canvas at top (presumably copies an inscription seen on the original canvas before it was relined): "Sir Toby Belch / And because thou art virtuous / Shall be no more cakes and ale? / Geo. H. Hall / New York / 1854."

Provenance: John Anderson, Jr., July 1906, $75

Condition: Glue-lined by Finlayson in 1932 onto a commercially prepared canvas with a ground. The lining is now in poor condition. The paint and ground are flaking from the original canvas.

Although Hall depicts daylight outside the window, the scene is set in Lady Olivia's house late at night, when the drunken singing of Sir Toby Belch, Sir Andrew Aguecheek, and Feste, the clown, attract Maria and a complaining Malvolio, Olivia's steward. Hall depicts only the figure of Sir Toby,

30

who, for a portly gentleman, dances nimbly while offering a retort to Malvolio: "Out o' tune, sir! Ye lie. Art any more than a steward? Dost thou think, because thou art virtuous, there shall be no more cakes and ale?" He concentrates on this merry life of cakes and ale, as he renders Sir Toby's red apple-cheek vitality, his expensive clothing, and the table set with a still life of fruits, wine, and a gleaming silver tankard. As Hall interprets the scene, Sir Toby's retort is without a trace of rancor, his twinkling eyes, wide grin, and carefree shrug with palms upward suggesting a benign and jovial extrovert. He also relies on bright colors to convey a sense of gaiety, even if his abilities to harmonize them are somewhat limited.

31

MALVOLIO CONFRONTING THE REVELERS
Twelfth Night II, 3
1855
Oil on canvas, 25¹/₁₆ × 30 in. (63.7 × 76.2 cm.)

Case no. 715

Signed and dated at lower left in red: "G. H. Hall / N.Y. 1855"

Provenance: William Matthews sale, Walpole Galleries, 17 November 1916, lot 254, $25

Condition: Glue-lined by Finlayson in 1932 onto another canvas prepared commercially with a ground.

31

Presumably inspired by Hall's picture of the previous year (no. 30), this painting is an elaboration on the same moment when Sir Toby Belch challenges Malvolio. Hall now includes all the characters and again emphasizes the pleasures of companionable drinking. Around the table from left to right are Sir Andrew Aguecheek, Feste, the expansively gesturing Sir Toby, and Maria, Lady Olivia's waiting woman. They all face Malvolio, who, having come to chastise them, stands at the far right in his nightgown and cap. A lute, a reminder of the boisterous singing, lies on the stool at the left, while the sparkling silver pitcher and well-stocked wine cooler refer to the lavish furnishings of this comfortable interior.

Domestic details in the manner of Hogarth offer a commentary on the moment depicted. The mantle consists of a relief sculpture of Venus with cupids, a reference to the role love plays in motivating so many of the characters in this amusing tale, including a foolish Malvolio, who stands beneath it. Hall also employs coarse Hogarthian humor in having Feste hold his glass of wine in such a way that its spilling contents offer a reminder of how quickly alcohol passes through the body.

William Hamilton (nos. 32–35)

Hamilton was born at Chelsea in 1750 or 1751 to a Scottish father who was to become an assistant to the architect Robert Adam. Adam sent Hamilton, when still quite young, to study in Italy, probably with Antonio Zucchi. Back in London in 1768, he continued with Zucchi and the following year entered the Royal Academy schools. He exhibited his first picture at the Royal Academy in 1774, was made an associate member ten years later, and a full academician in 1789. A prolific artist, who generally preferred the pleasant and charming to the grand, he executed numerous narrative pictures, history paintings, portraits, book illustrations, and decorative art for furniture, windows, and carriages. He was second only to Robert Smirke in the number of paintings he executed for Boydell's Shakespeare Gallery. Highly respected in his lifetime, he died in London on 2 December 1801.

32 (Plate 7)

ISABELLA APPEALING TO ANGELO

Measure for Measure II, 2
1793
Oil on canvas, 65½ × 53 in. (166.3 × 134.6 cm.)

Case no. 1373

Signed and dated at lower right: "Wm. Hamilton RA 1793"

Provenance: Commissioned by James Woodmason for his Irish Shakespeare Gallery, which opened on 1 May 1793; Walpole Galleries, April 1925, $165

Exhibitions: Dublin, 1793, no. XXII; London, 1794–95, no. XXII

References: St. James's Chronicle, 28–30 January 1794, p. 4 (this and the companion picture described as "very excellent"); Hamlyn 1978, pp. 527, 529

Condition: The original canvas is a twill weave, from which all tacking margins have been removed. In 1932 Finlayson glue-lined it onto a pale green commercially grounded canvas. There is a medium-thick, buff-colored ground layer, and the paint layer ranges from very thin washes of color, with canvas weave clearly visible beneath, to areas of modeled impasto. There is abrasion in many of the thinly painted areas. Pentimenti reveal that the artist changed the position of Angelo's right knee. A comparison with the engraving shows some loss to the canvas along the bottom edge.

Engravings: J. Fit[t]ler, published on 1 August 1794 by Mr. Woodmason, London, 8 × 9⅝ in. (image)

Most of Hamilton's Shakespearean subjects were executed with specific projects in mind. He was responsible for six of the designs, engraved in 1785 and 1786, for John Bell's edition of Shakespeare's plays.[1] For Boydell he executed six large paintings, and eighteen of his works were engraved for the small series. He painted four pictures for Wood-mason's Irish Shakespeare Gallery, the Folger picture being one of two for *Measure for Measure.* These two works are the first known paintings to illustrate the play, having been executed before the Boydell pictures for *Measure for Measure,* a surprising fact in light of the play's popularity in the eighteenth century. The scene of Isabella pleading with Angelo, however, had appeared as a book illustration: in 1709 with Boitard's frontispiece and in Edward Edwards's design for Bell's 1774 edition.

Hamilton's painting shows Isabella before Angelo pleading for her brother's life. Angelo, deputy to Vincentio, Duke of Vienna, had been left in charge of the city during the Duke's absence, and, in his campaign to reform morals, he had decided to make an example of Isabella's brother Claudio, whose offense had been to impregnate his fiancée, Juliet. Isabella is seen with Lucio, a friend of Claudio, while behind the seated Angelo is the Provost, who is the keeper of the prison where Claudio awaits death. The companion piece, known only from the print after it (fig. 24), shows Isabella visiting Claudio in prison with the Duke, disguised as a friar, on the left and the Provost behind him. Isabella has come to tell her brother that she can secure a pardon for him only by sleeping with Angelo, for her an unthinkable demand. Claudio at first agrees that she should preserve her honor, but then weakens, and Isabella turns from him in disgust toward the religious Vanitas imagery of hourglass and Bible. The interiors are purposefully contrasted, an audience chamber in Angelo's house in the first picture and a grand, but oppressive, jail cell in the second.

Depictions of the pleading Isabella often show her kneeling in response to Lucio's instructions, "Kneel down before him, hang upon his gown." Hamilton, however, stresses her more heroic qualities. The grand sweep of her figure, which owes something to Fuseli's elongated anatomies, dominates the left portion of the composition, and the white fluted pilaster behind her reinforces a sense of stalwart purity. Her classicizing profile adds to her noble dignity, and Hamilton provides Isabella, a novice of a religious order, with an imposing costume made up of white drapery and a black headdress, the large dimensions of which are more clearly displayed in

Fig. 24. After William Hamilton, *Isabella Rebuking Claudio.* Engraving by J. Fit[t]ler, 1 August 1794.

the prison scene. This stark use of black and white contrasts with Angelo's purple throne, his persimmon doublet and slops over canions (tight-fitting breeches), and his green cloak.

Robert Smirke depicted this same scene from *Measure for Measure* for Boydell (fig. 25), and the similarity of Angelo's pose suggests that Smirke was aware of Hamilton's treatment. It is the contrasts, though, that are most revealing. Hamilton shows Angelo as a complex ruler, one who is thrown into confusion as his emotions catch him off guard, while Smirke is content to show him as purely evil and Isabella as a submissive victim. Smirke's treatment reverts to the theatrical characterization of this scene as performed during most of the eighteenth century, which stressed a more intimate, domestic confrontation. On 3 November 1783, Sarah Siddons portrayed Isabella in her first London performance in a Shakespearean role. Her characterization defied the conventional interpretation of the part, in that she brought to the role a sense of lofty and uncompromising morality. It is Siddons's inspired characterization of an energetic morality that so clearly underlies the Isabella found in both of Hamilton's pictures.[2] He presents Isabella as a neoclassical goddess in contrast to Smirke's appealing, but ineffectual, suppliant.

1. For Bell he executed one illustration for each of six plays: *Twelfth Night, The Comedy of Errors, I Henry VI, II Henry VI, Richard III,* and *Titus Andronicus.* The first four designs were engraved in a different format for Manley Wood's edition of Shakespeare's plays of 1806. Hamilton also exhibited two paintings from *The Tempest* at the Royal Academy, one in 1792 and one in 1793.

2. The costume may also owe a debt to Siddons. Under the influence of classical sculpture and a desire to adapt her style of acting to nobler and simpler lines, she was to abolish "the enormous head-gear, the hoops and flounces and train of a previous day" (Odell 1920, vol. 2, p. 93). For the influence of classical sculpture on Siddons, see James Boaden, *Memoirs of the Life of John Philip Kemble,* London, 1825, vol. 1, p. 425.

Fig. 25. After Robert Smirke, *Isabella Pleading with Angelo.* Engraving by J. Fittler, 29 September 1797.

33

THE DUKE OF YORK DISCOVERING HIS SON AUMERLE'S TREACHERY
Richard II V, 2
Late 1790s
Oil on canvas, 31³/₈ × 21³/₄ in. (79.7 × 55.3 cm.)

Provenance: Commissioned by Alderman John Boydell for the Shakespeare Gallery; sold by lottery 28 January 1805 and won by William Tassie; sold by Christie 20 May 1805, lot 9, as "*The Duke and Duchess of York and Aumerle*—finely drawn and coloured," bought by Henry Tresham, R.A., for 10 guineas (£10.10.0); Knott's Art Repository, 55 Yorkshire Street, Oldham (this information derived from printed label at top center of frame); purchased by John Anderson, Jr., from Messrs. Robinson & Fisher, London; John Anderson, Jr., sale, American Art Galleries, 6 April 1916, lot 18, as by Stothard, $110 plus 10 percent commission, Morris acting as agent

Exhibitions: London, Boydell, 1802, no. 122; London, Boydell, 1805, no. 65

References: Friedman 1976, p. 188, n. 380, and p. 224

Condition: A long zigzag tear running from Aumerle's cloak down through his legs and ending below the Duke of York's left knee was repaired in 1987. There is a strip measuring 1.5 centimeters along the bottom edge of the picture that was originally left unpainted, as was the case with Smirke's *Awakening of King Lear* (no. 58). At some point after this area was filled in, the painting was annotated in the lower right corner, "T. STOTHARD RA 1801."

Engravings: James Stow, published 4 June 1800 for 1802 Boydell edition of Shakespeare's plays, facing p. 96 of *King Richard II*

Seldom performed in the eighteenth century, *Richard II* was not a popular play among artists. It did receive, though, respectable coverage in the Boydell project: two large paintings, by Mather Brown and James Northcote, focus on scenes in which Richard is juxtaposed with his rival Bolingbroke. Hamilton painted the two pictures for the small series, the first showing Richard with his supporters after he has landed on the coast of Wales (now in Sir John Soane's Museum, London). The Folger painting is a later scene and is the only known depiction of this particular moment in the play. It shows the

33

Duke of York discovering his son's treachery on reading the incriminating document Aumerle has been carrying. The document reveals a plot to assassinate Bolingbroke, who, having deposed Richard, was soon to be crowned as king. Remaining loyal to the new ruler, York vows to expose this plot to restore Richard to the throne even at the cost of his own son's life. The Duchess pleas in vain for him to relent. The scene's innate drama is sufficient explanation for Hamilton's choice, but the artist may also have been responding to the con-

temporary political climate. In France, paintings such as Jacques Louis David's *The Oath of the Horatii* and *Lictors Returning to Brutus the Bodies of His Sons* dramatized the conflicts arising between family loyalties and duty to one's country, conflicts that were to be played out in the French Revolution. In choosing this moment from Shakespeare's play, Hamilton provides an English counterpart to these classical subjects that had been coopted by the French.

Hamilton employs histrionic gestures to convey the dramatic nature of the revelation, while Aumerle's upturned head with exposed nostrils is clearly borrowed from Henry Fuseli's similar characterizations. A pentimento reveals that Aumerle's left hand was originally lower, and it is now positioned slightly more prominently than before. The Duke's hands are unusually large, giving added emphasis to his surprised and outraged gesture.

The painting entered the Folger collection as by Thomas Stothard, based on the inscription in the lower right corner, "T. STOTHARD RA 1801." In his 1916 sale catalogue, Anderson triumphantly claimed to have discovered the annotation, undeterred by the facts that the Boydell engraving after the picture identified it as by William Hamilton and that the print was dated a year earlier than the date inscribed on the "Stothard" painting. On stylistic grounds, the Folger picture can be securely given to Hamilton, and during conservation in 1987, after it was determined that the inscription was a later and intrusive addition, it was removed.[1] The entire work had also been heavily toned with a brown glaze that would have originally been applied to impart a "Rembrandt glow." One suspects that both "improvements," the inscription and the varnish, were the work of Anderson.

1. The 1987 conservation report reads: "It [the signature] sat on top of the varnish and was easily removed with acetone. This last step in the restoration was carried out with the aid of a microscope at the Folger Conservation Laboratory, where it was readily visible that the paint used for the signature lay inside cracks which had formed in the original paint film, positive proof that the signature was an incorrect, later addition."

34 (Plate 2)
THE CAROUSING OF SIR TOBY BELCH AND SIR ANDREW AGUECHEEK
Twelfth Night II, 3
1792
Oil on canvas, $30^{15}/_{16} \times 22^{3}/_{16}$ in. (78.5 × 56.2 cm.)

Signed and dated at lower right: "Wm Hamilton RA / 1792"

Provenance: Commissioned by Alderman John Boydell for the Shakespeare Gallery; sold by lottery 28 January 1805 and won by William Tassie; sold by Christie 18 May 1805, lot 26, as "*Sir Toby, Sir Andrew, and Maria*—full of humour and possessing an admirable effect," bought by John Green for 13½ guineas (£14.3.6); Robert Hoe sale, American Art

Galleries, 17 February 1911, lot 66, $230 (price given in annotated copy of catalogue in the National Gallery Library), Wright acting as agent

Exhibitions: London, Boydell, 1795, no. 5; London, Boydell, *Small Pictures*, 1796, no. 6; London, Boydell, 1802, no. 111; London, Boydell, 1805, no. 34

References: Friedman 1976, p. 188, n. 380, and p. 225

Condition: The original canvas is lined onto a commercially prepared canvas with what may be an animal glue. There are a few small flake losses along the edges and in the red stockings of Aguecheek. There are also large patches of discolored retouching at the bottom right above the signature, in the upper right corner, and at the top center of the picture. From the wrinkled nature of the original paint surrounding these losses, the damage was probably incurred during a past lining procedure when a very hot iron was used and left in place for too long a time. The picture was most recently restored in 1988.

Engravings: J. Fittler, published 24 December 1793 for 1802 Boydell edition of Shakespeare's plays, facing p. 27 of *Twelfth Night*, $10^{3}/_{8} \times 6^{3}/_{8}$ in. (border of image and margin)

All three of Hamilton's paintings of *Twelfth Night* for Boydell's small series of pictures have survived.[1] The first, showing the meeting of Olivia and Viola-Cesario, is in the Victoria and Albert Museum, while the remaining two are in the Folger. In act II, scene 3, Sir Toby, a kinsman of Olivia, and Sir Andrew, a suitor, have been drinking and singing late into the night at Olivia's house. Feste, the clown, joins them, followed not long afterwards by Maria, Olivia's waiting woman. Malvolio, the steward, enters to complain bitterly about the noise. As soon as he leaves to inform against them, Maria hatches a plot to get even. Hamilton depicts Maria leaving to plant a letter that will fool Malvolio into thinking Olivia is in love with him. His main focus, however, is on the drunken condition of Sir Toby and Sir Andrew. He effectively contrasts the two figures, showing a portly, middle-aged Sir Toby, in an aggressive, swaggering pose, overshadowing an effeminate, slumping Sir Andrew, his callow companion. The feather in Sir Toby's hat and his pipe are jauntily erect, while Sir Andrew's are pointed downward. Sir Andrew's suit is also entirely yellow, a color that one soon learns Olivia abhors.[2]

Sir Toby's pose echoes that of the portrait of one of his and Olivia's ancestors hanging on the wall. Hamilton contrasts the martial dignity of the heroic, trim figure arrayed in armor in the portrait with the similarly posed drunken Sir Toby, whose appearance hardly adds to the family's honor. Empty bottles and wine glasses, evidence of Sir Toby's and Sir Andrew's revelry, are seen in the background. Near the beginning of the scene when the clown enters, he opens with a jest: "How now, my hearts! Did you never see the picture of 'we three'?" His reference is to the well-known painting of only two asses, the joke deriving from the fact that the spectator is the third ass of the painting's title. Hamilton wittily echoes the clown's humorous sally. Maria is placed well in the background so that the main focus is on the two foolish revelers, and the clown is left out of the composition entirely. Thus, the picture depicts two asses, and the viewer, with knowledge of the play's content, knows exactly where to find the third.

1. Hamilton also painted one of the two large pictures for *Twelfth Night*, and it may be the picture in the Somerset Maugham Collection at the National Theatre in London. The other large painting was executed by Ramberg and is in the Yale Center for British Art.
2. See II, 5, 218–20.

35

OLIVIA'S PROPOSAL
Twelfth Night IV, 3
ca. 1796
Oil on canvas, 30⅝ × 21⅝ in. (77.8 × 55 cm.)

Signed at lower right: "Wm Hamilton RA"

Provenance: Commissioned by Alderman John Boydell for the Shakespeare Gallery; sold by lottery 28 January 1805 and won by William Tassie; sold by Christie 18 May 1805, no. 25, as "*Sebastian, Oliver and Priest*—an elegant and fine specimen," bought by A. Paxton, Esq., for 9 guineas (£9.9.0); Hoe sale, March 1911, no. 66, $209

Exhibitions: London, Boydell, *Small Pictures*, 1796, no. 7; London, Boydell, 1802, no. 112; London, Boydell, 1805, no. 30

References: Friedman 1976, p. 188, n. 380, and p. 226

Condition: The tacking edges have been cut and the canvas has been lined onto a second canvas, probably using an aqueous glue adhesive. There are

several large losses of ground and paint along the bottom and right edges. A 5-inch scratch in the paint film, running diagonally to the left across the figure of Sebastian, was repaired in 1988.

Engravings: W. Angus, published 4 June 1794 for 1802 Boydell edition of Shakespeare's plays, facing p. 81 of *Twelfth Night*, 10½ × 6½ in. (border of image and margin)

In this scene Olivia proposes to Sebastian after having confused him with his twin sister, Viola, with whom she had fallen in love when she was disguised as Cesario. Sebastian, bewildered by all that has happened to him, accepts. Hamilton sets up an inexorable movement from left to right, leading Sebastian and the viewer toward the open door of the chapel where the priest will perform the ceremony. The scene takes place in Olivia's garden, and the dense, freely brushed foliage enhances the feeling of a sensuous, private setting. The influence of Fuseli's elongated figures seen from below is evident. Hamilton freely exaggerates anatomy for visual effect, particularly in the figure of Olivia, whose high waist and small head emphasize the sweeping grandeur of the fluid lines of her elongated legs and lower torso. The right arm of the priest, however, seems unusually oversized and clumsy. A surviving preparatory drawing (fig. 26) demonstrates that Hamilton made a number of changes in the final conception: Sebastian is seen in full profile; Olivia's dress has been simplified; and the priest moves more emphatically in the direction of the now truncated door of the chapel.

By 1790 for Boydell's large series of pictures, Hamilton had already painted the climactic last scene of *Twelfth Night* (V, 1), where the comic confusions are finally resolved (fig. 27). The grouping of the figures in the Folger painting distantly echoes that of the same figures in this larger composition, although Viola-Cesario is in the last, while it is her twin, Sebastian, who is in the former.

Angus's engraving after *Olivia's Proposal* curiously reverses the composition. It also opens up the sky at the top, presumably since in a black-and-white print too much foliage might appear overly claustrophobic.

Francis Hayman (nos. 36–37)

Hayman was born in 1708 in Exeter. He began work in London as a decorative artist and scene painter

at Goodman's Fields Theatre and Drury Lane Theatre, and may even have performed for a time as an
actor. He also designed around fifty pictures in
the early 1740s for the supper boxes at Vauxhall
Gardens and was later to add even more impressive
works to this popular London resort, then under the
proprietorship of Jonathan Tyers. In addition, Hayman excelled as a portraitist, as a painter of theatrical subjects, and as a book illustrator. He was also

an ambitious, if not always successful, history
painter. He became decreasingly active as an artist
in the last two decades of his life but was prominently involved in artistic affairs, serving as president of the Society of Artists. He went on to
become a founding member of the Royal Academy
and was appointed its librarian in 1770, a post,
largely honorary, in which he served until his death
on 3 February 1776.

35

Fig. 26. William Hamilton, *Olivia's Garden.* Pen and ink with wash. From the RSC Collection, with the permission of the Governors of the Royal Shakespeare Theatre ©.

36

THE PLAY SCENE FROM "HAMLET"
Hamlet III, 2
ca. 1745
Oil on canvas, 13¾ × 11⅝ in. (34.8 × 29.6 cm.)

Case no. 1688

Provenance: Betts, June 1927, £32

Exhibitions: New Haven, 1987, no. 38

References: Merchant, "Hayman's Illustrations of Shakespeare," *Shakespeare Quarterly* 9 (Spring 1958) p. 145, repr.; Merchant 1959, p. 47, repr.; Kalman A. Burnim, "Eighteenth-Century Theatrical Illustrations in the Light of Contemporary Documents," *Theatre Notebook* 14 (Winter 1959–60), p. 54; Paulson 1982, p. 63; Karen Newman, "Hayman's Missing *Hamlet*," *Shakespeare Quarterly* 34 (Spring 1983), pp. 77–78, repr.

Condition: Hayman painted this picture on top of another composition, or at least a portion of one. When the painting was restored in 1987, two heads emerged in the drapery just above the head of Claudius. This first picture was on the horizontal axis (with the draperies at the left). The heads, however, have been again painted over in order not to

Fig. 27. After William Hamilton, *Olivia Procuring the Priest's Testimony.* Engraving by F. Bartolozzi, 29 September 1797, 19¾ × 24¾ in.

intrude on the design of the completed vertical composition.

Versions: Drawing, pen and ink and gray wash, for Sir Thomas Hanmer's edition of *The Works of William Shakespeare*, ca. 1740–41, 8½ × 5¾ in., interleaved in vol. 6, FSL (the engraving after the drawing does not reverse the image); oil on canvas executed for Jonathan Tyers for the Prince of Wales's Pavilion at Vauxhall Gardens, ca. 1745, location unknown; oil on canvas, ca. 1745, location unknown, repr. Merchant 1959, pl. 8a, sometimes identified as the Vauxhall picture

The moment chosen is Claudius's startled reaction to the performance of *The Murder of Gonzago.* To the left of Claudius is Polonius, the Lord Chamberlain, and seated to the right of the throne is Gertrude, Queen of Denmark and Hamlet's mother. The play-within-the-play is at the lower left, where one sees the nephew assassinating the player-king by pouring poison into his ear. Opposite in the right foreground reclines Hamlet beside a seated Ophelia. Standing behind her is Hamlet's friend Horatio, who has been instructed to watch closely Claudius's reaction to the play.

Hayman had first illustrated the play scene for Hanmer's edition of Shakespeare (fig. 28), and soon thereafter, about 1745, painted it as one of four Shakespearean scenes decorating the Prince of Wales's Pavilion at Vauxhall Gardens. The Folger picture is thought to be the *modello* for this now missing canvas.[1] This scene from *Hamlet* seems to have been selected with Frederick, Prince of Wales, specifically in mind. From 1733 until his death in 1751, Frederick was increasingly the focus of the opposition to his father, George II. It is not too strong to say that both the king and queen detested their son. The tension between Hamlet, Prince of Denmark, and Claudius, King of Denmark, was an apt expression of the bitter feelings being played out in the Hanoverian court.[2]

From the Hanmer illustration to the Folger picture, there are important changes in composition. In the first conception, the king's dais is positioned in the left foreground, his throne awkwardly oriented outward, while Hamlet and his party are on the right, with the play-within-the-play enacted upstage in the center. The Folger painting contracts the composition, pulling together more closely all three groupings, and places the king at center stage

with the performance of *The Murder of Gonzago* at the left. This last arrangement is thought to be a more accurate reflection of the actual stage practice of this period,[3] and Brian Allen suggests that Garrick, who advised Hayman on other Shakespearean compositions, may have been responsible for this change as well.[4] Certainly the new arrangement makes the guilty reaction of Claudius the central focus. All the figures look at him except for Ophelia, who has eyes only for Hamlet. Claudius is the only spectator looking at the play-within-the-play, although the statue in the niche behind Polonius seems also to gaze in that direction. Perhaps Hayman intends this as a statue of Hamlet's father, so that the victim as well as the assassin are riveted by the action of the mock play.

Ophelia is shown holding her fan, a prop that plays a role all its own in the history of performances of this scene,[5] while Claudius and Hamlet clutch their swords, indicative of the violent resolution to come. Hamlet, the melancholy Dane,

Fig. 28. Francis Hayman, *The Play Scene from "Hamlet."* Pen and ink and wash.

wears black, while Ophelia's dress, a virginal white, offers a dramatic contrast. Only Claudius, the actual king, wears royal purple; the player-king, though wrapped in an ermine robe and shown with a stage crown, wears plainer dress.

1. Brian Allen, who is the most knowledgeable writer on Hayman, identifies the Folger picture as the *modello* for the Vauxhall picture (catalogue to New Haven, 1987, p. 114). Newman, however, feels the Vauxhall painting is the version in which the figure of Hamlet is absent.

2. The other three paintings for the pavilion were *Lear in the Storm*, the scene in *Henry V* in which Henry scornfully rejects the French Herald's demand for ransom, and Miranda startling at the sight of Ferdinand from *The Tempest*. They may also have been specifically chosen with Frederick in mind. Surely a scene from the life of Henry V, the hero-king, was selected in part because he had already been the main protagonist in two of Shakespeare's earlier plays, *I Henry IV* and *II Henry IV,* where of course he appears as a sympathetic Prince of Wales. Just as Prince Hal went on to become, as Henry V, the example of what a king should be, Frederick (although he died before his father) was often promoted by his supporters as embodying the ideal of the Patriot King. The scene from *King Lear* shows the king gone mad, but in the context of the Prince of Wales's Pavilion the focus may have been as strongly on Edgar, an outcast who was the lawful heir of the Earl of Gloucester. Prince Frederick, like Edgar and Cordelia, must have also felt he had been egregiously treated by his father. Finally, the scene from *The Tempest* focusing on Miranda and Ferdinand offers a highly flattering image of a prince.

3. See Merchant 1959, p. 47, and Burnim 1959–60, pp. 53–54. Newman argues that the Hanmer version is the one that reflects stage practice at this time (1983, p. 73).

4. Catalogue to New Haven, 1987, p. 114.

5. See Sprague 1944, pp. 157–58, and Burnim 1959–60, p. 54.

37

FALSTAFF REVIEWING HIS RECRUITS

II Henry IV III, 2

1760s

Oil on canvas, 40$\frac{1}{8}$ × 48$\frac{1}{4}$ in. (101.6 × 122.5 cm.) (original remaining canvas), 40$\frac{3}{4}$ × 49$\frac{3}{16}$ in. (present size of lining)

Provenance: Col. W. B. Molony; his sale, Puttick and Simpson, 18 March 1927, lot 25, as by Fuseli; bought from Thomas, $50 (Thomas, who has not yet been identified, may have been acting as Folger's agent at the sale).

Exhibitions: Possibly the version exhibited in London at the Society of Artists in 1765, no. 49; Amherst, 1959, as by Fuseli(?)

References: Paulson 1982, pp. 42, 47, 157, n. 40, repr. p. 184 (pl. 23), as present location unknown;

Brian Allen, *Francis Hayman,* exhibition catalogue, 1987, pp. 22–23, 145, 179 (no. 142), repr. p. 21

Condition: At one time the canvas was mounted on a stretcher with diagonal crossbars in the corners. The canvas retains the outline of these crossbars in cracks in the paint and ground. The canvas was most recently conserved in 1988.

Versions: Drawing, pen and ink and gray wash, for Sir Thomas Hanmer's edition of *The Works of William Shakespeare,* ca. 1740–41, 8$\frac{1}{2}$ × 5$\frac{3}{4}$ in., interleaved in vol. 8, FSL (the engraving after the drawing reverses the image); oil on canvas, early to mid-1760s(?), 20$\frac{1}{2}$ × 23$\frac{1}{2}$ in., City Art Gallery, Birmingham, England; oil on canvas, early to mid-1760s(?), 39$\frac{1}{4}$ × 49$\frac{1}{4}$ in., National Gallery of Ireland, Dublin; print after missing oil on canvas, engraved by W. W. Ryland and published 25 March 1776; drawing, black chalk with white highlights on buff paper, early to mid-1760s(?), 7$\frac{3}{8}$ × 9$\frac{5}{8}$ in., Yale Center for British Art, New Haven

Hayman executed several versions of this subject, exhibiting paintings of this scene at the Society of Artists in 1761 and again in 1765. His first version was for Sir Thomas Hanmer's edition of Shakespeare's plays, published in 1743–44 (fig. 29). Hanmer's instructions to the artist have survived:

A room in a country-Inn, where two Justices of peace Shallow and Silence are sitting at a table upon the business of impressing Souldiers for Falstaff. Shallow a lean meagre pert coxcomb, Silence a heavy stupid blockhead. Their Clerk with pen and paper at the lower end of the table. Falstaff sits upon a chair near them with his arm over the back of the chair, and with an air of importance: his Corporal Bardolfe and a scrub page waiting behind him. At some distance two Constables attend with their staffs in their hands, having brought five fellows with them to be press'd into the service, viz: Mouldy, Shadow, Wart, Feeble, and Bulcalf, all shabby poor-looking rogues, one of them standing forwarder than the rest as under examination.[1]

The Folger painting differs from the Hanmer print in a number of respects. The format is horizontal rather than vertical, and, to streamline the composition, the clerk and one of the constables have been dropped. Falstaff's pose is more imperious, and

37

it is Shallow who now throws his arm over the back of the chair. Bardolph, with his red bulbous nose, guzzles his wine in such a manner that even the servant is amusingly astonished. These figures are placed on a dais, Hayman now more clearly differentiating between the rulers and the ruled. The artist presents the motley recruits in the same order as Shakespeare: from right to left are Ralph Mouldy, his hand raised in alarm; Simon Shadow, whose face cannot be seen and whose light gray coat befits his name; Thomas Wart, uncomfortably resting on a seat with Francis Feeble behind. In the foreground the Constable wrestles with a reluctant Peter Bullcalf, much of the humor arising from the discrepancies in their size and age, the smaller man valiantly attempting to bring forward the larger reluctant youth.

> *Falstaff.* Yea, marry, let's see Bullcalf.
> *Bullcalf.* Here, sir.
> *Falstaff.* 'Fore God, a likely fellow! Come, prick me Bullcalf till he roar again.
> *Bullcalf.* Oh Lord! good my lord captain,—

> *Falstaff.* What, dost thou roar before thou art prick'd?
> *Bullcalf.* Oh Lord, sir! I am a diseased man.

Of the surviving versions the Folger painting seems to be the latest, making it the final resolution of the composition. The painting closest in size and composition is the Dublin version (fig. 30), and both dramatize the tension between the two groups. In the Folger painting Bullcalf pulls more forcibly away from Falstaff, taking the Constable with him, and the more pronounced diagonal of the receding wall also helps to break up the rigid confines of the box-like setting.

Hogarth had depicted this scene in the late 1720s, but, as Ronald Paulson has pointed out, his interpretation of Falstaff is bitingly accusatory. Falstaff is shown accepting the bribes, and Hogarth's emphasis on the corrupt nature of his use of power is presumably a veiled allusion to the contemporary practices of Sir Robert Walpole.[2] Hayman's interpretation, on the other hand, emphasizes the swaggering glutton. Falstaff was recognized as a persona

II.^d Part of KING HENRY IV. Act. 3. Sc. 5.

Fig. 29. After Francis Hayman, *Falstaff Reviewing His Recruits.* Engraving by H. Gravelot, 8¼ × 5¾ in. (image).

of the artist, in that Hayman himself was of Falstaffian size and temperament. Writing in 1813, one reviewer remarked, "*Apropos,* the humour of Hayman, *jocularly satirical,* and sometimes *affectedly morose,* was something similar to that of the fat knight his favourite."[3] When Johan Zoffany executed his painting *The Academicians of the Royal Academy* (fig. 31), which he exhibited in 1772, he consciously echoed Hayman's pose for Falstaff by showing the artist seated toward the left-hand side with legs spread, stomach protruding, and arms bowed out at his sides.[4] Furthermore, just as Hayman shows Falstaff inspecting the physical suitability of his recruits, Zoffany shows Hayman inspecting the Royal Academy's "recruits," two male models stripping down at the right.

1. Quoted from Marcia Allentuck, "Sir Thomas Hanmer Instructs Francis Hayman: An Editor's Notes to his Illustrator (1744)," *Shakespeare Quarterly* 27 (Summer 1976), p. 310.
2. See Paulson 1982, pp. 36–47.
3. Anonymous review of Northcote's *Life of Reynolds* in the *European Magazine* 64 (November 1813), p. 415, quoted in catalogue to New Haven, 1987, p. 21.
4. Brian Allen was the first to point out this connection.

Fig. 30. Francis Hayman, *Falstaff Reviewing His Recruits.* Oil on canvas, 39¼ × 49¼ in. National Gallery of Ireland, Dublin.

Fig. 31. Johan Zoffany, *The Academicians of the Royal Academy.* Oil on canvas, 39³/₄ × 58 in. Copyright reserved to Her Majesty Queen Elizabeth II.

Francis Hayman, after

38

FALSTAFF'S COWARDICE DETECTED
I Henry IV II, 4
Mid-eighteenth century
Oil on canvas, 10³/₈ × 14³/₈ in. (26.4 × 36.5 cm.)

Case no. 1780

Provenance: Betts, May 1928, £18, purchased as a scene from *The Merry Wives of Windsor* by Hayman

References: Highfill 1973–, vol. 12, p. 241 (no. 13)

Condition: Finlayson lined the canvas in 1932.

Engravings after original: C. Grignion, published 4 April 1743 by Thomas Bowles, 10¹/₄ × 13¹⁵/₁₆ in., inscribed with verse: "When Henry in Disguise had rob'd the knight, / He hack'd his Sword, & swore 'twas done in Fight. / The Prince declares the whole—Sr. John can frame / No instant Falshood to elude his Shame— / At length, cries he—'Should I've my Prince withstood, / 'The Lyon knows by Instinct Royal Blood— / 'I knew thee Hal, soon as

thou cams't in Sight— / 'Twas Loyalty, not Fear, that wing'd my Flight.-"; undated engraving published by Robert Sayer.

The scene is the Boar's Head Tavern, where the Prince and Poins are listening to Falstaff's claims of having fought a gang of rogues, whose number is constantly increasing. Falstaff has hacked his sword in order to help verify his tale. The servant Francis appears at the right holding a glass and bottle, while two of Falstaff's three cohorts (Bardolph, Peto, and Gadshill) can be seen drinking at the left. Mistress Quickly is about to enter through the open door.

Hayman's original painting, executed for Vauxhall Gardens, has not survived. The print after it (fig. 32) demonstrates that his Falstaff wears the standard theatrical attire for the period: a ruff is about his neck, while his headgear and that of Mistress Quickly are old-fashioned. Hayman employs a simple, symmetrical composition set within a stage-box setting. The figures' proportions, at least as revealed in the print, are somewhat awkward, as Falstaff is oversized as compared to his companions.

The Folger painting is approximately the same size as the print and is surely a copy based on it

38

Fig. 32. After Francis Hayman, *Falstaff's Cowardice Detected*. Engraving by C. Grignion, 4 April 1743.

rather than on the original canvas. Its color scheme, therefore, probably bears little relationship to the Vauxhall picture: Poins, to the viewer's left of Falstaff, wears a brown coat; Falstaff wears a lilac coat, blue waistcoat, and yellow breeches; Prince Hal, a blue-green coat, pink waistcoat, and yellow breeches. The copyist has also left out or altered certain details: the plates seen through the doorway on the shelf are missing, the light still streaks down from the upper left but the corner of the window given in the print has been excluded; only one sheet of paper is attached to the wall at the right and its perspective is awkwardly managed; the barrel is too small and the chair too large; and the sconce or candlestick holder on the left side is angled left-ward rather than to the right, as in the print, where it leads the viewer's eye back to the center.

William Salter Herrick

Little is known about the life of William Salter Herrick, whose name suggests he may have been related to another artist represented in the collection, William Salter (see no. 55). Herrick first surfaced in 1852, when he exhibited at the Royal Academy. He continued to exhibit there almost annually until 1874, after which time he submitted works only in 1877 and 1880. In addition, he participated seven times at the British Institution from 1857 until 1867. In the beginning he exhibited primarily portraits, but later, when attempting literary subjects, showed a marked predilection for the type of picture falling into the category of the Keepsake Beauty. From Shakespeare alone, he exhibited Imogen, Beatrice, Portia, Olivia, Viola, Ophelia, Juliet, and Rosalind. *Hamlet in the Queen's Chamber* was his first picture drawn from a Shakespearean tragedy and was presumably his first departure into the realm of "high art." Herrick must have been disappointed with the results, as, after this time, when he undertook one of the tragedies, he preferred subjects that revolved around bittersweet heroines such as Desdemona, Ophelia, and Juliet.[1] The last picture of which there is a record is a painting of Rosalind that he executed in 1886 and donated to the Shakespeare Birthplace Trustees in Stratford-upon-Avon.[2] It is yet another winsome beauty, demurely fetching in contrast to the gothic horror of his earlier illustration to *Hamlet*.

1. Folger purchased two of Herrick's paintings from *Othello* (see D33 and D34).

2. This gift was soon transferred to the Shakespeare Memorial and is given a full-page reproduction in its catalogues of 1896 and 1898.

39 (Plate 18)
HAMLET IN THE QUEEN'S CHAMBER
Hamlet III, 4
ca. 1857
Oil on canvas, 45 × 62 in. (114.1 × 157.6 cm.)

Case no. 2032

Provenance: Michelmore, February 1930, £150

Exhibitions: London, Royal Academy, 1857, no. 498, as "The chamber scene from 'Hamlet'"; Amherst, *Shakespeare*, 1951

References: "The Exhibition of the Royal Academy," *The Art Journal*, 1 June 1857, p. 173

Condition: Finlayson glue-lined the picture onto a commercially prepared canvas with a ground in 1932, slightly flattening the impasto in the process. There are extremely wide separation cracks in the dark areas that have been repainted, but in places a red ground shows through.

The scene in the Queen's chamber had proved a popular one for artists. It was the moment chosen by Boitard for the first illustration of *Hamlet*, executed for the frontispiece to the 1709 Rowe edition, and Francis Hayman executed the first painting of this scene in the second half of the 1750s in a canvas depicting Spranger Barry as Hamlet and Mrs. Mary Elmy as Gertrude.[1] In all, the subject is recorded at least fifteen times.[2]

Herrick's painting, following precedent, depicts Hamlet reacting to his father's Ghost, who is seen only by him. It is the moment after he has confronted his mother and has slain the hiding Polonius, who had responded to Gertrude's cries. Herrick places Hamlet at center stage, his histrionic pose perhaps derived from the theater. His costume is a simplified version of the tunic and cape adopted at this time by the actor Charles Kean. Hamlet's mother is seated at the left; he first pushed her into the chair near the beginning of the scene when she attempted to leave. Then, having killed Polonius, he commands, "Peace! Sit you down."

The setting is the Queen's closet, an anteroom to her bedroom. In his film version of *Hamlet* released in 1948, Laurence Olivier placed the action in Gertrude's bedroom, effectively underscoring the hero's denunciation of his mother's licentious behavior, but Herrick's setting is the traditional one demanded by the text. He does, however, introduce two unusual features. The Queen would appear inappropriately to be at her devotional, as an illuminated book is open on the table beneath a crucifix, and the room itself is unexpectedly extended on the right, the passage leading to a view of a clear night sky. Gertrude's right hand and knee recline downward, her left hand and knee upward, leading the viewer's eye, along with her gaze, to Hamlet, whose dramatic, diagonal pose focuses the viewer's attention on the elusive, transparent form of the Ghost at the far right. Polonius lies unobtrusively beneath the arras, Hamlet's sword, only discreetly bloodied, pointing to his body.

Herrick's picture received only one brief notice in the various reviews of the exhibition: "The ghost is a very felicitous conception; the shadowy phantom realises Hamlet's descriptions of his father. Hamlet is also successful, but the queen is a failure. The apartment and the auxiliary composition are unexceptionable." The reviewer's negative reaction to the treatment of the Queen may be due to the lack of idealization in her features, a surprising defect in light of Herrick's interest in depicting conventional female beauty, and to the fact that she is too small in scale. Hamlet, on the other hand, with his long blond hair and drooping mustache, is a fitting nordic hero. The transparent Ghost belongs to the realm of history painting rather than the theater, and while Herrick was not the first to depict him as a "shadowy phantom," his is a dramatic and compelling representation.[3] Apparently in accordance with stage tradition, the Ghost is shown almost invariably dressed in the same armor in which he makes his first appearance in the play, but Herrick, attentive to Hamlet's line, "My father, in his habit as he lived!" presents him in a robe instead of a suit of armor and gives him a crown in place of a helmet.

1. Reproduced in catalogue to New Haven, 1987, p. 116, no. 41.
2. See Altick 1985, p. 302.
3. As the print after the now missing painting demonstrates, Henry Liverseege, for one, showed the Ghost as transparent in his picture exhibited at the Royal Academy in 1831. Liverseege's painting illustrated the same moment as Herrick's, the line in the exhibition catalogue reading, "Do you not come your tardy son to chide?"

James Clarke Hook

Born on 21 November 1819, Hook was admitted as a student at the schools of the Royal Academy in 1836. In 1845 he was awarded the gold medal for history painting and the next year the traveling prize, which enabled him to study in France and Italy until the Revolution of 1848 forced him to return home from Venice. He first exhibited at the Royal Academy in 1839 and exhibited continuously from 1844 until 1902, even sending back paintings during his travels on the Continent. He was elected an associate member of the Royal Academy in 1850 and a full academician in 1860. At first he primarily painted subjects drawn from literary sources, but beginning in 1856 he turned to coastal scenes. As a marine painter his style became more naturalistic, and it was Ruskin's praise of his painting *"Luff, Boy,"* exhibited in 1859, that firmly established his reputation. He died on 14 April 1907.

40 (Plate 17)
OTHELLO'S DESCRIPTION
OF DESDEMONA
Othello IV, 1
ca. 1852
Oil on panel, 31 × 21 in. (78.6 × 53.3 cm.)

Case no. 1444

Signed at lower right: "J C HOOK." A piece of paper in pen and ink, perhaps in the artist's hand, is glued to the back of the panel at upper left: "Othello's description of Desdemona. / —An admirable musician! O, she / will sing the savageness out of a bear!— / Of so high and plenteous wit and / invention! / Othello Act 4th. Scene 1st. / Painted by Jas C Hook A.R.A. / Tor Villa / Campden Hill / Kensington" (Tor Villa is the house that Hook had just built for himself).

Provenance: Michelmore, July 1925, £100. (A printed text, listing this picture as no. 14, has been cut out and pasted on the back of the panel at lower left. The entry may well be clipped from an auction catalogue.)

Exhibitions: London, Royal Academy, 1852, no. 210

References: The Times, 14 May 1852, p. 6; *The Art Journal*, 1 June 1852, p. 169; *The Athenaeum*, 3 July 1852, p. 129; *The Dictionary of National Biography*, London, Supplement (1912; reprinted 1927), vol. 2,

p. 294, this painting and two others cited as the best-known pictures of his early period; Altick 1985, p. 307

Condition: The panel has been prepared with a fine gesso surface, which has been painted over smoothly. There is no evidence of repaint or other restoration.

Versions: A small oil sketch on panel (9½ × 6¾ in.) was sold at Sotheby's Belgravia on 19 November 1974, lot 139, repr. It was inscribed on its reverse: "[to] P. F. Poole A.R.A. from J. C. Hook."

Hook took particular delight in *The Merchant of Venice* and *Othello.* He exhibited a painting of Lorenzo and Jessica, his first of a Shakespearean subject, at the British Institution in 1845. In 1847 he sent back from Florence *Bassanio Commenting on the Caskets* for exhibition at the Royal Academy, and, after his return to London, exhibited *Othello's First Suspicion* in 1849, *The Defeat of Shylock* in 1851, and *Othello's Description of Desdemona* in 1852. In this last year he also exhibited *Olivia and Viola* from *Twelfth Night* at the British Institution. These were his only exhibited Shakespearean works,[1] and, with the exception of *Olivia and Viola,* reflect his fascination with Venice.[2] This fascination extended not only to subject matter but also to style, as Hook's rich, lush color at this period owes a strong debt to paintings of the Venetian Renaissance. Indeed in 1852, when Hook exhibited the Folger picture along with a scene from Boccaccio, the critic for the *Times* was led to complain, "Mr. Hook pursues without variety the course he adopted in former years, and seems so enamoured of Venetian colouring that his only book might be Othello or Portia, and his life be spent in a gondola. We earnestly hope for newer things from an artist of so much feeling for colour and sentiment."[3] *Othello's Description of Desdemona* was Hook's last picture of a Venetian subject.

In act IV, scene 1 of *Othello,* Iago skillfully orchestrates the Moor into such a passion that he resolves to kill Desdemona. Yet, even as Othello lashes out at his wife's "betrayal," his memories of her sterling qualities keep intruding. Hook paints Othello's recollection of her entrancing musical abilities: "an admirable musician! O! she will sing the savageness out of a bear. Of so high and plenteous wit and invention!" The setting, a Venetian garden with a white marble fountain and decorated archway, is an earthly paradise of which Desdemona is the center, physically and morally elevated above Othello. It was customary to show Desdemona playing an instrument as she sings, and Hook provides her with a lute. Lost in an enchanted reverie, she does not look at Othello, perhaps suggesting the psychological gulf that ultimately separates this pair despite the depth of their passion. She wears a pale blue silk dress with white highlights and a purple trim or mantle, and a purple bodice over a white blouse. Each color is enlivened with a variety of hues, the individual brushwork creating a richly textured pattern. Pearls and flowers are intertwined in her hair. Othello's hose is a dull red, while his gown is brown, a color that links him with his own reference to the savage bear. The sword at his side is a reminder of this violent potential. The conception of music soothing savage passions is a familiar one: the most relevant earlier subject of this type is that of David singing and playing the harp for a disturbed Saul. As with this Old Testament subject, the spellbinding music can only postpone, rather than cure, the eruption of crazed violence.

The theme of the Garden of Love was popular in the Venetian Renaissance, but its roots go back to earlier Northern European art. The garden offers a walled, protected environment, an earthly paradise where fecund nature flourishes. The fountain is a typical feature of such settings: related to the Fountain of Youth, its water is life-giving and its pulsating rhythms are also associated with Desdemona's music. The gate behind it, however, strikes an ominous chord. With its attached herms, reclining figures, and urns, it marks an exit to a world beyond the garden that presages death. Certainly, there is no mistaking the meaning of the cypress that rises up behind the two lovers, its gloomy, forceful vertical dwarfing that of the bright fountain. Because of its dark foliage and its inability to grow again from its roots once it is cut, this tree has been linked with death since classical times and today is still frequently to be found in cemeteries. Here it foreshadows the couple's fall from grace, Thanatos and Eros once again inextricably linked. It may also be intended as an ominous pun on Cyprus, the island where the two lovers will meet their tragic deaths.

1. In 1875 Hook exhibited *Hearts of Oak* at the Royal Academy with a quote from *King John* in the catalogue: "What England, hedged in with the main, etc." While perhaps inspired by Austria's lines in the play (II, 1), this marine picture is not, strictly speaking, an illustration to Shakespeare.

2. The artist also exhibited *A Dream of Venice* at the Royal Academy in 1850 and *The Rescue of the Brides of Venice* in the following year, two non-Shakespearean scenes that are also inspired by his interest in this city.

3. *The Times*, 14 May 1852, p. 6.

Arthur Boyd Houghton

Houghton, whose father was employed by the East India Company, was born in India in 1836, but his family returned to London the following year. His father, intending for him a career as a surgeon, enrolled him in medical school when he was sixteen, but after two years Houghton was allowed to pursue his own interests, enrolling in Leigh's General Practical School of Art in 1854. He studied there, at the Antique School of the Royal Academy and the "Langham," and in 1861 began to exhibit at the Royal Academy and the British Institution. Having lost one eye in a childhood accident, Houghton was more successful with line than with oils, the strain on his one good eye giving him difficulty with color. In view of his abilities as a draftsman, it is not surprising that he increasingly turned to book and magazine illustration for financial support, and it is this work for which he is best known today, including the remarkable illustrations for the Dalziels' *Arabian Nights* of 1863–65 and the illustrations executed for the *Graphic* while on a seven-month tour of the United States in 1869–70. He married in 1861, but his wife died just three years later. Increasingly turning to drink for relief from depression and anxiety, he died on 25 November 1875 at age thirty-nine.

41

SIR TOBY BELCH COMING TO THE
ASSISTANCE OF SIR ANDREW AGUECHEEK
Twelfth Night, IV 1
ca. 1854
Oil on panel, 11¾ × 15¾ in. (29.8 × 39.7 cm.)

Case no. 1901

Provenance: Parsons & Sons, March 1929, £35 (asking price), bought with Cruikshank drawing for £85, which represented approximately a 13 percent discount

References: Paul Hogarth, *Arthur Boyd Houghton: Introduction and Check-List of the Artist's Work*, London, 1975, p. 19 (no. 1); Hogarth, *Arthur Boyd Houghton*, London, 1981, repr. p. 15

Condition: The panel is sightly warped, and its edges are beveled on the verso. It was conserved in 1991, when the flaking paint surface was secured to

41

the white gesso ground. Fallen chips, particularly along the upper edge, were reattached, and some in-painting, based on an old photograph, was necessary to replace a few missing portions. A pen-and-ink label attached to the upper center of the verso reads, "Toby Belch coming / to the assistance / of Aguecheek."

Paul Hogarth believes the Folger picture to be an early work, dating it to around 1854, when Houghton first embarked on his career as an artist. The choice of a Shakespearean scene conforms to the type of subject encouraged by James Mathews Leigh, Houghton's first art teacher. The artist's dependence on line is evident in this sketchily rendered scene. He also becomes caught up in incidental details such as the patterns formed by the branch and its shadow placed at the figures' feet.

Until now the painting has been identified as showing Sir Toby Belch, Viola, and Sir Andrew Aguecheek in the scene from *Twelfth Night* in which Viola, disguised as Cesario, and Aguecheek are baited into fighting a duel. As a woman, Viola is not trained for such combat, nor is she aggressive in temperament. Aguecheek too fears his opponent, and the humor arises at the squaring off of two such reluctant adversaries. The moment had long attracted artists: Francis Wheatley had exhibited a theatrical conversation piece of this subject at the Society of Artists as early as 1772, and in 1843 Frith had exhibited an amusing rendering at the British Institution. Houghton, however, illustrates the next scene in which Sebastian, rather than Viola-Cesario, is Aguecheek's opponent, a subject that George Clint had exhibited at the Royal Academy in 1833.

The setting is a pastoral village, with Olivia's inviting estate glimpsed through the impressive gates on the right. Houghton delights in exaggerating aspects of Elizabethan costume for humorous effects, the bulbous trunk-hose contrasting with spindly legs. Sir Andrew's trunk-hose is more baggy than swollen, unlike the puffed-up dress of the two aggressive males, and his sword hangs between his legs like the tail of a cowed dog. Sebastian's dress is somewhat effeminate, with his V-neck doublet exposing a shift with a ruff collar. It is of course the gender confusion that gives this and the preceding duel scene their comic edge. Sebastian, who is

thought to be Viola-Cesario, is expected to be timorous, but instead acts forcibly.

In *Twelfth Night* the expectations one places on sexual identity lead to comic situations. Near the end of his career in 1871, Houghton became mesmerized by the role women played in the Commune in France. The "masculine" traits displayed by these grim and heroic fighters are far removed from the light-hearted humor of the role reversals Houghton had earlier found in Shakespeare's play.

Frank Howard

Howard, the son of the royal academician Henry Howard (1769–1847), was born in London, probably in 1805. He studied art with his father and at the Royal Academy schools and was an assistant of Sir Thomas Lawrence. He began his public career with two paintings from Shakespeare's history plays that appeared at the British Institution in 1824. He exhibited at the Royal Academy the following year, and, except for a hiatus in the mid-1830s, continued to exhibit regularly at both institutions until 1846. In 1827 he published his first in a series of outline engravings of subjects based on Shakespeare's plays. This work, entitled *The Spirit of the Plays of Shakspeare, Exhibited in a Series of Outline Plates Illustrative of the Story of Each Play*, was completed by 1833. Soon after this he published a number of art manuals, along with a memoir accompanying the publication of the lectures his father had given as Professor of Painting at the Royal Academy. Beginning in 1843, he participated in the competitions for cartoons of pictures proposed for the decoration of the new Houses of Parliament. Sometime in the 1840s, his career only marginally successful, Howard moved to Liverpool. He again found patronage difficult to secure and supplemented his income by teaching and by working as a theater critic for a newspaper. He died in Liverpool on 30 June 1866.

42

PORTIA PRONOUNCING SENTENCE
The Merchant of Venice IV, 1
ca. 1830–31
Oil on canvas, 28 × 36 in. (71.2 × 91.5 cm.)

Case no. 1730

42

Provenance: Betts, November 1927, £50, as by Daniel Maclise

Exhibitions: London, British Institution, 1831, no. 416

References: "Critical Notices: Exhibition of Pictures at the British Institution," *Library of the Fine Arts,* vol. 1, 1831, p. 161 (mentioned briefly)

Condition: The canvas is torn at the left center, and the paint surface suffers throughout from wide separation cracks.

The painting is based on Frank Howard's print entitled *Portia Giving Judgment* (fig. 33), published on 1 June 1828. The engraving was the fifteenth image in a series of eighteen Howard executed of the play, a series that was published, along with illustrations to the other plays, in the artist's book *The Spirit of the Plays of Shakspeare.* Of the 483 designs involved in the total project, Howard exhibited only two at the Royal Academy: in 1828 "Bottom and Titania; one of a series of designs illustrative of Shakespeare, publishing in outline, etc." (no. 594) and in 1830 "Portia pronouncing sentence; one of a series of designs published in outline, etc." (no. 69). In 1831 Howard exhibited a painting of the latter scene at the British Institution (no. 416), and presumably this is the Folger picture. The work's measurements are given in the catalogue as 38 by 46 inches. If one subtracts 10 inches from both height and width, five inches being a plausible depth for a large frame, these measurements are identical to those of the Folger picture.

The subject is the play's climactic scene when Shylock, about to carve out his pound of flesh from Antonio's exposed breast, is unexpectedly thwarted by Portia at the last moment. At the left Antonio kneels with his shirt stripped away, waiting to pay the forfeiture for his inability to pay back Shylock the three thousand ducats. He had borrowed the money on Bassanio's behalf, and it is Bassanio who now supportively crouches beside him. Their friend Gratiano presses forward to mock the stunned moneylender, who has been immobilized by Portia's verdict. At the right on an elevated platform is the presiding Duke of Venice. In front of him is Portia disguised as Balthasar, a doctor of laws who has come to Venice for this one proceeding. Holding the bond in her left hand, Portia addresses Shylock.

Fig. 33. Frank Howard, *Portia Giving Judgment*. Engraving, 1 June 1828.

Having granted him the right to execute the terms of the bond, she then snatches away his victory by narrowly focusing on a literal interpretation of its content:

Tarry a little; there is something else.
This bond doth give thee here no jot of blood;
The words expressly are "a pound of flesh."
Take then thy bond, take thou thy pound of
  flesh;
But, in the cutting it, if thou dost shed
One drop of Christian blood, thy lands and goods
Are, by the laws of Venice, confiscate
Unto the state of Venice.

With few exceptions, all eyes are focused on her. But one of the law clerks seated at the table looks at Shylock, and "he" is presumably the disguised Nerissa.

The painting follows closely the print, although there are minor differences. For example, the positioning of Portia's hands is altered and the Venetian lion that appears on the cloth hanging behind the Duke is transferred to the tapestry added as a covering for the scribes' table in the painting. Given the print's abbreviated, outline style, Howard's tendency of stereotyping the male figures proves tolerable, but in the painting these heads produce a numbing sameness.

Aspiring throughout his series to the exalted level of high art, Howard went to great pains to disassociate himself from theatrical practices: "I have in no instance consulted theatrical effect, or what would be adapted to the stage; but have only considered how I could best produce, by pictorial representation, the same impression on the mind as is excited by reading the poet."[1] Yet this particular image may in fact be constructed around stage business. In performances of *The Merchant of Venice* from at least the time of Cooke in the late eighteenth century to that of Irving in the late nineteenth, Shylock often dropped his knife or scales or both at the moment of Portia's triumph, the crash underscoring the dramatic tension.[2] Although it is difficult to be certain, since Howard had already shown the scales lying on the floor along with Shylock's hat in the preceding engraving, *The Court of Judgment* (no. 14 in the series), it would appear that the scales have just crashed to the floor as Portia pronounces her sentence.

1. Frank Howard, *The Spirit of the Plays of Shakspeare*, London, 1833, vol. 5, "Postscript," pp. 1–2.
2. See Sprague 1944, p. 29.

George Jones, attributed to

Jones, whose father was a mezzotint engraver, became a student at the Royal Academy in 1801 at age fifteen. He was already exhibiting works in the annual exhibitions by 1803, and, inspired by Wellington's Peninsular campaign against the French, he joined the militia, serving in the Army of Occupation in Paris after Waterloo. Not surprisingly, military subjects became a favorite with Jones, and in 1820 the British Institution awarded him a premium of a hundred guineas for his picture of Wellington leading the advance at Waterloo. Jones was elected an associate member of the Royal Academy in 1822 and a full member in 1824. He was later to serve as its librarian and then as keeper. Over the years he exhibited numerous works at the Royal Academy and the British Institution. His favorite text was the Bible; of the 221 works he showed at the Royal Academy, only one was from Shakespeare, a scene from *The Tempest* exhibited in 1864 (no. 666). Jones died in London on 19 September 1869.

43

HAMLET IN THE QUEEN'S CLOSET
Hamlet III, 4
ca. 1830
Oil on panel, 12 × 9⁷⁄₈ in. (30.5 × 25 cm.)

Case no. 1925

Provenance: McGirr, September 1929, $36 (bought with West's *Lear and Cordelia*)

Condition: The paint surface suffers from separation cracks and the vertical splitting of the panel. The panel is incised on its verso: "BROWN / 163 / HIGH HOLBORN."

The picture was acquired as the work of the English artist George Jones, and its thickly painted passages of rich, Rembrandtesque highlights against a dark background are typical of Jones's style in works such as *Esther Approaching Ahasuerus* (Worcester Museum of Art), exhibited at the Royal Academy in 1828, and *The Burning Fiery Furnace* (Tate Gallery, London), exhibited at the Royal Academy in 1832, both of which are also executed on panel. Yet the relatively poor quality of the figures' hands and faces in the Folger painting gives one

pause in firmly attributing this work to Jones.

The scene is the Queen's closet, where Gertrude recoils from her son's acerbic comparison of the sterling qualities of his murdered father, her late husband, with the wicked deficiencies of his uncle, the murderer himself who has replaced him in the Queen's affections. Hamlet uses as a point of departure for his comparison of the two men a portrait of each, and in eighteenth-century performances it was apparently customary to have him refer to paintings hanging on the wall. Here, as is typical of later performances, he holds a small picture while chastising his mother for her inconstancy. Gertrude, resplendently dressed, recoils at the sight of the proffered image, beseeching her son to speak no more. Hamlet's sword, which he had unsheathed to kill Polonius, lies on the floor at the lower right, a reminder of the earlier, violent assault.

The Ghost, who commandingly towers above the two, makes his appearance in order to deflect Hamlet's anger at his mother, instructing him to offer comfort to the shaken Queen and not to forget the real villain in this tragedy. Both Hamlet and his mother react in astonishment: Hamlet to his father's Ghost, his outstretched right arm in alignment with that of his father's pointing gesture,

43

indicative of their common bond and purpose, the Queen to the picture held by Hamlet, which presumably contains an image of her late husband. Gertrude is oblivious to Hamlet's sighting of the Ghost, and the painter relishes the dramatic irony of each looking at, and reflecting on, images of Hamlet's father, yet each focused on a different source.

G. Jones

Because of the signature at the lower right, this painting has been attributed to the Royal Academician George Jones (1786–1869). The signature may indeed be correct, but it is obviously another Jones who is the author of this crude work. A G. Jones, listed as a miniature painter living at 38 Leicester Square, exhibited a portrait of Napoleon at the Royal Academy in 1832; G. Jones, living at 2 Radcliffe Terrace, Goswell Road, exhibited a landscape watercolor at the Society of British Artists in 1835; and G. Jones, at G. Smetham, 120 Adelaide Road, exhibited *Disaster* at the same society in 1888–89. It is unlikely, however, that the Folger picture was executed by a professional painter.

44

FALSTAFF AND FORD AT THE GARTER INN
The Merry Wives of Windsor II, 2
1864
Oil on panel, irregular, 5³/₄ × 8¹/₈ in. (14.7 × 20.5 cm.)

Signed and dated in red at lower right: "G. JONES. / 1864"

Accession no. 202156

Provenance: Gift of Herbert Kleist, Cambridge, Mass., September 1969. (When Kleist, a retired member of the staff of Harvard's Widener Library, donated this painting, he wrote that he thought he had acquired it ten to fifteen years earlier at the Goodwill store in Boston.)

Falstaff sends love letters to Mistress Page and Mistress Ford, which his go-betweens, Nym and Pistol, in an act of betrayal, take instead to their husbands. Ford, disguised as a Mr. Brook, then approaches Falstaff to test his wife's faithfulness. His story is that he wants Falstaff to seduce Mrs. Ford

in order that he might use her fall from grace to his advantage in pressing his own assault on her virtue. Falstaff, with a draught of sack sitting beside him, a present from Mr. Brook, eagerly looks on as Ford pushes a bag of money toward him, his payment for the planned seduction. Ford offers the money with one hand, while his clenched fist held behind his chair indicates his true feelings.

The design for this picture is based on a book illustration that bears the initials "CG" and is engraved by Gouters.[1] This title page, in turn, goes back to Orrin Smith's wood engravings from designs by Joseph Kenny Meadows, first published in 1840, which show the figures reversed, with Ford on the left and Falstaff on the right and the gutter of the book between them. Jones's design is closer to the title page than to Meadows's conception, and he has inserted a table between the two men and either discarded or rearranged such details as the canes to accommodate this addition. Jones's version is unable to sustain the humorous intensity of the original conception, and the addition of an environment for the figures is too crudely managed to do anything other than detract from this confrontation.

1. The title page is located in ART File S528m4, no. 136. If it was published later than 1864, then the date and the signature on the Folger painting are both called into question.

Sir James Dromgole Linton

Throughout his career Linton worked in both watercolors and oils, but he was best known as a watercolorist. He was born in London on 26 December 1840. From an early age he desired to become an artist, but his father, concerned with the difficulties of succeeding in this profession, insisted on his learning a trade, apprenticing him to a firm of glass-stainers. However, until he was twenty-one Linton also studied at J. M. Leigh's Art School. He exhibited for the first time in 1863 at the Society of British Artists, and his first appearance at the Royal Academy came two years later. In 1867 he married and was elected a member of the Institute of Painters in Water-Colours. For a time he also supplemented his income by working as an illustrator for the *Graphic*. He received official recognition when awarded the Gold Medal for a drawing at the Philadelphia International Exhibition in 1873. Toward the end of the 1870s he began to work more

44

frequently in oils, receiving in 1879 a commission
for his most famous series of paintings, *Incidents
in the Life of a Sixteenth-Century Warrior.* In 1883
he was elected president of the newly formed Institute of Painters in Oil Colours, and the following
year he took over the presidency of the Royal Institute, formerly the Institute of Painters in Water-
Colours. His success as an administrator led to a
knighthood in 1885. Linton served as president of
the Royal Institute until 1898 and again from 1909
until his death in 1916. His contemporaries found
in his work the unusual combination of the decorative splendor of the great Venetians, such as Ver-
onese and Tintoretto, with the precise handling of
such seventeenth-century Dutch painters as Ter-
borch and Metsu.

45

PORTIA

The Merchant of Venice IV, 1
ca. 1895
Oil on canvas, 50⅛ × 28 in. (127.3 × 71 cm.)

Monogram in lavender letters in lower right corner:
"JDL"

Provenance: Source unknown; the file card lists the
purchase price as £75.

Exhibitions: London, Institute of Painters in Oil
Colours, *A Catalogue of the 13th Exhibition*, 1895–
96, no. 281, as "Portia," repr. pl. i, price listed as
£105

Condition: The painting is executed on a medium-
weight, tabby-weave canvas preprimed with a layer
of white ground. The paint film is folded over the
edges of the stretcher on three of its four sides,
suggesting the work was first executed on an un-
stretched canvas. The picture was restored in 1991,
perhaps for the first time, when two tears were repaired, a square-shaped one at the bottom center of
Portia's cap and an irregular one in her robe 19½
inches from the bottom and 6 to 7 inches from the
left-hand edge. At this time the canvas was also
cleaned, lined, and attached to a new stretcher.

Linton executed a number of images illustrating
The Merchant of Venice in both oil and watercolor.
In this exhibited picture of 1895 he shows Portia in
three-quarter length disguised as Balthasar, a doctor
of law who has come to the Venetian court to help
resolve Shylock's demand for a pound of Antonio's
flesh, the forfeiture stated in the bond between the
two antagonists. Portia wears a red velvet brocaded
robe with deep sleeves trimmed in ermine, and
a black cap. At her side she holds a handsomely
bound portfolio, presumably containing her legal

ently the first to introduce red robes into the theater, and both Baldry's and Millais's paintings are based on her actual costume.[2]

In its format and reflective mood, Linton's interpretation is indebted to that of his two predecessors, but the depiction of a handsome female in a moment of quiet meditation was already a well-established part of his repertoire, as indeed it had been for Victorian painting as a whole. Linton may even have seen his painting as an opportunity to improve on that of his more illustrious colleague. Millais had begun his canvas as the study of a model in a Greek dress, only later to transform it into Portia after having borrowed Ellen Terry's costume. His Portia, presumably because of her genesis as a Greek girl, would never have fooled anyone as to her sex. Linton at least attempts a Portia who might be convincing as a young man. In addition, he seems to have attempted to disassociate his characterization from that of Ellen Terry's by modeling his heroine on the features of her celebrated rival, the American actress Mary Anderson (fig. 35).[3] Ultimately, his *Portia* is more convincing as an interpretation of the character in Shake-

brief, a prop that may have been borrowed from the theater: Helen Faucit introduced in the nineteenth century the stage business of Portia's reading from a legal text beginning at the line, "It is enacted in the laws of Venice . . . ."[1] In Linton's painting Portia's ring, a gift from her husband, Bassanio, which will play a role in the plot, is prominently displayed on her right hand.

Portia was a popular heroine in Victorian culture, and in the late nineteenth century the great actress Ellen Terry defined this role for her contemporaries. G. W. Baldry's *Ellen Terry as Portia* of 1885 (Garrick Club, London) and Sir John Everett Millais's *Portia* (fig. 34) of 1886 were two important images indebted to Terry's conception painted just a decade before Linton's interpretation. All three paintings show Portia in three-quarter length wearing red garments. Traditionally her legal robes were black (see, for example, nos. 42 and 82), but Terry was appar-

speare's play than is Millais's, but it is inferior as a picture. The stolid handling of the paint and unflattering shading of the nose make for a more prosaic image totally lacking in the lyrical grace and color harmonies of Millais's painting.

1. See Sprague 1944, p. 26.
2. Baldry's painting is a theatrical portrait, but in Millais's, only the costume is derived from Terry's performance. See Lucy Oakley's article "The Evolution of Sir John Everett Millais's *Portia*" for reproductions of both works (*Metropolitan Museum Journal* 16 [1981], pp. 181–94). Although the column in Millais's painting, as Oakley remarks, is a vestige of the grand-manner portrait, it also is intended to echo Shylock's comment on Portia-Balthasar, "I charge you by the law, / whereof you are a well-deserving pillar" (IV, 1, 238–39). Working in Venice, Henry Woods executed his painting of Portia in 1887 for the Graphic Gallery of Shakespeare's Heroines. Now in the Laing Art Gallery, this picture is reproduced in the catalogue to Buxton 1980, p. 69.
3. It is unlikely that Anderson posed for Linton. Already retired from the stage, she in fact had never played this particular role as she feared comparison with Terry's popular rendition. Ironically, Anderson may have been the inspiration for Millais's *Portia* in its earlier state as the figure of a Greek girl.

Henry Liverseege, after (nos. 46–48)

A Manchester artist, Liverseege was born on 4 September 1803. Drawn to painting at an early age, he first attracted notice when he exhibited at Manchester in 1827 three small pictures of banditti. In the following year he exhibited at the Royal Academy in London, and a year later began to exhibit as well at the Society of British Artists and the British Institution. Suffering for some time from poor health, Liverseege died on 13 January 1832. Apparently largely self-taught, he never mastered the technical refinements of painting but was appreciated for his ability to express character and to tell a story. He was also an amateur performer, and his experience as an actor obviously aided him as an artist. His favorite authors were Shakespeare and Cervantes. His canvases tended to be relatively small, and in their conception look back to seventeenth-century Dutch painting.

46

THE GRAVE-DIGGER
Hamlet V, 1
ca. 1832
Oil on canvas, 18¼ × 14 in. (46.5 × 35.5 cm.)

Case no. 1701

Provenance: Holoway, June 1927, bought as by Robert Smirke

Exhibitions: Amherst, *Shakespeare*, 1951, as by Smirke

Condition: Finlayson lined the canvas in 1932.

Related works: The original painting was exhibited at the Society of British Artists in 1831 as "The Grave-Digger" (no. 78). It is presumably the painting that sold at Christie's on 23 May 1980, lot 64, which was signed and dated 1830 (oil on panel, 17 × 13¼ in.). A smaller, unsigned version (oil on canvas, 11³⁄₁₆ × 8¾ in.) is in the Manchester City Art Gallery. A copy of the picture signed "Thos Webster," deaccessioned by the Yale Center for British Art, was sold at Sotheby on 18 November 1981, lot 149 (oil on board, 11¾ × 8¾ in.).

Engravings after original: John Charles Bromley, 1 November 1832, entitled "The Grave-Diggers," 10½ × 8⅜ in. (ART Vol. f18); an undated engraving marked "J. Andrews dirext." and "E. Hobart Sc.," 5¹³⁄₁₆ × 4¹³⁄₁₆ in. (image) (ART File S528h1, no. 60, pt. 2); a photograph of the above was published in 1900 in the Connoisseur Edition of the Shakespeare Rare Print Collection, issued for subscribers to *The Eversley Shakespeare*, part 9, no. 8 (ART Vol. e58). This print is wrongly captioned, "From a painting by E. Hobart."

In 1831 Liverseege exhibited two pictures from *Hamlet*, one serious, the other comic: the closet scene at the Royal Academy and *The Grave-Digger* at the Society of British Artists. The *Times* critic praised the artist, noting that in *The Grave-Digger* he "caught the true humour of the characters, and expressed it with great skill."[1] The Folger painting is a copy after this latter work, perhaps based on the engraving.

The grave-diggers open the fifth act of the play, where, pausing in their work of excavating a grave for Ophelia, they exchange humorous sallies. While critics often objected to the low humor introduced into so solemn a scene, the two clowns were extremely popular with the majority of nineteenth-century audiences. Liverseege deliberately contrasts the two grave-diggers, one young, tall and lanky, and dressed in dark clothes, the other old, squat and broad, and dressed in a light-colored coat. Their ungainly appearance adds to the scene's humor, as does Liverseege's choice of a punning title. The artist depicts the moment when the first digger, who is presumably the older man with the spade, queries the second, "What is he that builds stronger than either the mason, the shipwright, or the carpenter?" The boards at the bottom right surely allude to the second digger's answer of the "gallows-maker," but of course the correct response is "a grave-maker," for "the houses that he makes last till doomsday." Liverseege frames the two men in a church doorway as Ophelia is being buried in consecrated ground despite speculation that her death was a suicide, and references to churches are also part of the imagery invoked by the first digger's riddle. Perhaps because it might strike too somber a note, the artist leaves out the grave itself, which the text makes clear has already been begun.

The Folger picture is a copy of high quality that differs only in incidental details from the painting and the print after it. For example, the wry, pinched face of the figure on the left has been softened; the red cloth at lower left is mounded higher; and the pattern of the jagged upper edge of the drain has been made more regular.

1. *The Times*, 28 March 1831, p. 3.

46

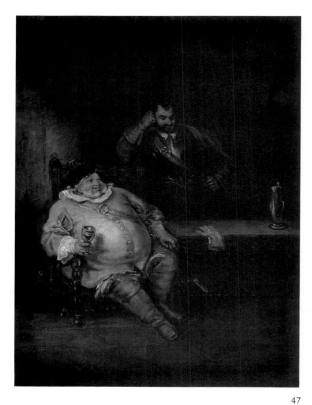

47

48

FALSTAFF AND BARDOLPH

I Henry IV III, 3

After 1833

Oil on canvas, 12 × 10 in. (30.5 × 25.4 cm.)

Provenance: Source unknown. The work was photographed, presumably for the dealer, by A. C. Cooper. On the back of the photograph are written the painting's dimensions, the name "D. Wilkie," and "15 guineas less 10% [or 18%]." Below this "Hamilton" has also been written in. Presumably, though, the painting was bought as by David Wilkie.

Condition: The canvas has never been lined.

Liverseege depicted Shakespearean subjects more than those of any other author, and the collection of prints issued shortly after his death includes one entitled *Falstaff and Bardolph* (fig. 36). This print almost certainly reproduces the painting mentioned as his last work in an obituary published shortly after the artist's death: "The picture left on his easel (Sir John Falstaff), of which the right hand and arm are the only parts approaching to completion, give promise that the whole would have been a decided improvement on all his former efforts. He

47

FALSTAFF AND BARDOLPH

I Henry IV III, 3

After 1833

Oil on canvas, 15¾ × 12 in. (40.1 × 30.6 cm.)

Provenance: Anderson, January 1921, as by J. M. W. Turner. This painting was sold along with two watercolors, also said to be by Turner, for $1,000. Anderson wrote that he thought he had acquired this work from the collection of John E. Parsons. He does not say to whom the work was then attributed, but he was the one to identify it as by Turner. He later "discovered" Turner's signature on the upper portion of the sword scabbard (Anderson to Folger, 8 January 1921).

Condition: The canvas has been lined, and the paint surface is in good condition, although there are noticeable separation cracks along the top and left side and some damage appears in both left-hand corners.

Engraving after original: J. Bromley, published 31 August 1833, 10 × 7¹⁵⁄₁₆ in.

48

Fig. 36. After Henry Liverseege, *Falstaff and Bardolph*. Engraving by J. Bromley, 31 August 1833.

anticipated finishing it with enthusiasm, for he trusted to make it his 'great work.'"[1] In any event, the print is now the only remaining image of Falstaff by Liverseege.

The two Folger pictures are by different hands, and stylistically no. 47 is closer to works securely attributed to Liverseege. The figures are approximately the same size in both versions, although no. 47, the larger of the two, includes more background. In this version Falstaff wears a black hat with gold trim, a yellow doublet with red slashed sleeves, and a red belt. In the smaller version he sports a red hat with gold trim; the slashed sleeves are green; and the belt is a brownish yellow, close in color to the doublet. Bardolph's wardrobe also changes from a brown doublet to a green one.

1. *The Athenaeum*, 21 January 1832, p. 48.

Rev. Matthew William Peters

Peters's life was unusual in that he pursued two professions, that of a painter and that of a clergyman, and was successful at both. His parents were Anglo-Irish, and although he was born in 1742 on the Isle of Wight, he grew up in Dublin. His education was directed toward his taking orders in the Church of England, but, demonstrating a flair for art, he was also sent to the School of Design to study under Robert West and then to London to the painter Thomas Hudson. In 1759 he won a premium at the Society of Arts, and three years later the Dublin Society sent him to study in Italy, where in 1763 he was elected a member of the Florence Academy. Back in London in 1765 he became a member of the Society of Artists, exhibiting portraits there until 1769, when he also began to exhibit at the Royal Academy. He was elected an associate member of the Royal Academy in 1771 and six years later was made a full academician. He traveled in France and Italy from 1772 to 1776, spending two years in Venice studying coloring. In 1779 he studied at Oxford for the church and was ordained a priest in 1782; soon thereafter he again studied in France. Some of his earlier works, under the influence of Jean Baptiste Greuze, had depicted tantalizing women in various states of undress, but in 1782 he exhibited at the Royal Academy a work more appropriate to his other profession—*An Angel Carrying the Spirit of a Child to Paradise*. Peters increasingly withdrew from painting as he advanced in his ecclesiastical career. He last exhibited at the Royal Academy in 1785 and resigned his membership in 1788, having served as its chaplain from 1784. Despite giving more time to his ecclesiastical career, Peters was still a major contributor to the Boydell Shakespeare Gallery, executing five large paintings (see no. 50), and was the single largest contributor to the rival Irish Shakespeare Gallery, executing six canvases from five plays.[1] Woodmason clearly found his participation desirable not only because some of his Boydell pictures were popular but also because he was one of the few artists who could claim to be from Ireland. Marrying in 1790 at age forty-eight, he continued to prosper, leaving a sizable fortune to his family when he died on 20 March 1814.

1. The six paintings were *The Apparition Scene* from *II Henry VI*, *Imogen before the Cave of Belisarius* from *Cymbeline*, *The Storm Scene* and *The Confrontation between Prospero and Caliban* from *The Tempest*, *Charmian and the Soothsayer* from *Antony and Cleopatra*, and the Folger's *The Death of Juliet*.

49 (Plate 8)

THE DEATH OF JULIET

Romeo and Juliet V, 3
1793
Oil on canvas, 65³/₄ × 52³/₄ in. (167.2 × 134.1 cm.)

Case no. 1677

Provenance: McLaughlin sale, Christie's, 18 February 1927, lot 157, 42 guineas, bought by Smart; Parsons, May 1927, £80

Exhibitions: Dublin, 1793, no. IX; London, 1794–95, no. IX

References: Lady Victoria Manners, *Matthew William Peters, R.A.*, London, 1913, p. 57; Salaman 1916, p. 25; Hamlyn 1978, pp. 522 and 529, no. IX, repr. as "Juliet stabbing herself"; Waterhouse 1981, p. 278, as "The Suicide of Juliet"; Kestner 1986, p. 14, repr. in color p. 11

Condition: A comparison of the painting to the print after it shows that the canvas has been cut down slightly. The whole of Romeo's boot, for example, is visible in the print. The print also shows lettering on the edge of the tomb, lettering that is no longer visible in the painting: "ARIA[?] CAPULETTA. VER." Parts of the picture have been overpainted. The piece of Juliet's drapery covering Paris's head is a later addition. It is the wrong color and obscures too much of Paris's face. According to the photograph the dealer sent Folger to pique his interest, there was even more overpainted drapery in the painting then than now. The picture has also suffered from solvent abrasion. The two middle fingers of Juliet's left hand have been damaged as well as the head of the tomb effigy. The shafts above Juliet's head are also no longer clearly defined.

Engravings: R. Rhodes, published 1 January 1817 by John Murray, 9³/₄ × 7¹³/₁₆ in. (image)

The subject of Juliet stabbing herself is perhaps Peters's finest painting. As was so often the case, a beautiful woman is his focus, but she is now at the center of a scene of high-minded tragedy where the charge of frivolousness leveled at some of his other works could no longer apply. Some of the painting's details are more clearly seen in the print after it (fig. 37) than in the canvas itself. The engraver Rhodes, however, took some liberties with the design, altering, for example, the angle of Juliet's dagger. The blade in the print extends down the center of her arm, insuring that in the black-and-white im-

Fig. 37. After Rev. Matthew William Peters, *The Death of Juliet.* Engraving by R. Rhodes, 1 January 1817, 9³/₄ × 7³/₄ in. (image).

age its edge would not be confused with that of the arm itself.

The scene is the tomb of the Capulets, where both Romeo and Paris had come to visit the grave of Juliet, whom they believed to be dead. There the two fight, and the body of the slain Paris lies at the left. Wishing to join Juliet in death, Romeo takes poison, the empty cup lying beside him. When Juliet awakens from her drugged sleep to find her husband dead, she prepares to kill herself. As the Watch approaches, led by Paris's Page, she utters her last words: "O happy dagger! This is thy sheath; there rust, and let me die." Paintings depicting the Tomb Scene were not uncommon, but the actual moment showing Juliet poised with her dagger had been executed only three times before. It served as the frontispiece to the 1709 edition of the play (fig. 38) and was engraved by Anthony Walker in the last of a series of five prints illustrating *Romeo and Juliet*, apparently first published in 1754 (fig. 39).[1] Peters's painting, however, invites comparison with the almost contemporary picture by Joseph Wright

of Derby (fig. 40), a work that was well known as it
had been rejected by Boydell and was then exhibited
at the Royal Academy in 1790. After a quarrel with
the Academy, Wright reworked and exhibited it at
the Society of Artists the following year. Concentrating on gesture rather than expression, Wright
shows Juliet from behind as she reacts to the approach of the Watch, whose shadow appears on
the door to the tomb.[2] The two lovers are somewhat dwarfed by the ambiguous space of the dark
interior. Juliet's raised hand, recalling Garrick's expressive gesture in Benjamin Wilson's painting of
the Tomb Scene (see fig. 67), is the picture's central
focus. In contrast, Peters makes his figures monumental, and his sources are to be found in such
grand-manner subjects as the Death of Lucretia, a
scene of Roman virtue, and the Pietà, one of Chris-

Fig. 38. After François Boitard, *The Death of Juliet.* Engraving by
Elisha Kirkall, 1709, 6½ × 4 in. (image).

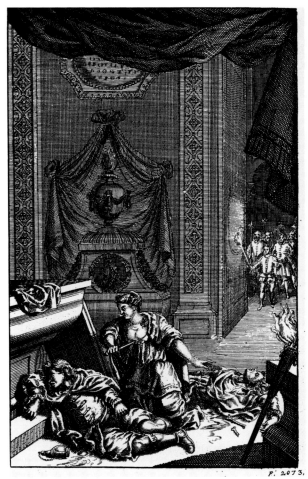

Fig. 39. Anthony Walker, *The Death of Juliet,* 1754. Engraving, 8¼
× 5⅝ in. (image).

tian sentiment. Juliet, dressed in her white funeral
shroud and bathed in warm light, looks heavenward
with wet, gleaming gray eyes, her pathetic gaze recalling images of Baroque saints, and Peters's adaptation of Christian imagery to a secular subject
effectively intensifies the scene's emotional content. As in the two earlier engravings, he shows the
Watch approaching in the distance, finding drama
in the radical changes in scale. Paris's body at the
left, unobtrusively positioned beneath the effigy of
a Capulet ancestor, is unusually small, but the artist's only false note is in his difficulty with Juliet's
anatomy, her left knee extending out too far in an
effort to accommodate her lover's body.

1. The series by Walker deserves more attention than it has received. Four of the preparatory drawings are in the Huntington
   Library and Art Gallery and three of these are dated 1753.
   Walker exhibited four of his scenes from the play in the first exhibition held at the Society of Arts in 1760 (no. 128). While it
   has been stated that "There is no indication that any of the
   prints were published until 1795, thirty years after Walker's
   death" (Robert Wark, *Drawings from the Turner Shakespeare,*
   San Marino, Calif., 1973, p. 49), one of the Folger prints, the Bal-

Fig. 40. Joseph Wright of Derby, *The Tomb Scene*. Oil on canvas, 70 × 95 in. By permission of the Derby Museums and Art Gallery.

cony Scene, bears the publication date 15 January 1754. H. A. Hammelmann writes that the prints were intended for a quarto edition of Shakespeare to be published by Lowndes ("Anthony Walker: A Gifted Engraver and Illustrator," *Connoisseur* 163 [July 1968], p. 172), but it is of interest that the lines accompanying the Tomb Scene belong to Garrick's version of the play and not to Shakespeare's.

2. Judy Egerton explains the low position of the shadow on the door as the result of the figure being in the act of ascending a stair (see the exhibition catalogue *Wright of Derby*, Tate Gallery, Grand Palais, Metropolitan Museum of Art, 1990, p. 124). The low point of view, however, is rather the result of the Watch's lantern hanging from atop the long staff that the shadow shows him holding. The dramatic use of the shadow is of course meant to intimate death, and the positioning of the staff here recalls the figure of Death with his spear in Wright's earlier painting *The Old Man and Death*, now in the Wadsworth Atheneum, Hartford. As in that painting, the person whom Death visits is free to choose whether or not to accept him.

Rev. Matthew William Peters, after

50

FALSTAFF HIDING IN THE BUCKBASKET
Merry Wives of Windsor III, 3
Early nineteenth century
Oil on canvas, 22⁷/₈ × 17 in. (58.1 × 43.2 cm.)

Case no. 1386

Provenance: Maggs, March 1925, £105 for this and D31, as by William Hamilton

Condition: Finlayson lined the canvas in 1932.

Original painting: Peters's original canvas was painted for Boydell's Shakespeare Gallery and was first exhibited in 1791 (no. LVII). It is now in the Museo de Arte de Ponce, Fundacion Luis A. Ferré, Ponce, Puerto Rico (98 × 70 in.)

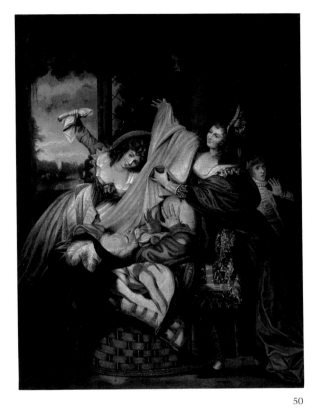

50

Engravings after original: P. Simon, published 24 December 1793, 25½ × 18⅛ in. (21⅞ × 15⅝ in., image)

Condition: Relined by Finlayson, 1932.

Peters executed five works for the large series of paintings for Boydell's Shakespeare Gallery: *Mrs. Page and Mrs. Ford Reading Falstaff's Love-Letters* (also engraved for the small series) and *Falstaff Hiding in the Buckbasket* from *The Merry Wives of Windsor, Hero and Ursula with Beatrice Listening in the Garden* (also engraved for the small series) from *Much Ado about Nothing*, and *Queen Katherine, Wolsey, and Campeius* and *The Baptism of Princess Elizabeth* from *Henry VIII.* Peters's scenes of attractive women, dressed in fancy laces in comic situations, proved the most popular of his paintings. Mr. Folger bought copies of two of these works, *Falstaff Hiding in the Buckbasket* and *Hero and Ursula with Beatrice Listening in the Garden* (see D31). When offering the paintings to Folger, Maggs wrote, "The two Paintings in question are though not necessarily by Peters, certainly by a contemporary and exceedingly clever artist, most

probably by W. Hamilton, R. A. (1751–1801), who exhibited Shakespearian and Historical Pictures from 1774."[1] When Folger queried the price, which he felt was high for copies, Maggs replied, "As these subjects were the greatest favourites, there was consequently a demand for them, and Boydell employed Hamilton (who was a celebrated R. A.) to make replicas in a smaller size, suitable for ordinary galleries."[2] There is no evidence to document this last statement, and the crude modeling suggestive of the light and dark contrasts of an engraving indicates that the Folger copy is after Simon's reproductive print rather than the original painting. In addition, the painting shows a view of Windsor Castle from the window, while the print, like the Folger work, depicts only a boat on the Thames, without Windsor in the background.[3]

Peters's original conception was a highly successful one, combining the self-conscious charms of the two women, Mrs. Ford and Mrs. Page, with the ridiculous situation of the fat knight about to be covered up in dirty linen. At the right, Robin, Falstaff's page, anxiously awaits the approach of Mr. Ford, who, accompanied by friends, is determined to search the house for his wife's supposed lover.

1. Maggs to Folger, 5 February 1925, Folger file.
2. Maggs to Folger, 6 March 1925, Folger file.
3. The painting is reproduced in black and white in the catalogue to Montgomery, 1985–86, no. 49. This change from the painting to the print was presumably made because Windsor Castle already appears in the background of *Mrs. Page and Mrs. Ford Reading Falstaff's Love-Letters,* and Boydell or the artist wished to introduce more variety into the series of prints.

Sir Joshua Reynolds, studio of

Reynolds was the most successful English painter of his generation. Born on 16 July 1723 at Plympton Earle, Devonshire, where his father, Rev. Samuel Reynolds, was the master of the Free Grammar School, he arrived in London in 1740 to begin an apprenticeship with another Devonshire artist, Thomas Hudson. He worked as a portrait painter in London and Devonshire until 1749, when he sailed with Commodore Keppel to the Mediterranean, arriving in Rome in April 1750. After studying the old masters abroad, he settled permanently in London in 1753 and was soon recognized as the city's most eminent painter. On the foundation of the Royal Academy in 1768, he was elected its president and in the following year was knighted by the king.

Reynolds also aspired to a career as a writer, and his *Discourses*, delivered in his capacity as president of the Royal Academy, have long been recognized as classic statements on academic theory. Through his writings and his art, Reynolds helped popularize the grand style. His portraits were often highly intellectual, elevating their sitters through an idealizing style, allegorical subject matter, and quotations from historical painting and antique sculpture. Given Reynolds's prominence, Boydell was determined to secure his participation in his Shakespeare Gallery, paying him for one picture his highest fee of 1000 guineas. (Benjamin West was the only other artist to receive a similar sum.) Reynolds seldom ventured into history painting, but for Boydell he painted *The Death of Cardinal Beaufort* for the large series (it was also engraved for the small one) and the Salvatorian *Macbeth in the Witches' Cave* (see fig. 10). For the small series, he painted *Puck*, a type of subject he had often explored in his fancy pictures of children. The Boydell pictures were among his last. Ill and almost blind, Reynolds died on 23 February 1792.

51

THE DEATH OF CARDINAL BEAUFORT

II Henry VI III, 3
ca. 1790?
Oil on board, 16³/₄ × 12¹³/₁₆ in. (42.5 × 32.5 cm.)

Provenance: Acquired by John Anderson, Jr., from Henry Dale, Reading, Berkshire; Anderson sale, American Art Galleries, 6 April 1916, lot 76, $260 plus 10 percent commission, Morris acting as agent

Exhibitions: Amherst, 1950, no. 16, as by Reynolds; Washington, 1976–77, no. 17, as by Reynolds

References: Art in America, December 1950, pp. 225–26 (reprint of Amherst exhibition); repr. in *A Brush with Shakespeare* (catalogue to Montgomery, 1985–86), fig. 7, as the engraving by Caroline Watson; Martin Postle, "The Subject Pictures of Sir Joshua Reynolds," Ph.D. diss., Birbeck College, London University, 1989, Catalogue, p. 32, no. 4

Condition: Comparison with the original indicates that this version has been cut down, particularly at the bottom.

Original painting: Commissioned by Alderman Boydell and exhibited in 1789 at the opening of his Shakespeare Gallery (no. 23). Acquired by the Earl of Egremont in 1805, this painting (93 × 56 in.) is still at Petworth.

Engravings after original: Caroline Watson, 25 March 1790 (first state) and 1 August 1792, 19⁷/₈ × 15³/₈ in., for Boydell's large series of prints (the demon behind the Cardinal's pillow has been removed in this second state); Andrew Grey, 4 June 1801, 10⁵/₈ × 6⁹/₁₆ in. (image and margin), for Boydell's small series

Related works: A version (oil on canvas, 92¹/₂ × 64¹/₄ in.) was bequeathed to the Shakespeare Memorial Gallery, Stratford-upon-Avon, by Henry Graves in 1892; a sketch (oil on canvas, 48³/₄ × 65¹/₄ in.) is in the Dulwich Gallery, London; and a small copy (27¹/₂ × 21 in.), which Postle feels dates from the nineteenth century, is in the Holburne of Menstrie Museum, Bath. The painting was frequently copied in the nineteenth century. Graves and Cronin mention, for example, that copies on a smaller scale were made by twelve different artists in 1823 when the picture was exhibited at the British Institution: Salter, Sargeant, Wright, Omon, Bridges, Davis, Elton, Johnson, Middleton, Fowler, Hayter, and Miss Drummond (see *A History of the Works of Sir Joshua Reynolds*, 4 vols., London, 1899–1901, vol. 3, p. 1146). In *Art in America* it is suggested that the painting called a "small copy" which was sold in the Thomas Phillips sale, Christie's, 9 May 1846, no. 6, may be the Folger painting.

Although the *Henry VI* trilogy was rarely performed, as a source of English history it proved a popular subject for painters for Boydell. One of the most famous and controversial paintings of the entire gallery was Reynolds's *Death of Cardinal Beaufort*. The King and the Earls of Salisbury and Warwick are present at the Cardinal's deathbed, where he is haunted by his sins, particularly the murder of Duke Humphrey. Reynolds pays close attention to the text, visualizing Warwick's observation, "See, how the pangs of death do make him grin!" The King attempts to rouse him: "Lord Cardinal, if thou think'st on heaven's bliss, / Hold up thy hand, make signal of thy hope.— / He dies, and makes no sign. O God, forgive him!" The King raises his own arm, while, in contrast, the Cardinal's hangs downward, his fist clenched in agony. The swags of drapery, as in a portrait, lend dignity to the scene, but these bed curtains are also a part

51

of the scene's imagery: "Close up his eyes and draw the curtain close." Reynolds also dared to visualize the King's earlier comment, "O, beat away the busy meddling fiend / That lays strong siege unto this wretch's soul, / And from his bosom purge this black despair!" The demon Reynolds placed behind the Cardinal's pillow provoked so much criticism that a second state of the large print was made with it removed. The Petworth painting itself was re-touched in order to obscure the devil,[1] but, while difficult to see, the demon is present in the Folger

sketch. As was pointed out at the time, the composition pays homage to Poussin's *The Death of Germanicus,* a copy of which the artist owned, yet Reynolds skillfully adapted the horizontal format, usual for a deathbed scene, into a compacted verti-cal one.

In 1916, when selling the sketch that Folger bought, John Anderson, Jr., wrote in his sale cata-logue that the painting is signed on the bed-cover "J. Reynolds," making it "one of only three known examples bearing Sir Joshua's signature, the others being *Mrs. Siddons as the Tragic Muse* and *Lady Cockburn and her Children.*" He notes that some of the letters are indistinct—they are in fact nonexistent—and audaciously claims that this picture is the original for Boydell and that the large painting at Petworth was made at a later date.

While Anderson's claims for the Folger picture are extravagant fantasies, the work itself should not be too quickly dismissed. Martin Postle, who is publishing a book on Reynolds's history paintings, speculates that "the Folger picture may be a reduced copy made in Reynolds's studio, although one cannot completely rule out the possibility that it was done in the early 19th century."[2] The work differs in small details from the original and the prints after it, as, for example, in the case of the longer loop to the cord hanging from the Cardinal's hat and the more generalized treatment of the drapery. Whether a studio creation or a later one, it is a spirited interpretation rather than a prosaic transcription.

1. For an interesting discussion on this detail, see Albert S. Roe, "The Demon behind the Pillow: A Note on Erasmus Darwin and Reynolds," *The Burlington Magazine* 113 (August 1971), pp. 460–70. Postle convincingly argues in his dissertation that the demon was overpainted.
2. Letter from Martin Postle to the author, 28 January 1991.

John Francis Rigaud

Rigaud was born on 18 May 1742 in Turin, then part of the Kingdom of Savoy. He first studied painting under Claudio Francesco Beaumont and worked for a number of years in Florence, Bologna, and Rome. On the completion of his studies, he first settled in Paris but soon moved on to London in 1771. He worked in a variety of media and attempted a wide range of subjects, including history painting, decorative painting, popular subjects aimed at the print trade, and portraiture. He was elected a full academician by the Royal Academy in 1784, and in 1795 was appointed Historical Painter to King Gustavus IV of Sweden and made a member of the Royal Academy of Stockholm. He died on 6 December 1810 at Packington Hall, Warwickshire, the home of the fourth earl of Aylesford, his most sympathetic patron.

52

CONSTANTIA REVEALING HERSELF TO HER FATHER
Chaucer, "The Man of Law's Tale"
ca. 1788
Oil on canvas, 14⅛ × 18¹/₁₆ in. (35.9 × 45.8 cm.)

Provenance: Parsons, May 1928, £33 less 10 percent, as Angelica Kauffmann's *Lear and Cordelia*

Exhibitions: Washington, 1976–77, no. 13, as Angelica Kauffmann's *Cordelia and King Lear*

Condition: The original canvas is a twill weave and has been glue-lined onto a new canvas and attached to a new wooden stretcher, presumably when it was restored in 1953. The paint has suffered slightly from solvent abrasion, and there is some repaint in the red robe and in the green curtain. There are also a few separation cracks, the most notable running vertically to the left of the woman with both hands raised above Constantia.

Versions: The Folger picture is either a preparatory study for the large painting commissioned by Thomas Macklin for the British Poets' Gallery or a reduced copy by Rigaud for the engraving after it. It is more likely the latter, as the image in the print (14 × 17⅛ in.) is almost identical in size to the Folger painting. The Macklin painting, which measures 240.1 by 330.2 centimeters, was shown in the 1981 Summer Exhibition at the Heim Gallery, London, no. 20. It is now at Spencer House, London.

Engraving after the Macklin painting: Francesco Bartolozzi, published 30 November 1799, 17 × 19⅞ in. (platemark). Stephen Rigaud, the artist's son, writes that Bartolozzi lent his name to the print even though "it hardly contains a stroke of his masterly hand" (Rigaud, *Facts and Recollections* [see note 2 below], p. 79).

Thomas Macklin, inspired by the example of Boydell's Shakespeare Gallery, proposed in 1787 to commission artists to execute a hundred paintings illustrating the texts of British poets. The Poets' Gallery opened the following year, and Rigaud's picture, which was an illustration to Chaucer's "The Man of Law's Tale," was among the works that had already been completed. The Folger canvas is most likely a reduced copy for the engraving after it.

The text that Rigaud used was not Chaucer's but

rather a modern retelling by Henry Brooke, published in 1741.[1] The painting depicts a Roman emperor presiding at the festival he has consecrated to the memory of his daughter Constantia, whom he believes to have been slain several years earlier in Syria. The soldiers who have laid waste to the offending Syrian kingdom have only recently returned and form part of the celebration along with numerous Roman ladies. Constantia, however, had escaped Syria only to encounter new difficulties in England after having been shipwrecked on the Northumbrian coast. She had married the British king Alla and had borne him a son, but her evil mother-in-law conspired to have her and her son Mauritius set adrift on the ocean. Seized by pirates, they had arrived in Rome as slaves and had only recently been reunited with Alla, who had just undertaken a pilgrimage to the holy city. In the painting Constantia drops to her knees from her chair as she announces to her grieving father that she is still alive, the revelation surprising even her husband, who had not known of her royal birth. Following the text closely, Rigaud shows Alla, who holds his son, at the emperor's left and Constantia at his right. The emperor, in response, is about to fall on his daughter's neck, while a soldier in the background at the left is already alerting the multitude of this happy reunion, for, "Wing'd as an Arrow from some vig'rous Arm, / Through *Rome's* wide City flew the glad Alarm." The text also mentions "ceaseless Clamours and extended Hands," and Rigaud repeats this gesture liberally. The Roman matron with both hands raised above Constantia is perhaps intended as her mother, though she is not mentioned in the text. The model for this figure was the artist's wife, as can be seen in portraits of Mrs. Rigaud.[2] Since this Roman emperor was Christian, the artist also places a cross above the imperial eagle on the standard that forms part of the trophy mounted to the left of the curtain.

52

Rigaud's own comments on his difficulties with the picture have survived:

A large picture eleven feet by eight from Chaucer; painted for Mr. Macklin, for his intended plan of publishing sets of prints from the English Poets. He called and settled the price with me, a little before Mr. Alderman Boydell; which induced me to execute his picture first. It represents Constantia; being returned to Rome, and throwing herself at her Father's feet; there is a variety of attendants of different ages and characters. Her husband and her Son are also introduced. I studied this picture much and it is brilliant of colour, and has also a broad mass of light, and yet there is a something upon the whole that I do not like, and will require time for me to discover; it seems to me that there is a want of clearness; and the light, though broad, is cut in a strange manner about the chair; The drapery of the Emperor, behind the head of Constantia is too much of the scarlet, it should have more broken tints in it, and that I believe I shall do, when an opportunity offers. The figures and expression of the Emperor and Constantia *are happily hit*. It is taken from the Canterbury Tales;—the Man of Law's tale, modernized by Mr. Brook. It came back in December [1788]; I glazed, I harmonised, and made some alterations in it.[3]

His complaints about the large picture do not apply to the sketch because of the difference in scale. The scarlet drapery of the emperor remains a largely undifferentiated red, as various tints on this scale would be inappropriate. What seems to have eluded Rigaud in the gargantuan format required of the exhibited picture works effectively in this more decorative rendering.

1. See George Ogle, *The Canterbury Tales of Chaucer modernis'd by several hands*, London, 1741, vol. 2, pp. 104–98.
2. See, for example, Rigaud's *Self-Portrait with Family*, ca. 1784–86, repr. in Stephen Francis Dutilh Rigaud, *Facts and Recollections of the XVIIIth Century in a Memoir of John Francis Rigaud Esq., R.A.*, abridged and edited with an introduction and notes by William L. Pressly, *Journal of the Walpole Society* 50 (1984), fig. 3.
3. Ibid., p. 79.

George Romney (nos. 53–54)

Romney enjoyed a distinguished career as a portrait painter, but his passion was for literary subjects and Shakespeare was a favorite author. Born on 15 December 1734 in Lancashire, he studied with the itinerant painter Christopher Steele from 1755 to 1757. Leaving behind in Kendal a wife and two children, he arrived in London in 1762, winning premiums from the Society of Arts in 1763 and in 1765. He exhibited at the Free Society from 1763 until 1769, one of the works from the first year being a scene from *King Lear*. He switched his allegiance from 1770 to 1772 to the Society of Artists, and in 1773 traveled to Rome, returning to London two years later. Inspired both by the art of the old masters and by his contact with other artists then studying in Rome, such as Fuseli and Thomas Banks, Romney returned with renewed energy to literary subjects. His work in this area was confined largely to drawings. He obsessively reworked these compositions, sometimes on a large scale, but seldom completed them in oil. Anxious and reclusive in personality, Romney withdrew from his fellow artists, refusing to exhibit at the Royal Academy. His circle of friends revolved more around literary figures, the most influential of whom was the poet William Hayley. Romney was present at the dinner in 1786 at which the idea for the Boydell Shakespeare Gallery was born, and his son in fact claims his father was the one who proposed this ambitious project. Romney contributed four paintings to the gallery. The scene from the opening of *The Tempest* was his first, a bifurcated composition that unhappily attempts to juxtapose Prospero and Miranda on shore with the men on board the foundering ship at sea. His *Cassandra Raving*, closely tied to the conventions of the full-length portrait, is a more successful composition. In a departure from the types of work normally commissioned by Boydell, Romney also executed for the gallery his *Infant Shakespeare* (see no. 176) and in a similar vein *Shakespeare Nursed by Tragedy and Comedy*.

53

MACBETH AND THE WITCHES
Macbeth IV, 1
1785
Oil on canvas, 29½ × 24¹⁵⁄₁₆ in. (74.9 × 63.3 cm.)

Case no. 1929

53

There is a two-line inscription at the left of Macbeth's right foot. The top line is extremely difficult to read, and it was assumed in the 1977 restoration to be a signature. If this is the case, it seems unlikely that it spells "Romney." Two expert cipherers, independently of one another, concluded that the word is "Febr." The inscription, therefore, reads, "Febr / 1785."

Provenance: Parsons & Sons, June 1929, £42.10.6

Exhibitions: Amherst, 1950, no. 19; Amherst, *Shakespeare,* 1951; Washington, 1976–77, no. 19; San Francisco, 1979–82, repr. in color p. 168; Montgomery, 1985–86, no. 55

Condition: The canvas suffers from extensive solvent abrasion in an early restoration. It was relined and freshly inpainted in 1977. The canvas has a cream-colored ground, and pentimenti are visible around the hands of several of the figures.

Romney completed few history paintings, and it is difficult to be certain that this canvas is indeed by him. In its light tonalities and delicate touch, it departs from a larger work such as his *Infant Shakespeare* (no. 176), yet the abstracted, curving bodies of the witches are extremely characteristic of his style, lending support to the traditional attribution. The canvas appears to be dated February 1785, a time that fits well into the chronology of Romney's career. In this period he was attending readings given by two of his close friends, John Henderson, the actor, and Thomas Sheridan, the actor, writer, and teacher of elocution, both of whom were members with him in the Unincreasables Club, a small dining and literary group whose membership was limited to eight.[1] Presumably *Macbeth* was one of the texts they used, as Romney's son links his father's painting *Henderson as Macbeth* (see no. 124) with Henderson's performance at these readings.[2] Yet no. 53, while also presumably inspired by the actor's recitation, is not in the conventional sense a theatrical conversation piece. Romney does not paint a performance of Henderson in the role of Macbeth, but rather the terrifying passions evoked by his interpretation.

The artist creates a scene of hellish mystery. The background is a murky brown, and such witches' paraphernalia as a human skull and a horse's skull, from which a serpent crawls through an eye socket, are at the lower left. The witches, all of whom share the same emaciated, pointed features, perform within a magic circle sketched on the ground. Macbeth's dress is similar to that worn by Henderson in no. 124: a red cape over armor with a claymore at his side. Here, however, he wears a green kilt, whereas in the portrait he appears to be wearing a pleated tunic trimmed in green.

Macbeth turns away in horror at the sight of the last scene conjured up by the witches, in which eight kings parade in front of him. Only the last two are completely visible, with the very last king holding a scepter and a mirror. Banquo's ghost follows behind, pointing to his heirs as he looks toward Macbeth, who ordered his murder.

The two cowled figures between Macbeth and the vision have been misidentified as "the spirits of Banquo and probably Duncan."[3] As already noted, Banquo is part of the glowing vision projected behind and above the witches. Instead, one of the figures must be Hecate, the deity of ghosts and magic. She is often shown as three separate figures as she reigns in heaven and earth and in the underworld, and perhaps Romney here is only doubling, rather than tripling, her form.

1. The readings were given in the Lenten season of 1785 (Ash Wednesday fell on 9 February and Easter on 27 March).
2. See Romney 1830, p. 166.
3. Amherst, 1950; see *Art in America* 38 (December 1950), p. 229.

54 (Plate 9)
Study for TITANIA, PUCK, AND THE CHANGELING
A Midsummer Night's Dream II, 1
1793
Oil on cardboard mounted on canvas, 10³/₄ × 14 in. (27.3 × 35.7 cm.)

Beneath the frame is attached a small box containing a mourning ring in memory of Lord Nelson. Inscribed to the left: "THIS PICTURE WITH THE MOURNING / RING IN MEMORY OF LORD NELSON / WAS GIVEN TO JOHN BRAHAM / BY LADY HAMILTON." To the right: "LADY HAMILTON AS TITANIA, / WITH PUCK & THE CHANGELING. / PAINTED BY G. ROMNEY, / THE ORIGINAL SKETCH." A photograph of the picture made in 1927 showing an earlier frame with a similar inscription is in the Witt Library, London.

Provenance: Presented to Lady Hamilton by the artist?; presented to John Braham by Lady Hamilton; Braham sale, Christie's, 9 February 1889, lot 40, bought by Samuel, £94.10.0; Raphael sale, Christie's, 29 May 1927, lot 91, £304.10.0, bought by F. Sabin; bought by Folger from Wells, March 1928, $3850

Exhibitions: Amherst, 1952; Washington, 1985

References: Romney 1830, p. 234; Fink 1959, p. 88

Condition: The surface has been squared off in faint blue lines for transfer. The squares are approximately 1⁵/₁₆ inches a side. Ultraviolet light reveals a fair amount of retouching in the sky and in the foliage in the background.

Versions: The larger picture, for which this work is a preparatory sketch, is in the National Gallery of Ireland, Dublin. See Ward and Roberts's list of sketches of this subject that appeared in the Romney sale held at Christie's on 27 April 1807 (1904, p. 195).

Engravings: For prints after the Dublin picture, see Ward and Roberts 1904, p. 195. The earliest of these prints was by Edward Scriven and published on 1 December 1810 by Longman & Co. It appears in John Britton's *The Fine Arts of the English School* (London, 1812).

A Midsummer Night's Dream was a favorite of Romney, and his "fancy pictures" that focused on this play were not commissioned works but were executed for his own pleasure. He concentrated on Titania; her world of magic, though not without its storms, is a fairyland that is far different from the evil magic to be found in *Macbeth* (see nos. 53 and 124).

Titania, Puck, and the Changeling is a beautifully executed sketch for a larger, unfinished painting in the National Gallery of Ireland. It is inspired by Puck's speech describing the fight between Oberon and Titania over who is to have custody of a changeling.

> For Oberon is passing fell and wrath,
> Because that she as her attendant hath
> A lovely boy stolen from an Indian king.
> She never had so sweet a changeling;
> And jealous Oberon would have the child
> Knight of his train, to trace the forests wild;
> But she perforce witholds the loved boy,
> Crowns him with flowers, and makes him all her
>   joy.

A bewitching Titania confronts the spectator at the right, while on the left lies the changeling with Puck "in wanton merriment, seeking to bind his feet in flowery fetters."[1] The three figures form a gracefully undulating chain from left to right, Puck and Titania extending beyond the picture frame on each side. The setting is an Indian beach, India being the home of fairyland, and Romney captures the sense of joyous celebration centered around the child. Fairies fly above the infant, and the central figures of the woman and child have been interpreted as a fairy transporting the changeling.[2] The fairies, several of whom hold their hands to their head, strike an ominous cord, a reminder of the ensuing fight between Titania and Oberon over the infant.

In the play Titania is associated with the moon and the night, her classical parallel being Diana. But in Romney's interpretation dawn floods the canvas,[3] and the classical parallel is with Venus and Cupid, the seaside setting reinforcing this association. The changeling is in an unusually provocative pose; only the difference in ages between him and Titania (as with Cupid and Venus) enables Romney to escape censure. It is this combination of innocence with wanton abandon that makes the images so compelling.

The subject is one of three episodes that Romney painted from this play, and all the depictions are interrelated. *The Indian Woman* shows the votaress of Titania, pregnant with the child who becomes the changeling, sporting on an Indian beach.[4] Romney discreetly shows only the woman's drapery billowing in the wind, her stomach not protruding, and to the left is the small, protected figure of Titania curled up in a cloth held by attendant fairies. Between them are two figures that echo the pose of Puck and the changeling in the Folger painting. A third scene shows Titania in the same position preparing for sleep as the fairies at her command sing and dance, chase bats, and kill cankerworms to prepare their queen for a restful sleep.[5] The National Gallery of Ireland picture was bought by Sir John Leicester in the Christie's sale of 27 April 1807. It has a distinguished history, having been consistently praised throughout the nineteenth century. The earliest accounts, however, do not mention the painting in connection with Lady Hamilton. The first time she is identified as Titania is in William Carey's description of 1819,[6] but, once made, this identification has never been challenged. The subject of Titania, Puck, and the changeling is the only one of the series from *A Midsummer Night's Dream* in which Titania is depicted on a large enough scale that such an identification is warranted. The fact that the Folger picture was at one time in the possession of Lady Hamilton helps confirm her association with the figure of Titania.

Romney could be said to have been obsessed by Lady Hamilton, and he was hardly the only one on whom she cast a spell. Born Amy Lyon in 1765 (she soon changed her name to Emma Hart), she rose from provincial, impoverished beginnings to an exalted position, a progression not unlike Romney's own. She first sat to the artist on 13 April 1782, when she was the mistress of the Hon. Charles Greville, and she posed for around three hundred sittings before leaving in 1786 for Naples, where she lived with Sir William Hamilton, Greville's uncle. She last posed for Romney in 1791, when she and Sir William returned to London for their wedding. Later she became the mistress of Admiral Nelson, even having a child by him, and was to die a penniless alcoholic in Calais in 1815, her protectors, Sir William and Nelson, both having predeceased her.

John Romney, the artist's son and biographer, dates "those various unfinished pictures, representing *Titania* under different circumstances, and in different attitudes," to around the time his father painted *The Indian Woman* in the winter of 1793–94.[7] But because a letter from the artist to his brother James dated 8 April 1793 speaks of the picture of the Indian woman as having been completed, the other Titania pictures are normally dated to this year as well.[8]

If the Folger sketch was executed in 1793, then Lady Hamilton could not have posed for the picture. Yet, she was clearly the inspiration for Titania's features. It is possible that the sketch was executed earlier, at a time when she was posing for the artist, but it is just as likely that Romney in 1793 was relying on previous sketches of his favorite model. Painted on the frame is a provenance stating that the work was a gift from Lady Hamilton to John Braham.[9] Braham, a celebrated singer, had tutored Nelson's wife in music in 1795 and a few years later was a frequent visitor to Nelson's residence in Leghorn when both men were in Italy. In the spring of 1802, he sang at least once at Merton, the country estate Nelson had bought for Emma, who also performed alongside the singer. On 7 December 1805, not long after Nelson had died at Trafalgar, Braham performed in a commemorative melodrama-ballet entitled *The Naval Victory and the Triumph of Lord Nelson on the Memorable 21st October 1805*. It seems plausible, then, that Emma would have given Braham, who was a friend as well as an admirer of both her and Nelson, this sketch accompanied by a mourning ring.[10]

1. William Carey, *A Descriptive Catalogue of a Collection of Paintings by British Artists, in the Possession of Sir John Fleming Leicester, Bart.*, London, 1819, p. 55.
2. "W. H. W." in *The Fine Arts of the English School; Illustrated by a Series of Engravings, from Paintings, Sculpture, and Architecture of Eminent English Artists*, ed. John Britton, London, 1812.
3. The streaks of light have also been interpreted as a rainbow.
4. Reproduced in the catalogue to Waterloo, 1985, fig. 24.
5. Reproduced in 1961 exhibition catalogue *George Romney: Paintings and Drawings*, held at Kenwood, no. 37. In 1795 Romney also executed for Lord Egremont a family portrait of a lady as Titania, with her four children as fairies shooting arrows at bats.
6. Carey, *Descriptive Catalogue* (see note 1 above), p. 55.
7. Romney 1830, p. 234.
8. The letter is mentioned in Ward and Roberts 1904, p. 195.
9. While there is no evidence that Emma and Romney saw one another after 1791, they were in correspondence and Nelson had contact with the artist, so there was ample opportunity for a sketch of 1793 to have passed from Romney to the muse who

had inspired his composition. It is also possible that Lady Hamilton purchased this work at the sale of the artist's effects held at Christie's on 27 April 1807.
10. John Mewburn Levien specifically notes, "After Nelson's death Lady Hamilton gave Braham a handsome mourning ring, with a lock of Nelson's hair in it" (*Six Sovereigns of Song*, London, n.d., p. 13, n.).

William Salter

Salter, a history painter and portraitist, was born in 1804 at Honiton in Devonshire. From 1822 to 1827, he was a pupil of James Northcote, another Devonshire artist who himself had studied under Sir Joshua Reynolds. He next spent five years in Florence and studied in Parma, and was elected to the academies in both cities before returning to London in 1833. Eight years later Salter privately exhibited his most famous picture, *The Waterloo Banquet at Apsley House*, to great acclaim. The painting, on which he had worked for six years, showed one of the annual banquets the duke of Wellington held at his London home to celebrate the English victory. He exhibited at the British Institution from 1822 until 1852 and at the Royal Academy from 1825 to 1845, but his closest ties were with the Society of British Artists. He began exhibiting there in 1836, became a member in 1846, and later served as its vice president. By the time of his death in London on 22 December 1875, he had exhibited 101 works at the society. His subject matter was eclectic, including portraits, Italian peasant subjects, sentimental genre, mythological scenes, biblical scenes, and pictures based on English history. He turned to Shakespeare relatively late in his career, *Othello's Lamentation* of 1857 being his first exhibited painting of a Shakespearean subject, but he went on to exhibit five other scenes from his plays in addition to a study of a Moor's head that was presumably related to Othello.

55

OTHELLO'S LAMENTATION
Othello V, 2
ca. 1857
Oil on canvas, 45½ × 56½ in. (115.5 × 143.4 cm.)

Case no. 1750

Signed at lower left: "W. Salter M A F. [Member of the Academy of Florence]"

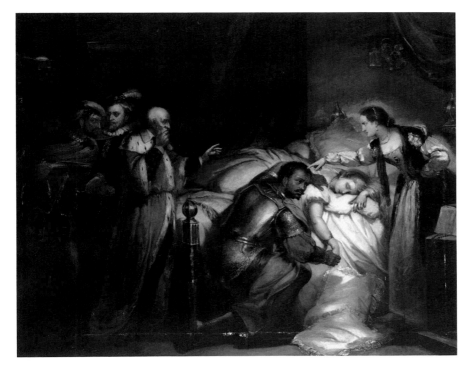

55

Provenance: Collection of W. D. MacKenzie, Fawley Court, Henley-on-Thames; his sale, Christie's, 26 April 1918, lot 153, as "Othello Lamenting over the Body of Desdemona," bought by Pickering, £7.7.0; Parsons, January 1928, £45

Exhibitions: London, Society of British Artists, 1857, no. 187, as "Othello's lamentation—Iago, Montano, and Gratiano. £210. 'Emilia. Nay lay thee down and roar, / For thou hast killed the sweetest innocent / That e'er did lift up eyes.' Act 5th. Scene 2nd."

References: The Athenaeum, 28 March 1857, p. 410; *The Illustrated London News,* 4 April 1857, p. 320; *The Art Journal,* 1 May 1857, p. 143

Condition: The canvas has been lined, presumably by Finlayson in 1932. The paint and white ground are actively flaking at the edges, and there are cracks in the paint surface that correspond to an earlier stretcher.

Engravings: wood engraving, ART Vol. b54, vol. 19, p. 139: OTHELLO'S LAMENTATION.—FROM A PAINTING BY T. SALTER IN THE EXHIBITION OF THE SOCIETY OF BRITISH ARTISTS (appears to be clipped from a magazine such as the *London Illustrated News).*

The last scene of *Othello,* in which the Moor kills his innocent wife, was the most frequently illustrated scene from the play. Several moments proved popular: Othello in contemplation as he approaches the sleeping Desdemona, his wife pleading for mercy, the murder itself, Iago stabbing Emilia, and Othello killing himself. Salter's painting is the first, however, to show Othello's lamentation.[1] After Emilia discovers the Moor's evil deed, her cries summon Montano, the former governor of Cyprus, who is followed by Gratiano, Desdemona's uncle, and Iago, Emilia's husband. Under Emilia's questioning, Iago's villainous machinations start to come to light. Salter depicts Othello at the moment he begins to realize he has been misled into believing his wife guilty of adultery, falling down with the agonizing cry, "O! O! O!" Emilia responds,

> Nay, lay thee down and roar;
> For thou hast kill'd the sweetest innocent
> That e'er did lift up eye.

Iago has already tried to silence her, and as she continues to expose him, he prepares to stab her. Though at first restrained by Gratiano, he soon succeeds.

The setting is a bedroom in the castle at Cyprus, a

Venetian coat of arms over the bed. A devotional is open on the stand with a crucifix at the right, a reminder of Desdemona's virtuous character and of her positive response to her husband's query, "Have you pray'd to-night, Desdemon?" Light plays an active role in this scene beginning with Othello's soliloquizing to the candle, "Put out the light, and then put out the light." Salter spotlights the main characters but without giving the light's source, and a darkening moon is seen through the archway at the left, Othello twice referring to the moon as an omen of terror and madness. Othello was shown on stage dispatching his wife in a variety of ways, including strangulation, stabbing, and smothering her with a pillow. Salter adopts the last method of execution, as shown by the pillows scattered about the bed and floor. He incorrectly, though, shows Iago clutching at his dagger, Gratiano's admonition making clear his first reaction is different: "Fie! / Your sword upon a woman?" Othello is typically portrayed as a dark-skinned European. Frank Howard had earlier justified such a presentation with the racist defense, "The physiognomy of the negro would entirely prevent the nobleness of the character being expressed." He went on to add, "Moreover, it is wrong, as OTHELLO is a native of Barbary, and not of the coast of Guinea."[2] What is surprising, though, is that Salter makes Iago almost as dark as the Moor.

The painting employs a range of bright, but not always felicitous, colors, including Othello's purple shoes and stockings, red cloak, and sleeves of reddish purple. He is positioned against the bright yellow of the bedspread, and his dark skin is contrasted to the deathly gray pallor of Desdemona, who is already turning into "monumental alabaster." Salter also has difficulty with scale and anatomical proportions, Montano for one being too small in relationship to the other figures, while Othello's left arm forms an awkward appendage. One critic felt compelled to unleash a devastating critique of the artist's insufficiencies:

Let who will lament for the Moor, we lament for Mr. Salter, who has painted (and *sold*) one of the most fantastic and absurd parodies on Shakspeare ever perpetrated. A more womanish bit of stage-*millinery*, a completer set of wooden-headed, tottery, imbecile lay-figures were never daubed with red and blue. Strip the broken-backed, puzzle-twisted Othello,—the second-

childhood Brabantio [Montano is meant],—the shaky, spineless, gristle-legged attendants, and we should be driven into torrents of laughter at the impossible anatomies. If clever, flashy armour and yellow and purple can atone for such a hospital of pictorial disease, the purchaser may be satisfied.[3]

The overall conception is indeed less than satisfactory. The overlapping of Emilia's finger with Othello's head is an unhappy juxtaposition, and the ultimate effect is to make her appear to be scolding a naughty miscreant rather than unfolding for Othello a series of painful and grotesque revelations.

Salter was undaunted by the reaction to his first attempt (the fact that he had sold the painting surely offered encouragement), and he exhibited another scene from *Othello* the following year, now known from a wood engraving after it (fig. 41). Depicting Othello and Desdemona in confrontation with her father Brabantio, it serves as a pendant to the Folger picture, and even allowing for inaccuracies on the part of the engraver, the artist's difficulties with scale are still very much in evidence, Brabantio's hands belonging to a different species from those of his daughter.

1. While Salter's is the first known painting of this subject, the German artist Moritz Retzsch had executed a print of the closely related moment of Emilia's exposing of Iago. Earlier in 1829, Frank Howard had issued the print *Emilia Undeceiving Othello* as part of his series of illustrations to this play, but he concentrates on Iago stabbing his wife.
2. Frank Howard, *The Spirit of the Plays of Shakspeare*, London, 1833, vol. 5, "References Descriptive of the Plates: Othello."
3. *The Athenaeum*, 28 March 1857, p. 410. The critic for the *Illustrated London News* was only mildly disapproving of Salter's picture, while the *Art Journal* faintly praised it.

Michael William Sharp

Sharp is thought to have been born in London, but the year is uncertain. A pupil of Sir William Beechey, he also attended the Royal Academy schools. He exhibited regularly at the Royal Academy from 1801 until 1828 and at the British Institution from its opening in 1806 until 1830. His earliest subjects were portraits, but he soon gravitated toward genre subjects, often injecting a touch of humor. In 1809 he won a premium of fifty guineas at the British Institution in the class of subjects of "Familiar Life" for his painting *The Music*

THE MOOR OF VENICE.——"OTHELLO," Act I.; Scene III.
(AFTER A PICTURE BY W. SALTER, IN THE SUFFOLK-STREET EXHIBITION.)

Fig. 41. After William Salter, *The Moor of Venice*. Wood engraving.

Master. In 1813 he settled in Norwich, where he studied with John Crome, but was back in London by 1820. His paintings proved popular and were often engraved. The last painting that he exhibited—the only one, in fact, in the last decade of his life—was the Folger picture from *The Taming of the Shrew*, which was shown at the Royal Academy in 1836. Sharp died in Boulogne four years later.

56

PETRUCHIO AND THE TAILOR
The Taming of the Shrew IV, 3
1835
Oil on canvas, 26⅝ × 22⅝ in. (67.7 × 57.5 cm.)

Case no. 1771

Signed and dated at lower left in black: "M. W. SHARP / 1835"

Provenance: Holoway, February 1928, £35

Exhibitions: London, Royal Academy, 1836, no. 220, as "Taming of the Shrew.—Act iv, Scene 3. 'Petruchio. Thy gown? why aye, Come, tailor, let's see't, etc.'"

References: The Times, 11 May 1836, p. 7, and 13 May 1836, p. 6

Condition: The original canvas, a tabby weave, was glued-lined on to a commercially prepared canvas with a ground by Finlayson in 1932. The paint has been moderately applied and has typical stress cracks throughout. The surface has been solvent-abraded, and large separation cracks have been repainted in the upper section. Sharp shortened the handle of the whip, the pentimento revealing how far it originally extended.

Shakespeare's *The Taming of the Shrew* fared poorly in its performances. In 1667 a much inferior adaptation called *Sauny the Scot* was performed by John Lacy. In 1756 Garrick introduced a condensed version entitled *Catherine and Petruchio*, and this was the play still being performed when Sharp executed his picture in 1835. In Garrick's version the scene occurs in the beginning of act III, before Hortensio has entered. Sharp takes pains in the Royal Academy catalogue to cite the original act and scene as written by Shakespeare, and his inclusion of Hortensio is another indication that he intends to illustrate the play as originally written.

As part of his plan to tame his bride, Petruchio orders new clothes so they can visit her father's house. Yet when the haberdasher and the tailor show their garments, of which Katherina wholeheartedly approves, Petruchio only finds fault and dismisses each of the tradesmen in turn. In the

56

painting, Grumio, Petruchio's servant, is at the far left, and the tailor kneels beside his gown while defending his work by pointing with his shears to the written specifications. The cap for which the haberdasher was dismissed lies in the lower left corner next to the gown. Petruchio is elegantly dressed in black with red netherstocks, a red plume in his hat, and with red in the slashes of his sleeves and upperstocks. He points to the offending dress with a whip, a stage prop that was popular in nineteenth-century performances, where it was intended to suggest Petruchio's physical as well as mental dominance over his wife. A bejeweled and puzzled Katherina attempts to restrain her husband with one hand, the other held to her mouth.[1] A sleek

greyhound cringes at his agitated master's feet, while Hortensio literally backs up his friend at the right.

The setting is a grand one, the room well lighted by large windows with delicate gothic tracery. Rosettes adorn the coffered ceiling, and the room opens up on the right onto a similar interior.

Samuel Redgrave, in his *Dictionary of Artists of the English School*, accused Sharp of "a tendency to vulgarity." The phallic shears the tailor holds are large, in keeping with the scene's bawdy humor, but Sharp also plays on class distinctions. The three aristocratic figures to the right are elegantly attired and physically attractive, in decided contrast to the dwarfish servant Grumio and the rail-thin tailor, whose face is grotesque with its inflamed nose and caricatured features. It is a comic rendering, calculated to appeal to class prejudice.

1. This last gesture was probably prompted by Thomas Stothard's interpretation of this same subject as seen in Heath's engraving of 1 May 1803.

Robert Smirke (nos. 57–71)

Smirke was born at Wigton, near Carlisle, on 15 April 1752. His father brought him to London when he was thirteen and apprenticed him to a heraldic painter. In 1772 he became a student at the Royal Academy and began to exhibit at the Society of Artists in 1775. He exhibited sporadically at the Royal Academy from 1786 until 1813. He was elected an associate member of the academy in 1791 and a full academician two years later. In 1804 he was elected its keeper, but, because of his republican sympathies, King George III refused to sanction his appointment. A painter of humorous and sentimental scenes, often on a modest scale, he was frequently employed as a book illustrator. He was also the most prolific of all the artists working on the Boydell Shakespeare Gallery. Smirke died in London on 5 January 1845.

57 (Plate 3)

FALSTAFF REBUKED
II Henry IV V, 5
ca. 1795
Oil on canvas, 31¼ × 21⅞ in. (79.4 × 55.5 cm.)

Case no. 1090

Provenance: Commissioned by Alderman John Boydell for the Shakespeare Gallery; sold by lottery 28 January 1805 and won by William Tassie; sold by Christie 17 May 1805, lot 6, as *"The King rebuking Falstaff—painted in a fine clear tone of colouring,"* bought by John Mehux for 13 guineas (£13.13.0); Joseph Pyke as of 1891; Michelmore, October 1922, £125 (£250 for this picture and no. 85).

Exhibitions: London, Boydell, 1795, no. 16; London, Boydell, 1796, no. 18; London, Boydell, 1802, no. 126; London, Boydell, 1805, no. 105; London, Whitechapel (St. Jude's), 1891, no. 145?; London, Grafton Gallery (Musical), 1892, no. 85 (for preceding two items, see Graves 1913); Amherst, 1959

References: Friedman 1976, p. 212, n. 415, and p. 236; Altick 1985, pp. 289–90

Condition: The paint is thinly applied on a white ground, and there are small areas of inpainting throughout.

Engravings: Joseph Collyer, published 4 June 1795, for 1802 Boydell edition of Shakespeare's plays, facing p. 119 of *II Henry IV,* 10½ × 6⅜ in. (image and margin); a later outline engraving by Starling, 4⅛ × 2¾ in. (image)

The newly crowned King Henry V stands at the left, his head dramatically silhouetted against the banner of St. George. He pauses on a raised walkway covered with a reddish orange cloth and sprinkled with flowers. A page holds his long train. At the king's command, the Lord Chief Justice admonishes Falstaff. The king himself is about to launch into his famous speech, beginning, "I know thee not, old man; fall to thy prayers. How ill white hairs become a fool and jester!" Accompanying Falstaff are Shallow, Pistol, and Bardolph, and in the distance, thinly painted, looms an almost spectral Westminster Abbey. Smirke leaves off the top portions of the west towers, which were not completed until the eighteenth century. The Abbey is partially obscured by puffs of smoke, presumably caused by the firing of guns in a salute to the king. Smirke executed five pictures for Boydell illustrating *I Henry IV,* two for the large series and three for the small, all but one of which are concerned with the play's comic subplot. For *II Henry IV* he executed only two pictures, the Folger painting and one depicting an earlier moment when the dying king confronts his son, a work now known only from the engraving after it (fig. 42). The two images are clearly related, the prince being chastised in the first and Falstaff adopting a similarly contrite pose when he is chastised in his turn by the prince who is now king.

Many early critics approved of King Henry V's renunciation of his former companion and even applauded Sir John's being taken away to the Fleet Prison at the play's end, a fitting retribution for his immorality. By the late eighteenth century, however, Falstaff increasingly attracted defenders. Writing in 1777, Maurice Morgann felt his generosity and humor outweighed his defects: "we can scarcely forgive the ingratitude of the Prince in the

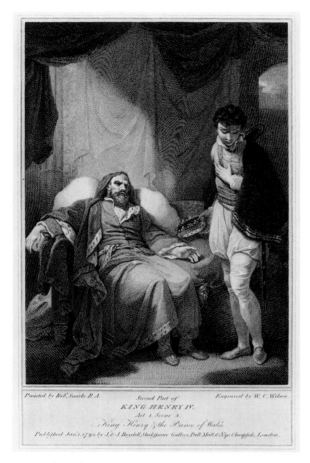

Fig. 42. After Robert Smirke, *King Henry IV and the Prince of Wales.* Engraving by W. C. Wilson, 1 January 1795.

new-born virtue of the King, and we curse the severity of that poetic justice which consigns our old good-natured delightful companion to the custody of the *warden,* and the dishonours of the *Fleet.*"[1] Clearly Smirke shares this view: Falstaff is sympathetically portrayed, his pose echoing the sincere repentance shown by Prince Hal in the earlier scene.

Recently, Altick faulted Smirke's "attempt to fit a familiar comic character into a conventional high-art triumphal scene."[2] Yet, nothing in the artist's characterization is out of place in the context of high-minded history painting. Only Bardolph's inflamed nose at the far right strikes a less than ennobling note. If the painting is to be faulted, it is not in Smirke's rendering of Falstaff, but rather in his depiction of King Henry V, who here is too

callow a youth to have effected his old friend's conversion.

1. Quoted in Stuart M. Tave, *The Amiable Humorist,* Chicago, 1960, p. 127.
2. Altick 1985, p. 290.

58

THE AWAKENING OF KING LEAR
King Lear IV, 7
ca. 1792
Oil on canvas, 31 × 20¹⁵⁄₁₆ in. (78.7 × 53.2 cm.)

Provenance: Commissioned by Alderman John Boydell for the Shakespeare Gallery; sold by lottery 28 January 1805 and won by William Tassie; sold by Christie 18 May 1805, no. 11, as *"Lear, Cordelia and Kent*—a charming and elegant Picture," bought by Crome, Esq., for 10 guineas (£10.10.0); Michelmore, February 1922, £125 (£250 for this picture and no. 86)

Exhibitions: London, Boydell, 1795, no. 30; London, Boydell, *Small Pictures,* 1796, no. 33; London, Boydell, 1802, no. 155; London, Boydell, 1805, no. 42

References: Friedman 1976, p. 212, n. 415, and p. 236

Condition: A large scratch across the bottom of Cordelia's robe (visible in the photograph) and an old zigzagging tear 22 inches long across the middle of the painting were repaired in 1988. In the arch at the upper left, Smirke had originally included a leaded window pane, which he then painted out with clouds and a blue sky.

Engravings: Anker Smith, published 6 October 1792 for 1802 Boydell edition of Shakespeare's plays, facing p. 113 of *King Lear,* 10³⁄₈ × 6³⁄₈ in. (image and margin); a smaller print by M. F. Geisler, 5⁷⁄₈ × 3³⁄₄ in. (image and margin); an outline engraving by Starling, 3⁷⁄₈ × 2⁷⁄₈ in. (image)

Beginning in the 1760s, *King Lear* proved a popular play for artists for over a hundred years. Boydell's Shakespeare Gallery contained three large paintings: Fuseli's scene of Lear banishing Cordelia, West's *Lear in the Storm,* and James Barry's painting of Lear agonizing over the body of Cordelia before his own heart breaks. For Boydell, Smirke executed all three of the small pictures illustrating the play: the first shows Cordelia and the King of France leaving Goneril and Regan (fig. 43); the sec-

58

ond Edgar as Poor Tom encountering Lear, Kent, and the Fool in the storm; and the third, the Folger picture, showing the reunion of Lear and Cordelia. The last is the only one of the three to have survived. The subjects for the large series of paintings emphasize King Lear, while Smirke's small series places a greater emphasis on Cordelia, a not inap- propriate response given her popularity as a heroine in the eighteenth century.

In the play the scene takes place in a tent in the French camp before the climactic battle, with Lear asleep in a bed. The moment of Lear's awakening was the subject of numerous book illustrations and paintings. The first was Gravelot's frontispiece to

Fig. 43. After Robert Smirke, *Cordelia Departing from the Court.* Engraving by W. Sharpe, 6 October 1792.

molten lead." Yet, by retaining the throne rather than a bed, Smirke suggests the king's still imposing dignity. The interior is a simple one in keeping with the solemnity of the scene, and its architecture deliberately recalls the setting depicted in the first scene, when Cordelia leaves her father's court, beginning the tragic unfolding of Lear's downfall. The story has now come full circle, with daughter and father reunited at the beginning of the denouement.

59

STEPHANO CONFRONTING THE MONSTER
The Tempest II, 2
ca. 1798
Oil on canvas, 30³/₄ × 21¹⁵/₁₆ in. (78.0 × 56.9 cm.)

Case no. 1123

Fig. 44. After Charles Reuben Ryley, *The Awakening of King Lear.* Engraving by Heath, 1 April 1786.

Theobald's 1740 edition showing Lear asleep on a throne in am impressive interior. Closer in date to Smirke's conception is Charles Reuben Ryley's neoclassical illustration of 1786 for Lowndes's *New English Theatre* (fig. 44). Ryley accurately shows Lear in a tent, half reclining and half sitting on a chaise longue. The physician stands to the left with a concerned Kent to the right. Smirke clearly knew Ryley's composition, but he makes important changes, as the grouping of his figures is more carefully controlled. A diagonal beginning in the lower left corner rises up through the body of Cordelia to Lear's head and ends with the head of Kent. This compact right-angle triangle is balanced by the vertical of the physician on the left. Smirke captures Lear's anxious befuddlement on awakening: "Thou art a soul in bliss; but I am bound / Upon a wheel of fire, that mine own tears / Do scald like

Provenance: Commissioned by Alderman John Boydell for the Shakespeare Gallery; sold by lottery 28 January 1805 and won by William Tassie; sold by Christie 17 May 1805, no. 26, as *"Trinculo and Caliban*—admirably composed and painted,"* bought by Dr. Westrop for 11 guineas (£11.11.0); collection of D. Levin in 1910; Michelmore, February 1923, £125

Exhibitions: London, Boydell, 1802, no. 86; London, Boydell, 1805, no. 97; London, Whitechapel Art Gallery, *Shakespeare Memorial and Theatrical Exhibition,* 1910, no. 148, as "The Tempest"; Amherst, *Shakespeare,* 1951; Amherst, *The Tempest,* 1951

References: Friedman 1976, p. 212, n. 415, and p. 238

Condition: Judging from the engraving after this painting, the canvas has been trimmed on all four sides. A restoration of 1988 helped to repair the abrasion of the paint film, due to a heavy-handed cleaning in the past that particularly damaged the sky.

Engravings: W. C. Wilson, published 23 April 1798 for 1802 Boydell edition of Shakespeare's plays, facing p. 53 of *The Tempest;* a later outline engraving by Starling, $4^{1}/_{8} \times 2^{7}/_{8}$ in. (image).

Versions: Smirke executed a variation on this composition for a later publication (see following entry for information on this work).

Caliban, returning with a bundle of firewood that can be seen in the lower right corner, stretches out on the beach at the approach of the shipwrecked Trinculo, whom he mistakes for a spirit sent to torment him by Prospero. Despite Caliban's unsavory appearance and smell, Trinculo, fearing the approach of a second storm, takes shelter under his cloak. Stephano, another survivor of the shipwreck, happens along to discover what to him, in an inebriated state, is a four-legged monster. Stephano, the butler of the King of Naples, had ridden to shore from the shipwreck on a butt of sack, which he then secured. He carries now a portion of the wine in what he describes as a "bottle, which I made of the bark of a tree with mine own hands." Smirke, as did many of his contemporaries in the theater,[1] interprets the bottle as a keg. Pouring some of its contents out for Caliban, Stephano turns startled to hear a second voice emerge from

the hybrid monster, that of Trinculo, whose head is at the other end. Caliban, tasting the "celestial liquor" for the first time, soon becomes drunk himself and pledges to serve the butler, whom he mistakes for a god. On first spying Caliban, Trinculo had debated whether he was a man or a fish, but, as was frequently the case with English artists of this period, Smirke presents him only as a brutish human.

Smirke's conception is a comic masterpiece. This scene had been depicted earlier in Edward Edwards's book illustration published on 1 March 1773 for John Bell's edition of Shakespeare,[2] but Edwards's design, with the two castaways standing at the left watching a guzzling Caliban at the right, lacks the tight focus of Smirke's composition, with its skillful concentration of the narrative and effective integration of the figures. In Smirke's painting, the butler, colorfully attired in a red turban, orange jacket, and white trousers with orange stripes, straddles the darker four-legged monster to form the apex of a bizarrely heroic pyramid. He looks down at Trinculo on one end, while at the other Caliban looks up at the keg he is holding. These three are placed within a brooding seascape that effectively conveys Trinculo's description of the approaching storm: "Here's neither brush nor shrub to bear off any weather at all, and another storm brewing; I hear it sing i' th' wind. Yond same black cloud, yond huge one, looks like a foul bombard [black leathern jug] that would shed his liquor." Open on the left-hand side, the painting is closed at the right, where liquid flows from both the keg and the cloud.

1. See Sprague 1944, p. 42.
2. The Folger also owns an interesting political satire of the Prince of Wales and his cronies that is based on Edwards's design. Entitled *Reynard's Hope,* it was published by J. Brown on 15 April 1784 (ART File S528t2, no. 107).

A Series of Twelve Panels (nos. 60–71)

ca. 1820–25
Oil on panel, pencil underdrawing and border

Five of the six panels from the second set (nos. 64, 68, 69, 70, 71) are initialed in brown paint at lower right "RS." The initials in each case are clearly a later addition placed on top of the old varnish.

Provenance: Set of six (nos. 60, 61, 62, 63, 66, 67), Maggs, November 1923, £52.10.0, as by Stothard; set of six (nos. 64, 65, 68, 69, 70, 71), Maggs, November 1924, £52.10.0, as by Smirke

Exhibitions: Four of the paintings were in the *Henry IV* exhibition held at Amherst in 1959 as painted by Stothard. Nos. 60 and 61 were in this group, and presumably the other two were nos. 62 and 63, since Falstaff also appears in *The Merry Wives of Windsor.*

Condition: The panels are of oak with the grain running vertically and vary in thickness from ¹/₁₆ to ³/₈ inches. Each is painted in grisaille (shades of brown, yellow, and blue-gray with white) over an ivory-colored gesso ground. The panels were presumably bought with the ground already prepared, as several bear a gesso stamp (a circular design 1 inch in diameter with scalloped edges). They were most recently restored in 1988.

The twelve panels at the Folger Shakespeare Library are the only ones known to have survived from a series that originally numbered forty works. Given their small size and monochromatic execution, they were obviously intended from the beginning as designs for engravings, and it is from the engravings that one can reconstruct the entire series. Smirke executed five designs for each of eight plays: *The Tempest, Merry Wives of Windsor, Taming of the Shrew, Twelfth Night, Measure for Measure, I Henry IV, A Midsummer Night's Dream,* and *Romeo and Juliet.* The first four plays were published by Rodwell and Martin, Bond Street, London, in 1821 and 1822. Each play also had a title page illustrated with a vignette. Apparently, the remaining illustrations were only published independently of the text. The engravings for *Measure for Measure* were published by Rodwell and Martin in 1822 and 1823 and the engravings for the remaining three plays by Hurst, Robinson & Co. and R. Jennings in 1825. This last company published all forty engravings together with a title page that reads *Illustrations to Shakespeare by Robert Smirke, R.A.* Some of these scenes were reproduced in later editions in engravings of inferior quality.

Because of the similarity in concept and execution, the panels were presumably executed at approximately the same time, even though the scenes were not engraved all at once. Smirke may have executed the designs for *The Merry Wives of Windsor*

first, since in these images he employed heavily incised lines, a practice he soon abandoned. In terms of execution, the two scenes from *I Henry IV* are among the best, and they may well have been among the last executed.

60

60

FALSTAFF INSTRUCTING BARDOLPH
I Henry IV IV, 2
5⁷/₈ × 4⁵/₈ in. (14.9 × 11.7 cm.)

Condition: Maggs noted that five of the works in the first set (this panel and nos. 61, 62, 63, and 66) had "pasted on the backs in contemporary MS, the quotation from the scene depicted." Unfortunately, none of these notations have survived. They may have been discarded and replaced by typed labels when the works were reframed by Mickelson's in the early 1960s. The original frames were described by Maggs as contemporary gold ones. There are numerous cracks in the gesso ground, but the paint layer, which is thin with some impasto, is in reasonable condition.

Preparatory drawing: Pen and brown ink with brown wash and bodycolor over pencil with gum,

6⅛ × 4½ in., Paul Mellon Collection, Yale Center for British Art, New Haven

Engravings: Charles Heath, 4⅛ × 3⅛ in. (image), published by Hurst, Robinson & Co. and R. Jennings, London, 1825

Marching with his troops to Shrewsbury, Falstaff tells Bardolph to go ahead to Coventry to buy him a bottle of sack. One of the lead soldiers making up his ragged regiment walks with his legs wide apart, recalling Falstaff's rumination, "the villains march wide betwixt the legs, as if they had gyves [fetters] on; for indeed I had the most of them out of prison."

61

61
FALSTAFF STRUGGLING
WITH HOTSPUR'S BODY
I Henry IV V, 4
5¹³⁄₁₆ × 4⅝ in. (14.7 × 11.7 cm.)

Condition: The panel is thin (¹⁄₁₆ in.) and has been covered on both sides with a very fine fabric and then coated with ivory-colored gesso. The gesso has flaked badly on the reverse, and there are some losses on the front of the panel. There is some abrasion and tiny flaking losses in the paint film.

Preparatory drawing: Falstaff Dragging away the Body of Hotspur, pen and brown ink with brown wash and bodycolor over pencil with gum, 6⁷⁄₁₆ × 4¹⁵⁄₁₆ in., Paul Mellon Collection, Yale Center for British Art, New Haven

Engravings: Charles Heath, 4⅛ × 3⅛ in. (image), published by Hurst, Robinson & Co. and R. Jennings, London, 1825

Falstaff, in the climactic battle of the play, feigns death in order to escape from the Earl of Douglas. As soon as Prince Hal leaves after having slain his noble adversary Hotspur, Falstaff takes up the body, claiming he had been the vanquisher. Before taking on this burden, Falstaff had stabbed Hotspur in the thigh in case he too had been feigning death. Smirke chooses not to focus on the bloody violence implicit in the scene; not even a sword is to be found nearby. He also plays down Falstaff's size in this one instance in order to make his task of taking up Hotspur's body all the more difficult. In the theater, actors playing Falstaff often stretched out the action, tumbling about with the body before finally hefting it into position.[1]

1. See Sprague 1944, pp. 90–91. After audiences tired of this particular piece of buffoonery, some actors abandoned it altogether, having soldiers carry off the body.

62

ANNE PAGE'S INVITATION TO SLENDER
The Merry Wives of Windsor I, 1
5⁷/₈ × 4¹¹/₁₆ in. (14.9 × 11.9 cm.)

Condition: The forms are outlined by deeply incised lines, and the paint layer has shrunk away from these lines. Incised lines that have been overpainted reveal that Slender's right arm was originally extended, balancing his left. There is abrasion, particularly at the upper left and right, and scattered small flaking losses.

Preparatory drawing: Anne Page and Slender, pen and brown ink with brown wash and bodycolor over pencil with gum, 7⁵/₁₆ × 4⁷/₁₆ in., Paul Mellon Collection, Yale Center for British Art, New Haven

Engravings: Charles Heath, 4¹/₈ × 3¹/₈ in. (image), published by Rodwell and Martin, London, 1821

Slender is shown awkwardly responding to Anne Page's invitation to come into dinner. Smirke first illustrated this popular subject for a book illustration engraved by Isaac Taylor in 1784 entitled *Slender's Bashfull Behaviour to Ann Page.* He also executed this same scene for Boydell (see no. 72), and there is a later engraving by Portbury after another of his designs. No. 62 differs from all these interpretations: the Grecian purity of Anne Page's dress contrasts with her usual depiction in Elizabethan attire, and even the architecture is rendered with a greater starkness.

63

FALSTAFF HIDING IN THE BUCKBASKET
The Merry Wives of Windsor III, 3
5⁷/₈ × 4⁹/₁₆ in. (14.9 × 11.5 cm.)

Condition: The forms are outlined by deeply incised lines, and the paint layer has shrunk away from these lines. A gesso stamp appears at upper right. The Page's left arm was originally placed higher on the railing.

Engravings: Charles Heath, 4¹/₈ × 3¹/₈ in. (image), published by Rodwell and Martin, London, 1821

Mistress Ford and Mistress Page trick Falstaff into hiding in the foul linen in the buckbasket. Robin, Falstaff's young page who is in on the plot, watches from the landing. Falstaff, in a complicated pose, twists around to look up the stairwell in anxious

63

expectation of the arrival of Mistress Ford's jealous husband. In Falstaff's pose, Smirke would seem to allude to the celebrated Hellenistic sculpture of Laocoön. The contrast of Falstaff with the heroic Trojan priest, who is flanked by his two sons, is of course intended as bathos, and Smirke is careful to make the reference subtle rather than heavy-handed.

64

LYSANDER DECLARING HIS
PASSION TO HELENA
A Midsummer Night's Dream II, 2
5¹³/₁₆ × 4³/₈ in. (14.8 × 10.6 cm.)

Annotated on verso: "Eng. by C. Pye 5/28 1824"

Condition: The panel is chamfered one inch on left reverse and bottom. The clothing of Lysander and Helena has undergone deep shrinkage cracking overall.

Preparatory drawing: Pen and brown ink with brown wash and bodycolor over pencil with gum, 6¹/₂ × 4³/₈ in., Paul Mellon Collection, Yale Center for British Art, New Haven

64

65

PUCK'S REPORT TO OBERON
A Midsummer Night's Dream III, 2
5⅞ × 4⅝ in. (14.9 × 11.7 cm.)

Condition: The clothing, particularly of Oberon, has undergone shrinkage cracking. There are two vertical cracks through the gesso layer on the left-hand edge. The first begins ⅜ inch from the left upper corner and extends over half the length of the panel. The second begins 1¾ inch from the bottom left corner and extends vertically over half the length of the panel. There are deep horizontal scratches at the top and bottom of the picture, both of which have been overpainted. A gesso stamp at upper left has tear-shaped damage near its center.

Preparatory drawings: A drawing showing Oberon standing (B1977.14.3468) and one showing him seated (B1977.14.3469; fig. 45) are in the Paul Mellon Collection, Yale Center for British Art, New Haven.

Engravings: Edward Finden, 4¼ × 3⅛ in. (image), published by Hurst, Robinson & Co. and R. Jennings, [London], 1825

Engravings: C. Pye, 4⅛ × 3⅛ in. (image), published by Hurst, Robinson & Co., Pall Mall, and R. Jennings, Poultry, [London], 1825 (listed on engraving as "Act 2 Sc 3")

Puck, who has been sent by Oberon to anoint the eyes of Demetrius with a love potion that he might return Helena's love for him, mistakes one sleeping Athenian couple for the other, sprinkling Lysander's eyes instead. Smirke depicts the moment when Lysander, awakened by Helena, falls madly in love with her as the first person he sees after having been anointed with the potion. The startled Helena grimaces, thinking he is cruelly teasing her, while Lysander's beloved Hermia continues to sleep in the background. Smirke does little to distinguish between the two maidens, though it is clear from the text that Helena, a "painted maypole," is tall and fair, while Hermia is much shorter and darker in complexion.

65

Puck is shown telling Oberon how he has suc-cessfully carried out all of his instructions. Smirke worked through at least two compositions before settling on this design. In the first drawing he shows Oberon standing with Puck kneeling and fairies dancing to the left. The second drawing (fig. 45) shows Oberon seated and the dancing fairies re-placed with quietly attentive ones. In the Folger picture, Oberon is more regally presented in an ermine-lined robe, holding a staff, and, in a reversal of the first conception, he now sits while Puck stands. A small brook separates the two main fig-ures, and the bewitching moon is given greater prominence by the exclusion of one of the branches of the tree.

Fig. 45. Robert Smirke, *Oberon and Puck.* Pen and brown ink with brown wash and bodycolor over pencil with gum, 6³/₄ × 4³/₈ in. Yale Center for British Art, Paul Mellon Collection.

66

67

**KATHERINA'S FIRST MEETING
WITH PETRUCHIO**
The Taming of the Shrew II, 1
5¹³/₁₆ × 4⁷/₈ in. (14.8 × 12.4 cm.)

Condition: The panel is split at the left edge, caused by a framing nail. The paint layer is extremely abraded in the background. The gesso stamp at upper left has been overpainted.

Engravings: Charles Heath, 4¹/₈ × 3¹/₈ in. (image), published by Rodwell and Martin, London, 1821

Maggs Brothers sold this work as showing Grumio and Katherina in act IV, scene 3, a scene that Smirke did execute for this series. However, the subject here is from an earlier moment in the play, Petruchio's courting of Katherina. Petruchio displays an animated grace as he attempts to win Katherina, who, in contrast to Petruchio, appears like an unmovable statue, as she only begrudgingly responds to his courtship.

66

BOTTOM IN THE FOREST
A Midsummer Night's Dream IV, 1
5⁷/₈ × 4¹/₂ in. (14.9 × 10.9 cm.)

Condition: The panel is chamfered one inch on its back left-hand edge. There is deep shrinkage cracking in Bottom's cloak and hair. His right foot has been only partially filled in.

Engravings: W. Greatbatch, 4 × 3¹/₁₆ in. (image), published by Hurst, Robinson & Co., Pall Mall, and R. Jennings, Poultry, [London], 1825

Bottom awakens to find himself alone in the forest, the four lovers just disappearing from view at the far right. He begins immediately to muse on his dream. Although Smirke ably captures Bottom's sense of exuberance and his plebeian nature, Maggs Brothers incorrectly identified the subject as Oberon in act II, scene 1.

67

68

68

**KATHERINA'S CHASTISEMENT
OF BIANCA AND THE WIDOW**
The Taming of the Shrew V, 2
5⅞ × 4⅝ in. (14.9 × 11.7 cm.)

Condition: Detailing in the urn in the lower left corner has been lost through abrasion. The shading behind the man seated at right appears now almost as if it were a chair back.

Engravings: J. Romney, 4⅛ × 3⅛ in. (image), published by Rodwell and Martin, London, 1821

This scene concludes the play. After a banquet at Lucentio's house, the three women retire. Defending himself against the others' taunts, Petruchio wagers that his wife is the most obedient of the three. When the women are summoned one by one, only Katherina returns to the table. She then brings in the other two women and lectures them on their duty to their new husbands, as the men look on in surprise and admiration. Her figure is now lithe and supple in contrast to the pose she had assumed in the earlier scene of her first meeting with Petruchio.

69

PROSPERO SUMMONING ARIEL
The Tempest I, 2
5¹³⁄₁₆ × 4⁹⁄₁₆ in. (14.8 × 11.6 cm.)

Condition: There is a small impact damage to the gesso at a point on Miranda's left leg above her ankle. The gesso ground is also damaged in the two left corners. Overall, the paint layer is thin and in poor condition, with large losses and much overpaint. Only traces of the vine extending out from the cliff at its top can now be seen.

Preparatory drawing: Prospero and Ariel, pen and brown ink with brown wash and bodycolor over pencil with gum, 5¹⁵⁄₁₆ × 4¹³⁄₁₆ in., Paul Mellon Collection, Yale Center for British Art, New Haven

Engravings: F. Engleheart, 4⅛ × 3⅛ in. (image), published by Rodwell and Martin, London, 1821

Having caused his daughter Miranda to fall into a deep slumber, Prospero summons the spirit Ariel, who is seen silhouetted against the bright sky. Partially turned away from the viewer, Prospero strains toward his spry servant, the placement of the sleeping Miranda between them setting up an effective tension. The bold, yet graceful, outlines of the preparatory drawing are lost in the painting's more pedestrian rendering.

69

70

FERDINAND PROCLAIMING
HIS LOVE TO MIRANDA
The Tempest III, 1
5³/₄ × 4¹/₂ in. (14.6 × 10.9 cm.)

Condition: The paint layer has serious, bitumen-like shrinkage cracking, particularly in and around the figure of Miranda and in Ferdinand's cloak.

Engravings: Charles Heath, 4¹/₁₆ × 3¹/₁₆ in. (image), published by Rodwell and Martin, London, 1821. (Two trees have been added to the background: one at the far left and one behind Prospero. Ferdinand's hat has also been added lying on the ground beside him. Prospero looks downward and his hands are clasped together.)

Ferdinand and the artless Miranda confess their love for each other, while Prospero, made invisible by his magic cloak, looks on unobserved. Miranda's pose of bashful coyness is typical of illustrations of this scene, even if it does not conform all that well to Shakespeare's characterization. The figures and the background undergo slight alterations from the oil sketch to the engraving. In the engraving the left-hand side is closed by a bush and the limb of a slender tree; the hill on the right is replaced with shrubs and a tree that rises behind Prospero; Ferdi-nand's hat lies on the ground in the center foreground and he is again equipped with a sword; Prospero's hands are clasped; and Miranda's dress is slightly altered, though her pose remains virtually the same. Perhaps in this instance the Folger picture is only the penultimate design, Smirke having produced a final version in the form of either another oil on panel or a drawing.

71

STEPHANO DEMANDING TRINCULO'S GOWN
The Tempest IV, 1
5³/₄ × 4¹/₂ in. (14.6 × 10.9 cm.)

Condition: There is visible pencil underdrawing. The paint layer is thinly applied. It is a little abraded, but on the whole is in good condition.

Preparatory drawing: Pen and brown ink with brown wash and bodycolor over pencil with gum, 6³/₄ × 4¹/₂ in., Paul Mellon Collection, Yale Center for British Art, New Haven

Engravings: E. Portbury, 4¹/₈ × 3¹/₈ in. (image), published by Rodwell and Martin, London, 1821 (Ariel is clearly a woman in the engraving, although this is not necessarily Smirke's intent).

71

Fig. 46. Robert Smirke, *Stephano Demanding Trinculo's Gown.*
Pen and brown ink with brown wash and bodycolor over pencil
with gum, 6¾ × 4½ in. Yale Center for British Art, Paul Mellon
Collection.

Fig. 47. After Robert Smirke, *Stephano Demanding Trinculo's
Gown.* Engraving by E. Portbury, 1821.

Caliban has persuaded Stephano with Trinculo's
help to kill Prospero so that Stephano might rule
the island in his place. Ariel, after having led
the three through briars and thorns into a scum-
covered pond, has, at Prospero's command, placed
glittering clothes for them on a line in front of Prospero's cell.[1] Trinculo tries on a garment fit for a
king, but Stephano, who would be ruler, demands
he give it to him. Caliban, aware of the danger they
are in, urges the two to forget the clothes and enter
into Prospero's cell to kill the old man as quickly as
possible. In the bottom margin of his preparatory
drawing (fig. 46) Smirke sketched out alternate
heads for the bestial Caliban, and the painting follows more closely the baldish, ape-like appearance
rendered in the margin. In the play, Ariel and Prospero both observe the trio but are invisible to them.
Smirke shows Ariel only, since, perched on top of a
cloud, it is easier to think of him as unseen. In both

the drawing and the picture Ariel's sex is somewhat
ambiguous, as he is given a full chest. Although
spirits may change their sex, one presumes Smirke
meant, for consistency's sake, that Ariel be seen as
a male, but one cannot entirely blame Portbury, the
engraver of this scene, for unambiguously rendering
him as a woman (fig. 47).

1. Sprague points out, "When in IV, I, Prospero bids Ariel hang the
   glistering apparel 'on this line,' editors and actors have been at
   odds as to his meaning. Having decided that clotheslines were
   unpoetical, and ascertained that 'a line' might mean a lime tree,
   the editors have been satisfied to believe that Prospero refers to
   a lime tree here" (1944, pp. 43–44). He goes on to give examples
   of how performances in the eighteenth and nineteenth centuries
   were content to use the "unpoetical" clothesline, and in his design Smirke follows the theatrical tradition over that of the editors.

Robert Smirke, after

72

ANNE PAGE INVITING SLENDER TO DINNER
The Merry Wives of Windsor I, 1
Early nineteenth century
Oil on canvas, 22 × 18 in. (58.9 × 45.7 cm.)

Case no. 1405

Provenance: Maggs, April 1925, £42, as by Smirke

Exhibitions: Washington, 1976–77, no. 20, as by Smirke

Condition: The canvas has never been lined.

Original painting: A fragment of the canvas showing only the figure of Anne Page (42 × 25 in.) is all that has survived. It is in the Royal Shakespeare Theatre Picture Gallery.

Engravings after original: J. P. Simon, published 24 December 1793 for the large series of prints, 22 × 16 in. (image); M. Haughton, published 4 June 1801 for the 1802 Boydell edition of Shakespeare's plays, 10 × 6⅛ in. (image and margin). The image proved popular enough that it was engraved on a smaller scale at least five more times.

The scene is before the door of Anne Page's house, where she invites Slender, her awkward suitor, to dinner. Slender's servant Simple stands behind him.

Robert Smirke executed this subject for Boydell, and two engravings were made, one for the large series of paintings and one for the small. Only a fragment of Smirke's canvas survives, showing the figure of Anne Page. She is dressed in black over white with a white lace ruff, a red heart with gold trim hangs down by her side, and her cuffs and veil are gray. In the Folger picture, however, her ruffs are white and her veil red with a hint of stripes. This version is almost certainly after one of the Boydell prints rather than the painting. In the small print the gate on the left has five vertical slats, while in the large one it has four. The Folger picture also shows four slats but its proportions are slightly different and it varies in small details from either engraving.

72

Carl Ferdinand Sohn, after

Sohn was born in Berlin on 10 December 1805 and in 1823 entered the Berlin Academy, where he studied under Wilhelm Schadow. He followed Schadow to Düsseldorf in 1826 and in 1830 traveled with him to Italy. In 1832 Sohn himself was teaching at the Düsseldorf Academy of Art and six years later was made a professor. He is best known for his portraits and history paintings. In this last category he executed two popular works from Shakespeare, both from *Romeo and Juliet*. The first was a painting of 1836 of Romeo departing from Juliet, which was purchased by the Berlin banker Frankel. It is the picture on which the Folger painting is based, and it was followed in 1838 by a scene of the Capulet ball. After a distinguished career in Düsseldorf, Sohn died in Cologne on 25 November 1867.

73

ROMEO AND JULIET
Romeo and Juliet III, 5
After 1836
Oil on tin, 10⅜ × 8⅛ in. (26.3 × 20.6 cm.)

Case no. 1029

73

Provenance: Acquired shortly before 6 February 1922, when it appears in case no. 1029

Condition: The work is abraded at its edges from the frame, and a gold ground shows through. There are several scratches on the paint surface. One of the most severe runs from the column at the left through Juliet's left arm and throat. There is another at lower right extending from the horizontal crease in Juliet's dress through the floor almost to the right-hand edge.

Engravings after original: Gustav Luederitz, 16³/₈ × 11⁵/₈ in. (image) (ART Vol. b55, vol. 3); T. S. Engle-heart, 4¹³/₁₆ × 3⁷/₁₆ in. (image) (ART File S528n1, no. 52)

The departure of Romeo and Juliet, along with the earlier balcony scene, which is its counterpart, were among the most popular in the play. That a German artist should have chosen to execute a scene from *Romeo and Juliet* is not surprising, given its popularity on the Continent. Sohn's painting was engraved twice, once by Luederitz in a large, detailed print, and once by Engleheart in a smaller format. The Folger painting is based on the smaller print, for it glosses over some of the details visible in Luederitz's larger and more accurate reproduction.

The tin support gives the paint surface an enamel-like finish. Juliet, wearing a yellow brocaded dress over a long white nightgown, kneels on a red cushion. Romeo's red fur-trimmed tunic lacks the floral brocade found in the large print and which can easily be misread as shadows in the small one. The arriving dawn, which signals the lovers' separation, is rendered as a dull gray, presumably since the painter had only a black-and-white model to follow.

The composition has been expanded on all four sides. In Sohn's painting, as rendered in the prints, the column on the left is bisected by the frame, closing the composition, and only the portion of the bed with the bolster is visible at the right. The effect of pushing the figures further back into the interior mutes some of the tension found in the original design. Romeo's anguished features are also muted, his bland face masking his emotions.

Frank Stone

Born in Manchester on 22 August 1800, Stone first followed his father's example by working as a cotton spinner. He did not begin studying as a painter until he was twenty-four, and in 1831 he moved to London to pursue his career as an artist, where initially he was best known for his watercolors. He made his public debut at the Society of British Artists in the 1833–34 exhibition. Beginning in 1835 he exhibited works at the British Institution, where he won a premium of fifty guineas in 1841. With the exception of 1855, when apparently he was briefly residing in France, Stone exhibited every year at the Royal Academy from 1837 until 1860. He was best known for his "love pictures," subjects of young lovers bordering on mawkish sentiment. The *Art Journal* critic elaborated on this type: "The pictures to which we refer possessed that peculiar attractiveness which was almost sure to command a large amount of admiration from those who are readily pleased with pretty faces, elegant figures, and a certain kind of sentiment that is patent to the most casual and careless observer."[1] Stone, however, turned to more serious subject matter when he exhibited a distraught Ophelia singing before the Queen at the Royal Academy in 1845. In 1848 he submitted the biblical subject of Christ and the sisters of Bethany, and in 1851 his painting of Bassanio reading the letter, for which the Folger picture is a

study and which led to his election to the Royal Academy as an associate member later that year. He died in London on 18 November 1859 from heart disease.

1. *The Art Journal* 1850, p. 334.

74
Study for BASSANIO RECEIVING THE LETTER ANNOUNCING ANTONIO'S LOSSES AND PERIL
The Merchant of Venice III, 2
ca. 1850–51
Oil on panel, 6⅞ × 9 in. (17.3 × 22.7 cm.)

Case no. 1388

Provenance: Maggs, February 1925, £42

Condition: The paint and ground are well attached except for a few chips and scratches at the top corners.

While the present whereabouts of the exhibited picture is unknown, a wood engraving reproducing it (fig. 48) demonstrates that there are only minor differences between it and the preparatory sketch in the Folger collection. Stone's use of an oil study may have been a departure from his normal practice warranted in this instance by the ambitious scope of the project. *Bassanio Receiving the Letter* was the cornerstone in the artist's campaign for greater professional respectability and gained for him an associate membership in the Royal Academy.[1] The reaction of a character to a letter, usually a love letter, was a staple of Victorian painting, and Stone himself had already executed subjects of this type. This picture elevates such a narrative ploy by its association with Shakespeare, and one contemporary critic aptly classified it as a "domestic historical" painting,[2] a history painting but one not too far removed from the category of genre. Costume and setting take on greater importance, and the composition also is far more ambitious in its use of multiple figures than Stone had been used to employing.

This particular moment had been painted before, most recently by Gilbert Stuart Newton for the Royal Academy exhibition of 1831,[3] and one reviewer commented on Stone's audacity: "This subject is well calculated for the exhibition of the artist's speciality. It was a bold thing to venture on the identical subject which Mr. Stuart Newton had

74

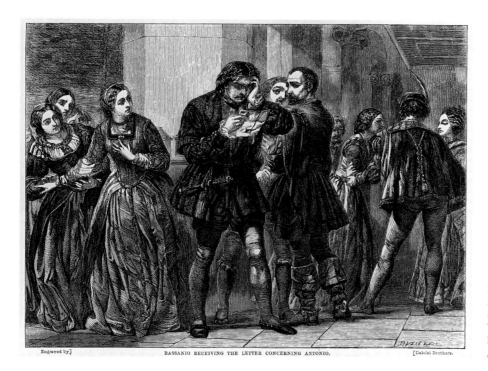

Fig. 48. After Frank Stone, *Bassanio Receiving the Letter concerning Antonio.* Wood engraving by the Dalziel brothers in the *Art Journal* 1856, p. 333.

dealt with in that excellent work which is now an ornament of the Sheepshanks Gallery."[4] Stone's effort, while adopting Newton's tripartite division, is a more complex composition with a stronger emotional impact. In splitting the two lovers with the caskets placed between them, he relied on the more dramatic solution of an earlier painting by William Hamilton, published in a print of 1 January 1803 (fig. 49). Bassanio, having just made the correct choice of the caskets and thus securing Portia's hand in marriage, is depicted reacting in astonished horror to the letter revealing the disastrous news of Antonio's predicament. Antonio, the merchant of Venice, had given his bond as security to the moneylender Shylock so that Bassanio could have funds sufficient to court Portia. The three months stipulated in the bond have passed, and, none of his ships returning, Antonio must pay the forfeiture—a pound of his own flesh. Bassanio stands in the center of the composition, while Portia with her atten-

Fig. 49. After William Hamilton, *Bassanio Reading the Letter.* Engraving by J. Heath, 1 January 1803.

dants at the left immediately senses her lover's anguish. Alongside Bassanio completing the central group of figures are Gratiano, his close friend, and Salerio, the booted gentleman with spurs who has just arrived from Venice with the letter. These two are shown clasping hands in accordance with Gratiano's salutation, "Your hand, Salerio." The couple Lorenzo and Jessica had accompanied Salerio, and they are shown in the group on the right being greeted by Nerissa, a group that is as yet unaware of Bassanio's disturbed reaction.

The Folger painting has little of the architectural detail found in the wood engraving after the exhibited picture. Rather, Stone was more concerned with working out the relationships among the figures in terms of composition and color, and even on this small scale he effectively captured a sense of warm sunlight flooding the chamber. In the central group only Bassanio's red stockings stand out, an enlivening splash of color that is echoed in Lorenzo's red dress at the right. In the final picture, Stone narrowed the distance between the two main protagonists but, in doing so, de-emphasized the caskets, leading one critic to complain of the Royal Academy picture, "we think there is a want of sufficient allusion to the casket exhibition."[5] Stone also decided to darken Bassanio's sleeves in order to give more contrast to his hand and the letter. At the right, Nerissa's and Jessica's faces are less obscured in the final design, and Lorenzo's stance is given a more picturesque emphasis with an ornate cord added to the middle of his cloak.

1. The reviews were invariably positive. See *The Builder,* 10 May 1851, p. 292; *The Athenaeum,* 24 May 1851, p. 559; *New Monthly Magazine,* May 1851, pp. 49–50; and *The Art Journal,* 1 June 1851, p. 160. The painting sold at Christie's a few years later for £241.10.0, the second highest price paid for one of Stone's pictures at auction in his lifetime (30 March 1855, lot 62).
2. *The Builder,* 10 May 1851, p. 292.
3. This painting, in the Victoria and Albert Museum, London, is reproduced in Altick 1985, p. 131 (pl. 102).
4. *The Athenaeum,* 24 May 1851, p. 559.
5. Ibid.

Thomas Stothard (nos. 75–78)

Stothard was born on 17 August 1755 in the tavern operated by his father in Long Acre, London. An only child, he received a good education and in 1770 was apprenticed to a Spitalfields silk weaver. Befitting his beginnings as a craftsman, his art was always closely tied to the lucrative trade in mass-produced luxury items. One of his first employers was Josiah Wedgwood, for whom he created designs for ceramics, and he was later to create designs for silverwork. He was also one of the most prolific designers for book illustrations of his generation, turning out both drawings and oils for the book trade. Stothard enjoyed a high reputation with his contemporaries: elected an Associate in 1791, he became a full Royal Academician three years later. He also served as the academy's librarian from 1812. Not surprisingly, given his work as a book illustrator, Stothard was often called upon to illustrate Shakespeare's plays. He executed three paintings for Boydell, one of the designs being engraved in both the large and small series of prints. While Shakespeare was for him a favorite author, Coxhead, one of his biographers, disparaged his production in this area: "The artist's work for Shakespeare has not much distinction, and the student who would wish to see the best only of his art, would lose comparatively little if this portion, large in bulk as it is, were for any reason withheld from him."[1] The Folger Falstaff paintings certainly contradict this assessment. Stothard was best known for his sentimental subjects, exhibiting a delicate grace, and his most successful Shakespearean works are his depictions of comic scenes on a small scale. Having outlived his wife and most of his children, he died on 27 April 1834.

1. Coxhead 1906, p. 95.

75 (Plate 14)
FALSTAFF DESCRIBING THE FIGHT AT GADSHILL
I Henry IV II, 4
ca. 1827
Oil on panel, 8½ × 5¾ in. (21.6 × 14.6 cm.)

Case no. 1983

Provenance: From earl of Effingham collection (according to Folger file card); Maggs, November 1929, £19.16.0 for pair

Condition: The paint surface, applied on to a gessoed panel, is in good condition with no flaking.

Related works: Earlier, Stothard had executed a similar design of this scene with Falstaff seated for a print by J. Neagle, published on 21 January 1804 by George Kearsley.

76
FALSTAFF AND DOLL TEARSHEET
II Henry IV II, 4
ca. 1827
Oil on panel, 8⅜ × 6 in. (21.2 × 15.3 cm.)

Case no. 1983

Provenance: Collection of J. E. Taylor, London, by 1894; label of Thomas Agnew & Sons at the top back of the panel indicates that this work at some point passed through the hands of this London dealer; Maggs, November 1929, £19.16.0 for pair (the play is incorrectly identified in the Folger files as *The Merry Wives of Windsor* III, 3).

Exhibitions: London, 1894, no. 245, as "Falstaff"

Condition: The paint surface suffers from overpainting and separation cracks. At one point when it was behind glass, some mold also began to develop.

Engravings: Engraved by S. Davenport for the title page to the 1827 edition of Shakespeare's plays published by Thomas Tegg, London.

The two paintings would seem to be pendants, although only one (no. 76) was engraved, appearing on the title page of Thomas Tegg's 1827 edition *The Dramatic Works of Shakspeare*.[1] They are the last of three separate projects that Stothard undertook in illustrating the two parts of *Henry IV*. The first involved three engravings for Manley Wood's 1806 edition of Shakespeare, and the second two scenes for Pickering's 1825 edition. None of the subjects repeat themselves, and all seven feature Falstaff as their main protagonist.[2]

Executed shortly after the Pickering illustrations, the Folger pair marks the last time Stothard concentrated on the fat knight. It is also the only time he shows a smiling Falstaff. Although purporting to discuss all his Falstaff illustrations, Anna Eliza Bray in her biography of Stothard, published in 1851, more accurately describes the Folger pair:

His *Falstaffs* are not merely gross, fat old men (as they are commonly painted) whose belly alone says, "I am Jack Falstaff." Nothing can be finer than his discrimination in portraying the knight of "sack and sugar," of mirth and wit, and good humour and knavery. True it is, that in Stothard's *Falstaffs* he strongly preserves the characteristic of the sensualist, but it is re-

76

fined upon by the air of the gentleman who had known the company of a prince, and the manners of a court. What archness is there in the look, what intelligence in the sly and laughing eye; what a ready playfulness, yet never wholly divested of cunning, does he convey to the entire expression of the head and face. Never but in one instance does this most amusing of knights betray (in Stothard's delineation of him) an unguarded and weak expression; and that is where *Doll* sits on his knee, and he asks her of what

stuff she will have kirtles. There even his wit and caution is over-mastered by the cunning of woman; and *Doll* plays with his poll, covered with thin white hairs, as recklessly as did Dalilah with the locks of Samson.[3]

Both scenes are set in the Boar's Head Tavern, but the two are deliberately contrasted, the first bright with a radically simplified background, the other dark with a few simple details of the interior. Both scenes had already proved popular with artists, the scene with Doll having been chosen as early as 1709, when Boitard produced the first illustrations for the two plays.

The scene from *I Henry IV* overflows with sparkling energy, as Stothard's predilection for opulent colors, deriving from his admiration for Rubens and Titian, is given free rein. The colorful garments of the figures are set against a light, neutral background. Falstaff is typically dressed in a yellow doublet. He also wears a bright red cape and colorful, wispy feathers in his dark blue hat. With sword and shield in his hands, he regales the Prince and Poins with his invented account of the fight at Gadshill. Bardolph is at the right with two other companions, one of whom is completely eclipsed, except for a foot, by Falstaff's great girth.

In the companion painting, Falstaff is again dressed in a yellow doublet but now with rose sleeves and pants, and is seated on a brown chair, his sword still in his hand after he has just chased away Pistol. Doll Tearsheet, wearing a pink dress and an Elizabethan peaked hat, caresses him. To the right stands a watchful Hostess, whose one hand is grasped by a lecherous Bardolph while the other maintains a grip on her keys. To the left, disguised as drawers or waiters, are the Prince and Poins, who have come to spy on Falstaff. To the extreme left, the musician, who has just been summoned, plays a flute.

Falstaff entreats, "Sit on my knee, Doll." In Stothard's rendering she is somewhat awkwardly perched on his thigh, only her right leg crossing over his left one. This arrangement permits more of Falstaff's ample waist to be shown, but more to the point, Stothard evokes a conventional image for sexual compliance. The leg of one lover slung over the other has a long history in Western art as an erotic motif, and in employing it Stothard is not so much attempting a naturalistic portrayal of Doll's action as he is a symbolic one, discretely suggesting the carnal relationship between the two.[4]

The Prince's comments on Doll's caresses are hardly flattering: "Look whe'er the wither'd elder hath not his poll [head] claw'd like a parrot." Yet Stothard's design reminded Bray of Samson and Delilah, a comment that not only calls attention to Falstaff's weakness for women but also associates him and Doll with a biblical prototype. While this allusion may not be what Stothard intended, he does imbue his scene with refined geniality that is not necessarily a part of the text. In both works, as

Bray pointed out, the debauched knight retains the air of a courtly gentleman.

1. If Tegg had a choice between the two images, it would not be surprising that he chose the second, as Smirke's version of the first scene had just been published in 1825 in the series of prints discussed in nos. 60–71.
2. For the Wood edition, published by George Kearsley, Stothard executed Falstaff acting the role of the king (*I Henry IV* II, 4), Falstaff confronting the Chief Justice (*II Henry IV* II, 1), and Falstaff driving out Pistol (*II Henry IV* II, 4). For Pickering he chose Falstaff and his confederates being robbed in their turn by Prince Hal and Poins (*I Henry IV* II, 2) and Falstaff choosing his recruits (*II Henry IV* III, 2).
3. Anna Eliza Bray, *Life of Thomas Stothard, R.A.*, London, 1851, p. 113.
4. For sacred and secular uses of the slung-leg motif, see Leo Steinberg's "The Metaphors of Love and Birth in Michelangelo's *Pietàs*," in *Studies in Erotic Art*, New York and London, 1970, pp. 231–335.

77

MARINA SINGING BEFORE PERICLES
Pericles V, 1
ca. 1825
Oil on canvas, 23 × 17 1/8 in. (58.5 × 43.4 cm.)

Case no. 1679

Provenance: William F. Robinson as of 1876; bought from Parsons & Sons, May 1927, £45

Exhibitions: London, Royal Academy, *Exhibition of Works by the Old Masters, and by Deceased Masters of the British School*, 1876, no. 95, as "Scene from *Pericles, Prince of Tyre*"

Condition: The canvas was lined by Finlayson in 1932. There is some damage to the paint surface, particularly along the top.

Engravings: A. Fox, published by W. Pickering, 1825 (ART File S528p1, no. 16, copies 1 and 2)

This is, for Stothard, a relatively large painting. Ironically, the design was used for one of the small, exquisite engravings illustrating William Pickering's 1825 edition of Shakespeare, but the composition does not suffer in being reduced to this scale.

Stothard was most successful in painting young, pretty women. This scene from *Pericles* follows stage directions added in the eighteenth century which place Pericles in a "close pavilion" (that is, tent) on the deck of his ship. Thus, what appears to be a column behind the king is most likely the base of a large mast, around which rich cloth is draped to form an enclosure. At the beginning of this scene, Helicanus, an attending lord, describes to Lysimachus, the governor of Mytilene, where the ship has weighed anchor, how the king has not spoken to anyone for three months, burdened as he is by the loss of his wife and daughter. At Lysimachus's suggestion, Marina, an accomplished maiden, is brought on board to see if she can rouse the king from his melancholy state. Accompanied by a young lady, she sings to the depressed monarch. When she eventually captures his attention by telling him her tragic story, Pericles joyfully realizes that Marina is his own daughter whom he had presumed dead.

Although *Pericles* was printed in quarto during Shakespeare's lifetime with his name on the title page, the play was excluded from the First Folio, and its authorship has long been a matter of dispute. Many authorities feel Shakespeare had a hand in writing only the last three acts. In the entire

77

eighteenth century the play was performed only
three times, all in August 1738, and then only in
George Lillo's adaptation entitled *Marina*, which
consists of a rewriting of acts III through V. Not surprisingly in light of the play's critical reputation,
illustrations are rare. Though there were a few
attempts at book illustrations, the Folger painting
may be the first canvas portraying a scene from *Pericles*. One has to wait until 1852 for an exhibited
picture from this play—Paul Falconer Poole's *Marina Singing to Her Father, Pericles*, exhibited at the
Royal Academy (no. 411).

Even book illustrations from this play are comparatively rare. Boitard provided a frontispiece for
the 1709 edition, but the play was excluded from all
subsequent illustrated editions, including Boydell's,
until Harding's edition of 1799, which contained
three designs by R. K. Porter. Fuseli and Stothard
were the first to illustrate the moment when Marina sings before her father. Fuseli's design was executed as a frontispiece for the play in Chalmer's
1805 *Shakespeare*, the print being dated 9 March
1804. At about the same time Stothard designed
two scenes for Manley Wood's 1806 edition, both
focusing on Marina, the first showing her with a
basket of flowers on a stormy sea lamenting, "Aye
me! Poor maid, Born in a tempest," and the second,
published on 29 April 1804, showing the same
scene as illustrated in the Folger picture.

The 1804 engraving (fig. 50) and the Folger painting differ substantially.[1] The print, influenced by
neoclassical tastes, is all verticals and horizontals.
The figures are statuesque, Marina's head in profile,
her body parallel to the picture plane, and the setting austerely simple. Pericles himself comments
on Marina as "wand-like straight" and "in pace another Juno," and Stothard captures a sense of her
imperial classical beauty. The Folger painting, on
the other hand, replaces the rigidity of the earlier
work with a graceful and sentimental interpretation. A softer Marina, wearing a wreath of flowers
and playing a more primitive lyre constructed from
a tortoise-shell, looks heavenward as she sings, her
willowy body forming an elegant S-curve. The gentle lines of the draperies provide a harmonious setting, and the curve of the drapery on the left is even
continued in the line of the outer garment worn by
her attendant. As with Hook's later painting of Desdemona playing for Othello (no. 40), music is used
to soothe and charm. A troubled Pericles, pushed
somewhat into the background, is already begin-

Fig. 50. After Thomas Stothard, *Marina and Pericles*. Engraving by
C. Armstrong, 29 April 1804.

ning to respond to Marina's sweet and entrancing
presence.

1. Despite the pronounced differences between the two works,
Coxhead curiously writes of the Pickering engraving, which is
based on the Folger picture, "The same design as in Kearsley's
edition [George Kearsley was the publisher of the 1806 Wood
edition]" (1906, p. 101).

78

THE VINTAGE

ca. 1833–34
Oil on canvas, 31 × 23¼ in. (78.9 × 59.1 cm.)

Case no. 563

Provenance: Stothard sale, Christie's, 17–19 (19)
June 1834, lot 106, as "THE VINTAGE, *full of beauti-
ful character*"?; Samuel Rogers's sister by 1841?;
J. E. Taylor by 1894; sold as from Taylor's collec-

tion, Christie's, 4 April 1913, lot 56, as *The Seven Ages of Man*, bought by Folger, £17.17.6, Quaritch acting as agent.

Exhibitions: London, British Institution, *Catalogue of Pictures by Italian, Spanish, Flemish, Dutch, French and English Masters*, 1841, no. 169, as "The Vintage"?; London, 1894, no. 233, as "The Seven Ages of Man"; Washington, 1976–77, no. 22, as "The Seven Ages of Man"

Condition: The paint was applied with little impasto, and this has been flattened in a past lining. It was last lined by Finlayson in 1932.

Engravings: J. Goodyear, published November 1834 for the Proprietor by Whittaker, $4\frac{1}{4} \times 3\frac{1}{8}$ in. (image)

Purchased as *The Seven Ages of Man*, the engraving after the painting gives its correct title as *The Vintage*. The print was published in November 1834, several months after Stothard's death in April. Though small, it was never used as a book illustration, and A. C. Coxhead doubts it was ever intended as such.[1] That the engraving is posthumous and the corners of the canvas are unfinished suggest that the painting was one of Stothard's last works. Throughout his career, he had been attracted to the pastoral as a genre, depicting a number of times the theme of the vintage and bacchanalian dances. The genesis of the central motif of the mother with her two children can be found in one of Stothard's designs for Samuel Rogers's *The Pleasures of Memory*. The 1810 edition, published by Cadell, contains thirty-four vignettes by Stothard engraved on wood by Luke Clennell, and one of these designs (fig. 51) is incorporated into the later painting, though reversed and with the swirl of drapery below the cradled child omitted. The theme of the vintage is now grafted onto that of mother and children. The sole male, his ruddy flesh and dark hair contrasted with that of the fair-skinned and blond mother, reaches to pluck one of the bunches of grapes growing in the vine overhead.

Two complementary themes are introduced in the woman at the right holding a distaff and the old woman resting with her crutch at lower left. The woman with the distaff sounds a note of feminine domesticity, but she also recalls the Fate Clotho, who holds the thread of life. That she looks out at the viewer, the only figure to do so, invites the

Fig. 51. After Thomas Stothard, *Mother with Children*. Wood engraving by Luke Clennell (greatly enlarged).

viewer to contemplate his or her own mortality. The old woman underscores this sense of transience in that she with the children and the adults evokes the Three Ages of Man, not the Seven Ages that suggested a relationship to Shakespeare's *As You Like It*.

The painting is filled with a Rubensian vitality, the mother's delicate pink dress contrasted with the darker, more robust colors surrounding her. Yet the picture's celebration of the harvest and of wholesome motherhood is tempered by its bittersweet reflection on the transience of life and pleasure. In this it again recalls the "pleasing melancholy"[2] to be found in Rogers's poem *The Pleasures of Memory*.

Stothard, characterized by his contemporaries as sweet and gentle, had a troubled old age. His eldest son was killed in a shooting accident in 1801; his second son died suddenly in 1821; and his third son suffered a paralytic stroke the following year. His wife died in 1824, and he himself was severely injured when struck by a cab in 1833. Nevertheless, the painting is a decorous celebration of life, faintly tinged with sadness, offering a fitting capstone to the artist's productive career.

1. Coxhead 1904, p. 219.
2. This phrase is used in the "Analysis of the First Part" of Rogers's poem.

Thomas Stothard, manner of (nos. 79–80)

Acquired from the same dealer, a little over a half-year apart, these two paintings are by the same hand and the dealer probably obtained them from the same source. Each was attributed to Stothard, but they fall far below his standard. Stothard was one of the most influential artists of his generation in reviving an interest in the works of the early eighteenth-century French painter Antoine Watteau. Stothard offered his own interpretations of Watteau's pictures, beginning with his painting *Sans Souci*, exhibited at the Royal Academy in 1817, and he continued to promote his personal conception of this artist's work throughout his career. He often placed his Watteauesque paintings in a medieval context illustrating, for example, an author such as Bocaccio, and the creator of the Folger paintings in choosing a Renaissance literary source with a garden setting is close to Stothard's example, as is his use of panel instead of canvas as a support.[1] These images, with their gentle humor and attempts at courtly elegance, are interesting products, albeit awkward ones, of the Watteau revival in nineteenth-century England.[2]

1. In its dimensions and in the relationship of the figures to the landscape background, the first painting is close to one attributed to Stothard that sold in the Devitt sale, Christie's, 16 May 1924, lot 165 (*A Party of Ladies and Gentlemen in a Garden*, oil on panel, 13 × 26½ in.; repr. in the Witt Library, London).
2. For a study of the influence of Watteau on English art, see Selby Whittingham, "What You Will; or Some Notes Regarding the Influence of Watteau on Turner and Other British Artists," *Turner Studies* 5 (Summer and Winter 1985), pp. 2–24 and 28–48.

79

THE PERFORMANCE OF THE NINE WORTHIES

Love's Labour's Lost V, 2
Oil on panel, 14¼ × 26⅝ in. (36.1 × 67.7 cm.)

Case no. 1729

Provenance: Parsons, October 1927, £45, as by Stothard

Condition: There is some paint flaking at the right, and there are cracks in the panel and separation

79

80

cracks in the paint surface. Five vertical braces with canvas strips are glued to the sides across the back of the panel.

Five of the characters in *Love's Labour's Lost* agree to stage a play of the Nine Worthies in front of the King of Navarre and the Princess of France and their companions. The figures at the left appear to be Costard, who plays Pompey the Great, Holofernes as Judas Maccabeus, the diminutive page, Moth, as Hercules, and Don Adriano de Armado as Hector of Troy. The audience at the right is composed of the four couples. Ferdinand, the King of Navarre, is surely the figure seated at the right who strikes a grand pose, and he exchanges glances with the princess, who still holds her mask.

The two standing figures in the center are more puzzling. The figure in white wears the costume of Pierrot, a comic figure from the Italian commedia dell'arte. Pierrot is traditionally masculine, and in the painting he (or she) is being wooed by a male figure in black. The pairing would seem to be that of Comedy and Tragedy. *Love's Labour's Lost*, of course, closes with the songs of Spring and Winter, and this duality is implied in the figures as well.

80

OLIVIA GREETING CESARIO
IN THE GARDEN
Twelfth Night III, 1
Oil on panel, 16³/₈ × 19¹³/₁₆ in. (41.7 × 50.3 cm.)

Case no. 1802

Provenance: Parsons, May 1928, £35.2.0 (£39 less 10 percent), as by Stothard

Condition: Two vertical braces support the back of the panel. It appears that another brace has broken off at the far right.

To the left stands Viola-Cesario. Olivia, accompanied by Maria, looks adoringly toward "him." In the play Feste, the fool, exits the garden just before Olivia's appearance, but, as he is described as holding a tabor (a drum like a tambourine without jingles), his presence in the painting helps confirm that the scene is indeed from *Twelfth Night.* To the far right stand Sir Andrew Aguecheek and a portly Sir Toby Belch.

The artist's technical abilities are limited. The figures are awkwardly rendered; the characterization of Viola-Cesario seems particularly unfortunate. Spatial relationships are also poorly articulated. For example, Sir Andrew's left arm is in advance of Sir Toby, while Sir Toby's right leg projects beyond Sir Andrew's left one. The background is only vaguely rendered, and it is not clear to where the steps lead. Olivia and Maria have perhaps emerged from a portal in the brown wall, as an indistinct light blue area appears behind Olivia's head.

Thomas Sully (nos. 81–82)

After Gilbert Stuart's death in 1828, Sully was recognized as America's leading portrait painter. He was born on 19 June 1783 at Horncastle in Lincolnshire, England, to parents who were actors. The family moved in search of work to America in 1792, eventually settling in Charleston, South Carolina. He showed an early interest in painting, and at age sixteen, having fought with his brother-in-law who was giving him lessons, he traveled to Richmond to live with his eldest brother, Lawrence, who was a painter primarily of miniatures. Two years after Lawrence's death in 1804, Sully married his widow, adopting her three children and eventually fathering six more. In 1807 the family settled in Philadelphia, then the largest city in the United States. Sully, however, traveled frequently to other cities in search of commissions, and on two occasions, in 1809 and 1837, journeyed to London for extended stays. He played a prominent role in the cultural life of Philadelphia, and given his theatrical background, it is not surprising that some of his best works were portraits of actors in character or pictures of scenes from plays. Sully died in his home in Philadelphia on 5 November 1872.

81

MACBETH IN THE WITCHES' CAVE
Macbeth IV, 1
1840
Oil on canvas, 29 × 24 in. (73.5 × 60.9 cm.)

Case no. 1086

Inscribed on back of canvas at lower right: "Macbeth in the Witches' Cave / Begun 1822—Finished 1840 / TS [the two letters are squeezed together]"

Provenance: Rosenbach, October 1922, $892.50

Exhibitions: Amherst, 1950; Amherst, *Shakespeare,* 1951

References: Biddle and Fielding 1921, no. 2404: "MACBETH. Painted from a Shakespearean sketch made in 1822. Painting begun Oct. 9th, 1840, finished Oct. 18th, 1840. Size 29″ × 24″. Price $100.00"

Condition: A hard, gray lead layer in oil was applied as a ground to the original canvas. In general, the oil paint is moderately applied with impasto only in areas of white lead. The paint has been noticeably solvent-abraded, particularly at the upper left, and Macbeth's hands and legs have been overcleaned and overpainted. There are paint losses at the lower right beneath the cauldron and at the upper left. The whole bottom edge of the canvas has been repainted. The original canvas at some point, probably by Finlayson in 1932, was lead-lined on to a commercially prepared canvas with a ground. The backing was removed in 1988, exposing the original inscription.

Sully kept a register listing the vast majority of the works he executed. The Folger painting is simply entitled *Macbeth,* and this painting and a picture of Lady Macbeth executed in 1836 were the only works he did of this play.[1] According to the register, the artist began work on the painting on 9 October 1840 and finished nine days later. He valued the painting at $100, a relatively low price (*Lady Macbeth,* for example, was listed at twice this amount). The register entry also states that the work was painted from a Shakespearean sketch made in 1822; obviously it was a composition he had long had in mind.

The rendering is more dramatic than is usual for Sully, and this essay in the horrific and the sublime departs from his more sentimental and conventionally stylish compositions. It is also more freely painted than is usual for the artist, who obviously felt liberated by the bold subject matter, which, at least initially, was conceived independently of any patron. The fire at the lower right consists of crude slabs of red and orange paint, and the smoke engulfing the rest of the composition obscures detail. The witches are roughed in with sketchy, energetic strokes, and the figures are so summarily treated that their identity is debatable. The Amherst exhibition catalogue cites the witches as appearing to the left of Macbeth with "the ghost of Banquo in the background." More likely, however, Sully shows

only one moment, the appearance of the helmeted head; this is the first apparition, Banquo being summoned up later in the scene with the fourth apparition. In this reading, the hooded figure to the right of Macbeth is the third witch, as only two are shown huddled at the left.

Macbeth is dramatically posed, seen from behind. Though startled, he confronts the head, seemingly less alarmed than the witches themselves. He wears armor over a white blouse, beneath which is a tan kilt patterned in aquamarine and red stripes, a large feathered bonnet on his head. Drapery falls across his left arm, lending even greater solidity to his firm stance. The helmeted head, even more terrifying with its visor down obscuring its features, offers a counter-diagonal to Macbeth's pose.

Sully's conception may look back to Edward Edwards's design for John Bell, published on 1 March 1773 (fig. 52), and he may also have known William

Fig. 53. William Marshall Craig, *Macbeth and the Apparition of the Armed Head*, ca. 1820. Pen and sepia and gray ink, gray wash, and watercolor, 11¹/₁₆ × 8¹⁵/₁₆ in. Yale Center for British Art, Paul Mellon Fund.

Fig. 52. After Edward Edwards, *Macbeth in the Witches' Cave*. Engraving by W. Burne, 1 March 1773.

Marshall Craig's watercolor of about 1820 adapted from it (fig. 53). Sully, however, transforms these pedestrian sources into a work of tense excitement, Macbeth positioned in a taunt diagonal and lit by flashes along his side. Sully's dramatic rendering was also inspired by Fuseli's example,[2] but he employs none of Fuseli's anatomical distortions. Ultimately, he rejects a purely visionary treatment for one more closely rooted in reality, and one suspects his scene also owes a debt to the theater. The armored head appears above and behind the cauldron, much as in stage productions, where the helmeted figure rose through a trap-door, its body obscured by the smoke. Not everyone apparently approved of the close juxtaposition of the apparition with the cauldron. Already in the late eighteenth century, James Sayer had issued a print (fig. 54) critical of one of Kemble's productions. Shakespeare appears in the form of the Westminster Abbey statue to complain, "Pray Sir dont boil my Spirits in this manner[.] some of them are of ye Lobster kind & will boil red[.] the Cauldron is in[s]tead for the purpose of Incantation not as a Stew pot for Ghosts[.]

Pray open your Trap doors and let them rise in a more natural Way." One again sees in this print that the depiction of Macbeth from behind in a recoiling diagonal is a stock device presumably in the theater as well as in art, but Sully's forceful, statuesque handling of this pose is superior to that of his predecessors.

1. For Lady Macbeth, see Biddle and Fielding 1921, no. 2405.
2. See in particular Fuseli's image of the soldier discovering Caius Marius, reproduced in Schiff 1973, no. 934.

82 (Plate 15)

PORTIA AND SHYLOCK

The Merchant of Venice IV, 1
1835
Oil on canvas, 38 × 29 in. (96.5 × 73.6 cm.)

Case no. 1629

Initialed and dated in lower left corner of bond: "T. S. 1835." Inscribed at top of bond, which, as held, is rotated 90 degrees to the right: "MDXXII / Bond / Gratiano / Shylock." In 1976, the conservator

Robert Scott Wiles recorded the following on the reverse of the lining fabric, where it had been copied during a previous restoration: "Portia . . . Be merciful. Take thrice thy money. Bid me tear the bond. Shylock—When it is paid according to the tenour. vide Merchant of Venice Act 4 Scene 1 ??1835."

Provenance: Painted for Edward L. Carey of Philadelphia; in 1921 owned by A. H. Halberstadt, Pottsville, Penn.; bought by Folger, January 1927, $2,000, Wells acting as agent.

Exhibitions: Montgomery, 1985–86, no. 61, repr. in color

References: Biddle and Fielding 1921, p. 379, no. 2514; *The Art News: An International Pictorial Newspaper* 25 (5 February 1926), repr. p. 1 (caption reads, "Recently sold by Gabriel Wells to an American collector")

Condition: The canvas was relined in 1976. There is a slight cupping in the paint surface, but there is also little evidence of loss or overpainting.

Fig. 54. [James Sayer], *An Apparition of an Armed Head Rises.* Etching and aquatint.

Engravings: Engraved by J. B. Forrest for a book illustration, according to Biddle and Fielding.

Preparatory study: Biddle and Fielding record a study measuring 20 by 17 inches for a large painting of Portia and Shylock, which, begun in June 1835, was abandoned (no. 2515).

Portia and Shylock was one of several paintings Sully executed for the Philadelphia collector Edward L. Carey. Born on 6 April 1805, Carey was the son of Mathew Carey, who built up the most prominent publishing and bookselling firm in the United States. Edward, while joining the family business, avidly pursued a career as a collector and patron of the arts, eventually being elected president of the Pennsylvania Academy of the Fine Arts on 2 June 1845. He died, however, less than two weeks later. The first picture Sully painted for Carey was *Frances Anne Kemble as Beatrice* (Pennsylvania Academy of the Fine Arts; Biddle and Fielding 1921, no. 955), a theatrical portrait in a Shakespearean context that he executed from 22 September to 7 October 1833. This was followed by *Lady Reading in Bed* (no. 2379; 10 July 1834–8 January 1835) and then by the Folger *Portia and Shylock* (14 November–4 December 1835). Sully presented to Carey a small *Juliet Arisen from the Tomb* (no. 2352) begun on 7 January 1836 and completed just four days later, and also painted for him in that same year *Lady Macbeth* (no. 2405; 29 August–5 September 1836) and *Isabella* (Pennsylvania Academy of the Fine Arts; no. 2346). Sully began *Juliet* (no. 2351) for Carey on 14 December 1836 but did not complete it until 2 June 1840, after he had returned from his second stay in England. On his return to America, he also painted for this patron *Nurse and Child* (no. 2460) and *Child in Contemplation* (no. 2135). The paintings are heavily weighted toward Shakespearean heroines[1] and can be seen as a response to the English actress Fanny Kemble's appearance on the Philadelphia stage; Sully's portrait of her as Beatrice, painted for Carey, was one of a number of portraits he executed of her in character. While *Portia and Shylock* is not a theatrical portrait, one suspects that the performances of Fanny Kemble and her father, Charles, in these roles are an underlying source of inspiration. Sully listed its price at $400, the highest of any of the above pictures, and he must have considered it the most ambitious and successful of this group.

The Folger picture focuses on the play's climactic scene, when Shylock, the Jewish moneylender, has come to demand payment of his bond. Antonio, the merchant of Venice, had secured a loan from Shylock for his friend Bassanio, who was in need of money to woo the wealthy Portia. His ships overdue and presumed lost, Antonio cannot repay the loan and now must pay the forfeiture stated by the bond, a pound of his own flesh. Portia, disguised as Balthasar, a doctor of laws, attempts to talk Shylock out of collecting the stated forfeit, and Sully depicts the moment when she cajoles, "Be merciful; / Take thrice thy money; bid me tear the bond." Shylock, though, remains adamant, replying, "When it is paid according to the tenour." Curiously, Sully has inscribed Gratiano's name on the bond along with Shylock's. Gratiano, a friend of Bassanio, plays a role in this scene, but one suspects Sully confused Gratiano with Antonio.[2] Shylock is shown holding both the scale and knife in his right hand,[3] Portia in the middle offering to tear the bond, and presumably at the far right in profile is Bassanio and behind him Antonio or Gratiano, who for Sully seem to be one and the same.

In representing Shylock, Sully avoids caricature. The moneylender is a stern, patriarchal figure of imposing dignity. Portia, representing gentle mercy, literally stands between him and his prey. Shylock, who relies on his legal rights, looks at the bond, while Portia, who represents human qualities, looks at him. The heads of Antonio and Bassanio are closely juxtaposed with Portia's, yet cast in shadow; they reinforce, rather than detract from, the focus on her. Portia is literally surrounded by an all-male world, one that demands strict adherence to the law. She triumphs only by interpreting the law in its most literal sense, but Sully's focus is not on her eventual triumph but on her giving and compassionate nature. She is the supplicating, tender female within the hard, cruel world of masculine values.

Sully composes the scene in terms of the close-up, intimate view of a portrait painter. The composition is densely packed, Shylock's body being cropped at the left and a part of Bassanio's head being cropped at the right. The composition is locked in place by a diagonal shaft of light emanating from the sky at the upper left: it beams down on the gleaming back of Shylock's bald head and the red lining of his garment, on the face and shoulders of Portia and her delicately posed hands holding the white bond, and finally on the colorful flashes of Bassanio's blue cloak and yellow waist-coat in the lower right corner.

1. Sully also painted at this same time *Miranda* (no. 2421) and, when in England, exhibited *Isabella* and *Beatrice* at the British Institution in 1838.

2. Perhaps Sully was attracted to the name "Gratiano" because of its associations with "gratia," the Latin word for love or grace.

3. The knob of the object Shylock is holding protrudes from his right hand. Given its tilted curvature, it appears to be the end of the hilt of a knife. It is also possible that this is intended as the top of the support for the scales, one arm of which is clearly visible. Biddle and Fielding in their brief description of the painting refer only to "Shylock with his scales" standing beside Portia. In this interpretation, the knife, which gives Shylock a more demonic character, is not shown.

Frederick Weekes

Weekes grew up in Pimlico in London, the second son of the sculptor Henry Weekes, the successful Royal Academician. He was one of three sons who pursued painting, none of whom enjoyed the professional success of their father. Weekes first exhibited at the British Institution in 1854; his inaugural effort was a scene from Shakespeare of Touchstone and Audrey in act III, scene 3 of *As You Like It.* He continued to exhibit at the British Institution until 1867, at the Royal Academy from 1861 to 1871, and at the Society of British Artists from 1863 to 1892–93, many of these later works being watercolors rather than oils. He also exhibited at the New Water-Colour Society in addition to other galleries. He specialized in battle scenes, often drawing his subject matter from earlier times.

83

FALSTAFF AND BARDOLPH
I Henry IV III, 3
ca. 1855–57
Oil on canvas, 18¾ × 15⅛ in. (47.7 × 38.4 cm.)

Case no. 1798–99

Signed in red at lower right: "F WEEKES." (the "F" is superimposed over the "W")

Provenance: Michelmore, June 1928, £20 (see Michelmore's *A Catalogue of Shakespeareana,* with notes and preface by Falconer Madan, [1927], no. 702, asking price £125, as from *The Merry Wives of Windsor*)

Condition: The canvas has never been lined.

The Michelmore catalogue identifies this scene as the opening of act III, scene 5 in *The Merry Wives of Windsor,* with Falstaff commanding Bardolph to buy him a quart of sack after his unceremonious dumping in the Thames. Far more plausible is the identification of the scene with the confrontation between Falstaff and Bardolph in the Boar's Head Tavern in *I Henry IV,* a popular subject with painters. The two trade insults, with Bardolph joking about Falstaff's size: "Why, you are so fat, Sir John, that you must needs be out of all compass, out of all reasonable compass, Sir John." Bardolph's pointing toward Falstaff's belly, to which the knight's own hand draws attention, supports this reading. Falstaff in turn launches into his brilliant asides on Bardolph's red nose.

The painting's stretcher has an old paper label in pen and ink pasted on its back at the upper center. Difficult to cipher, it appears to read, "F. Weekes. / 14 Moreton Terrace / Belgrave Road / Pimlico." When Weekes exhibited at the British Institution in 1854, his address was given as 29 Lower Belgrave Place, just a few doors from his father's house. The next time he exhibited was in 1857, when he is listed at 14 Moreton Place, from which he had moved by the following year. Thus, the Folger picture must be an early work created around 1857. It has a hard-edged metallic quality, more the work of an illustrator than of an accomplished painter. The choice of colors also is infelicitous, with olive green dominating. The careful treatment of the details for the objects and costumes, however, reveals Weekes's life-long concern with historical accuracy.

Weekes returned to the subject of Falstaff a few years later, exhibiting at the Society of British Artists in 1865 *Falstaff Vows to Marry Mrs. Quickly* from *II Henry IV.* He exhibited two other scenes from Shakespeare, both from *As You Like It.*[1] While he was normally drawn to scenes of picturesque warriors, his forays into Shakespeare always centered on comic characters, and in *Falstaff and Bardolph* he obviously relished the opportunity of developing the fat knight's exaggerated pose and expression.

1. *Touchstone and Audrey,* British Institution, 1854, no. 506, and *Touchstone, William, and Audrey,* Society of British Artists, 1865, no. 177.

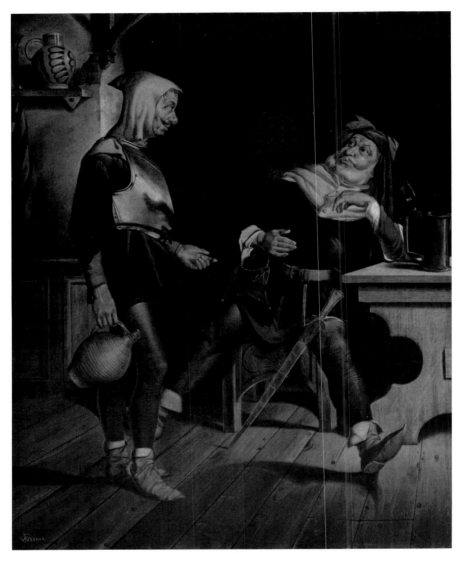

83

Benjamin West

West was the first American artist to gain international fame. Born just outside Philadelphia on 10 October 1738, he left America in 1760 for Rome, the first American painter to make this trip to what was then the Western world's artistic capital. He stopped in London in 1763 on his way back to the Colonies, but finding a responsive audience, he made the decision to remain. West's neoclassical history painting *Agrippina Landing at Brundisium with the Ashes of Germanicus* of 1768 secured for him the patronage of King George III. In that same year he became a founding member of the Royal Academy. On the death in 1792 of Sir Joshua Rey-nolds, the academy's first president, West took over the presidency, serving in this capacity, with the exception of one year, until his own death on 11 March 1820. He was a prolific painter of historical subjects, and his *The Death of General Wolfe*, executed in 1770, proved an influential adaptation of the great style to a modern subject. As Historical Painter to the King, he worked on a number of important projects, including subjects drawn from the classical past, medieval history, and biblical illustrations. West was present at the dinner in 1786 when the idea for the Boydell Shakespeare Gallery was born. He and Reynolds received the highest fees paid by Alderman Boydell, West contributing two major pictures.

84 (Plate 10)

KING LEAR AND CORDELIA
King Lear IV, 7
1793
Oil on canvas, 19 × 23⁹/₁₆ in. (48.1 × 59.9 cm.)

Signed and dated at lower left: "B. West, 1793 -"

Provenance: Painted for George Bowles (died 1817) of Wanstead (this information is derived from a printed label in the middle of the upper portion of the back of the frame: "B. West, P.R.A., 1792 [inaccurate date] / The Death of King Lear [inaccurate] / 19 in. by 24 in. / Engraved in Boydell's edition of Shakespeare [inaccurate] / From the Wanstead House Collection"); in the collection of Lt. Col. Willoughby Pitcairn Kennedy, who retired in 1906 to Lynedoch, W. Byfleet, Surrey, and died on 7 August 1928 (this information is derived from a label on lined paper in pen and ink at the lower left of the back of the frame: "No. 16. Drawing room / Death of King Lear by / B. West R. A. / Propt. Col. W. P. Kennedy"); purchased by Folger from McGirr, September 1929, $540

Exhibitions: London, Royal Academy, 1794, no. 17, as "Cordelia making herself known to her father, King Lear"

References: "A Correct Catalogue of the Works of Benjamin West, Esq.," *La Belle Assemblée or Bell's Court and Fashionable Magazine* 4 (1808), Supplement, p. 19 ("The Grecian Daughter defending her father from the tyrant—Its companion, the Couch scene of King Lear and his Daughter," painted for Mr. Bowles of Wanstead); John Dillenberger, *Benjamin West: The Context of His Life's Work*, San Antonio, 1977, p. 188, no. 497; Helmut von Erffa and Allen Staley, *The Paintings of Benjamin West*, New Haven and London, 1986, p. 276, no. 215

Condition: The original canvas, now missing its tack-over edges, was lined at some early date and again in 1976. The paint surface has been solvent-abraded, and there is extensive repaint, particularly in the drapery at the top, in the figures of the two women at the left, and in the separation cracks.

Versions: Painting (42 × 56½ in.) ca. 1784, bought by Peter, duke of Courland, Mitau, and Berlin, now unlocated (von Erffa and Staley 1986, no. 212) but known from a print by Daniel Berger of 1791; painting owned by Henry E. Huntington Library and Art Gallery, San Marino, Calif. (42½ × 57 in.) similar in composition to Berger print, though cropped at edges, repr. in von Erffa and Staley 1986, no. 213; painting (18½ × 23½ in.) unlocated, von Erffa and Staley 1986, no. 214, presumably the image reproduced in Richard Earlom's mezzotint of 1 January 1799 (18 × 22¹⁵/₁₆ in.)

Related studies: Von Erffa and Staley mention that West's son Benjamin sold a drawing entitled "King Lear and Cordelia" in 1839; one drawing of this subject, dated 1783, is in the British Museum and another is in the Toledo Museum of Art. A related composition is found in three drawings entitled "Esau selling his Birthright for a Dish of Pottage" in the Pierpont Morgan Library, New York.

Engravings: Richard Earlom, published in 1799, after one of the earlier versions

West illustrated five scenes from Shakespeare, more than from any other English writer. Some exist in more than one version, and all are drawn from the tragedies. His first work was *Romeo and Juliet*, which bears the date 1778. This was followed by what was apparently his first version of *Lear and Cordelia*, around 1784, now known only from a print after it (fig. 55).[1] Both of these paintings were purchased by the German duke of Courland. Then came two works painted for Boydell, *Lear in the Storm* of 1788 and *Ophelia before the King and Queen* of 1792. Finally, for the Royal Academy exhibition he submitted a sketch entitled *Macbeth and the Witches* in 1793 and the Folger picture the following year.

Scenes from *King Lear* were popular throughout this period, and the subject of Lear awakening had been treated in both paintings and book illustrations. The Folger picture would seem to be West's fourth and final version of *Lear and Cordelia*. Like the earlier versions, it shows Lear awakening, troubled and disoriented, as Cordelia, her classical profile silhouetted against the sky, lovingly attends him. The gentleman at the right is either the doctor or Kent, both of whom figure prominently in the scene. The identity of the two women at the left has proved troublesome to establish. Of the version sold to the duke of Courland, von Erffa and Staley point out, "The title used for the subject in the early lists of West's works, 'King Lear and His daughters,' establishes that the two female figures standing behind Cordelia are Goneril and Regan (and they could hardly be anybody else), but Goneril

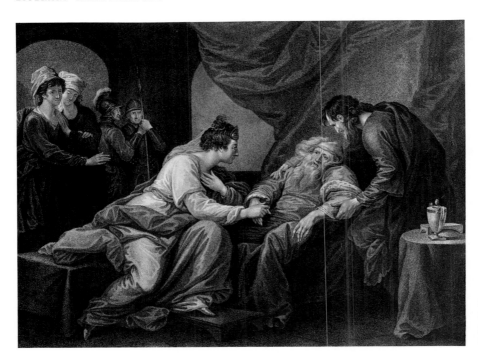

Fig. 55. After Benjamin West, *König Lear und Kordelia.* Engraving by D. Berger, 15¹/₈ × 18³/₈ in., 1791.

and Regan should not appear in this scene . . . . It would seem either that West was extremely careless, or that he deliberately sought to create a generalized sense of the play rather than exact delineation of a specific passage from it" (p. 274). Neither explanation is convincing. Given the two women's sympathetic reactions, it would seem more likely that they are attendants of Cordelia, who after all is the queen of France, and it is not the painting that is in error but rather the title "King Lear and His daughters," which did not appear until two decades after the first picture was executed.[2] The Folger version is closer in conception to a painted-over proof of Earlom's mezzotint (fig. 56) than it is to the other earlier versions. The mezzotint was not published until 1799, but proofs could have been pulled considerably earlier, and the painted-over proof bears a date of 1792. If this date is correct, then, as von Erffa and Staley suggest, the painted-over proof could have served as a preliminary sketch for the Folger version. Yet, the Folger picture differs in a number of details from all of these earlier attempts. The two soldiers standing in front of the pier have been dropped, a removal warranted by the small size of the canvas. To give more dignity and emphasis to the pier, West replaced its simple detailing with an engaged column on a tall

plinth. This substitution is visually satisfying even if the column is architecturally out of scale with the flanking arches. West also discarded as anatomically awkward the hand of Kent or the doctor that had rested on Lear's right shoulder. In addition, the orthogonal lines formed by the squared-off pavement now position the viewer in front of Cordelia, whose pose carries the eye from left to right to focus on the distressed old king. Overall there is a more expressive nervous energy in the rendering than had appeared in the earlier works. To take only one example, the fingers of Lear and Cordelia are now spindly and eloquently mannered.

West executed the Folger *Lear and Cordelia* for George Bowles, a wealthy collector. He also painted for Bowles a companion picture *The Grecian Daughter Defending Her Father* (fig. 57), dated 1794, and the two pictures were exhibited together at the Royal Academy that same year. The pendant shows a moment from the final scene of Arthur Murphy's play *The Grecian Daughter,* first performed in 1772. It focuses on the loving concern of Euphrasia, who, like Cordelia, comes to her father's aid. Euphrasia throws herself between the aged Evander and the tyrant Dionysius, who has come to kill him. In contrast to *Lear and Cordelia,* this scene of filial virtue has a happy ending: it is Dionysius who is slain

Fig. 56. Benjamin West ?, oil sketch over mezzotint by Richard Earlom of West's *Lear and Cordelia*. From the RSC Collection, with the permission of the Governors of the Royal Shakespeare Theatre ©.

Fig. 57. Benjamin West, *The Grecian Daughter Defending Her Father*, 1794. Oil on panel, 19 × 23 in. Collection of the Newark Museum, purchase 1956, John J. O'Neill Bequest Fund.

while Evander, the rightful king of Syracuse, regains his throne. The two works, small in scale,[3] energetic in execution, and with dramatic, irrational architectural backdrops, offer a sensational pairing in which a contemporary drama set in ancient Greece and a Jacobean drama set in ancient Britain are seen as universalizing statements on the same theme.

1. The Folger impression of this print may be unique, as the authors of *The Paintings of Benjamin West*, published in 1986, state that none is known to exist.
2. The title first appeared in the list of West's paintings published in *Public Characters of 1805*.
3. In 1795 Bowles commissioned two subjects drawn from English history from John Francis Rigaud: *The First Interview of King Edgar and Elfrida* and *Lady Elizabeth Grey Petitioning King Edward IV for Her Husband's Lands*. Given their modest size (20¾ × 29¾ in. each), it may be that Bowles preferred works on a small scale. It is also of interest that these two paintings feature scenes in which women are again prominent protagonists. Beginning in 1782, Bowles had been particularly fond of the work of Angelica Kauffmann, and, not surprisingly, a number of her pictures for Bowles also emphasize heroines.

Richard Westall (nos. 85–86)

Westall was born in Hertford on 2 January 1766. He was apprenticed to a silver engraver in London in 1779, studying evenings at a school of art. By 1784 he felt himself ready to exhibit a portrait drawing at the Royal Academy. He entered its schools the following year. Early in his career he was best known for his watercolors and also became a noted book illustrator, second only to Thomas Stothard in productivity. From 1790 to 1794 he shared a house with the promising young painter Thomas Lawrence; he was elected an associate member of the Royal Academy in 1792 and a full academician two years later. Along with Stothard and William Hamilton, he was among the most prolific contributors to the Boydell Shakespeare Gallery: there are five engravings after his pictures for the large series and eighteen for the small one.[1] Westall, however, never found a market for his historical pictures, and his primary source of income remained watercolors and book illustration. While these works proved popular with the public, critics complained of his mannered style, which relied too heavily on formulaic stereotypes of female beauty. Throughout his career, he exhibited steadily at the Royal Academy, 313 works in all, and from 1806, the year of its founding, to 1834, he was also a frequent exhibitor at the British Institution. Impo-

verished late in life by ill-advised speculation in old pictures, he died on 4 December 1836 at age seventy-one.

1. One of Westall's subjects, his painting from *Cymbeline* of Imogen before the cave, was engraved for both the large and small series of prints. As the picture is listed in the Boydell catalogues only with the small series, it would appear that it was never executed on a large scale and that Boydell had the small picture act as a model for both series of engravings.

85

WOLSEY DISGRACED

Henry VIII III, 2
1795
Oil on canvas, 31¾ × 21½ in. (80.6 × 54.4 cm.)

Case no. 1090

Initialed and dated at lower right: "R. W. 1795"

Provenance: Commissioned by Alderman John Boydell for the Shakespeare Gallery; sold by lottery 28 January 1805 and won by William Tassie; sold by Christie 17 May 1805, no. 13, as "*Wolsey disgraced and receiving the discovered Paper from Henry the VIIIth*—very fine," bought by John Mehux, Esq., for 15 guineas (£15.15.0); Michelmore, October 1922, £125 (£250 for this picture and no. 57)

Exhibitions: London, Boydell, 1795, no. 22; London, Boydell, *Small Pictures*, 1796, no. 25; London, Boydell, 1802, no. 135; London, Boydell, 1805, no. 112

References: Friedman 1976, p. 198, n. 388, and p. 240

Condition: The impasto was indented in an early lining, and the surface also suffers from drying cracks and areas of abrasion. The painting was most recently conserved in 1987, when it was cleaned, retouched, and relined in an effort to repair some of the earlier damage.

Engravings: W. C. Wilson, published 29 September 1796, for 1802 Boydell edition of Shakespeare's plays, facing p. 76 of *King Henry VIII*, 10⅝ × 6½ in. (border of image and margin)

Westall executed four scenes from *Henry VIII* for Boydell, one for the large series and three for the small series. Cardinal Wolsey appears in two of these works, in the Folger picture and in the large painting which showed him entering the Abbey of Leicester to die, a scene that is described in the play

85

rather than enacted. The Folger painting depicts the earlier moment of Wolsey's downfall. As Lord Chancellor of England and the most influential member of Henry's court, Wolsey had wielded enormous power and in the process had considerably advanced his own fortunes. But letters he intended for the pope entreating him to interfere with the king's divorce of Queen Katharine and a paper listing his

many possessions had miscarried, finding their way into Henry's hands. In their next meeting the king gives signs of his displeasure, and on leaving the room he hands the incriminating documents to Wolsey to read. Soon the noblemen, who had left with the king, return to deliver Henry's order that the cardinal surrender to them the Great Seal that accompanies the office of Lord Chancellor. Wolsey, knowing he is lost, still shows defiance, refusing to surrender his badge of office to any but the king himself. Westall shows Cardinal Wolsey seated at the left, pointing to the purse containing the Great Seal. At the right stand the Dukes of Norfolk and Suffolk and the Earl of Surrey, his enemies who demand its return. Behind them at the far right stands a sympathetic Lord Chamberlain. The faces are not nearly so generalized as in the following work, *Shylock Rebuffing Antonio*, and it would appear that, when possible, Westall based his heads on engravings of the historical figures.[1]

The scene takes place in the antechamber to the king's apartment, and Westall envisions an expansive and impressive interior. Earlier in this same scene, the king had sat in the chair Wolsey now occupies. In placing Wolsey in this same regal seat, Westall suggests the cardinal's overweening pride and worldly ambition, but also his dignity and strength.

1. Wolsey's features were well known from a number of prints, and the right-hand figure in the row of the three noblemen is based on an engraving published on 27 November 1792 by S. Harding of a portrait of Charles Brandon, duke of Suffolk, then in Horace Walpole's collection.

86 (Plate 4)

SHYLOCK REBUFFING ANTONIO

The Merchant of Venice III, 3
1795
Oil on canvas, 32$^{1}/_{16}$ × 21$^{1}/_{16}$ in. (81.5 × 53.5 cm.)

Case no. 1056

Signed and dated at lower right: "R. Westall 1795"

Provenance: Commissioned by Alderman John Boydell for the Shakespeare Gallery; sold by lottery 28 January 1805 and won by William Tassie; sold by Christie 17 May 1805, no. 8, as "*Antonio conducted to Prison*," bought by Crome, Esq., for 9$^{1}/_{2}$ guineas (£9.19.6); Michelmore, February 1922, £125 (£250 for this picture and no. 58)

Exhibitions: London, Boydell, *Small Pictures*, 1796, no. 47; London, Boydell, 1802, no. 103; London, Boydell, 1805, no. 113; Washington, 1976–77, no. 23

References: Friedman 1976, p. 198, n. 388, and p. 242, as "*Antonio conducted to Prison*"

Condition: The tacking edges have been cut, and the painting glued to a second canvas probably in the nineteenth century. There is an old tear, irregularly shaped and 5 inches long, in the upper left quadrant of the picture which had been repaired and the loss filled in an early restoration. There is abrasion to Shylock's face and to the signature. Visible in the background is a pentimento of Venice as seen from the Piazzetta.

Engravings: J. Parker, published 1 December 1795 for 1802 Boydell edition of Shakespeare's plays, facing p. 63 of *The Merchant of Venice*, 10$^{1}/_{2}$ × 6$^{1}/_{2}$ in. (border of image and margin); there are also a small engraving by F. C. Bock and outline engravings by Starling and A. T. Aikman.

Only two subjects for *The Merchant of Venice*, both executed by Westall, were painted for Boydell's small series of pictures. In this scene, Antonio, who is unable to repay the loan of three thousand ducats, approaches Shylock to ask that he reconsider the stipulated forfeit of a pound of flesh. The figures are all walking in the same direction, but Shylock dramatically looks back, dismissing Antonio with contempt: "I'll have my bond; I will not hear thee speak." Antonio is flanked by his friend Salarino, the close juxtaposition of their heads suggestive of his support, and by the jailer, who stands in shadow suggestive of his grim duty as demanded by the bond. Shylock's imperious left hand dominates Antonio's beseeching gesture, while his clenched right hand parallels the jailer's fist clenching the sword that will enforce the bond. To the left is the entrance to Shylock's house, and the fact that the window is opened is surely intended as an allusion to Jessica's elopement.[1] The disposition of the figures is similar to that in *Wolsey Disgraced* (no. 85): the main protagonist is alone at left, the others bunched at right, and, as first envisioned, with the architectural background insistently separating them.

As the pentimenti make clear, Westall had originally employed as a background a view of Venice from the Piazzetta looking north. The figures were shown standing at the southeast corner of the Doges' Palace, the corner column with its sculpted figure above bisecting the picture space. Just above Shylock's extended left arm can be seen the southern portico of the Basilica San Marco. The roof line of the Libreria Vecchia is at the left, the Campanile towering above it. The dominating presence of the Doges' Palace was appropriate in this play about jus-

Fig. 58. After Edward Edwards, *I'll Have My Bond.* Engraving by Sharpe, 1 October 1782.

tice as wielded by the state, and the basilica, with its overtones of mercy, is positioned between the head of the Jew and those of the Christians.

This moment of confrontation had been depicted in an earlier design by Edward Edwards for Lowndes's *New English Theatre* (fig. 58). Westall may have been following Edwards's example when he chose the Piazzetta as a background, but his rendering, in contrast to Edwards's, is topographically accurate, providing a great deal of information within a small format. He undoubtedly made good use of prints of Venice and may even have seen Canaletto's painting *The Piazzetta: Looking North*, which was then, as now, in the royal collection. One can only speculate as to why he painted over his first background. The artist may have been concerned that the architectural background threat-

ened to overwhelm the figures, detracting from the drama of this encounter. In addition, the stage directions specify only that the scene take place on a Venetian street; by placing the action before Shylock's house, the image is better integrated with some of the play's earlier scenes and such earlier Boydell pictures as Smirke's large painting set in the interior of Shylock's home.

1. The opposition of shuttered to opened windows is emphasized in act II, scene 5, where Shylock directs Jessica, "Lock up my doors . . . / . . . stop my house's ears, I mean my casements" (lines 29 and 34). Launcelot Gobbo, however, immediately contradicts him, whispering to Jessica: ". . . Mistress, look out at / window, for all this; / There will come a Christian by, / Will be worth a Jewess' eye" (lines 40–43).

Francis Wheatley

Wheatley, the son of a master tailor, was born in London in 1747. In 1762 he was awarded the first of two premiums from the Society of Arts and began to exhibit at the Society of Artists in 1765, winning a prize from this society in the following year. He was elected a member of the Society of Artists in 1770 and in 1778 began to exhibit at the Royal Academy. Although he was successful as as painter of portraits and landscapes, his expenses outstripped his income. He became involved with the wife of a fellow artist, John Alexander Gresse, and in 1779 left with her for a four-year stay in Dublin in order to escape his difficulties. On his return to London, he found a market for idealized scenes of rustic genre and illustrations to contemporary literature. His most famous series is the *Cries of London*, paintings of sentimental genre that were exhibited at the Royal Academy from 1792 to 1795 and were widely known from the engravings after them. Influenced by the example of John Hamilton Mortimer, Wheatley had in 1772 exhibited a theatrical conversation piece at the Society of Artists of the dueling scene in *Twelfth Night*; yet it was for Boydell that he created most of his Shakespearean paintings—thirteen in all, twelve of which were engraved. The Royal Academy was late in acknowledging his abilities, but he quickly rose from an associate member, a position to which he was elected in 1790, to a full member the following year. Despite his success, he was plagued by debts and for a number of years before his death on 28 June 1801 was racked by poor health.

87 (Plate 5)

**HELENA AND COUNT BERTRAM
BEFORE THE KING OF FRANCE**
All's Well That Ends Well II, 3
1793
Oil on canvas, 30 or 31 × 21³/₄ in. (78.5 × 55.3 cm.)

Case no. 1168

Provenance: Commissioned by Alderman John Boydell for the Shakespeare Gallery for 20 guineas;[1]
sold by lottery 28 January 1805 and won by William
Tassie; sold by Christie 18 May 1805, no. 9, as *"The
King, Helena and Lords,"* bought by a Mr. Salteri
for 5 guineas (£5.5.0); Michelmore, July 1923, £125
(£250 for this painting and a work by Cattermole)

Exhibitions: London, Boydell, *Small Pictures,* 1796,
no. 43; London, Boydell, 1802, no. 109; London,
Boydell, 1805, no. 36; a photograph of the painting
was included in the exhibition *Francis Wheatley
RA, 1747–1801,* held at the Aldeburgh Festival of
Music and the Arts, 15–25 June, and Leeds, City
Art Gallery, 8 July–8 August 1965, no. 104, as "The
King, Helena and Lords"; Washington, 1976–77, no.
24

References: Mary Webster, *Francis Wheatley,* London, 1970, no. 101; Friedman 1976, pp. 178 and 242,
repr. pl. 97

Condition: In 1932, Finlayson glued this work onto
a commercially prepared, preprimed canvas. The
picture has been severely abraded in the upper left
quadrant and in the background around the king's
legs. The original tacking edges have been cut off in
a previous restoration. It was most recently conserved in 1988.

Engravings: Luigi Schiavonetti, published 1 September 1797, for 1802 Boydell edition of Shakespeare's plays, facing p. 35 of *All's Well That Ends
Well,* 11³/₁₆ × 6³/₄ in. (border of image and margin)

　　In the eighteenth century *All's Well That Ends
Well* was not particularly popular with either audiences or artists. Wheatley, however, was clearly
drawn to this play, executing four paintings, three
for Boydell and one for Woodmason; in each case he
was the only artist who chose to illustrate this
work. His first picture shows the final scene in
which Helena confronts Bertram. Painted for Boydell, it was already on exhibit by 1790. The Folger
picture is one of two painted for Boydell's small series, the other showing the conversation between

Fig. 59. After Francis Wheatley, *The Princess Showing Rosaline
Her Presents from the King.* Engraving by W. Skelton, 4 June 1793.

Helena and the Countess of Rousillon in act I,
scene 3. Thus, for Boydell, Wheatley chose to nar-
rate the play through scenes centering on Helena.
His picture for Woodmason illustrated an aspect of
the subplot involving Count Bertram and Parolles,
showing Parolles ambushed in act IV, scene 1, a subject that had already proved a favorite of book illustrators.

　　In the Folger painting, the King of France, as a re-
ward for restoring him to health, grants Helena
the husband of her choice. Passing over four lords,
Helena picks the young man with whom she is in
love, Bertram, Count of Rousillon. Offended by her
low birth, Bertram at first rejects Helena but then,
temporarily at least, yields to the king's command.
The grouping is compact, with the figures intimately clustered about the king. Wheatley's instincts are decorative rather than grand, as he
presents an elegant and inoffensive confrontation
on a domestic scale. Hand gestures are emphasized,

and Helena, despite Bertram's ill-tempered rejection, remains elegantly calm. Her pose and, to some extent, even her gown are a reprise of those of the princess in Wheatley's illustration of act V, scene 2, for *Love's Labour's Lost* (fig. 59),[2] the artist obviously being content to repeat what he felt was a successful attitude.

Interestingly, the painting differs significantly from the print (fig. 60). Wheatley, Boydell, or Schiavonetti, the engraver, obviously thought the original conception could be improved upon. In the painting three bearded lords are ranged behind Bertram, but in the print their heads are no longer lined up in a row extending down Bertram's arm. Instead, only two more distant heads are visible, and they are now possibly intended to represent Lafeu, an elderly lord, and Parolles, a companion of Bertram, rather than the other eligible bachelors. In

addition, in the painting only one guard appears with a halberd behind Helena, while in the print another halberd is added along with two heads, more firmly anchoring this side of the composition. One change Schiavonetti made is clearly a misreading of Wheatley's intentions. In the painting the king's cloak falls over the arm of the chair so that only a portion of the arm is visible. In the print, this portion of the chair is incorrectly interpreted as a steep pyramid whose sharp point would have made sitting an adventure.

1. The receipt, dated 28 October 1793, reads, "Received from Messrs. Boydell eighty-four pounds for four pictures from 'All's Well' and 'Much Ado,' in full" (Anderson Collection, Royal Academy Catalogues, 1793, British Museum Print Room).
2. The reproduction is of the print after the painting, but the painting itself was at one time in the Folger collection (see D59).

Francis Wheatley, after

88

JAQUENETTA APPROACHING SIR NATHANIEL WITH BEROWNE'S LETTER
Love's Labour's Lost IV, 2
Early nineteenth century
Oil on canvas, 30 × 24⅞ in. (76.2 × 63.2 cm.)

Case no. 1798

88

Fig. 60. After Francis Wheatley, *Helena and Count Bertram before the King of France*. Engraving by L. Schiavonetti, 1 September 1799.

Annotated and dated at lower left: "F Wheatley / 1792[?]"

Provenance: Appeared in Michelmore catalogue *Shakespeareana Illustrated* [1923?], no. 45, as by Wheatley, repr. in color, asking price £250; it is not known when Folger purchased it from Michelmore.

Original painting: The Boydell picture dates to around 1792. Its present whereabouts is unknown.

Engravings after original: J. Neagle, 4 June 1793

Wheatley painted this scene for Boydell's small series of pictures. Despite the date and "signature" on the Folger picture, it is only a copy and, considering its dull handling, is assuredly after the print rather than the painting. Wheatley painted two scenes from this play for the small series; the other scene (in this case, the original canvas) was also purchased from Michelmore by Folger, although it is no longer in the Library's collection (see D59).

The painting shows Jaquenetta asking Sir Nathaniel, a country curate, to read the letter given to her by Costard. Holofernes, the schoolmaster standing next to Sir Nathaniel, is the one who discerns that Costard has delivered the wrong letter, as this one is from Lord Berowne to Rosaline, one of the ladies attending the Princess of France.

John Masey Wright (nos. 89–91)

Although he began his career as a painter, Wright made his name primarily as a watercolorist. He was born in London on 14 October 1777. His father wanted him to follow him in his profession as an organ builder, but the boy insisted on becoming an artist. At age sixteen he observed Thomas Stothard in his studio; later he worked for a time as a scene designer and for Thomas and Henry Aston Barker as a painter of panoramas. In 1812 he exhibited for the first time a picture at the Royal Academy, showing six more works until 1818.[1] He exhibited regularly at the British Institution from 1817 to 1823 and again in 1830 and 1836. Wright began exhibiting at the Society of Painters in Water Colours (the "Old Water-Colour Society") in 1824, the year in which he was made an associate; full membership followed a few months later. With the exception of 1854, he exhibited every year from 1824 until 1864, sometimes as many as a dozen works.[2] In addition, in 1835, the only year he exhibited at

the Society of British Artists, all five works were watercolors. In the 1820s and 1830s, Wright frequently illustrated books and literary annuals, and he taught as a drawing master, opening a fashionable practice that attracted members of the nobility. Shakespeare was his favorite author, and the Folger has a collection of 122 of his watercolors which, though purchased in 1920, has a provenance going back to at least 1898. Given the varied quality of these works, one suspects that some are by his pupils. In later years, Wright struggled to find employment and received gifts from the Old Water-Colour Society and in 1858 a life annuity from the Royal Academy. He died on 13 May 1866. While a number of watercolors and drawings which can firmly be attributed to him have survived, this is not the case with his work in oil.[3] His is an oeuvre that still needs to be reconstructed, and, ironically, the three paintings ascribed to him here were purchased as by different artists, while the two signed works have been demoted to attributions.

1. As in the case of Richard Cook, there has been confusion in the literature over which paintings were by John Masey Wright and which by an artist with the same last name. The best account of Wright's career is to be found in John Lewis Roget's *A History of the "Old Water-Colour" Society* (London, 1891, vol. 1, pp. 535–39, and vol. 2, pp. 204–05), where a solution to this problem is offered.

2. The total number of works Wright exhibited at this society fluctuates in the literature. The obituary in the *Art Journal* (6 [1 February 1867], p. 56) mentions that "nearly one hundred and forty were shown in their annual exhibitions." Roget (*History,* vol. 2, p. 204) offers the more more modest figure of 111. Two complications are that in the early catalogues Wright is listed as "T. M. Wright," and one suspects that his work is sometimes confused with that of John William Wright, who began to exhibit watercolors in 1831. Is the "Una—a Sketch" exhibited in that year (no. 217) as by "J. M. Wright"—at a time when John Masey was almost invariably cited as "T. M. Wright"—by him or by J. W. Wright, who exhibited this same subject in 1839 (no. 124)? If one accepts the 1831 *Una* as J. M.'s work and an earlier work of 1827, recorded as by F. M. Wright, as his as well, his works exhibited at the Society of Painters in Water Colours total 116.

3. A signed painting entitled *The Ghost,* presumably the work Wright exhibited at the Royal Academy in 1813, was auctioned at Sotheby on 21 March 1979 (lot 64) and was photographed at that time; a print of the photograph is on file at the Witt Library, London. Unfortunately, the signature cannot be seen in the photograph, making impossible a comparison with the signatures in nos. 92 and 93. In 1899 the third duke of Wellington acquired Wright's *The Battle of the Pyrenees* and *The Battle of Vittoria,* which also date to around 1813 and are now at Stratfield Saye House (see F. G. Burrett, "John Massey Wright (1777–1866)," *The Old Water-Colour Society's Club Annual Volume* 54 [1979], p. 45).

89

89

MISTRESS FORD AND FALSTAFF
The Merry Wives of Windsor III, 3
ca. 1810s?
Oil on canvas, oval, 12 × 15⁷/₁₆ in. (30.5 × 39 cm.)

Case no. 1730

Provenance: Betts, October 1927, £45 (price for pair) as by Angelica Kauffmann

Exhibitions: Amherst, 1950, no. 15, as "Mistress Page and Falstaff" by Kauffmann; Washington, 1976–77, no. 15, as "Mistress Page and Falstaff" by Kauffmann

Condition: Unlike its damaged companion, this canvas, which has never been lined, is in fair condition, although its surface has been badly solvent-abraded, particularly in the figure of Mrs. Ford and in the background at the right.

90

JULIET AND THE NURSE
Romeo and Juliet II, 5
ca. 1810s?
Oil on canvas, oval, 12¹/₁₆ × 15¹/₁₆ in. (30.8 × 38.3 cm.)

Case no. 1730

Provenance: See above.

Exhibitions: Washington, 1976–77, no. 14, as by Kauffmann

Condition: The painting, which has been lined, has been severely damaged in the past. More than three-quarters of the surface is covered with repaint, little of the original design elements remaining.

The scene from *The Merry Wives of Windsor* has traditionally been identified as "Mistress Page and

Falstaff," but it clearly shows Falstaff wooing Mrs. Ford, with Mrs. Page listening at the door, waiting to cue Robin as to when he should enter with her on his heels. As preplanned, the two will burst in to announce Mr. Ford's imminent arrival to search the house for his wife's suspected lover. The painting hanging on the wall between Mrs. Ford and Falstaff, like the painting in *Romeo and Juliet*, plays a role in the drama. A male portrait, it is surely of Mr. Ford, and acts as a reminder that he will soon enough come between the pair.

The paintings were purchased as by Angelica Kauffmann (1741–1807) but are later and by a lesser hand. It is on the basis of watercolors in the Folger collection of this same subject that the painting *Mistress Ford and Falstaff* and therefore its companion as well can be given to Wright. Three watercolors, and particularly the one that is ini-

tialed "JMW," are all close variations on this same composition.[1]

The scene from *Romeo and Juliet* shows Juliet's nurse after she has returned, several hours later than expected, with news from Romeo as to if and when they are to be married. She teases Juliet by making her wait for the news, complaining at length about her fatigue and various aches and pains. The stage directions place this scene in the Capulets' orchard, but artists often portray the meeting indoors. Robert Smirke was the first artist to depict this moment, which was to prove popular, in a painting executed around 1796 for Boydell's Shakespeare Gallery. Smirke showed both figures seated, while Wright seats only the nurse, a pleading Juliet standing beside her. The Folger painting also depicts the nurse with a truly agonized expression, the humor lying in the parallel between her

90

suffering and that of a female saint in the picture hanging on the wall behind her.[2] As was customary, Juliet is shown attempting to coax an answer from the nurse; later in the century, Ellen Terry was to take a different approach, portraying Juliet as angry over the nurse's stalling tactics.[3]

The choice of subject from *The Merry Wives of Windsor* was obviously made to harmonize with the more common depiction of Juliet and the nurse. Painted as decorative ovals, the scenes may have been intended to be engraved. Both match a "beauty" with a "beast," though it is the beast who does the wooing in the one and the beauty who cajoles in the other. The two scenes work well as pendants, although the pairing of the two plays is odd.

1. The signed watercolor is ART Box W951 no. 114 and the other two are nos. 113 and 115. I would like to thank Catherine Johnson for bringing them to my attention. In 1827 Wright also exhibited *Falstaff and Mrs. Ford* at the exhibition of the Society of Painters in Water Colours (no. 345). This was one of twenty-seven watercolors, each by a different artist, commissioned by a lady for an album. In later years he exhibited scenes from this play whose subjects are unspecified (1833, no. 141; 1843, no. 180; and 1864, the last year in which he exhibited, no. 338).
2. In 1842 Wright exhibited at the Society of Painters in Water Colours an unspecified scene from *Romeo and Juliet* (no. 209); in 1843 *Juliet and Nurse* (no. 277), which showed the moment in act IV, scene 5, when the nurse is unable to awaken her mistress; and in 1848 *Juliet and the Nurse* (no. 267), a subject without any other identification.
3. Sprague 1944, p. 304.

91

MERCUTIO BIDDING FAREWELL TO JULIET'S NURSE

Romeo and Juliet II, 4
ca. 1820s?
Oil on canvas, 18 × 13⅞ in. (45.7 × 35.7 cm.)

Case no. 1702

Provenance: Parsons, July 1927, £35, as by Stothard

Condition: Pentimenti reveal that both of the buildings at the right have been moved farther to the right. The painting was cleaned by Finlayson in 1932. The surface suffers from wide separation cracks.

Acquired as by Stothard, the picture is here attributed to his pupil John Masey Wright. The painting, in its somewhat feeble highlights and in its treatment of heads and hands, is similar to nos. 89

and 90, though the fact that the scene is now outdoors gives a different dimension to the background. Yet again it is a watercolor that offers the best confirmation of this new attribution. Wright depicted the nurse's servant greeting his mistress in this same scene,[1] and the pose and dimensions of the nurse in the watercolor are identical to those of the painting. The buildings also recede in a similar fashion, with the same funneled chimney positioned on one of the roofs. After the popular actress Mary Ann Davenport played the nurse in Fanny Kemble's debut as Juliet in 1829, artists were for a time particularly attracted to scenes of this character,[2] but Wright, as seen in works such as no. 90, had already exploited the nurse's comic potential.

The scene is a street in Verona, where the nurse has gone in search of Romeo to arrange his clandestine marriage with Juliet. Accompanied by her servant, Peter, the nurse encounters Romeo with his friends Mercutio and Benvolio. Mercutio, after his bawdy exchange with the nurse, departs in mock-courtly fashion: "Farewell, ancient lady; farewell, [*singing*], 'lady, lady, lady.'" Wright conceives him leaving arm in arm with Benvolio as a teasing reference to young lovers. The nurse's reaction is one of huffy disdain. Earlier Mercutio had announced her bustling, self-important entrance with the line, "A sail, a sail!" and in the painting she indeed is a formidable sight in her large, billowing white dress. Next to her at the far left stands an amused Romeo, patiently waiting his turn to talk. Mercutio had greeted him, "Signior Romeo, *bonjour!* There's a French salutation to your French slop," and Wright accurately shows Romeo, alone of the characters, wearing baggy breeches. He has shifted the buildings on the right-hand side farther to the right, opening up more of the light, powdery sky. The painting effectively captures the scene's light-hearted banter and the gaiety of new love, a brief interlude before the unfolding of the tragic denouement.

1. See ART Box W951, no. 31. This is perhaps the watercolor *The Nurse and Peter*, or one related to it, exhibited at the Society of Painters in Water Colours in 1825 (no. 112) illustrating the line, "Peter, take my fan, and go before."
2. See Altick 1985, p. 295.

92

John Masey Wright, attributed to
(nos. 92–93)

92

PETRUCHIO AND THE HABERDASHER
The Taming of the Shrew IV, 3
ca. 1830s?
Oil on canvas, 17½ × 15 in. (44.5 × 38.3 cm.)

Case no. 1667

Signed at lower right: "J M WRIGHT" (extremely
faint and positioned in a declining arc)

93

PETRUCHIO AND THE TAILOR
The Taming of the Shrew IV, 3
ca. 1830s?
Oil on canvas, 17½ × 15 in. (44.5 × 38.3 cm.)

Case no. 1667

Signed at lower right: "J M WRIGHT" (the lettering is
again extremely faint; only the "W," "G," and "H"
of the last word can be made out)

Provenance: Holoway, April 1927, £30 (for pair)

Exhibitions: Washington, 1976–77, no. 25 (either
this painting or its companion)

Condition: Both paintings were glue-lined onto a
commercially prepared canvas with a ground by
Finlayson in 1932. In both cases the paint has been
applied moderately, with little impasto. The paint
layers are in relatively good condition, with areas of
loss filled and repainted.

This pair, more tightly rendered and with a higher
finish than the previous three, does not at first
glance appear to be by the same hand. Yet given the
"signatures" and similarities in the use of theatrical gestures and doll-like heads, one hesitates to re-
ject Wright entirely as their creator.[1] His drawings
show a versatility in style that could also extend to
his oils.

The two paintings form a curious pair. The first
illustrates the moment when Petruchio rejects the
haberdasher's hat:

> Why, this was moulded on a porringer;
> A velvet dish. Fie, fie! 'tis lewd and filthy.
> Why, 'tis a cockle or a walnut-shell,
> A knack, a toy, a trick, a baby's cap.
> Away with it! come, let me have a bigger.

93

The haberdasher is at the far left; next to him, against the back wall, the astonished tailor approaches holding a gown; Katherina takes a step toward her husband with Hortensio at her side; and at the far right are two ragged servants, the figure between them probably Grumio. The second painting focuses on the confrontation between Petruchio and the tailor. The cast of characters is greatly reduced, as only Katherina, backed by a servant, stands between the two men. The comedy here is built around the figure of the tailor, whose elegant clothes contrast with his ungainly stance, unflattering, thick glasses, and ridiculously long tape.

The pictures are identical in size, yet they are like two opposing approaches to the same scene. In the first picture Katherina's dress is as tattered as that of the servants, and Petruchio wears plain black attire. In the second, Petruchio's outfit is comically overdone, while Katherina sports a fancy new gown. Even the interiors change to match the moods: in the first the decor is stark and the room without furniture; the second shows a curving wall with pilasters and decorative detailing over the paneled doors.

If the two paintings are read as a connected narrative, the second shows Petruchio and Katherina wearing the new clothes brought by the tailor; it is the moment when the two men are at odds over the interpretation of Katherina's remark, "Belike you mean to make a puppet of me." But the principals never actually change their attire in this scene. By contrasting the plain and tattered dress and the equally plain interior with the fancy dress and setting, perhaps the artist is attempting to visualize Petruchio's sentiment, "For 'tis the mind that makes the body rich." The tailor with his thick glasses has difficulty seeing even the appearance of things, while Petruchio, using the mind's eye, can at any one moment see more than one reality.

1. Wright exhibited two watercolors from *The Taming of the Shrew* at the Society of Painters in Water Colours, an unspecified subject in 1832 (no. 235) and the *Induction to Taming a Shrew* in 1833 (no. 416).

Lee Woodward Zeigler

Zeigler was born on 6 May 1868 in Baltimore, where he was a pupil at the Maryland Institute. From 1910 to 1918, he was director of the St. Paul Institute School of Art in Minneapolis, which awarded him a gold medal in 1915. He had success as an illustrator, executing designs for de luxe editions of Charles Kingsley, Jane Austin, Balzac, and Gautier. He also executed a number of altarpieces for churches throughout America and created several large decorative programs. In Baltimore he painted the large mural *Maryland* for the Maryland Institute and eighteen panels illustrating Edmund Spenser's *The Faerie Queene* for the reading room of the Enoch Pratt Free Library, a project that he proposed in 1929 but did not complete until 1945. His home, "Fanewood," overlooked the Hudson River near Newburgh, New York. He died on 16 June 1952, seven years after completing the Pratt Library murals, his most ambitious project.

94

ANTONY APPROACHING CLEOPATRA, MEÏAMOUN LYING DEAD AT HER FEET
Théophile Gautier, "Une nuit de Cléopâtre"
ca. 1900
Oil on canvas, 16 × 22½ in. (40.9 × 57.5 cm.)

ART Box Z45 1

Signed at lower left: "Lee Woodward Zeigler"

Provenance: Anderson Galleries, 18–19 (19) January 1917, lot 289

Condition: Sold as 17½ by 24 inches in a dark oak frame. At an early date the canvas was removed from its stretcher. The tacking edges were trimmed, with only a portion surviving at the bottom of the right side. The canvas was supported by a piece of stiff cardboard on the verso, on which was written in Mr. Folger's hand: "Antony & Cleopatra / Original monotone by / Lee Woodward Zeigler / Frontispiece "One of Cleopatra's / Nights" / No. 289 Anderson sale / Jan. 18, 1917." Paint is missing from a rubbed patch beneath the foot of the approaching Mark Antony.

Engravings: Photogravure frontispiece to *The Works of Théophile Gautier*, translated and edited by F. C. de Sumichrast, New York, 1901, vol. 8, with the caption, "'By Hercules, my lovely Queen, though I travelled fast, I see I have come too late,' said Marc Antony.—Page 284." (This is the 24-volume edition. When the series was published in 12 volumes, this frontispiece was one of the plates that was dropped.)

94

Born in 1811, Gautier, a leader of the romantic movement, was still a young man when his "Une nuit de Cléopâtre" (One of Cleopatra's nights) was published in 1838. The first English version of this tale, translated by Lafcadio Hearn, appeared in 1882, ten years after the French writer's death. Zeigler's illustrations after Gautier, however, were among those executed for Prof. F. C. de Sumichrast's edition of the complete works, published between 1900 and 1903. The Folger canvas, thinly painted in the background, was executed in grisaille in order that it might more easily be reproduced in photogravure. It was one of a dozen "original monotones" by Zeigler sold at auction in 1917 illustrating the works of Gautier, and it was the only one of the group depicting this story. It is the only painting that Folger knowingly bought as illustrating a text other than Shakespeare's. Although the tone of Gautier's decadent story of a sterile love is different from anything Shakespeare wrote, Folger presumably perceived the French writer's world as an extension of the one the Bard had created in his play *The Tragedy of Antony and Cleopatra*. Indeed, Gautier relies on his reader's familiarity with such earlier accounts, inserting Mark Antony at the end without bothering to explain his relationship to the queen.

Gautier tells the story of Cleopatra's dalliance with the twenty-year-old youth Meïamoun, who desired her at any cost. Intrigued by his courage and the promise of new pleasure, she grants him a single night into which a life-time of sensual delights are compressed. As dawn breaks, reality intrudes, and Meïamoun, swallowing poison from a horn vase, falls dead at Cleopatra's feet. Zeigler shows the story's final moment when Mark Antony, announced by four mounted officers, three of whom can be seen but only the shadow of the fourth, approaches the queen on her throne.

"You see yourself the time has come. It is day, the hour when fair dreams vanish," said Meïamoun. Then at one draught he emptied the fatal cup and fell as if struck by lightning. Cleopatra bowed her head, and within her cup a burning tear, the only one she ever shed, joined the melted pearl.

"By Hercules, my lovely queen, though I travelled fast, I see I have come too late," said Mark Antony, as he entered the banquet hall. "Supper is over—but what is this body lying on the flags?"

"Oh, nothing," said Cleopatra, smiling. "A poison I was trying; to use if Augustus should take me prisoner. Will you not, my dear lord, sit down beside me and watch these Greek buffoons dance?" (pp. 283–84)

Zeigler includes archeological details to conjure up the exotic nature of ancient Egypt, placing an ornate throne at the right with sphinxes, hieroglyphs, and burning brazen tripods dimly seen in the background. Cleopatra had earlier described Egypt as "truly frightful,—everything sombre, enigmatical, incomprehensible. . . . I am terrified by its architecture and its art" (p. 237). It is a threatening and funereal land, where colossal basalt sphinxes "obstinately fix their stony glare upon Eternity and the Infinite" (p. 238). As described by Gautier, the banquet hall is three colossal stories high, with the sky for its roof. In conjuring up this magnificent setting, he invokes the English painter John Martin, and earlier he had compared Cleopatra's orgy to Belshazzar's feast. Indeed, Martin's painting *Belshazzar's Feast*, well known through prints after it, is the prototype for Gautier's megalomaniacal setting. Yet ultimately Zeigler was more strongly influenced by the work of the French academician Jean Léon Gérôme than by Martin. His main emphasis is on the figures rather than the architecture and, like Gérôme's *Death of Caesar*, first exhibited at the Salon of 1859, his composition is anchored on one side by a throne and a dead body, with, under the influence of photography, the pavement rapidly receding to an impressive wall of a large interior.[1] Curiously, his execution of the horses is superior to that of the human protagonists, and the figure of Antony is only a feeble echo of the nude martial statue of Pompey positioned high on a plinth in Gérôme's work.

1. A version of Gérôme's painting (7 ft. 2 in. × 10 ft. 5 in.), now lost, was easily available to Zeigler, as the Corcoran Gallery of Art in Washington, D.C., purchased it from the artist on 4 October 1873. The smaller version now in the Walters Art Gallery in Baltimore was before 1917 in a private collection in New York. Zeigler could also have known the composition through engravings. Appropriately in the context of the Folger picture, Gautier himself had praised Gérôme's design (see "A travers les ateliers," *L'Artiste* 14 [16 May 1858], p. 177).

Francesco Zuccarelli

Zuccarelli was born in 1702 in Pitigliano, Italy, a town near Orvieto. He probably trained in Florence and by around 1730 was in Venice, where he was influenced by the work of Marco Ricci. Enjoying the favor of English collectors and encouraged by Con-

sul Joseph Smith, he journeyed to London in the autumn of 1752. Zuccarelli was well received as a landscape painter, but after a decade he held a sale of his remaining pictures and was back in Venice before the end of 1762. By 1765 he had returned to London, where he received the support of George III. He exhibited at the Free Society in 1765 and 1766 and then switched his allegiance to the more prestigious Society of Artists, where he exhibited in 1767 and 1768. At the end of this last year he became a founder member of the Royal Academy, where he showed pictures in the first three annual exhibitions from 1769 to 1771. Returning to Venice in 1771, he was elected president of the Venetian Academy the following year. A biblical subject by him appeared in the Royal Academy exhibition of 1773, and in 1782 he exhibited a mythological subject at the Free Society. Not long after becoming president of the Venetian Academy, he retired to Florence, where he died in 1788.

95 (Plate 1)

MACBETH MEETING THE WITCHES
Macbeth I, 3
1760
Oil on panel, 31⁹/₁₆ × 56¼ in. (81.7 × 142.5 cm.)

Case no. 1431

Signed and dated at lower center beneath Banquo's right foot: "Zuccarelli fecit [possibly 'fecet'] / 1760." (This inscription, uncovered in a 1988 restoration, is not recorded in the previous literature; the last two digits are difficult to read and are open to interpretation; "1768" has also been suggested.)

Provenance: Richard Grosvenor, first earl Grosvenor, was the picture's first owner and may have commissioned the work; by descent to the duke of Westminster, Grosvenor House, Park Lane, London; sold by him to Rosenbach in 1925; bought by Folger, July 1925, $2850

Exhibitions: Amherst, *Shakespeare*, 1951

References: John Young, *A Catalogue of the Pictures at Grosvenor House, London*, London, 1821, p. 41 (no. 128); Anna Jameson, *Companion to the most celebrated Private Galleries of Art in London*, London, 1844, pp. 262–63; G. F. Waagen, *Treasures of Art in Great Britain*, London, 1854, vol. 2, p. 173, misattributed to Richard Wilson; Michael Levey,

"Francesco Zuccarelli in England," *Italian Studies* 14 (1959), pp. 6–7

Condition: The one-piece oak panel has been thinned to ¼ inch and stained a dark brown. Marks made by the planing of the wood are clearly visible in the sky. Two identical oak slats, 30½ × 3½ × ½ inches, have been added to the reverse of the panel as structural restraints and are fastened by paired screws in slotted holes to accommodate possible movement. The screws enter 3½ × 2 × ⅛ inch wood blocks, which in turn are glued to the original panel. The vertical oak slats are located 15½ inches from each side and are 18 inches apart. Two short wooden strips (³⁄₁₆ inches thick) have been glued parallel to the grain at the left and right edges of the panel in an attempt to restrain cracks emanating from the edges along the grain. One (5 × ¾ in.) is located 14½ inches from the bottom on the left and the other (3¼ × ¾ in.) 7⅜ inches from the bottom on the right.

Engravings: An etching, 2¼ × 3⅞ in., appears in Young's 1821 *A Catalogue of the Pictures at Grosvenor House,* facing p. 41.

Related works: A painting (37 × 47 in.) signed and dated "Fran. Zuccarelli, fecit . . . 1760 in Londra" sold at Christie's, 14 December 1956, lot 52. This is the painting that was engraved by William Woollett in a print published on 20 December 1770, one state of which gives William Lock as the picture's owner; a canvas (27 × 36 in.) at the Royal Shakespeare Theatre, Stratford-upon-Avon, is similar in composition to the Lock version but is inferior in quality; Levey mentions that a picture of this subject by Zuccarelli appeared in a London sale of 1761, and one of the versions was exhibited at the Society of Artists in 1767 (no. 196), as "Macbeth meeting the Witches"; there is a pen-and-ink drawing (16 × 21 in.) at Stourhead which is related to the Lock version.

Standing on either side of the central axis in mannered poses, Macbeth and Banquo confront the three witches. They are returning in a storm from the battlefield where they had defeated the King of Norway and those traitorous Scots who had joined him. Their destination is the royal palace at Forres, where Duncan, King of Scotland, waits to receive them. The first witch hails Macbeth as Thane of Glamis, the title he had inherited from his father,

the second as Thane of Cawdor, a title which, unbeknownst to him, has just been bestowed by the king, and the third greets him with the truly astounding acclamation, "All hail, Macbeth, that shalt be King hereafter!" Banquo queries his friend, "Good sir, why do you start, and seem to fear / Things that do sound so fair?" But at the same time he comments on Macbeth's trance-like state, and goes on to question the witches about his own future. It is not entirely clear in the painting which figure is which, but one assumes that Banquo is the astonished figure nearer to the witches and the central witch is pointing to Macbeth, who stands farther to the right. Since the third witch had announced the two men's arrival with the couplet, "A drum, a drum! / Macbeth doth come," the army can be assumed to be not far behind, and Zuccarelli shows soldiers at the far right, two of whom hold the generals' horses. Banquo wears a red tartan, while Macbeth is in green, the same color worn by the buffeted troops.

From 1760, the year in which public exhibitions were first held, until 1830, the meeting of Macbeth and Banquo with the witches was the fifth most popular Shakespearean subject with artists, and the related scene of Macbeth at the witches' cave was the second most popular.[1] William Dawes exhibited a painting of the latter subject at the Society of Artists in 1760, and Zuccarelli painted his picture of the meeting in the same year. Surprisingly, in light of its subsequent popularity, Zuccarelli's is the first depiction of this subject in either painting or book illustration.

Zuccarelli executed several versions of Macbeth and the witches, but the Folger picture is almost certainly the first. It also stands somewhat apart from the others in its composition. Apparently dated 1760, it may have been commissioned by Sir Richard Grosvenor, afterward first earl Grosvenor, who was the painting's first owner. Though Grosvenor was just twenty-nine years old in 1760, he was already an active patron and collector, having in 1758 approached Hogarth with a commission. In that instance the project ended in a small scandal, as Grosvenor, who had left the subject up to the artist, bowed out when he did not approve of the completed canvas of Sigismunda. Since the painting of Macbeth departs from Zuccarelli's usual preference for decorative pastorals, one suspects the subject was of Grosvenor's choosing. If he commis-

Fig. 61. After Francesco Zuccarelli, *Macbeth Meeting the Witches*. Engraving by William Woollett, 20 December 1770. Yale Center for British Art, Paul Mellon Collection.

sioned this work, he certainly would not have wanted to repeat the Hogarth fiasco of leaving so important a decision solely to the artist's discretion. In any event, the painting proved so successful that Zuccarelli painted another version dated the same year, which Woollett engraved ten years later (fig. 61). He also exhibited this or another version of the painting at the Society of Artists in 1767. Writing in 1821, John Young was to claim precedence for the Grosvenor-Folger painting: "This is the original Picture; but an objection being taken to its shape by Woollet, his Print was engraved from a repetition, in the Collection of the late Mr. Purling." Anna Jameson was also to complain that the Grosvenor painting was "ill proportioned." Given its unusually elongated shape, it may well have been intended for a particular place, such as over a mantel, and such a specific function again suggests it was a commissioned piece. While the composition lacks the concentrated focus of the design reproduced in the print, it does offer in its place a majestic panorama.

Macbeth Meeting the Witches is Zuccarelli's sole attempt at an epic landscape featuring a literary subject in the sublime setting of a terrifying storm. For his model he looked back to seventeenth-century Italianate storm scenes, in particular to one

of Gaspard Dughet's paintings of a storm that was in England at least by 1742, when it was engraved by John Wood.[2] Dughet's *Storm* features a similarly structured landscape with wind-blown trees and arching, massed cloud formations. It even contains the bolt of lightning striking and setting fire to a distant castle that can be seen in the Lock version. Of course, in following this Roman tradition Zuccarelli departed radically from Shakespeare's text, where Macbeth and Banquo meet the witches on a heath, a barren wasteland that offers an appropriate backdrop for Macbeth's evil and destructive ambition. In doing so, he also falls back on aspects of the pastoral tradition with which he was most familiar. Aside from the storm, the landscape is inviting, a fertile land where nature is normally in harmony with man, and the standard staffage is present in the herdsman on horseback in the middle distance at the left and the shepherd at the right.

In his later versions, Zuccarelli slightly increases the scene's emotional content. In the Grosvenor-Folger picture, Macbeth and Banquo strike patrician poses; even the dark ambition of Macbeth does not detract from the nobility of the ruling class. Superbly rendered, these figures are superior in execution to Zuccarelli's usual portrayals. In the later works, though, Banquo's pose is slightly more de-

monstrative and the witch at the far left more dramatically positioned, as she now holds aloft her
staff entwined with a serpent. The lightning too is
more prominently featured, and a banner whipping
in the wind is added to the troops at the right.

In contrast to contemporary stage practice and to
contemporary imges of the play, Zuccarelli is the
first to show his characters attired in traditional
Scottish dress.[3] Macbeth and Banquo are wrapped
in the belted-plaid or great kilt (*filleadh mór*), fixed
by a clasp to the left shoulder, and wear tartan
stockings and a round bonnet (now called the Bal-
moral) to which sprigs are attached, this last touch
characteristic of Highland dress.[4] They are armed
with breastplates, dirks, and basket-hilted clay-
mores. After the Jacobite Rebellion of 1745, Highland dress was prohibited,[5] and it may well be
that its banishment was the spur that induced Zuccarelli to recreate it with such detailed care. Outside of exempted regiments in the English army,
where the little kilt was worn, painting was one of
the few places that kilts could be displayed.

In the nineteenth century Zuccarelli's works often
came under attack for their artificiality. In *Macbeth
Meeting the Witches*, the conventions of pastoral-
ism and of the seventeenth-century Italianate storm
scene are curious choices for conveying the sinister
horror of Shakespeare's confrontation. Yet, the ex-
periment remains an intriguing one. It is one of
Zuccarelli's most original and exotic achievements
and, given the several versions, was obviously one
that excited his contemporaries as well.

1. See Dotson 1973, p. 505.
2. For a reproduction of Dughet's work, see the exhibition catalogue *Gaspard Dughet, Called Gaspar Poussin, 1615–75*,
   Greater London Council, The Iveagh Bequest, Kenwood, 1980,
   p. 65 (pl. 19). The catalogue also offers a helpful discussion of the
   relationship of Woollett's print after Zuccarelli's Lock version to
   Dughet's picture and his pioneering efforts in the genre of land
   storms.
3. In 1757 actors in Scottish dress had appeared on the Edinburgh
   stage, but it was not until Macklin's 1773 production that something other than contemporary theatrical attire was attempted
   on the London stage. Even then, Macklin did not wear a kilt.
   See M. St. Clare Byrne, "The Stage Costuming of *Macbeth* in
   the Eighteenth Century," in *Studies in English Theatre History*,
   London, 1952, pp. 52–64.
4. Commenting on the version of the painting at Stratford-upon-
   Avon, Altick interpreted the bonnets as plumed hats, remarking
   they were "suggestive of the commedia dell'arte and Watteau"
   (1985, p. 35).
5. The Proscription Act of 1746 was not repealed until 1782.

96

Anonymous (nos. 96–105)

96

CELIA AND ROSALIND DEPARTING
FROM ORLANDO
As You Like It I, 2
ca. 1840s
Oil on tin, 7¹⁵/₁₆ × 6⁵/₈ in. (20.2 × 16.9 cm.)

97

ROMEO AND JULIET
Romeo and Juliet III, 5
ca. 1840s
Oil on tin, 7¹⁵/₁₆ × 6⁵/₈ in. (20.2 × 16.8 cm.)

Provenance: Richard Mansfield sale, Anderson Galleries, 7–8 (?) May 1926, lot 150, $25 for pair plus 10
percent commission, Rosenbach acting as agent. (In
the sale catalogue the works are described as "Early
Victorian School. Two Shakespearian Subjects. One
representing 'Romeo and Juliet'; the other, 'Much
Ado About Nothing.' On copper.")

Condition: Both works are abraded at the edges
from the frame, particularly at top and bottom.
Each has a gold ground. In no. 96 there is paint loss

97

to the left of Rosalind's right hand. In no. 97 there is a damaged spot to the left of Romeo's right foot and a star-shaped cracking pattern on the left side ⅝ inch from the edge and 3 inches from the top.

The first picture was bought as illustrating a scene from *Much Ado about Nothing*. More plausibly, it illustrates an early moment in *As You Like It*, when Orlando, victorious over the wrestler Charles, is approached by the two cousins Celia and Rosalind, both of whom admire his comely appearance and courage in the fight.

> *Rosalind.* Gentleman,
> [*Giving him a chain from her neck.*]
> Wear this for me, one out of suits with Fortune,
> That could give more, but that her hand lacks
>   means.
> Shall we go, coz?
> *Celia.* Ay. Fare you well, fair gentleman.

If this is the moment depicted, Orlando demurely gives Celia a good-bye kiss on the cheek, as Rosalind slips the chain from around her neck.

The second painting shows Romeo's departure from Juliet. Like the first picture, it is a somewhat idiosyncratic interpretation. Romeo's rope ladder is nowhere in sight, nor do the two seem to be on a

balcony.[1] Juliet also is shown as uncharacteristically reserved.

The artist is of modest talents. Lacking decisive characterization, his figures seem interchangeable. The moustaches are somewhat out of place on both Orlando and Romeo, and the female figures are most noteworthy for their tiny feet and hands. The workmanship seems German rather than English. As there were a number of German and French works in the Mansfield sale, from which Folger acquired these paintings, one can presume that Mansfield traveled extensively on the Continent and acquired this pair there.

1. The setting may reflect stage convention, as Odell points out that in Garrick's version, "the parting of the lovers at dawn is not in Juliet's chamber, but with the garden-set, the unhappy pair being shown at Juliet's window, not even, I suspect, in a balcony" (1920, vol. 1, p. 344). Also see Sprague 1944, p. 308.

98

FALSTAFF AT THE BOAR'S HEAD TAVERN
I Henry IV II, 4
ca. 1840
Oil on canvas, 17⅛ × 23⅞ in. (43.5 × 60.7 cm.)

Case no. 1650

Signed and dated at lower left: "Webster 1840" (last digit is uncertain)

Provenance: Barnard, April 1927, £10, incorrectly identified as Prince Hal impersonating the king and Falstaff impersonating the prince

Exhibitions: Amherst, 1959, as by Webster

Condition: Lined by Finlayson in 1932, the canvas is now brittle and is beginning to buckle at the corners.

Falstaff is depicted, sword in hand, as he boasts about how he valiantly fought against a band of men whose number keeps increasing with the telling. All of the figures smile or laugh at his invented tale.

The painting is signed "Webster" and apparently dated "1840." The signature is intended as that of Thomas Webster, a successful Victorian painter specializing in scenes of children. Webster was born on 20 March 1800 in Pimlico and, abandoning a musical career, entered the Royal Academy schools in 1821. He first exhibited at the Royal Academy in 1823 and was made an associate in 1840 and an aca-

98

demician six years later. In a long career he exhibited only one painting from Shakespeare, a picture of Malvolio, Olivia, and Maria from *Twelfth Night*, first at the Society of British Artists in 1825 and then the following year at the British Institution. The gentle humor and genre elements of the Folger picture are typical of his compositions. However, the looser technique and clumsy passages make it doubtful that this painting is by him.[1] The conservator Charles Olin, examining the painting in 1985, challenged the authenticity of the signature itself. He felt it was almost certainly a later addition, as it is in an area where the paint has been abraded. If the signature is false, the reliability of the date is also called into question, but 1840 is not an implausible assumption. The artist has not yet been identified, but Olin tantalizingly pointed out that there was an inscription at lower right beginning with the letter "F" that was deliberately removed by solvent action and painted over.

1. One curious feature is the relationship of the stone floor to the wooden one. Because Bardolph's right foot is cut off, it is clear that the stone is a step above the wood. Yet the placement of Prince Hal's left foot clearly indicates that at that point they are at the same level. The handling of Prince Hal's sausage-like legs is also unsatisfactory.

99

FALSTAFF IMPERSONATING THE KING
I Henry IV II, 4
ca. 1840s
Oil on canvas, 10¼ × 11⅞ in. (26 × 30.2 cm.)

Case no. 1838

Provenance: Parsons, September 1928, £22.10.0, as by Sir Robert Kerr Porter (bought at same time as *Shylock*, no. 102, and Hamilton, no. D29). Entitled in the Folger files "Falstaff at Boar's Head Tavern."

Exhibitions: Amherst, 1959, as "Falstaff at the Boar's Head Tavern" by Porter

Condition: The painting is executed on a pre-primed canvas. Wide separation cracks had been covered by colored glazes from a past restoration. The canvas was most recently restored in 1991, when a small hole punched above Falstaff's left elbow was repaired. The paint film was cleaned and inpainted and the canvas relined.

The Folger painting depicts the popular subject of Falstaff's impersonation of King Henry IV, as he prepares the prince for his coming interview with his father. Falstaff has just given his blustering account of having fought off a small army after the robbery at Gadshill, and a cape, sword, and masks from the robbery anchor the painting's left corner, while a buckler leans against the chair. The text makes clear that Falstaff seizes on a humble joined stool as his throne, a detail the artist ignores in favor of a more impressive piece of furniture. Sir John holds a dagger as a scepter (some artists chose to depict him holding the dagger by the blade with the hilt uppermost). The cushion he uses as a crown has slipped off behind his head in conformance with the prince's observation, "thy precious rich crown [is taken] for a pitiful bald crown!" At the far right an awkward Prince Hal appears to be performing a curtsy to the counterfeit king. The room at the Boar's Head Tavern is described as having tapestries, and an impressive hunting scene is shown hanging on the wall, perhaps alluding to how these two protagonists take turns in stalking one another as each impersonates the king.

This picture proved small enough that Edwin Parsons mailed it to Folger on approval without having first solicited his opinion with a photograph. Folger replied on 8 December 1927, "I am sorry that it does not appeal to me sufficiently to make me feel like keeping it, so I am returning it to-day by mail." Obviously he changed his mind, and Parsons's in-stinct to send the painting before receiving authorization proved a wise one. The dealer identified the artist as Sir Robert Ker Porter, yet what little is known about Porter's career offers little support for this assertion.

Born in Durham in 1777, Porter grew up in Edinburgh. Brought by his mother to London, he entered the Royal Academy schools in 1790, won a silver palette from the Society of Arts in 1792, and by the following year was already receiving important commissions. In 1800 he captured the public's imagination with his painting *The Storming of Seringapatum*, a panorama that was 120 feet long, the first of several enormous battle pictures. He exhibited every year at the Royal Academy from 1792 until 1805 and also contributed four paintings to the small series of pictures for the Boydell Shakespeare Gallery. In 1804 he departed for Russia to take up an appointment as historical painter to the czar. He traveled extensively, publishing books on his trips lavishly illustrated with his own sketches. In 1826 he accepted an appointment as British consul in Caracas, Venezuela. He returned to England in 1841 and died on 3 May 1842 while visiting his daughter in St. Petersburg.

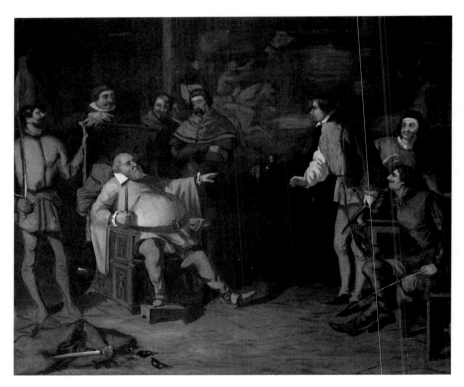

99

On stylistic grounds the Folger picture appears to date from around the 1840s. It is unconvincing as the work of an artist trained in the late eighteenth century and has none of the grandiloquence of Porter's earlier scenes for Boydell. Its subject matter also does not conform to the types of pictures for which he was known in his later years: portraits, views, religious subjects, and battle scenes.

100

FALSTAFF AND BARDOLPH
I Henry IV III, 3
Early nineteenth century
Oil on canvas on panel, 15¹/₈ × 12³/₁₆ in. (38.5 × 30.9 cm.)

Inscribed at lower left: "David Wilkie" (the last four letters are very faint)

Provenance: Collection of Alexander Cecil Fenton, Bayonne, N.J.; John Anderson, Jr., sale, American Art Galleries, 6 April 1916, lot 30, as by Sir David Wilkie, $100 plus 10 percent commission, Morris acting as agent

Condition: A vertical split runs down the center of the panel between the two figures, and there are repaired splits in the canvas running around all four edges.

The painting is signed "David Wilkie" at lower left, and it was sold in the John Anderson, Jr., sale in 1916 as indisputably his work. Born in 1785, Wilkie, who was Scottish, first studied at the Trustees' Academy in Edinburgh. Moving to London in 1805, he gained early success with his paintings of Scottish peasant life, which were strongly influenced by Dutch genre painting. He was made an associate member of the Royal Academy in 1809 and an academician just two years later. A trip to Spain in 1825, where he studied works by artists such as Velázquez and Rubens, dramatically accelerated his progress from a painter of carefully crafted pictures to one who favored large compositions emphasizing bold brushwork and rich colors. Wilkie was to die in 1841 while returning from a trip to the Near East. In his catalogue entry, Anderson placed the Folger painting in this context.

A decidedly original conception of the fat knight. Believed to be the only Shakespearean subject painted by Wilkie, as no other can be traced.

100

Painted in his first style, previous to his visit to Spain. He afterwards adopted a new style, somewhat Spanish in character.

This example shows the effect of daylight in an interior, in producing which he is said often to have come near to equaling Van Ostade.

Anderson's entry is almost as humorous as the painting it pretends to describe. The work, of course, has nothing to do with Wilkie's art, and the signature is a false addition. The image, though, is a comic rendering of Falstaff and Bardolph, executed in the same spirit as an earlier lively caricature simply signed "K" and dated to 1785 (fig. 62). Both works show the verbal sparring between the two men, Falstaff attacking his companion's flaming red nose and Bardolph his friend's large stomach. Both place the two antagonists in a simple interior whose space is measured by receding floorboards. Both stress the incongruity of the figures, the one fat, the other thin, although the Folger painting refrains from overly exaggerating Bardolph's red nose. The creator of this work, however, finds humor in manipulating the conventions of perspective and scale: the floorboards at times widen rather than contract as they recede; the chair and the painting on the wall are ridiculously small; and the tiny window at the right is burdened with an oversized curtain.

Fig. 62. J. Kay, *Henderson as Falstaff and Charteris as Bardolph.* Etching and aquatint, 1785, 7¹/₈ × 6¹/₄ in.

101

KING LEAR
King Lear IV, 6
1874

Oil on canvas mounted on board, 30 × 25 in. (76.2 × 63.5 cm.)

Case no. 1880

Signed (signature now scratched out) and dated "1874" beneath Lear's left shoulder

Provenance: Louis A. D'Aras, apparently shortly before 13 February 1929, when the following heading appears in the case listings for no. 1880: "Papers to go with Sully: Kemble as Lear," $325.

Condition: The canvas suffers from several complex tears. Much of the impasto in the head and straw was flattened in an early lining, and early work on the canvas also resulted in areas of abrasion and of crude overpainting. In 1976 the work was relined, the old repaint removed, and new inpainting introduced to harmonize with the original paint. Beneath this surface is a thinly applied cream-colored ground.

When Folger acquired this picture, it bore Thomas Sully's signature and was dated to 1832. The dealer even enclosed a clipping that reproduced a related painting said to be by Sully sold in the Harned sale of 1917 (fig. 63).[1] When the painting was restored in 1976, the date of 1832 proved to be fugitive, having been placed over the varnish. A date of 1874 then appeared beneath Lear's left shoulder, and above it one could see where a signature had been scratched out. Just enough of the signature's configuration remains to make it a valuable part of any test that a candidate must pass in order to be recognized as the painting's creator.

Lear is shown with straw in his hair wearing an ermine-trimmed robe of regal purple. He looks woefully heavenward, his hair and beard streaming out in the wind. The Harned picture was clearly the point of departure, the figure being portrayed with the same deep-set eyes and bulbous nose. The Folger painting, however, is in no way a copy, but is rather a free interpretation, very different in character. The paint is loosely and thickly applied, giving a sense of crackling energy. The robe is now opened and its contours softened so that the viewer's attention is more exclusively focused on Lear's an-

Fig. 63. Thomas Sully, attributed to, *King Lear.* From Harned sale, Henkels, Philadelphia, 28–29 May 1917, lot 66.

101

guished head, which does not even have a neck for support.

The concept of showing only Lear's head and shoulders, his hair streaming in the wind, was already old by the nineteenth century. The Harned picture was based on Reynolds's ideal head of Lear of about 1780, which was well known through engravings (fig. 64).[2] Reynolds, in his turn, had been inspired by John Hamilton Mortimer's etching of the head of Lear published on 15 March 1776, and Mortimer's conception had been influenced by that of James Barry in his picture of Lear and Cordelia exhibited at the Royal Academy in 1774 (see fig. 2). The heads by Mortimer and Reynolds show Lear in the storm, illustrating act III, scene 2, while the Harned and Folger paintings, with the addition of the straw in the king's hair, transfer the action to act IV, scene 6.[3]

1. The clipping in the Folger file does not have a source, but fortunately the identical clipping in the Witt Library, London, gives as the source the catalogue of the Harned sale held at Henkels in Philadelphia on 28 and 29 May 1917.

2. A sketch for Reynolds's *Lear*, the head facing to the viewer's left, is reproduced in the catalogue to Montgomery, 1985–86, no. 54. There is a mezzotint, said to be by Marchi, after Reynolds, and the print by W. Sharp was published in two editions, on 1 July 1780 and 1 May 1783.

3. An earlier image of Lear adorned with straw was sold at Sotheby, New York, on 8 January 1981, lot 76. It is recorded as by Richard Westall and entitled, probably incorrectly, *David Garrick as King Lear.*

Fig. 64. After Sir Joshua Reynolds, *King Lear.* Engraving by William Sharp, 1 July 1780, 6³/₈ × 5⁷/₁₆ in.

the seal from off my bond, / Thou but offend'st thy lungs to speak so loud." The scale for weighing a pound of Antonio's flesh sits on the desk beside him.

103

TITANIA CARESSING THE DROWSY BOTTOM
A Midsummer Night's Dream IV, 1
Early nineteenth century
Oil on canvas, 17 × 14¹/₈ in. (43.3 × 35.8 cm.)

Case no. 1709

Provenance: Parsons, September 1927, £16, as by Cawse

Exhibitions: Amherst, 1952, as by Cawse

Condition: The canvas has a thin, buff-colored ground. In 1932 it was relined by Finlayson and in 1988 was cleaned and inpainted.

On 30 June 1927, Folger replied to Edwin Parsons's offer of this painting, "Before I could decide on this piece I would like to know the name of the artist. Can you give me this information?" Parsons was happy to oblige, writing on 19 July, "I believe this picture to be by John Cawse whos[e] name appears

102

102

SHYLOCK
The Merchant of Venice IV, 1
Early nineteenth century
Oil on canvas, 15 × 12¹/₂ in. (38.2 × 31.8 cm.)

Case no. 1838

Provenance: Parsons, September 1928, £15 less 10 percent, as by Smirke (bought at same time as nos. 99 and D29)

Acquired as by Robert Smirke, this picture on both a technical and interpretative level is by an artist of limited ability. It is a nineteenth-century depiction of Shylock as caricatured villain without any of the humanity afforded him in the play. The "portrait" of Shylock is independent of any one moment enacted on stage, although its ingredients are drawn from the trial scene. While fondling the blade of his knife, Shylock gleefully gloats over his bond, attached to which is the red wax seal, to which he refers in the lines, "Till thou canst rail

103

on the back of the canvas." The canvas was relined in 1932, and no name is recorded. In any event, on stylistic grounds this lyrical treatment of Titania and Bottom cannot convincingly be ascribed to Cawse.

Angry with his wife for not having given him the changeling he desires, Oberon caused her to fall in love with the monstrous Bottom, the weaver who has been given an ass's head. The painting shows Titania in a deep woods kissing Bottom, having just placed a garland of flowers around his neck. Bottom, more asleep than awake, assumes an awkward pose. Titania's crown is now a butterfly, she having put off her queenly crown and scepter in her bewitched state. Oberon, who is about to undo his

spell, is seen approaching at the far right, a mischievous Puck gesturing at his side.

This particular moment in the play had proved popular, appearing in the Boydell Shakespeare Gallery and the Irish Shakespeare Gallery as well as in book illustrations. In the first decades of the nineteenth century, it also appeared several times at the Royal Academy: H. W. Pickersgill exhibited *Titania Caressing Bottom* in 1815, Henry Singleton *Titania Caressing the Drowsy Bottom* in 1823, George Francis Joseph *Titania Caressing the Drowsy Bottom* in 1824, Edmund Cotterill a sculpture of Titania, Bottom, and Sprites in the same year, and Frank Howard an outline drawing of Bottom and Titania in 1828. Unlike many of the other artists, the creator of the Folger painting forgoes the humor to be found in this scene, concentrating instead on the charms of infatuation.

104

ARIEL LEADING CALIBAN BY A CHAIN [?]
The Tempest II, 2?
Nineteenth century
Oil on panel, 8³/₈ × 10⁵/₈ in. (21.2 × 27 cm.)

Case no. 765

Annotated at lower right: "W. Blake"

Provenance: William W. Phillips sale, Walpole Galleries, New York, 14 March 1918, lot 147, as "Ariel and Caliban?" by William Blake, $85, bought by Wells (price given by the *New York American*, 15 March 1918); bought by Folger, 19 March 1918, $175, as by Blake

Exhibitions: Amherst, *The Tempest*, 1951, as by Blake (?); Washington, 1976–77, no. 26, as Artist Unknown, formerly attributed to William Blake

References: Letter from Geoffrey Keynes to E. E. Willoughby, 1 September 1943, FSL; Martin Butlin, *The Paintings of William Blake*, New Haven and London, 1981, vol. 1, p. 610, mentioned in no. 848

Condition: The panel is approximately ¼ inch thick with open ducts. It is split vertically 6½ inches from the left at the top down to 6 inches from the left bottom. In the past the paint surface has been overcleaned and heavily repainted.

A winged spirit, dressed in a red tunic with crescent moons and what may be stars, holds a wand in his right hand and a chain in his left, to which is attached an angry nude figure. This wild man's ears are unusually large, suggesting a monster such as Caliban. The monster's form is entirely enclosed by the dark hills behind, while the angelic sprite is silhouetted against the sky, offering another contrast of their natures. The subject is uncertain. While there is no moment in *The Tempest* when Ariel leads Caliban in chains, this could well be the intended subject, as Caliban complains about being tortured by Prospero's spirits:

Plate 1. Francesco Zuccarelli, *Macbeth Meeting the Witches*, 1760 (no. 95).

Plate 2. William Hamilton, *The Carousing of Sir Toby Belch and Sir Andrew Aguecheek*, 1792 (no. 34).

Plate 3. Robert Smirke, *Falstaff Rebuked*, ca. 1795 (no. 57).

Plate 4. Richard Westall, *Shylock Rebuffing Antonio*, 1795 (no. 86).

Plate 5. Francis Wheatley, *Helena and Count Bertram before the King of France*, 1793 (no. 87).

Plate 6. Henry Fuseli, *Macbeth Consulting the Vision of the Armed Head*, 1793 (no. 24).

Plate 7. William Hamilton, *Isabella Appealing to Angelo,* 1793 (no. 32).

Plate 8. Rev. Matthew William Peters, *The Death of Juliet*, 1793 (no. 49).

Plate 9. George Romney, Study for *Titania, Puck, and the Changeling*, 1793 (no. 54).

Plate 10. Benjamin West, *King Lear and Cordelia*, 1793 (no. 84).

Plate 11. Henry Fuseli, *Ariel,* ca. 1800–1810 (no. 28).

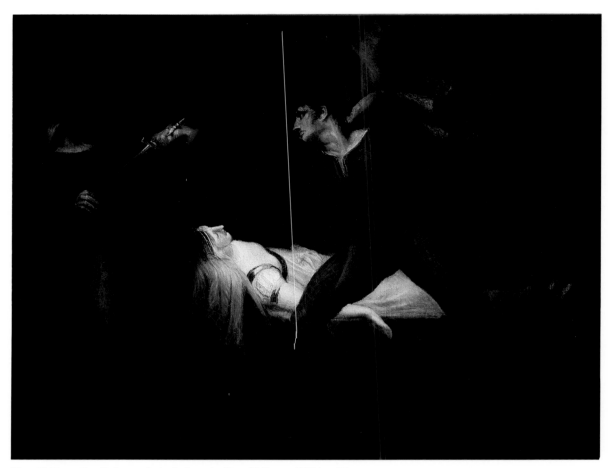

Plate 12. Henry Fuseli, *Romeo Stabs Paris at the Bier of Juliet,* ca. 1809 (no. 27).

Plate 13. Henry Fuseli, *Faery Mab,* ca. 1815–20 (no. 29).

Plate 14. Thomas Stothard, *Falstaff Describing the Fight at Gadshill*, ca. 1827 (no. 75).

Plate 15. Thomas Sully, *Portia and Shylock*, 1835 (no. 82).

Plate 16. Friedrich Brockmann, *Portia and Nerissa,* 1849 (no. 4).

Plate 17. James Clarke Hook, *Othello's Description of Desdemona*, ca. 1852 (no. 40).

Plate 18. William Salter Herrick, *Hamlet in the Queen's Chamber*, ca. 1857 (no. 39).

Plate 19. Thomas Francis Dicksee, *Anne Page*, 1862 (no. 20).

Plate 20. William Powell Frith, *Olivia Unveiling*, 1874 (no. 23).

Plate 21. Nathaniel Dance, *David Garrick*, 1774 (no. 106).

Plate 22. Robert Edge Pine, *David Garrick*, ca. 1780 (no. 120).

Plate 23. Thomas Sully, *Charlotte Cushman*, 1843 (no. 125).

Plate 24. Anonymous, *Sir Thomas Overbury* [?] (formerly Janssen Portrait of Shakespeare), early 1610s (no. 160).

ÆTATIS. SVÆ. 47.
Aº 1612.

Plate 25. Anonymous, *The Ashbourne Portrait of Shakespeare/Sir Hugh Hamersley*, 1612 with nineteenth-century alterations (no. 165).

Plate 26. Thomas Sully, *Portrait of Shakespeare*, 1864 (no. 170).

Plate 27. George Romney, *The Infant Shakespeare Attended by Nature and the Passions*, ca. 1791–92 (no. 176).

Plate 28. George Gower, *The Plimpton "Sieve" Portrait of Queen Elizabeth I*, 1579 (no. 187).

Plate 29. After Daniel Mytens, *Henry Wriothesley, Third Earl of Southampton*, after 1620 (no. 189).

Plate 30. After Paul van Somer ?, *Elizabeth Wriothesley, Countess of Southampton*, after 1620 (no. 190).

Plate 31. Nicholas Hilliard, *Lettice Knollys, Countess of Leicester*, ca. 1595–1600 (no. 193).

Plate 32. Isaac Oliver, *William Herbert, Third Earl of Pembroke*, 1611 (no. 194).

Plate 33. Peter Oliver, *Henry Frederick, Prince of Wales*, early 1610s (no. 195).

Plate 34. Thomas Nast, Study for *The Immortal Light of Genius*, 1895 (no. 201).

. . . His spirits hear me
And yet I needs must curse. But they'll nor
  pinch,
Fright me with urchin-shows, pitch me i' th'
  mire,
Nor lead me, like a firebrand, in the dark
Out of my way, unless he bid'em.
(II, 2, 3–7)

The picture was bought as by William Blake, but, despite the "signature" at lower right, it seems unlikely that he played any role in its creation. As early as 1943, Geoffrey Keynes wrote to E. E. Willoughby, the Library's chief bibliographer, that he and the collector Graham Robertson felt that, based on the evidence of excellent photostats of this work, they could not accept the picture as by Blake. In the more recent catalogue of the artist's work, Martin Butlin writes that the picture "does not seem to be by Blake, unless by some faint chance it is an almost entirely overpainted work originally by him."

  Interest in fairies played a strong role in nineteenth-century culture, and the Folger painting may well be by an artist, yet to be identified, who was a devotee of the popular genre of fairy painting and whose work was later mistakenly assigned to Blake. Yet, since the picture is heavily overpainted, more may have been involved in its transformation into a Blake than just the addition of the artist's name.[1]

1. At approximately this same time Folger purchased forged drawings said to be by Blake. They were part of a larger collection discussed in J. E. Robinson's article "An Unknown Collection of Portraits by William Blake; The Genius of the Pre-Raphaelite Movement" (*Arts and Decoration* 8 [1918], pp. 100–105, 130).

105

UNKNOWN SUBJECT
Late eighteenth or early nineteenth century
Oil on canvas, 39½ × 29 in. (100.4 × 73.9 cm.)

Case no. 926

Provenance: Private owner represented by Walters, December 1920, $100 plus 10 percent commission

Exhibitions: Washington, 1985, as "Scene from Shakespeare's *King John*"

Condition: Lined by Finlayson in 1932, the canvas was most recently cleaned in 1985 in preparation for the Kemble exhibition.

105

In a letter of 13 November 1920, Curtis Walters offered this painting to Folger, describing it as a portrait of Kemble in the role of King John. Walters was so certain that he had formerly seen engravings after this picture that would give the artist's identity that he did not hazard an attribution. After seeing the work, Folger replied, "It seems to me that while the painting may be intended by the artist to depict Kemble, it cannot be painted from life as it is so poor a portrait of Kemble. Indeed, I am not entirely clear that it is a Shakespeare scene." The painting may well be a theatrical portrait, although, if this is the case, the identity of the central figure is uncertain. Of the Kembles, the dimpled chin most closely resembles that of John Philip. The other figures, however, belong to the idealizing genre of history painting rather than to theatrical portraiture. Curiously, they all are placed in a line at the very top of the picture, their glowing presence suggesting Rubens as a model.

  In a letter of 29 November, Walters cited "Alfred Becks, former curator of the Dramatic collection of Harvard," as his source for identifying the subject as from *King John.* He had earlier listed the characters as Constance with an attendant, King John, the Duke of Austria, and King Philip. Philip, the king of France, had been prepared, with the support of Austria, to go to war with John, the English king, in order to replace him with Constance's son Arthur, who he felt was the rightful heir to the throne, but the two kings then made peace between themselves with the proposed marriage of Philip's son to John's niece. In Beck's interpretation, the painting shows the moment when Constance confronts the two monarchs, crying out, "Arm, arm, you heavens, against these perjur'd kings! / A widow cries; be husband to me, heavens!" Yet one wonders why Philip's tent, where the scene takes place, has a paved floor, why Philip holds a document, and why his clothes are so unlike those of a king. The Elizabethan costume of the central figure also does not conform to normal stage attire for King John. The painting could as easily depict the last scene of *Measure for Measure,* where Mariana and Isabella confront Angelo, whose wicked conduct is publicly exposed before the Duke and others. But Folger's first response, "I am not entirely clear that it is a Shakespeare scene," may have been correct after all.

II Theatrical Portraiture

The genre of the theatrical portrait embraces a wide variety of paintings, ranging from portraits of individuals to multifigured scenes of actors engaged in particular performances. At one end of the spectrum are portraits of actors appearing in everyday dress, like any other middle-class sitter. The earliest portraits of actors in English art, including Shakespeare's own time, are of this type. One of the more famous examples is the painting of Shakespeare's friend Richard Burbage, now in the Dulwich College Picture Gallery, London. Among the Folger Library's earliest examples of this type are the paintings after Lewis's *Peg Woffington* (no. 117) of 1753 and Gainsborough's *Sarah Siddons* (no. 110) of about 1785. In addition, there are three important paintings of Garrick: those by Nathaniel Dance (no. 106), Robert Edge Pine (no. 120), and the studio of Reynolds (no. 121). Garrick did more than any other actor to elevate the status of his profession, and the fact that theatrical portraiture flourished during his career offers testimony to his success. The three portraits of him, unlike those of the two actresses, contain allusions to his intellectual prowess in the inclusions of a book or manuscript.

Portraits of actors in the costume of a particular character begin in the late seventeenth century. Two famous examples are John Michael Wright's triple portrait of about 1668–70 of John Lacy attired for different roles, painted for Charles II and now at Hampton Court, and Sir Godfrey Kneller's *Anthony Leigh in the Part of Dominic in the "Spanish Friar"* of 1689 (National Portrait Gallery, London). The earliest such painting in the Folger collection is the work by or after James McArdell of about 1750, showing James Quin as Falstaff (no. 118).

Hogarth, in his pictures of the prison scene from John Gay's *The Beggar's Opera*, executed between 1728 and 1731, became the first English artist to paint his conception of a play in performance. *The Beggar's Opera* was the most successful play of the eighteenth century. First performed at Lincoln's Inn Fields on 29 January 1728, it proved so popular that the manager, John Rich, was able to build from its profits a new theater in Covent Garden, which opened in 1732. Rich commissioned two of the six paintings Hogarth executed of this scene. The fifth and final version (fig. 65)[1] shows a grander setting than the earlier designs, an idealized version of the projected Covent Garden Theatre. Distinguished members of the audience are in the boxes along the sides of the stage, and in Hogarth's treatment they become an important part of the subject matter. In the play, Polly Peachum, who kneels at the right in the painting, pleads with her father, the corrupt lawyer, to save the enchained highwayman Macheath. Peachum is played by Lavinia Fenton, who is the lover of

Fig. 65. William Hogarth, *The Beggar's Opera*. Oil on canvas, 23¼ × 30 in. Yale Center for British Art, Paul Mellon Collection.

the Duke of Bolton, who watches the performance at the far right beneath the pointing finger of the lustful satyr directly above him. Thus, the actress turns from her stage lover toward her real lover, as though to illustrate Shakespeare's line "all the world's a stage."

Hogarth's conception of *The Beggar's Opera*, of course, is closely related to his painting *Falstaff Examining His Recruits* executed about the same time, yet it breaks new ground in depicting a staged performance. In its portrayals of actual people, it also has roots in the conventions of the conversation piece, a type of group portrait in which the sitters are usually informally posed on a small scale in familiar surroundings. As an example of "performance painting," the pictures of *The Beggar's Opera* also look forward to Hogarth's modern moral subjects, the first of which, *The Harlot's Progress* of 1731, was composed of a series of six pictures unfolding a story in six acts.[2]

The first great picture of a Shakespearean performance, arguably one that has never been equaled, is also the work of Hogarth: it is the depiction of David Garrick as Richard III (fig. 66), the role in which the actor first gained fame when he performed it at Goodman's Fields on 19 October 1741.

Hogarth was not the first to depict Garrick in the tent scene after he has seen the ghosts of his victims, but he was the first to elevate the genre of theatrical portraiture, giving the picture the heroic simplicity and grandeur of a history painting. More than a portrait, it becomes a work illustrating the national past that raises Garrick to the role of a tragic villain.

Hogarth's depiction of Garrick is based on well-established pictorial conventions. Painters had long been concerned with how to render emotions, creating a visual language of gesture and expression that would reveal to the viewer the figure's soul. But in late seventeenth-century France, under the influence of rationalistic academic doctrines, there was a strong movement to codify the passions, to reduce them to formulas that would "scientifically" detail what were considered to be universal expressions of human emotions.[3] In English translations, books such as Charles LeBrun's *A Method to learn to Design the Passions* of 1701 and Gerard de Lairesse's *The Art of Painting in All its Branches* of 1738 offered a repertoire for the painter in his attempts to capture an attitude. In Hogarth's painting of Garrick, the raised right hand with the fingers spread wide is the proscribed gesture for sur-

Fig. 66. William Hogarth, *David Garrick as Richard III*, 1745. Oil on canvas, 75 × 98½ in. The Board of Trustees of the National Museums and Galleries on Merseyside (Walker Art Gallery, Liverpool).

prise. This telling gesture is made all the more significant by its placement above the exact center of the composition. In addition, Garrick's face delineates a combination of the expressions for horror and admiration (that is, amazement).[4]

Hogarth's formulation was so successful that when Francis Hayman and Nathaniel Dance painted portraits of Garrick as Richard III, they felt it necessary to choose a different moment to illustrate (see no. 107). It was not until William Hamilton exhibited his picture of Kemble at the Royal Academy in 1788 (see no. 112) that an artist dared to take up Hogarth's subject. Hamilton abandons Hogarth's attempt to define in classicizing terms a combination of passions, rendering instead a scene of emotional drama where action is more important than academic decorum.

Whether Hogarth's characterization of Garrick faithfully reflects how the actor actually performed this scene is debatable. What is certain, however, is that actors as well as painters were students of the passions as defined by contemporary psychological and physiological theories, each sharing a formal language of gesture and expression. Thomas Betterton, who dominated the London stage from the Restoration until his death in 1710, is quoted as saying

the actor should study history painting "because the knowledge of the Figure and Lineaments of the Persons represented will teach the Actor to vary and change his Figure."[5] On 3 August 1749, the drama critic Aaron Hill wrote Garrick a highly flattering letter which, while hardly unusual in its sentiments, again ably reflects the perceived bond in the eighteenth century between acting and painting. After comparing Garrick's creativity to that of the *"painter, statuary* or *engraver,"* Hill goes on to christen him a *"life-painter."* He invites Garrick to study French prints, whose quality has been perfected by an understanding of *"history pieces,* and *fine statues,* of antiquity," in that they could "furnish [an] infinite *supply* of *hints,* to so compleat a *judge* of *attitudes."* Yet, he adds, "I say *hints,* because, in many of the very *finest* of 'em all, there are *defects,* which *you* could rectify. . . . [Y]ou cannot fail to draw a *proof* from that remark, how much the *painters* may improve, by copying Mr. *Garrick,* and what little room there is, for *his* improving, by the *painters."*[6]

The gestures and expressions of the pictorial language of the passions often now appear highly rhetorical and artificial, but in the eighteenth century they were considered to express fundamental truths about human emotions. Garrick's ability to find the right formulations for an emotion as perceived in terms of academic rules helped define his acting style for his contemporaries as naturalistic. George Taylor provides an excellent summation of how this approach to acting contrasts with modern sensibilities:

What I think this interpretation of behaviour in terms of passion also explains, is the practice of eighteenth-century actors of making isolated and individual points, rather than seeking the overall development of the character. The actor who could convey one specific passion in a single line or gesture caused the whole audience to applaud that one "stroke of nature," unlike a modern audience which watches the gradual unfolding of a personality through the development of the action of a play, withholding their applause until the whole process, or life of the performance, has been completed.[7]

A number of images of Garrick in performance have survived, and while it is always difficult to know exactly how much of the portrayal is Garrick's and how much the painter's, these pictures at least give some clues as to his acting style. Beginning in the early 1750s, Benjamin Wilson created a series of three paintings showing Garrick in some of his most famous roles—Romeo, Hamlet, and Lear. A version of the earliest in the series, *Mr. Garrick and Miss Bellamy in the Characters of Romeo and Juliet* (fig. 67), is dated 1753[8] and commemorates one of the most famous duels in theater history. On 29 September 1750 Drury Lane and Covent Garden opened competing productions of *Romeo and Juliet*, Garrick and Mrs. Bellamy performing at the first theater and Spranger Barry and Mrs. Cibber at the second. Wilson, of course, shows the Drury Lane production with Garrick, who had rewritten parts of the last act, performing his own lines. Garrick was not the first to rewrite the play so that Juliet and Romeo have a last moment together in the tomb, but his version proved the most satisfactory and dominated the stage until Charlotte Cushman returned to the original text almost a hundred years later. In Garrick's version, Romeo, believing Juliet to be dead, breaks into the Capulet tomb to take the poison by her side, concluding with lines that blend Shakespeare's text with Garrick's own:

No more! Here's to my love! Eyes look your last;
Arms take your last embrace; and lips do you
The doors of breath seal with a righteous kiss.
Soft! soft! She breathes and stirs!

Fig. 67. Benjamin Wilson, *David Garrick and George Anne Bellamy in "Romeo and Juliet,"* 1753. Oil on canvas, 54⅝ × 72½ in. Yale Center for British Art, Paul Mellon Collection.

The awakening Juliet then speaks, "Where am I? Defend me, powers!" to which the dying Romeo replies, "She speaks, she lives! And we shall still be blessed!"[9] Wilson depicts this dramatic reunion showing both figures reacting in amazement. Garrick's pose is carefully calculated to find a definitive conception for this moment. Garrick's solution is similar to the pose that the actor William Powell strikes in the scene from *Hamlet* where the hero first encounters his father's Ghost (no. 128). The language of gestures, which was thought to describe universal attitudes in an objective manner, would seem to have led to a repertoire of conventional poses for specific situations.

Shakespeare found new champions on the London stage in the remarkable Kemble family, in particular John Philip Kemble and his sister, Sarah Siddons. These actors replaced Garrick's brand of naturalism with a style that stressed grandeur and dignity, minimizing action and embracing a loftier tone of speech. Paintings such as Thomas Lawrence's *Kemble as Coriolanus* (see no. 114) and *Kemble as Hamlet* (see no. 115) are, in the artist's words, "a sort of half-history picture." Lawrence's conception is more aristocratically imposing than Hogarth's of Garrick as Richard III. All four of his paintings of Kemble portray the actor as hero, majestically overwhelming his public. Lawrence's portraits may not be entirely accurate in their portrayals of Kemble's acting style—indeed, this may never have been the artist's intention—but they do capture the sense of the actor as demigod, no longer, as Garrick had been, a man among men.

With the exception of Garrick, actors did not seem to grasp fully the publicity value of the theatrical portrait. Although happy to sit for an artist of reputation, they rarely instigated the sittings. The painters, on the other hand, not only found such subjects topical and obviously dramatic, but they could expect profits in the form of prints after their paintings. Few theatergoers could afford the painting itself, but, particularly as reproductive techniques developed, the prints proved eminently affordable souvenirs. Many of the Folger paintings are in fact based on these reproductions rather than on the originals. The existence of these copies underscores the popularity of the genre itself: paintings were turned into prints only to be turned back into paintings, albeit ones generally of poor quality. For many, quality was clearly less of an issue than

having a memento of an actor in a favorite part.

By the middle of the nineteenth century, photography was also placed in the service of the theatrical portrait. Photographs not only stood on their own, but wood engravings could be made after them, ensuring their dispersal on a wide scale in journals and other publications. Number 131 illustrates this progression: Miss Glyn first posed as Lady Macbeth for the photographer; this image was transformed into a print, which in its turn became the basis for a painting. While such images helped satisfy a demand, obviously most of the artists supplying these works would not be found in the upper echelons of their profession. The use of photography also introduced a note of realism, so that even if the actors struck the same heroic poses of the previous generation, their translation into paint was not as successfully managed. Painting at the end of the eighteenth century and beginning of the nineteenth, Lawrence transformed Kemble into a sublime historical fiction. Gabriel Harrison's 1872 painting of Edwin Forrest as Lear (no. 113) is instead rooted in photography, and despite the impressively stormy sky and dramatic pose, the image never rises to the heroic level of Lawrence's conceptions. These later images contain more of the actor and less of the character they are portraying.

In the Romantic period, theater architecture changed decisively. In Garrick's day, the actors performed for the most part on a large forestage, allowing them to inhabit the same space as their audience. But the new designs greatly expanded the size of the audience, making a sense of intimacy difficult, and reduced the forestage, making the actors still more remote. Thus, the Kembles' heroic acting style and the new architectural space of the theaters themselves worked hand in hand to distance actor from audience. The introduction of gas lighting in 1817 further changed this relationship. With the audience now in darkness and the stage lighted, the separation was complete, the audience looking at the performers framed by the proscenium arch. This pictorial mode of staging was in part a response to the influence that painting had exerted on the theater, an influence that of course could also flow in the other direction.

In embracing a more pictorial aesthetic, John Philip Kemble stressed the whole over the parts, attempting to blend the various elements into a harmonious dramatic illusion. James Boaden, his friend and biographer, stressed the kinship between the actor's approach and that of painting: "As to Mr. Kemble, though he never handled the pencil, he had a great affection for the art, and well understood how far it could be serviceable to his own."[10] Kemble was the first to stress historical accuracy, researching costume and scenery. The pictorialism and historical realism that led to the spectacle style of the Victorian stage have their origins in his productions.

In the second half of the nineteenth century, managers vied with one another in creating sumptuous productions. Great expense was bestowed on costume designs and sets in an effort to achieve beautiful stage pictures of a recaptured past portrayed with historical accuracy. At times the plays seemed little more than an excuse for grandiose spectacles that threatened to make the text an irrelevancy.

Alfred Roffe's painting *Macbeth's Murder of Duncan* (no. 123) was inspired by Henry Irving's 1888 production of this play. In 1853 Charles Kean had firmly set *Macbeth* in eleventh-century Scotland, and his was the first Shakespearean revival to include a scholarly disquisition in the playbill.[11] Irving went to even greater pains to create the illusion of Scotland in the eleventh century. Hawes Craven was the principal scenic designer, and the artist Charles Cattermole created 408 costumes for the production. The collections of the British Museum and the South Kensington Museum (now the Victoria and Albert Museum) were carefully researched to make the details as historically accurate as possible. The scenes consisted of seventeen tableaux, some, such as the banquet scene (see fig. 83), involving "recreations" on an impressive scale.

Roffe's painting does not slavishly reproduce any one set from the play; rather, in its placement of the figures within a large Romanesque interior, in its Celtic costumes and furniture, and in its dark spaces with Rembrandtesque highlights, it is inspired by Irving's production. Furthermore, the figure of Macbeth is pure Irving. George Odell points out how alien the actor's interpretation was to the traditional view of Macbeth's character: "For better or worse, certain traditions have grown up about the character, and most of these Irving was bound to violate. For instance, he was not able to look big and warlike, his voice was rasping and nasal, quite incapable of coping with the 'big' speeches, and in every way he suggested the ascetic, intellectual vi-

sionary, rather than the bluff warrior. Hence he was forced to portray Macbeth as a neurasthenic, madly driven by ambition to a murder planned in his mind even before the encounter with the witches; a cowardly, conscience-smitten criminal."[12] Roffe depicts Macbeth in Irving's image. Gone is the generalized pose that Garrick had hoped to achieve, epitomizing a statuesque grace in harmony with the pictorial rhetoric of the old masters. In its place is an idiosyncratic posturing, as a gaunt, spindly Macbeth creeps and lurches across the stage. The rational, classicizing world inhabited by Garrick has been replaced by a romantic one stressing the singular and individual over the general.

Roffe's painting is itself an anomaly. It is a painting of a performance, but, ironically, one that was never performed, since in *Macbeth* the murder takes place offstage. The painting thus offers a fitting climax to the tradition of theatrical portraiture. It is an imagined depiction of an unseen action, but one that is nonetheless rooted in a particular production. Irving's interpretation of Macbeth, the man, and his staging of Macbeth's world proved so strong for Roffe that the scene could only be conceived in this context. The visual traditions of painting and of the theater are here conjoined.

1. The sixth painting in the series, executed in 1731 and now in the Tate Gallery, is a replica of the fifth.

2. In his autobiographical notes, Hogarth specifically compared his paintings to the theater: "I wished to compose pictures on canvas similar to representations on the stage, and further hope that they will be tried by the same test, and criticized by the same criterion. . . . I have endeavoured to treat my subjects as a dramatic writer: my picture is my stage, and men and women my players, who by means of certain actions and gestures are to exhibit a dumb show."

3. For helpful discussions of the passions in both painting and acting, see Brewster Rogerson, "The Art of Painting the Passions," *Journal of the History of Ideas* 14 (January 1953), pp. 68–94, and George Taylor, "'The Just Delineation of the Passions': Theories of Acting in the Age of Garrick," in *The Eighteenth-Century English Stage*, ed. Kenneth Richards and Peter Thomson, London, 1972, pp. 51–72.

4. This description follows Alastair Smart's excellent analysis of Hogarth's painting is his article "Dramatic Gesture and Expression in the Age of Hogarth and Reynolds," *Apollo* 82 (August 1965), pp. 90–97.

5. Quoted in Alan S. Downer, "Nature to Advantage Dressed: Eighteenth-Century Acting," *Publications of the Modern Language Association of America* 58 (1943), p. 1028.

6. *The Works of the Late Aaron Hill*, London, 1753, vol. 2, pp. 385–86.

7. Taylor, "'Just Delineation,'" p. 60.

8. For a discussion of the various versions of Wilson's painting

and the prints and enamels after them, see Iain Mackintosh, "David Garrick and Benjamin Wilson," *Apollo* 121 (May 1985), pp. 314–20.

9. *The Plays of David Garrick*, edited with commentary and notes by Harry William Pedicord and Frederick Louis Bergmann, Carbondale and Edwardsville, Ill., 1981, vol. 3, pp. 141–43.

10. James Boaden, *Memoirs of the Life of John Philip Kemble*, London, 1825, vol. 1, p. 425.

11. Michael R. Booth, *Victorian Spectacular Theatre, 1850–1910*, Boston, London, and Henley, 1981, p. 48.

12. Odell 1920, vol. 2, p. 384.

Nathaniel Dance

Born in London on 18 May 1735, Dance was the son of George Dance the elder, an eminent architect. He studied for a time with Francis Hayman and then had the opportunity of a lengthy sojourn in Rome, where he arrived in May 1754 and remained until at least the end of 1765. Dance painted a number of conversation pieces of his countrymen making the grand tour and also sent back to London a history painting entitled *The Death of Virginia*, which, exhibited at the Society of Artists in 1761, was a seminal work in the formation of the neoclassical style. After his return to London one of the works Dance exhibited was a painting illustrating the scene in Shakespeare's play *Timon of Athens* (see fig. 6), in which Timon, seated at the mouth of his cave, scornfully gives gold to Alcibiades and the two prostitutes who accompany him. It is the first Shakespearean picture that can be called a history painting, and it is not surprising that it should be a subject from one of Shakespeare's plays set in classical antiquity. Dance was a founder member of the Royal Academy but stopped exhibiting after 1776. His social aspirations supplanted his desire for professional acclaim, and, living the life of a gentleman after an advantageous marriage, he was eventually made Sir Nathaniel Dance-Holland in 1800. He died on 15 October 1811.

106 (Plate 21)

DAVID GARRICK
1774
Oil on canvas, 30 × 25⅛ in. (76.2 × 63.8 cm.)

Signed in yellow paint at lower left on edge of book: "N. DANCE" (last letter difficult to see; may be written in script). Inscribed in black paint at top of book page: "MACBETH." Annotated in black at lower right: "Anno: 1774. This Portrait of my dear, & worthy friend / DAVID GARRICK Esqr. (painted by Mr. / N: Dance of London) was presented to me / by Himself: & is, in my own opinion, as / well as every other persons; allow'd, to be / the most true, & striking, likeness; of that great / Man, that ever was painted. John Taylor."

Provenance: Gift of David Garrick to John Taylor; Taylor sale, Christie's, 14 March 1840, lot 31, bought by Wilson, £19.8.6; collection of Sir Henry Irving; his sale, Christie's, 16 December 1905, lot 118; Christie's, 15 June 1923, lot 135, as the property of a Lady; bought by Folger, April 1926, from Walters, who had acquired the painting from Meagher, another dealer (until now the provenance of no. 137 has been wrongly ascribed to this painting)

Exhibitions: Amherst, *Shakespeare*, 1951

References: George Winchester Stone, Jr., *The Journal of David Garrick*, New York, 1939, frontispiece; Fink 1959, p. 62 (pl. 16); review of Fink by Dorothy Adlow, *The Christian Science Monitor*, 4 May 1960, p. 6 repr.; George Winchester Stone, Jr., ed., *The London Stage 1660–1800*, Carbondale, Ill., 1962, part 4, vol. 1, repr. facing p. 176; Anglesea 1971, p. 164; David Goodreau, *Nathaniel Dance*, exhibition at Kenwood, 1977, no. 28; G. W. Stone, Jr., and George M. Kahrl, *David Garrick: A Critical Biography*, London and Amsterdam, 1979, p. 303; *The Plays of David Garrick*, ed. Harry William Pedicord and Frederick Louis Bergmann, Carbondale and Edwardsville, Ill., 1980, vol. 1, frontispiece

Condition: Finlayson's lining of 1932 was replaced in 1977. An old large tear to the left of the figure was refilled and inpainted at that time.

Versions: The Folger picture is itself a replica or version of Dance's portrait of Garrick executed for William, first earl of Mansfield, the present location of which is unknown. This is possibly the painting which sold at Christie's, 23 October 1969, lot 33, as "Zoffany, portrait of David Garrick," bought by Proctor-Pearson for 220 guineas. A drawing of Garrick by Dance, dated 16 March 1771, which formed the basis for the Mansfield portrait, is in the National Portrait Gallery, London. A drawing, much closer to the final conception, is in the William Salt Library, Staffordshire.

Engravings after original: The portrait is reversed
and is in an oval format ($2^3/_8 \times 1^7/_8$ in.) in an elaborate frame, engraved by J. Hall and published 1 December 1773 for John Bell, who also published a
copy of this print by T. Cook in 1786.

Garrick, the son of an army captain, was born in
Hereford on 19 February 1716/17. In 1737 he traveled to London in the company of his tutor, Samuel
Johnson. He worked as a wine merchant along with
his brother Peter, but his interest in the theater already had a strong hold on his time. His first play,
Lethe, was performed in 1740, and he made his London debut as an actor in 1741 (see no. 107 below).
Garrick's success was immediate. He went on to
dominate the stage as an actor and from 1747 also
managed the Theatre Royal, Drury Lane. Shakespeare's plays always formed an important part of
his repertoire. He was the driving force behind the
jubilee held to celebrate the bicentennial of Shakespeare's birth at Stratford-upon-Avon in 1769 (five
years after the appropriate date). He retired from
the stage in 1776 and, dying on 20 January 1779,
was buried in Westminster Abbey.

Garrick first met Dance when visiting Rome,
writing on 2 January 1764, "the Painter is a great
Genius, & will do wt he pleases when he goes to
London."[1] The Folger picture is a version or replica
of Dance's now lost portrait of Garrick painted for
Lord Mansfield soon after he had completed his
Garrick as Richard III (see no. 107). As its inscription makes clear, it was a gift from Garrick to John
Taylor, the landscape painter, who was born in Bath
about 1745, dying in 1806.[2] It is significant that the
book which Garrick holds is identified as *Macbeth.*
From 1672 until Garrick's day, Sir William Davenant's reworking of this play was performed in preference to the original. Davenant had turned the
drama into a lavish spectacle, adding more singing
and dancing. He also introduced elaborate machin-
ery that enabled the witches to fly, and made the
character of the witches more comic than terrifying. The outlines of Macbeth's character were also
softened, playing down his violent cruelty. On 7
January 1744, Garrick introduced his staging of
Macbeth, a bold attempt to restore much of the
original, but, knowing his audience's expectations,
even he did not dare to undo all of Davenant's innovations and added lines of his own so that Macbeth
would die onstage. The choice of being associated

Fig. 68. Raphael, *Tommaso Inghirami.* Isabella Stewart Gardner
Museum, Boston.

with *Macbeth* may well have been the sitter's, for
Garrick was proud of his interpretation of this play,
his first effort to return to Shakespeare's original
text, and Robert Edge Pine was also to depict him
holding a copy of *Macbeth* in his portrait of ca.
1776 (see fig. 79).

Garrick's flushed face stands out from the somber
background, and the bright red vest with animated
gold trim also highlights the center of the composition. His forehead, the seat of intellect, is illuminated, and his eyes sparkle as he looks into the
light in a moment of inspired meditation. As an
image of genius, this portrait follows a conventional format, one that ultimately goes back to
Raphael's *Portrait of Fedra Inghirami* (fig. 68).
Dance does not present Garrick as an actor, stage
manager, or writer, but instead focuses on the private man in intimate communion with the Bard.

1. Quoted in Stone and Kahrl 1979, p. 303.

2. In the sale of Garrick's effects at Christie's on 23 June 1823, the following work was noted: "John Taylor, Esq. of Bath. An oval landscape and waterfall (presented to Mr. Garrick by this amateur artist) as appears by an inscription on the Picture" (lot 31). Stone and Kahrl mention that Taylor presented his picture to Garrick in response to some complimentary verses Garrick had composed for him (1979, pp. 457–58). It seems reasonable to assume that Garrick responded by giving Taylor his portrait. Dance's signed receipt of 1775 made out to Garrick for framing the portrait for Taylor has survived (see Rackett sale, to be held at Phillips, London, 19 March 1992, lot 15).

Nathaniel Dance, after

107

DAVID GARRICK AS RICHARD III

Richard III V, 4
After 1772
Oil on canvas, 49½ × 32⅞ in. (125 × 85 cm.)

Case no. 1507

107

Provenance: Brought from England to America by an unnamed owner in 1924 (see Walters's letter to Folger, 19 March 1926); acquired by Meagher and sold to Walters (see Meagher's letter to Folger, 8 May 1926, in Barker file); bought from Walters, April 1926, $350 (an impression of the mezzotint after the original was included in the price)

Exhibitions: Washington, 1976–77, no. 2, as by Dance

References: Anglesea 1971, p. 163; London, The Iveagh Bequest, Kenwood, *Nathaniel Dance, 1735–1811*, 1977, no. 29; Burnim 1984, p. 189 (repr.), as a smaller version presumably by Dance

Original painting: Royal Academy, 1771, oil on canvas, 93 × 59 in., Stratford-upon-Avon Town Council. Other copies of the original can be found at the Central Museum and Art Gallery, Northampton; by H. R. Morland, the Garrick Club, London (34¼ × 23 in.); Hurst House, Carmarthenshire (36 × 24 in.); W. Somerset Maugham Collection, National Theatre, London (25¼ × 16½ in.); and the Collection of Mr. and Mrs. E. Hal Dickson, Mr. and Mrs. James R. Duncan, and Mr. and Mrs. Frank W. Rose, San Angelo, Tex.

Engravings after original: J. Dixon, 28 April 1772, published by John Boydell, 25 × 15⁹⁄₁₆ in. There are also several engravings made in the nineteenth century.

Garrick made his debut in London on 19 October 1741 at Goodman's Fields in the role of Richard III. The play as performed was from Colley Cibber's adaptation of Shakespeare's *Richard III* (V, 8 in this version). The moment is when the king cries out, "A Horse! a Horse! My Kingdom for a horse!"

Garrick had already been depicted in this role, first by Thomas Bardwell in 1741 (Russell Cotes Art Gallery, Bournemouth), then by Hogarth in 1745 (see fig. 66), and finally by Hayman in 1760. Not surprisingly, since Hayman was his teacher, Dance's interpretation is most closely attuned to this earlier work. Yet Dance's conception is even more heroic, Garrick having both figuratively and literally grown in the role, as he strikes a grander pose and displays a more ample figure.

This rather poor copy of Dance's painting of 1771 was sold to Folger as the original. Given its stark modeling and lack of subtlety in the blending of tones, it was clearly copied from the print rather than from the painting. The silhouette of the hair, for example, reflects the brittle, stringy characterization found only in the mezzotint. As would be expected, the colors differ from the painting: Richard's robe, for example, is red rather than purple and his boots a bright tan rather than muted toward gray. Some of the detail found in the original and in the print has also been omitted. Most of the detailing of the anachronistic Star of the Order of the Garter, which was not introduced until the reign of Charles I, has been left out, and the group of soldiers above the raised sword at left has been omitted entirely.

George Dawe

Dawe, the son of a London engraver, was born in 1781. In 1796 he became a student at the Royal Academy, and seven years later won a gold medal for his picture *Achilles Rejecting the Consolations of Thetis.* In 1809 he was elected an associate and in 1814 a Royal Academician. Two years later he exhibited *Miss O'Neill as Juliet,* which, too late for the Royal Academy's annual exhibition though already included in the catalogue, was exhibited by lamplight at the artist's house in order that it might be viewed under the same conditions as applied to the stage. The painting's success encouraged Dawe to abandon history painting in favor of portraiture. From 1819 until 1828 he was in Russia, painting for Emperor Alexander portraits of officers who had fought against Napoleon. On a second trip to St. Petersburg in 1829 he fell ill, dying in the fall of that year after his return to London.

108
Study for MISS O'NEILL AS JULIET
Romeo and Juliet II, 2
ca. 1816
Oil on canvas, 25 × 18⅛ in. (63.6 × 46 cm.)

Case no. 1769

Provenance: Parsons, March 1928, £33.15.0

Exhibitions: Washington, 1985.

Condition: The painting, which required only minor adjustments, was restored in 1985 in preparation for the Kemble exhibition.

Exhibited painting: The picture is listed in the Royal Academy catalogue for 1816 as no. 199: "Miss O'Neill in the character of Juliet. Scene, a Garden (Juliet appears above in the balcony). 'See how she leans her cheek upon her hand, etc.'" There is a photograph of a painting, which could be the original, on file at the Witt Library, London, where it is listed as in a private collection in Wales.

Engravings after exhibited painting: G. Maile, May 1816; H. Dawe, 1 June 1839, published by Ackermann, 14⁷⁄₁₆ × 10⁹⁄₁₆ in.

Born in 1791, Eliza O'Neill was the daughter of an Irish actor. Her London debut came at Covent Garden on 6 October 1814 in the role of Juliet, a performance that met with an enthusiastic reception. Though highly popular, particularly as a tragedian, she retired from the stage in July 1819 and later that year married William Wrixon Becher, an Irish member of Parliament. When Becher was created a baronet on the coronation of William IV in 1831, Eliza became Lady Becher. Never returning to the stage, she died in 1872.

Dawe clearly found the subject of melancholy and distressed women to be a profitable one. The first painting he exhibited at the Royal Academy was from the Bible: *Naomi and Her Daughter* (1804, no. 273), which was accompanied in the catalogue by the verse, "Orpah wept and departed, but Ruth clave unto her mother-in-law." In 1810 when he turned to Homer, he picked a scene of Andromache imploring Ulysses to spare her son's life (no. 4). When selecting a subject from contemporary literature, he chose Coleridge's poem "Love," where the maiden Genevieve listens to "a soft and doleful air" (Royal Academy, 1812, no. 220). He also depicted two remarkable contemporary anecdotes, one showing a mother rescuing her child from an eagle's nest (Royal Academy, 1813, no. 1) and the other, exhibited posthumously, of a mother screaming for her lost infant as they both drown in a shipwreck (British Institution, 1833, no. 102). Although *Miss O'Neill as Juliet* differs from these others in that it is a theatrical portrait, in mood and intention it certainly is at home among these images of doleful women.

This moment from the play was extremely popular in the nineteenth century. John Opie had depicted it in a painting exhibited at the Royal Academy in 1803 (no. 44: "See how she leans her

108

cheek upon her hand"). An enamel by Henry Bone
after Opie's picture was exhibited soon thereafter
(1805, no. 428), and two years before Dawe, Thomas
Phillips had exhibited *Miss Stanley in the Character of Juliet* (1814, no. 93: "Scene on the balcony.
'What's in a name? etc.'"). The Folger also owns a
drawing by Harlow, signed and dated 26 August
1811, entitled *Miss B. Q. Brown as Juliet.*

Dawe shows Miss O'Neill wearing a virginal
white gown with gold brocade and leaning against a
massive balustrade. Her standing, crossed-leg pose
with head resting on one hand was a common type.
Dawe may even have intended an association with
Peter Scheemaker's statue of Shakespeare in Westminster Abbey, where the Bard is similarly depicted. Celebrated for her classical beauty, Miss

O'Neill is posed in profile. The abundant red drapery of fashionable portraiture almost threatens to take over. Two light sources for this nocturnal scene are given, the full moon and an oil lamp at upper left. When viewed by candlelight, as at the artist's house, the picture must have been doubly effective.

Dawe includes a large flower at the lower right. Flowers, of course, are associated with traditional Vanitas imagery (as is the burning lamp), but this particular plant is more exotic than most. It is the blue passion flower and is surely derived from the engraving of January 1800 published by Robert Thornton for his ambitious botanical work *The Temple of Flora*. A passion flower is a highly appropriate symbol for the love of Juliet and Romeo.[1] Thornton points out that this flower blooms and dies within only three days, and he compares it to Christ's Passion, yielding an even more profound association with tormented love.

1. Dawe was not alone in using such a motif. A painting of Lady Essex as Juliet in the Renwick Gallery, Washington, D.C., contains a similar detail. This work is listed as by a follower of Sir Thomas Lawrence and dated ca. 1810–15. It may, though, be slightly later, this artist having been influenced by Dawe rather than the other way around.

Thomas Gainsborough, after (nos. 109–10)

Though decidedly different in temperament, Gainsborough and Reynolds were the two outstanding portrait painters working in England in the late eighteenth century. In contrast to Reynolds's studied idealization of his sitters, Gainsborough offered a lyrical and seemingly more spontaneous approach. Baptized on 14 May 1727 in Sudbury, Suffolk, Gainsborough arrived in London about 1740, studying apparently with Gravelot and Hayman in the St. Martin's Lane Academy. He returned to Sudbury in 1748, then settled in Ipswich in 1752, moving to Bath in 1759. From the beginning of his career he worked as a landscape painter as well as a portraitist, though he never received as much encouragement in the former genre. His early landscape style was heavily influenced by the realism of Dutch seventeenth-century painting, but later he turned more to the poetical examples of Rubens and Watteau. Even when in the provinces, he kept up his London contacts, first exhibiting at the Society of Artists in 1761 and becoming a founder member of the Royal Academy near the end of that

decade. In 1774 he moved back to London but exhibited only sporadically at the Royal Academy as he was dissatisfied with the placement of his pictures. His portrait style, refined by his study of Van Dyck, proved popular and secured for him, in noticeable contrast to Reynolds, the patronage of the royal family. Gainsborough died in London on 2 August 1788.

109

DAVID GARRICK LEANING ON
A BUST OF SHAKESPEARE
After 1769
Oil on canvas, 45 × 29^{15}/$_{16}$ in. (114.3 × 75.9 cm.)

Case no. 1565

Provenance: Michelmore catalogue *Shakespeareana Illustrated*, [1923?], no. 42, as by John Hoppner after Gainsborough, repr. in color, £400 asking price; bought by Folger shortly before 20 September 1926, $1,000

109

Exhibitions: Washington, 1976–77, no. 12, as by Hoppner

References: Fink 1959, p. 63 (lists two paintings of Garrick by or after Gainsborough, but both entries refer to this one painting); Anglesea 1971, p. 172, as by Hoppner; Burnim 1984, p. 211, as by Hoppner

Condition: The canvas was lined by Finlayson in 1932.

Original painting: 1766–69, 92½ × 60 in., hung in Town Hall, Stratford-upon-Avon, and destroyed by fire in 1946

Engraving after original: Mezzotint by Valentine Green, published 2 April 1769 by John Boydell, 23⅞ × 15⅛ in.

Other copies: Sotheby, 2 May 1962, lot 152, bought by Rich, £60 (48½ × 35 in.); collection of Edgar Monet, Bournemouth (45 × 30 in.); head and shoulders only, Shakespeare Birthplace Trust (3 × 2½ in.). Anglesea also records what is said to be a finished sketch by Gainsborough in the collection of G. B. Fisher (24 × 16 in.).

The first work Garrick commissioned from Gainsborough was a full-length portrait, where he was shown leaning on a tall plinth supporting a bust of Shakespeare. The painting was exhibited at the Society of Artists in 1766. Apparently it was this same picture that Gainsborough, with Garrick's approval, reworked and sold to the Corporation of Stratford in 1769 after it had requested a portrait of the actor for the Shakespeare Jubilee. The picture, destroyed in a fire of 1946, depicted Garrick in a pose that deliberately echoed Shakespeare's in Scheemaker's statue executed for Westminster Abbey.

The dealer Michelmore attributed the Folger copy to John Hoppner (1758–1810), but it would be unfair to blame Hoppner for this crude performance, a copy almost certainly after Valentine Green's mezzotint rather than the original painting. Not only is the Folger picture technically deficient, conveying little of Gainsborough's genius, but it is also an inaccurate rendering: for example, the river should run behind Garrick; the base directly beneath the bust of Shakespeare should bow inward at the back rather than outward; and the ivy, symbolic of eternal fame, should not continue all the way up the plinth.

110

110

SARAH SIDDONS

After 1785

Oil on canvas, 30 × 24⅞ in. (76.1 × 63.2 cm.)

Provenance: Collection of Augustin Daly (on exhibit in Daly's Theatre in New York); Daly sale, Anderson Galleries, 27 November 1912, lot 62, Smith acting as agent

Exhibitions: Washington, 1985

Condition: The painting was lined by Finlayson in 1932 and was last restored in 1985. The surface contained extensive repaint, some of which was removed and replaced with new inpainting at that time.

Original painting: Oil on canvas, 49¾ × 39¼ in., perhaps begun 1783, finished 1785 and exhibited at the Royal Academy, now in the National Gallery, London

Sarah Siddons, one of the theater's great tragedians, was born on 5 July 1755. She was the eldest child of Roger and Sarah Kemble, who were also the parents of several other distinguished actors, including John Philip Kemble. As the daughter of an actor, Sarah was exposed to the stage at an early age and, overcoming her parents' reluctance, married a fellow actor, William Siddons, in 1773. Garrick engaged her for her London debut at the Theatre Royal, Drury Lane, on 29 December 1775. However, her career did not flourish and Garrick did not renew her contract for the next season. After noted triumphs in the provinces, she returned to the London stage on 10 October 1782 in Garrick's version of Southerne's *Isabella; or, The Fatal Marriage,* immediately establishing herself as a great performer. Her first Shakespearean role in London was Isabella in *Measure for Measure,* which she performed on 3 November 1783. Tall in stature with imposing features, she was particularly accomplished in roles requiring dignified grandeur and impassioned power. She retired from the stage on 29 June 1812 in her celebrated role of Lady Macbeth, and after that time only appeared in benefits, the last of which occurred in 1819. She died on 8 June 1831.

Executed on a three-quarter-length canvas (30 × 25 in.), the Folger picture is a copy of the head and shoulders of Gainsborough's portrait of Sarah Siddons, a half-length canvas (50 × 40 in.) which he exhibited at the Royal Academy in 1785 (fig. 69).

Fig. 69. Thomas Gainsborough, *Mrs. Sarah Siddons,* 1785. Oil on canvas, 49³⁄₄ × 39¹⁄₄ in. Reproduced by Courtesy of the Trustees, The National Gallery, London.

Gainsborough shows Mrs. Siddons in fashionable contemporary attire seated against a muted, though still dazzling, crimson drapery. Gainsborough is said to have remarked of the sitter, "Damn the nose, there's no end to it," and the Folger picture with its concentration on the head does nothing to minimize this feature.

The Folger file card lists this picture as "from Mrs. Folger's house," making it one of the few paintings that was not put into storage after its purchase. Its massive gold frame also indicates how highly it was valued. Its importance, though, is one of association, as it inadequately reflects the excellence of the original, even though it is a far better work than the "Hoppner" copy after Gainsborough (see no. 109). It is faithful in its coloring, but it lacks the painterly brushwork of the original, a deficiency that is particularly evident in the powdered hair. The darker curls cascade down onto the shoulders in an undifferentiated mass without any of Gainsborough's dynamic brushwork.

James Green, after

Born in 1771 at Leytonstone, Essex, Green entered the Royal Academy schools in 1791 and began to exhibit at the Royal Academy two years later. Best known for his portraits, he worked in a variety of media, including watercolor, miniature painting, and oil. Although he spent most of his career in London, he died at Bath in 1834.

111

GEORGE FREDERICK COOKE AS IAGO
Othello III, 3
After 1801
Oil on canvas, 30⁵⁄₈ × 25 in. (77.8 × 63.7 cm.)

Provenance: Source unknown. This work has been confused with a watercolor of this subject bought from John Anderson, Jr. (see ART Box C772, no. 2, X-Large).

References: Highfill 1973–, vol. 3, p. 466 (no. 31), as Richard III by an unknown artist; Don B. Wilmeth, *George Frederick Cooke: Machiavel of the Stage,* London, 1980, p. 288, as Richard III by an unknown artist

Exhibitions: Washington, 1985, as "Cooke as Iago" by Green

111

Condition: The ground is cream-colored. Finlayson in 1932 glue-lined the original canvas to a preprimed canvas.

Original painting: Royal Academy, 1801, no. 127, as "Mr. Cooke in the character of Iago"; now in the Garrick Club, London, 49½ × 39½ in.

Engravings after original: Mezzotint by James Ward, 21 April 1801; an engraving by an anonymous artist of about the same date is mentioned in Highfill 1973–, vol. 3, p. 465.

According to his own account, Cooke was born on 17 April 1756, but he may well have been born three years earlier and not in London as he maintained, but in Berwick-upon-Tweed or Dublin. For years he was a popular actor in the Midlands and in Dublin, but it was a long time before he was offered an acceptable major engagement in London. Throughout his career, heavy drinking led to frequent absences from the stage, and his personal affairs were often chaotic. Obviously, Cooke's reputation gave London managers pause. Having finally been signed by the Covent Garden Theatre in 1800, he enjoyed a London triumph in the role of Richard III on 31 October. Attracted by a lucrative contract, he sailed for New York in October 1810 to become the first major British actor to perform in America. His de-

but was again a great success, but his drinking soon became even more unrestrained. He died on 26 September 1812 of cirrhosis of the liver and was buried in the Strangers' Vault of St. Paul's Church. On his visit to America in 1820–21, Edmund Kean, an admirer of Cooke, had his body (or at least those parts not kept as souvenirs) removed to the center of the cemetery, where he erected a monument to his memory.

Cooke was best known for his portrayal of Richard III, and the Folger painting was acquired with this identification. The painting, however, is based on James Green's conception of Cooke as Iago (fig. 70).[1] Cooke had played Iago at least as early as 1792, and in his first season at Covent Garden, he made his London debut in this role on 28 November 1800. Green's painting was exhibited in the spring of 1801 at the Royal Academy, and James Ward's mezzotint after the painting was published on 21 April of that year. Green's painting illustrates Iago's speech to Othello beginning, "O beware, my Lord, of jealousy."[2] This same line accompanies an earlier print of the actor Robert Bensley in the role of Iago published on 15 November 1775 for Bell. Where Bensley strikes a histrionic pose, his left hand raised high,

Fig. 70. After James Green, *George Frederick Cooke as Iago.* Mezzotint by James Ward, 21 April 1801, 16³/₁₆ × 12¹/₄ in.

his right held out at his side, as he lunges to his left, Cooke's portrayal, as characterized by Green, is far more subdued. Clearly the actor took his cue from earlier passages in this scene spoken by Othello to Iago:

> And didst contract and purse thy brow together,
> As if thou then hadst shut up in thy brain
> Some horrible conceit.
> . . . I know thou'rt full of love and honesty,
> And weigh'st thy words before thou giv'st them
>   breath,
> Therefore these stops of thine fright me the
>   more.

Cooke's Iago is the cunning confidant whose every response is quietly measured.

The Folger painting, which is probably based on Ward's mezzotint, expands on Green's three-quarter-length format to show Cooke in full length in an elaborate setting. The costume, as in Green's painting, is a martial one—a red tunic decorated with gold and black.[3] The cloak, however, is now blue, the original having been red, and the black hat and hair are now a dark brown. The scene is staged within the garden of the Cyprian castle, but the fanciful setting in the picture lacks coherence: for example, the column at right, enveloped at its top in red drapery, is unrelated to the rest of the structure; the shadows are inconsistent; and the courtyard behind shows a trabeated colonnade in front and arcuated ones at the side and rear. In Green's original conception, Othello's presence is implied beyond the frame. In the Folger painting, Iago seems to stand alone and his crucial lines—"O, beware, my lord, of jealousy! / It is the green-ey'd monster which doth mock / The meat it feeds on"—are rendered more as a soliloquy than as an ironic warning to the Moor.

1. The painting (49½ × 39½ in.) is in the Garrick Club, London.
2. This line appears in the 1807 British Institution catalogue, when Green exhibited a painting of Iago, which was possibly the Royal Academy picture. The dimensions of the British Institution picture were given as 60 by 50 inches; perhaps the extra ten inches are accounted for by the frame. When the Royal Academy painting was listed in *Mathews's Gallery of Theatrical Portraits* of 1833, this line was included in the entry.
3. William Ridley's engraving after J. Corbett of 31 December 1800 for the *Monthly Mirror* also shows Cooke as Iago. Interestingly, the costume, a mixture of classical and Elizabethan elements, differs from the one portrayed by Green.

William Hamilton

112

JOHN PHILIP KEMBLE AS RICHARD III
Richard III V, 3
ca. 1787
Oil on panel, 21⁷⁄₈ × 18¼ in. (55.5 × 46.5 cm.)

Inscribed on the garter on the left leg: "MAL" (the rest of the motto "Honi soit qui mal y pense" is illegible, thereby emphasizing the word for "evil").

Provenance: Purchased Stonehill, June 1947, $15, as by Stothard

Exhibitions: Washington, 1985, repr. p. 11

Condition: The panel split in two when it was shipped to the Folger in 1947. The work was rejoined for the 1985 exhibition, but the vertical crack running through the entire panel which passes close to Kemble's right shoulder remains clearly visible. A rectangular crack is just to the left of this at the center top of the panel. Another vertical crack runs from the top edge to Kemble's right knee, roughly paralleling the edge of the right-hand side of the tent opening. A smaller crack is at the upper left, 2½ inches from the left-hand edge.

Exhibited painting: London, Royal Academy, 1788, no. 22, now in the Raymond Mander and Joe Mitchenson Theatre Collection (2.18 × 1.55 m.)

Versions: A small version is in the Dyce Collection, Victoria and Albert Museum, London. Another was in the collection of the American Shakespeare Festival Theatre before it was sold at Sotheby Parke Bernet, 15 January 1976, lot 107. It is now in a private collection in California (see Geoffrey Ashton, "Paintings in the Mander and Mitchenson Theatre Collection," *Apollo* 114 [August 1981], p. 92, n. 5).

Engravings after original: Bartolozzi, 1789 (trimmed impression, ART Vol. b8, no. 69)

John Philip Kemble was the leading actor on the London stage between the retirement of Garrick and the rise of Kean. He was particularly noted for his productions of Shakespeare's plays, and, celebrated as a tragedian, he was most successful in roles demanding heroic dignity. Born on 1 February 1757, he was from a distinguished family of actors, not the least of whom was his elder sister, Sarah

Siddons. He performed as a boy in his father's company, but his father, intending him for the priesthood, also made certain he received a strong classical education. Kemble, however, resisting his father's wishes, embarked instead on a career as an actor in 1776. He first appeared in London at Drury Lane on 30 September 1783 in the role of Hamlet. In the season of 1788–89, he undertook the management of the theater and, leaving Drury Lane in 1802, soon acquired an interest in the Covent Garden Theatre. His last appearance occurred on 23 June 1817 in his popular role of Coriolanus. He died on 26 February 1823.

Kemble portrayed Richard III at Drury Lane in 1783. He was not to play this role again until the autumn of 1788, after William Smith, who normally acted the part, had retired. Kemble was never celebrated for his villainous roles, and he seemed constitutionally ill-suited to the role of the tempestuous, deformed Richard. His later performances were compared unfavorably, first to those of his rival, George Frederick Cooke, and then to those of Edmund Kean. Yet, his 1783 performances must have made a substantial impression, as he was painted in this role by Gilbert Stuart around 1786 and it was just two years later that Hamilton exhibited his portrait. In 1780 Hamilton had exhibited at the Royal Academy a painting of Sarah Siddons in the character of the Grecian Daughter (see cat. 84), but he seems to have placed particular importance on the theatrical portrait of 1788. Although he exhibited almost every year at the academy, he had shown nothing the year before, and his painting of Kemble was the only work he exhibited in 1788. Clearly he wished to concentrate attention on this work, and surely it is no coincidence that he became a full academician soon thereafter.

For his performance, Kemble reworked Colley Cibber's version of Shakespeare, and his tent scene occurs in act V, scene 5. Hamilton shows Kemble as Richard on Bosworth Field, the night before his battle with the Earl of Richmond, starting from his sleep, having been visited by the ghosts of his victims. The artist's conception pays conscious tribute to Hogarth's 1745 painting of Garrick as Richard III (see fig. 66). Although Hogarth's is a portrait of an actor in character, it elevates the tent scene to the level of a heroic history painting in the grand style. Not only does Hamilton align himself with the artistic lineage of Hogarth, but he shows Kemble

following in the tradition of Garrick. Hamilton's conception, however, does differ in important points from his predecessor's, as he abandons Hogarth's majestic grandeur in favor of a more emotional portrayal. He chooses an interior view, positioning Richard and the viewer inside the tent, thereby creating a more intimate setting while bringing the viewer closer to the figure. He also gives Richard a more dynamic pose, the figure, as well as the bed, forming a dramatic diagonal. Seen now within a tight vertical format, the pose is greatly exaggerated: the left knee is raised high, the right arm thrusting farther outward, the hand lighted from behind with its palm in shadow, and the head turned dramatically to the viewer's left in counter to the figure's thrust toward the right. The Hamilton Richard, with agitated hair and tightly knitted brow, recoils in horror at the sight of the ghosts, while the Hogarth Richard focuses on the figure's inner turmoil as he awakens in stunned disbelief. What is a vision seen from within in the one becomes externalized in the other. Apparently, Kemble's acting of this celebrated scene was far more physically active than Garrick's had been, anticipating Edmund Kean's dynamic interpretation.

The Folger painting differs significantly in its color scheme from the larger, exhibited picture. It is not a preparatory sketch but rather a finished work in its own right that explores interesting variations on the original theme. In the Folger version the tent is entirely red, this bright background working well on a small scale, and more of the tent is included along the left-hand edge. In the larger painting, the inside of the tent has been rendered as a muted green, with red playing a more prominent role in the costume. The robe, excepting the sleeve, and the trunk hose or slops are red with blue strips edged in gold, whereas the sleeve and doublet are gold. In the Folger sketch, the robe and slops are gold and the doublet red.

Gabriel Harrison

Harrison had many interests, including the theater, photography, painting, and writing. Born on 25 March 1818 in Philadelphia, he moved with his family six years later to New York. He became enamored with the theater when, at age fourteen, he first saw Edwin Forrest perform. He wrote his first play at age eighteen and in 1838 made his professional debut as an actor at the National Theatre in Washington, D.C., in the role of Othello. He opened a general store in New York in 1843 but soon became a force in the cultural life of Brooklyn. In 1853 he founded the Brooklyn Dramatic Academy and opened the Park Theatre ten years later. He also organized one of the first American opera companies. Earlier he had experimented with daguerreotypes and throughout his life painted portraits and landscapes. He died in Brooklyn on 15 December 1902.

113

EDWIN FORREST AS KING LEAR

King Lear IV, 6
1872
Oil on paper pasted on board, 19³⁄₄ × 15¹⁄₄ in. (50.2 × 38.7 cm.)

ART Box H319, no. 2

Inscribed at lower left center: "1872"; at lower right: "EDWIN FORREST, AS LEAR / By Gabriel HARRISON"

Provenance: Anderson Auction Company, 27 April 1905, lot 9, "Edwin Forrest as King Lear," $11, bought by Little (presumably this work); when Folger acquired this painting is not known, but the Folger file card lists him as having paid $18.

Condition: The sheet of paper that has been attached to the illustration board stops two inches short of the bottom.

Edwin Forrest was America's first actor with an international reputation. Born in Philadelphia in 1806, he early showed a desire to become a performer and had the opportunity in 1825 to work in Albany with Edmund Kean, who helped him sharpen his skills. On 23 June 1826 Forrest made a triumphant debut in New York in the role of Othello. His subsequent career was marred by his temper and suspicious nature. In 1849 his public quarrel with the English actor Macready (see no. 119) led to a violent riot on the part of his supporters in the streets of New York, and in 1851 he began an acrimonious suit against his wife for divorce. One of his most celebrated roles late in his career was King Lear. His biographer writes that Forrest's Lear was "the sublimest in spiritual power and

113

tragic pathos" of all his characterizations.[1] Forrest died on 12 December 1872, the same year that Harrison executed this painting.

Harrison knew Forrest extremely well. He wrote to his first biographer, "I have seen Forrest act more than four hundred times. I have sat at his feet as a pupil artist learning of a master artist."[2] Harrison later published his own book on the actor, and of the pictures he reproduced he writes, "The illustrations of Forrest are from a set of photographer's negatives, found in the Forrest Home, never before published, and worked up with appropriate backgrounds by the writer. The likeness of Forrest and the costumes are carefully preserved in every particular."[3]

The photographs from which Harrison worked are by Matthew Brady.[4] Harrison reproduces as his frontispiece Brady's photograph of Forrest in contemporary dress, dating it to 1858. As all the photos show Forrest in the same studio setting, which had a fluted column on the right with drapery and an octagonally patterned floor, it seems likely that they all date from the same time. The Folger Library also possesses a Brady photograph dated 1866 of Forrest as Hamlet retouched by Harrison, which clearly documents his working method. The studio

Fig. 71. Photograph after print of Matthew Brady's *Edwin Forrest as King Lear.*

painted, thereby more closely integrating figure with ground. Harrison also simplified the figure's costume and paraphernalia, attempting to create a more unified and imposing design. The series forms an interesting dialogue between the uses and limitations of photography versus painting as seen within a nineteenth-century context.

Harrison's comments on Forrest's depiction of Lear in the storm indicates the sublimity the artist was trying to capture:

His opening scene in the third act amidst the storm with his grand figure towering, and in a rage of exclamations equal to the frenzy of the night, was a dramatic picture that exalted the admiration of his audience beyond description.

"And thou, all-shaking thunder,
Strike flat the thick rotundity o' the world."

was given with a height of voice and pose of body that were the zenith of grandeur:

background is painted over up to the contour of the figure, and the ruff of a sleeve is touched up in white.

The Brady photograph of Forrest as Lear (fig. 71) shows the actor's raised left arm supported by a stand. Even so, the sheaf of straw in his hand is somewhat blurred as he could not hold this pose without some movement.[5] In his book of 1889, Harrison includes his depiction of Forrest as Lear signed and dated 1871 (fig. 72). It is presumably identical in technique to his Hamlet of 1866. He entirely painted over the background and made only slight alterations to the figure, as in the case of the windswept beard and the shortened straw sword.

In these works Harrison was attempting to retain the realistic accuracy of the photograph, while replacing the studio backdrop with a setting appropriate to the character, but there is an inherent awkwardness in the contrast between the realism of the photograph and the artifice of the painted, illusionistic setting. The Folger painting is an attempt to overcome this tension. It retains the dimensions of the photograph and the scale and positioning of the figure, but the entire surface is

By Gabriel Harrison.

FORREST AS KING LEAR,

"Ay, every inch a King!"

Fig. 72. Gabriel Harrison, *Edwin Forrest as King Lear.* Painted over a Brady photograph and reproduced in Harrison's *Edwin Forrest: The Actor and the Man* (Brooklyn, 1889).

"Rumble thy fill! fight whirlwind, rain and fire!"

All these explosive expletives were rendered in the expression of frightful anger.[6]

Harrison's setting, dark and foreboding, is intended to convey this cataclysmic energy. The pose of Lear, however, is from a different moment in the play. Brady photographed Forrest as Lear at the moment he replies to Gloucester's question, "Is't not the King?"[7] Holding aloft his straw scepter and wearing a handmade crown, Lear majestically replies, "Ay, every inch a king! When I do stare, see how the subject quakes." In Harrison's rendering, Forrest-Lear is intended to stare down the storm itself.

1. William Rounseville Alger, *Life of Edwin Forrest*, Philadelphia, 1877, vol. 2, p. 780.
2. Quoted in ibid., p. 543.
3. Gabriel Harrison, *Edwin Forrest: The Actor and the Man*, Brooklyn, 1889, p. 8.
4. The Folger has prints after fourteen of Brady's photographs, one a portrait of Forrest in contemporary attire and the others portraits of the actor posed in the costumes of various characters.
5. In 1877 Alger reproduced this image in his book in the form of an engraving (without the stand) by G. H. Cushman (vol. 2, facing p. 780).
6. Harrison, *Forrest*, p. 121.
7. It is of interest to note the similarity of Brady's photograph to a London photograph of Charles Kean as Lear made in 1858 (reproduced in A. L. Rowse's *The Annotated Shakespeare*, New York, 1978, vol. 3, p. 374). The Brady-Forrest pose was obviously a stock type, and in 1858 the Philadelphia artist Peter Frederick Rothermel had also painted this moment from the play in similarly dramatic terms, though he included the figures of Gloucester and Edgar. A painting of this scene by the Belgian artist J. B. Wittkamp (1820–85) was in the same Philadelphia collection, that of Joseph Harrison, Jr., as the Rothermel *Lear* (see Philadelphia, Frank S. Schwarz & Son, *A Century of Philadelphia Artists*, Philadelphia Collection XXXVII, Summer 1988, pp. 62–64).

Sir Thomas Lawrence, after (nos. 114–15)

Known for his virtuoso technique and rich color, Lawrence was the most successful portrait painter of his generation. Born on 13 April 1769 at Bristol, he demonstrated a precocious talent that his father promoted from an early age. He first exhibited at the Royal Academy in 1787, settling in London in that same year. On Reynolds's death in 1792, he was appointed Painter-in-Ordinary to the King and was voted a full academician in 1794. In 1820, he succeeded Benjamin West as president of the Royal Academy, a position he held until his own death on 7 January 1830.

114

114

JOHN PHILIP KEMBLE AS CORIOLANUS
Coriolanus IV, 5
Early 1800s
Oil on cardboard, 10⅝ × 8¹¹⁄₁₆ in. (27 × 22 cm.)

Case no. 1798

Annotated on verso in brown ink on shaped paper pasted in center: "Finely Painted / Portrait / of / John Kemble / as / Coriolanus." Beneath this in a different hand is a "signature" with flourishes apparently written over an earlier, fainter inscription: "Henry Harlowe [last word or words no longer legible; possibly a date that has been written over 'Lawrence']."

Provenance: Michelmore, June 1928, £15 (part of a group of ten works purchased from *Shakespeareana Catalogue;* this was no. 407, asking price £75)

Exhibitions: Washington, 1985, as by Harlow

References: Highfill 1973–, vol. 8, p. 377 (no. 92), as by Harlow

Condition: The painting is executed in oil on heavily gessoed and varnished cardboard. Two small losses of paint and ground were repaired in the face in 1985. A tiny network of cracks is visible in the dark areas.

Original painting: London, Royal Academy, 1798, no. 225, now in the Guildhall Art Gallery, London, 113 × 70 in.

Engravings after original: Stipple engraving by R. M. Meadows, 1805; mezzotint by H. Dawe, March 1838; mezzotint by W. O. Burgess, 11 March 1839

Related works: A sketch was in the Lawrence sale, Christie's, 15 May 1830, lot 20. Its present whereabouts is unknown. A copy of the Guildhall painting by Washington Allston is in the Players Club, New York, and another copy is in the Dyce Collection of the Victoria and Albert Museum, London.

The role of Coriolanus may well have been John Philip Kemble's most successful, yet it was not among his early repertoire. Not until 7 February 1789, after he had undertaken the management of the Drury Lane Theatre, was his *Coriolanus* first seen. It was primarily a mixture of Shakespeare with James Thomson's version. Kemble emphasized the cold grandeur inherent in this proud patrician, and his contemporaries enthusiastically responded to his stately characterization. When he returned to the Covent Garden stage on 15 January 1814 after a two-year absence, it was in this part, and he was greeted with a tumultuous reception. It was in this same role that he closed out his career, giving his final performance on 23 June 1817.

Thomas Lawrence knew the Kemble family well, his acquaintance going back to his boyhood in Bath. His four majestic full-length portraits of John Philip Kemble in character have established, as much as any critical commentary, the conception of Kemble's acting style as one of grandeur and a highly cultivated classicism. *Kemble as Coriolanus at the Hearth of Tullus Aufidius* (fig. 73), exhibited at the Royal Academy in 1798, is the first of this group; it was followed by *Kemble as Rolla in "Pizarro"* in 1800, *Kemble as Hamlet* in 1801, and *Kemble as Addison's Cato* in 1812. None of these portraits were commissioned, Lawrence painting them instead for reasons of prestige.

Coriolanus's name is a title bestowed upon him after he led the Romans to victory against the Volsces at Corioli. Appointed consul, he gave an arrogant acceptance speech so filled with contempt

Fig. 73. Sir Thomas Lawrence, *John Philip Kemble as Coriolanus at the Hearth of Tullus Aufidius.* Oil on canvas, 113 × 70 in. Guildhall Art Gallery, City of London.

for the people that his enemies persuaded the citizens of Rome to rescind the honor. After a struggle of wills, Coriolanus agreed to humble himself before the people, but his enemies provoked him into an outburst that led to his banishment. Seeking out his old enemy Tullus Aufidius, the leader of the Volsces, he placed his fate in his hands. Arriving at Aufidius's home unannounced, he revealed himself and offered to lead the Volsces against Rome. Lawrence depicts Coriolanus standing before a grand hearth awaiting his host.

From 1797 until 1806, political unrest fueled by economic depression and government repression during the wars with France led Kemble to withdraw *Coriolanus* with its decidedly inegalitarian hero. It was at this moment that Lawrence chose to inaugurate his series of portraits of Kemble with this work. The artist may have been in sympathy with Coriolanus's autocratic conduct, but he probably was responding less to political considerations than to Sir Francis Bourgeois' painting of Kemble as Coriolanus (fig. 74), exhibited at the Royal Academy the year before. Bourgeois shows Kemble's stage version, complete with the statue of Mars that he had introduced into Aufidius's hall. In contrast, Lawrence's hero fills the canvas. Seen from a low point of view, he towers above the spectator, haughty, commanding, fully self-contained and imperiously defiant even within his enemy's home. He is a romantic hero, or perhaps more accurately an antihero on a par with the devil in Lawrence's *Satan Calling His Legions*, also exhibited at the Royal Academy the year before. While at work on *Kemble as Coriolanus*, Lawrence wrote his friend Mrs. Boucherett describing the picture as "a sort of half-history picture."[1] In mixing the idealized realm of history painting with theatrical portraiture, Lawrence elevates Kemble, Shakespeare, and, not least of all, himself.

The Folger picture is a reduced version of the de-

Fig. 74. Sir Francis Bourgeois, *John Philip Kemble as Coriolanus*. By courtesy of the Trustees of Sir John Soane's Museum.

tail of Kemble's head and shoulders. The figure is no longer seen in context, the background consisting of a neutral brown. The concentration is on the piercing eyes, aquiline nose, slightly parted lips, unruly hair, the elegantly expressive hand, and the massive, agitated rhythms of the red cloak. The enlivening splashes of color in the bright patch of his clothing on his left shoulder is made up of gold, white, brown, and blue. The colors, however, do not match those of Lawrence's painting, where the cloak is green and the glinting strap across the shoulder a metallic blue-gray rather than gold. In the original a portion of the garment behind the left arm differs in color from the cloak itself. The hair of the Folger version also lacks the thick, massive locks of the original, and the head with its too red lips is not as forcibly rendered.

When selling the picture to Folger, Michelmore was confident that the work was by George Henry Harlow, a "signature" on the back confirming this attribution.[2] Born in London in 1787, Harlow entered Lawrence's studio as a young man. His high regard for his own talent led him to chafe under the conditions of his training, which consisted of a great deal of copying of Lawrence's work. After about eighteen months, the two men quarreled and Harlow left. There is no reason, however, to attribute to him this small-scale work, which is surely based on a print after the original painting.

1. D. E. Williams, *The Life and Correspondence of Sir Thomas Lawrence*, London, 1831, vol. 1, p. 197.
2. The Folger owns a black-and-red-chalk drawing by Harlow of Kemble as Coriolanus. It is a bust only, with the head facing forward and the eyes looking toward the upper left (ART Box H286, no. 1).

115

JOHN PHILIP KEMBLE AS HAMLET
Hamlet V, 1
Early 1800s
Oil on canvas, 30 × 19³/₈ in. (76.2 × 49.3 cm.)

Case no. 1798

Provenance: Michelmore, June 1928, £20, as by Harlow (part of a group of ten works purchased from *Shakespeareana Catalogue*; this was no. 406, asking price £105)

Exhibitions: Amherst, *Shakespeare*, 1951, as by Harlow; Washington, 1985, as by Harlow

115

References: Highfill 1973–, vol. 8, p. 378, mentioned in no. 104 as a copy after Lawrence

Condition: The painting was glue-lined by Finlayson in 1932. There are severe contraction cracks which follow the weave of the canvas over the entire surface of the painting excepting the figure.

Original painting: Royal Academy, 1801, no. 197, now at the Tate Gallery, London (120 × 78 in.)

Versions: Garlick offers a summary of the important versions: "Farington records, 12 March 1801, that Lawrence was painting the large figure of Hamlet 'from a small study'. This was probably the 'small version' lent by Sir Thomas Baring to the British Institution exhibition of 1830 (no. 33) and which belonged to the Earl of Northbrook in 1910. There are other recorded versions. Those which have the best claim to be autograph or studio are probably that which descended from Fanny Kemble to C. K. B. Wistar, Haverford, Pa., size unrecorded, and a head-and-shoulders, 30 × 25 (76.2 × 63.5),

now privately owned, which was presented by Lawrence to Miss Harriet Lee."[1] The Folger deaccessioned another reduced copy acquired from the Leverhulme sale; see D37.

Engravings after original: Mezzotint by S. W. Reynolds, 1805; according to Highfill, at least another thirteen engravers reproduced this painting.

Lawrence exhibited *Kemble as Hamlet*, his third portrait of the actor in a theatrical role, at the Royal Academy in 1801. Hamlet had long formed an important part of Kemble's repertoire. He had made his debut in this role at Leeds in 1779, at the Smock Alley Theatre in Dublin in 1781, and in London at the Drury Lane Theatre in 1783, opening his second season at Drury Lane in the same role. In 1803, for his first appearance at Covent Garden, where he had become an owner and manager, he again chose to appear in *Hamlet.*

Lawrence shows Kemble as Hamlet standing above the freshly dug grave awaiting Ophelia's body, the skull of Yorick, the court jester whom he had known and loved in his youth, in his hand. The gravedigger has just uncovered the skull and gives it to the prince, who then addresses his remarks to his friend Horatio standing at his side. Lawrence, concentrating on the image of Kemble, excludes the other participants. He shows the melancholy Dane contemplating the vanity of earthly existence, alone, silhouetted against the dark sky, the sun low on the horizon. Kemble was famous for his long pauses, and it seems likely that he held such a meditative pose, his eyes looking heavenward, before launching into his speech, "Alas, poor Yorick! I knew him, Horatio; a fellow of infinite jest, of most excellent fancy." The gentleman who first purchased the painting intended it for a church altarpiece, but his offer was refused by the bishop of the diocese.

The Folger painting is a reduced copy of the original, the second one Folger had purchased of this famous picture (see D37). The dealer Michelmore listed it in his sale catalogue as by Harlow, but even he hedged in the entry's text: "It is in all probability from the brush of that eminent artist, George Henry Harlowe, and was doubtless painted in Lawrence's studio soon after Sir Thomas had finished the original." Harlow may well have copied Lawrence's picture, but this perfunctory copy is surely by another hand.

1. Kenneth Garlick, *Sir Thomas Lawrence: A Complete Catalogue of the Oil Paintings,* Oxford, 1989, p. 216.

Thomas Lawrence, manner of

116
**MACREADY [?] IN THE
CHARACTER OF A KING**
ca. 1820s
Oil on canvas, 30 × 25 in. (76.2 × 63.4 cm.)

Annotated at lower left in gold paint: "J. Opie" (the varnish layer has not been removed in the area of the "signature").

Provenance: Collection of Evert Jansen Wendell; his sale, American Art Galleries, 21 October 1919, lot 4853, $148, as a painting of Edmund Kean in the character of Richard III by J. Opie

Condition: The painting has been previously lined with a wax-resin-like adhesive to a canvas of similar tabby weave.

The earlier identification of the figure as Kean as Richard III seems unlikely and the original attribution to Opie untenable. It is plausible, however, that this is the portrait of an actor in the role of a king, possibly William Charles Macready (see no. 119), judging from the similarity of the sitter's features to images such as John Jackson's *Portrait of Macready as Macbeth* (fig. 75).

John Lewis, after

Lewis, though apparently an English artist, spent most of his career in Ireland. He was a scene

116

Fig. 75. John Jackson, *Portrait of Macready as Macbeth*. From the RSC Collection, with the permission of the Governors of the Royal Shakespeare Theatre ©.

painter at Smock Alley Theatre in Dublin from 1750 to 1757, when Thomas Sheridan was the manager. He is, however, best known as a portrait painter; his earliest dated portrait was executed in 1740 and his latest in 1769.

117

MARGARET "PEG" WOFFINGTON
ca. 1753
Oil on canvas, 30 × 25 in. (76.4 × 63.5 cm.)

Provenance: Collection of Augustin Daly (on exhibit in Daly's Theatre in New York); Daly sale, Anderson Galleries, 27 November 1912, lot 54, as by Jackson, repr., $115 plus 10 percent commission, Smith acting as agent

Exhibitions: Washington, 1976–77, no. 29, as by Artist Unknown, formerly attributed to John Lewis

References: New York Times, 28 November 1912; Fink 1959, p. 213

Condition: Lined by Finlayson in 1932 and restored in 1953.

Versions: The National Gallery of Ireland has a portrait by Lewis of Peg Woffington signed and dated at the lower left of the painted oval: "Jn Lewis April 1753." It is approximately the same size (29 × 24 in.) as the Folger canvas and was purchased in London at Christie's in 1907, having been put up for sale by a Mr. Barrett of Temora, Frankfort, Queen's Co. In 1913, Walter G. Strickland recorded an identical portrait, also signed and dated 1753, as being in the possession of Mrs. Agar, Stanton House, Highworth, Wiltshire. In 1905 W. J. Lawrence described as the original portrait a work in which the hat and cloak are dove-colored. This picture was then in the possession of a Dalkey lady (Lawrence, "A Mysterious Woffington Portrait," *Connoisseur* 11 [February 1905], p. 83). The Royal Dublin Society also owns an unsigned and undated copy of the portrait which was bequeathed to it early in the nineteenth century by Thomas Pleasant as by Reynolds. Lawrence first described the hat and cloak in this picture as dark blue ("The Real Peg Woffington," *Connoisseur* 8 [January 1904], p. 44) and later as green ("A Mysterious Woffington Portrait," p. 83); The National Portrait Gallery, London, acquired a portrait signed and dated 1753, which was sold at Christie's, 25 May 1984, lot 118.

Engravings after original: Mezzotint by Michael Jackson, reverses composition (this is presumably the source of the attribution to Jackson in the 1912 sale catalogue).

Margaret Woffington was born in Dublin around 1714. Her father received a pauper's burial in 1720, and her mother supported the family by hawking fruits and vegetables. She first performed at the Smock Alley Theatre in Dublin on 12 April 1737 as Ophelia. Other roles followed, including in 1740 what was to prove to be her most popular characterization, that of Sir Harry Wildair in *The Constant Couple*. She first appeared in London at the Covent Garden Theatre on 6 November 1740 and in the next year was engaged at Drury Lane. In the three seasons 1751 to 1754, she performed again in Dublin. It was during that time that Lewis painted her portrait, and he also executed a portrait, dated to the same year, of Thomas Sheridan, the theater's manager (now in the National Portrait Gallery, Lon-

117

don). Woffington was back in London in the fall of 1754. Her health already in decline, she collapsed in a performance given on 3 May 1757. It was to be her last, though she did not die until 28 March 1760.

Woffington has been described as one of the most beautiful actresses of the English theater, and her powers to captivate did not end at her death. Augustin Daly (1838–99), the American playwright and producer, was enamored of her, publishing a privately printed biography in 1888. The Folger picture was one of several in his collection.[1] He wrote of Woffington's appearance:

Probably none of the portraits painted of her by contemporaneous artists, famous or obscure, render absolute justice to the charms of Woffington. In most of them . . . we may discover the dreamy yet laughing black eyes, with their gracefully pencilled arched brows, the aquiline and delicately moulded nose, the well rounded coquettish chin; the pouting witchery of the ever-parted lips, the wonderful lithe and willowy figure, the slender hand and taper fingers for which she was noted. She wore her hair without powder, brushed carelessly back to expose the white forehead, nearly always with a

Fig. 76. John Lewis, *Margaret Woffington*, 1753. Oil on canvas, 30 × 25 in. National Portrait Gallery, London.

cap thrown gracefully on her head, or a lithe flat garden hat worn negligently, as we see her in most of the mezzotints of John Faber, of Michael Jackson and of James McArdell.[2]

The portraits in the National Gallery of Ireland and in the National Portrait Gallery, London (fig. 76), are securely attributed to Lewis, although they differ slightly from one another, particularly in the backgrounds. The Folger picture, in its turn, differs from both of these works but is closest in its details to the National Portrait Gallery picture. More prosaic in its rendering, it is still a satisfying transcription of Lewis's conception.

1. In the first Daly sale of 1900, two other portraits of Peg Woffington were sold: Augustin Daly sale, American Art Galleries, 19–21 (19) March 1900, lot 724, Portrait of Peg Woffington by Hogarth from the collection of Lord Lonsdale; and lot 728, Portrait of Peg Woffington, attributed to Hogarth. These two paintings are perhaps the ones listed in Fink 1959, p. 212. One of them also may have been the work sold at the Fifth Avenue Auction Rooms, 10–13 (13) 1909, lot 901, as "Portrait in oil—Peg Woffington, from the Augustin Daly sale."
2. Augustin Daly, *Woffington: A Tribute to the Actress and the Woman*, 2 vols., New York, 1888, vol. 1, p. 15.

James McArdell, attributed to

McArdell was one of the greatest mezzotint engravers of the eighteenth century. Born in Dublin in 1728 or 1729, he settled in London in 1746. While he did engrave a few works after his own designs, most of his prints were reproductive, and he is particularly well known for his prints after portraits by Sir Joshua Reynolds. He died on 1 June 1765, when he was only thirty-seven years old.

118

JAMES QUIN AS FALSTAFF
I Henry IV II, 4
ca. 1750
Oil on canvas, 21 × 15½ in. (53.3 × 39.5 cm.)

Inscribed on paper at lower left: "Capon 2.4 / Sack 7.0 / Bread .½"

Provenance: Anderson, March 1911, $150, as by Hayman (receipt is in C Deck correspondence)

References: New York, 1964, mentioned in entry no. 41 as by McArdell; Highfill 1973–, vol. 12, p. 241 (no. 16), as by McArdell

Condition: The primary support is a tabby-weave canvas, from which the tacking edges have been cut off. In 1932 Finlayson glue-lined the original canvas onto a commercially prepared ground. Falstaff's hat has been damaged and extensively repainted.

Version: What was described as "an amateur copy" either after the Folger picture or McArdell's mezzotint was owned by the American Shakespeare Festival Theatre by 1964. It was sold at Sotheby Parke Bernet on 15 January 1976, lot 142.

Born in London on 24 February 1692/93, James Quin spent part of his childhood in Ireland. He first performed on stage in Dublin and was performing in London as early as 1715. He was to remain a commanding figure even after the appearance of Garrick, whose style of acting dated his own. His most popular role was Falstaff. Retiring at the end of the 1750–51 season, Quin returned to act Falstaff in *I Henry IV* in two benefits for a friend, in 1752 and 1753. He died at Bath on 21 January 1766.

When Folger purchased *James Quin as Falstaff* it was said to be by Francis Hayman. However, as early as the 1932 appraisal of the collection, the painting was attributed to McArdell, presumably

118

because the second state of the print reproducing this subject bears the inscription, "J. McArdell delin. et fecit" (fig. 77).[1] Yet, the attribution of the painting to McArdell must remain tentative, as there are no known pictures securely attributed to him with which the Folger painting can be compared. In addition, the Folger picture is not identical with the print.

McArdell had published his print of Quin as Falstaff by 1751,[2] and the picture probably dates to

this same time. Yet, the conception was not a new one. John Laguerre had published an etching *The Stage Mutiny* in 1733 in which he showed the actor John Harper as Falstaff in the same pose and in a similar costume. Hayman's conception of Falstaff in *Falstaff's Cowardice Detected* (see fig. 32) is in the same vein, and the colors worn by Hayman's Falstaff in *Falstaff Reviewing His Recruits* (no. 37) are identical to those worn by Quin as Falstaff in the Folger picture. This conception proved so pop-

Fig. 77. James McArdell, *Mr. Quin in the Character of Sir John Falstaff*. Mezzotint. Harvard Theatre Collection.

ular that it continued to appear in a variety of contexts: Patrick O'Brian used it in his print *The Theatrical Steel-Yards of 1750*, published on 27 April 1751; it was used as a design for china numerous times beginning around 1750; and it even appears on a playing card of 1757, as the design of Thomas Foubert.[3] McArdell, however, was the first to isolate Falstaff. Yet, his Falstaff is hardly alone. Looking directly outward, he now blusters just for the viewer.

1. The second state of the print, published by Robert Sayer, is posthumous. The first state, published by McArdell, did not identify the artist or engraver.
2. *James Quin as Falstaff* was advertised for sale in Ireland, along with other of McArdell's prints just imported from London, in *Faulkner's Journal* for September 1751.
3. Raymond Mander and Joe Mitchenson illustrate and discuss many of these works in their article "The China Statuettes of Quin as Falstaff," *Theatre Notebook* 12 (Winter 1958), pp. 54–58. Foubert's playing card, the five of spades, is inscribed, "Invt. et Delin. Londini Thos. Foubert 1757" (an impression is in the FSL, ART Vol. d94, no. 91b).

John Neagle, after

Neagle, a Philadelphia portrait painter and son-in-law of Thomas Sully, was born in Boston on 4 November 1796, when his parents were visiting that city. Interested in painting from an early age, he attended a drawing school operated by Pietro Ancora and was apprenticed when he was fourteen to Thomas Wilson, a coach and ornamental painter. Later he took lessons from the portraitist Bass Otis, who had arrived in Philadelphia from New York in 1812. By 1817 Neagle was listed in the city directory as a portrait painter, but, leaving briefly in search of patronage, he traveled as far away as New Orleans before returning in 1819 to settle permanently in Philadelphia. In 1826, he married one of Sully's stepdaughters, and his art—not surprisingly, given Sully's preeminent position in his hometown—was influenced by that of his father-in-law. His first great success was his painting *Pat Lyon at His Forge*, which he exhibited at the Pennsylvania Academy in 1827. A respected member of the Philadelphia art community, Neagle died on 17 September 1865, having suffered from paralysis for a number of years.

119
WILLIAM C. MACREADY AS MACBETH
After 1827
Oil on canvas, 30 × 25 in. (76 × 63.4 cm.)

Case no. 828

Provenance: Collection of Evert Jansen Wendell; his sale, American Art Galleries, 21 October 1919, lot 4859, $12, as "Attributed to Naegel"

Condition: Finlayson lined the canvas in 1932.

Engraving after original: Asher B. Durand, published by Thomas T. Ash, Philadelphia, 1827

William Charles Macready, born in 1793 in London, was the son of an Irish actor and manager. His stage debut came in Birmingham on 7 June 1810, and he first performed in London at Covent Garden on 16 September 1816. He traveled to America on three occasions, arriving on his first trip in September 1826. It was during this stay that John Neagle painted his portrait in his favorite role as Macbeth. On his third trip to America in 1848, Macready was not so well received. Accusations by the American

119

actor Edwin Forrest that Macready had conspired against him when Forrest had performed in London led to the worst riot in theater history. On 10 May 1849, a xenophobic mob, numbering around fifteen thousand, surrounded the theater where Macready was performing. Troops had to be called out to restore order, and a number of the rioters were killed in the fighting. Macready was again appearing as Macbeth in this, his last American performance. The actor retired from the London stage in 1851 and died in 1873.

In 1826 Neagle executed a series of sixteen portraits of actors in character for Francis Courtney Wemyss, an actor-manager, and Mr. Lopez, a prompter, which were engraved for A. R. Poole's *The Acting American Theatre.*[1] The present whereabouts of Neagle's portrait of Macready is unknown, but the crudely painted Folger work, which shows Macready posed before a stone wall and wearing a green tartan, is presumably after the 1827 print.

1. See the catalogue for Montgomery, 1985–86.

Robert Edge Pine

The son of a prominent engraver, Pine was born in London probably as early as the 1720s. In 1760 and again in 1763 he won first prize at the (Royal) Society of Arts, in both cases for works drawn from British history. Despite such successes, he was not a founding member of the Royal Academy, and his quarrelsome nature led him to resign from the Society of Artists in 1772. On his brother's death that same year, he moved to Bath, returning to London in 1780. Pine exhibited at the Society of Artists from its foundation in 1760 until he fell out with its president in 1771. He then exhibited at the Royal Academy in 1772, 1780, and 1784. His exhibited works covered a range of genres, including history painting. The majority, however, were portraits; a number of these were theatrical portraits, and those which were engraved proved popular. He held a one-man exhibition of Shakespearean painting in the Great Room at Spring Gardens in 1782. Finding his talents insufficiently appreciated and being sympathetic to the American cause, he moved to the United States in 1784. Settling in Philadelphia, he was highly prolific in his last few years, attempting a series of works depicting scenes from the American Revolution. He died on 12 November 1788. Many of his paintings were destroyed in a fire in 1803 in Bowen's Columbian Museum in Boston.

120 (Plate 22)

DAVID GARRICK
ca. 1780
Oil on canvas, oval, 29¾ × 24⅝ in. (75.5 × 62.6 cm.)

Case no. 1372

Provenance: Collection of Arthur Tooth; his sale, American Art Galleries, 19 February 1925, lot 24, $320 plus 10 percent commission, Rosenbach acting as agent

References: Anglesea 1971, p. 194

Exhibitions: Pine exhibited a portrait of Garrick at the Royal Academy in 1780 (no. 82), possibly the Folger picture.

Condition: The painting has been lined and attached to an oval stretcher. The impasto was flattened in a past lining, and the paint surface also suffers from solvent-abrasion and overpainting.

Versions: Portraits of Garrick by Pine of varying degrees of quality are numerous. They range from the simple bust in an oval at the Elizabethan Club in New Haven (27 × 21½ in.) to more elaborate compositions such as the one at the National Portrait Gallery, London (fig. 79). The Folger painting, however, is the only one I have seen in which Garrick is shown holding a book with fluttering pages. The closest image to it is a portrait (27 × 22 in.) sold at Sotheby on 14 February 1962, lot 172, showing Garrick positioned as he is in the Folger painting but wearing an open-neck shirt and holding in his right hand an opened book whose page is labeled "MAC-BETH." The hand is unobtrusively positioned at the lower edge of the composition and the book lacks the animation of the one in the Folger picture. For a list of Pine portraits of Garrick, see Anglesea 1971, pp. 193–95. Robert Stewart's file on Pine at the National Portrait Gallery, Washington, mentions additional works at the Huntington Library and Art Gallery, the New York Public Library, and the New-York Historical Society. Graves, in *A Century of Loan Exhibitions,* also records a portrait from Christ Church, Oxford, exhibited in 1906, and Gulian C. Verplanck published a portrait in 1857, then belonging to A. M. Cozzens, that possibly is to be identified with one of the above works (see *Garrick: His Portrait in New York, Its Artist and History,* New York, 1857). This work, with Garrick's left hand pressed to his breast, is identical in type to one in the Garrick Club.

While Pine surely found a responsive market for his pictures of Garrick, the frequency with which he painted the actor suggests a fascination that went beyond simple economics. Pine shared Garrick's passion for Shakespeare, having exhibited numerous paintings from the plays at Spring Gardens in London in 1782 and again in 1784 in Philadelphia in what was the first one-man art exhibition to be held in America. Pine painted Garrick at least twice in character: as Don Felix in *The Wonder,* dated 1777 and now in the Garrick Club, and as Jaques in *As You Like It,* exhibited at the Royal Academy in 1780. On 4 April 1779, shortly after the actor's death, he published a print of his death mask, to which he added the eyes. In addition, he commemorated his retirement in a canvas entitled *Mr. Garrick's Resigning the Stage,*[1] and executed a monumental allegorical picture, 8 by 7 feet, of Garrick speaking his ode to Shakespeare to a statue of the Bard surrounded by various figures from the

Fig. 78. After Robert Edge Pine, *David Garrick Speaking the Ode to Shakespeare.* Engraving by Caroline Watson, 1 March 1783, 24¼ × 17⅝ in.

plays, a work now known from the engraving after it (fig. 78).

Pine also painted a portrait of Garrick (fig. 79), engraved as early as 1776,[2] in which the actor is shown seated at a table, a copy of *Macbeth* held in his left hand and his right clenched and held close to his heart as he looks off into the distance in rapt meditation. Anglesea has called this image "the most overtly 'romantic' of the non-theatrical portraits of Garrick,"[3] and it is this head on which the majority of the other portraits are based, including the large picture where the actor speaks his ode.

The many portraits of Garrick based on this image vary enormously in quality, so much so that Robert Stewart suspects that Pine's daughters helped in the manufacture of the weaker ones. The Folger version is perhaps the finest, a bravura performance that on grounds of quality has the best claim to be the picture exhibited at the Royal Academy in 1780. Executed in an oval, it simplifies the design of the earlier 1776 picture, editing out the chair and the table with its contents. Garrick is shown with piercing, brown eyes, his face a model of intense concentration. He holds an unspecified text in his right hand, its agitated pages taking on a life of their own. The pamphlet's vivid three-dimensional presence, its fluttering pages also conveying the idea of winged thought, pushes the sitter, who is clad in a dark plum-colored coat, into the background. A critic who signed himself "M. M." complained of the earlier portrait that Pine, "whose greatest defect was ill-drawing, painted and engraved Garrick humpback, and though told in time determined to let him go so."[4] The softening of the outline of the sitter's left shoulder and the extension of the right in the Folger picture mitigates the fault found in the National Portrait Gallery painting.

1. This picture and Garrick speaking his ode were in the lottery of Pine's work held in 1789, an advertisement for which is reproduced in Robert G. Stewart's exhibition catalogue *Robert Edge Pine: A British Portrait Painter in America, 1784–1788*, National Portrait Gallery, Washington, 1979, p. 117.
2. The print by W. Dickinson was published in 1778, but a proof is dated 1 December 1776.
3. Anglesea 1971, p. 100.
4. Quoted in William T. Whitley, *Thomas Gainsborough*, London, 1915, p. 189.

Fig. 79. Robert Edge Pine, *David Garrick*. Oil on canvas, 35 × 28 in. National Portrait Gallery, London.

Sir Joshua Reynolds, studio of

121

DAVID GARRICK
ca. 1776–79

Case no. 2039

Oil on canvas, 29½ × 24¼ in. (75 × 61.5 cm.)

Inscribed at the top of the paper facing Garrick: "Prologue"

Provenance: Belonged in 1779 to Sir Thomas Mills (according to Graves and Cronin); the marquess of Lansdowne, Lansdowne House, Berkeley Square, London; Lansdowne sale, Christie's, 7 March 1930, lot 65, 950 guineas plus 10 percent commission (£1097.5.0), as by Reynolds, Wells acting as agent

Exhibitions (always exhibited as by Reynolds): London, British Institution, *Catalogue of Pictures by Italian, Spanish, Flemish, Dutch, French, and English Masters*, 1861, no. 148; London, 1869, no. 607; Birmingham, Museum and Art Gallery, *Loan Collection of Portraits by Sir Joshua Reynolds, Thomas Gainsborough . . . and Other Artists*, 1900, no. 17; Amherst, *Shakespeare*, 1951 (a photograph of this last exhibition confirms it was this picture and not no. 122 or no. 135 that was on loan)

References: G. F. Waagen, *Treasures of Art in Great Britain*, London, 1854, vol. 2, p. 152, "The portrait of Garrick is very characteristic"; Charles Robert Leslie and Tom Taylor, *Life and Times of Sir Joshua Reynolds*, London, 1865, vol. 2, pp. 149–50, "Sir Joshua had very lately finished his portrait of Garrick for the Thrale Gallery—the head now in the Lansdowne Gallery, with the thumbs placed together, and the bright speaking face, with its lambent eyes turned full on the spectator"; Algernon Graves and William Vine Cronin, *A History of the Works of Sir Joshua Reynolds*, London, 1899, vol. 1, p. 348; Sir Walter Armstrong, *Sir Joshua Reynolds*, London and New York, 1900, p. 207; Wayne C. Smith, "Folger Shakespeare Library Exhibit at Amherst College," *The Springfield Sunday Republican*, 25 February 1951, as "now thought to be a copy of Reynold's [sic] portrait by either Copley or Stuart"; letter from Charles Morgan to Louis Wright, 13 March 1951, in "Loan File," FSL (quoted in text); Fink 1959, p. 64; Anglesea 1971, p. 203;

Highfill 1973–, vol. 6, p. 85 (no. 42); Stone and Kahrl 1979, repr. p. 637; Burnim 1984, p. 208, repr. p. 210

Condition: In a letter of 13 March 1951 to Louis B. Wright, the Folger's director, Charles Morgan, who had mounted an exhibition at the Mead Art Museum, wrote that three of the paintings borrowed from the Folger had been in the most precarious condition and were relined and completely cleaned. The Reynolds portrait was one of these works. In contrast to the original, the bottom edge of the table projects forward near the center, forming a corner, rather than extending across the entire front parallel to the picture plane. This would seem to be the result of the canvas having been pulled here by the tacking, a distortion that was reinforced by the addition of highlights. There is a broad patch of white paint beneath the word "Prologue" that may also have been added.

Original painting: Painted for the Thrales and exhibited at the Royal Academy in 1776; sold at Christie's, 24 November 1972, lot 140, bought by Lawson

Related works: A replica that was presented to the third duke of Dorset in 1780 is at Knole. In addition to the two works at the Folger are ones in the National Portrait Gallery, London; the Garrick Club;

121

the Hereford City Museum; and the collection of the late Lord Olivier (see Highfill 1973–, vol. 6, pp. 85–86 [no. 42]).

Engravings after original: Mezzotint by Thomas Watson, 14³⁄₄ × 11 in., published by Watson and Dickinson, 1779. This was the first of many. A list is given in Highfill 1973–, vol. 6, p. 86. Graves and Cronin incorrectly list the prints as being after the Lansdowne version.

Reynolds knew Garrick well, even writing a biographical sketch of his famous contemporary. He admired the actor but was highly critical of the man, feeling Garrick had sacrificed too much in the pursuit of shallow fame. After characterizing him as "unfit for the cultivation of private friendship," Reynolds continued, "Garrick died without a real friend, though no man had a greater number of what the world calls friends. Garrick had no friends to whom he gave orders that he was always at home, except to his doctors, of which he had two sorts, one sort administering for his body, the other for his diseased mind—in other words, his vanity. The first were generally quacks and the others sycophants."[1] The artist created four different conceptions of Garrick, painting him first in the allegorical portrait *Garrick between Tragedy and Comedy,* exhibited at the Society of Artists in 1762, then in character in 1768 as Kitely in Ben Jonson's play *Every Man in His Humor,* next in a portrait with his wife exhibited at the Royal Academy in 1773, and finally in a portrait painted for the Thrales' library at Stretham (fig. 80). The Folger picture is a version of this last work.

The Thrale portrait, which was exhibited at the Royal Academy in 1776, was one of thirteen that Reynolds executed for Henry and Hester Thrale, a series that included portraits of other illustrious contemporaries such as Samuel Johnson, Oliver Goldsmith, Edmund Burke, and the artist himself. Reynolds's final portrait of Garrick shows him seated at a desk looking out reflectively, his hands folded over a sheet of paper on which "Prologue" has been written across the top. Earlier Hogarth had depicted Garrick in a canvas, now in Her Majesty's Collection, pausing over a prologue he is writing for Samuel Foote's play *Taste* while his wife playfully comes from behind to snatch away his pen. Reynolds, however, does not show Garrick writing a specific prologue, nor in fact does he show him

Fig. 80. Sir Joshua Reynolds, *David Garrick,* RA 1776. Photograph: A. C. Cooper.

writing at all. Garrick's last performance was given on 10 June 1776, shortly after the Thrale portrait had been exhibited at the Royal Academy in the spring. The portrait commemorates an ending instead of a beginning. Reynolds may well have had in mind Shakespeare's phrase, "what's past is prologue" (*The Tempest* II, 1), and, if so, he must have relished the irony that in this case the illustrious past leads only to unproductive retirement.[2] The sitter's decision to embark on this new phase of his life renders him mute as both an author and actor.

The Folger picture has a distinguished pedigree, taking it back to 1779, and sometimes has even been confused with the Thrale portrait. Only once has this painting been challenged as not being by Reynolds. In 1951, when the portrait was on loan for an exhibition at Amherst College, Charles Morgan, the exhibition's organizer, wrote Wright, the Folger's director, "The one certain thing is that it cannot be by Reynolds, but suggests either the hand of Stuart or Copley when they were both newly arrived in England and very probably employed in the Reynolds' atelier." The attribution to Stuart or Copley is fanciful, but I share Morgan's doubts that the picture is entirely by Sir Joshua. It is a drier, more pedestrian rendering than the Thrale original, but, given its provenance, surely came out of the artist's studio and involved his participation. It differs from its model in that the overall impression is less elegant and more stolid. The hands, rotated toward the sitter, show more fingers and deemphasize the decorative pattern of the negative space formed by the juxtaposed thumbs. The sitter's gaze is more focused as he invites contact with the viewer: the pensive man in his study has given way to a more receptive and convivial one.

1. *Portraits by Sir Joshua Reynolds,* with introduction and notes by Frederick W. Hilles, Melbourne, London, and Toronto, 1952, p. 87.
2. It should be remembered that "what's past is prologue" occurs in a negative context in Shakespeare as well. It forms part of Antonio's appeal to Sebastian to kill his own brother.

Sir Joshua Reynolds, after

122

DAVID GARRICK
Early nineteenth century
Oil on canvas, 12 × 10 in. (30.5 × 25.5 cm.)

Case no. 1389

Inscribed at top of the paper facing Garrick: "Prologue"

Provenance: Robson through Wells, October 1924, £100. In a letter of 10 September 1924 to Gabriel Wells, Robson & Co. Ltd. claims that this painting was sold at Christie's early in 1901 (May given in a later note) and that the lot number is on the old strainer.

References: Anglesea 1971, p. 205, as a copy; Highfill 1973–, vol. 7, p. 85, n. 42, as a copy

Condition: The canvas has never been lined.

Related works: See no. 121.

This is a crude copy, presumably after one of the many prints reproducing Reynolds's Thrale portrait (see fig. 80). While Folger apparently accepted Robson & Company's description of it as "a fine and genuine portrait," its authenticity was challenged from the beginning of the Library's history: the 1932 appraisal of the collection listed it as only at-

122

tributed to Reynolds. Even this nomenclature is too optimistic. Reynolds had nothing to do with this poor work.

Alfred Roffe

The painting is signed "A. Roffe," and when Michelmore sold this picture to Folger, he gave the artist's name as "A. J. Roffe," mentioning that he exhibited at the Royal Academy in 1845. There is no such artist listed in any of the academy's exhibitions, and perhaps Michelmore was thinking of William John Roffe, who at least has "J" as a middle initial and did exhibit a picture in 1845. A. Roffe is surely the Alfred Roffe who exhibited a study at the Society of British Artists in 1879 (no. 454). In the catalogue he is listed at a London address: 18 Giesbach Road, Upper Holloway. Christopher Wood also mentions that an Alfred F. Roffe exhibited six landscapes from 1872 to 1883.[1] In this last year Alfred Roffe also exhibited at the Royal Institute of Oil Painters, and his address is given as c/o Thames Side, Windsor, Berkshire. Roffe appears to have been from a family of artists, but little is known about any of its members,[2] a particularly surprising omission in his case, given the ambitious size of the Folger canvas. Yet, many of the painting's elements, such as the figures' hands, are awkwardly rendered, and it is possible that for Roffe, painting was more a hobby than a profession.

1. Christopher Wood, *The Dictionary of Victorian Painters*, Woodbridge, Suffolk, 2d ed., 1978. Wood does not say where the works were exhibited, but they did not appear in the main exhibitions held at the Royal Academy, the British Institution, or the Royal Society of British Artists.

2. There is a reproductive engraving of a seventeenth-century portrait of a woman in the British Museum Print Room signed "Alfred Roffe Sc." (folder c.18*). The manuscript catalogue gives the engraver's year of birth as 1769, too early for the painter of the Folger canvas. In addition, there is an Alfred T. Roffe who was described as a miniature painter in the Royal Academy catalogue of 1822 and exhibited a work of unspecified medium in the 1829 exhibition of the Society of British Artists. In *Art Sales*, Graves lists him as flourishing from 1822 until 1859 (Graves 1918–21, vol. 3, p. 82).

123

MACBETH'S MURDER OF DUNCAN
Macbeth II, 2
ca. 1888
Oil on canvas, 51½ × 71½ in. (131.7 × 181.5 cm.)

Case no. 1705

Signed in black at lower left: "A. ROFFE" (the signature is below the line at the bottom where the canvas at one time was folded back and used as a tacking edge).

Provenance: Michelmore, August 1927, £75

Exhibitions: Amherst, *Shakespeare*, 1951, as "The Murder of the Grooms"

Condition: In 1932 Finlayson glue-lined this work onto a commercially prepared canvas with a ground. It appears that at some time the bottom edge of the original canvas was folded back about

123

two inches and used as a tacking edge. Olin wrote in 1985, "The design of the impasto underneath does not coincide with the present painting, indicating there may be an entire painting beneath." This seems unlikely, but there are passages where pentimenti are clearly visible, demonstrating that certain details have been altered. For example, the legs of the stool have been thinly painted over those of the sleeping guard at left so that a double image is now present.

Sir Henry Irving was the greatest actor-manager since David Garrick and the first actor to be knighted, an indication of how far the theater had come in terms of respectability. He was born John Henry Brodribb on 6 February 1838 at Keinton Mandeville in Somerset, his family moving to London when he was ten. He first performed professionally in 1856 but did not achieve prominence as an actor until 1871, when appearing in *The Bells* at the Lyceum Theatre in London. He is best remembered for his reign there as actor-manager from 1878 to 1903, with Ellen Terry as his leading lady. Irving demanded absolute control over his productions, his cast having to fit within his overall conception of a play. He always had his critics, many objecting to his idiosyncratic mannerisms and his peculiar pronunciation, but he also had a mesmerizing power that overshadowed his technical deficiencies. In his last years he suffered financial difficulties and died on 13 October 1905 in Bradford while on a farewell tour. As befitting his stature, he was buried in Westminster Abbey.

Irving followed his successful portrayal of Hamlet, his first Shakespearean role at the Lyceum, with Macbeth, which opened on 25 September 1875. This production, though running for 80 performances, received a poor critical reception. Irving next performed *Macbeth* in a production opening on 25 December 1888. Running for 151 performances, it came in for much of the same criticism. Irving rejected the usual interpretation of Macbeth as a bold warrior, undermined by witches and an evil wife, in favor of a more flawed character, one who himself conceives the murder of Duncan and whose conduct is craven and weak. A caricature of Irving as Macbeth (fig. 81) captures a sense of the physical extravagance of his interpretation.[1] The 1888 production was distinguished for the lavishness of its costumes and sets. Care was taken

to research materials in the Victoria and Albert Museum and the British Museum to recreate the world of eleventh-century Scotland. Charles Cattermole worked on the costumes and properties, and Hawes Craven was the principal scenic artist. Two contemporary illustrations (figs. 82 and 83) give a sense of the ambitious scope of their collaboration.

Roffe's painting was presumably inspired by Irving's 1888 production. The skulking figure of Macbeth, who looks like an understudy for the hunchback of Notre Dame, has Irving's angular physique and bony features, though not the mustache he wore in both the 1875 and 1888 productions. The large cavernous space, with its massive pillars and Romanesque arches, is reminiscent of Craven's 1888 sets, and the dramatic lighting would seem to be influenced by Irving's innovations in stage lighting, the actor's effects often being described as Rembrandtesque.

MR. HENRY IRVING AS "MACBETH."

Fig. 81. *Caricature of Sir Henry Irving as Macbeth.* Colored wood engraving, 7 × 4½ in. (image).

Fig. 82. J. Jellicoe and H. Railton, *"Macbeth" at the Lyceum Theatre.* Wood engraving by J. Swain in the *Illustrated Sporting and Dramatic News,* 5 January 1889.

While Roffe's painting is indebted to Irving's 1888 production, it is in no way a record of that performance. Shakespeare has Duncan murdered offstage, and Sir Edward R. Russell's review leaves no doubt that Irving did as well:

But of all the scenes the most effective is the court of Macbeth's castle [see fig. 82], where he sees the air-drawn dagger, and where practically the central tragedy of the play is performed, though with great art kept out of sight of the audience. It is of irregular construction, built in the style wherein Norman architecture began to put on decoration, but fully retained its rounded masses and rugged strength. . . . On the left is a round tower-like structure suggestive of a spiral stairway. Against this Lady Macbeth leans her back restlessly while the murder is in progress.[2]

Outside the theater there is a pictorial tradition of showing Macbeth murdering Duncan that dates back to the eighteenth century. Macbeth is usually seen approaching the sleeping king or departing from his corpse.[3] One example, close in time to Roffe's picture, is a watercolor (fig. 84) by Charles Cattermole, the designer of Irving's costumes.[4] Roffe's conception combines the two traditions, that of the theater with that of history painting, in effect imagining what Irving's staging might have looked like if extended to this scene.

The canvas is thinly painted in parts, particularly in the upper corners, and patchy networks of closely juxtaposed colors, as in the hanging shield, enliven its surface. Curtains hang from the massive pillars, and through the archway on the left the space opens up to reveal another vaulted chamber, a massive pillar in its center. Macbeth's purple garment is similar in color to the king's ermine-lined robe, a reference to his usurpation of the throne. Surrounded by his spotlighted victims and pushed to the back of an ominous void, Macbeth is himself menaced by his unholy act.

1. This caricature is dated ca. 1888 in *Shakespeare: The Globe and the World* (see San Francisco, 1979–82, p. 171, no. 13) and 1875 in Ashton 1990, p. 126.
2. Quoted from Austin Brereton, *The Life of Henry Irving,* New York and London, 1969 (reprint of 1908 edition), p. 143. The review was first published in the *Liverpool Daily Post.*
3. The earliest image of Macbeth murdering Duncan occurs in Henry Fuseli's drawing, executed in Rome ca. 1777–78, showing a number of scenes drawn from the play (see Schiff 1973, no. 476). It appears several times in book illustrations. The first time is Henry Singleton's design for *The Shakespeare Gallery,* the print by C. Taylor bearing the publication date 1 June 1792 and the line, "I've done the deed:—did I not hear a noise?" Macbeth is again seen leaving the king's chamber in W. H. Worthington's image engraved for the Miniature Classics series in 1823. In a print by C. Rolls that would appear to be of around the same date, Henry Courbould shows Lady Macbeth in the foreground, with a glimpse in the background of Macbeth poised ready to strike the sleeping king. A print of Macbeth pausing before murdering Duncan by John Howard was published on 1 May 1827, and a scene of him enacting the murder by Moritz Retzsch appeared in 1833. In 1808 Benjamin Robert Haydon began work on a large painting, commissioned by Sir George Beaumont, showing Macbeth the instant before he murdered Duncan. This painting, now lost, was exhibited at the British Institution in 1812.
4. A version of this watercolor is at Stratford-upon-Avon. Because the scene does not occur in the play, it is incorrectly identified as *Banquo's Ghost* in the book *Pictures and Sculpture from the Royal Shakespeare Theatre Picture Gallery,* London, n.d.

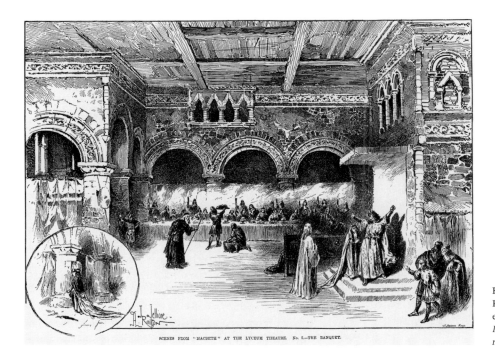

SCENES FROM "MACBETH" AT THE LYCEUM THEATRE. No. 5.—THE BANQUET.

Fig. 83. J. Jellicoe and H. Railton, *The Banquet*. Wood engraving by J. Swain in the *Illustrated Sporting and Dramatic News*, 5 January 1889.

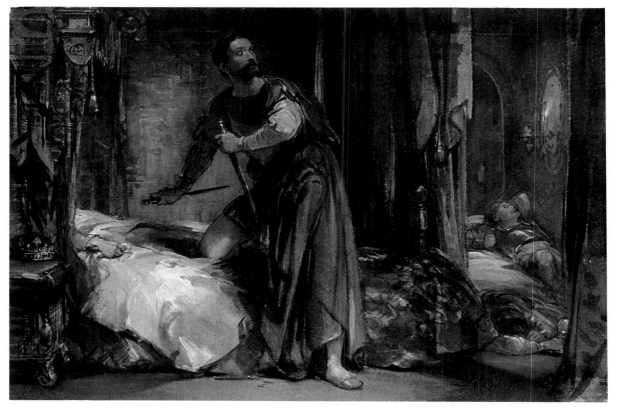

Fig. 84. Charles Cattermole, *The Murder of Duncan*. Watercolor, 8 × 11¾ in.

George Romney

124

JOHN HENDERSON AS MACBETH
Macbeth I, 3
ca. 1787
Oil on engraving mounted on canvas, 16¾ × 20½
in. (42.5 × 52 cm.)

Case no. 1727

Provenance: Montmartre Gallery, October 1927, $50, as "Charles Kean as Macbeth" by Thomas Stothard

Exhibitions: Washington, 1985, as George Romney's *John Henderson as Macbeth*

References: Northampton, Mass., Smith College Museum of Art, *The Drawings of George Romney,*

1962, pp. 26–27, as a small oil sketch that shows the whole of the original composition; Highfill 1973–, vol. 7, p. 262 (no. 39), as a version of the original canvas; Waterloo, 1985, catalogue, p. 62, as a replica on a small scale

Condition: Lined by Finlayson in 1932. When it was conserved in 1985, it was discovered that the paint had been applied over an engraving. In a raking light, the ridges of the engraved lines can be clearly seen in many passages of the painting.

Related works: Romney's painting of Henderson as Macbeth (54½ × 64½ in.) was won by W. J. Long in a raffle held for members of the Unincreasables Club after Henderson's death. This work was last recorded in the Long sale, Christie's, 28 June 1890, lot 116, 250 guineas. A smaller version (34½ × 27¼ in.), acquired from the Charles Mathews collection, is in the Garrick Club, London. Romney also appar-

124

ently executed Henderson as Macbeth as a single figure in several versions (this is assuming these works were not cut down). See Ward and Roberts 1904, p. 76; Highfill 1973–, vol 7., p. 262; and catalogue to Waterloo, 1985, no. 22. In a notation of April 1959 in the Folger file, Patricia Milne Henderson also lists a number of drawings related to this work: "There is probably an earlier composition sketch for this subject in the Witt Collection Romney sketch-book No. 1848 fol. 30, there two of the witches are about a cauldron. This composition is reversed on fols. 31 verso, 32, & 32 verso. In the Fitzwilliam Museum, Cambridge, there is 1. a sheet with pencil sketches for the portrait (L.D. 115) there in a series of 3 figure sketches Henderson first appears wearing a bonnet and then bare headed. The verso shows a composition sketch which includes the actor bare headed and the witches at the right. 2. a pencil sketch of the three witches (M.D. 27)."

Engravings after original: John Jones, 19 May 1787, 16¹/₈ × 19³/₄ in., first state in Fitzwilliam Museum, Cambridge (c.s. 37), published with full inscription on 1 December 1787. Smaller engravings also appeared: J. Hopwood's print to *The Cabinet*, 1807; Ino Kennerley's print to Oxberry's *Dramatic Biography*, 1826; and one published by Gebbie and Husson Co. Ltd. in 1888.

Romney and Henderson knew one another well, both belonging to the Unincreasables Club, which consisted only of eight members. Henderson sat to Romney five times in 1780,[1] but John Romney, the artist's son, writes that the picture of Henderson as Macbeth "was painted about the time when Thomas Sheridan and Henderson had their Public Readings."[2] These readings were given in Freemasons' Hall in the Lenten season of 1785, and thus this picture and no. 53 would both seem to have been inspired by Henderson's performance, as presumably *Macbeth* was one of the works he read. The painting was not a commissioned work, as it was eventually raffled at the Unincreasables, each member, including Romney, putting in ten guineas toward its purchase.[3]

John Romney described the painting as a Bolognese half-length,[4] a reference to Baroque paintings of the Bolognese school that bring the figures close to the picture plane, cutting them off above the knee. This allows for a close-up portrait of Hender-

son, and Banquo is enshrouded and pushed off to the left so that his figure does not intrude.

John Romney states that the witches were based on actual models: "The prototype of all Mr. Romney's visionary beings was nature." He identifies one of them: "Mr. Romney being present at one of those recitations [at Freemasons' Hall], was so forcibly struck with the countenance of a man staring with all his attention at Sheridan, that he could not refrain from studying it carefully as an appropriate representation of a witch's face; and having on his return home sketched it on canvas, he afterwards introduced it into the picture of Henderson."[5] Charles Mathews identified the other two witches as portraits of the actor Charles Macklin (1699–1797) and the writer "Anthony Pasquin," a pseudonym for John Williams (1761–1818).[6]

An engraving reproducing this painting was first published on 19 May 1787 (fig. 85), and the Folger picture is actually painted over an impression of this print. Certain details, such as the army in the background, have been entirely painted out. Given the vigor and strength of the overpainting, it seems likely that it was done by the artist himself. Obsessive reworking of subjects was typical of Romney's practice, and in this sketch he seems most interested in experimenting with dramatic lighting effects. The prophetic hand and head of the foremost witch are silhouetted against the apocalyptic glow of the setting sun, which is about to be overwhelmed by the darkening sky.

Romney must have felt a special sympathy for this image of his departed friend. Henderson was best known for his portrayals of Falstaff, his rotund features providing the necessary padding for the part, and Romney executed him in this role as well. But Henderson is transformed and ennobled in Romney's presentation of the actor as Macbeth. The artist was fascinated by this play, but one assumes so was the actor. In a book published the year after Henderson's death, John Ireland wrote that the actor's reading "comprehended all books upon apparitions, illusions of the devil, and visions,"[7] and the sale catalogue of Henderson's library supports this claim, as it contains numerous entries, often with more than one book, concerned with witchcraft, demonology, and magic.[8] Ireland suggests that this lifelong fascination arose from an incident that happened when Henderson was eight,

Fig. 85. After George Romney, *John Henderson as Macbeth*. Mezzotint by John Jones, 19 May 1787. By courtesy of the Trustees of the British Museum, London.

his brother ten. Their mother, deeply depressed, left the house one morning. When she had not returned by the evening, the two boys went in search of her. They became lost, but, after sitting down to cry, they saw a light. When they walked toward it, the light moved and, following it, they came to a body of water upon which it vanished. At that spot they found their mother lost in reflection. Presumably Henderson's belief in the supernatural was not unlike that of Shakespeare's audience: for him the witches in *Macbeth* were very real indeed.

1. The days on which Henderson is recorded as having sat to Romney are 13, 18, 24, 29 October and 23 December 1780.
2. Romney 1830, p. 166.
3. Ibid., p. 168. The exhibition catalogue *George Romney in Canada* (Waterloo, 1985) notes a reference to a 5-guinea subscription under the date 14 September 1786 (pp. 61–62).
4. Romney 1830, p. 166.
5. Ibid., pp. 166–67.
6. *Catalogue Raisonnée of Mr. Mathews's Gallery of Theatrical Portraits*, London, 1833, p. 23 (no. 52). Both Macklin and Williams were known for their difficult personalities, and one presumes that their inclusion as witches was not intended as flattery. The fact that all the witches are male conforms to one

stage tradition, although Romney does depict them as women in no. 53.
7. John Ireland, *Letters and Poems by the Late Mr. John Henderson with Anecdotes of his Life*, London, 1786, p. 272.
8. *A Catalogue of the Library of John Henderson, Esq.*, T. and J. Egerton, Booksellers, 20–25 February 1786, nos. 214–30, 365–86.

Thomas Sully

125 (Plate 23)
CHARLOTTE CUSHMAN
1843
Oil on canvas, 20¼ × 17¼ in. (51.4 × 44 cm.)

Accession no. 5055

Provenance: Commissioned by Charlotte Cushman; by descent to her nephew and adopted son, Edwin Charles Chusman; by descent to his wife; by descent to their son, Victor N. Cushman; by descent to his wife, who was the daughter of Sen. Joseph Benson Foraker of Ohio; gift of Mrs. Victor N. Cushman, 24 September 1936

Exhibitions: Washington, D.C., National Gallery of Art (now National Museum of American Art), National Museum Building, *Exhibition of Early American Paintings, Miniatures and Silver*, 5 December 1925–3 January 1926, no. 68

References: Leach 1970, p. 133, repr. following p. 178

Condition: A brown-paper tape covers the tacking edge, extending 3/16 inch over the front of the painting and 1½ inch over the back of the stretcher. "Thomas Sully, 1844" is written in pencil on this paper tape in the upper left corner. The work underwent restoration in 1953 and again in 1976.

Versions: Biddle and Fielding note that three portraits are listed in the artist's register. The first (no. 404) was begun on 1 March 1843 and finished on 27 April 1843; it is listed as a head (20 × 17 in.) and valued at $80. The second (no. 405) was painted for a Mrs. Gardette; after noting that it was begun on 28 June 1843, the register lists it as "Expunged." The third (no. 406) was the portrait painted for Mrs. Gardette in place of the one expunged; begun on 21 July 1843, it was finished on 29 July; a head, it was also valued at $80. The only other version known to have survived is owned by the Library Company of Philadelphia (20 × 17¼ in.).

Charlotte Cushman was the first American actress to achieve an international reputation. Born on 25 July 1816 in Boston, she first embarked on a career as a singer. When her voice failed at age nineteen during an appearance in New Orleans, she immediately turned to acting, performing successfully as Lady Macbeth. Engagements in New York and Albany followed, and in the 1842–43 season she was the leading actress and stage manager at the Walnut Street Theatre in Philadelphia. Encouraged by the English actor Macready, she determined to try her luck in London. Arriving in November 1844, she made her debut on 14 February 1845. After several productive years in London and the provinces, she returned to the United States in August 1849. Back in England in 1852, she announced her retirement, the first of many such farewells. From 1857 she alternated between living in America and living in Rome, and in the last years of her life she gave public readings in America, the last on 2 June 1875. She died in Boston on 17 February the following year.

Charlotte Cushman first met Sully in Philadelphia during the 1842–43 season. She may well have been introduced to him through their mutual friend, the actress Fanny Kemble, who had been painted by Sully numerous times. Soon Charlotte was an intimate friend of the family, and she and Rosalie, Sully's daughter who was two years younger, became the closest of friends. In 1843 Charlotte commissioned a portrait of herself, which Sully began on 1 March and completed on 27 April. The artist in his register mentions beginning a copy of this painting on 28 June 1843 for a Mrs. Gardette, but, having expunged this first effort, he completed his next attempt on 29 July. In addition to the Folger picture, there is a version of the portrait in the collection of the Library Company of Philadelphia. This last work was a bequest of 1892 of Anne Hampton Brewster, a friend of Charlotte Cushman from the 1840s in Philadelphia who, like the actress, later lived in Rome. The Folger portrait is the more dramatic of the two, its colors slightly more varied and providing greater contrast.

In correspondence to the Frick Art Reference Library, Mrs. Victor Cushman commented on the Folger painting, which was then still in her and her husband's possession:

The portrait we have of Charlotte Cushman by Sully was painted in Philadelphia about 1844 and was called by her "A Study." My husband's father was her nephew and also her adopted son and this portrait was always in Miss Cushman's home. My mother-in-law married Edwin Charles Cushman, the nephew, in 1863 and went to Rome to live with Miss Cushman.

They always occupied the same house—I mean the three lived together—until 1876 when Miss Cushman died. Mrs. Cushman prized this portrait very highly as she adored Miss Cushman.

Charlotte Cushman went to England to act in 1845 and she told my mother-in-law that she sat for this portrait a little before that.[1]

A tape on the painting's tacking edge is misleadingly inscribed, "Thomas Sully, 1844," but Mrs. Cushman's letter makes clear that this date was only approximate, as she was told that the painting was executed a little before Charlotte's departure for England in 1845 (she actually left in 1844). Thus, there is no reason to challenge the Folger's portrait's claim to being the first version painted for Charlotte in 1843, although it is still unclear how Anne Brewster obtained her version.[2]

Upon receiving her portrait in 1843, Charlotte

overpaid Sully by ten dollars (he had valued the work at eighty dollars). When the artist returned the overpayment to her, she wrote a note that reads in part: "Dear Mr. Sully—had I have <u>overpaid</u> you twenty times it could not half <u>repay</u> the obligations I should be under to you for the most excellent terms you have put me upon with my unfortunate '<u>Mug</u>' for I have established it in my mind as a settled fact <u>that I am beautiful</u>. Can you wonder that I should have made a blunder under such a mona-mania [sic]?"[3] Other portraits and daguerreotypes of the actress reveal Sully's conception to be a heavily idealized image, a typical response on the artist's part. Even Fanny Kemble had not been entirely pleased with Sully's having turned her into a conventional beauty. Writing to a friend on 8 January 1838, she relates how the artist was to paint her again, since the first portrait had been judged unsuitable. She was pessimistic, though, that he would succeed: "I do not feel very sanguine about it for Sully's characteristic is delicacy rather than power, and mine may not be power, but is it is certainly not delicacy."[4]

Both the Folger and the Philadelphia versions show Cushman with her head tilted slightly downward, as she turns and looks out at the viewer with a coy smile. She wears a blue dress with a broad white collar, and a red scarf trimmed with gold stitching is tied around her head. The shape of the collar and the headdress depart from ordinary American attire of this period. The suggestion has been made that the portrait shows Cushman as Juliet.[5] Yet while there is no evidence in contemporary illustrations of this play to support such a reading, it would seem likely that Sully is portraying Cushman in theatrical costume representing a character that remains to be identified. As with many of Sully's portraits, the face is tightly painted, with the brushwork in the background only loosely applied, reinforcing the sense of freshness and spontaneity found in the pose.

1. Quoted in letter of 9 May 1925 from Ethelwyn Manning, Frick Art Reference Librarian, to George M. Abbott, librarian at the Library Company of Philadelphia. The Frick Art Reference Library restricts access to the original correspondence, but I would like to thank Selma Kessler of the Library Company of Philadelphia for providing me with copies of their letters.
2. In her journal under 14 December 1874, Mrs. Brewster mentions a visit by a Mrs. Shipley, who asked to see her portrait of Charlotte Cushman, which she had last seen some thirty years earlier in her music room in Philadelphia. Thus, Brewster would appear to have had her version from almost the time Sully

painted it. One of the acquaintances that Brewster mentions in her journals is Dr. C. D. Gardette, who is surely the writer Charles D. Gardette. This friendship opens up the possibility that there might be a connection between her version and the one recorded in the artist's register as painted for a Mrs. Gardette. I would like to thank Denise M. Larrabee, Curator, Women's History Collection of the Library Company of Philadelphia, for sending me this information.
3. Autograph note in the Harvard Theatre Collection, Harvard College Library, Cambridge, Mass.
4. Frances Ann Kemble, *Records of Later Life*, New York, 1882, p. 81.
5. See Monro H. Fabian, *Mr. Sully, Portrait Painter*, Washington, D.C., National Portrait Gallery, 1983, no. 65 (the Philadelphia version).

Wilhelm Trautschold

Carl Friedrich Wilhelm Adolph Trautschold was born in Berlin on 2 June 1815. He trained in the Düsseldorf Royal Academy of Art, and in 1843 was appointed Professor of Art at the University of Giessen. Two years later he left for Liverpool, having been invited to stay at Seaforth Hall. In 1849, while living in an apartment in Seaforth, he exhibited a painting of the playwright James Sheridan Knowles (now in the National Portrait Gallery, London) at the Royal Academy. He married in the following year and returned to Germany but settled in London in 1856, where he continued his career as a portraitist. Retiring to Munich in 1874, he died on 7 January 1877.

126

CHARLOTTE CUSHMAN
ca. 1847
Oil on canvas, 18¼ × 14 in. (46.3 × 35.5 cm.)

Accession no. 5056

Inscribed in gold on book at lower right: "POEMS / BY / ELIZA CO [only half of the 'O' is legible, the rest of the letter and the word having been cut off]"

Provenance: Gift of Mrs. Victor N. Cushman, 24 September 1936

References: Margaret Trautschold Hayford, *C. F. Wilhelm Trautschold, 1815–1877: A Preliminary Catalogue Illustrated*, privately printed in U.S.A., 1980, pp. 5 and 18, no. 60–90

Condition: The paint surface is starting to crack and separate from the ground. The canvas, which has never been lined, is stamped on the verso: "PREPARED BY / CHARLES ROBERSON / 51 LONG ACRE LONDON."

126

Charlotte Cushman left for England on 6 October 1844. Once established, she sent for her family, and she and her sister Susan, who was six years younger, resumed performing together. The two sisters were a great success in their London debut on 30 December 1845, Charlotte playing Romeo opposite Susan's Juliet. One of the admirers Susan attracted was James Sheridan Muspratt (1821–71), the son of James Muspratt (1793–1886), the wealthy founder of the alkali industry in Lancashire. When performing in Liverpool in December 1846, the two sisters attended a lavish New Year's ball at Seaforth Hall, the nearby Muspratt estate. Susan and James Sheridan were soon engaged and married on 22 March 1848.

Because of their interest in chemistry, the Muspratts spent time in Germany, and James Muspratt commissioned from the German artist Trautschold a portrait of his son Frederic, which was painted in Giessen. Pleased with the result, the senior Muspratt invited Trautschold to come to Seaforth Hall in 1845 as his artist-in-residence. Clearly, Traut-

schold would have painted Charlotte around the time that she and Susan first became so intimately associated with this Liverpool family.

Trautschold depicts Charlotte holding a red book whose title shows it to be poems by Eliza Cook. Meditatively looking into the distance, Cushman is obviously portrayed musing on thoughts conjured up by the poems written by her new English friend. It is, though, a discrete reference, available only to those who knew the poet, as most of Cook's last name is covered by Charlotte's thumb. Cook, who, like Rosalie Sully, was two years Charlotte's junior, had met the actress soon after her arrival in London. When Charlotte set up a house for herself and her family, Cook also moved in. Cook wrote poems to Charlotte,[1] and she in her turn was portrayed by Trautschold in two lithographs. Back in America, Rosalie was devastated when she learned that the actress had found a new friend.

Although painted within just a few years of one another, there is a marked difference between Trautschold's dark, more labored portrait of Cushman and Sully's seductive image (no. 125), the one working in a stolid, middle-class German tradition, the other in an English aristocratic one (albeit transplanted to democratic America). Yet the difference between the two images is not just stylistic: the sitter herself had changed in those few years. Upon her arrival in England, Charlotte made friends with a number of prominent feminists, of whom Cook was, for her, the most influential. Cook's bold example led Charlotte to dress in more masculine attire, and Trautschold depicts her in a black satin dress, cut somewhat like a suit, with a white blouse, resembling a man's shirt, finished off with a scarf tied like a bow tie. Soon images of Cushman abandon the lace frills on her shirtfront, lending an even more austere and masculine touch to her appearance.[2]

1. Her poem "To Charlotte Cushman, on seeing her play 'Bianca' in Milman's Tragedy of 'Fazio'" can be found in *The Poetical Works of Eliza Cook*, London, 1870, pp. 364–65.
2. See, for example, William Page's portrait of 1853 at the National Portrait Gallery, Washington, D.C.

127

Richard Westall, attributed to

127

VOLUMNIA PLEADING WITH CORIOLANUS
Coriolanus V, 3
ca. 1800
Oil on canvas, 30⅛ × 25⅜ in. (76.5 × 64.3 cm.)

Case no. 1952

Provenance: Parsons & Sons, September 1929,
£35.18.0, as by William Hamilton

Exhibitions: Washington, 1976–77, no. 11, as by
William Hamilton

Condition: Elizabeth Steele, who restored this
painting in 1988, wrote at that time concerning its
condition: "During cleaning, it became apparent
that damage to the paint film was severe and perva-
sive throughout the picture. In some areas, certain
elements of the composition appeared rough and
sketchy after the varnish and old restorations were
removed. The sketchiness in these areas strongly
resembles under painting which may suggest

Fig. 86. After Gavin Hamilton, *Volumnia Pleading with Coriolanus*. Engraving by J. Caldwell, 4 June 1803.

that the artist never fully completed the picture, whereas, other parts of the composition emerged after cleaning as quite complete. For this reason it may be postulated that this picture was actually never finished by the artist, perhaps because of the large cracks which developed by using a slow drying paint such as bitumen. A continuation of the history of the painting may be that someone at a later date finished the picture some years after the artist had put it aside unfinished. . . . Complete removal of all of the old restorations was not carried out because so little of the original paint was found extant."

The painting depicts the banished Roman Coriolanus seated on his throne-like chair in front of his tent pitched before the walls of his native city. He has returned to Rome as the leader of the enemy Volscian army and is accompanied by the Volscian general Tullus Aufidius, who stands behind him to the right. From the city comes a procession of women to plead with him to spare Rome. His wife, Virgilia, and his son Marcius touch his cloak. They are followed by an imposing Volumnia, Coriolanus's mother, who makes her appeal, while in front of her kneels Valeria, a friend of Virgilia. David George was the first to point out that the scene is based on John Philip Kemble's production of Shake-

speare's play. In his production (see no. 114), a mixture of Shakespeare's text with James Thomson's version, this moment occurs in act V, scene 1, instead of scene 3. Thomson added the character of Volusius, a friend of Aufidius, and while it is not unusual to find two soldiers next to Coriolanus in illustrations of Shakespeare's text, the soldier next to Aufidius in the Folger painting is surely this extra character. The lines, which are a condensation of those in the original text, are the ones uttered by Volumnia to her son, who is still seated in Kemble's version, though standing in Shakespeare's:

> He turns away:
> Down ladies; let us shame him with our knees.
> Nay, behold us:
> This boy [Marcius], that cannot tell what he
>   would have,
> But kneels, and holds up hands, for fellowship,
> Does reason our petition with more strength,
> Than thou hast to deny't.

Coriolanus wavers and eventually gives in, making peace with Rome and thereby sealing his fate with the Volces, who soon assassinate him.

This scene had long proved a favorite one for artists. François Boitard chose to illustrate the pleading women before Coriolanus in his frontispiece of

1709 (see fig. 5), even though his design was inspired, not by Shakespeare's play, but by Poussin's painting based on Plutarch.[1] He was followed by Gravelot in his illustration to the 1740 edition and by Hayman in 1744. Working in Rome, Gavin Hamilton also chose this moment for his history painting executed for Boydell, first exhibited in 1791 (fig. 86). The Folger painting, however, appears to be the first image to show Coriolanus seated.[2] It focuses on his agonizing choice as he strikes a meditative pose that must reflect Kemble's characterization. While Coriolanus's well-chiseled features and lengthy sideburns recall those of Kemble and Volumnia's features those of Sarah Siddons, Kemble's sister who played opposite him, the figures are idealized, and this painting is more accurately described as a history painting inspired by Kemble's production than as a literal rendition of a specific performance.

Appropriately, given its subject matter, the painting is conceived in a neoclassical style with statuesque, bulky figures arranged in frieze-like fashion across the foreground. The work was purchased as by William Hamilton, but, even given the fact that the artist might have altered his style to conform to the classical subject, the painting does not resemble his oeuvre. The attribution is made more difficult in that the painting may have originally been left unfinished, only to have been completed by another hand. In its weighty stoicism, however, it more closely resembles the work of Richard Westall in paintings such as *The Sword of Damocles* (fig. 87) than compositions by William Hamilton and is here tentatively ascribed to his hand.

1. For a helpful discussion of the influence of Poussin's conception, including a print illustrating Kemble's staged version, see Merchant's chapter "A 'Coriolanus' after Poussin, 1709" in his book *Shakespeare and the Artist* (Merchant 1959).

2. In the engraving of this scene published by Harding in his 1799 edition of the play, Coriolanus is shown standing, and he also stands in Henry Howard's design engraved in 1805 for Longmans's edition, published in 1807 (vol. 2, p. 197). It would be interesting to see the following works, now missing, originally shown at public exhibition in London: John Bacon's clay model *Interview between Coriolanus and Volumnia*, Free Society, 1762, no. 172; Fileter N. Stephanoff, *Interview of Coriolanus with His Family in the Camp of the Vollci*, Royal Academy, 1781, no. 262; Henry Singleton, *The Mother of Coriolanus, His Wife, and the Principal Matrons of Rome, Interceding with Him to Withdraw from the Siege of that Capitol*, Royal Academy, 1802, no. 267; Henry Corbould, *Coriolanus* ("Nay, behold us! this boy, etc."), Royal Academy, 1808, no. 272; and Thomas Clement Thompson, *Coriolanus* ("Aufidius and you Volsces, mark, for we'll hear naught from Rome in private."—Act V, scene iii).

Fig. 87. Richard Westall, *The Sword of Damocles*, 1811. Oil on canvas, 30 × 24 in. Private collection, England. Photograph: Courtauld Institute of Art.

Benjamin Wilson

Wilson was born at Leeds on 21 June 1721, the youngest of fourteen children. In London, he obtained a clerkship at the Registry of the Prerogative Court in Doctors' Commons but also continued an early interest in painting. In addition, he began to undertake experiments in electricity. Having spent three weeks in Dublin in 1746, he lived there from 1748 to 1750, working as a portrait painter. On his return to London, he divided his time between painting and scientific experimentation, publishing his research on electricity. He was to become a Fellow of the Royal Society in 1756, and his scientific interests continued to occupy him through the remainder of his life. As early as around 1751–52, he executed the theatrical conversation piece *David Garrick as Romeo and George Anne Bellamy as Juliet in the Tomb Scene from "Romeo and Juliet"* (see fig. 67). This was the first of three such pictures, the other two now known only from the prints after them, *Garrick as Hamlet* being engraved in 1754 (fig. 88) and *Garrick as King Lear in the Storm* in 1761 (see D25). He painted a portrait of Shakespeare (see fig. 121) for Garrick for the Shakespeare Jubilee of 1769. A favorite of the duke of York, Wilson served for a time as manager of his private theater. He did not marry until 1771, having obtained the financial security of his appointment as "Painter to the Board of Ordnance." Enjoying a substantial income and a position of social prominence, Wilson executed few paintings in his late years. He died in London on 6 June 1788.

128

WILLIAM POWELL AS HAMLET ENCOUNTERING THE GHOST

Hamlet I, 4
ca. 1768–69
Oil on canvas, 49½ × 45⅝ in. (126.4 × 116 cm.)

Provenance: Collection of Sir Henry Irving; his sale, Christie's, 16 December 1905, lot 103, $110, as "Hamlet and his Father's Ghost: David Garrick, in the Character of Hamlet" by Zoffany

Exhibitions: Amherst, *Shakespeare,* 1951, as Zoffany's "Hamlet and the Ghost"

References (all citations are as by Zoffany, with Garrick as Hamlet): Fink 1959, p. 64; Highfill 1973–, vol. 6, p. 94 (no. 165), vol. 7, p. 191, and vol. 11, p. 143 (no. 5) (identity of Hamlet as Garrick questioned in vols. 7 and 11); Burnim 1984, p. 196 (repr.)

Condition: The original canvas is a closed tabby weave. Although the tacking edges have been cut unevenly, the canvas seems to be the original size. It has been torn in several places. The original canvas has been glue-lined to another canvas in a past restoration, presumably before it was purchased by Folger. Wrinkling of the paint from excessive oxidized oil is evident throughout. The surface has been extensively repainted.

Early illustrations to *Hamlet* most frequently revolve around confrontations between the hero and his father's Ghost. The supernatural visitations obviously appealed for their dramatic possibilities, and it is the prince's response to the Ghost's de-

mands for vengeance that propels the play. The first illustration to the play, François Boitard's frontispiece to Rowe's 1709 edition, depicts the closet scene where the Ghost appears to Hamlet, though invisible to his mother. A few decades later in his frontispiece to Theobald's 1740 edition, Gravelot depicted Hamlet's first confrontation with the Ghost, showing the moment when his friends attempt to restrain him from following. Then Benjamin Wilson, in a now lost painting engraved in 1754 (fig. 88), showed Garrick as Hamlet reacting to the Ghost's appearance. The Folger painting chooses this last moment as well. The time is just past midnight, as the moon, shining from behind clouds, inexplicably lights up Hamlet's entire face and portions of the other figures. The setting, according to the stage directions, is a platform, where cannon are mounted on the ramparts, before the castle at Elsinore. The Folger painting, however, shows Hamlet and his companions emerging from a drawbridge, presumably a typical stage setting in the eighteenth century, as Gravelot had earlier used

Fig. 88. After Benjamin Wilson, *David Garrick as Hamlet,* 1754. Mezzotint by James McArdell.

128

this same arrangement. In the Folger picture, Hamlet, still wearing the customary black clothes of mourning, is supported by Marcellus, a uniformed officer, at the left, and Horatio, his friend and fellow student, at the right. The Ghost at the far right appears entirely in armor, as the text requires, and holds a truncheon of command in keeping with other eighteenth-century depictions.[1] The moment is the pause between Horatio's exclamation on sighting the Ghost, "Look, my lord, it comes!" and Hamlet's response, "Angels and ministers of grace defend us!" In the picture Marcellus and Horatio look to their friend, while Hamlet is fixated only on the Ghost, who slowly turns as he prepares to beckon the prince to follow him. Wilson's earlier depiction of Garrick as Hamlet showed ships beyond a fortress wall, echoing the ocean imagery in Horatio's speech:

What if it tempt you toward the flood, my lord,
Or to the dreadful summit of the cliff
That beetles o'er his base into the sea,
. . . .
The very place puts toys of desperation,
Without more motive, into every brain
That looks so many fathoms to the sea
And hears it roar beneath.

Though difficult to make out because of its poor condition, the Folger picture appears to show water and a boat in the middle ground between the two major protagonists.

The picture was purchased as by Johan Zoffany and was identified as Garrick in the character of Hamlet. Zoffany, born near Frankfurt, Germany, in 1733, arrived for the first time in London in 1760. He worked for a time for Benjamin Wilson, who

Fig. 89. John Hamilton Mortimer, *William Powell, His Wife and Two Daughters*, 1768. Oil on canvas, 95.1 × 120.5 cm. Garrick Club, London.

is said to have exploited his talents, but was rescued by Garrick, for whom, beginning in 1762, he painted a number of works. Zoffany left London for Florence in the summer of 1772 and did not return until late 1779. Obviously, if the attribution and identification are to be accepted, the painting must date between 1762 and 1772. There are, however, problems with both the attribution and identification. To start with the latter, it was first pointed out in print in 1982 that the figure of Hamlet does not look like Garrick.[2] Neither the head nor the slender figure resembles Garrick as he appeared in the 1760s. A convincing argument can be made for the painting's representing William Powell in the starring role.[3] Powell's features as rendered, for example, by John Hamilton Mortimer in his group portrait *William Powell, His Wife and Two Daughters* (fig. 89), exhibited at the Society of Artists in 1768, closely conform to those of Hamlet in the Folger picture. Powell performed Hamlet on only four occasions, all at Covent Garden: 25 April 1768, 16 and 27 February, and 31 March 1769. Born in 1735 or 1736, he was around thirty-three years old at the time of these performances. In all four performances, Robert Bensley played the Ghost, and, while little can be seen of the Ghost in the Folger picture, his long nose is an unhappy characteristic of Bensley's features. The head of Horatio is more clearly rendered, and it closely resembles surviving images of Thomas Hull, who played this part.[4]

Powell came to London from Hereford and worked

in the City countinghouse of Sir Robert Ladbrooke. Despite a successful apprenticeship, he felt irresistibly drawn to acting, and in 1763 Garrick groomed him as his replacement while he and his wife left for a grand tour of the Continent. Powell made his debut on 8 October 1763 and was enthusiastically received, enjoying popular acclaim for the rest of his career. He acted in *Hamlet* for the first time on 16 May 1764, but only as the Ghost, not wishing to compete with his mentor in one of his most popular roles. In 1767 Powell abandoned Garrick and Drury Lane for Covent Garden, where he became manager and part owner. It was here, out of Garrick's shadow, that he first attempted the role of Hamlet. Yet it is clear from descriptions of Garrick in this part that Powell did not venture far from his mentor's highly acclaimed interpretation. As rendered in the Folger picture, Powell's staging seems the counterfeit of Garrick's as described by the German critic Lichtenberg:

Suddenly, as Hamlet moves towards the back of the stage slightly to the left and turns his back on the audience, Horatio starts, and saying: "Look, my lord, it comes," points to the right, where the ghost has already appeared and stands motionless, before any one is aware of him. At these words Garrick turns sharply and at the same moment staggers back two or three paces with his knees giving way under him; his hat falls to the ground and both his arms, especially the left, are stretched out nearly to their full length, with the hands as high as his head, the right arm more bent and the hand lower, and the fingers apart; his mouth is open: thus he stands rooted to the spot, with legs apart, but no loss of dignity, supported by his friends, who are better acquainted with the apparition and fear lest he should collapse. His whole demeanour is so expressive of terror that it made my flesh creep even before he began to speak. The almost terror-struck silence of the audience, which preceded this appearance and filled one with a sense of insecurity, probably did much to enhance this effect. At last he speaks, not at the beginning, but at the end of a breath, with a trembling voice: "Angels and ministers of grace defend us!" words which supply anything this scene may lack and make it one of the greatest and most terrible which will ever be played on any stage.[5]

Obviously there was considerable continuity in eighteenth-century acting styles. Powell's success was short-lived: he died of pneumonia on 3 July 1769 in Bristol.

In the scale of the figures to the setting, in the moonlight effects, and in the dry, pedestrian handling of the paint, the picture resembles other works by Wilson. The question arises, though, as to why he would paint Powell, Garrick's chief rival. At this time the painter and Garrick remained on good terms. Wilson executed Shakespeare's portrait for the actor (see fig. 121) for the Shakespeare Jubilee of 1769, and even accompanied the Garricks to Stratford-upon-Avon on this occasion.[6] Yet it is also true that Johan Zoffany had supplanted Wilson as Garrick's favorite painter of theatrical conversation pieces, and the Folger picture suggests that Wilson was now considering doing for Powell's career what he had earlier done for Garrick's, though, given Powell's untimely death, this picture remains one of a kind.

1. There was textual justification for showing the Ghost holding a truncheon, for Horatio, in describing to Hamlet the Ghost's appearances to Marcellus and Bernardo, specifically states, "Thrice he walk'd / By their oppress'd and fear-surprised eyes, / Within his truncheon's length . . . " (I, 2).
2. The Highfill entry (1973–, vol. 7) on William Havard refers to "a painting by Zoffany which supposedly depicts Garrick meeting the Ghost in *Hamlet*, though the figure of Hamlet does not much resemble Garrick" (p. 191). It is also of interest that Anglesea does not include the Folger picture in his catalogue of paintings depicting Garrick.
3. I would like to thank Geoffrey Ashton for suggesting this identification to me.
4. Burnim wrote in 1984: "In addition to Garrick as Hamlet, it [the Folger picture] depicts [Astley] Bransby as the Ghost, [Ellis] Ackman as Marcellus, and either [William] Havard or [John Hayman] Packer as Horatio." These identifications are less convincing than those of the cast surrounding Powell. One reason it is difficult to tell in the Folger picture whether or not Horatio was played by Havard or Packer, both of whom performed with Garrick, is that the figure looks like neither.
5. George Christlob Lichtenberg to the editor of the *Deutsches Museum*, 1 October 1775, in *Lichtenberg's Visits to England*, translated and annotated by Margaret L. Mare and W. H. Quarrell, Oxford, 1938, p. 10. Not everyone was enamored of Garrick's solution. Earlier in 1757 the *Theatrical Examiner* had offered the criticism, "The start at the ghost in the play of Hamlet may be picturesque, but it is grossly absurd to see a man fling himself into so exact an attitude, which it is impossible for him to remain steady in, without two supporters" (quoted in Sprague 1944, p. 138).
6. Wilson even takes credit for suggesting to Garrick the lucrative staging of the Jubilee performance back in London (see the typescript of Wilson's memoir of ca. 1783, the property of J. W. Hulton, in the National Portrait Gallery Archives, London, pp. 52–53).

Anonymous (nos. 129–34)

129

ELIZA WALSTEIN [?] AS ROSALIND
As You Like It III, 5
After ca. 1815
Oil on panel, 4½ × 3⅛ in. (11.5 × 7.8 cm.)

Case no. 150

Inscribed on verso: "Mrs. Siddons as / 'Rosalind' / 1799" (formerly transcribed as "N.C. Scetty sings / 'Rosaccind' / 1799")

Provenance: Source unknown

Condition: The grain of the panel runs vertically and the back edges have been beveled. Reframed by Michelson's in 1959.

Rosalind flees the court of her uncle to seek safety in the Forest of Arden. Traveling with her cousin Celia and Touchstone, she assumes masculine dress as a disguise. The small Folger painting depicts an actress in the role of Rosalind wearing brown rustic

129

attire. She stands against a black background on a shallow brown foreground strip, onto which she casts a small shadow. Often Rosalind is shown holding a bear-spear, but the Folger figure appears to be holding an arrow, perhaps an allusion to act III, scene 5, where Silvius evokes such imagery in his lament to Phebe: "Then shall you know the wounds invisible / That love's keen arrows make." Of course, no sooner has he said this than Rosalind's words and eyes pierce Phebe's heart, the shepherdess having mistaken her for a man.

The Folger image is too slight to allow a positive identification with a specific actress, but an inscription on the back identifies it as Mrs. Siddons in 1799. Rosalind, however, was not one of Siddons's successful roles. She first performed the part in London at Drury Lane on 30 April 1783, and her last performance, at least before 1799, was on 7 June 1786. Dorothy Jordan's successful debut in the role on 13 April 1787 was apparently too effective to challenge. Anna Seward, in a letter of 20 July 1786,

Fig. 91. W. Heath, *Miss Walstein as Rosalind*. Engraving, 18 June 1815, 11¼ × 8⅜ in.

complained of Mrs. Siddons's appearance, "Then her dress was injudicious. The scrupulous prudery or decency, produced an ambiguous vestment, that seemed neither male nor female."[1] A critic in the *Morning Post* was also displeased: "Her hussar boots with a gardener's apron and petticoat behind, gave her a most equivocal appearance which rendered Orlando's stupidity astonishing in not making a premature discovery of his mistress."[2] An engraving (fig. 90) showing Mrs. Siddons as Rosalind holding a shepherdess's staff confirms these accounts of her effeminate costume, which does not match the attire seen in the Folger work. This picture instead more closely resembles in its characterization of the figure's dress and long nose a print of the actress Eliza Walstein published on 18 June 1815 (fig. 91). Walstein had made her London debut at the Drury Lane Theatre on 15 November 1814. Though not identical to the image in the print, there are enough similarities to warrant discounting the inscription and changing the original identification.

Fig. 90. Anonymous, *Mrs. Siddons as Rosalind*. Engraving, 5¼ × 3½ in. (sheet of paper).

1. Anna Seward, *The Swan of Lichfield*, London, 1936, p. 91.
2. Quoted in Linda Kelly, *The Kemble Era*, New York, 1980, p. 54.

Anonymous, American school?

130

SARAH SIDDONS AS QUEEN KATHARINE

Henry VIII II, 4
After 1817
Oil on canvas, 31⁷/₈ × 21³/₄ in. (81 × 55.1 cm.)

Case no. 332

Provenance: Old National Theatre, Boston; purchased from C. F. Libbie & Co., Boston, shortly before 26 June 1905 (date of case number)

Exhibitions: Washington, 1985

Condition: Finlayson glue-lined the original canvas onto a commercially prepared canvas in 1932.

Original painting: George Henry Harlow, *The Court Scene for the Trial of Queen Katharine*, oil on canvas, 63 × 86 in., first exhibited at the Royal

130

Academy in 1817 (no. 17), now owned by the Trustees of the Morrison Picture Settlement

Engravings after original: Mezzotint by George Clint, 22¹/₂ × 30¹/₄ in., published by W. Cribb, 1819; engraving for French market by Jazet

John Philip Kemble first offered his production of *Henry VIII* in the autumn of 1788, reviving a play that had fallen out of favor. His sister, Sarah Siddons, offered an electrifying portrayal of Queen Katharine. George Henry Harlow saw her perform this role at Covent Garden in 1806 and may well have seen her in later years. His painting of Siddons in the trial scene (fig. 92), exhibited at the Royal Academy in 1817, proved so popular that it in its turn became a model for the staging of productions throughout the nineteenth century.

The scene is a hall in Blackfriars, where Katharine of Aragon has been brought in a hearing of the divorce case instigated by her husband, King Henry VIII. Guiltless, she is to be judged by the scheming Cardinal Wolsey and the weak Cardinal Campeius, who has just arrived from Rome. After an elegant plea to her husband, the queen asks for a delay until she can receive council from her native land. Wolsey dismisses her request,supported by Campeius. Harlow focuses on the subsequent moment when Katharine, brushing aside Campeius, points to Wolsey, the play's villain, and chillingly intones, "Lord Cardinal, / To you I speak."

Harlow's characterization of Siddons at this moment proved so popular that prints of her alone were published, some of which focus only on her from the waist up. While the pointing gesture links Katharine to Wolsey, the fact that she looks away makes it easier for her to be excerpted in this manner. The Folger painting is a free interpretation, presumably from one of the prints. The costume differs from the original, allowing for greater contrast, as a white satin underskirt is combined with a purple bodice and train; the interior is entirely made up; and the figure resembles a scarecrow more than the beleaguered queen of England. The artist also chose to deemphasize the actress's strong chin in order to play up her doleful eyes and expressive eyebrows.

According to the file cards, *Sarah Siddons as Queen Katharine* is one of three paintings Folger purchased in 1905 that had hung in the Old National Theatre, Boston. The other two were *Isabella*

Fig. 92. George Henry Harlow, *The Court Scene for the Trial of Queen Katharine.* Oil on canvas, 31½ × 41 in. From the RSC Collection, with the permission of the Governors of the Royal Shakespeare Theatre ©.

Glyn as Lady Macbeth (no. 131) and *Vandenhoff as Coriolanus* (D60). No photograph of *Vandenhoff* has survived, but, since they come from the same source and are equally bad, *Siddons* and *Glyn* may well be by the same hand.

131

ISABELLA GLYN AS LADY MACBETH
Macbeth I, 5
After 1850
Oil on canvas, 35¾ × 29 in. (90.7 × 73.5 cm.)

Case no. 332

Provenance: Old National Theatre, Boston; purchased from C. F. Libbie & Co., Boston, shortly before 26 June 1905 (date of case number)

Condition: Finlayson lined the canvas in 1932.

Born in 1823 in Edinburgh, Isabella Glyn was raised in a Presbyterian family that was opposed to the stage as a career. Yet, as a young woman in London, she performed in amateur theatricals and went briefly to Paris with her husband to study acting. On her return to London in 1846 she was given instruction by Charles Kemble and as a tragedian was

one of the last of the Kemble school. Her London debut came at the Olympic on 26 January 1848, and beginning with the 1848–49 season she starred at Sadler's Wells. In 1851 she gave the first of her Shakespearean readings, and in time the recitals became more frequent than her performances in plays. Perhaps it was the readings she gave in Boston in 1870 that led to the inclusion of her portrait in the Old National Theatre. She died in London in 1889.

The Folger painting is a copy of a wood engraving showing Miss Glyn in the role of Lady Macbeth (fig. 93). The wood engraving, in its turn, is based on a daguerreotype by Paine of Islington. The date of the wood engraving is presumably 1850, the year in which Glyn turned twenty-seven, as she appears in an identical pose, only with a different background, in a print published in the December 1850 issue of *Tallis's Dramatic Magazine.*[1]

The moment depicted is Lady Macbeth's first appearance in the play. After reading her husband's letter, she begins a soliloquy indicating her resolve that the witches' prophecy should come true. *Tallis's Dramatic Magazine* describes the actress's interpretation:

131

Fig. 93. *Miss Glyn as Lady Macbeth.* Wood engraving from a daguerreotype by Paine of Islington.

Our artist has portrayed Miss Glyn in the part of Lady Macbeth, at the important moment when she first conceives the murder of Duncan:–

Glamis thou art, and Cawdor; *and shalt be What thou art promised.*

To this prophetic intimation, Miss Glyn gives a startling emphasis—sudden, vehement, and oracular. The effect is all the more startling from the natural and level manner in which she reads the letter, and the breathless astonishment with which she lights upon the weird sisters' prediction—"Hail, king that shalt be!" In such passages, Miss Glyn knows the value of long pauses; and having the entire confidence of the audience, is, upon right occasions, able to make the most of them. Her singularly expressive forehead, with her large and lustrous eyes, aid her in commanding attention.

Glyn's conception of this role is based on the one established by Sarah Siddons. Westall had portrayed Lady Macbeth for Boydell's Shakespeare Gallery (fig. 94), and the grand passion displayed in his work presumably owes a debt to Siddons's powerful interpretation. Harlow painted Siddons in this role in

a pose that is even closer to the one adopted by Glyn.[2] Since Harlow's painting, however, is a theatrical portrait, his heroine does not grimace as does the figure in Westall's history painting. The wood engraving of Glyn shows her scowling intensely. Based on a photograph, it lacks the idealization found in either Westall's history painting or Harlow's portrait, but the Folger copy after the wood engraving, despite its primitive crudeness, attempts to soften Glyn's features.

1. *Tallis's Dramatic Magazine,* London and New York, December 1850, facing p. 37.
2. One version of Harlow's *Mrs. Siddons as Lady Macbeth* (23¼ × 14½ in.) is in the Garrick Club, London. A larger version (94½ × 58 in.) at Bob Jones University, Greenville, S.C., is discussed and reproduced in the catalogue to Montgomery, 1985–86, no. 30.

Fig. 94. After Richard Westall, *Lady Macbeth with a Letter.* Engraving by J. Parker, 4 June 1800.

132

SARAH SIDDONS AS LADY MACBETH
Macbeth II, 2
ca. 1790–1810
Oil on canvas, 29 × 24 in. (73.6 × 60.9 cm.)

Case no. 1709

Provenance: Parsons, September 1927, £45, as by Smirke

Exhibitions: Amherst, *Shakespeare,* 1951, as by Smirke; Washington, 1985, as by Smirke

References: Fink 1959, as by Smirke

Condition: In 1985 some discolored repaint in the figure of Lady Macbeth and in Macbeth's right leg and foot was removed. An old tear found on Macbeth's right thigh above the knee was also inpainted. Finlayson's lining of 1932 was retained.

Although acquired as by Robert Smirke, on stylistic grounds this picture is clearly not by him, the artist having a pronounced predilection for large, mannered hands, the extremities smoothly rendered as if sculpted in wax. The painting was said to depict Sarah Siddons as Lady Macbeth, and, while the features are generalized, this identification is plausible. It is the role for which the actress was most famous, having first performed it in London on 2 February 1785. She chose to appear in it in her farewell performance of 29 June 1812 and also several times afterwards in benefits.

The painting is loosely based on a print by de Loutherbourg (fig. 95), dated 9 August 1784 and conceived before Siddons's London triumph. With wind-blown hair, agitated dress, and his face obliterated by pockets of light and shadow, Macbeth is more dramatically rendered than in the print. The obscurity of his features clearly indicates that no

Fig. 95. After de Loutherbourg, *Macbeth and Lady Macbeth.* Engraving by F. Bartolozzi, 9 August 1784.

132

particular actor is intended,[1] but the expressive eyebrows and long nose of Lady Macbeth may well represent Sarah Siddons. Yet it is not so much in the features as in the characterization of this Lady Macbeth that one most clearly sees Siddons's imprint. The agitated, winsome beauty of de Loutherbourg's interpretation gives way to a commanding woman of statuesque bearing and penetrating stare. Pentimenti reveal that her head originally inclined toward Macbeth, a pose closer to the print's characterization, but the painter's final rendering shows her haughtily defiant.

In 1809, Prof. George Joseph Bell of the University of Edinburgh left detailed notes on a performance Siddons gave in Edinburgh. The moment depicted in the play is just after Macbeth has committed the murder and, returning from the chamber, is now undone by his deed. Lady Macbeth queries her husband, "Why did you bring these daggers from the place? / They must lie there. Go carry them; and smear / The sleepy grooms with blood." Macbeth replies, "I'll go no more. / I am afraid to think what I have done; / Look on't again I dare not." Lady Macbeth then takes charge: "Infirm of purpose! / Give me the daggers. The sleeping and the dead / Are but as pictures; 'tis the eye of childhood / That fears a painted devil. . . ." It is here that Bell writes of Siddons's performance, "Seizing the daggers very contemptuously."[2] Following de Loutherbourg's lead, the Folger painting shows the characters grasping only one dagger, the other lying at bottom center, but the painting amply conveys Siddons's imperious contempt for her husband's faltering remorse.

1. Interestingly, de Loutherbourg's conception was later adapted to show Cooke in the role of Macbeth, a print of which was published on 28 November 1803. In this version Lady Macbeth remains as before. The Folger painting, of course, reverses the process, making Lady Macbeth a particular actress and Macbeth her foil.

2. See H. C. Fleeming Jenkin, *Mrs. Siddons as Lady Macbeth and as Queen Katharine*, no. 3 in Papers on Acting, published for the Dramatic Museum of Columbia University, New York, 1915, p. 55, n. 42.

133

133

ACTOR IN THE CHARACTER OF OTHELLO
Late nineteenth century
Oil on paper mounted on cardboard, 13⅝ × 9⅜ in. (34.7 × 23.8 cm.)

Provenance: Gift of Mrs. William M. Hanney, 7 March 1942

The picture shows a brown-skinned man with dark curly hair, a moustache, and a small goatee beneath his lower lip. He is wearing a short-sleeve red tunic with gold trim. A fluid light-brown wash composes the background.

The image is tightly compressed, and the figure's left shoulder and arm have been barely sketched in. Given that the character is in costume, is dark-skinned, and wears an intense, troubled expression, the identification with Othello seems likely. It is doubtful, however, that the generalized features can be identified with a particular actor.

134

EDMUND KEAN AS SIR GILES OVERREACH
Philip Massinger, *A New Way to Pay Old Debts*
ca. 1816
Oil on panel, 15⅛ × 11¼ in. (38.4 × 28.4 cm.)

Case no. 1798

Provenance: Michelmore, June 1928, £10, as "Edmund Kean as Richard III" by Henry Edridge

Exhibitions: Washington, 1985, as Kean as Richard III by Edridge

Condition: The mahogany panel is ¾ inch thick with vertical graining. A small batten strip has been joined to the panel along the bottom edge using the tongue-and-groove method.

Born in London in 1787 and abandoned early on by his mother, Edmund Kean was forced to perform from a young age. However, he postponed his appearance in a leading role on the London stage until 26 January 1814, when he was scheduled to perform at Drury Lane as Shylock. The management, regretting having signed him, stoically waited for the debacle, but Kean, playing to a house that was less than a third full, electrified the audience, becoming overnight a sensation. Public opinion eventually turned against him in 1825, when a scandal broke

134

over his affair with the wife of a prominent banker and alderman of the City of London. He rode out the storm in England and America, but his heavy drinking also took a toll on his professional abilities. He died on 15 May 1833.

Kean was most celebrated for his impassioned performances in tragic roles, particularly his characterizations of Richard III, Othello, Hamlet, and King Lear. When the Folger painting was acquired, it was said to show Kean in the role of Richard III, a misidentification that may well have been intentional,

since the dealer Michelmore knew that Folger, one of his more dependable clients, would only be interested in the painting if it was related to Shakespeare. The picture in fact depicts Kean in the role of the villainous Sir Giles Overreach in Philip Massinger's *A New Way to Pay Old Debts*, the most durable of Jacobean plays after Shakespeare's own. There are several depictions of Kean in the costume for this role (see, for example, fig. 96) that confirm this identification. Sir Giles stops at nothing in his amassing of power and fortune, and he is distin-

Fig. 96. T. Wageman, *Mr. Kean as Sir Giles Overreach.* Engraving.

guished from most villains by his lack of hypocrisy in carrying out his ruthless machinations. In the late eighteenth century, Henderson, Kemble, and Cooke all enjoyed success in this role, but by all accounts Kean's performances were especially thrilling. He first acted this part on 12 January 1816, and it instantly became the most popular of his non-Shakespearean characters. Women are said to have screamed and run in hysterics from the theater, and Lord Byron was thrown into a convulsive fit when confronted with the actor's overwhelming intensity. George Clint's celebrated painting of Kean as Sir Giles attempting to slay his own daughter (fig. 97) proved so popular on its exhibition at the Royal Academy in 1820 that a guard rail had to be placed around it.

The Folger painting, on the other hand, is more in the nature of an intimate sketch. The costume's colors offer dramatic contrasts of orange and olive green, and the figure of Kean is boldly outlined in strong accents, a violet highlighting the left side of the legs, with blue around the arms and torso. The figure's forceful pose captures some of the intensity of Kean's performance, and one suspects that the artist, as presumably did the actor, plays on the character's name, in that Kean as Sir Giles is shown energetically overreaching.

Michelmore ascribed the painting to Henry Edridge (1769–1821), who specialized in portraiture, primarily in the medium of pencil. Yet there is no evidence, other than the dealer's statement, to warrant such an attribution. Although no securely attributed oil sketch by Edridge survives to which the Folger picture can be compared, his portrait drawings are fastidious and precise, their static poses hardly suggestive of the energy embodied in the Folger sketch.

Portraits Formerly Identified as Actors
Sir Joshua Reynolds, attributed to

135
UNKNOWN MAN
Oil on canvas, 26⅞ × 20⅞ in. (68.3 × 53 cm.)

Provenance: Collection of Augustin Daly (on exhibit in Daly's Theatre in New York); Daly sale, Anderson Galleries, 27 November 1912, lot 49, repr., $1,000 plus 10 percent commission, Smith acting as agent

References: New York Times, 28 November 1912 (mentions that it brought the highest price paid at Daly sale); Burnim 1984, p. 206 (doubts both attribution and identification)

Condition: A restoration undertaken in 1988 revealed that the image purchased by Folger in 1912 had been almost totally repainted in an earlier restoration. Two or three layers of resinous repaint covered the background, shirt, and coat of the sitter. The face had suffered the least, but here too there were heavy applications of resinous glazes and sienna repaint that covered the darker, modeled tones in the flesh. Extensive gray repaint covered abrasion losses in the hair, and the face itself had originally

Fig. 97. George Clint, *Edmund Kean as Sir Giles Overreach*, RA 1820. Oil on canvas. Garrick Club, London.

135   135 (before restoration)

been fuller. The canvas had been prepared with a thick ground which has the appearance of red lead and had been lined at least once. On the verso was a thin, hard gray material with characteristics of white lead.

In the 1912 auction of the collection of paintings that had hung in Daly's Theatre in New York, Reynolds's portrait of Garrick (see no. 135; before restoration) brought the highest price. It obviously had attracted its share of admirers, yet its quality was poor. As early as 1950 in his report on the Folger collection, Maurice Block challenged its authenticity: "There is no valid reason to accept the attribution either as to subject or artist in this case. A proper label would be 'Portrait of an Unknown Man by a Follower of Reynolds.'" The painting had little about it that was of the eighteenth century, much of the original surface having been crudely overpainted. It showed the sitter in a wine-red coat with matching vest, his torso parallel to the picture plane and his face in three-quarter view looking to the viewer's left.

During the 1988 conservation, a different image was found underneath. This design, however, was severely damaged, and one presumes its poor state

was the reason that an earlier restorer had taken such liberties in repainting it. The recent restoration also involved by necessity a great deal of overpainting, but it attempts to be faithful to the outlines of the original. Because so little remains of the work in its first incarnation, it is difficult to be certain who the artist is, but the original attribution to Sir Joshua Reynolds cannot be ruled out. The figure's torso is now turned to the side at an angle slightly more acute than that of the head. The coat is blue, and underneath it can be glimpsed a tan vest. There are, however, anomalies: the informality of the shirt collar seems out of place with the rest of the attire, and the coat's buttoned lapel is also an odd feature.

Anonymous (nos. 136–37)

136

UNKNOWN BOY
Early nineteenth century
Oil on canvas, 20 × 16⅛ in. (50.3 × 41 cm.)

Case no. 828

Provenance: Collection of Evert Jansen Wendell; his sale, American Art Galleries, 21 October 1919, lot 4871, $60, as a portrait of Sarah Siddons attributed to Opie

Exhibitions: Washington, 1976–77, no. 16, as by Opie of Mrs. Siddons

References: Fink 1959, p. 181, with the comment, "There is doubt as to whether or not this is Mrs. Siddons."

Condition: Lined by Finlayson in 1932.

The painting was purchased as a portrait of Sarah Siddons by John Opie. Neither the identification nor the attribution can be correct. Surely the sitter is a young boy, and it has been suggested that it depicts Master Betty (1791–1874), a child star who made his first appearance on 19 August 1803 in Belfast and then in London on 1 December 1804. As much as one would like to see this portrait remain within a theatrical context, given the sitter's thin face and jutting chin, the identification with William Henry West Betty seems unlikely.

136

137

137

UNKNOWN MAN [DAVID GARRICK?]
ca. 1760s
Oil on canvas, 30⅛ × 25⅜ in. (76.6 × 64.4 cm.)

Case no. 1190

Provenance: Collection of W. Lockett Agnew; his
sale, Christie's, as a portrait of Garrick by Dance;
acquired by Wells from Harry Spurr (the above information is contained in a letter from Wells to
Folger, 18 December 1923); bought by Folger from
Wells, December 1923, $550, as by Dance

References: Fink 1959, p. 64, as Garrick by Zoffany;
Highfill 1973–, vol. 6, p. 89 (no. 68), lists as by Zoffany but adds, "The identification of Garrick as
sitter is questioned."

The sitter, wearing a powdered wig, red coat with
a blue-green lining, and a red vest, sits at a table
with an unidentified book held casually in his left
hand. Pausing in his reading, he looks out at the
viewer, the color of his eyes matching that of his
coat's lining.

This portrait was attributed first to Zoffany, then
to Dance.[1] When he acquired the painting, Folger
chose to discard the later attribution, accepting
Zoffany as the painter.[2] Neither Dance nor Zoffany

seems a likely candidate, and it is even possible
that the artist was not of the British school.

The sitter has traditionally been described as Garrick, but this identification seems unlikely. Block,
in compiling his list of the Folger paintings in 1950,
was the first to question it: "The facial contours,
and the sensuous mouth do not tally with the features as registered in the fine portraits of Garrick
in this collection by Reynolds, Pine and Dance,
and the drawings of Gainsborough." On stylistic
grounds the Folger portrait would not appear to
date before the 1760s, and while there are some re-
semblances to Garrick, especially as he appears in
Arthur Pond's portrait engraved in 1745 (fig. 98), the
sitter of the Folger picture is too young to represent
a man who would have then been well into his forties.

1. At the upper middle of the stretcher is a piece of paper on which
   is written in pen, "David Garrick / by Zoffany." "Zoffany" is
   scratched out in pencil and added below it, also in pencil, is
   "Dance." Penned on a piece of paper at bottom center of the
   stretcher is another attribution to Dance. The reference is again
   to Dance in the catalogue entry glued to the frame at upper
   right. This attribution has led to a great deal of confusion in the
   Folger records between this painting and Dance's *Garrick* (no. 106).
2. In the Case Lists (no. 1190) the painting is recorded as "Portrait
   Garrick, by Zoffany. Z's name crossed off, and Dance's sub-
   stituted; but tho't wrong by H. C. F."

Fig. 98. After Arthur Pond, *David Garrick.* Engraving by J. Wood,
29 April 1745.

Miniatures

James Ferguson

According to Samuel Redgrave, Ferguson was a prodigy. Born on 25 April 1710 to poor parents in Banffshire in northeastern Scotland, he learned to read by hearing his father instruct his older brother. He developed, largely on his own, an interest in mathematics and gained a knowledge of astronomy from observing the sky while tending the sheep of the farmer for whom he worked. Showing an ability at drawing, he was sent by friends to Edinburgh to study. There and then in London, he supported himself by drawing miniatures, while continuing to pursue his interests in astronomy. On 27 November 1746 he advertised his new address in a London newspaper: "Mr. Ferguson limner in China ink, has removed from Compton Street to the White Perriwig next door to the Golden Ball in Gt. Pultney St. near Golden Sq. where he draws pictures as usual for nine shillings or goes abroad to do them for ½ guinea."[1] A prolific artist, he died in London on 16 November 1776.

1. *Daily Advertiser*, 27 November 1746, quoted in Daphne Foskett, *A Dictionary of British Miniature Painters*, New York, Washington, 1972, p. 269.

138

MARGARET WOFFINGTON
Mid-eighteenth century
Pencil and india ink on vellum, oval, 2³/₁₆ × 1³/₄ in. (5.5 × 4.4 cm.) (sight)

Provenance: Collection of Lord Henniker; collection of Francis Wellesley, no. 23 in his privately printed catalogue; Wellesley sale, Sotheby, 28 June– 2 July (29) 1920, lot 327, £4.5.0, Quaritch acting as agent

References: Janet Camden Lucey, *Lovely Peggy*, Watford, Herts., 1952, p. 257 (mentions photograph in British Museum of Ferguson miniature, presumably a photo of the Folger picture)

Condition: Some staining, particularly across the upper right side. Mounted in a deep wooden frame with ring at top.

Ferguson is best known for his plumbago drawings, of which the Folger miniature is a good example. Plumbago miniatures are graphite drawings on

138 (enlarged)

vellum. Continental in origin, they proved popular in England in the seventeenth century and in the first half of the eighteenth. These monochrome miniatures provided a cheap alternative to the more elaborate works in watercolor, but the use of vellum as a support gave them a status over small-scale drawings on paper. Often the identity of Ferguson's sitters has been lost, but the traditional identification of the Folger miniature as Peg Woffington is plausible in light of other portraits of this celebrated actress.

Woffington, shown half-length, wears a décolleté bodice with lace-edged fichu tied at her bosom with a bow, a lace mobcap tied with a bow under her chin. The costume, pose, and characterization are similar to those of a miniature in the Fitzwilliam Museum, though the latter sitter is more portly and her hair does not show behind her neck.[1] Clearly, Ferguson's approach to portraiture was somewhat formulaic, which, given his output and the small size of his medium, is unsurprising.

1. See Bayne-Powell 1985, p. 82 (no. 3731).

John Howes, after Cipriani

John Howes entered the Royal Academy schools in 1770, winning a silver medal in 1772. The following year he exhibited his first work at the Royal Academy, the head of an old man in enamel. He continued to exhibit until 1793, and many of his pieces were classified as enamels or miniatures. According to Waterhouse, he also painted portraits on the scale of life and occasional pastorals in the manner of Wheatley. Initially his exhibited subject matter consisted primarily of portraiture, but he increasingly attempted historical subjects, including scenes from Shakespeare. One presumes that many of these productions were after the work of other artists.

Giovanni Battista Cipriani was born in Florence in 1727. Arriving in Rome in 1750, he moved on to London in 1756 with the support of the English architect Sir William Chambers and the sculptor Joseph Wilton. Settling permanently in London, he married a wealthy English lady in 1761 and was one of the founding members of the Royal Academy in 1768. A highly successful decorative painter in a fashionable neoclassical style, he also exhibited paintings, primarily of classical subjects, at the Royal Academy from its first exhibition in 1769 until ten years later. One of his designs, not carried out, was for a monument to David Garrick, showing the actor in a pose and dress reminiscent of Scheemaker's statue of Shakespeare in Westminster Abbey (the drawing is in the Witt Collection, Courtauld Institute, no. 1418). He died of rheumatic fever on 14 December 1785.

139

DAVID GARRICK UNVEILING A HERM OF SHAKESPEARE AND THE EPHESIAN DIANA
1777
Enamel, circular, 4⅝ in. diameter (11.7 cm.)

Signed and dated at base of herm: "I Howes Pinxt. / 1777." Inscribed on verso: "The Incorporated Actors belonging to the Theatre Royal, Drury Lane, humbly beg leave to present their perpetual president, David Garrick Esqr. with this medal; in testimony of their gratitude for his having raised and supported by his excellent performance on the stage, and finally established by an Act of Parliament obtained by his interest, and at his sole expence the Theatrical Fund hoping he will conde-

scend to accept it, as a small memorial of their respect and affection for him as a man, of their admiration of his unequalled talents as an actor, as well as an acknowledgment of the high sense they entertain of the honour and happiness they enjoyed under the direction of a manager, whose virtues and abilities have so long & so justly been encouraged and applauded by the united voice of the public, March 25, 1777." Inscribed on verso of metal piece at bottom: "Purchased at Mr. Garrick's sale in 1823 and presented by the committee of the Covent Garden Theatrical Fund to their treasurer, Iohn Fawcett, Esq., in grateful testimony of his valuable and unparalleled services in supporting and bringing to a state of perfection an institution (commenced by Garrick) by which numbers of his profession will be secured from poverty in their latter days and in whose gratitude the name of Fawcett must ever hold a place equally honorable to its possessor as to humanity.

'A gift keeps even measure with the heart
And doth expand in worth and efficacy
As 'tis received.'

       March 10th, 1824"

Inscribed on verso of ribbon at top: "W. Abbott, C. Connor, C. Farley, C. Mathews, R. Jones, J. Sinclair, T. Yates, C. Taylor, C.(?) Young, D. Edgerton, Sec." (These men formed the Committee of the Covent Garden Actors' Fund.)

Provenance: Presented to David Garrick by the Incorporated Actors of the Theatre Royal, Drury Lane, 25 March 1777; Garrick sale, Christie's, 23 June 1823, lot 77, bought by Rainey for £27.6.0; presented by the Committee of the Covent Garden Theatrical Fund to John Fawcett, its treasurer, 10 March 1824; when Folger acquired it is not known.

Exhibitions: London, Royal Academy, 1777, no. 186, as "The honorary medal presented to David Garrick, Esq., by the incorporated actors of Drury Lane Theatre, painted in enamel from a drawing by Mr. Cipriani"; San Francisco, 1979–82, repr. p. 185

References: The London Packet, 25–28 April 1777, p. 1 (favorable mention which is reprinted in the *Morning Chronicle,* 28 April 1777, p. 2); Basil S. Long, *British Miniaturists,* London, 1929, p. 227; Piper 1964, p. 32 (repr.); Anglesea 1971, pp. 98, 184, and 256

139

Condition: There are nicks in the surface near the middle of the base of the herm and to the right of Garrick along the same line. The enamel is mounted in a thin gold frame surmounted by a metal gold ribbon shaped as a bow with a ring at top center, and below is an elaborately decorated crescent. The entire piece measures 7¼ inches in height.

Long interested in a fund for retired, indigent actors, Garrick, on nearing his own retirement, lobbied Parliament to pass a bill incorporating the Theatrical Fund for actors, their widows, and children. The bill was enacted in March 1776, and in March of the following year the actors of the Drury Lane Theatre presented him, as a token of their appreciation, with an enamel medallion designed by

Cipriani and executed by Howes. Although the gift honors Garrick as a benefactor, the image itself has nothing to do with charity but celebrates instead the actor's and Shakespeare's genius. Presumably, the implication is that the playwright and his interpreter had raised English drama to such a high level that its practitioners were worthy of public support.

Garrick, in classical attire, the outer garment a regal purple, appears as a new Roscius. Togaed contemporary figures were more likely encountered in the eighteenth century in sculpture, but in the context of this presentation piece Garrick's costume is not inappropriate. In one hand the actor holds a mask of tragedy, his own smile suggesting his comedic talents, and with the other hand he pulls back a green drapery to reveal the double herm of Shakespeare and the Ephesian Diana.[1] Shakespeare points to his temple, underscoring his imaginative intellectual powers. Despite the heavily classicizing nature of the work, he remains in Jacobean attire, unalterably himself. The Ephesian Diana represents exuberant fertility, making Shakespeare abundant Nature's twin. Her hair cropped short and mounted with a crown, an acorn necklace around her neck, multiple breasts protruding from her chest, a lion resting on her extended arm, and her waist encircled by animals, she is closely based on surviving antique statuary.[2]

Interestingly, Cipriani's design uses many of the same elements found in John Hamilton Mortimer's frontispiece (fig. 99) executed for Evan Lloyd's *An Epistle to David Garrick* of 1773.[3] At the right in Mortimer's etching, a more naturalistic, but still multibreasted, Ephesian Diana leans against Shakespeare's sarcophagus while crowning Genius, who personifies the glories of Garrick as Roscius. Mortimer employs the language of classical allegory; Cipriani, on the other hand, introduces portraiture into a conception that is not far removed from a historical portrait such as Sir Joshua Reynolds's *Three Ladies Adorning a Term of Hymen* (Tate Gallery, London), exhibited at the Royal Academy in 1774, where contemporary figures masquerading as the Three Graces adorn a term set off by drapery. Yet the Cipriani-Howes medallion creates a bizarre mixture in pedantically insisting on an archeologically precise Ephesian Diana, while giving Garrick classical apparel and Shakespeare van Dyckian dress. Horace Walpole apparently felt the work failed on the level of both allegory and portraiture,

Fig. 99. John Hamilton Mortimer, *Frontispiece to Evan Lloyd's "Epistle to David Garrick,"* 1773. Etching, 8¾ × 7⅞ in. (image).

as he scribbled in his copy of the Royal Academy exhibition catalogue, "very bad and unlike." Walpole's is too harsh a judgment, but one can sympathize with his unhappiness over the medallion's conceit.

1. Charles Reuben Ryley may have been thinking of Cipriani's design when he created a frontispiece showing Shakespeare writing at a table and gazing on the Ephesian Diana, who is unveiling herself to him. Ryley's drawing was engraved by Widnell and appears in volume 3 of *The Plays of Shakespeare*, published by Ogilvie and son in London in 1798.
2. Engraved examples of statues of the Ephesian Diana can be found in Bernard de Montfaucon's *L'Antiquité expliquée*, Paris, 1722, vol. 1, pls. 93 and 94. Animals that encircle her waist are traditionally stags, bulls, lions, horses, goats and rams. Exactly what Howes or Cipriani intended is unclear, goats possibly coming the closest.
3. Mortimer signed this print with an "M," difficult to make out, in the lower left corner.

Joseph Inchbald, attributed to (nos. 140–41)

Inchbald, born around 1735, was an actor who also aspired to be an artist. He made his London stage debut at Drury Lane on 8 October 1770. The following spring he met Elizabeth Simpson, marrying her on 9 June 1772. That fall he and his wife joined an acting company in Scotland, but, meeting with little success, he decided to pursue full-time his interest in portrait painting. On 2 July 1776 he and his wife left Edinburgh for Paris, where he planned to devote a year to the study of painting. The plan, though, was soon abandoned, the Inchbalds returning to England and performing in a number of provincial towns. Inchbald died at age forty-four on 6 June 1779.

140

ELIZABETH INCHBALD

ca. 1772–79

Watercolor on ivory, circular, irregular, 1⅝ in. diameter (4.2 × 4.1 cm.)

Case no. 1266

Provenance: Mrs. Elizabeth Inchbald; inherited by her nephew George Huggins; by descent from Mrs. Huggins (George's wife?) of New House Farm, Beaulieu, New Forest, to her cousin Frances Croucher in 1874; by descent to her daughter Agnes Croucher in 1893; sold Sotheby, 18–19 (18) March 1909, lot 22, £5.5.0 (the miniatures formed part of a collection of materials by or about Mrs. Inchbald; the catalogue

contains Father George Huggins's guarantee that all items are genuine and come from the actress); the entire lot offered to Folger by American Art Galleries for $400 and acquired by July 1924

Condition: This miniature and the following were originally mounted on a single piece of cardboard and were secured by thread. This miniature was on the right side and beneath it in pen and ink was inscribed: "Mrs. Inchbald."

Elizabeth Simpson was born near Bury St. Edmunds in Suffolk on 15 October 1753. In April 1771 she ran away to London, where she soon sought the protection of members of her family. Here she met Joseph Inchbald, who was eighteen years her senior. In April of the following year she returned to London, marrying Inchbald on 9 June. Long attracted to the stage, she joined her actor-husband on tour, making her debut on 4 September 1772 in the role of Cordelia in Bristol. In October 1780, over a year after the death of her husband, Mrs. Inchbald appeared in London at the Covent Garden Theatre. Realizing that her acting career held only limited promise, she left the stage at the end of the 1788–89 season determined to succeed as a writer. Extremely prolific, she wrote a number of successful plays and novels before her death on 1 August 1821. Although she burned her autobiography, James Boaden's *Memoirs of Mrs. Inchbald* is based on her diaries, some of which have survived.

The miniature portrays Mrs. Inchbald at a young age, presumably in her mid-twenties, as the hair style is one that was popular from the mid- to late 1770s. Executed before she had obtained fame, this work is the earliest known portrait of her.

The Folger miniature is not a polished performance, and Joseph Inchbald, an amateur who could not succeed as a professional, seems a likely candidate as its creator. No works firmly attributed to him have been found, but Boaden affirms that he painted portraits of his wife on a number of occasions. Not until 1777, however, did he manage a portrait to his satisfaction: "His wife's beauty had constantly foiled him [as an artist], but at Canterbury the difficulty was surmounted; he got a likeness with which they were both pleased."[1]

1. James Boaden, *Memoirs of Mrs. Inchbald*, London, 1833, vol. 1, p. 86.

140 (enlarged)

141 (enlarged)

141

ROBERT INCHBALD

ca. 1770s

Watercolor on ivory, oval image on rectangular piece of ivory with clipped corners, $1^{11}/_{16} \times 1^{1}/_{2}$ in. (4.6 × 3.8 cm.)

Case no. 1266

Provenance: Same as no. 140

Condition: See no. 140. On the cardboard beneath the position where the miniature had been placed is the following inscription: "Master Inchbald / who died in childhood."

The sitter in the miniature is clearly a young boy. He wears a child's costume, consisting of a blue-red jacket with a lace collar and broad-brim hat. The work is not a pendant to the miniature of Mrs. Inchbald (though at one time paired on the same mount, they differ in scale and background), but it appears to be by the same amateurish hand. The following description is given in a list of the materials that were contained in the lot sold in 1909: "Two miniatures painted on ivory one of herself [Mrs. Inchbald] & one of her only child who died in childhood."[1] The statement, presumably made by

Agnes Croucher, is in error. Mrs. Inchbald never had any children of her own. When she married Joseph, he had two illegitimate sons: George, who was already an adult, and Robert. Surely Joseph Inchbald practiced on his son as well as his wife, and if the sitter is a Master Inchbald, it can only be Robert. As such, it is the only known portrait of him. Robert accompanied his father and stepmother after their marriage, acting in juvenile parts such as Fleance in *Macbeth*. Boaden writes that the relationship between Mrs. Inchbald and her stepson was not always a happy one, the actress arranging for him separate lodgings on their return from Glasgow to Edinburgh.[2] In 1774, however, he reports, "The boy Bob is now become more agreeable. She goes seldom either to the play or rehearsal, and in the evening plays at cards with him, while Mr. Inchbald is otherwise engaged."[3] Robert's career in the theater was short, and for the remainder of his life he seems to have found work as a musician.[4] He did not die young as stated in the list of materials included in the sale catalogue, outliving even his stepmother, who refers to him in her will as "the person calling himself Robert Inchbald, the illegitimate son of my Late husband."[5]

1. Folger MS, Y.d. 592 (13). The list itself of course formed part of the lot, and this information was repeated in the Sotheby catalogue.
2. Boaden, *Memoirs*, vol. 1, pp. 45–46.
3. Ibid., p. 53.
4. See Highfill 1973–, vol. 8, p. 86.
5. Folger MS, Y.d. 592 (9).

Rosalie Sully (nos. 142–43)

The daughter of the painter Thomas Sully, Rosalie was one of twelve children. Sarah, her mother, had had three children by her first husband, Thomas's brother Lawrence, before he died. After she and Thomas were married, they had nine children together, of which Rosalie, born on 3 June 1818, was the seventh. Rosalie, trained by her father, showed promise as an artist. In October 1839 she exhibited five landscapes at the Apollo Association in New York. She also specialized in miniatures, and at least two of these were copies after her father's portraits.[1] She died on 8 July 1847.

1. Theodore Bolton mentions only one miniature by Rosalie, a copy after her father's portrait of her mother (*Early American Portrait Painters in Miniature*, New York, 1921), and no. 143 is also a copy after a work by her father.

142 (enlarged)

142

CHARLOTTE CUSHMAN
1844
Watercolor with tempera on ivory, oval, 2 × 1½ in.
(5.2 × 3.9 cm.)

Accession no. 5057

There are faint traces of an inscription, now illegible, along the right-hand side above the sitter's shoulder.

Provenance: Painted as a gift from the artist to the sitter; by descent to Charlotte Cushman's nephew and adopted son, Edwin Charles Cushman; by descent to his wife; by descent to their son, Victor N. Cushman; by descent to his wife; gift of Mrs. Victor N. Cushman, 24 September 1936

References: The five miniatures given in the Cushman bequest are mentioned in four different sources. The earliest is composed of a printed list cut from a catalogue and pasted on a scrap of paper entitled, "List [illegible word] to Loan Collection in Newport" (FSL MS, Y.d. 531 [4]). The owner is given in this text as Mrs. E. C. Cushman, who is the

wife of Edwin Charles Cushman, the nephew and adopted son of Charlotte. The following items recorded in this list are relevant to the works in the Folger:

18   *The Misses Sully,* by Sully.
19* *Head of Mrs. Fanny Kemble,* by Sully.
20* *Miss Charlotte Cushman,* by Sully.
21* *Miss Charlotte Cushman,* copied by Watkins.
22* *Miss Charlotte Cushman,* by Sully.
23* *Mrs. Muspratt,* by Watkins.
24   *Miss Cushman's Mother,* by Watkins.
34   *Miss Cushman's Sister.* [crossed out in pencil]
35* *Study of an Eye,* by Mrs. Young.
      [Asterisk denotes entries marked in red pencil]

A manuscript entitled "Contents of this box—Sep. 29. 1917" [Y.d. 531 (3)] mentions three relevant works: "Study of C.C.-'s eye," "Miniature of Fanny Kemble her[?] hair," "Charlotte Cushman—Rose Sully," this last entry being the first time Rosalie Sully is distinguished from her father, Thomas. All of the objects bequeathed by Mrs. Victor Cushman are mentioned in the FSL *Annual Report* for 1936–37, but a more accurate list is contained in the ledger with accession numbers. The accession numbers were not written on the objects, so the works as catalogued here are an attempt to match each miniature with its correct entry.

Condition: The brown in the hair is severely cracking with some flaking. The coating used in the finely hatched, light brown background may be watercolor mixed with egg tempera. It shows evidence of shrinkage causing a splotching effect, which may also be the result of air bubbles. The miniature is in a gold frame, on the back of which are locks of hair decorated with gold thread and a pearl ornament. The small clump of hair to the left is a light brown, in contrast to the darker brown hair composing the other clusters. One possibility is that the light hair is Rosalie's and the dark hair is Charlotte's. Neither shade of hair matches that of the bracelet in no. 143. The case is mounted as a brooch.

Charlotte Cushman enjoyed a special friendship with Rosalie Sully, who was just two years younger; each woman was passionately devoted to the other.[1] Charlotte's diary entries for 1844 are filled with references to her friend, of letters written and letters received when they were apart, and Charlotte was consumed with longing thoughts of Rosalie when crossing by ship to England in late October of that year.[2] Soon, though, Rosalie was devastated by reports from London that someone else had supplanted her in her friend's affections, but one of her surviving letters, written to Charlotte on 11 May 1845, offers proof of the enduring strength the relationship held for her:

> The matting and summer covers in the parlour do so forcibly bring to mind the many happy hours <u>we</u> two have passed there together and the melancholy change that a twelve month has made in my life—our sofa occupies the same place opposite the back-room door as it did last summer but now instead of passing there hours of sweet companionship with you I often throw myself upon it alone and heart broken—praying fervently for death to end my misery—and yet there is not a being in the world that has the least idea of what I feel, for outwardly I am the same as ever, save that I am often <u>more quiet</u>. . . . I am as fondly your's as I was the 6th of July last[.] that pledge I still wear—were my feelings towards you the least changed I should remove it from off my finger for I never deceive either in word or action—since your absence the <u>bracelet</u> has never been <u>unclasped</u>.[3]

The Folger miniature is undoubtedly one of the gifts Rosalie had given in her turn to her closest friend. It is recorded in the accession ledger as "Miniature in oil of Ch Cushman, gold frame . . . Mrs. [Victor] C[ushman]. thinks by Sully but possibly daughter Rosalie." Less polished than Thomas's works, the miniature is undoubtedly by Rosalie, and Leach, Cushman's most recent biographer, identifies it with Rosalie's miniature portrait of Charlotte that became for the actress a special treasure.[4] As with other of the Sully miniatures, it was a highly personal memento that was mounted so that it might be worn. In this instance, there is no evidence that Rosalie was following a portrait first executed by her father. The miniature is surely entirely of her own design. Cushman, posed against a gray-and-brown background, is shown faintly smiling, her large, luminous brown eyes dreamily unfocused. She wears a blue dress over a white blouse pinned at the neck with an oval cameo. Unlike her father (see no. 125), Rosalie refused to transform her friend into a conventional beauty.

1. Not everyone was happy with the intensity of their bond. Leach sums up the evidence: "Charlotte's vague diary notations and

an inference in one of Rosalie's letters suggest an affectionate regard between them that was not universally approved, though the written endearments that passed between them said nothing that might not have appeared in any number of Victorian expressions of female friendship" (1970, p. 114). One of those who disapproved was Charlotte's mother, who wrote her daughter when she was in England, "I wish you would not mention the Sullys to me in your letters. The spirit in which you do it is most painful to me" (quoted on p. 153).
2. See Charlotte Cushman Diary for 1844–45, Rare Book and Manuscript Library, Columbia University Libraries, New York.
3. Rosalie Sully to Charlotte Cushman, 11 May 1845, Charlotte Cushman Papers, Library of Congress, Washington, D.C., vol. 14, 3970.
4. Leach 1970, pp. 114 and 412, n.

143
FRANCES ANNE KEMBLE
1844
Watercolor on ivory, oval, 1^9/$_{16}$ × 1^1/$_4$ in. (4 × 3.2 cm.) (sight)

Accession no. 5061

Provenance: Presented by the artist to Charlotte Cushman; by descent to her nephew and adopted son, Edwin Charles Cushman; by descent to his wife; by descent to their son, Victor N. Cushman; gift of Mrs. Victor N. Cushman, 24 September 1936

143 (enlarged)

References: See no. 142.

Exhibitions: Washington, 1985; New York, Grolier Club, *The Terrific Kemble,* 17 February–2 April 1988

Condition: Some retouching is evident under raking light, and there are air bubbles in the hair and a small amount of flaking. The entry in the accession records reads, "mounted in [rose] gold, as a bracelet, of Fanny Kemble's hair." The hair is medium brown and consists of four rows of double knots. Engraved on the back of the case: "Charlotte from Rosalie / July 23rd. 1844 [the date is Charlotte Cushman's birthday]."

Fanny Kemble was born on 27 November 1809 in London to actor Charles Kemble, who was the brother of the more celebrated actors Sarah Siddons and John Philip Kemble. After being educated in France, Fanny made her debut at Covent Garden, where her father was a proprietor, on 5 October 1829. In 1832 she came to America with her father, touring for two seasons from New York to New Orleans. She was in Thomas Sully's studio as early as November 1832 and first sat to him on 10 March 1833. Sully was to paint her on numerous occasions, but often from recollection rather than life. She and Sully's wife, Sarah, were close friends. Though an acclaimed actress, Kemble disliked the exhibitionism of the stage, and she retired two weeks after her marriage to Pierce Butler of Germantown, Pennsylvania. From this time her energy often went into writing, and over the years she produced a number of books. Her husband's income came from his Georgia plantation, and after spending the winter of 1838–39 there, Kemble recoiled from the horrors of slavery. She became increasingly estranged from her husband, and in 1846 left him completely to return to the London stage. In 1849 her husband successfully ended a divorce suit against her. Kemble supported herself primarily through her brilliant public readings of Shakespeare both in England and America. She died in London on 15 January 1893.

The Sullys had known Kemble from the time she had first arrived in Philadelphia. Of their children, one imagines that Rosalie in particular felt a special bond with the actress, as her middle name was Kemble; her father had obviously christened her in honor of Fanny's illustrious family long before he had ever heard of its latest celebrity.

The case holding the Folger miniature is engraved on its back, "Charlotte from Rosalie / July 23rd. 1844." It was Rosalie's present to her close friend on the actress's twenty-eighth birthday. According to Cushman's diary, on 6 March 1844 Rosalie had given her a miniature of Fanny Kemble. On 16 July she mentions, "Bracelet from Rose and note answered."[1] It is possible that this bracelet of 16 July is the one in the Folger, the birthday present having been given a week early. The present is either a second miniature of Kemble or is the one first given on 6 March but now mounted and engraved. The hair composing the band of the bracelet is cited as Kemble's in the accession records, and it does match fairly well the color of her hair as rendered in the miniature.

The present was an appropriate one, for Cushman and Kemble were also close friends, having first met in the fall of 1840. By 1844 their friendship had become intense, as Cushman sought to assist her friend in securing a divorce from her husband, even volunteering to collect evidence of his infidelities. The friendship ultimately did not survive the strain of Cushman's involvement in Kemble's personal af-

Fig. 100. Thomas Sully, *Frances Anne Kemble,* 1832. Oil on canvas, 30 × 25 in. Abbott Lawrence Fund, courtesy Museum of Fine Arts, Boston.

fairs, but the Folger miniature offers a striking memento of their friendship.

Rosalie Sully's miniature is based on the portrait her father painted of Kemble in 1833, a work now in Boston (fig. 100).[2] This painting hung in the Sully home, and on 27 May 1835 Kemble had mentioned it when writing her friend Harriet St. Leger, who had been disappointed with another portrait Sully had painted of the actress: "He pressed upon my acceptance for you, a little melancholy head of me, an admirable and not too much flattered likeness; but as he had given that to his wife, of whom I am very fond, of course I could not deprive her of it."[3] Rosalie, though of course condensing the image, followed her model closely: Fanny is shown with brown eyes and brown hair and a tan collar, but the background is now blue rather than gray. Rosalie also slightly elongated the actress's features, presenting her as even more austere than in the original. Of all Sully's portraits, Kemble felt that this likeness alone did not unduly flatter her, a fault she found in most of the artist's work, and, as we have seen, she characterized the image as melancholy. The line of her neck eloquently extended, her head turned to one side, she appears moodily reflective, the rendering bringing out her qualities as a woman of character and high intelligence, attributes that surely appealed to her friends.

1. The diary, which covers only 1844–45, is in the Rare Book and Manuscript Library, Columbia University Libraries, New York.
2. At an unknown date Cushman approached Kemble for her permission to have Thomas Sully copy for her one of his portraits of Kemble (undated letter containing Kemble's positive response is in the FSL, C.c. [1]). Obviously, Rosalie's miniature was very much appreciated, and it may be after the very painting Cushman had wanted copied.
3. Frances Ann Kemble, *Records of Later Life*, New York, 1882, p. 13.

Thomas Sully, attributed to

144

SUSAN CUSHMAN
ca. 1843–44
Watercolor with bodycolor on ivory, oval, $1^7/8 \times 1^1/2$ in. (4.7 × 3.7 cm.) (sight)

Accession no. 5060

Provenance: Collection of Charlotte Cushman; by descent to her nephew and adopted son, Edwin Charles Cushman; by descent to his son, Victor N.

144 (enlarged)

Cushman; gift of Mrs. Victor N. Cushman, 24 September 1936

References: See no. 142.

Condition: Mounted as a brooch in a gold frame.

As an actress, Susan Webb Cushman, who was born in Boston on 17 March 1822, always lived in the shadow of her elder sister, Charlotte. Just before her fourteenth birthday she married Nelson M. Meriman of Boston but was soon abandoned by him with an infant, who grew up to become Charlotte's adopted son. She made her stage debut at age fifteen and was better noted for her attractive appearance than for her talent. She was part of the company when Charlotte was stage manager of the Walnut Street Theatre in Philadelphia in 1842–43, and soon followed Charlotte to London, where on 30 December 1845 she opened as Juliet to her sister's Romeo in a celebrated production of Shakespeare's play. In March 1848 she married J. Sheridan Muspratt of Liverpool and retired from the stage. She died in Liverpool on 10 May 1859.

One of the miniatures in the Cushman bequest is identified as depicting Susan rather than Charlotte, and this work seems the most likely. The sitter is more of a conventional beauty than the sitter depicted in the other two (nos. 142 and 145), and the suggestion of a cleft chin further sets her apart. Susan's eyes are gray, tinged with yellow; her hair is a dark brown; and one glimpses the fringe of her dress at lower left. She is posed against a mottled blue-gray background.

The accession ledger states of the Susan Cushman miniature, "Either by Thomas Sully or his daughter Rosalie." Presumably following the example of his brother Lawrence, Thomas Sully began his professional career painting miniatures. The majority of his pictures in this medium are early works, but Biddle and Fielding list some later miniatures, including two of Charlotte Cushman. The first (no. 2029), said to be painted about 1840, depicts her in *The Taming of the Shrew* and the second (no. 2030) in the character of Joan of Arc. There is no mention in Sully's register of any miniature of Susan Cushman, but the Folger painting is attributed to him here, rather than to Rosalie, on the grounds of its high quality.[1]

1. It is possible that the miniature is by William Henry Watkins. In an early list (see no. 142, References), there is a miniature recorded as "*Mrs. Muspratt,* by Watkins." Yet this work bears little stylistic resemblance to the other portrait attributed to Watkins (no. 145).

William Henry Watkins

In 1847 Watkins, a London painter, exhibited at the Royal Academy two miniatures, both of which were entitled simply *Portrait of a Lady* (nos. 790 and 882); he showed another (no. 937) the following year. It is possible that his miniature of Charlotte was one of these works. Watkins painted several portraits of the Cushman family; Mrs. E. C. Cushman's list (see no. 142, References) records a portrait by him of Charlotte's mother, Mary Eliza, and one of Mrs. Muspratt, Charlotte's sister. This portrait of Charlotte is listed as "copied by Watkins," raising the possibility that it is after another work.

145

CHARLOTTE CUSHMAN
Watercolor with bodycolor on ivory, oval, $3^{3}/_{16} \times 2^{1}/_{2}$ in. (8.1 × 6.5 cm.) (sight)

Accession no. 5058

Provenance: Collection of Charlotte Cushman; by descent to her nephew and adopted son, Edwin Charles Cushman; by descent to his wife; by descent to their, son Victor N. Cushman; gift of Mrs. Victor N. Cushman, 24 September 1936

145 (enlarged)

References: See no. 142.

Condition: There are some scratches on the paint surface, particularly noticeable in the background, and some abrasion on the lower right edge. The miniature is mounted in a brass frame with a ring at the top and backed with silk embroidered in a floral design.

The accession ledger lists a "miniature in oil of Ch. Cushman, by Watkins." Unlike the other miniatures of Charlotte (excluding the one of her eye, no. 146) and Susan, it is not stated to have a gold frame, and the frame of this particular image is brass. Furthermore, in technique and size it differs considerably from the works attributed here to the Sully family, and the dress Cushman is wearing suggests a date after her arrival in London, when she adopted more masculine attire. Cushman wears a light brown dress, shaded with hatchings in blue, purple, pink, and dark brown. A black bow is tied at her neck beneath the wide, loose collar of her white blouse. Her eyes are blue, her hair a dark brown, and she is placed against a blue background enlivened with extensive hatching that shades into brown at the bottom. Her elongated neck and slender torso give an awkward emphasis to her imposing head.

Mrs. Young

The accession records are frustratingly terse in cataloguing this work: "Miniature study of Ch. Cushman's eye, by Young." The Mrs. E. C. Cushman list, while offering less about the identity of the sitter, gives a little more information on the artist, listing her as "Mrs. Young." Of English painters, a J. Young, living at 7 Granby Street, London, exhibited a portrait of a member of the Scots Fusilier Guards at the Royal Academy in 1848 (no. 199). He or she painted miniatures, as one of Jane Shore, after a portrait at Ludlow Castle, was sold as by J. Young at Christie's on 25 October 1960.[1] This artist is a possible choice only because so little about him or her is known. Another possibility is that the artist is the American miniaturist Mary Eliza Young. Her birth date is unrecorded, but she married the artist Samuel Bell Waugh, who was born in 1814. While Miss Young became Mrs. Waugh, it is not incredible to speculate that she could have been incorrectly referred to as Mrs. Young in Mrs. E. C. Cushman's list. Whoever the artist, the Folger miniature was clearly executed by an accomplished professional.

1. See Daphne Foskett, *A Dictionary of British Miniature Painters*, New York and Washington, 1972.

146

CHARLOTTE CUSHMAN'S EYE

Watercolor with bodycolor on ivory, oval, $^{7}/_{8} \times {}^{11}/_{16}$ in. (2.3 × 1.8 cm.) (sight)

Accession no. 5059

Provenance: Collection of Charlotte Cushman; by descent to her nephew and adopted son, Edwin Charles Cushman; by descent to his son Victor N. Cushman; gift of Mrs. Victor N. Cushman, 24 September 1936

References: See no. 142

Condition: The miniature is mounted in a rectangular taped frame with a gold mat.

Miniatures focusing on the eye, either left or right, were not uncommon in the late eighteenth

146 (enlarged)

and early nineteenth centuries. In these works, the eye functions as a window into the sitter's soul. Obviously, the sitter cannot be identified from so small a portion of the face, but, given the Folger miniature's provenance, one accepts on faith that it portrays Charlotte Cushman's left eye. The eye is gray with luminous highlights, the eyebrow and hair a soft brown, the whole framed within an oval echoing the shape of the eye itself.

III Portraits of Shakespeare

One fifth of the Folger collection consists of portraits of Shakespeare, portraits that fluctuate dramatically in quality. It is testimony to the need for icons, where aesthetic questions are often irrelevant. For the Folgers themselves, this group formed the core of the collection. A number of these images were purchased as from life (one even showing the poet on his deathbed!), but none can now claim such a distinction.

  Born in Stratford-upon-Avon, Shakespeare was baptized on 26 April 1564, his birth date traditionally being placed on the 23rd. He was the third child and first son of John Shakespeare and Mary Arden. His father was chosen alderman in 1564 and in 1568 served as bailiff, the equivalent of mayor. John later, however, suffered debts and was eventually deprived of his alderman's gown. Shakespeare studied at the free grammar school at Stratford and around 1577 left to help his father, who apparently was then a butcher. In 1582 he married Anne Hathaway, eight years his senior. The wedding may have been forced on William to save Anne's reputation, as six months later she gave birth to a daughter, Susanna. In 1585 she delivered twins, Hamnet and Judith. Shortly afterwards Shakespeare left Stratford, eventually ending up in London.

  Shakespeare worked as an actor as a member of the earl of Leicester's company, with which he remained through its various transformations as the Chamberlain's Men and the King's Men, this last an honor awarded in 1603. By 1591 he was writing plays, producing over his career at least thirty-seven works. Among his earliest are the three parts of *Henry VI*, performances of which are recorded in 1592. In 1594 he acted before Queen Elizabeth, and in that year is also mentioned as one of the shareholders of the Lord Chamberlain's Company. He was one of the owners of the Globe Theatre, which opened in 1599, and in 1608 or 1609 joined his colleagues in purchasing the smaller, enclosed Blackfriars Theatre, which, unlike the Globe, could be used in the winter months. He also gained success as a poet, publishing *Venus and Adonis* in 1593 and *The Rape of Lucrece* in the following year, both of which were dedicated to Henry Wriothesley, earl of Southampton (see no. 189). His sonnets, though not published until 1609, were probably written at about this same time.

  As he prospered, Shakespeare helped relieve his family from its debts and in 1596 applied, in his father's name, to the College of Heralds for a coat of arms (see no. 202). The next year he bought New Place, then the largest house in Stratford. He did not settle there until 1611, though, even after this date, he continued to visit London frequently, purchasing a house in Blackfriars in 1613. Completing his will in March 1616, he died in Stratford on 23 April of that year, on his fifty-second birthday, if one accepts the traditional dating. His wife died in 1623, and his last descendant, Elizabeth, daughter of his eldest child, Susanna, died in 1670.

Although Shakespeare was appreciated by his contemporaries, both the man and his work enjoying success, he could not rise above his station: he was after all only a playwright, a profession that was still regarded as somewhat disreputable. Consequently, there was no great urge to leave an account of the man, and even a number of his plays were in danger of being lost to posterity. Antiquarians and critics only slowly began to record what they could discover about the life, and with the passage of time, as the facts had become few and far between, they had to be supplemented with heavy doses of fiction.

The desire to know what the poet looked like was an important part of the attempt to recover the man. Frustratingly, only two images can indisputably claim authenticity, the Droeshout engraving (see fig. 101) and the Stratford Bust (see fig. 106). Both of these works were posthumous, and neither is a distinguished work of art. Only one painting, *The Chandos Portrait of Shakespeare* (see fig. 110), was early on put forward as a life portrait, and it became the favored image of Shakespeare in the eighteenth century. Up to about 1770, memorial portraits and copies of the existing canon were all that was available to satisfy admirers of the Bard. As the century wore on, however, a view of writing as self-expression came to prevail, and this view that biography offered insights into an author's work intensified the desire to know Shakespeare the man. Not surprisingly, beginning in the late eighteenth century, a steady stream of images started to appear to supply this demand for more information about the National Poet. Now the canon itself was dramatically to expand. Some of these newly recovered images were created from scratch by forgers who wished to capitalize on this need. Yet these new images of Shakespeare usually bore a similarity to the surviving authoritative portraits, which, having been used as a guide, were then offered as proof of the new work's credibility. In other instances, authentic seventeenth-century portraits were christened Shakespeare (this may also have been the case with the earlier Chandos Portrait) and still other authentic portraits underwent altera-

tions to bring them more in line with the presumed likeness, often by simply enlarging the forehead.

All the types are represented in the Folger collection. There are early copies, fakes, altered seventeenth-century portraits, and seventeenth-century portraits that have simply been willed to be Will. Even when the sitter can no longer be identified as Shakespeare, the pictures have been retained in this section, as they form such an important part of the Shakespeare iconography. In the forefront of these works is the Janssen Portrait, a print of which was first published in 1770, the Felton Portrait, which surfaced in 1792, the Ashbourne Portrait discovered in 1847, and the Lumley Portrait, first exhibited in 1853.

While in Folger's lifetime the identity of the sitter was rarely seriously challenged, the attributions were often disputed. When in doubt, the two artists who were most frequently put forward as the creators were Richard Burbage and John Taylor. If these two men had not existed they would have to have been invented, and this in fact may well be the case with the latter. We owe John Taylor's name to George Vertue, who, writing in the early eighteenth century, attributed the Chandos Portrait to him, identifying him as an actor and close friend of the poet.[1] Although there is no evidence of an actor by that name, there was a Joseph Taylor (1586–1653) who was on the stage by 1610 but is not known to have painted. The life of Richard Burbage (1567?–1619) is much better documented. The son of an actor and theatrical manager, Burbage followed in his father's footsteps. He knew Shakespeare from at least 1594, had a financial interest in the Blackfriars and Globe theaters, and was celebrated as a tragedian, receiving acclaim in a number of Shakespeare's tragedies. Because he is also said to have painted, he has attracted the attribution of numerous portraits purporting to be of Shakespeare from the life.

In addition to copies, forgeries, and reworked and reidentified Jacobean portraits, the collection also includes memorial portraits executed by accomplished artists who wished to create their conception of this famous man. A certain power is granted to the artist in depicting an individual about whom little is known. The very absence of a satisfactory portrait from the life makes it possible for each artist to recast the subject in his own image: the creator must himself be created.

Memorial portraits of Shakespeare begin early: in the seventeenth century one could point to Soest's painting of Shakespeare, of which the Folger collection contains two variations, and to the Chesterfield Portrait now owned by the Shakespeare Birthplace Trust. In the eighteenth century it is in the area of sculpture that one encounters the best works of this type. In the nineteenth century paintings proliferate, and they expand to include pictures focusing on presumed incidences in Shakespeare's life, such as the Bard caught poaching or reading his work before Queen Elizabeth. Folger purchased no works of a narrative cast beyond pictures showing Shakespeare in his study. His passion, as with the artists he collected, was for exploring the character of the man through his physiognomy. His modern memorial portraits range from Sully's image of 1864 to Sartain's of 1907, to which Umberto Romano's dramatic characterization has recently been added. All of these artists were Americans by birth or by choice. By the late nineteenth century, one could argue that Shakespeare, the man, held an even stronger fascination for Americans than for the English. In the United States there was a stronger need to resurrect the great man than in the Old World, involving, as it did, a search for roots in a new land.

The English artist Thomas Gainsborough was perhaps the most articulate and candid in expressing what he felt was involved in painting a memorial portrait. Writing in 1768 to David Garrick, Gainsborough, who had apparently been given a commission by the actor, saw it as an opportunity rather than a burden. He wished to improve upon the original picture of Shakespeare, by which he presumably meant the Chandos Portrait or possibly the Droeshout engraving:

"Shakespeare shall come forth forthwith," as the lawyer says. Damn the original picture of him, *with your leave;* for I think a stupider face I never beheld, except D—k's.

I intend, with your approbation, my dear friend, to take the form from his pictures and statues, just enough to preserve his likeness past the doubt of all blockheads at first sight, and supply a *soul* from his works; it is impossible that such a mind and ray of heaven could shine with such a face and pair of eyes as that picture has; so, as I said before, damn *that*.[2]

Sully, Page, Hall, Sartain, and Romano would certainly have understood Gainsborough's excitement in attempting to conjure up the idea of the man, but not everyone would share their enthusiasm. Louis B. Wright, a former director of the Folger whose passions were books rather than paintings, replied on 27 February 1950 to a request from Charles Morgan for loans for an exhibition at Amherst: "You can of course have a Shakespearean portrait. None of them have any real validity and you can take your choice among these imagined images of the bard." It is precisely because they are imagined that they are important. Even the worst of the fakes offer insights into changing perceptions of the poet, and the best of the images offer glimpses into various interpretations of Shakespeare's genius. As Gainsborough maintained, the soul of the man, which itself changes from reader to reader and artist to artist, is ultimately of more interest than the record of a face.

1. George Virtue, "The Note-Books of George Vertue relating to artists and collections in England," *Journal of the Walpole Society* 18 (1930), p. 48.
2. Quoted in catalogue to Stratford-upon-Avon, 1864, p. 28. Gainsborough subsequently painted over his portrait of Shakespeare. X rays made at the instigation of Martin Postle have recently revealed this image beneath Gainsborough's 1780 portrait of Johann Christian Fischer now in the Queen's collection.

Droeshout Shakespeare

Martin Droeshout, an English printmaker of Flemish descent, supplied the engraving for the title page of the First Folio (fig. 101). He was only fifteen years old when Shakespeare died and just twenty-two when the First Folio was published in 1623. The engraving, the creation of a young artist of indifferent ability, unfortunately offers only a crudely executed likeness. Shakespeare wears a doublet with metal braid decoration and matching buttons. The strings and tassels of the stiffened, linen band have been left out, and the outline of the under-propper beneath this ruff is visible on the viewer's right-hand side. The edge of the band is presumably wired, and the band itself would also have been starched and pressed. The triangular "rays" emanating from the neck are "clocks" or pleats characteristic of bands of this period. The crudity of the representation, with its anatomical distortions in both head and body, has often been

Fig. 101. Martin Droeshout, *William Shakespeare.* Engraving, the Folio Title Page with Portrait, State II, 1623, 7⅝ × 6⅜ in. (image).

Fig. 102. Martin Droeshout, *William Shakespeare.* Engraving, the Folio Title Page Portrait, State I, 1623.

commented on, and the head, which is too large for the body, is also isolated by the ruff, so that it is implausibly suspended above the more two-dimensional rendering of the torso. The large dome of the head is the dominant feature, and in emphasizing the sitter's intellect the image happily conforms to most viewers' preconceptions of the appearance of genius.

The Droeshout image is itself variable. There are three states of the engraving from the time of the First Folio. The first (fig. 102), by far the rarest, shows a thinner mustache, no shadow on the collar to the viewer's right, and a different treatment of highlights on the hair, while the more common second and third states are virtually indistinguishable.[1] In addition, there are two states with only minor variations for the Second Folio of 1632, and the plate was heavily reworked for the Fourth Folio of 1685. Beginning as early as 1640 (fig. 103), numerous other prints, large and small, used the Droeshout engraving as a point of departure. Thus, artists who were drawn to the Droeshout Portrait

might be responding to one of a number of possibilities.

The engraving of 1623 was surely not executed from the life or from memory. Over the years those paintings that have been put forward as models for it have been challenged as having been based on the print rather than the other way around. Recently, however, *The Flower Portrait of Shakespeare* (fig. 104), which bears the date 1609 and is painted over an earlier picture of the Madonna and Child with St. John, has been resurrected as a possible candidate for the life portrait copied by Droeshout.[2] Earlier, M. H. Spielmann had suggested that Droeshout's model was not an oil painting but rather a " 'limning' of the poet—a portrait consisting of an outline drawing, with perhaps delicate flat washes of colour—as in a Hilliard miniature."[3] Spielmann also argued that since the first state of the engraving does not depict certain details present in both the second state of the print and the Flower Portrait, the Flower Portrait must postdate the print, having been based on the second state. Bertram and Cossa argue the evidence can just as plausibly be interpreted as suggesting that after pulling impressions of the first state, Droeshout, on comparing them with the Flower Portrait, then added elements that would make the engraving more faithful to its model. Spielmann's argument, however, seems more convincing. If the model had been a miniature or limning, once Droeshout enlarged the image in his engraving, he would have seen that it required additions to strengthen it. This seems more likely than the argument that he ignored so prominent a feature in the first state of the engraving as the shadow to the left side of Shakespeare's head, only to add it in the second after comparing it with his source.

1. For descriptions of the various states of the First Folio Page Portrait, see Charlton Hinman, *The Painting and Proof-Reading of the First Folio of Shakespeare,* Oxford, 1963, vol. 1, pp. 248–49.
2. See Paul Bertram and Frank Cossa, " 'Willm Shakespeare 1609': The Flower Portrait Revisited," *Shakespeare Quarterly* 37 (Spring 1986), pp. 83–96. For this picture's provenance, see entry for no. 147.
3. Spielmann 1924, p. 33.

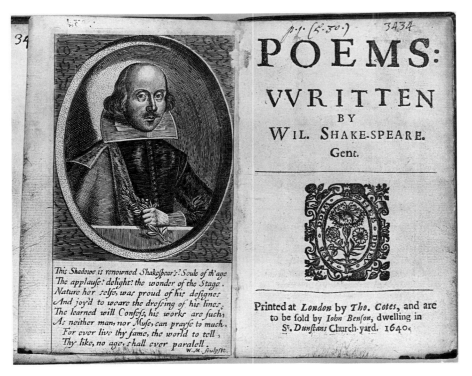

Anonymous (nos. 147–53)

147

THE BEADLE PORTRAIT OF SHAKESPEARE
Early nineteenth century
Oil on canvas, 30 × 23 in. (76.2 × 58.4 cm.), in elaborate Gothic frame with arched top

Accession no. 4204

Inscription: Coat of arms at upper left, partially cut off by arched top of frame

Provenance: By descent in 1873 to Virginia Bedell Topham of New York; bequeathed to William M. Simonson; sold by his widow, Clara L. Simonson of South Somerville, N.J., to the Library in February 1935 for $50

References: Clara L. Simonson Correspondence on file in the Library; FSL *Annual Report*, 1934–35, p. 21; Piper 1962, no. 5

Clara Simonson, the painting's last owner, supplied an ancient pedigree for this portrait. According to her account, it was purchased by Rev. Samuel

147

Beadle (1555–1615), rector of the Episcopal church at Wolverton, county of Suffolk. The portrait remained in the family in England, being passed down to the eldest married son, until 1873, when it was acquired by Mrs. Virginia Topham, an American relative of the English Beadles.[1] The picture was shipped rolled up to Mrs. Topham, and the Gothic frame was made in Philadelphia. After lengthy correspondence, Dr. Adams purchased the painting as a nineteenth-century work copied from

the engraving to the First Folio. The breadth of the moustache makes it clear that the image is based on a state of the engraving later than the first, where the moustache is thinner. The painting is listed in the Folger card file as a copy of *The Flower Portrait of Shakespeare* (see fig. 104) in the collection of the Royal Shakespeare Theatre Picture Gallery in Stratford-upon-Avon. H. C. Clements purchased the Flower Portrait around 1840, and it first attracted notice when he loaned it to the Memorial Picture Gallery in 1892. After his death in 1895, Mrs. Charles Flower purchased it and presented it to the Memorial. The Folger painting, however, was surely painted independently of the Flower picture, and their similarity is explained by their relationship to the Droeshout engraving. The Folger picture departs from the engraving and the Flower Portrait in that the embroidery and buttons on the doublet are muted so that the black of the doublet dominates; the bottom line of the collar is not as stiff; there is the suggestion of a beard at the tip of the chin; and the coat of arms is introduced at the upper left. It should be considered as another nineteenth-century attempt to provide an "old" portrait of Shakespeare compatible with the Droeshout type.

1. Mrs. Topham's maiden name was Bedell, the American branch of the family having altered the spelling.

148

THE BURBAGE PORTRAIT OF SHAKESPEARE
Early nineteenth century
Oil on panel, 23¼ × 14⅛ in. (59.0 × 35.8 cm.)

Case no. 836

Inscribed in gold letters on bottom panel:

> Howe speake thatte Browe soe pensive yet serene
> The lucidde Teare juste startynge to thyne Eyne
> Dost thou nowe dwelle onne Romeo's ill starr'd
>   love?
> Or doth the tortured Moore thy passion move?
> None so. Alasse! no more shalle phantasie's
>   Creature
> Adumbrate or enshroude the Poet's ffeatures
> To realle Illes hys frame nowe falles a Preye
> He feels approache the Ev'ninge of Lyfe's Daye
> And e'er another Dawne arise to cheere
> Lyfe's busie Sonnes: may droppe poore Wil
>   Shakspere.
> Sic cecinit Cygnvs Avoniae et Obiit 23 Aprilis
>   1616 Æts: 52

Provenance: According to the 1885 article in *Walford's Antiquarian,* the painting belonged to a Mr. Kinton, who died at Paddington in 1865 at age 91 (he had received it over 50 years earlier from a friend); given by Kinton to his medical attendant, who sold it to Mr. Grisbrook, a picture restorer; Sotheby, 7 December 1903, lot 8, £131, as the "Un-

known Portrait of Shakespeare," repr., bought by Moore; Sotheby, 8 December 1905, lot 567, £61, as the "Unknown Portrait of Shakspere," bought by Leach; offered to Folger by J. Pearson & Co. some years before 1919 sale; Sotheby, 28 July 1919, lot 264, as "the Burbage Portrait of Shakspere," £150, bought by Folger, Maggs acting as agent.

References: The Antiquarian Magazine and Bibliographer, August 1882, pp. 90–91 (also refers to an earlier notice in the *Artists' Critical Record*); *The Times,* 28 September 1885; "An Unknown Portrait of Shakspere," *Walford's Antiquarian* 8 (October 1885), pp. 157–59, repr.; Letter to the Editor from H. R. Forrest, *Walford's Antiquarian* 8 (December 1885), pp. 296–97 (questions painting's authenticity); W. Carew Hazlitt, *Shakespear: Himself and his Work,* 4th ed., London, 1912, pp. 158–59, head repr. facing p. 159; *Times Literary Supplement,* 8 August 1919; Letter to the Editor from M. H. Spielmann, *Times Literary Supplement,* 14–15 August 1919

Condition: The panel consists of five joined pieces: the main panel (16½ × 12 in., irregular), to which have been added thin vertical strips at either side (approximately 23¼ × 1 1/16 in.); a rectangular panel at bottom which perhaps split off from the main panel (6⅜ × 12 in.); and an inscribed panel screwed down over the bottom of the painting (7¼ × 12 in.). A parchment document with a red wax seal has been used to reinforce the back of the panel. The paint surface on the main panel suffers from severe vertical cracking. Paint has chipped off at the bottom fringe of the collar to the right of the neck and to the right of Shakespeare's left eye.

An eleven-line inscription in pen and ink, dated 1750, is attached to the back of the main panel at the top. Only a few words are now legible, but according to the transcription in the 1885 article in *Walford's Antiquarian,* it suggests that the poem accompanying the painting was written on the day Shakespeare died, encouraging one to presume that the portrait shows the poet at death's door.

There is a tradition that Shakspere, shortly before his departure, and in anticipation of that event, did at length, for the gratification of a much-valued Friend, submit to sit for his Picture. That this was the identical Picture the lines beneath sufficiently evince: the melan-

choly tone in which they are written, corresponding so emphatically with the characteristic traits of the Physiognomy, prove to demonstration that this must . . . Lymning (for Lymning it unquestionably is) and . . . infer from the Latin sentence 'Sic cecinit,' &c., that the prophecy contained in them was accomplished on the very day on which they were written. And . . . that this friend for whom the Picture was painted caused them to be inscribed in Letters of Gold under the Head. J. H. 1750.

The three Sotheby sale catalogues speculate that "J. H." was probably John Hathaway of Stratford-upon-Avon, who died in 1753, aged seventy-three.[1]

The 1885 article concluded that because the painting looks stiff and rigid, it must have been the work of an amateur, but William Carew Hazlitt later was more specific, attributing the painting to the actor Richard Burbage, and this was how it was sold in 1919. Hazlitt also provided an author for the verse, speculating it was the work of Shakespeare's relative Thomas Greene. He had no doubt that the picture showed Shakespeare on his deathbed, remarking, "There is that peculiar brilliance in the eyes notoriously premonitory of death."[2]

Folger was unhappy that, soon after his purchase of the work, the *Times Literary Supplement* questioned its authenticity, basing its argument on Spielmann's research. Spielmann followed up this notice with a long letter that opened by mentioning the "laughably fantastic price [paid] for such a production." He characterized the verse accompanying the portrait as "an amusing example of Wardour-street Elizabethan English," and he speculated that this picture was the work of the forgers Holder and Zincke. Folger wrote F. Wheeler of J. Pearson & Co. on 23 September 1919 querying if this was the portrait that Wheeler had offered to him earlier and, if so, whether it had ever been considered fraudulent. Wheeler replied on 23 September that Hazlitt, who had reproduced the work, considered it genuine and so did he. He continued, "We do not take Mr. Spielman seriously, nor do we appreciate his claim to be an expert in regard to portraiture."[3]

Of course, there is now no doubt as to which "experts" were correct. The poet's furrowed brow is closer to the romantic conception of melancholy genius than to seventeenth-century conven-

tions. The Burbage Portrait is most likely an early nineteenth-century fake loosely based on the Droeshout engraving. The goatee marks a departure from the engraving, but it was presumably suggested by the Stratford Bust (see fig. 106) or by pictures such as *The Strace Portrait of Shakespeare*, first engraved in 1811, that are derived from it.

1. The 1919 catalogue gives Hathaway's date of death as 1755.
2. Hazlitt, *Shakespear*, p. 159.
3. Letter from F. Wheeler to H. C. Folger, 23 Sept. 1919, Folger files.

149

THE BUTTERY PORTRAIT OF SHAKESPEARE
Nineteenth century
Oil on panel, 13 × 9¾ in. (33 × 24.7 cm.)

Coat of arms at upper left with inscription: "NON SANZ DROIOT"

Provenance: Discovered about 1850 by Charles Buttery, picture restorer to Queen Victoria; bought by William Russell, at whose death it was purchased by Horace Buttery and was in his possession by 1890; by 1896 owned by Ellis and Elvey, New Bond Street, London; Gilbert I. Ellis sale, Sotheby, 4 December 1902, lot 2283

Exhibitions: London, 1890, no. 393; Stratford-upon-Avon, Shakespeare Memorial, 1896, no. 62

References: Piper 1962, no. 42

Condition: The painting was cleaned in 1932, 1953, and 1970.

According to the 1902 Sotheby catalogue, "from its resemblance to the engraving by Droeshout it is conjectured that the painter of this [seventeenth-century] picture and the engraver must both have worked from a common original." David Piper felt it was more likely "a rather Teutonic fake of the 19th century." While closely basing his image on the Droeshout engraving, the artist still fails to capture its characterization. His most unusual additions are in his choice of colors: Shakespeare wears a red doublet with gold embroidery, and the blue-green background even shows through beneath the poet's arms. He also gives the poet a full moustache with the ends sweeping downward.

150

150 (before restoration)

150

THE FELTON PORTRAIT OF SHAKESPEARE

ca. 1792?

Tempera and oil (?) on panel, 10¹⁵/₁₆ × 8³/₁₆ in. (27.8 × 20.8 cm.)

Inscriptions: No inscription can now be seen on the verso, but according to George Steevens, writing in 1794, the panel was inscribed, "Guil. Shakspeare, 1597. R.N." Wivell records it as reading, "Gul. Shakspear / 1597-R-B." He notes that the inscription was painted in black and white, and he reproduces Richardson's transcription, which first was engraved on Trotter's print, and his own in his book of 1827 (facing p. 39).

Provenance: Placed on sale in the European Museum, London, by an anonymous gentleman; bought on 31 May 1792 by Samuel Felton of Drayton, Shropshire, and Curzon Street in Mayfair for 5 guineas; bought ca. 1794 by George Nicol for 40 guineas; according to Friswell (1864), it came into the possession of a Mr. Westmacott, a London solicitor who died in 1861 or 1862; Christie's, 30 April 1870, lot 96, as "part of an estate in course of administration under orders of the Court of Chancery," bought in at 50 guineas by Wrenfordsley (name in Graves, *Art Sales*); the Christie's 1922 sale catalogue states that George Nicol's collection was sold in 1873 and the Shakespeare head passed into the possession of Baroness Burdett-Coutts, thereby implying, without explicitly saying, that the baroness acquired it from the Nicol collection; Burdett-Coutts sale, Christie's, 4 May 1922, lot 131, £1522.10.0 plus 10 percent commission, Rosenbach acting as agent.

Exhibitions: London, European Museum, Fourth Exhibition and Sale, 1792, no. 359; for a time on exhibition at the Boydell Shakespeare Gallery; London, 1890, no. 389

References: The print seller William Richard's "Shakspeare" and "Proposals for the Publication of Two Plates from the Picture already described," London, 1794 (text actually written by George Steevens [FSL PR2929/S8/Cage]; reprinted in *European Magazine* 26 [October 1794], pp. 277–82); George Steevens, "Shakspeare," 10 November 1794, a leaf to be inserted after the Advertisement to the 1793 edition of Shakespeare (PR2929/S8b/Cage; reprinted in *European Magazine* 26 [November 1794], pp. 316–17); [George Steevens], "Shakspeare," 1794 (PR2929/S8a/Cage; reprinted in *European Magazine* 26 [December 1794], pp. 388–90); Isaac Reed, "Advertisement" to *The Plays of William Shakspeare*, notes by Samuel Johnson and George Steevens, revised and augmented by Isaac Reed, 5th ed., London, 1803, vol. 1, pp. v and 3; Satiricus Sculptor [William Henry Ireland], *Chalcographimania*, London, 1814, p. 99; James Boswell, Jr., "Advertisement" to *The Plays and Poems of William Shakespeare by the late Edmond Malone*, London, 1821, vol. 1, pp. xxvi-xxvii; Boaden 1824, pp. 81–112; Wivell 1827, pp. iv-v, 7–90, 119–22, 220–22, 246–47; review of Wivell, *London Literary Gazette*, 7 July 1827, p. 436; Wivell 1840, pp. 27–30; G. R. W., "On Some of the Presumed Portraits of Shakspeare," *The Builder* 13 [23 June 1855], pp. 296–97; Friswell 1864, pp. 46–52; Norris 1885, pp. 141–52; Spielmann 1906–07, pp. 25–28; Ogden 1912, p. 30; Spielmann 1910; Salaman 1916, pp. 6, 11, repr. p. 9; Spielmann 1921a; Spielmann 1922, p. 624 repr.; Spielmann 1924, p. 47; Piper 1962, no. 40; Marder 1963, pp. 198–201; Piper 1964, p. 36; Schoenbaum 1970, pp. 287–91; Schoenbaum 1981, pp. 184–88

Condition: The picture is executed on an oak panel with a vertical grain. There is a thin gray-colored gesso. Strips have been added to the panel on all four sides, extending the image considerably on the right and increasing the work's measurements to 15 by 12 inches. These additions were not included in the 1794 Trotter print (fig. 105). Either they were added later or were excluded by the engraver as clearly not being part of the original. The strips were removed by Michaels when he conserved the painting in 1979, since they were rigidly holding the original fragment and contributing to its cracking. The panel has a large vertical crack near its center running through the sitter's nose. This crack was remarked on by Boaden as early as 1824: "There was a splitting of the crust of the picture down the nose, which seemed the operation of heat, rather than age. I remember the difficult task Mr. Boydell described, when he afterwards, by softening the paint, and pressing with the pallet-knife, succeeded in fixing these warped and dissevered

parts to the oak pannel, on which they originally reposed." In 1827 Wivell reported it was "covered all over with dark spots, occasioned by being a long time in a damp place without varnish," and he pointed out that a crude repair had been made: "The extremity of the ruff, where the picture is cut off, has been repaired, and a small piece added, since it was discovered in the Minories." He also mentioned that two or three places about the size of a pea had been mended in the left cheek (meaning Shakespeare's left cheek) and the eye on the same side was a little rubbed, injuries that show up clearly in an X ray. At some point a mahogany bar was attached to the back of the panel as part of the repair for the vertical, central crack. As reported by Michaels, the portrait suffers from extreme abrasion, including most of the face except around the mouth, eyes, and the main structure of the nose.

Fig. 105. T. Trotter, *"Reconstruction" of Felton Portrait of Shakespeare*. Engraving, 1 November 1794.

Plate 1.   *T. Trotter Sculp.*

Guil Shakspeare.
1597 ℞

From the Original Picture in the Possession of M.ʳ Felton — Size of the Painting 11 by 8/4.
London Publish'd as the Act directs Nov.ʳ 1.ˢᵗ 1794 by W. Richardson Castle Street, Leicester Square.

The whole paint surface had formerly been painted over to hide this extensive abrasion and the severe damages. The background and dark hair color had been extended at the lower left to alter the design of the collar. The original line of the collar was obviously still visible in the nineteenth century, as, in his 1827 mezzotint reproducing this painting, Wivell interpreted it as the Bard's shoulder (the sole surviving impression of the mezzotint is reproduced in *Shakespeare Quarterly* 12 [1961], facing p. 318). As to the painting's age, Michaels left the question open, recording the date as "17th century (?)."

Engravings: Thomas Trotter, two engravings, published by W. Richardson, 1 November 1794, 5³/₄ × 4¹/₂ inches each (image): one print engraves the portrait as it is, adding in outline the missing portions as reconstructed from the Droeshout engraving, and the second print engraves in full the work as reconstructed; J. Godofroy, published by Richardson, 28 March 1796; J. Neagle (oval), 31 March 1803 for Isaac Reed's edition of Shakespeare; Charles Warren (oval), 1 May 1803; Warren from a drawing by John Thurston after the portrait, 22 July 1805 (oval, reverses the image); I. Thomson, ca. 1805; C. Warren, 1 May 1806, published by George Kearsley; Evans, 1806, published by Longman & Co. for Mrs. Inchbald's Theatre; Evans, published in Ballantyne's 1807 edition; J. Collyer, published by Longman & Co., 30 November 1810; William Holl, published by Isaac Reed, 26 December 1812; W. T. Fry, published by Longman & Co., 1819; Rivers after Thurston, published by Sherwin, 1 June 1821; Cosmo Armstrong, December 1822; J. Thomson, published by J. Robins & Co. 1827; John Cochran (for Wivell), 1827; unfinished mezzotint by Abraham Wivell, ca. 1827; G. Greatback, Felton Portrait identified as "The Burbage Portrait" in center of frontispiece with scenes by T. D. Scott for edition of Shakespeare's tragedies published by John Tallis & Co. ca. 1850; H. Wright Smith, ca. 1865; *Harvard Catalogue of Dramatic Portraits* also lists undated prints by W. & D. Lizars and J. Boyd. It lists another undated print by I. J. Penstone under works after Droeshout, but this engraving is also based on the Felton Portrait.

Related works: A drawing executed after the painting for Horace Walpole is also owned by the FSL. It enlarges the amount of the figure shown and is not completely accurate in its details. A copy of the painting is in the Royal Shakespeare Theatre Picture Gallery. It is said to have been painted by John Boaden in 1792. Another early copy was made for George Steevens by Josiah Boydell.

When it first came to light in 1792, the Felton Portrait, a fragment of a larger work, appeared different than it does today, the line of the collar being severely adumbrated at the left (see no. 150, before restoration). In addition, at some early point, the image was extended on all four sides, particularly on the right, thereby centering the head and extending the collar so that it ended in a straight line almost parallel to the one on the other side. The painting soon found an influential champion in the critic George Steevens, who, writing in 1794, proclaimed it as the sole surviving painting of Shakespeare. Steevens maintained that the picture was the original portrait, which had subsequently been severely cut down, from which Droeshout in 1623 and Marshall in 1640 had made their engravings (see figs. 101 and 103). He recorded an inscription on the verso dating the painting to 1597 and gave the initials of the artist as "R. N." He went on to give the provenance as supplied by J. Wilson, the owner of the European Museum, in a letter of 11 September 1792: "The Head of Shakspeare was purchased out of an old house known by the sign of the Boar in Eastcheap, London, where Shakspeare and his friends used to resort,—and report says, was painted by a Player of that time, but whose name I have not been able to learn." In 1794 Wilson elaborated to Steevens that "this portrait was found between four and five years ago at a broker's shop in the Minories, by a man of fashion, whose name must be concealed: that it afterwards came (attended by the Eastcheap story, &c.) with a part of that gentleman's collection of paintings, to be sold at the European Museum." Steevens allowed that this provenance was highly suspect and presumed that the portrait, if it ever was in the Boar's Head, must have been removed when the original building was destroyed in the Great Fire of London of 1666. Steevens employed the picture as a weapon with which to bash his rival Edmond Malone, who had done so much to support the claims of the Chandos Portrait (see fig. 110) as being from the life. He was also attracted to the painting's gentle characterization of the Bard, which he saw as an improvement on that conveyed in the First Folio.

Edmond Malone never accepted the portrait as genuine, and as early as 1814 William Henry Ireland challenged it in print, describing it as a snuff-taking German. Boswell, the son of Johnson's biographer, recounted in 1821 an even more damnable accusation: "There are not, indeed, wanting those who suspect that Mr. Steevens was better acquainted with the history of its manufacture, and that there was a deeper meaning in his words, when he tells us, 'he was instrumental in procuring it,' than he would have wished to be generally understood; and that the fabricator of the Hardiknutian tablet [a hoax Steevens had played in 1789 when he manufactured King Hardecanute's tombstone] had been trying his ingenuity upon a more important scale." Thus, the Felton Portrait was turned by Malone's supporters into a fabrication of Steevens, his principal challenger as a Shakespearean scholar. When three years later James Boaden weighed in with his study of Shakespeare portraits, the first book of its kind, the demolition of the Felton picture seemed complete. Boaden pointed out the inappropriateness of the spelling of Shakespeare's name and such inconsistencies with the Droeshout print as the form of the skull ("a very narrow egg in its shape"), the flattened nose, the painfully oblique eyes, and the misunderstood endings of the pleats. Boaden suspected it was an early picture whose reworkings were "aged" in an oven.

Abraham Wivell, a painter, followed up Boaden's book with one of his own published in 1827 in which he defended the authenticity of the Felton Portrait. Wivell uncovered a different reading of the inscription, one that permitted him to attribute the painting to Richard Burbage. He concluded the image shows the poet at age thirty-three in mourning for his only son, Hamnet, who had been buried in the previous year on 11 August 1596. Like Steevens, he also applauds the expression: "a calm benevolence, well suited to 'gentle Shakspeare.'" In a review of this book in the *London Literary Gazette* of 7 July 1827, Wivell was immediately attacked: "We have the most conclusive evidence that the Felton is a forgery; for it was altered and painted by John Crauch [Cranch], from a picture bought in a broker's shop in the Minories . . . ." Cranch, an amateur painter, had died in Bath in 1821 at age sixty-nine. It is interesting to note that the word "altered" is used, an acknowledgment that the original painting is an old one.

Writing in this century, Spielmann was also convinced that the painting had indeed been retouched to change the sitter to Shakespeare, and even felt the model for the transposition could be identified as William Sherwin's 1790 engraving after Droeshout for Asycough's edition of the plays. Like the Sherwin print, Spielmann felt the Felton Portrait incorrectly shows the moustache growing downward, and the curls of the hair on the sides of the head follow Sherwin's interpretation as well. Yet, at least in the picture's present state, it is difficult to confirm Spielmann's observations. While the painting could never have been the original on which the Droeshout engraving was based, the shape of the cranium for one being too different, it is related to the Droeshout image: the points of similarity are too close to be coincidental. It is possible that this is a Jacobean portrait of a now unknown sitter altered, using the print as a model, to more closely resemble Shakespeare. But, while there is evidence of extensive repainting, the features have remained basically the same. Given the misunderstandings of the shape and function of the collar even in its first incarnation in such details as the lack of an under-propper and the two edges forming only a single line where they are tied at bottom center, one suspects that it is entirely a production of the late eighteenth century that was intended to deceive its audience into believing it was from the life.

The straight line of the bottom edge of the collar may have been inspired by the Marshall engraving of Shakespeare (see fig. 103), in which the collar bows only slightly at one end. The original line of the collar at left in the Felton Portrait was painted over in an adaptation that may also have been influenced by the Marshall print, where the collar on the side of the face turned away from the viewer rises more steeply than it does in the Droeshout engraving. The Felton Portrait would thus seem to have been inspired by both the Droeshout and Marshall prints, and it is of interest that a faithful engraving after the Marshall by Delattre, dated 26 September 1786, had been published in Bell's 1788 edition of Shakespeare's plays just four years before the Felton Portrait "reappeared." Also just at this time there were precedents for showing Shakespeare with an enlarged, egg-shaped cranium.[1] Whether an altered early work or a fake made from whole cloth, the conception in its essentials is a product of the late eighteenth century, offering a luminescent, gentle Shakespeare, in which the close-up focus on the egg-shaped dome makes him seem an inhabitant of an extraterrestrial dimension.

1. See, for example, the engraved Shakespeare portrait by C. Knight of 1 February 1786 and the one by R. Field of about the same time, both after the Chandos painting (ART File S527, no. 41, pt. 2, and no. 35, copy 2).

151

PORTRAIT OF SHAKESPEARE
Nineteenth century
Oil on panel, 11½ × 9½ in. (29.3 × 24.1 cm.)

Case no. 1660

Provenance: Anderson Galleries, 27 April 1927, lot 307

References: Piper 1962, no. 41

Condition: The panel is split down its left-hand side.

Piper felt this portrait to be a "strange version of Chandos, date very uncertain," but it is more closely related to the Droeshout type. It also seems to reflect the influence of the Ely Palace Por-

151

trait. Unlike any of these images, however, Shakespeare is shown facing right and has been given an accordion-pleated ruff. One characteristic of the Droeshout print is that the sitter's left eye socket is considerably larger than his right, which is on the side of the head turned slightly away from the viewer. The artist of the Folger picture, in reversing the head from left to right, curiously retained the original imbalance so that the left eye socket, which is now farther from the viewer, is still the larger of the two. The Anderson Galleries of course sold the painting as a seventeenth-century portrait, but it is surely later.

Stratford Bust Shakespeare

The half-length statue of Shakespeare (fig. 106), most frequently referred to as a bust, forms the main part of the memorial erected in Holy Trinity Church, Stratford-upon-Avon, on the wall above Shakespeare's grave. The sculptor was Gheerart or Geraert Janssen (often anglicized as Gerard Johnson) and the work was in place by 1623, when it was mentioned in a poem by Leonard Digges composed for the First Folio. As a likeness, it obviously satisfied the playwright's family, who presumably had commissioned it. Yet, despite its secure position as an authentic portrait, the statue's unanimated, pudgy features have not spawned as many imitators as has the Droeshout engraving.

In this monument, Shakespeare wears a black gown faced with silk.[1] It is either sleeveless or the sleeves hang down at his side, and the gown is indicative of his role as a dignified citizen of Stratford. The doublet is red with gold buttons, decorative diagonal slashes across the chest, padded sleeves, and projecting wings on the shoulders.

1. A helpful discussion of Shakespeare's costume, to which this description is indebted, can be found in J. L. Nevinson's "Shakespeare's Dress in His Portraits," *Shakespeare Quarterly* 18 (Spring 1967), pp. 101–06.

Thomas Phillips

Phillips, a prolific portrait painter, was born at Dudley, Warwickshire, on 18 October 1770. After studying with Francis Eginton, a glass painter in Birmingham, he traveled to London in 1790, where he became a student at the Royal Academy the following year. He exhibited at the academy from 1792

Fig. 106. Gheerart Janssen, Monument to Shakespeare, Holy Trinity Church, Stratford-upon-Avon.

until 1846, and while his early works consisted primarily of history paintings, he soon devoted himself almost exclusively to portraiture. Elected an associate of the Royal Academy in 1804, he was made a full academician four years later. He served as its Professor of Painting from 1825 to 1832, and published in 1833 *Lectures on the History and Principles of Painting*. Phillips died in his residence in London on 20 April 1845.

152

THE STRATFORD MEMORIAL BUST
ca. 1816
Oil on panel, 26$^{1}/_{16}$ × 18$^{1}/_{4}$ in. (66.2 × 46.4 cm.)

Provenance: The Phillips picture is said in 1888 to have been in the possession of William Pearce of Bridge-street in Stratford-upon-Avon; its measurements are given as 18$^{1}/_{8}$ × 26 in. (see Halliwell-Phillips papers, FSL W.b.86, no. 12); gift of James G. McManaway, October 1975

Condition: The work is painted on an oak panel with a vertical grain, which, at an early date, split down its center. In a restoration of 1976 a dark shadow covering the figure's right arm, added apparently by a different hand in a different kind of paint, was removed.

Engravings: William Ward, published by J. Britton, 23 April 1816, 9 × 7 in.; W. T. Fry, published by T. Cadell and W. Davies, 1 November 1817; Francis Holl, published by Edward Moxon, 1857

From its inception, the purpose of Phillips's painting was presumably to serve as a model for the engraving after it, and the purpose of the engraving (fig. 107), as its caption makes clear, was to supply a true likeness of the Bard on the occasion of the bicentennial of his death. The painting, based on a cast made from the original by George Bullock, shows the figure in isolation, extracted from its memorial niche in Holy Trinity Church. The statue itself had been painted white in 1793 at the suggestion of the Shakespeare scholar Edmond Malone, who, in line with the then prevailing neoclassical aesthetic, thought he was returning it to its original condition.[1] Obviously, Bullock's cast was also white, and Phillips's painting is consequently executed in grisaille.

There is a discrepancy between the Folger painting and the print, where the front of Shakespeare's doublet is shown with decorative slashes not present in the painting. The painting may be a version of the original or it may have been rubbed and overpainted, thereby losing some of its details.

1. The monument remained white until 1861, when the attempt was made to restore it to its original colors.

Fig. 107. After Thomas Philips, *Bust of Shakespeare.* Engraving by William Ward, 23 April 1816.

Anonymous

153

THE DEXTER PORTRAIT OF SHAKESPEARE
Nineteenth century
Oil on panel, 15¹/₈ × 11¹/₂ in. (38.4 × 29.1 cm.)

Case no. 1996

Inscribed at top of paper on which Shakespeare is writing: "Merrie Wives of Windsor." (Elias Dexter's son also noted that the spines of the books on the shelves behind Shakespeare have titles, and he recorded the following: "Hamlet," "Terence in

Englyshe," "Doraster and Faunia," and "Fauna Romanorum." There is no evidence that this is the case. He may have been reading into the painted highlights on the spines words that simply do not exist.)

Provenance: Bought in or before 1864 by Elias Dexter, art dealer in New York City, from an unnamed lady to whom the painting had passed by descent; bought from Ella F. Dexter, Elias's granddaughter, then living in Brooklyn, through John Anderson, Jr., July 1906, $1500 plus commission. There is a curious twist to the story of Folger's acquisition of this painting, as so often is the case with objects with which John Anderson had been involved. Anderson negotiated the sale of the painting in 1906, but on 31 January 1910 he wrote Folger about a copy of the Dexter portrait: "In going over my personal possessions, strange to say, I have found a large painting of Shakespeare, and it proves to be a copy enlargement of the one which you purchased from Miss Dexter. It is undoubtedly a copy made in an amateurish way for his own purposes, by the former owner.—and, of course, belongs to you. What shall I do? Will I put my foot through it, or do you prefer to call and see it before coming to a decision?" Folger was in no hurry to collect this copy, as Anderson wrote again on 8 March reminding him to pick it up, yet it did eventually join the other painting. This copy, which measured 43 by 33 inches and was oil on canvas, was deaccessioned in 1964 (see no. D66) and its present whereabouts is unknown. Although it seems unlikely, there is the remote possibility, given Anderson's untrustworthiness, that the larger painting was the original and the smaller work catalogued here the copy. It would be interesting to know if the oil on canvas contained all of the inscriptions recorded by Elias Dexter's son.

References: Piper 1962, no. 7

Condition: Restored several times, the panel, approximately ¹/₄ inch thick, was rasped down to accommodate a cradle composed of five boards glued parallel to the ducts and five movable battens. A vertical crack runs through the panel about an inch left of the center. Another crack runs up the left edge starting about 2¹/₂ inches from the bottom, and there is a small crack running through Shake-

153

speare's left hand. Pentimenti indicate that buildings were painted out of the landscape, and there is
some repaint in Shakespeare's beard and collar.

Versions: See no. D66.

Along with this painting, Folger acquired notes
written by Elias Dexter's son,[1] remarking on the resemblance of this work to a portrait of Sir Henry

Wotton (fig. 108) and suggesting that the two images were by the same hand. Dexter's son even
went so far as to speculate that Wotton could have
written Shakespeare's plays. Noting the resemblance of the sitter's clothing to the Stratford Bust,
he also suggested that "the Stratford Bust was
painted from, if not entirely made from, this portrait." The painting found enough support as an au-

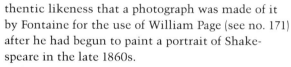

Fig. 108. Anonymous, *Sir Henry Wotton*. Oil on canvas, 49 × 39 in. National Portrait Gallery, London.

Fig. 109. Jodocus Hondius, attributed to, ca. 1583, finished by George Vertue, *Sir Francis Drake*. Engraving, 15½ × 12 in. National Portrait Gallery, London.

thentic likeness that a photograph was made of it by Fontaine for the use of William Page (see no. 171) after he had begun to paint a portrait of Shakespeare in the late 1860s.

The Dexter picture is more convincingly interpreted as a nineteenth-century portrait of Shakespeare that borrows the pose and setting of the chair and table from the Wotton portrait or an engraving after it and modifies the sitter's features and dress to conform more closely to the Stratford Bust, which also suggested the motif of pen and paper.[2] The artist took some pains to create an original conception of the poet, borrowing such motifs as the window at the left with the landscape beyond from Elizabethan portraiture. In this instance, the view is presumably that of Stratford with Holy Trinity Church. At the upper right of the painting is a medallion depicting Queen Elizabeth I, though the oval inexplicably floats amid the folds of the drapery. The artist may have had at hand an engraving such as that of Sir Francis Drake (fig. 109),

where a view through an arched window at the left is balanced by a coat of arms at the right.

1. Elias Dexter actually outlived his son. This information is contained in a letter of 9 March 1897 by Elias to Folger in which he also gives his age as 82 (Deck C File). The purpose of the letter is to offer for sale a collection of prints of Shakespeare and scenes associated with his life.
2. In the bust as it now appears and in the Dexter portrait, the wings joining Shakespeare's sleeves to his doublet are painted black, the same color as his robe. One would expect, though, that the wings were originally red, the same color as the doublet and sleeves of which they form a part.

Chandos Shakespeare

Whether the Chandos Portrait (fig. 110), an authentic Jacobean painting, actually depicts Shakespeare is now a subject of debate. However, it has a long and distinguished history as a likeness of the Bard and is a favorite model for Shakespeare portraitists. The sitter is shown in a painted oval. He is not presented formally, as his shirt collar is unbuttoned

Fig. 110. Anonymous, *Chandos Portrait of William Shakespeare*. Oil on canvas, 21¾ × 17¼ in. National Portrait Gallery, London.

and the strings of his collar are untied. He wears a black doublet, the wings of which are decorated with pickadill tabs, and he has a gold earring in his left ear. It is this last feature that often acts as a signature for the Chandos type. His eyes are a dark grayish color and his moustache brown. The forehead, as in the Droeshout engraving, again is unusually high, although here its ascent is not so vertical, as it slopes slightly backwards.

The Chandos Portrait's earliest origins are speculative. It is said to have been painted by a fellow actor, whom George Vertue in the eighteenth century identified as John Taylor.[1] No such actor is listed in any contemporary records, but there

was an actor named Joseph Taylor, whose career overlapped with Shakespeare's, although it is not known if he was also a painter. Taylor is said to have left the picture to Sir William Davenant, a poet, playwright, and theater manager who claimed to be Shakespeare's godson and/or illegitimate son. It was in 1747 that it came into the possession of James Brydges, later third duke of Chandos, and in 1856 was presented to the newly founded National Portrait Gallery by the earl of Ellesmere as the cornerstone of the museum's collection.

1. For detailed information about the painting and its history, see the entry on the Chandos Portrait in Strong 1969.

Anonymous (nos. 154–59)

154

THE SHAKSPERE PORTRAIT OF SHAKESPEARE
(Formerly "Kneller Portrait")
Early eighteenth century
Oil on canvas, 29½ × 24¾ in. (75 × 63 cm.); painted dark brown oval frame with laurel in all four corners

Case no. 1620

Provenance: George Shakspere, Coventry (died 1787); to his son Thomas Shakspere; to his daughter Rosa Shakspere; to the wife of her son, Mrs. Perkins of 12 Harewood Place, London (the provenance to this point is provided by Harry Spurr, a London dealer, who was involved in the negotiations with Folger); offered by Rosenbach on 6 January 1917; offered by Edwards on 1 June 1917; bought from Wells, September 1918, $2100

References: Wivell 1827, pp. 53–54, n. (mentions the painting had been in the Shakspere family's possession for more than a century and attributes the work to Jonathan Richardson); Piper 1962, no. 36

Condition: In 1979 the work was conserved but the old lining retained. Overpaint was removed, and

154

abraded areas in the background and in Shakespeare's coat were inpainted.

Sir Godfrey Kneller made a "copy" of the painting for the poet John Dryden sometime in the late seventeenth century. George Vertue first gave 1689 as the date when Kneller painted his copy for Dryden, then changed the date to 1698. As Dryden would appear to be referring to this gift in a publication of 1694, the first date would seem to be the correct one. At this time the Chandos Portrait was apparently owned by Thomas Betterton, the famous Restoration actor. The copy by Kneller is now owned by Earl Fitzwilliam, an ancestor of whom is thought to have purchased it from a relation of Dryden. The Fitzwilliam copy is in fact a version of the Chandos, as it enlarges the portion of the body shown (the canvas size grows from 21³/₄ by 17¹/₄ inches to 29 by 24 inches) and offers a more monumental and slightly embalmed image.

The Folger picture is a faithful copy of the Kneller version of the Chandos Portrait and seems to have been painted at an early date. Although the whereabouts of the Kneller copy was known when Wells sold his painting to Folger, the dealer still represented his canvas as being the actual portrait Kneller had painted for Dryden. Like the original painting, the Folger picture does not show the collar drawstrings in the Chandos Portrait. As the drawstrings are primarily the work of later restoration, they presumably were not easily visible when Kneller made his version.

155

THE GUNTHER PORTRAIT OF SHAKESPEARE
Eighteenth century
Oil on canvas (oval canvas attached to a rectangular one), 30 × 25¹/₂ in. (76.2 × 64.8 cm.) (sight)

Case no. 1209

Provenance: Charles F. Gunther, Chicago; bought from his estate by Oliver R. Barrett, Chicago; sold by Barrett, American Art Association, 12 April 1922, lot 752, as "very old and finely executed portrait, said to be 'the world's best portrait of Shakespeare,'" repr.

References: Piper 1962, no. 2

A letter from Oliver R. Barrett of Chicago to Mr. Folger of 19 January 1921 volunteers information

155

about Mr. Gunther's statements on the portrait: "I do remember, however, he stated that Mr. Quaritch [the London dealer] once came to see it and told him that he could secure a price which would seem fabulous for the picture. Mr. Gunther's idea was that this picture was painted by [Richard] Burbridge, but I do not find any signature on the painting itself." The painting, however, is a variation on the Chandos-Kneller theme, with a large branch of laurel placed at the bottom. This addition may have been inspired by William Marshall's engraving for the 1640 edition of Shakespeare's poems (see fig. 103), which, although based on the Droeshout print, shows Shakespeare holding a sprig of bay leaves positioned at the bottom of the oval composition. The large socket of the sitter's left eye suggests the artist was also looking at the Droeshout image.

156

THE LUMLEY PORTRAIT OF SHAKESPEARE
Eighteenth century
Oil on canvas, 17³/₄ × 14¹/₈ in. (45 × 36 cm.)

Case no. 1210

Provenance: According to the 1922 sale catalogue, sold with other pictures from Lumley Castle in

1785, but repurchased by the earl of Scarborough, the descendant of Lord Lumley who had inherited the collection; in 1807 bought by Ralph Waters, an artist of Newcastle; bequeathed to his brother Thomas Waters; sold by him to George Rippon of Waterville, North Shields, before 1853; bequeathed or sold to John Fenwick of Preston House, North Shields; bought in by Fenwick when he attempted to sell the painting at Christie's in 1874; sold by him to Baroness Burdett-Coutts in 1875 for 50 guineas, H. Wagner acting as agent; Burdett-Coutts sale, Christie's, 4 May 1922, lot 132, repr., 300 guineas; bought by Folger from Wells through Sabin, June 1922, $1750.

Exhibitions: New York, Crystal Palace, *Exhibition of the Industry of All Nations,* 1853, no. 5, as "Oil Portrait of Shakespeare, (Probably an early copy from the 'Chandos.')"; Stratford-upon-Avon, 1864, no. 123 (amended in pencil to "126"); London, 1890, no. 390

References: Spielmann 1910; Salaman 1916, p. 6, repr. p. 9; Spielmann 1921a; Spielmann 1921b, p. 428; Spielmann 1922, p. 624, repr.; Marder 1963, pp. 204–05

156

Condition: Cleaned by Finlayson in 1932; the painting was again cleaned and relined in 1979.

Engravings: Chromolithograph by Vincent Brooks, published by Henry Graves & Company, 1 July 1862, 17½ × 14 in. (an impression is in ART Vol. d99, vol. 9)

The 1864 exhibition catalogue gives the painting an impressive provenance, placing it in the collection of John, Lord Lumley, of Lumley Castle, Durham. Lord Lumley, a contemporary of Shakespeare who collected portraits of famous men, especially literary figures, died in 1609. The fact that the painting was not mentioned in the early Lumley inventories did not deter those who wished to establish this provenance. The claim was made that this painting had been misidentified in Stukeley's *Iter Boreale* of 1725, where the portrait was said to be of Chaucer. This "mistake" allows one to identify the painting with the portrait of Chaucer listed in the 1595 inventory of Lumley Castle, pushing the provenance all the way back to a time when Shakespeare was thirty-one years old.

The "documentation" on the early provenance raised doubts with Folger, and he did not purchase this work at the Burdett-Coutts sale. One wonders if he had read Spielmann's stinging appraisal of the painting in the *Illustrated London News* on 1 October 1921: "It is a striking, not very competent, portrait of a clumsy, heavy-jawed man, bearing some resemblance to the Chandos portrait, with no further evidence of the earring and the very suspicious 'ends' or strings of the 'band' (or collar), which incorrectly came over instead of under it." However, Gabriel Wells, the dealer who bought the painting, mounted a successful campaign to convince Folger of the work's importance. Frank H. G. Keeble, an art expert for the American Art Association, wrote Folger on 21 June 1922, "There is no doubt in my mind whatever, that this was painted by Shakespeare's erstwhile manager and confrere, Burbage. This portrait was known to me in England thirty-five years ago, and was then esteemed as presenting the actor in one of his freest moods." Despite such testimony, the portrait is more accurately described as an eighteenth-century portrait of Shakespeare based on the Chandos type, to which have been added the disproportional eyes of the Droeshout print. When the Lumley portrait was still in the possession of George Rippon, it was reproduced in a

Fig. 111. Overpainted chromolithograph by Vincent Brooks of *The Lumley Portrait of Shakespeare.*

relatively faithful chromolithograph by Vincent Brooks. Twice Mr. Folger purchased portraits of Shakespeare which were in fact the chromolithograph mounted on canvas, and in one instance touched up and varnished. The cost of this last "painting" (fig. 111) was $350.[1]

1. There is a file card written by Mrs. Folger that presumably describes this picture (18¹/₁₆ × 14⁷/₁₆ in.): "Sh Portrait, in oil, framed—Contemporaneous, 'Chandos' type—John Anderson Jr. thinks by Burbage or Taylor—Fine—Bought of John Anderson Jr., Mch, 1921." The receipt from Anderson is dated 15 April 1921. The second picture (18 × 14⁵/₁₆ in.) is almost certainly the portrait of Shakespeare that sold in the J. Parker Norris sale, American Art Galleries, 22 November 1922, lot 300. The Norris painting was described as after the Chandos Portrait, and its measurements (17¹/₄ × 14³/₄ in.) are roughly those of this picture. The Norris work was also sold with the painting *Shakespeare Arms* (no. 202). The measurements given for this last picture in the sale catalogue (23¹/₄ × 19¹/₂ in.) are also only approximate, and both it and this portrait have labels on the back identifying G. Sauter, manufacturer of looking glasses in Philadelphia, as the framer.

157

SHAKESPEARE SIGNBOARD

Late seventeenth or early eighteenth century
Oil on mahogany panel, oval, 37¹/₈ × 31¹/₄ in. (94.2 × 79.3 in.)

Provenance: Discovered in 1962 by the book dealer Jacques Vellekoop of E. P. Goldschmidt, London; came to America in the spring of that year; gift of Mary Hyde (now Lady Eccles), Four Oaks Farm, Somerville, N.J., October 1975

Exhibitions: New York, Pierpont Morgan Library, *Shakespeare's Four Hundredth Anniversary Exhibition,* 1964; San Francisco, 1979–81, repr. in color p. 86

References: Mary Hyde, "Shakespeare's Head," *Shakespeare Quarterly* 16 (1965), pp. 139–43; S. Schoenbaum, "Artists' Images of Shakespeare," in Werner Habicht, D. J. Palmer, and Roger Pringle, eds., *Images of Shakespeare: Proceedings of the Third Congress of the International Shakespeare Association, 1986,* Newark, Del., 1988, pp. 19–23; Gary Taylor, *Reinventing Shakespeare,* New York, 1989, fig. 7

Condition: On the back one can see traces where two braces, roughly 23¹/₂ by 5¹/₂ inches, were placed horizontally across the top and bottom of the panel, each secured by 8 nails. Two large iron eyes for hooks are still affixed to each side of the panel slightly above its center. Around the circumference, which is 1 inch thick, are 44 nail holes. In some cases, the nails are still there, and it would appear they held a rim that was part of a metal support. Modern accretions are staples and a screw with wire a little over 4 inches from the top.

Mary Hyde convincingly argues that this work must have served as a signboard. Such signboards were plentiful in England until the second half of the eighteenth century (a 1770 Act of Parliament banished them for good, with the exception of signs for inns). The large size of the head and the boldness of the execution would have made the image easily recognizable from a distance, and its painted frame, consisting of a yellow strip half an inch wide, would have meant it needed no other frame when mounted into a metal bracket.

When the signboard was rediscovered in 1962, it was immediately proposed that it had belonged to

157

the noted publisher Jacob Tonson. Tonson adopted *Shakespeare's Head* as a shop sign when he moved to new quarters in the Strand in 1710. It was an appropriate choice, as the year before he had published Rowe's edition of Shakespeare. The shop remained *Shakespeare's Head* until 1767, when it left the family's ownership and was changed to *Buchanan's Head.* In their publishing ventures, the Tonson family employed various versions of the Chandos Portrait in frontispieces to their works; in fact, the first engraving ever made of this painting

had been executed for Rowe's 1709 edition. Since the head in the sign is itself a variation on the Chandos theme, this supports its candidacy as the Tonson sign first put up in 1710. Yet, as Mary Hyde also makes clear, signs of *Shakespeare's Head* were popular throughout England, being employed by publishers other than the Tonsons as well as by countless inns and taverns. That the Folger painting is Tonson's actual sign seems a remote possibility, but one that cannot be ruled out.

158

The head is a crude departure from the Chandos type, while the two-dimensional torso with the cape across one shoulder, the other arm projecting out from the side, and the diagonally slanting buttons seem based on Marshall's frontispiece to Shakespeare's *Poems*, published in 1640 (see fig. 103). The entry in the Sotheby sale catalogue gives the following information: "One of four remarkable forgeries, believed to have been executed about a century ago by an unknown artist at Westminster." There seems no reason to doubt this assertion that

158

PORTRAIT OF SHAKESPEARE
Early nineteenth century
Oil on canvas, 30¼ × 22 in. (76.6 × 55.7 cm.)

Inscribed across the top in raised letters in black paint: "GVLIELMO SHAKSPERE"; underneath name at left: "Æt / 47"; underneath name at right: "Ao.D / 1611"

Provenance: Sotheby, 18 March 1909, lot 183, £2.2.0, Quaritch acting as agent

References: Piper 1962, no. 3

the picture is an early nineteenth-century forgery, and presumably the crudity of its execution was meant to increase its appearance of authenticity.

It seems to have proved a popular type, as a writer to the *Antiquarian Correspondence* in 1885 mentions having a portrait of Shakespeare on panel (17 × 13 in.) with an identical inscription in raised letters.[1] If the forger was indeed from Westminster, he would not need to have gone far for his Latinized spelling of Shakespeare's first name, for the inscription to the Scheemaker statue in the Poets' Corner of Westminster Abbey reads, "GULIELMO SHAKESPEARE."

1. A clipping of this letter is to be found in "Halliwell-Phillips Shakespeareana," FSL W.b.244.

159

PORTRAIT OF SHAKESPEARE
Probably early nineteenth century
Oil on panel, 13 × 11⅜ in. (33 × 28.8 cm.) (sight), framed in a mahogany or rosewood case with two doors

Case no. 1592

Provenance: Owned by Edwin H. Baverstock by 1864 (according to the 1864 exhibition catalogue, "This portrait was a bequest from one who highly

159

valued it, and who used to state that it had been in the family from whom he received it considerably more than a century"); Sotheby, 28 July 1926, lot 620, £170, bought by Gabriel Wells; bought by Folger, October 1926, $980

Exhibitions: Stratford-upon-Avon, 1864, no. 137 (amended in pen to "142"); Shakespeare Memorial Loan Exhibition, 1881 (according to card file, exhibited at Stratford 1881, possibly no. 60 or 84)

The head reverses that of the Chandos Portrait, transferring the ring from the left to the right ear. The attempt at a larger, more animated collar is disappointing, and while more of the body is shown than in the Chandos picture, the figure is still seen within a painted oval frame. The image has also been enshrined within a box with doors, a response to the ongoing deification of the Bard.

Janssen Shakespeare
Anonymous (nos. 160–64)

160 (Plate 24)
SIR THOMAS OVERBURY[?]
(Since its reappearance in 1770, this picture has most frequently been referred to as the Janssen Portrait of Shakespeare. Other titles it has borne are the Jennens Portrait of Shakespeare, the Ut Magus Portrait, the Hamilton, the Rupert, the Somerset, the Balstrode, and the Ramsden.)
Early 1610s, altered before 1770
Oil on panel, irregular, 22³/₁₆ × 17¹/₈ in. (55.9 × 43.4 cm.)

Accession no. 3155

Inscribed in upper left-hand corner: "Æte 46 / 1610." (The two small letters "te" have been misread as "fe," which would mean the painter AE made this work. However, "e" is an abbreviation for "is," and the word represented is "Ætatis." The inscription is executed in oil paint over the dark brown overpaint covering the background. Given the style and costume, the date 1610 may well be correct.)

Provenance: Acquired by Charles Jennens of Gopsel, Leicestershire, by 1770; by descent on Jennens's death in 1773 to Penn Assheton Curzon, who had married Jennens's niece; by descent to Lord

Howe, Curzon's successor?; purchased by Samuel Woodburn, a picture dealer, for the ninth duke of Hamilton, ca. 1809; at the duke's death in 1819 passed to his daughter, the wife of the eleventh duke of Somerset; by descent to the twelfth duke of Somerset in 1855; by descent to his daughter, Lady Guendolen Ramsden of Bulstrode, Gerrard's Cross, in 1885; by descent to Sir John Ramsden; his sale, Christie's, 27–30 May 1932, lot 65; bought from Sawyer, July 1932, £226.9.0. (Boaden speculates that the portrait was painted for Shakespeare's patron Henry Wriothesley, third earl of Southampton. Wivell offers a different version of its provenance. He maintains that, according to Samuel Woodburn, the son of the picture dealer who sold the painting to the duke of Hamilton, the work belonged to Prince Rupert, who left it to his natural daughter Ruperta, who married Emmanuel Scroopes Howes. Their descendants sold the painting to Mr. Spackman, a picture dealer, from whom Samuel Woodburn acquired the work, which he kept for about two years before selling it to the duke of Hamilton.)

Exhibitions: Amherst, *Shakespeare*, 1951

References: [George Steevens], *Critical Review* 30 (December 1770), p. 439, and 31 (January 1771), pp. 83–84; [Charles Jennens], *The Tragedy of King Lear, as Lately Published, Vindicated from the Abuse of the Critical Reviewers*, 1772, pp. 36–38; *Critical Review* 34 (December) 1772, p. 476; Boaden 1824, pp. 66–80, 188–206; Wivell 1827, pp. 91–118, 243–45; Wivell 1840, pp. 24–25; Henry G. Bohn, *The Biography and Bibliography of Shakespeare*, [London, privately printed, 1863], pp. 287–89; Friswell 1864, pp. 64–73; Norris 1885, pp. 122–40; Spielmann 1906–07, pp. 19–22; Spielmann 1909–10, pp. 230–37, 105–10, 151–58; Spielmann 1910, p. 450; Ogden 1912, pp. 30–31; Spielmann, *The Times*, 26 May 1932, p. 17, repr. p. 18; James Waldo Fawcett, *The Washington Star*, 28 August 1932; Barrell 1940; Piper 1962, no. 37; Marder 1963, pp. 201–02; Piper 1964, pp. 36–37; Schoenbaum 1970, pp. 283–85, repr. facing p. 265; J. Thomas Looney, *"Shakespeare" Identified in Edward De Vere, Seventeenth Earl of Oxford*, ed. Ruth Loyd Miller, 1975, vol. 2, p. 409, repr. in color; Schoenbaum 1981, pp. 180–84; David Piper, *The Image of the Poet*, Oxford, 1982, pp. 103–05, pl. 110; Gary Taylor, *Reinventing Shakespeare*, New York, 1989, fig. 20

160 (before restoration)

Condition: The panel consists of a single oak plank, apparently cut radially from the tree. At some point prior to 1770 the hairline was raised, the original hairline being restored in 1988. The ground is a thin cream-colored gesso. There are two severe vertical cracks. One runs from top to bottom on the right-hand side, passing the sitter's ear and curving gently at the bottom where it borders the sitter's left wing. The second crack is down the middle of the panel passing to the left of the figure's left eye. These cracks were visible early on, as they are commented on by both Boaden in 1824 (p. 194)

and Wivell in 1827 (pp. 108–09, n.). There is a third crack that starts at the top, 6½ inches from the left edge, and ends near the right eye. In 1909 Spielmann noted the repair of a damage about 2 inches long over the sitter's left eye. In 1932 the painting was damaged when it was shipped from England, a small nail in the frame scrapping the bottom edge of the paint surface in an area of about ³/₄ inch. The cradling consists of five vertical battens of irregular widths and spacing and five horizontal battens. Spielmann described it in 1909 as "on panel, very roughly hewn at the back and held together there by three strengthening uprights—not a recent addition—and strips of canvas glued against the two cracks" (p. 232).

Engravings: Mezzotint by Richard Earlom as frontispiece to Charles Jennens's 1770 edition of *King Lear,* 5⁷/₈ × 4¹/₂ in.; oval engraving by Gardner for the *Literary Magazine,* 1 June 1793 (reversed); mezzotint by R. Dunkarton, published by S. Woodburn, 1811, for *Characters Illustrious in British History;* mezzotint for Boaden by Charles Turner, 1 January 1824; engraving by T. Garner, published by John Bumpus, 1824; mezzotint after Earlom by Robert Cooper as frontispiece to 1825 edition of *The Works of William Shakespeare;* engraving after Dunkarton by Robert Cooper for John Bumpus's 1825 edition of Shakespeare; poster advertising the 1825 "London stage Edition" of *The Works of Shakespeare;* oval engraving after Cooper's mezzotint by J. Pass for the *Encyclopedia Londinensis* of 1827; engraving after Earlom by T. Wright for Wivell's *Inquiry* of 1827; engraving by James Hopwood, Jr., for the 1842 edition of Shakespeare for Baudry's European Library. (These images, along with six 19th-century French and Dutch prints, are reproduced in Spielmann's article.)

Versions: Spielmann lists the chief "copies" as the "Buckston" or "Duke of Kingston," which he believes to be early 18th century; the "Croker"; the "Staunton" (see no. 161); the "Duke of Anhalt," which is stated as having been executed in England in 1763–64; the "Earl of Darnley"; and the "Marsden."

Spielmann remarked in 1924, "As far as is known, up to 1790 no fabrications of portraits of Shakespeare, painted with deliberate intent to deceive, were known."[1] Surely he had in mind the Felton portrait as the work which inaugurated the legion of paintings that were painted (or overpainted) with the intention to deceive. The Felton, however, must now give way to the Janssen Portrait of Shakespeare (see no. 160, before restoration) as the first work fabricated to look like the Bard. An authentic Jacobean portrait, the Janssen had to be retouched only slightly in order to be rechristened. As recent cleaning has demonstrated, the hairline was at some point raised to resemble more closely Shakespeare's impressive dome.

Although it can no longer be considered a portrait

of the Bard, from 1770 until recently it played an important role in Shakespeare iconography. It clearly filled a deep-seated need, offering for two hundred years an interpretation of Shakespeare as an elegant and refined gentleman, sumptuously attired and sensitively portrayed. It was the Shakespeare his audience needed—the poet and playwright as aristocrat.

When the portrait first made its public debut in 1770, it was only the second painting, the Chandos being the first, to claim to be a portrait of Shakespeare from the life. Yet its entrance was made without fanfare, appearing with gentlemanly understatement as an engraved frontispiece to a 1770 edition of *King Lear,* which, though published anonymously, was by Charles Jennens, who included a dedication to himself. The print by Earlom (fig. 112) bore the caption, "From an Original Picture by Cornelius Jansen in the Collection of C. Jennens Esqr." Presumably, Jennens had only recently acquired the picture, as it is not mentioned in the description of his collection found in the 1761 *London and Its Environs,* nor in the 1766 *The*

Fig. 112. Richard Earlom, *William Shakespeare.* Engraving after Janssen Portrait.

English Connoisseur compiled by Thomas Martyn. One also presumes that the alteration was made to the painting shortly before it was sold to him.[2]

As soon as Jennens published his book, George Steevens greeted it scathingly, his attack extending even to the frontispiece, which he doubted was after a picture by Janssen or a portrait of Shakespeare. Later critics who had seen the picture rather than just the mezzotint after it were far kinder to the painting. In his book of 1824, Boaden accepted the work as by Janssen and endorsed the accuracy of the inscription, which dates the painting to 1610 and the sitter's age to forty-six. Three years later Wivell muddied the waters over the painting's provenance, but he too did not challenge its authenticity. Most subsequent writers, focusing on questions concerning attribution and provenance, ignored the question of the sitter's identity, everyone agreeing that it was the Bard. Writing in this century, Spielmann was the first after Steevens seriously to question whether this was actually a portrait of Shakespeare, but he too decided it was very likely a painting by Janssen, even though painted later than 1610.

Today the painting is in search of both an artist and a sitter. As to the first, Cornelius Janssen or Johnson (born in London, 1593, died in Utrecht, 1661) is not a contender. Even if the inscription can no longer be believed, a date of 1610 or slightly later is convincing in terms of the sitter's dress, and this is too early for Janssen, who, after training in Holland, returned to London about 1618.

As to the sitter's identity, Charles Wisner Barrell proposed in 1940 that this work was one of several portraits of Edward de Vere, the seventeenth earl of Oxford, altered to look like Shakespeare. Ruth Loyd Miller's 1975 edition of Looney's book on de Vere reported that Barrell, who had X rayed the painting, had also discovered that the inscription had originally read "1590," the year in which de Vere was forty years old (Spielmann had argued that the "6" in "Æte 46" in the painting's inscription had originally read "0"). No evidence I have seen supports a reading of the date as 1590, and despite Miller's assertion that "the 1590 date is confirmed by the Tudor rose design of the lace collar," the style of the sitter's dress in fact argues for a later date. A more plausible identification was put forward by David Piper in 1964. He pointed out that a version of the Folger picture, complete with the original hairline, appeared in 1947 from the Ellenborough

Fig. 113. Anonymous, *Sir Thomas Overbury* ? Oil on canvas, 22 × 16½ in. Private collection.

collection (fig. 113). This last portrait, he felt, should be identified as the painting of Sir Thomas Overbury that had earlier been recorded in the collection but was no longer there. He also pointed out that both the Folger picture and the Ellenborough version are in keeping with the authenticated portrait of Overbury in the Bodleian Library.

Sir Thomas Overbury, a poet and cultivated lover of literature, was born in 1581, being baptized on 18 June of that year. He graduated from Oxford at the end of 1598, whereupon, following his father's example, he entered the Middle Temple. Overbury's career flourished through his friendship with Robert Carr, a Scottish courtier at the court of James I, whose influence secured for Overbury a knighthood in 1608. Carr himself became Viscount Rochester in 1610, but he and Overbury soon quarreled when his friend disapproved of his plans to marry the divorced wife of the earl of Essex. Rochester, with the help of the earl of Northampton, who was the granduncle of Lady Essex, conspired to have James I offer Overbury a diplomatic appointment abroad to get him out of the way. Overbury balked, and it was then arranged to have him arrested and removed to the Tower of London on 26 April 1613. Here Lady Essex schemed to have her opponent poisoned. The poison, primarily white arsenic, gravely undermined Overbury's health, but he did not finally succumb until 15 September 1613. It was two years before evidence was forthcoming that he had been murdered. Overbury's reputation was only enhanced by the circumstances of his death. His poem on marriage "A Wife now the Widdow of Sir T. Overburye" inspired numerous tributes and imitations, including one by his friend Ben Jonson. If the Folger picture is indeed a portrait of him, which now seems the likeliest possibility, it has served as the portrait of two poets. Earlom's 1770 print reproducing the painting appeared with the inscription "Ut Magus" ("Like a Magician"), a reference to Shakespeare's talents, which could magically transform his audience from one realm to another (see no. 162). While the inclusion of "Ut Magus" was meant solely as a tribute to Shakespeare, it takes on an unintended irony in light of the painting's history, the picture magically transforming the sitter from one poet to the other.

1. Spielmann 1924, p. 46.
2. It should be noted that one of the versions after the Janssen Portrait has an inscription giving it a provenance that goes back to the early eighteenth century: "This Portrait of Shakespeare formerly belonged to the Marquis of Dorchester and was given by the late Duke of Kingston to his godson, Evelyn Rowland Cotton [died 1795], who left it to his Nephew, the Rev. R. R. Ward, the Natural Grandfather of the present owner, the Rev. R. G. Buckston [died 1903]" (quoted in Spielmann 1910–11, p. 153). Spielmann concluded on the basis of this pedigree that "it would seem that we here have proof that the picture was in the Kingston possession between 1706 and 1715" (p. 154). Obviously, though, the inscription was written well into the nineteenth century, and its accuracy is open to question.

161

THE STAUNTON PORTRAIT OF SHAKESPEARE

ca. 1770s
Oil on canvas, 30 × 25 in. (76.3 × 63.5 cm.), in painted brown oval frame

Case no. 1188?

Provenance: Father of William Staunton, Longbridge, Warwickshire, around 1777; sold by Staunton family to A. Whitcombe, Clarence Street, Cheltenham, and Stratford-upon-Avon, 1909;

bought by Folger from Sawyer, November 1923, £200

Exhibitions: Stratford-upon-Avon, 1864, no. 115 (amended in pencil to read 118), as painted by C. Jansen, lent by J. Staunton

References: Wivell 1827, Supplement, p. 37, n.; Wivell 1840, p. 24, n.; M. H. Spielmann, "The Janssen, or Somerset, Portrait of Shakespeare: The More Important Copies," *Connoisseur* 28 (November 1910), pp. 151–58, repr.; Piper 1962, no. 32

Condition: The canvas was relined, cleaned, and retouched in 1953.

This portrait is a variation on the Janssen theme. The image has been translated from panel to a larger-sized canvas, and to aid in the transition to the larger background, a painted oval frame has been added. There are a number of differences between the original and this version: the most obvious are that the sixteen buttons down the center of the doublet have been lengthened to nineteen and the pattern on the doublet is no longer as elaborate and the colors are more muted.

To the top of the frame has been affixed a plaque reading, "FROM THE PEEL COLLECTION," relating this picture to the portraits of statesmen and authors collected by Sir Robert Peel (1788–1850). Based on the photograph (admittedly of poor quality) and the description of the Staunton copy after Janssen offered by Spielmann in his article of 1910, the Folger painting can be identified with this work and the connection with Peel discounted.[1] Spielmann gives the measurements as 29 by 24½ inches; he counts nineteen buttons; and the photograph reveals enough about the positioning of the painted oval frame to demonstrate that it corresponds to the Folger picture. Even the shadow beneath the chin is visible in the reproduction. One might speculate that Sawyer sold the painting as contemporary with Shakespeare and was therefore eager to overlook its actual provenance.

Wivell is the first to mention the Staunton picture, in his book of 1827: "This gentleman [W. Staunton] has a very excellent copy of the Jansen portrait of Shakspeare, upon a three-quarter canvas [this is a standard canvas size measuring 30 by 25 inches], which is also painted in an oval, like that in Mr. Croker's possession, but with some trifling difference in the pattern of the doublet . . . . Mr. Staunton states to me, that this picture belonged to

his father about fifty years ago, and I think it cannot be much older than that." One surmises from this account that the copy was made not long after the Janssen original was engraved by Earlom in 1770. Spielmann raises one problem with this date in that he feels the Staunton painting is by the same hand that executed the Buckston or duke of Kingston's copy of Janssen, and he believes this last copy dates to near the beginning of the eighteenth century. If the Buckston and Staunton versions are by the same hand, it seems more likely that the Buckston provenance taking it back to about 1710 is in error.

1. Joseph Q. Adams, the Folger's first director, suspected as much, writing to Spielmann on 14 February 1933, "Will you be so kind as to tell me what you know of our copy of the Janssen portrait 'from the Peele Collection'? It has the nineteen buttons of the Staunton copy, and its measurements are virtually the same. Where is the Staunton copy now? Have you ever located the Croker copy?" If Spielmann replied, his letter is no longer on file.

162

PORTRAIT OF SHAKESPEARE
Probably early nineteenth century
Oil on panel, 7 × 5¼ in. (17.7 × 13.3 cm.)

Inscribed in ribbon banner above head: "UT MAGUS"

Provenance: First offered to Folger by Sotheran in 1909; Sotheby, 21 December 1910, lot 561, as "A Genuine Old Oil Panel Portrait of William Shakespeare, in a Lace Ruff, somewhat similar to the Chandos Portrait," £11.10.0, Mayhew acting as agent

References: Piper 1962, no. 31

Folger authorized the bookseller A. H. Mayhew to purchase this painting for him even though he had not had an opportunity to see the portrait, the auction being held in London while he was in New York. On its arrival, he realized it was a painting that he had already turned down when the dealer Sotheran had offered it to him in the summer of 1909 for nine pounds. He went on to muse in his letter to Mayhew of 26 January 1911, "It of course shows how difficult it is to purchase from a catalogue description. I am not at all sure that it was intended for Shakespeare."

The ribbon banner above the sitter's head marked UT MAGUS demonstrates that the Folger portrait is indeed intended as Shakespeare, as it is based on

Richard Earlom's print after the Janssen portrait published in 1770 (see fig. 112). The print, though not the painting it reproduces, bears this inscription, which translates into English, "Like a Magician." The quotation is from Horace's epistle to Augustus (book 2, epistle 1), and a translation of a portion of the passage from which it is excerpted reads, "a poet who tortures me with vain imaginings, who angers me, soothes me, fills me with false fears, is like a magician; one moment he carries me to Thebes, a moment later to Athens."[1] Thus, in 1770 Shakespeare is celebrated in portraiture as having the magical power to transport his audience. It is a discrete reference, whereas Umberto Romano, painting two centuries later (see no. 175), will make more implicit the image of the poet-magician.

The small size of the Folger painting also betrays its origin in Earlom's print. Its poor quality and summary treatment of its source help explain Folger's disappointment and his reluctance to accept it as an image of the Bard.

1. This translation is quoted from Spielmann 1909–10, p. 105.

162

163

PORTRAIT OF SHAKESPEARE
Nineteenth century
Oil on panel, 12 × 10 in. (30.4 × 25.3 cm.)

Inscribed across the top of the panel: "Gvls Shakespeare Ætat svae 40 D 1616 [?]"

Provenance: Sotheby, 6–9 (9) December 1905, lot 857

References: Piper 1962, no. 12

This portrait is another nineteenth-century image intended to appear as a contemporary likeness. David Piper describes it as a "conflation of Droeshout and ?Chandos mainly," and the collar may well be a lace-trimmed version of the Droeshout type. Yet the overall conception is closer to the Janssen type. It differs, however, from all of these models in that the ends of the moustache are extended, the shape of the lips is made fuller, and the doublet is an unrelieved black.

164

PORTRAIT OF SHAKESPEARE
Nineteenth century
Oil on paper mounted on an oak panel, 5⅛ × 4⁷⁄₁₆ in. (13.1 × 11.3 cm.)

Provenance: Source unknown

163

164

References: Piper 1962, no. 14

Condition: There is a vertical split in the panel and paper running through Shakespeare's right eye. It begins 1½ inches from the left-hand side at the top and ends 1¾ inches from the left-hand side at the bottom. Overall the surface is pitted and rubbed; particularly noticeable are damages to Shakespeare's forehead and below his left eye. The panel is ³/₁₆ inch thick, tapering off on the left-hand side.

Piper felt this work was "a very remote derivation from the Chandos," but it would seem to be more closely based on one of the prints after the Janssen type. The doublet is black with a red center strip, and the collar most closely resembles those in fashion in the reign of Charles I.

Ashbourne Shakespeare
Anonymous

165 (Plate 25)
THE ASHBOURNE PORTRAIT OF
SHAKESPEARE / SIR HUGH HAMERSLEY
1612, with nineteenth-century alterations
Oil on canvas, 47 × 37¼ in. (119.4 × 94.6 cm.)

Inscribed at upper left: "ÆTATIS SVAE. 47/ Ao: 1612 [later changed to 1611]"

Provenance: Bought before March 1847 in the London art market by Rev. Clement Usill Kingston of Ashbourne, Derbyshire; sold by Kingston to a Mr. Harvard of Attleborough for £80; at the latter's death (sometime before 1910) it was purchased by R. Levine of Norwich; sold by Levine's executors, Sotheby, 18–21 (20) June 1928, lot 568, repr., bought by Eustace Conway; Anderson Galleries, American Art Association, 16 December 1929, lot 36 (offered for sale by Conway but bought back in at $4,400); bought by Mrs. Folger from Conway, March 1931, $3,500, Scheuer acting as agent for Conway.

References: Friswell 1864, pp. 103–04; Norris 1885, pp. 166–71; M. H. Spielmann, "The Ashbourne Portrait of Shakespeare," *Connoisseur* 26 (April–May 1910), pp. 244–50, 38–42, repr. in color; Spielmann 1910; Ogden 1912, p. 32; Sir Sidney Lee, *A Life of William Shakespeare,* London, 1916, p. 534 n. (in a list of portraits falsely identified as Shakespeare); Eustace Conway, "The Ashbourne Portrait Again," *The Shakespeare Association Bulletin* 5 (October 1930), pp. 195–96; Barrell 1940, as of Lord Oxford; *Shakespeare Fellowship News-Letter* (American Branch), 1 February 1940, pp. 1–4 (cites some of the many newspapers and magazines that reported on Barrell's discoveries); Oscar James Campbell, "Shakespeare Himself," *Harper's Magazine* 181 (July 1940), pp. 172–85 (accepts Barrell's argument that original portrait was of Lord Oxford, but maintains this has no bearing on authorship question); William Smethurst, "The Ashbourne Portrait of Shakespeare," typescript at the Folger, 1943 (identifies the portrait as of Francis Trentham Arminger of Rocester Abbey and Westwood Leek, lord of Rocester and Denstone, Staffordshire); *Evening Star,* 2 July 1948; *Washington Daily News,* 2 July 1948; *Washington Post,* 2 July 1948, pp. 1 and 13; Letter to the Editor from Charlton Ogborn, *Time,* 9 July 1948; *Baconiana* 32 (Autumn 1948), p. 182; Bergen Evans, "Was Shakespeare Really Shakespeare?" *The Saturday Review of Literature* 32 (7 May 1949), p. 40; Dorothy and Charlton Ogburn, *This Star of England,* New York, 1952, pp. 699, 814–15, 864, 946, 1038–39, 1244 (as of Lord Oxford); Piper 1962, no. 35; Marder 1963, p. 204; Schoenbaum 1970, pp. 466, 604–05; J. Thomas Looney, *"Shakespeare" Identified in Edward DeVere, Seventeenth Earl of Oxford,* 3d ed., ed. Ruth Loyd Miller, Port Washington, N. Y.,

165, detail (1979, during restoration)

1975. vol. 2, pp. 411–29, repr. in color facing p. 416, as of Lord Oxford; *The Shakespeare Oxford Society Newsletter* (hereafter *SOSN*), Summer 1977, pp. 5–8; Spring 1979, pp. 1–2; Summer 1979, pp. 1–6 (for the first time as of Shakespeare/Hamersley); Fall 1979, pp. 5–7; *The Shakespeare Newsletter* 29 (November 1979), pp. 33–34; *SOSN*, Spring 1980, pp. 3–4; Schoenbaum 1981, pp. 188–91; William L. Pressly, "The Ashbourne Portrait of Shakespeare: Through the Looking Glass," forthcoming in *The Shakespeare Quarterly.*

Condition: Lined after having been purchased by Kingston. It would be difficult to say with absolute certainty when the painting underwent its metamorphosis from Hamersley to Shakespeare, but one suspects that Rev. Clement Kingston was the one who brought about this transformation. He certainly profited as the owner of this painting. Spielmann quotes a former pupil at Kingston's school as saying his teacher had been an artist. Thus, Kingston had the means as well as the motivation for undertaking this deception. In his article of 1940, Barrell reproduced an X-ray photograph

that shows the monogram "CK" to the lower right of the coat of arms. He interpreted this as evidence that Cornelius Ketel was the painting's creator. The whereabouts of Barrell's X rays are unknown, but the Folger possesses a set made by the National Gallery in 1948 or 1949 in preparation for the *Barrell v. Dawson* lawsuit. The monogram is only faintly visible on these X rays. Without Barrell's illustration it would in fact be impossible to read the marks as "CK" with any certainty, and the letters are no longer visible on the canvas itself. Assuming that Barrell did not strengthen the marks in his photograph and that the letters are as he depicted them, then one might speculate that they stood for Clement Kingston, who could not resist initialing his handiwork, even though he had to cover up the letters with overpainting. Restoration of the painting was undertaken in 1979–81, when the old glue-lining and varnish layers were removed. It was at that time that the partially scraped-off coat of arms at the upper left was exposed. Overall, a high degree of abrasion to the paint film was discovered. A restoration of 1988 cleaned all areas of the surface, repaired all tears, inpainted losses without obscuring some of the original alterations, and mounted the picture on a semirigid lining canvas. The coat of arms was left exposed in the condition in which it had been found; the remnants of the old date "1612" were left so that it can be seen beneath the "1611"; the sitter's ear, which had been covered with hair in imitation of the image in the Droeshout engraving, was left uncovered; and the line where the old forehead of Sir Hugh was made to expand into Shakespeare's large dome was left faintly exposed.

Engravings: G. F. Storm, 15 December 1847 (its three states are listed in Spielmann's article of May 1910, p. 42); wood engraving by Ebenezer Landells in the *Lady's Newspaper*, 6 August 1848, p. 117; steel engraving, unsigned and undated (all three prints are reproduced by Spielmann)

Versions: A copy, made from the mezzotint and inexact as to color, was reproduced in Spielmann's article of 1910 as in the possession of C. E. Graseman. Another copy, with an arched top, was owned by Charles Benck of Yonkers, N.Y., in 1977.

The portrait first surfaced in 1847 in the possession of Rev. Clement Usill Kingston, a second master at Queen Elizabeth's Free Grammar School at

Ashbourne, Derbyshire. Kingston wrote to Abraham Wivell, the writer on Shakespeare portraiture, on 8 March 1847 to inform him of his find, which he said he had bought in London after having been told of its existence by a friend. After viewing the work, Wivell endorsed its authenticity, citing it as "one of the most extraordinary discoveries of this age."

The subject is shown in a black doublet with an elaborate ruff and an ornate sword or dagger belt. In his right hand he holds a book with large red silk tie-ribbons, and in the center of the book is an intriguing design consisting of a mask(?) and crossed spears behind. His right arm rests on a skull placed on a table covered with a red cloth, the same color as the tie-ribbons. He wears a thumb-ring on his left hand and holds a glove with a richly embroidered gauntlet. Because of the presence of the skull and the elaborate nature of the dress—too fine for a playwright—the suggestion was put forward that Shakespeare is depicted in the character of Hamlet, but Spielmann, writing in 1910, correctly dismissed this notion as atypical of the conventions of Jacobean portraiture.

In 1937 the Folger Library permitted Charles Wisner Barrell to supervise the taking of X-ray and infrared photographs of this painting along with the Janssen Portrait. Barrell published an article in 1940 demonstrating that the painting had been significantly retouched. He went on to claim that the underlying image was that of Edward de Vere, seventeenth earl of Oxford, a claim he felt reinforced the argument that the earl was the real author of the body of work under Shakespeare's name.[1] While Barrell's assertion that the original portrait had been of the earl of Oxford has no basis in fact, he did reveal that the painting had been extensively retouched and that a coat of arms at the upper left had been overpainted. The conservator Peter Michaels removed the overpaint in 1979, and only then was it possible to identify the heraldry with any accuracy. The coat of arms (see no. 165, detail) consists of a shield on which are three rams' heads couped (cut off cleanly at the neck). At the top of the shield is a griffin perched on a helmet and holding a cross-crosslet fitchée gules. The Folger's staff identified this as the armorial coat of Sir Hugh Hamersley (also Hammersley, Homersley). In the scroll at the bottom of the coat of arms, only the last letters "MORE" are visible, but these fit in with Hamersley's motto "HONORE ET AMORE."

The inscription on the canvas identifies the sitter as forty-seven years old, and the date originally read 1612 before it was changed to 1611, the year in which Shakespeare turned forty-seven. Born in 1565, Sir Hugh Hamersley was forty-seven in 1612. He, however, did not have arms granted him until 1614: either the coat of arms was added at this slightly later date or was included in anticipation of the grant. Before his death in 1636, Sir Hugh held a number of important posts: he was Lord Mayor of London in 1627–28, Colonel of the City, President of Christ's Hospital, President of the Artillery Company, Governor of the Company of Russia Merchants and of those of the Levant, and of Merchant Adventurers of Spain, East India, France, and Virginia. Comparisons with other portraits of Sir Hugh are consistent with the identification of the Ashbourne portrait as having been originally of him.[2] The elaborate nature of the dress is also entirely appropriate, as is the skull, a memento mori commonly found in portraits of this period.

Thus, at some point a painting that began as a portrait of Sir Hugh Hamersley was altered to resemble Shakespeare. The coat of arms was partially scrapped out and then painted over, the date of the inscription changed from 1612 to 1611, the hair at the top of the head scrapped out and the forehead extended, and the hair over the ear lowered. The portrait can no longer be returned to its first state as too much of the original paint has been lost. The picture, therefore, remains a portrait of Shakespeare, né Sir Hugh.

1. Barrell's claims led to a lawsuit. On 25 July 1947, Giles E. Dawson, curator of books and manuscripts at the Folger, wrote to Meredith Underhill, a descendant of the Underhills of Stratford-upon-Avon, a critique of Barrell's article that read in part, "The plain fact is that we are unable to see any of the things he [Barrell] saw in the negatives. They just weren't there. If he can now produce pictures of these things, they must have been doctored up." Underhill triumphantly showed the letter to Charlton Ogburn, an officer in the Shakespeare Fellowship, a group founded in London in 1922 to support the claim that the seventeenth earl of Oxford was the real author of the body of work under Shakespeare's name. Ogburn persuaded Barrell to sue Dawson for $50,000 for libel. The story received a great deal of attention when it was carried by the Associated Press on 2 July 1948, but the suit was eventually dropped.
2. The Haberdashers' Company, Haberdashers' Hall, London, owns a full-length portrait of Sir Hugh Hamersley, a gift of his grandson in 1716.

Zuccaro Shakespeare
Anonymous

166

UNKNOWN MAN

(Formerly identified as Shakespeare; sometimes referred to as the Bath Portrait or the Archer Portrait of Shakespeare)
ca. 1615–20

Case no. 1526

Inscribed at upper right: "W Shakespeare"

Provenance: According to the 1922 sale catalogue, this picture was first referred to in an advertisement in a Bath newspaper in 1801, at which time it was attributed to the year 1602. It then passed into the possession of Mr. Archer of the Royal Library at Weymouth. In 1862 it was purchased by Mr. W. H. Wills, a well-known journalist, for Baroness Burdett-Coutts; Burdett-Coutts sale, Christie's, 4 May 1922, lot 133, repr., 300 guineas, bought by Wells, Sabin acting as agent; John L. Clawson sale,

166 (before restoration)

Anderson Galleries, 24 May 1926, lot 730B, repr., $1600, Rosenbach acting as agent.

Exhibitions: London, 1890, no. 391; Amherst, *Shakespeare,* 1951

References: The painting was reproduced for the first time in an English newspaper of 12 April 1905 (clipping of unidentified newspaper in Folger file); Spielmann 1911; Spielmann 1921a; Spielmann 1922, p. 624, repr.; Piper 1962, no. 26; Schoenbaum 1970, pp. 466–67

Condition: The oak panel is ¼ inch thick, with the wood grain running vertically. While the panel is probably the fragment of a larger painting, this piece had itself been enlarged at a later date. A restoration of 1988 revealed that there are serious losses of ground, and the surface of the wood also seems to be affected. The most serious losses are in the face. The whole lower half appears to have been deliberately defaced with very deep scratches, almost destroying the paint layer and ground of the chin, mouth, and beard.

When this painting reappeared in the nineteenth century (see no. 166, before restoration), it was attributed to Federigo Zuccaro (also spelled Zucchero and Zucharo), one of several works of a similar type ascribed to this Italian painter. Roy Strong demonstrated that these Zuccaro attributions were entirely fanciful, since this painter visited England in 1575 for not longer than six months.[1] Shakespeare, of course, was all of eleven in that year.

The Folger picture is an authentic Jacobean portrait that was overpainted in the nineteenth century to look like the artist's conception of Shakespeare. Only since the restoration of 1988 has it been possible to get back to something more closely resembling the original image. The Anderson Galleries catalogue offers a precise description of the portrait as it appeared in 1926: "The blue-gray eyes look out with directness from under finely arched brows; the high forehead is surmounted by soft and rather thin brown hair; the nose is thin and delicately aquiline; the moustache, pointed and shaved slightly above the centre of the upper lip; the pointed beard is close-cut; and there is a small tuft of beard just beneath the lower lip." A great deal has changed: the eyes are now tinged with brown and yellow in addition to gray; the pointed moustache and beard are more closely

166

cropped; the hair is a lighter color; and the bitumen that made the background and the doublet so dark has been removed, revealing a brownish red background and a green doublet embroidered on its wings in gold. The Christie's sale catalogue of 1922 mentioned that "a long chain ear-ring is suspended from his left ear." The reproduction in the catalogue is so small that this feature cannot be clearly seen. Wells must have had the earring overpainted, as it is not in the 1926 reproduction, although one can make out that there is something underneath the repaint. The 1988 restoration completely restored this feature, which appears not to be a chain but a strip of leather. The earring and the ruff suggest a date of about 1615–20.[2]

1. Roy Strong, "Federigo Zuccaro's Visit to England in 1575," *Journal of the Warburg and Courtauld Institutes* 22 (1959), pp. 359–60.
2. See Roy Strong's *The English Icon: Elizabethan and Jacobean Portraiture* (London and New York, 1969), where there are several portraits that support this date. In his portrait of 1613, Edward Sackville, fourth earl of Dorset, wears an elaborate earring, longer than those of earlier periods (no. 342). The portrait of Anne Clifford, ca. 1615–20, shows the sitter wearing an earring that consists of a long strap looped through the ear and tied into an elaborate knot from which hangs a pearl (no. 352). The ruff worn by an unknown lady from this same period (no. 362) also resembles the one in the Folger painting.

167

Vroom Shakespeare
Anonymous

167

UNKNOWN MAN
(Formerly identified as Shakespeare)
Seventeenth century with later overpainting
Oil on panel, 24¼ × 18⅜ in. (61.6 × 46.6 cm.)

Accession no. 3979

Provenance: Collection of the Earl De Montalt of Dundrum, co. Tipperary (1817–1905)?; bought by Mrs. Folger from Paul S. Van Baarn, a New York antique dealer acting (in bad faith) for the Newhouse Galleries, New York, April 1934, $5,000; presented to the Library by Mrs. Folger, June 1934

References: William Shakespeare by Hendrik Cornelisz Vroom, 1566–1640, privately printed, n.d.; *North Shore Daily Journal,* Great Neck, Long Island, 27 July 1934, p. 1; Piper 1962, no. 27

Condition: The panel, now cradled, is split down both sides. A small strip (1⅜ in.) has been added at the top. There are several chips in the paint exposing the white ground beneath: one is in the sitter's collar to the left of his moustache and three others are in his black doublet.

On 18 June 1934, presumably at the same time she presented the portrait, Mrs. Folger gave to the Library a booklet describing this picture. It is privately printed, has only four pages of text, gives no author's name, and a photograph of the painting serves as its frontispiece. According to the early accession records, the booklet had been a gift of Mr. Van Baarn, the dealer from whom Mrs. Folger acquired the portrait. Obviously, Van Baarn prepared this production as part of an elaborate advertisement for the painting.

The booklet states that the portrait is of Shakespeare at age thirty-nine, which would date the picture to 1603–04, and was painted by Hendrik Cornelisz Vroom, who had come to England in 1600 to execute the cartoons for the series of tapestries depicting the defeat of the Spanish Armada. These tapestries were commissioned by Charles Howard of Effingham (from 1597 earl of Nottingham), who was the Lord Admiral of the English navy. Since Lord Nottingham had contact with Shakespeare, the author feels it reasonable to presume that Nottingham commissioned the portrait of the Bard. The only provenance given is that "in the course of time this portrait passed from the collection of Lord Nottingham into the collection of the Earl of Montalt from whom the foregoing history was received."

Lord Howard, in fact, commissioned the tapestries in 1592, and they were completed three years later. There is no evidence that, when he was working on the cartoons, Vroom ever left Haarlem, instead working from charts, drawings, and engravings sent over from England. His friend and fellow artist Karel van Mander, however, does mention a later visit by Vroom to London in his book *Het Schilder-Boeck,* first published in 1604: "One time when he travelled from Zandvoort to England he went to see the Admiral and introduced himself as the designer of the tapestries of the Fleet, whereupon he received one hundred guilders as a present."[1] Yet there is no reason to believe that the Folger picture is by Vroom, who did not regularly paint portraits, or that the sitter is Shakespeare. David Piper even challenges its antiquity: "rather odd, perhaps something of 16th century underneath modern paint." The only information in the book describing the painting that might be accurate is the statement that the portrait once belonged to the earl of Montalt, by which is presumably meant the earl De Montalt of Dundrum, co. Tipperary, who lived from 1817 to 1905.

1. Quoted in M. Russell, *Visions of the Sea: Hendrick C. Vroom and the Origins of Dutch Marine Painting*, Leiden, 1983, p. 93.

Memorial Portraits

Soest Shakespeare
Anonymous (nos. 168–69)

Gerard Soest, a painter from Westphalia, came to London about 1656 and his portrait of Shakespeare (fig. 114) was probably painted shortly after his arrival. It is an early example of a memorial portrait and may be based in part on the Chandos Portrait. David Piper writes, "It appears to be of a living sitter of that time, dressed in a later 17th century conception of early 17th century costume, and there is a story of such a (now lost) portrait having been painted of a later actor said to resemble Shakespeare closely. This portrait may well reflect a tra-

Fig. 115. After Gerard Soest, *William Shakespeare*. Engraving by J. Simon.

dition in living memory, early in the second half of the 17th century, of the poet's appearance."[1] The eyes are narrower than in the Chandos and Droeshout renderings, the cheekbones more pronounced, and the color of the face fairer than in the swarthy Chandos head. The painting possesses a convincing vitality, but it presents a sitter who differs substantially from the earlier likenesses or supposed likenesses.

John Simon's mezzotint (fig. 115) of about 1731 helped to insure the Soest portrait a wide audience.[2] The Folger paintings are in fact from the print rather than from the painting it copies. The print of course reverses its model and places the sitter within an oval format. Yet it differs in small details as well: it emphasizes the errant curl where the hair is parted; the eyebrows undulate; the cheekbones are softened; and the beard ends in a well-defined point. More significantly, the overall impression is altered, Shakespeare taking on a more melancholic, sensitive expression.

1. Piper 1964, p. 14.
2. The print measures 13⅝ × 9¾ in., and it bears the caption, "Done from a Capital Picture in the Collection of T. Wright

Fig. 114. Gerard Soest, *William Shakespeare*. Shakespeare Birthplace Trust, Stratford-upon-Avon.

Painter in Covent Garden." The spelling of the artist's name is given as "Zoust." A later print after this one was executed by T. Burford, and another by W. Holl was published by Wivell in 1827.

168

THE COSWAY PORTRAIT OF SHAKESPEARE
Probably late eighteenth century
Oil on circular panel, 7½ in. diameter

Provenance: Augustin Daly sale, American Art Galleries, 19 March 1900, lot 723, bought by Folger, Wells acting as agent

Exhibitions: Said to have been exhibited at Stratford-upon-Avon in 1864, but this cannot be confirmed, as the entries in the Tercentenary catalogue are too summary to make a positive identification possible.

References: Piper 1962, no. 21

Mounted on the board covering the back of the picture is a printed text, parts of which are repeated in the 1900 auction catalogue, that offers documentation about the work:

This portrait is one of the most charming representations of our Great Dramatist—it is believed to be by an Italian artist. It is called the *Cosway Portrait* as it came from the celebrated collection made by Cosway, the Royal Academician, in

168

Stratford Place, and was sold at his sale, which took place soon after his death in 1821; it was bought by my late uncle and has been in our family ever since. It was exhibited at Stratford-upon-Avon in 1864, and is mentioned in *Wivel's Portraits of Shakespeare*, published about 50 years, and in *Hain Friswell's Life-Portraits of Shakespeare*, published in 1864.

Unfortunately, the source of this text has not yet been found, and the information is suspect. Boaden, Wivell, and Friswell record a portrait of Shakespeare that had been owned by the artist Richard Cosway but was attributed to Zucchero (Zuccaro). Their descriptions and the engraving in Wivell, however, demonstrate it is an entirely different image.[1] In discussing the Soest portrait of Shakespeare, only Wivell mentions a painting which he says was executed by Cosway: "There is in the possession of Mr. Booth, Bookseller, a small copy, in oil, by Mr. Cosway from the above picture, or print, which was purchased at his sale for nearly the sum of twenty pounds. The artist has taken some liberties, one in particular, by making the out-line of the nose quite straight."[2] If the author of the text on the back of the Folger picture was thinking of the Cosway-Booth picture, his reference to an Italian painter as its creator may have been due to his conflating this image with *The Cosway Portrait of Shakespeare* said to be by Zucchero.

Whatever the Folger picture's provenance, it is clear that it is a work based on the Simon mezzotint after Soest. Shakespeare wears a black doublet and is posed against a green background. It is a small, intimate rendering, with the focus on the head. If the highlight at the bottom of the right ear is intended as an earring, it would be a detail suggested by the Chandos Portrait.

1. See Boaden 1824, pp. 60–65; Wivell 1827, Supplement, pp. 17–19; and Friswell 1864, p. 90.
2. Wivell 1827, p. 162, n. For Boaden's discussion of the Soest portrait, see 1824, pp. 134–41, and for Friswell's, 1864, pp. 87–90.

169

THE ZOUST PORTRAIT OF SHAKESPEARE
Probably early nineteenth century
Oil on copper, 8⅛ × 7⁷⁄₁₆ in. (20.6 × 18 cm.)

Case no. 553

Provenance: Gregory, November 1912, £12.2.3 (£15 less 20 percent)

169

References: Piper 1962, no. 13

Condition: "Shakespeare" is cut into the copper on the verso.

The painting was listed in George Gregory's *Illustrated Catalogue of Rare Mezzotint and Other Engravings, Etchings, Etc.* of 1912 (no. 378) as the painting by Zoust rather than as after it. It would appear to have been part of a series, along with portraits of Francis Beaumont and John Fletcher, which were offered for sale by Gregory at this same time.

Thomas Sully

170 (Plate 26)
PORTRAIT OF SHAKESPEARE
1864
Oil on canvas, 20⅛ × 17¹/₁₆ in. (51.1 × 43.3 cm.)

Case no. 1398

The lining canvas is annotated in black ink on its back: "Shakespeare / Copied from Engravings / TS 1864." Presumably this annotation repeats information on the back of the original canvas.

Provenance: By descent to Dr. Matthew Woods, whose family purchased the painting for $3000; sold at auction in Philadelphia for $1100; bought by Sessler $1300 (above information from Sessler correspondence in Folger file); bought by Folger from Sessler, December 1924, $1500

References: Matthew Woods, *Rambles of a Physician: or, A Midsummer Dream,* Philadelphia, 1889, vol. 1, p. 218, repr. on p. 219 with the following caption: "SULLY'S 'THREE THOUSAND DOLLAR SHAKESPEARE' IN POSSESSION OF THE AUTHOR), PAINTED BY THAT ARTIST FROM HIS COLLECTION OF NEARLY 400 PICTURES OF SHAKESPEARE, AND WHICH HE MAINTAINED 'CONTAINED THE EXCELLENCIES OF ALL, AND THE FAULTS OF NONE'"; Biddle and Fielding 1921, no. 1570

Condition: The original canvas was glue-lined, apparently by Finlayson in 1932, onto another canvas with a commercially prepared ground. There is a small tear in the sitter's left collar and a small puncture to the left of the center of the head. The work was conserved in 1988.

In the last two decades of his life, Sully was not always able to sustain the high standards of his earlier work, and he suffered a decline in patronage. His last notation of a price increase was made on 10 August 1841, and from about 1855 he increasingly adjusted his prices downward.[1] With fewer commissions for portraits of his contemporaries, Sully showed an increasing interest in painting posthumous portraits of famous men. In 1871, his last full year as an artist, he painted at least thirty-two pictures featuring George Washington, and the last painting recorded in his register, probably never completed, was a head (20 × 17 in.) of "Michael Angelo from a print." This is exactly the way in which he had earlier approached the task of portraying Shakespeare.

Sully painted two portraits of Shakespeare. His register notes that he began one, copied from the Chandos type, on 19 August 1865 and completed it two and a half weeks later on 5 September, placing on it an evaluation of fifty dollars.[2] While engaged on this work, he executed another head of Shakespeare that he notes was "painted from an engraving." This study, which is the Folger portrait, was begun on 30 August and finished just five days later. Consequently, Sully valued it at the lower price of thirty dollars. The information written on the back of the canvas—"Copied from Engravings"—suggests the work is a composite, yet it is clear that the Soest type was the primary source.

The Folger painting certainly does not suffer from its rapid execution. Sully must have been chafing under the more painstaking effort and dashed off this work, which is all of a piece. The head has a soft focus, individual details being blurred, although the nose does cast a pronounced shadow.

The portrait is not so much an attempt to transfer Shakespeare from the medium of prints to oils as an effort to convey a sense of his personality. Sully offers a sensitive, refined image tinged with sadness, placing Shakespeare within the tradition of melancholy genius. In this he follows Simon's mezzotint after Soest's painting, but one suspects that a print after one of Van Dyck's portraits of Charles I may also have provided a source of inspiration, as the thin, elongated head, pointed beard, and pensive expression are a part of Van Dyck's image of royalty.

1. See Monroe H. Fabian's exhibition catalogue *Mr. Sully, Portrait Painter*, National Portrait Gallery, Washington, 1983, p. 17.
2. See Biddle and Fielding 1921, no. 1571.

William Page

Page was born in Albany, New York, on 23 January 1811, but his family moved to New York City when he was nine. After a brief, unsuccessful stint in a law office, he returned to his first love of art, in 1825 studying with James Herring and in the following year with Samuel F. B. Morse and at the National Academy of Design, where in 1827 he won a prize for life drawing. After briefly considering a career as a Presbyterian minister, he worked as a portrait painter in Albany, but soon returned to New York, where he was elected to the National Academy in 1840. During the middle of that decade he worked for four years in Boston and departed for Europe in 1850, where he lived in Florence and then in Rome. He resettled permanently in New York in 1860 and was president of the National Academy from 1871 to 1873. He died in his home on Staten Island on 1 October 1885.

171

PORTRAIT OF SHAKESPEARE
1873
Oil on canvas, 27 × 21 in. (68.6 × 53.3 cm.)

Inscribed at lower left next to arm: "WP. 3d Shke / 1873." Inscribed in pen and ink on a page glued to upper center of blind stretcher: "Studio Building, 57 W. 10th St: / New York March 22nd '73 / My dear Sarah Shaw the / head of Shakespeare, which you / saw in my studio, and which I am / still at work on, was painted / for a gentleman, to whom, I have / written, to come and see it, no less / than twice he having neglected / to do so I consider myself at lib- / erty to do what I will with the / picture. Would you like to / have it, or Frank? I thought / befor I attempted otherwise to dis- / pose of it I ought to let you know / as you seemed interested in it—Hope / Mr Curtis is better Ever your friend / Wm Page." (Page moved into the Studio Building in 1867. Sarah and her husband, Frank, whose full name was Francis George Shaw, were close friends and patrons of the artist.)

Provenance: According to Page, commissioned in 1868, possibly by Theodore Tilton; offered by the artist to Mrs. Francis George Shaw on 22 March 1873; presented to the Metropolitan Museum of Art in 1903 by Mrs. Francis George Shaw; Metropolitan Museum sale, American Art Association, February 1929, lot 59 (a portion of a Metropolitan Museum label is still on the frame at lower right); bought by Folger from Union Square Book Shop, May 1929, $625

References: Joshua Taylor, *William Page: The American Titian*, Chicago, 1957, p. 257, no. 47 (Taylor gives the early provenance but did not know the painting's present whereabouts); Piper 1962, no. 6

Condition: The oil paint is thinly applied without impasto. There appears to be extensive repaint in both the figure and the background. The canvas was lined apparently by Finlayson.

The depiction of Shakespeare was Page's consuming passion near the end of his life. He began work in 1868 on two portraits, *The Head of Christ* and *Shakespeare*, "because," as he wrote, "*I believed in them.*"[1] But he also, at least initially, had the support of Theodore Tilton, the editor of the *Independent*. Tilton received the finished *Christ*, but by

the time *Shakespeare* was nearing completion he seems to have lost interest in the project. On 2 May 1872, Page sent a letter to his friend: "I wrote you a note last Saturday saying the picture of Shaks- was done, and that I wanted the ballance due on it to pay my rent. it was only yesterday I learned where you were—now I am compelled to ask you to send me a check for the three hundred and fifty, the ballance on the picture—do it if possible for I am in a very tight place. Judge Daly wants to borrow the picture for the occasion of the unveiling of Wards statue and I told him I would ask you if he can have it for that day."[2] The eventual disposition of this portrait is unknown, but, undaunted, Page continued to work on his project.

The inscription on the Folger picture marks it as the artist's third attempt at portraying Shakespeare, and a note glued to the verso reveals that it was almost completed as of 22 March 1873. It was not, however, to be his last. Page went on to paint *Shakespeare Reading*, which he exhibited on more than one occasion, beginning with the 1874 exhibition at the National Academy. This work eventually found its way into the Folger collection but has since been deaccessioned (see D52). From the beginning of this project Page also worked on sculptures of Shakespeare's head, of which only photographs of the final plaster have survived.

It was from the teachings of Christ and the writings of Shakespeare that Page felt their identities and even their appearance could be discovered, for the inner man stood revealed in the face: "A true likeness shows one inside out . . . . The soul is photographed upon the face . . . . The great portraits of Raphael and Titian are soul tale-bearers, no less than the 'terza rima' of Dante or the 'Sonnets' of Shakespeare."[3] In the case of Shakespeare, some documentation as to his appearance already existed, mainly in the form of the Droeshout print, the Stratford Bust, and the Chandos Portrait, but, ironically, this material was more limiting than helpful. Finding it difficult to reconcile the various likenesses, Page turned to the Darmstadt death mask, which, recently having come to light, was said to be of Shakespeare.[4] Here was the "reality" that could guide Page in creating his "soul tale-bearer" of the Bard. When working on the Folger painting he had only seen photographs of the death mask, but he made a pilgrimage to Germany to see the holy relic for himself in September 1874, a visit

that confirmed for him its authenticity and renewed his faith in his quest to capture the Bard's spiritual portrait. In 1875 he published "A Study of Shakespeare's Portraits" in *Scribner's Monthly*, and the article was reprinted the next year as a small book.

The Folger portrait is severe, yet penetrating. Shakespeare, wearing a black doublet, is positioned against a brown background that harmonizes with his auburn hair and yellow-brown eyes. Page's celebrated kinship with Titian, though subdued, is still in evidence. The limited palette allows the vitality of the sitter's face to shine through, his cheeks and lips a rosy red. Even the brushstrokes ringing the head in the background remain visible, responding to the sitter's presence with their own animating rhythms. The primary model is still the Chandos Portrait, the angle of the head, the shape of the thin beard, the upturned moustache, some hair remaining on top of Shakespeare's head, and the disposition of the collar and its tie strings having been derived from this source. Nothing so distracting as the earring, however, is allowed to intrude. Yet, the overall impression differs considerably from that of its source. The shape of the head is fuller, its features more determined, and the eyes are now unfocused, as the figure, an image of noble meditation, turns within itself, exhibiting a quiet strength.

1. William Page. "A Study of Shakespeare's Portraits," *Scribner's Monthly* 10 (1875), p. 558.
2. Page to Tilton, 2 May 1872, Historical Society of Pennsylvania, microfilm reel P20 538, Archives of American Art, Washington, D.C.
3. "Shakespeare's Portraits," p. 573.
4. For a more recent discussion of the death mask, see F. J. Pohl, "The Death-Mask," *Shakespeare Quarterly* 12 (Spring 1961), pp. 115–25.

George Henry Hall

172a

SHAKESPEARE COMPOSING
WHILE LOOKING OUTWARD
1794
Oil on canvas, 10 × 8 in. (25.4 × 20.4 cm.)

Signed and dated above the left hand: "Geo. Henry Hall / '94."

172

172b

SHAKESPEARE COMPOSING WHILE LOOKING UP TO HIS RIGHT
Oil on canvas, 10 × 8 in. (25.3 × 20.3 cm.)

Signed and dated above left hand: "Geo. Henry Hall / 1891 [or 1894?]"

172c

SHAKESPEARE COMPOSING WHILE LOOKING UP TO HIS LEFT
Oil on canvas, 10 × 8 in. (25.3 × 20.3 cm.)

Signed and dated above right hand: "Geo. Henry Hall / '93 [or 1894?]." (The last digits of the dates in this work and no. 172b are difficult to cipher. Since the "4" is clearly legible in 172A, the presumption is that all three panels may date to this year, as they appear to have been done at the same time.)

Provenance: In the possession of John Anderson, Jr., as of 1914; sold to Winston H. Hagen by 1916; when and how Folger acquired these pieces is not known.

Exhibitions: New York, Grolier Club, *Catalogue of an Exhibition Illustrative of the Text of Shakespeare's Plays as Published in Edited Editions,* 1916, no. 431a

References: Piper 1962, no. 8

Related works: Two drawings: 3 February 1896, 19³/₈ × 15¹/₈ in., and 13 February 1896, 19⁵/₁₆ × 15¹/₁₆ in.; 1896 painting at Stratford, 50 × 40 in. (For a replica of this last picture, see no. D28.)

In all three depictions, Shakespeare, wearing a plum-colored doublet and trunk hose, is shown pausing in inspired reverie while he writes. Such a conception is not unusual for poets and writers, and Benjamin Wilson was the first to use it for depicting Shakespeare when he executed his picture for the Shakespeare Jubilee of 1769 (see fig. 121). Wilson's conception proved highly popular in the nineteenth century, Hall's works being three late variations on this theme. Hall, however, deliberately avoided defining the study beyond depicting a relatively simple chair and table, the background remaining unobtrusively neutral. His conception emphasizes Shakespeare as a learned author, a stack of books rising up from the floor. In each canvas, a rose and bud, a Vanitas motif, lie on a book on the table.

A letter of 17 March 1914 from John Anderson, Jr., to Folger indicates that the three pictures passed through the dealer's hands: "Incidentally, I think you will in time regret it if you pass by those fine little paintings by Geo. H. Hall. The one in Stratford is out of reach, and, personally, I consider these the more desirable. It is a successful attempt to portray the poet and dramatist with the inspiration fresh upon him." The painting in Stratford out of Folger's reach was the portrait of Shakespeare that Hall painted in 1896 and donated to the Memorial Gallery at Stratford in 1901 (fig. 116). The three small pictures can be considered as preparatory to it.

Hall based his "official" portrait on the middle of the Folger designs. The two, however, differ in small

Fig. 116. George Henry Hall, *William Shakespeare*, 1896. Oil on canvas, 50 × 40 in. From the RSC Collection, with the permission of the Governors of the Royal Shakespeare Theatre ©.

Fig. 117. George Henry Hall, *William Shakespeare*, 13 February 1896. Black and white chalk, 19⁵/₁₆ × 15¹/₁₆ in.

details: in the Stratford painting the flowers have been dropped, less of the shirt is showing, and the tie cords have been deleted. More importantly, the angle of the head and direction of the gaze have been slightly altered, the head's final conception being based on a drawing executed in Rome on 13 February 1896 (fig. 117). Together the three Folger pictures read like snapshots of genius at work. There is an easy informality implied in their scale that is no longer present in the Stratford painting.

In the nineteenth century, *The Tempest*, Shakespeare's last comedy, was often read as a personal allegory, with the Bard playing the role of Prospero. One rendering of this concept is to be found in Thurston's design engraved for the title page published on 20 March 1812 for volume 1 of Thomas Tegg's edition of the plays (fig. 118). The vignette shows Prospero with Ariel, but the allusion, placed as it is as a preface to all the plays and not just to *The Tempest*, is to Shakespeare himself, with Ariel performing the role of the Muse of Inspiration. Hall too had in mind Shakespeare as Prospero, for he penned Prospero's famous speech to Ferdinand on a

preparatory drawing (fig. 119) executed on 3 February 1896:

> The cloud capp'd towers, the gorgeous palaces,
> The solemn temples, the great globe itself.
> Yea, all which it inherit, shall dissolve,—
> And, like the baseless fabric of a vision,
> Leave not a rack behind. We are such stuff
> As dreams are made of, and our little life
> Is rounded with a sleep.

Interestingly, his transcription of these lines from act IV, scene 1 follows, in part, the textual adaptation that appears on Scheemaker's monument to Shakespeare in Westminster Abbey, thereby placing his work within the context of this distinguished memorial.[1] In the Stratford painting, Hall also inscribed "MONTAIGNE / ESSAIS" on the spine of the book on the top of the pile. Shakespeare knew John Florio's translation of Montaigne's *Essays*, published in 1603, as it has been shown that Gonzalo's discourse in *The Tempest* on the ideal commonwealth, which would embody a state of innocent nature, is indebted to one of these essays (no. 30).

Hall's Shakespeare is certainly not concerned with commercial success; rather, he is shown musing on the Golden Age as portrayed by Montaigne and on the insubstantial nature of this or any vision, even of life itself.

1. Shakespeare's text reads, "And, like the baseless fabric of this vision, / The cloud-capp'd towers, the gorgeous palaces, / The solemn temples, the great globe itself, / Yea, all which it inherit, shall dissolve / And, like this insubstantial pageant faded, / Leave not a rack behind. We are such stuff / As dreams are made on, and our little life / Is rounded with a sleep." The Westminster Abbey memorial reads, "The Cloud capt Tow'rs The Gorgeous Palaces / The Solemn Temples. / The Great Globe itself, / Yea all which it Inherit, Shall Dissolve / And like the baseless Fabrick of a Vision / Leave not a wreck behind."

Fig. 119. George Henry Hall, *William Shakespeare*, 3 February 1896. Black and white chalk, 19³/₈ × 15¹/₈ in.

Fig. 118. After John Thurston, Title Page. Engraving by Rhodes, 20 March 1812.

Anonymous

173

THE PALMER PORTRAIT OF SHAKESPEARE
Late nineteenth century
Oil on panel, 13⁹/₁₆ × 9³/₄ in. (34.4 × 24.7 cm.)

Case no. 715

Provenance: Bought by A. M. Palmer from George Fawcett Rowe; Anderson sale, 9 November 1916, lot 31, $25 plus 10 percent commission, Smith acting as agent

This portrait follows fairly closely the Chandos as a model, but it is more freely painted than other works of this type, particularly in the fluid treatment of the background. On the verso of the panel appears the following imprint: "G. ROWNEY & CO. / Prepared / Mahogany Panel / London / 52 RATHBONE PLACE." In choosing a panel so clearly marked, the artist had no intention to deceive. However, a print after the Chandos Portrait was subsequently pasted over the imprint, and at that

173

point the intent may have been to transform the portrait from a modern interpretation of the Chandos type to an "old" image closer in date to Shakespeare's lifetime.

William Sartain

Born in Philadelphia on 21 November 1843, Sartain received instruction in drawing and engraving from his father, John. He had already produced a print by 1864, but, deciding on a career as a painter, in 1867 he attended classes at the Pennsylvania Academy of the Fine Arts and studied for a year with Christian Schussele. In 1868 he went to Paris, where he studied at the Ecole des Beaux Arts and under Léon Bonnat. He went on to travel extensively throughout Europe before settling in New York City in 1877. Two years later he began teaching at the Art Students' League at Cooper Union and the following year was made an associate academician of the National Academy of Design. Well received by critics, particularly for his landscapes, he was

awarded a number of medals throughout his career at various expositions. He died on 25 October 1924.

174
PORTRAIT OF SHAKESPEARE
1907
Oil on canvas, 24 × 20¼ in. (60.9 × 51 cm.)

Signed lower right: "w. SARTAIN"

Case no. 1185

Provenance: Bought by Eustace Conway from the artist in April 1907; bought by Folger from Conway, October 1923, $400

References: Piper 1962, no. 18

Condition: Despite its date of 1907, the canvas appears to have been lined by Finlayson in 1932.

Eustace Conway, a lawyer, had inherited his interest in Shakespeare from his father, Moncure D. Conway, also a lawyer and an avid admirer of the Bard. Eustace Conway purchased the canvas directly from the artist, and he may well have commissioned the piece. Sartain saw to it that the work was framed before sending on the painting, and the frame, which is from the New York firm of E. A. Milch Inc., is one of the most substantial in the collection. It cost $38.50 in 1907, and, toned in gold leaf, it harmonizes with the yellow-green tonalities of the painting.

Sartain wrote Conway on 9 April 1907, "I have slightly toned the forehead to the color of [the] lower face . . . and it has made an improvement in it."[1] The forehead is still in a brighter key than the rest of the head, suggesting a radiating intelligence. After Conway sold the painting to Folger, Sartain wrote, "I think I struck the character while closely adhering to the *authentic* data." Of course, he is referring to his primary model, the Droeshout engraving, whose awkward proportions have been only partially corrected. Sartain did "cheat" on the amount of collar beneath the chin, so that the head would not appear so detached from the torso, and the figure is given more room on all four sides. The moustache with its upturned ends and the goatee are borrowed from the Stratford Bust. The doublet itself is conceived as a deep red with a lighter red for the trim, the color probably having been suggested by the red doublet Shakespeare wears in the bust. The artist avoided a sharp focus, the head and

174

torso appearing slightly blurred, as if seen through the haze of memory.

1. Sartain's correspondence concerning the painting is on file at the FSL.

Umberto Romano

Romano was born on 26 February 1905 in Bracigliano, a town near Salerno, Italy. When he was nine, his family emigrated to America, settling in Springfield, Massachusetts. Drawn to art at age five, Romano was singled out early as a promising talent. Upon graduation from the Classical High School in Springfield, he attended the National Academy of Design, and in 1926 and 1927 studied at the American Academy in Rome. His first one-man show was held in New York at the Frank K. M. Rehn Galleries when he was only twenty-three years old. He married Clorinda Corcia on 12 June 1941. He was renowned as a teacher as well as a painter, having founded the Romano School of Art (Gallery on the Moors) in East Gloucester, Massachusetts, in 1933. Throughout his career he received numerous prizes, and his works are represented in the permanent collections of a number of major institutions. A resident of New York, he died on 27 September 1982.

175

SHAKESPEARE RECITES SHAKESPEARE
ca. 1960s
Oil on canvas, 50⅛ × 40⅛ in. (127.3 × 101.9 cm.)

Signed lower left: "Umberto Romano"

Provenance: Gift of Mrs. Clorinda Romano, widow of the artist, and Robin Romano, their son, December 1984

References: Umberto Romano, *Great Men*, New York, Dial Press, 1979, p. 70 (repr. in color)

Shakespeare is shown in three-quarter length, his right hand raised in an elegant, rhetorical gesture. He is dressed in black, wearing a white shirt with a lawn collar and lacy cuffs. His body dissolves into the background at the edges, and, reflecting the influence of abstract expressionism, drips of brown and orange-red paint energize the black portions of the surface. The figure is surrounded by a shifting blue background, with blues also dominating the face. The textures differ throughout, with heavy impasto in and around the head and with the stained canvas showing at the outer edges.

175

The theme of genius fascinated the artist. Throughout the 1960s, he worked on a series of paintings that were published in 1979 under the title *Great Men*.[1] The series, as constituted in the book, numbers forty pictures arranged by title in alphabetical order. While the members of this select group often transcend types, they fall roughly into the following categories: religious leaders (nine), rulers and statesmen (seven), philosophers (five), writers (five), artists (five), musicians (four), scientists (four), and explorers (one). Twelve of the portraits are of twentieth-century figures, but all five of the writers date from earlier periods. In addition to Shakespeare, they are Dante, Cervantes, Voltaire, and Dostoevsky.

In *Great Men* the Folger painting is simply entitled *William Shakespeare*, in keeping with the book's format, but a pencil notation on the stretcher provides a more elaborate title offering a suggestion of a narrative: "Shakespeare Recites Shakespeare." The artist's widow feels the notation on the stretcher "was the preferred title—suggesting the living Shakespeare rather than a portrait of a dead hero."[2] Shakespeare is depicted as sorcerer, magically transporting the viewer, his audience. While the swarthy head is reminiscent of the Chandos type, it now takes on a sinister power. Romano captures the feel of a demiurge who exhibits the electrifying force of a rival to the Creator.

1. The date for this series is supplied by Clorinda Romano in a letter to the author of 17 January 1990. The review of Romano's exhibition at the Franz Bader Gallery in Washington in the *Sunday Star* of 25 February 1962 lists a few of the portraits of famous men, which helped to inaugurate the series, but, since the portrait of Shakespeare is not among them, it was presumably executed later.
2. Letter from Mrs. Romano of 17 January 1990.

Allegorical Portraits

George Romney

176 (Plate 27)

THE INFANT SHAKESPEARE
ATTENDED BY NATURE AND THE PASSIONS
ca. 1791–92
Oil on canvas, 56½ × 80⅞ in. (143.5 × 203 cm.)

Case no. 1717

Inscribed in sky at upper center: "SHAKSPERE"

Provenance: Painted for Alderman John Boydell for the Shakespeare Gallery; sold by lottery 28 January 1805 and won by William Tassie; sold by Christie, 18 May 1805, lot 41, as "*The Infant Shakespear—Poetically composed, tastefully drawn, and charmingly coloured,*" bought by Michael Bryan (1757–1821), picture dealer and author of *Biographical and Critical Dictionary of Painters and Engravers*, for 62 guineas (£65.2.0); collection of Thomas Chamberlayne by 1848; by descent to his grandson Tankerville Chamberlayne (1843–1924) of Cranbury Park, Winchester; bought 1905 by Norman Forbes-Robertson (1858–1932), the actor and brother of the celebrated actor Sir Johnston Forbes-Robertson; Christie's, 19 May 1911, lot 121, £420, bought by Gilbert. (A scrawling handwriting in white can be found in a number of places on the stretcher. Of those passages that are legible are the following two: "Scrimgeour Esq." and "May 19–11." This date is of course that of the Christie's sale, and the most logical candidate for this surname is Rev. John C. Scrimgeour, the editor of three plays by Shakespeare, published in 1914, 1916, and 1921. Presumably, Scrimgeour had some involvement with the painting at this point.). Bought August 1927 by Folger through Wells, £10,500 ($51,074.94).

Exhibitions: London, Boydell, 1792, 1793, 1794, 1796, not numbered but placed at end of the paintings listed for these years in the Boydell Shakespeare Gallery catalogues as "*The Infant Shakespeare, Attended by Nature and the Passions.* Nature is represented with her face unveiled to her favourite Child, who is placed between Joy and Sorrow.—On the Right-Hand of Nature are Love, Hatred, and Jealousy; on her Left-Hand, Anger, Envy, and Fear"; London, Boydell, 1802, no. 87; London, Boydell, 1805, no. 138; London, British Institution, *Catalogue of Pictures by Italian, Spanish, Flemish, Dutch, French and English Masters*, 1848, no. 118; London, British Institution, *Catalogue of Pictures by Italian . . . and English Masters*, 1863, no. 182; London, Grafton Galleries, *Exhibition of a Special Selection from the Works by George Romney*, 1900, no. 61, and *Exhibition of a Second Selection from the Works by George Romney*, 1900–1901, no. 46 (both times the painting is listed as *Shakespeare Nursed by Tragedy and Comedy*); Washington, 1976–77, no. 18; San Francisco, 1979–82, repr. in color p. 186; Montgomery, 1985–86, no. 56

Fig. 120. George Romney, *Nature Unveiling to the Infant Shakespeare.* Cartoon, 50⅛ × 40¼ in. The Board of Trustees of the National Museums and Galleries on Merseyside (The Walker Art Gallery, Liverpool).

References: Romney 1830, pp. 146, 147, 152, 174–75, 219; Hamilton 1831; Redgrave 1878, p. 367; Lord Ronald Gower, *Romney and Lawrence,* New York, 1882, pp. 16–18; Hilda Gamlin, *George Romney and his Art,* London and New York, 1894, pp. 86–88; Ward and Roberts 1904, vol. 2, p. 194; Arthur Bensley Chamberlain, *George Romney,* 1910 (reprint: Freeport, N. Y., 1971), pp. 142, 147, 170–71, 268–69, 352–53, 362; Salaman 1916, p. 20; *New York Times,* 19 September 1927, p.24; *New York American,* 20 September 1927, p. 5, repr.; *New York Herald Tribune,* 27 September 1927, p. 16, repr.; *The* *Times Weekly Edition,* 29 September 1927, repr.; *Illustrated London News,* 1 October 1927, repr.; *Washington Post,* 3 October 1927, repr.; Edgar Wind, "Humanitätsidee und Heroisiertes Porträt in der Englischen Kultur des 18. Jahrhunderts," *Vorträge der Bibliothek Warburg* 9 (1930–31), p. 190 (mistakes Stratford version for original); T. S. R. Boase, "Illustrations of Shakespeare's Plays in the Seventeenth and Eighteenth Centuries," *Journal of the Warburg and Courtauld Institutes* 10 (1947), p. 107; Friedman 1976, pp. 135–38, 234 (repr.); Yvonne Romney Dixon, "The Drawings of George Romney in the Folger Shakespeare Library," Ph.D. diss., University of Maryland, 1977, pp. 47, 49, 60–67, 314–15

Condition: The engraving reveals that the canvas has been cut down slightly on all four sides, particularly at top and bottom. The uppermost wingless angel in the engraving at the upper right of Shakespeare's name is no longer visible in the painting. The head that appears above Jealousy is only faintly visible, and some of the definition of Nature's cloak has been lost, the engraving showing a zigzagging line, the energizing shape of a lightning bolt connecting Nature's head with that of Shakespeare. The original canvas is a twill weave, and it is attached to two desiccated animal-glue linings. A recent examination reveals two possible tears: measuring from the lower left corner, one is $46^{1/2}$ inches up by 14 inches over, the other 16 inches up by 67 inches over. Two pronounced vertical cracks extend from top to bottom at $53^{1/4}$ and 58 inches from the left-hand margin; these seams are covered with fill material. The use of bitumen has created disfiguring cracks. Overcleaning has created significant paint loss, particularly in the darker areas, and the entire surface suffers from the excessive application of overpaint applied on at least two occasions. When the painting was on exhibit in New York in *A Brush with Shakespeare,* a vandal made a series of irregular scratches across the buttocks of the figure of Sorrow or Tragedy. The scrapes, now repaired, extended through the varnish and paint films into the ground, but did not cut the canvas itself.

Engravings: Benjamin Smith, published by J. & J. Boydell, 29 September 1799, $19^{5/8} \times 24^{7/8}$ in.; the picture was also engraved in outline on a small scale by Starling and Normand *fils.*

Preparatory drawings: Romney was a prolific draftsman and numerous sketches survive that are related to the theme of the birth of Shakespeare. It is, however, often difficult to pin these works down to a specific painting. Of the drawings in the Folger, those that are possibly preparatory to *The Infant Shakespeare* are the following: ART Vol. ca. 60.101 (verso), 60.102 (verso), 60.103 (verso), and ART Flat b7.70. A drawing of the three passions on the right is reproduced in *The Drawings of George Romney,* Smith College Museum of Art, Northampton, Mass., 1962, pl. 21.

Versions: A sketch (oil on panel, $18^{1/2} \times 24$ in.) is in the Royal Shakespeare Theatre Picture Gallery, Stratford-upon-Avon.

Executed for the Boydell Shakespeare Gallery, this painting was on exhibit by 1792. Yet Romney's interest in the subject of Shakespeare as an infant predates the gallery. At least as early as 1783 he was at work on sketches of the birth of Shakespeare[1] and apparently even earlier on sketches of Nature unveiling herself to the infant (fig. 120), a scene inspired by lines in Thomas Gray's poem "The Progress of Poesy," first published in 1757.

> Far from the sun and summer-gale,
> In thy green lap was Nature's Darling laid,
> What time, where lucid Avon stray'd,
> To him the mighty Mother did unveil
> Her aweful face: The dauntless Child
> Stretch'd forth his little arms, and smiled.

Gray's conception of Shakespeare as an untutored genius, with Nature rather than Learning as his inspiring muse, was a favorite one of the eighteenth century.

The Folger painting adds to this conceit of Nature's unveiling her awful face the idea of the infant attended by the Passions, an idea which, as confirmed by the artist's son,[2] was inspired by William Collins's poem "The Passions: An Ode for Music," first performed in 1750.

> When Music, Heav'nly Maid, was young,
> While yet in early Greece she sung,
> The Passions oft to hear her Shell,
> Throng'd around her magic Cell,
> Exulting, trembling, raging, fainting,
> Possest beyond the Muse's Painting . . . .
>
> (lines 1–6)

Romney substitutes Shakespeare, the incarnation of Poetry, for Music, and his painting is of course on one level an answer to Collins's criticism in the last line quoted of painting's limitations.

Romney gives prominence to two of the Passions, Joy to the left of the infant as seen from the viewer's perspective, and Sorrow to the right, figures that double as Comedy and Tragedy. On the left-hand side are seen Love and Hate: the two figures are closely aligned, Hate's right arm paralleling Love's left. Above them hovers Jealousy, who, in Collins's poem, alternately courts both emotions. A fourth figure, now only dimly seen, is above Jealousy, and this is surely Pale Melancholy, whom Collins links with the other three. On the right-hand side, Anger, "his Eyes on fire" (line 21), aggressively bears down on the child, while Envy is coupled with Fear, who "back recoil'd" (line 19).

John Romney rightly compared this picture to Correggio's work in terms of its coloring, design, and use of chiaroscuro. There is a glowing warmth to its striking contrasts of light and shadow, and much of its inspiration lies in Correggio's religious painting. Shakespeare becomes a secular divinity and the Passions are adoring or respectfully wary worshipers. The infant is clearly associated with the Christ Child, as beams of light, surrounded by adoring angels, burst through the clouds. In the middle of the radiant glow appears Shakespeare's name, another example of the Word made flesh.

The model for the child was said to be the son of a guardsman, an infant whom Romney used in several other pictures. Looking out with a solemn gaze, he is the only figure in the painting to make eye contact with the viewer, and some have found his grave demeanor disconcerting, one critic remarking, "The naked babe, who remains quite unmoved in the midst of this nightmare of the passions, is almost amusing in his stolidity."[3] This stolidity should be interpreted instead as melancholy, the melancholy born of genius, and, beginning with Wind's article of 1930–31, critics have pointed out the similarities between Romney's *Infant Shakespeare* and Reynolds's *The Infant Johnson* and *The Infant Hercules*, two other pensive babies whose massive, square heads and brooding melancholy features give promise of greatness to come.[4]

Romney's conception of a great man as a pensive infant may indeed be based on Reynolds's, but the work's sobering mood is also in tune with that of its two poetic sources. Gray traces poetry's historical development only to lament, "Oh! Lyre divine, what daring Spirit / Wakes thee now?" (lines 112–13). Collins is even more plaintive: "Why, goddess, why, to us denied, / Lay'st thou thy ancient lyre aside?" (lines 97–98). For Romney, as in Gray's poem, Shakespeare's birth brings genius to England's shore, but in the eighteenth century his promising legacy is seen as having gone unfulfilled. Ultimately, *The Infant Shakespeare* is as much a lament as a celebration.

Romney went on to contribute to the Gallery *Shakespeare Nursed by Comedy and Tragedy*, an intimate scene of only three figures. In light of romanticism's cult of childhood, it is not surprising that images of Shakespeare as an infant were to prove extremely popular with other artists as well, but only Fuseli was to come close to the power of Romney's first conception.[5]

1. See Patricia Jaffe's exhibition catalogue *Drawings by George Romney*, Cambridge, 1977, pp. 37–38 (no. 61).
2. Romney 1830, p. 174.
3. Chamberlain, *Romney*, p. 352.
4. For a discussion of Reynolds's images in the context of melancholy genius, see Carey McIntosh, "Reynolds's Portrait of the Infant Johnson," in W. H. Bond, ed., *Eighteenth-Century Studies in Honor of Donald F. Hyde*, New York, 1920, pp. 279–96.
5. Fuseli's painting was exhibited at the British Institution in 1806 (see Schiff 1973, no. 1202). Some of the other artists who depict Shakespeare as an infant are Charles Smith, Edward Francis Burney, Angelica Kauffmann, Richard Westall, William Hamilton, Mather Brown, Richard Cook, Henry Singleton, and George Cruikshank.

Anonymous

177

APOTHEOSIS OF SHAKESPEARE
Early nineteenth century
Oil on paper on canvas, 21³/₄ × 16¹/₈ in. (55.2 × 40.9 cm.)

Provenance: Arthur Dean of Birmingham, England, by 1881; the Folger file card lists the source as simply "From Mrs. Folger's house"

Exhibitions: A label in pen and ink on paper pasted at the bottom center of the stretcher gives the following information: "Lent to the Shakespeare Memorial / Exhibition 1881 by Arthur[?] Dean, 16 Weaman Street, / Birmingham, To be returned to him in about / 3 months from this date April 12th 1881." *The Catalogue of Pictures, Drawings, &c., Exhibited in the Gallery of the Shakespeare Memorial, Stratford-on-Avon, April, 1881* lists only one entry that, because of its nonspecificity, could correspond to this work: "84 Portrait—Shakespeare." There is also a printed fragment at the bottom of the frame that suggests the work was exhibited elsewhere: "338 Early English School: A Portrait of Shakespeare."

References: Piper 1962, no. 4

177

Fig. 121. Benjamin Wilson, *William Shakespeare.* Painted for the Town Hall, Stratford-upon-Avon, and destroyed in a fire of 1946. Photograph: National Portrait Gallery Archive, London.

Condition: The paper consists of a center piece that has been enlarged with strips on all four sides.

This crude but vigorous interpretation of the deified Bard is based on Benjamin Wilson's painting of Shakespeare in his study given to the Town Hall, Stratford-upon-Avon, by David Garrick on the occasion of the Shakespeare Jubilee of 1769. Wilson's painting was destroyed in the fire of 1946, but a photograph of it has survived (fig. 121). Wilson shows Shakespeare in Van Dyck dress, seated in his study and pausing in the act of writing. The Folger artist has simply adapted this design to a new context, one in which Shakespeare is exalted to the rank of an immortal. Holding a book and a quill pen—a curious combination in that one presumes the book represents a published text—the poet is posed within a glory of clouds. Faint rays can be seen issuing from his head. He turns to his left, looking upward in a moment of inspiration. The brown cape over his shoulders has a red lining, the same color as the slashed portion of the sleeve of the green doublet. The red trim down the front of the doublet does not match up with the center of the collar, and the collar itself bunches up around the neck. The large right eye socket is poorly integrated into the face, and the anatomy in general is unconvincing.

Miniatures

Droeshout Shakespeare
Dante Gabriel Rossetti

Rossetti was born in London in 1825, his father being an Italian refugee who was Professor of Italian at King's College. After having studied in art schools, Rossetti became briefly a pupil of Ford Madox Brown in 1848, and later that year joined with William Holman Hunt and John Everett Millais and four others to form the Pre-Raphaelite Brotherhood, an attempt to reform art by returning to nature and the purity of "primitive" painting before the time of Raphael. Soon abandoning the meticulous execution prescribed by his colleagues, he turned from painting to watercolors, his subject matter often being drawn from Dante, with whom he closely identified, and the Arthurian legends. He married his model, Elizabeth Siddal, in 1860 and was strongly affected by her death from an overdose of laudanum two years later. From this point in his career he returned to oils, focusing on languid, sensual images of women, representatives of what became known as a Pre-Raphaelite type. Throughout his life he considered himself more a poet than a painter, and in the English school only Blake surpasses him in his ability to produce at the highest level in both of these arts. After years of decline, Rossetti died in 1882.

178

PORTRAIT OF SHAKESPEARE
ca. 1865
Watercolor with gouache on ivory, oval, $2^{7}/_{16} \times 1^{7}/_{8}$ in. (6.1 × 4.7 cm.) (sight)

PR2842/1709/Copy 3/Ex. Ill.

Signed at left center: "D.G. / Rossetti"

Provenance: Gift from Rossetti to William Joyce (the book is inscribed on the back of the frontispiece: "William Joyce Esq / from / Yours faithfully / D G Rossetti / 4 Dec 1865"); bought by Folger from Thorp, 1929

Condition: The miniature is mounted in a brass frame on the cover of a book—volume 7 of Rowe's 1709 edition of *The Works of Shakespeare,* containing *Venus and Adonis, Tarquin and Lucrece, Poems on Several Occasions.* A drawing by Rossetti is also glued to the back of the frontispiece, with an inscription on the page opposite: "This pen and ink drawing / by Rossetti represents / Vincennes / the death of the Duke / of Engheim in which / Rossetti's friend, Joyce / was much interested."

The drawing is a reduction of the portrait of Shakespeare found in the Droeshout print to the size of a miniature, the dominant art form of Shakespeare's England. It shows Shakespeare, with auburn hair, wearing a black doublet with gold trim and posed against a blue background. Although a minor effort on Rossetti's part, it turns an otherwise undistinguished volume of Rowe's 1709 edition into a miniaturized version of the First Folio, with the image of the poet introducing the text.

Anonymous (nos. 179–82)

179

PORTRAIT OF SHAKESPEARE
Probably nineteenth century
Watercolor with touches of gouache on ivory, $3^{7}/_{16} \times 2^{5}/_{8}$ in. (8.7 × 6.6 cm.)

Provenance: Sotheby, 17–20 (20) July 1916, lot 892a, £3

Condition: The miniature is behind glass but unframed. It is backed with paper and taped around the edges.

This and the following work are so close in technique and color that one presumes they are by the same hand. Shakespeare wears a black doublet with purple undertones; some brown and blue appear in the white ruff; he is shown with brown hair and pink cheeks. Stippling is used to animate the background.

178 (enlarged)

179 (enlarged)

180

PORTRAIT OF SHAKESPEARE
Probably nineteenth century
Watercolor with touches of gouache on ivory, 3¼ ×
2½ in. (8.2 × 6.4 cm.) (sight)

Provenance: Bought from Millard, May 1916, £10

Condition: The work is under glass in a thick gold
frame.

181

PORTRAIT OF SHAKESPEARE
1769?
Enamel on copper, oval, 1⅝ × 1⅜ in. (4.2 × 3.4
cm.) (sight)

Case no. 1535

Provenance: Said by Rosenbach to be made for the
Jubilee of 1769; bought from Rosenbach, May 1926,
$275 (for this and the following miniature)

Condition: The enamel is in a gilded brass frame
mounted in a wooden box lined with red velvet.
Penned on a piece of paper glued to the back of
the box: "Shakespeare / from the / Chandos Portrait / Enamelled on Copper, / William Beford [or
William B. Ford']"

181 (enlarged)

180 (enlarged)

182

PORTRAIT OF SHAKESPEARE
1769?
Enamel on copper, oval, $2\frac{1}{2} \times 1^{15}/_{16}$ in. (6.3 × 5 cm.)

Case no. 1535

Provenance: Said by Rosenbach to be made for the
Jubilee of 1769; bought from Rosenbach, May 1926,
$275 (for this and the preceding miniature)

Condition: Mounted in a gilded brass frame.

Chandos-Chesterfield Shakespeare
Anonymous

183

**THE CLOPTON-WINGFIELD
PORTRAIT OF SHAKESPEARE**
Watercolor on ivory, $5\frac{1}{4} \times 3^{7}/_{8}$ in. (13.3 × 9.8 cm.)

Case no. 272

Provenance: Collection of Major W. Clopton-
Wingfield; sold Sotheby, 7 December 1901, lot 1449

Condition: Backed with paper, on which is a pencil
drawing of the bust of a lady in a bonnet; the paper
is inscribed at upper right: "William Goar [re-
mainder cut off by edge; there is an unintelligible
word beneath]." The miniature is mounted on
brown velvet and is boxed.

The artist's rendering is based on Gaspard Du-
change's engraving of Benoit Arlaud's portrait of
Shakespeare, which appears in some copies of
Rowe's 1709 edition of Shakespeare's works opposite signature a, vol. 1. Although he shows the
figure only from above the waist and with just a
moustache, Arlaud's primary source of inspiration
may well have been *The Chesterfield Portrait of
Shakespeare* (Shakespeare Birthplace Trust, Stratford-
upon-Avon), a memorial portrait of around the
1660s and 1670s which, though presumably based
on the Chandos Portrait, offers a more magisterial
and expansive image of Shakespeare seated with
a book, the grand folds of his large cloak adding
to the work's baroque drama.
The creator of the Folger miniature greatly simplifies the details in the Arlaud-Duchange engraving, making Shakespeare more youthful in the

182

183

184

185

process. He also somewhat haphazardly positions the sitter's buttons and reduces the classicizing cloak seen in the print to a schematic diagram.

Janssen Shakespeare
Anonymous

184

PORTRAIT OF SHAKESPEARE
Probably nineteenth century
Enamel, irregular oval, $2^5/_{16} \times 1^7/_8$ in. (5.8 × 4.7 cm.)

Case no. 1529

Inscribed across center of verso: "Wm. Shakspeare."
Dated on verso at lower right: "1626."

Provenance: Bought from Sawyer, April 1926, £50 (Sawyer told Folger he purchased this work from Sotheby).

Condition: There is a small crack at lower right. The enamel is mounted in a silver frame set with pieces of enamel and glass.

Shakespeare is shown wearing a blue doublet with brown trim. The dark background is similar in color to the trim. Since this image is based on *The Janssen Portrait of Shakespeare* (no. 160), which did not resurface until 1770, the 1626 date is obviously false. In addition, enamel painting was not introduced into England from the Continent until the eighteenth century.

Welbeck Abbey Shakespeare
Anonymous

185

PORTRAIT OF SHAKESPEARE
After 1721
Watercolor with white gouache in ruff on ivory, oval, $3^3/_4 \times 2^{15}/_{16}$ in. (9.6 × 7.4 cm.) (sight)

Inscribed at top in a ribbon-scroll: "WILLIAM SHAKE-SPEARE"

This work is based on George Vertue's 1721 en-graving (fig. 122) of a miniature then in the posses-

Fig. 122. Engraving by George Vertue of *The Welbeck Abbey* or *Harleian Miniature of Shakespeare*, 1721.

sion of Edward Harley, later earl of Oxford. Vertue executed his print for Alexander Pope's edition of Shakespeare published by Jacob Tonson. The artist of the Folger miniature has retained the engraved surround, a creation of Vertue, even depicting the wreath of bay leaves and the inscribed ribbon-scroll above. The identification of the sitter in the Welbeck Abbey or Harleian miniature as Shakespeare has often been challenged.[1]

1. For a discussion of the Welbeck Abbey miniature, see M. H. Spielmann, "The 'Welbeck Abbey' or 'Harleian' Miniature of Shakespeare: The 'James I. Type,'" *Connoisseur* 35 (January 1913), pp. 3–10, and Richard W. Goulding, *The Welbeck Abbey Miniatures*, Oxford, 1916, pp. 79–80 (no. 46).

IV Portraits of Shakespeare's Contemporaries

Of the thirteen works in this section, only two were acquired by Folger. Isaac Oliver's miniature *William Herbert, Third Earl of Pembroke,* bought in 1903, was the fourth painting he purchased and the first that was not a portrait of Shakespeare. But after this auspicious beginning, he acquired only the portrait identified as of Ben Jonson and attributed to Isaac Oliver. The remainder of the works were acquired by the Library after Folger's death. Their acquisition, though obviously on a much smaller scale, parallels the growth of the book collection, the Library having early on expanded its scope to include a wider variety of books in the Elizabethan and Jacobean periods than had been included in Folger's interests. The Library purchased five paintings and miniatures in the 1930s and early 1940s, four of them portraits of members of the family of King James I and one a portrait of John Dryden by Jonathan Richardson. The motivation for these acquisitions was more historical than aesthetic. Since then the collection of portraits of Shakespeare's contemporaries has expanded entirely through gifts, including the important pair of portraits of the third earl of Southampton and his wife and the splendid Hilliard miniature of Lettice Knollys.

Paintings from the preceding section also need to be mentioned in this context, as some of the portraits of Shakespeare are in part or in whole portraits of his contemporaries. As already mentioned, the Vroom Portrait is surely of an unknown contemporary who was re-christened Shakespeare. The Janssen Portrait, the Ashbourne, and the Zuccaro all began life as a portrait of a contemporary that was later physically altered in an effort to recreate Shakespeare, and in two of these cases the identity of the original sitter has been recovered. The Ashbourne Portrait unquestionably was first a picture of Sir Hugh Hamersley, and the Janssen Portrait has, with a fair degree of certainty, been identified by David Piper as Sir Thomas Overbury. Since this last painting in a recent restoration was returned closer to its original appearance, it now arguably belongs in this section rather than in the one on Shakespeare. However, it has been retained in the earlier section because it played so important a role in Shakespeare iconography and more appropriately accompanies some of the many images of Shakespeare that it helped to create.

John De Critz, the Elder, after

De Critz was born in Antwerp around 1552/53. He was brought to England in 1568 as part of the exodus of Flemish intellectuals after the arrival of the Spanish duke of Alva in the Low Countries. By the end of the century, he was one of the leading portrait painters in London, and in 1603 he became Serjeant Painter to James I. Despite his success, his work has proven difficult to identify. He died in London on 14 March 1642.

186

QUEEN ELIZABETH I
After 1620
Oil on panel, 4⁵/₁₆ × 3⁷/₁₆ in. (11 × 8.7 cm.)

Inscribed in gold at top center: "ELISABETH"

Provenance: Purchased by John J. Cunningham of the National Sculpture Society, New York, in a village west of London; on loan to the FSL from April 1948 and given in December 1965

Exhibitions: Washington, 1979–81, repr. in color p. 106

186 (enlarged)

Condition: The paint surface has chipped at the edges where it has rubbed against the frame. The oak panel consists of two pieces, the smaller one (3¹/₈ × 2⁵/₈ in.) being inserted into the larger piece framing it. The panel is beveled on the back across both pieces, the flat inner surface measuring 2¹/₂ by 1³/₈ inches. There is a red wax seal in the lower right corner of the flat surface extending into the beveled edge.

Original painting: The portrait of Queen Elizabeth thought to be by John De Critz is now known only through the engravings after it. The Folger painting is based on the print by Magdalena and Willem van de Passe, 6¹/₄ × 5³/₄ in., published in Henry Holland's *Herωologia* of 1620.

Born in 1533, Queen Elizabeth I was the daughter of Henry VIII and Anne Boleyn. Her mother was executed when Elizabeth was less than three years old. She ascended the throne in November 1558 after having survived the reign of her half-sister, Mary, who for a time had had her imprisoned. She was well educated, and her reign was marked by political astuteness and a tough practicality. Elizabeth surmounted several crises, including the challenge to her throne that came from her cousin, Mary, Queen of Scots, and the threat of invasion by the Spanish Armada in 1588. Vain and susceptible to flattery, she encouraged a cult that idolized her in such guises as the divine Gloriana and the Virgin Queen. She enjoyed adorning herself in sumptuous dresses and jewelry, and her love of expensive finery was reflected in court portraiture. Dying on 24 March 1603, she dominated the period in which Shakespeare came of age, and he paid tribute to her more than once, as in *A Midsummer Night's Dream*, where Oberon describes to Puck seeing Cupid shoot an arrow:

> . . . A certain aim he took
> At a fair vestal throned by the west,
> And loos'd his love-shaft smartly from his bow,
> As it should pierce a hundred thousand hearts;
> But I might see young Cupid's fiery shaft
> Quench'd in the chaste beams of the wat'ry moon,
> And the imperial vot'ress passed on,
> In maiden meditation, fancy-free.
>
> (II, 1, 157–64)

Fig. 123. After John de Critz, *Queen Elizabeth I.* Engraving by Magdalena and Willem van de Passe.

The Folger painting is based on a print of Queen Elizabeth (fig. 123) that was published in Henry Holland's book *Herωologia* of 1620. The print, almost certainly executed by Magdalena and Willem van de Passe, is thought to go back to a drawing by Isaac Oliver which itself was based on a painting by John De Critz.[1] The style of Elizabeth's costume dates the conception of the original image to the 1590s, during the last years of Elizabeth's reign, and, as with other portraits of this period, the queen is depicted as eternally youthful, unmarked by her advanced years. Like its model, the Folger painting is small, its size, though not its medium, relating to the tradition of miniature portraits.

Having based the image on a black-and-white print, the Folger painter presumably chose his or her own colors. Elizabeth is shown with reddish brown hair arranged in tight curls and waves. She wears an open ruff, standing high and radiating outward. Her dress is red, the bodice cut low and square, as was the fashion for young virgins, and it is patterned with gold thread, pearls, and other

jewels. Hanging from a pearl necklace is a pendant whose most prominent feature is a gold crescent moon, a reference to Elizabeth as Cynthia or Diana, the moon goddess. Tributes to this aspect of the cult of Elizabeth began as early as about 1586–87 and were meant not only as a reference to the queen's virgin purity but even more to her influence over water, exalting her as the ruler of a maritime empire.[2]

The artist of the Folger portrait simplified many of the print's details as can be seen, for example, in the treatment of the queen's hair. Certain awkward passages, such as the almost missing left ear, are the result of imperfections that were already present in the print. A more significant difference between the two images is that the Folger painter omits the orb and scepter; the resulting slightly different angle in the positioning of the lower arms is awkwardly managed. This alteration has the effect of making the queen less regal, thereby presenting a more intimate, attractively accessible image.

1. This information is contained in marginalia and notes to be found in various copies of the *Herωologia*. It is published in Arthur M. Hind, *Engraving in England in the Sixteenth and Seventeenth Centuries*, Cambridge, 1955, p. 153, no. 9. An even more immediate source for the print is Renold Elstrack's engraving of this same image, published in Holland's *Basiliωlogia* of 1618. The 1620 engraving, however, depicts Elizabeth with an even younger, blander countenance than does the 1618 version, and it is the 1620 interpretation that the Folger painting follows.
2. See Strong 1987, p. 127.

George Gower

Of gentle birth, the artist was from the family of Gower of Stettenham, Yorkshire. Born around 1740, he was practicing as a portrait painter in London by 1573, the date of his portraits of Sir Thomas Kytson and his wife (Tate Gallery, London). His self-portrait, dated 1579, the same year as the "Sieve" Portrait, contains a convoluted inscription beneath which is a compass (the two-pronged instrument for describing circles or transferring measurements), a symbol of the artist's craft, out-weighing his coat of arms.[1] The inscription indicates that Gower now resumes his God-given talents as a painter after "youthfull wayes" had enticed him to neglect his abilities, and his artistic skills add to his family's reputation. He was appointed Serjeant Painter for life to Queen Elizabeth I on 5 July 1581, and three years later he and Nicholas Hilliard unsuccessfully attempted to secure a monopoly on the production of images of the queen, Gower holding the right to portraits and prints and Hilliard to miniatures. No documented works by Gower of the queen have survived, but on stylistic grounds Roy Strong identified the other version of this type as by him[2] and, on seeing the Plimpton Portrait in October 1991, confirmed it to be by Gower as well. The artist died in London, where he was buried on 30 August 1596.

1. The painting is catalogued in Roy Strong, *The English Icon*, London and New York, 1969, no. 113. Ellis Waterhouse glosses the inscription in his book *Painting in Britain 1530–1790*, London, 1953, p. 21.
2. See Strong 1987, p. 95.

187 (Plate 28)

THE PLIMPTON "SIEVE" PORTRAIT OF QUEEN ELIZABETH I
1579
Oil on panel, 41⅛ × 30 in. (104.4 × 76.2 cm.)

Inscriptions: Above the globe at upper left: "TVTTO VEDO & / MOLTO MANCHA [last two letters are joined]" ("I see everything and much is lacking"). Above the royal arms at upper right: "E R." On the royal coat of arms: "HONI SOIT QV . . . I MAL Y PENSE" and "SEMPER EADEM." Beneath the arms: "STA[last two letters are joined]NCHO RIPO / SO & RIPOSATO / AFFANO 1579" ("Weary I rest and, having rested, I am still weary," from Petrarch's *Trionfo d'Amore*, IV, l. 145). On the rim of the sieve running along the upper left quadrant: "ATERA [portion obscured by overpainting] MAL DIMORAINSELA" ("A terra il ben mal dimora in sella"—"To earth the good, bad remains in the saddle").[1]

Provenance: Acquired by George Arthur Plimpton by 1930; by descent to his son Francis T. P. Plimpton; promised by Mrs. Francis T. P. Plimpton to the Folger Shakespeare Library

References: "Club Notes," *The Bulletin of the Needle and Bobbin Club* 14 (1930), p. 54, repr. p. 55; Roy C. Strong, *Portraits of Queen Elizabeth I*, Oxford, 1963, p. 66, no. 43 (repr.); Strong 1969, vol. 1, p. 110; Frances A. Yates, *Astraea: The Imperial Theme in the Sixteenth Century*, London and Boston, 1975, p. 114, n. 2; Strong, *The Cult of Elizabeth*, Wallop, Hampshire, 1977, p. 153; Walter Oakeshott and [Constance] Anson Jordan, "The Siena Portrait of Queen Elizabeth I," *Apollo* 74 (October 1986), pp.

308–09; Strong 1987, p. 95; Elizabeth W. Pomeroy, *Reading the Portraits of Queen Elizabeth I*, Hamden, Conn., 1989, p. 52

Versions: Strong lists two other versions, one of which, now missing, is described by George Vertue in the eighteenth century (see Strong 1963, p. 66). Strong discusses the surviving version at length in his book *Gloriana* of 1987, where it is recorded as in the possession of Lane Fine Art Ltd., London (it is now in a private collection in Florida). Its measurements (34 × 24 in.), medium (oil on panel), and provenance are corrected from his earlier listing.

Related works: A series of other works, dating from about 1580 and slightly later, also show Elizabeth holding a sieve in her left hand, though she now turns to the viewer's left. In addition, she is shown with a symbolic pillar. The most famous of this group is the Siena Portrait (Pinacoteca di Siena, oil on canvas, 49 × 36 in.), which, according to Jordan, was recently discovered to be by the Antwerp painter Quentin Massys the Younger ("Representing Political Androgyny," p. 164).

Elizabeth holds a sieve in her left hand, and in her right she holds a tan glove, while resting her hand on the arm of a black chair with gold trim. The figure is boldly rendered without subtle transitions, and it inhabits a shallow and constricted space, the shelf on which the globe rests, for example, being only suggested rather than fully articulated. The queen is an icon commanding reverence, and, as Roy Strong observed, her face and headdress are approved images, having been derived line for line from the earlier Darnley Portrait of Elizabeth now in the National Portrait Gallery, London.[2] The color scheme matches that of the other surviving version.[3] Elizabeth wears a red dress embroidered with gold and silver thread, every detail of her sumptuous adornment precisely delineated. A transparent, olive-gray mantle with gold parallel bars descends from her headdress. Her sleeves are a creamy white patterned with gold thread, and the pearly grays of her ruff and cuffs help set off the pale complexion of her face and slender, elegant hands.

The "Sieve" Portrait is the first visual expression of two important interrelated themes: Elizabeth's emergence as the orchestrator of imperial expansion and as the Virgin Queen, wise in her purity

and free of entanglements that marriage in a patriarchal society would bring. The globe, paralleling
the coat of arms, of course signifies her imperial
ambitions, and in the Plimpton version, it is the
southern hemisphere that is emphasized, with Af-
rica on the right and an even more crudely shaped
South America on the left. While Europe is dwarfed
by her southern neighbor, England is, unsurpris-
ingly, prominently displayed. Obviously the queen
and her country, the two being synonymous, are
beginning to covet the empires of Portugal and
Spain, and at least one ship can be seen sailing on
the globe in a westerly direction. The inscription
over the globe—"I see everything and much is
lacking"—refers to empire building on a global
scale, and, as Strong has pointed out, this addition
to the iconography of monarchy owes a debt to the
vision of a British Empire founded on sea power articulated by John Dee in his book *General and Rare
Memorials Pertayning to the Perfect Arte of Navi-
gation,* published in 1577.[4]

The entire image, including the emphasis on the
imperial idea, is inspired by Petrarch, whose writings were seen by the Elizabethans as supporting
their Protestant ideals. The inscription "Weary I
rest and, having rested, I am still weary" is taken
from Petrarch's *Triumph of Love,* where those ruled
by Cupid are subject to "the vain imaginings and
foolish hopes of lovers."[5] *The Triumph of Love* is
followed by *The Triumph of Chastity,* and Elizabeth, by holding a sieve, is shown to have surmounted love's pitfalls through her virginal status,
for the sieve is the symbol of the Vestal Virgin Tuccia, who is a member of Petrarch's second triumphant procession. Tuccia had proven her chastity by
carrying water in a sieve from the Tiber River to the
Temple of Vesta, and the virginal sieve became one
of the queen's favorite symbols. The inscription on
the sieve—"To earth the good, bad remains in the
saddle"—is more problematical. Presumably it refers to the sieve's sifting process, which separates
out the good from the bad, paying homage to Elizabeth's wisdom, although ironically it reverses the
concept of the sieve's ability to retain its contents
when held by a virgin.[6]

The use of Italian inscriptions not only harks back
to Petrarch, but also indicates Elizabeth's emergence into an international arena. Her overall form,
with her arms stiffly bent at the elbows, aggressively occupies space. She fills the composition,

and the circular shape of the sieve she holds is related to that of the globe, again reaffirming the ambitious dimensions of her aspirations. In a later
image of the queen, the Armada Portrait, one version of which is at Woburn Abbey, also apparently
by Gower, the globe replaces the sieve and the composition itself expands horizontally under the pres-
sures of the queen's inflated dress. While Gower,
among others, created an impressive imperial
iconography for the queen, this was one instance
when the reality was eventually to live up to its
propaganda.

1. The inscriptions and their meanings in parentheses come from
Roy Strong, *Portraits of Queen Elizabeth I,* Oxford, 1963, p. 60,
and Constance Jordan, "Representing Political Androgyny:
More on the Siena Portrait of Queen Elizabeth I," in Anne M.
Haselborn and Betty S. Travitsky, eds., *The Renaissance English
Woman in Print,* Amherst, 1990, p. 166.
2. Strong 1987, p. 95.
3. I would like to thank the Lane Fine Art Gallery for supplying a
color photograph of the work formerly in its possession.
4. Strong 1987, p. 99.
5. Strong 1963, p. 66.
6. The use of "saddle" in the quotation opens up the possibilities
of interpretation. Yates sees it in a more negative light: "On
earth the good has difficulty in remaining in the saddle (or in
command)" (1975, p. 116), and along similar lines Pomeroy suggests one reading as the "good falls while the bad is elevated or
remains in power" (1989, p. 52). Jordan reads into it some stimulating, though strained, observations on Elizabeth's manipula-
tion of sexual politics. For her, it is an intentionally enigmatic
image: "The idea of virginity it symbolizes is contradicted by
the image of sexual passion, of riding, or of being in the saddle . . . . The sieve symbolically enfolds its opposite, just as the
virgin Elizabeth symbolically enfolds a sexually potent prince
who rides and commands" ("Representing Political Androgyny," pp. 167–68).

Michiel Jansz van Miereveld, after

Born in Delft in 1567, Miereveld trained there and
in Utrecht. Although he attempted history painting
early in his career, he was most successful as a portraitist. He continued throughout his life to reside
in Delft but also worked at The Hague, the seat
of government for the United Provinces, where
he painted the members of the house of Orange-
Nassau and their court. His matter-of-fact renderings proved popular; according to Joachim Sandrart,
he oversaw a large workshop that eventually turned
out over ten thousand portraits before his death in
Delft in 1641.

188

ELIZABETH, QUEEN OF BOHEMIA

After 1623

Oil on panel, irregular, 12⅛ × 10¼ in. (30.8 × 25.9 cm.)

Provenance: Collection of the Rt. Hon. Viscount Feilding, Newnham Paddox, Rugby; Feilding sale, Christie's, 1 July 1938, lot 90, sold with portrait of Mary King, widow of Sir William Meredyth and first wife of William, third earl of Denbigh, a painting dated to ca. 1630 and also attributed to Miereveld; bought by Leggatt Brothers, London; sold to B. F. Stevens & Brown Ltd., London, who then sold the paintings to the FSL, August, 1938. While both paintings were received, the portrait of Mary King remains untraced.

Exhibitions: San Francisco, 1979–81, detail repr. in color p. 127

Condition: The vertically grained panel appears to be oak. The paint and its thin white ground suffer from buckling cleavage as a result of movement of the panel caused by changes in humidity. In 1977 this buckling was corrected, some of the old repaint removed, and areas of loss filled and inpainted.

Elizabeth was the eldest daughter of James VI of Scotland (afterwards James I of England) and Anne of Denmark. Born in 1596, she traveled to England in 1603 on her father's accession, residing at court from 1608. On St. Valentine's Day 1613, she married the German Protestant Elector Palatine, Frederick V, a welcomed occasion for celebration after the death of her brother, Prince Henry, with whom she had been particularly close. "Lady Elizabeth's Men," formed in the winter of 1610–11, performed as part of the festivities, as did Shakespeare's company, which presented a number of the Bard's plays. Elizabeth left England with her new husband, arriving in Heidelberg in June 1613. In time she bore him thirteen children, and the English monarch George I of the House of Hanover was their grandson. In 1619 they were crowned king and queen of Bohemia, but the Thirty Years War soon forced them out of both Prague and the Palatine electorate, Elizabeth living in exile at The Hague from 1621. Frederick died in 1632, but Elizabeth did not return to England until 1661, dying on 13 February of the following year. She was celebrated by her countrymen as a champion of Protestantism.

Fig. 124. Michiel Jansz van Miereveld, *Elizabeth, Queen of Bohemia.* Reproduced by permission of His Grace, The Duke of Norfolk. Photograph: Courtauld Institute of Art.

Miereveld painted Elizabeth more than once, beginning soon after her arrival at The Hague. The portrait type to which the Folger work belongs dates to these first years, as it was engraved by W. J. Delff in 1623. Elizabeth ordered copies of her portraits as favors for supporters, as in the case of her friend Sir Thomas Roe, to whom she wrote in August 1621, "I will send you my picture, as soon as I can have it done, for you know, I am sure, that Michael of Delft is very long in his work."[1] A signed full-length portrait of this early type is in Arundel Castle (fig. 124), but there are also works on a smaller scale by both the artist and his workshop.

One suspects, though, that the Folger portrait is by neither Miereveld nor his studio. In its details and oval format, it comes closest to the Delff print of 1623 and is presumably an early image based on it rather than on one of the paintings. It also somewhat idealizes the queen's features, deemphasizing her long face and strong jaw.

1. Quoted in London, National Portrait Gallery, *The Winter Queen: Elizabeth, Queen of Bohemia and Her Family*, 1963, no. 68.

Daniel Mytens, after (no. 189)
Paul van Somer, after? (no. 190)

Mytens, a Dutch artist, was born probably in Delft around 1590. He was influenced by both Jan Antoniz Ravestyn and Michiel van Miereveld and became a master in the Guild of St. Luke at The Hague in 1610. Mytens had arrived in England by 1618 and was employed by the Crown two years later, becoming Court Portrait Painter in 1622. He was the best of the court portraitists before Van Dyck entered the service of Charles I in 1632. He retired to The Hague in the early 1630s and died there around 1647.

Van Somer was born in Antwerp around 1577/78 and had settled in London by December 1616. He was made a court portrait painter the following year. Possibly trained in Holland, he developed a style similar to that of Mytens. He died in London after only a few years, being buried on 5 January 1622.

189 (Plate 29)
HENRY WRIOTHESLEY,
THIRD EARL OF SOUTHAMPTON
After 1620
Oil on canvas, 45 × 36 in. (114.3 × 91.5 cm.)

Inscribed at lower left in yellow: "Earl of Southampton"

190 (Plate 30)
ELIZABETH WRIOTHESLEY,
COUNTESS OF SOUTHAMPTON
After 1620
Oil on canvas, 45 × 35 in. (114.4 × 91.5 cm.)

Inscribed at lower left beside the pearl bracelet: "Countess of Southampton"

Provenance: The pair purchased in September 1950, by John F. Fleming, an associate of the Rosenbach Company, from a Mrs. Henry Mostyn, then living in Riverdale, Md., who was thought to be a direct descendant of the countess of Southampton; collection of Mr. and Mrs. Paul Mellon; first loaned to FSL by Paul Mellon in January 1960 and given on 22 May 1980

Exhibitions: Detroit Institute of Arts and Richmond, Virginia Museum of Fine Arts, *The World of Shakespeare, 1564–1616*, 1964, nos. 13 and 14, as "attributed to Jan Antoniz Ravesteyn"

References: Strong 1969, vol. 1, p. 301 (no. 190 only)

Versions of no. 189: Roy Strong feels the original portrait "is probably the head and shoulders (on panel) in the collection of Earl Spencer, Althorp, which is signed by Mytens and dated 1618 (?)."[1] Altogether, five head-and-shoulders versions are known; and half-length versions can be found in the National Portrait Gallery, London; in the Wingfield Digby Collection, Sherbourne Castle; and a small copy at Hodnet Hall, Shropshire. Three-quarter-length versions, like the Folger painting, are at Hardwick Hall; Gorhambury (Earl of Verulam); Master's Lodge, St. John's College, Cambridge; and Alex Wengraf Limited, London, this last a work formerly in the collection of Earl Howe.

Versions of no. 190: According to Strong, this is the only type of the countess of which multiple images exist. Although the original has not been identified, he feels it is possibly by van Somer. There are two versions showing her seated, three-quarter length: the one at Welbeck Abbey shows her turned to the viewer's left, the one at Sherbourne Castle to the right. Two other versions show the figure more than slightly half-length, turned to the right, with her right hand touching an ornament at her breast: one is again at Sherbourne Castle and the other in the National Portrait Gallery, London.

Henry Wriothesley was born on 6 October 1573, becoming third earl of Southampton on the death of his father just eight years later. Educated at St. John's College, Cambridge, he exhibited early a passion for literature and was known for his patronage of poets and playwrights. Among those who sought his favor was Shakespeare, who dedicated his poem *Venus and Adonis* to him in 1593 and the following year *Lucrece*. This second dedication is far warmer than the first, and even allowing for Elizabethan conventions of address, suggests a certain intimacy. In his biography of 1709, Nicholas Rowe states, on the authority of Sir William Davenant, that Southampton gave Shakespeare a thousand pounds, which, if even partially accurate, indicates a strong bond between the two men. Southampton has long been a candidate for the Fair Youth whom Shakespeare addresses in his sonnets.

Southampton's career was eventful. Possessed of good looks and high spirits, he was soon noticed by Queen Elizabeth, but he ran afoul of her favor when he secretly married one of the queen's waiting women, Elizabeth Vernon, after she became pregnant. On the discovery of their indiscretion, both husband and wife spent a short time in prison. Southampton's friendship with the earl of Essex, his wife's first cousin, led to more serious trouble, when he joined Essex in a failed revolt against the queen's ministers on 8 February 1601. Southampton had literally set the stage for the revolt by engaging Shakespeare's company to enact *Richard II*, with its story of the deposition of a king, the night before. While Southampton was among those convicted of treason, instead of being beheaded, he had his sentence commuted to life imprisonment. He was, however, soon set free when James I ascended the throne in 1603 and was given a number of high honors along with being recreated earl of Southampton. His hot temper, though, kept him from positions of the highest responsibility, and much of his energy consequently was devoted to colonial expansion. He and his eldest son died of fever on a military expedition to the Low Countries in 1624.

Born apparently in January 1573, Elizabeth Vernon was the daughter of John Vernon of Hodnet in Shropshire. She was introduced to the court by her first cousin, Robert Devereux, second earl of Essex, a favorite of Queen Elizabeth, and was appointed a maid of honor to the queen. She became involved with Southampton as early as 1595, secretly marrying him in 1598, thereby forfeiting the queen's favor. Long outliving her husband, the countess gave refuge to Charles I at Titchfield in 1647 after his escape from Hampton Court and may even have lived on after this incident for another eight or nine years.[2]

The Folger portrait of the earl is one of a number of versions of this type. Southampton is shown in armor in three-quarter length, his right arm akimbo and his left hanging by his side. His hair is a graying brown, his eyes blue. He wears a falling ruff of point lace, point-lace cuffs, and gray gloves. The thumb of his right hand does not point upward as in some versions, although the canvas is rubbed in this area and may have been reworked. An elaborate sash embroidered with gold and silver threads with a few red passages crosses over his right shoulder. Underneath a blue ribbon supports the George of the Order of the Garter. His sword hangs at his left from a gold embroidered sword belt, and the end of the scabbard can be only faintly seen projecting from behind the figure on the other side. To the sitter's left is a table covered by an oriental carpet on which sit a plumed helmet, a staff, and gauntlet. Strong points out that this image reflects a standard Dutch formula for military portraits as seen in works by Ravesteyn, to whom the Folger paintings were once attributed, and Miereveld. This authoritative, martial pose was appropriate for Southampton, who had earlier served on several military expeditions with Essex.

The countess wears a black dress decorated with a regular pattern of black beads. The upper part of the bodice and sleeves are slashed over scarlet. Her eyes are brown, her hair a light brown. A large pearl earring, with a cord, hangs from her left ear. On her hand she wears a circlet of pearls with lace behind, and a rose and red, blue, and yellow berries are placed in her hair to the viewer's right. She wears a falling lace ruff and point-lace cuffs over a band of crimson. A double-chain necklace hangs over her shoulders with a jeweled *S* and pendant pearl at its center. At her waist is a V-shaped silver girdle decorated with jewels and gold trim. Her left arm rests on a red chair studded with brass nails. On her wrist she wears a bracelet composed of linked jeweled *S*'s and a gold ring on her little finger. A pearl bracelet of three rows is on her right wrist, and in her hand she appears to hold a black-feathered fan. This painting may well be directly based on the missing original, as some of its details agree with one version and some with another.

While there are numerous versions of both portraits, both even appearing in the same collection, as far as is known this is the only time the two images were painted to be seen as a pair. Beyond matching their sizes, the artist made adjustments to the portrait of the countess to harmonize the two. The Folger portrait is the only three-quarter-length version to show the countess standing rather than seated in a chair, so that she will complement the pose of her husband. Both works have red objects positioned in the lower right corner, the carpet in one and the chair, which is green in other versions, in the other. The countess's fan, formerly red, is now black in order not to unbalance the two paintings. It is a skillful merger of the two types, even the positioning of the countess's arms being slightly adjusted in order that they might reflect, without parodying, those of her husband.

1. Strong 1969, vol. 1, p. 299. In addition to Strong, one should consult Richard W. Goulding's article "Wriothesley Portraits" for a list of images of both sitters, though the Folger paintings are not included (*Journal of the Walpole Society* 8 [1919–20], pp. 16–94).

2. The date of the countess's death is given as "?1655/6" in Alan and Veronica Palmer's *Who's Who in Shakespeare's England*, Brighton, 1981.

Peter Oliver, after

Peter Oliver was the eldest son of the celebrated miniaturist Isaac Oliver. Born around 1589, he grew up in London in the parish of St. Anne Blackfriars, where he worked closely with his father, his style and Isaac's being indistinguishable before the latter's death in 1617. He married the younger sister of his father's third wife, and when Isaac died, he inherited the business, continuing to work for the court. Increasingly he turned away from portraiture to the production of copies of history paintings, reflecting a more intellectual patronage. He died in 1647.

191

BEN JONSON
Mid-eighteenth century
Oil on canvas, 8³⁄₈ × 6³⁄₈ in. (21.2 × 16.2 cm.)

Provenance: Gift of the Trustees of the Cleveland Museum of Art in memory of Mr. and Mrs. James Parmalee, 11 November 1940

Jonson, poet and dramatist, was born in Westminster in 1572. Though raised in poor circumstances, he was educated at Westminster School and may have gone on to attend St. John's College, Cambridge. He served in the military in Flanders, but, returning to London around 1592, he embarked on a career in the theater. Of a violent temper, he killed a fellow actor in 1598 in a duel or brawl. In that same year, his play *Every Man in His Humour* was performed by the Lord Chamberlain's Men, with

Shakespeare playing one of the parts. A number of Jonson's comedies and tragedies were performed by Shakespeare's company, including *Volpone*, *Epicoene*, and *The Alchemist*. Jonson was also involved with writing masques for the court. His quarrelsome nature, the pointed satire in his plays, and his conversion to Catholicism (later recanted) led to serious difficulties with the authorities on more than one occasion. Suffering in his last years from ill health and declining patronage, he died on 6 August 1637 and was buried in Westminster Abbey.

As part of a series published in Birch's *Heads of Illustrious Persons of Great Britain* (1743), Houbraken engraved in 1738 a portrait of Ben Jonson said to be after a painting by Isaac Oliver (fig. 125). This image proved popular, being engraved a number of times in smaller and less elaborate formats, and the Folger painting is probably after one of the prints that reverses the head as seen in Houbraken's design. Houbraken, in his turn, had reversed the head as seen in the painting. In an article published in 1906, Sir Richard R. Holmes wrote that the miniature which he believed to be Houbraken's model was not by Isaac Oliver but

191

Fig. 125. After Isaac Oliver, *Ben Jonson.* Engraving by Houbraken, 1738.

rather by his son, Peter Oliver. Furthermore, the miniature does not represent Ben Jonson but probably is an image of one of Peter's younger brothers.[1] Yet even if the original model is not Jonson, that is who the artist of the Folger picture set out to paint, and this work forms a part of the Jonson iconography, just as portraits of Shakespeare based on false models are still indispensable in understanding critical perceptions of the man and his work. The Oliver type, as executed here, presents a more cultured, sensitive gentleman than does the robust image descended from the authoritative Blyenberch type (see fig. 126). Jonson wears a regal purplish red cloak. He turns toward the viewer, his dark eyes set off against his expansive, highlighted brow. The original oval shape of the image is retained, as a painted brown frame encompasses the figure.

1. See Sir Richard R. Holmes, "The English Miniature Painters Illustrated by Works in the Royal and Other Collections," *Burlington Magazine* 9 (May 1906), p. 110, repr. plate 2, fig. 5.

Anonymous

192
UNKNOWN MAN
(Formerly identified as Ben Jonson)
Seventeenth century with later overpainting
Oil on panel, 22½ × 17⅜ in. (57.2 × 44 cm.)

Case no. 753

Provenance: Collection of Comte de Lautreppe, 9 rue Pasquier, Paris; by descent to Miss Ada Oliphant Murdoch, The Rockingham, Broadway and 56th Street, New York, as of April 1916;[1] bought by Folger from Smith, December 1917, $500

Exhibitions: Amherst, *Shakespeare,* 1951, as Jonson by Isaac Oliver; San Francisco, 1979–81, repr. in color p. 176 as "Ben Jonson attr. to Isaac Oliver"

References: Strong 1969, vol. 1, p. 184

Condition: The panel appears to be mahogany. It is ³⁄₁₆ inch thick and is beveled on the back along its edges. There are two severe vertical splits along the grain of the wood: one starts 3¼ inches from the left bottom and ends 4 inches from the left top; the other begins 13¼ inches from the left bottom,

192

Fig. 126. After Abraham van Blyenberch, *Ben Jonson*. Oil on canvas, 18½ × 16½ in. National Portrait Gallery, London.

ending 13 inches from the left top. The panel has been prepared with a thin white ground. The original paint surface has suffered extensive losses from cleavage caused by movement of the panel and solvent abrasion from past cleanings. The picture has been repainted at least twice.

There are two contemporary references to paintings of Jonson: the poet refers in his *Works* to one by Sir William Borlase, and one by Abraham Blyenberch is listed in 1635 in the collection of the second duke of Buckingham.[2] Neither work has survived, but there are numerous copies of the Blyenberch type (see, for example, fig. 126). Abraham van Blyenberch worked in London from 1617 until 1621, and his conception of Jonson is the yardstick by which other purported portraits must be measured. The sitter in the Folger painting has similar dark brown hair, and his hairline and beard conform to the same pattern. He is seen against a brown background and wears a plain black doublet with buttons, his dress and appearance in keeping with John Aubrey's description of the poet: "He was (or rather had been) of a clear and faire skin; his habit was very plaine."[3] His eyes, though, are blue rather than dark as in the Blyenberch type. But more significant is the difference in overall impres-

sion. Even at second-hand, the Blyenberch type conveys a sense of vigorous intelligence, the head bulky and powerful, the mood one of profound reflection. The Folger sitter offers in contrast a bland mask. The sitter is inoffensively handsome, without the charged emotions and florid bulk of the Blyenberch Jonson. Heavily reworked, the Folger picture is in any case only an approximation of the sitter, who remains to be identified.

1. This information is contained on the back of old photographs of the Folger painting in the archives of the National Portrait Gallery, London. A printed text in French was removed from the back of the painting itself, reinforcing the likelihood of its having been in a French collection. This text concerns an account of Horace Walpole's description of Oliver's work, including his portrait of Ben Jonson. An old pen-and-ink inscription was also removed from the back of the Folger picture that more clearly links the painting to Walpole's account: "Benjamin Johnson by / Isaac Oliver. / This picture is noticed by Horace Walpole in his anecdotes / of painting in England collected by Vertue / published at Strawberry Hill / 1761 / There is good authority / for its authenticity R.L.F." Walpole in fact seems to have been referring to the Oliver portrait of Jonson reproduced in Houbraken's engraving (fig. 125), and there is no authority, good or bad, to link the Folger painting with Jonson, Oliver, or Walpole, other than the note itself.

2. The most recent summary of the images of Jonson can be found in Strong 1969, vol. 1, p. 184.

3. *"Brief Lives," chiefly of Contemporaries, set down by John Aubrey,* ed. Andrew Clark, Oxford, 1898, vol. 2, p. 14. For further remarks by Aubrey on Jonson's appearance, see no. 197.

Miniatures

Nicholas Hilliard

Hilliard, the greatest miniature painter of his generation, helped shape posterity's view of the Elizabethan age. Born in 1547 to Richard Hilliard, an Exeter goldsmith, he was sent to Geneva with the Bodley family in 1557 to escape Queen Mary's persecution of Protestants. Returning soon afterwards, he was apprenticed in 1562 to Robert Brandon, Queen Elizabeth's goldsmith. Though trained as a goldsmith and jeweler, he excelled at limning, and the queen, who was in search of a native-born court artist, first sat to him in 1572. Four years later, Hilliard left for an extended visit to France in order to study the Continental masters. The 1580s proved to be his most productive decade, but in the 1590s he encountered competition from other limners, many trained by him, who were then coming into favor. Hilliard found himself increasingly in financial difficulties, and, although he was always capable of inspired pieces, in general the quality of his production declined. By the time of his death in January 1619, he had been eclipsed by his more popular rivals.

193 (Plate 31)

LETTICE KNOLLYS, COUNTESS OF LEICESTER

ca. 1590–95

Watercolor on vellum, oval, 1¹³⁄₁₆ × 1½ in. (4.5 × 3.8 cm.) (sight)

Accession no. 231301

Provenance: Acquired from D. S. Lavender Antiques Ltd., London, by an anonymous donor, January 1987

Versions: An inferior copy, listed as "School of Nicholas Hilliard," is in the Fitzwilliam Museum (see Bayne-Powell 1985, p. 120).

Condition: The painting is backed with cardboard and mounted in a contemporary gold frame with spiral cresting.

The sitter wears a black-and-white dress with black cloak, all trimmed in gold. Across her shoulders lie a heavy gold chain and pendant, both of which are set with jewels. Her blond, curled hair is dressed high with a circlet of rosettes composed of elaborate jewels. On her cloak to her left is a blue-green leaf trimmed in gold. The background consists of a crimson curtain, and the dress and use of the curtain as a backdrop suggest a date near the end of the sixteenth century.

Hilliard did not work from drawings, preferring to paint *ad vivum*, and the closely observed details of this miniature suggest it was painted directly from the life. Typically of Hilliard, the portrait, an abbreviated half-length framed in an oval, is rendered in line in a flat, two-dimensional field. The emphasis on strong decorative patterns allows the dress to compete with the sitter's face, providing an image of sumptuous splendor.

A poor copy of this miniature is in the Fitzwilliam Museum, indicating that the sitter was of some social standing. This copy is identified only as of an unknown lady, but the Folger work was acquired with the identification of Lettice Knollys. The likeness agrees with other portraits of the countess,[1] and one might surmise that the leaf on the sitter's cloak is intended as a pun on her name.[2]

If the identification is correct, it is the only portrait of her by Hilliard to have survived.

Lettice was the daughter of Sir Francis Knollys, Treasurer of the Household to Queen Elizabeth. Sir Francis and members of his family left England during the Marian persecutions, and it seems likely that the Knollys' associations with Hilliard began as early as 1557, when they were all in Geneva. Lettice's first husband was Walter Devereux, later first earl of Essex, but soon after his death in 1576 she married Robert Dudley, earl of Leicester, who was rumored to have poisoned Essex in order to arrange the marriage. Leicester, the favorite of Queen Elizabeth, who for a time contemplated marrying him herself, was a man of considerable influence at the court and one of Hilliard's most important patrons. Four of Hilliard's seven children, in fact, were given names that suggest that members of Leicester's family may have acted as godparents: Francis, baptized on 24 December 1580, could have been named after Sir Francis Knollys; Lettice Hilliard was baptized on 25 May 1583; Penelope Hilliard, who bore the name of one of Lettice's daughters, on 31 October 1586; and Robert, who had the name of both Lettice's husband and her first-born son, on 30 March 1588. Leicester died on 4 September 1588, some saying he had been poisoned by Lettice, who had fallen in love with Sir Christopher Blount, a friend of her oldest son. She and Blount were married before the end of the year, but her third husband was executed along with her eldest son, Robert Devereux, second earl of Essex, when in 1601 they attempted to overthrow Queen Elizabeth's councilors. After this tragedy, Lettice lived in retirement until her death in 1634.

1. For a portrait of ca. 1585 of Lettice Knollys by George Gower, see Strong 1969, p. 180 (no. 133).
2. The leaf resembles vaguely the delicate, upper leaves of the Sauoie lettuce as illustrated in John Gerard's *The Herball or Generall Historie of Plants* (London, 1597, vol. 1, p. 240). The leaf, however, is too generalized to make a precise identification possible. The name Lettice is an Anglicized form of Letitia, which comes from the Latin for joy.

Isaac Oliver

Oliver was the great successor to Hilliard. Together they dominate the English portrait miniature. Oliver was born in Rouen to the goldsmith Pierre Olivier sometime in the first half of the 1560s. He was, however, in London by 1568. While the documentary facts on Oliver's life are sparse, his training appears to be Continental rather than English, though he worked for a time with Hilliard. His emphasis on a command of chiaroscuro and a scientific use of perspective placed him outside Hilliard's Elizabethan aesthetic. He presumably studied at some point in France and in the Low Countries, and it is known that he visited Venice in 1596. In his miniatures he employed a variety of sizes and shapes, and in addition to these works he also painted on a large scale. He was the first artist working in England to elevate drawings to works of art in their own right and turned to mythological and religious subjects as well as portraiture. By 1605 he was appointed "painter for the Art of Limning" to Queen Anne of Denmark and may have revisited Italy in 1610. He was buried in London on 2 October 1617.

194 (Plate 32)
WILLIAM HERBERT, THIRD EARL OF PEMBROKE
1611
Watercolor with bodycolor on vellum, oval, 2⅛ × 1¹¹/₁₆ in. (5.3 × 4.3 cm.) (sight)

Signed with monogram and dated at left center: "I" with superimposed "O" / "1611" (the last digit is difficult to read and has been interpreted as a zero)

Provenance: A Mr. Anderson by 1865; Collection of W. E. Bools, Enderby House, Clapham, bought for £50 at an unspecified date; Bools sale, Sotheby, 22–27 (22) June 1903, lot 1435, £56 plus 10 percent commission, Sotheran acting as agent

Exhibitions: London, South Kensington Museum (now Victoria and Albert), *Catalogue of the Special Exhibition of Portrait Miniatures on Loan at South Kensington Museum,* June 1865, no. 298, as "William Herbert Third Earl of Pembroke. Signed and dated 'I.O.1610.'"; San Francisco, 1979–81, repr. pp. 122 and 177 (image reversed)

Condition: The miniature is executed in watercolor, with bodycolor used in the lace and gold paint on the earring. The surface suffers from some flaking. The work is mounted in a black carved wooden frame, consisting of an oval within a rectangle. Two fragments of playing cards were re-moved as backing for the miniature. They appear to be the Seven of Hearts and a face card, probably a Queen or Jack.

William Herbert, third earl of Pembroke, was born at Wilton on 8 April 1580. He succeeded to the earldom on the death of his father on 19 January 1601. His relationship with Queen Elizabeth, already lukewarm, was severely strained when he refused to marry a maid of honor bearing his child. His career at court, however, was revived on the ascension of James I, and Pembroke greatly enhanced his financial position when he married in 1604 Lady Mary, the wealthy daughter of the seventh earl of Shrewsbury. Although an adviser to the king, he lacked the ambition and will to achieve his full potential in the governance of state affairs. The nephew of the poet Philip Sidney and himself a poet on a minor scale, Pembroke took delight in associating with, and supporting, men of letters. He was also a generous benefactor to Oxford University, where he was chancellor from 1617 until his death on 10 April 1630. The editors John Heminge and Henry Condell dedicated the First Folio of 1623, the first collected edition of Shakespeare's plays, to Pembroke and his brother Philip. Pembroke certainly had known Shakespeare, and, given his earliest name, William Herbert, he has at times been identified as the "W. H." of Shakespeare's sonnets. This association, however, is now generally discounted, as it seems highly unlikely that the two men were close friends, nor would Lord Herbert later have been addressed by his youthful name. The fact that Pembroke had been appointed Lord Chamberlain in 1615, giving him the responsibility of overseeing the production and publishing of plays, is sufficient to explain the dedication of the First Folio to him.

The miniature depicts Pembroke with gray eyes, a thin blond beard, and auburn hair falling over a white lace whisk collar. Backed by a red curtain, he wears a black slashed doublet. Around his neck is the blue ribbon of the Order of the Garter, and from his left ear hangs a gold earring with leather straps.

Peter Oliver

195 (Plate 33)
HENRY FREDERICK,
PRINCE OF WALES
Early 1610s
Watercolor with bodycolor, gold-trimmed garnet, on vellum, oval, 2 × 1⅝ in. (5.1 × 4 cm.) (sight)

Accession no. 4880

Provenance: Collection of Henry Yates Thompson; his sale, Sotheby, 2–4 (2) July 1941, lot 125, repr., £28; bought by FSL from Stevens & Brown, £75, September 1941

Exhibitions: San Francisco, 1979–81, repr. p. 122, as "attributed to Peter Oliver"

Condition: Bodycolor is used in the ruff and gold-trimmed garnet in the decoration. The surface suffers from peeling and is abraded along the edge. The miniature is mounted in a gold frame with spiral cresting. On the back of the case is engraved, "Prince Henry / Son of James 1st."

Henry Frederick was born on 19 February 1594, the first child of James VI of Scotland and his wife, Queen Anne. When only about a year old, he was entrusted to the hereditary guardianship of the earl of Mar over the strenuous objections of his mother. Queen Anne refused to journey to London in 1603 for the coronation of her husband and herself until the prince was allowed to accompany her. In 1605 Henry matriculated at Magdalen College, Oxford, and was created prince of Wales five years later. He proved popular as the heir to the throne, was supportive of his friends, and made a bold defense of Sir Walter Raleigh. He also gave promise as a distinguished patron of the arts, at an early age already overshadowing his parents. Even more enthusiastically than his mother, he preferred the miniatures of Oliver to those of Hilliard. He died of typhoid fever at St. James's Palace on 6 November 1612, just eighteen and a half years old.

The prince, posed before a blue curtain, is wearing damascened armor over a cream-colored doublet trimmed in gold. His blond hair is swept back over his forehead, and his eyes are gray. The vivid blue ribbon around his neck is that of the Order of the Garter, but it is difficult to see the decoration he is wearing.

While this portrait has been traditionally identified as of Henry, one must offer the caveat that he and his younger brother, Charles, duke of York, who was eventually crowned as Charles I, looked very much alike and their portraits are often confused. They shared the same broad forehead, long, thin face, and fair, upswept hair. If it is a portrait of Charles, who was born in 1600, it is likely that it shows him sometime between his investiture as Knight of the Garter in 1611 and his brother's death the following year,[1] but, for lack of conclusive evidence, the old identification of the sitter as Henry is retained here.

The miniature's style is convincing as an early work of Peter Oliver, when he was employed by his father, Isaac. He worked from models created by his father, executing portraits of both princes. Those of Henry Frederick were in particular demand after his premature death.

1. In a letter to the author of March 1990, Dr. Jill Finsten suggests this as the most plausible dating if the portrait is of Charles, an identification to which she is inclined. For images of the young prince, see Margaret R. Toynbee, "Some Early Portraits of Charles I," *Burlington Magazine* 91 (1949), pp. 4–9.

Jonathan Richardson

A Londoner, born around 1665, Richardson was apprenticed against his will by his stepfather to a notary. Following his own inclination after the death of his stepfather, he became the pupil of the portrait painter John Riley, whose niece he was to marry. Richardson enjoyed a successful career, becoming the leading native-born portrait painter working in England in the first four decades of the eighteenth century. He is also remembered for his critical writing on art, including *An Essay on the Theory of Painting* (1715), *An Essay on the whole Art of Criticism in Relation to Painting* (1719), *A Discourse on the Science of a Connoisseur* (1719), and, with his son, *An Account of Some of the Statues, Bas-Reliefs, Drawings, and Pictures, in Italy* (1722) and *Explanatory Notes and Remarks on Milton's Paradise Lost* (1734). His dated drawings indicate that he was extremely active as a draftsman from the late 1720s, when he had more leisure time. Enfeebled by a stroke a few years before his death, he died on 28 May 1745.

196 (enlarged)

196

JOHN DRYDEN
ca. 1730s
Pencil on vellum, oval, 3¼ × 2⅝ in. (8.2 × 6.6 cm.)
(sight)

Inscribed at upper right: "1697"

Provenance: Collection of Francis and Minnie Wellesley, no. 443 in their privately printed catalogue;
Wellesley sale, Sotheby, 28 June–2 (1) July 1920, lot
652, £7, bought by Dobell; bought by FSL from
P. J. Dobell, summer 1939 (listed in a manuscript
catalogue entitled "Dryden Collection," dated
March 1939)

Exhibitions: London, Victoria and Albert Museum,
*Catalogue of a Collection of Miniatures in Plumb-
ago, Etc., Lent by Francis Wellesley, Esq.*, 1914–15,
no. 42, repr. pl. 9 as after Kneller (also appears in
list of illustrations as attributed to Richardson)

Condition: Mounted in a rectangular case with a
silver frame.

Born on 9 August 1631, fifteen years after the
Bard's death, John Dryden is not a contemporary of

Shakespeare, but, through his contact with William
Davenant, who claimed Shakespeare as his god-
father and apparently even his natural father, the
poet must still have been for Dryden almost a living presence. In his preface to his adaptation of *The
Tempest,* Dryden credits Davenant for having first
taught him to admire Shakespeare, at a time when
Shakespeare's reputation was inferior to that of
playwrights such as Ben Jonson. Kneller's "copy" of
The Chandos Portrait of Shakespeare of course
hung in Dryden's study (see no. 154), and the writer
thanked the artist in his poem "To Sir Godfrey
Kneller" of 1694.

> *Shakespear* thy Gift, I place before my sight;
> With awe, I ask his Blessing e're I write;
> With Reverence look on his Majestick Face;
> Proud to be less, but of his Godlike Race.[1]

Dryden was indeed of the same godlike race: a successful playwright for the Restoration stage, a distinguished poet who, for a time, was poet laureate,

Fig. 127. After Godfrey Kneller, *John Dryden*. Engraving by George
Vertue, 1730.

a great satirist, and a celebrated translator particularly well known for his work on Virgil. After his death on 1 May 1700, he was buried in the Poets' Corner of Westminster Abbey.

Richardson's portrait of Dryden is a plumbago miniature. Like many of his drawings, it is not *ad vivum*. Instead, it is based on Sir Godfrey Kneller's rendering of the poet now in Trinity College, Cambridge. Kneller's portrait was painted in 1697, probably for the publisher Jacob Tonson as one of the earliest canvases executed for the Kit-cat Club series.[2] It was engraved several times, and one presumes Richardson used one of these prints as a model rather than the painting itself, as the prints have already transformed the image into line. In addition, in the painting Dryden faces left, and in some of the engravings (see, for example, fig. 127), the head is reversed as in Richardson's design. The "1697" that appears on the drawing obviously refers to the date Kneller executed his canvas rather than to the date of the drawing itself. In the miniature, Richardson concentrates only on the sitter's head and shoulder, the painting showing Dryden in half-length holding a laurel wreath in one hand. Richardson also ignores the mole on Dryden's cheek, which, in any case, in the print is barely visible.

Kneller, born in 1646 in Lübeck, was a generation older than Richardson. Arriving in England in 1676, he dominated English art until his death in 1723.

He was honored with a knighthood in 1692 and made a baronet in 1715. In adapting Kneller's *Dryden* to the format of a plumbago miniature, Richardson was honoring the Dutch artist as well as the poet.

1. *The Poems of John Dryden*, ed. James Kinsley, Oxford, 1958, vol. 2, p. 860.
2. Apparently the date of 1697 was only recently uncovered. In the 1971 National Portrait Gallery catalogue *Godfrey Kneller*, J. Douglas Stewart gives the date as ca. 1698, but in his more recent book *Sir Godfrey Kneller and the English Baroque Portrait*, he lists it as signed and dated 1697 (Oxford, 1983, p. 103, no. 244).

Anonymous (nos. 197–99)

197

BEN JONSON

Late eighteenth or early nineteenth century
Watercolor and bodycolor on ivory, oval, 1½ × 1¼ in. (3.7 × 3.1 cm.) (sight)

Accession no. 220700

Provenance: Gift of Robert Butman, Haverford, Penn., December 1980

Condition: The color has been scratched away in order to create white highlights in the eyes; mounted in a deep wooden frame.

In 1711 George Vertue engraved a portrait of Ben Jonson said to be by the Dutch painter Gerard Honthorst. The location of Vertue's model is not known, but this portrait type exists in a number of versions (see, for example, fig. 126), all of which are related to a painting of Jonson by Abraham van Blyenberch rather than Honthorst, who was in London only once for a few months in 1628 and never painted Jonson. For the frontispiece to the first volume of the 1716 edition of *The Works of Ben Jonson*, Vertue executed a print (fig. 128) similar to the first but with small variations such as the absence of a cloak and the addition of tie strings to the collar. The Folger miniature is after this later conception.

Jonson wears a black doublet; his hair and beard are a dark brown; his eyes are brown; and his head is set against a mottled brown background. Jonson was not a handsome man, Aubrey reporting that he "had one eie lower than t'other, and bigger,"[1] and the Blyenberch type shows him with a wart close to

197 (enlarged)

Fig. 128. After Abraham van Blyenberch, *Ben Jonson*. Engraving by George Vertue, frontispiece to PR2600 1716 Cage v. 1.

his nose on his left cheek (reversed in Vertue's engraving). The Folger miniature, in part because of its small size, leaves out such flaws, emphasizing instead the forceful, large head with its halo of energized hair.

1. *"Brief Lives," chiefly of Contemporaries, set down by John Aubrey*, ed. Andrew Clark, Oxford, 1898, vol. 2, p. 14.

198

KING JAMES I

ca. 1620?

Watercolor with bodycolor on vellum, oval, 1⅝ × 1⅜ in. (4 × 3.4 cm.) (sight)

Accession no. 4147

198 (enlarged)

199

ANNE OF DENMARK

ca. 1620?

Watercolor with bodycolor on vellum, oval, 1⅝ × 1⅜ in. (4 × 3.4 cm.) (sight)

Accession no. 4148

Provenance: Anderson Galleries, 19–24 November 1934, lot 736 (no. 196), as by Hilliard, $100; lot 737 (no. 197), as by Hilliard, $90, G. A. Plimpton acting as agent

Exhibitions: San Francisco, 1979–81, repr. p. 122, as "attributed to Nicholas Hilliard"

References: FSL *Annual Report*, 1934–35, pp. 20–21

Condition: (No. 198) There is some flaking, and areas along the edge have been retouched, particularly at the upper left. Mounted in a gold frame with spiral cresting. (No. 199) Bodycolor is used in the lace, eyes, and jewelry and gold paint for the earring. There is some flaking and the edges have been abraded by the frame. The gold frame is surmounted with spiral cresting.

199 (enlarged)

Born on 19 June 1566 in Edinburgh Castle, the only son of Mary, Queen of Scots, and Henry, Lord Darnley, James was crowned James VI of Scotland on his mother's abdication in 1567. Mary was eventually executed twenty years later by order of her cousin Queen Elizabeth, and James, next in line to the English throne, was crowned James I of England on the Virgin Queen's death in 1603. A lover of theater, on his arrival in London he assumed patronage of the Lord Chamberlain's Men, Shakespeare's company, which by royal patent became the King's Men. Not surprisingly, the company was to perform more frequently at court during his reign than under Elizabeth's. A scholar in his own right, James published several books. In personality somewhat dour and pedantic, frequently at odds with Parliament, unenthusiastic in his support of Protestantism and conciliatory toward Catholic Spain, James never enjoyed the popularity of Elizabeth. He died on 27 March 1625 and was succeeded by his only surviving son, Charles I.

Born in Jutland on 12 December 1574, Anne was the daughter of King Frederick II of Denmark and Norway. On 20 August 1589 she was married by proxy to James, the two meeting for the first time on 19 November of that year in Norway, where the king sailed, eager to meet his bride. Her first-born was Henry Frederick (see no. 195), and she went on to give birth to six more children, few of whom survived infancy. Anne relished her role as the queen consort after she and her husband were crowned in London. She spent liberally, leaving large debts on her death on 2 March 1619. She was particularly interested in indulging her passions for building and for court entertainments. The English masque, marked by the collaboration of Ben Jonson and Inigo Jones, flourished under her patronage, and the queen herself performed in these masques as a dancer. Her involvement in state matters was limited, as she did not enjoy a close relationship with her husband. Though born a Lutheran, she was attracted to Roman Catholicism, an inclination that was discouraged and viewed with displeasure by many of her Scottish and English subjects.

The traditional identifications of the Folger portraits as James I and his queen are possible, although they cannot be proven as the depictions are not based on any of the canonical types. Shown with blond hair and a pointed beard, the hatless monarch is posed before a red curtain. He wears a black doublet with a white floral pattern, and the style of his collar dates his attire to around 1620. Positioned against a neutral blue-gray background, Queen Anne appears all the more radiant. She is shown wearing a standing wired lace collar and a low-cut décolleté red dress that also dates to around the time of her death. Her jewelry consists of a single strand of large pearls and a pearl earring, and her hair is crowned with a circlet of red, blue, yellow, and white flowers. Her thin, long, pointed nose is her most characteristic feature and supports the portrait's identification.

The two miniatures are by the same hand, but they cannot be by Nicholas Hilliard, to whom they were ascribed when they were acquired. They are executed with a dense coarseness uncharacteristic of his modeling, and, as the painting of the king does not conform to any of the types established by Hilliard, they also cannot be described as after any of his images.

V Shakespeareana

As Shakespeare became deified, his devotees required pilgrimage sites and relics. The Shakespeare Jubilee of 1769 firmly established Stratford-upon-Avon as a Mecca for the believers. The house on Henley Street, where the Bard was said to have been born, acquired a special importance. It was first depicted in an engraving in the *Gentleman's Magazine* for July 1769 and throughout the nineteenth century was featured in a variety of media. The Folger painting of the house is based on an elaborately decorated print issued for the tourist trade. In his painting, Nast actually visits the sanctum sanctorum, where one sees a ghostly worship service in progress. The *Coat of Arms* is a reminder of the poet's social status, of his hard-won right to bear heraldic arms. The many portraits of Shakespeare, catalogued in a separate section, are yet another example of Shakespeareana, and the Folger Shakespeare Library also has numerous relics to accompany these painted tributes, including objects carved from the famous Mulberry Tree, said to have been planted by Shakespeare himself, and carvings from Herne's Oak, a tree made famous by *The Merry Wives of Windsor*. Plaster casts, porcelains, and works in silver are among the wide variety of other objects rounding out these many manifestations of bardolatry.

J. T. Clark, after

The only information on this artist comes from the print on which the Folger painting is based. Published in 1849, the print simply states that it is from an original drawing by J. T. Clark. He or she was presumably a minor figure, as no artist by this name exhibited in London or America during this period.

200

THE HOUSE IN WHICH SHAKESPERE WAS BORN
After 1849
Oil on panel, 11¾ × 15¾ in. (30 × 40.2 cm.)

Case no. 1146

Inscribed on both sides of the signboard: "THE IMMORTAL / SKAKE-SPERE [letters after "P" difficult to see] / WAS BORN IN THIS HOUSE [last words difficult to read]"

Provenance: Samuel Rogers?; collection of Baroness Burdett-Coutts; Burdett-Coutts sale, Christie's, 4–5 (5) May, 1922, no. 250, as by George Vincent; Michelmore, June 1923, £150, as by Vincent ("G. Vincent." is lettered on the back of the panel at lower right; Michel-

200

more published this work in his sale catalogue *Shakespeareana Illustrated*, [1923?], no. 34, repr. as frontispiece).

Condition: The panel is approximately ¼ inch thick at the edges. Since the edges are beveled about 1 inch, the center of the panel is around ³/₈ inch thick. The panel is nicked in two places at the right, ½ inch and 2 inches from the bottom. The reverse of the panel has been prepared with a white gesso that is now dark gray. The recto has been prepared with a white ground that is well attached. The paint has been applied thinly and is solvent-abraded. The paint surface is cracked throughout, and there are two old horizontal cracks in the upper right side in the sky about 2½ inches down. The painting was last cleaned by Finlayson in 1932.

Engraving after original: T. H. Ellis, "The House In Which Shakspere Was Born at Stratford upon Avon Warwickshire From an original Drawing [by J. T. Clark] in 1849," published by T. H. Ellis, 11 × 14¾ in. (image), 17½ × 23⅝ in. (including margins with vignettes). There is also a lithograph by Annie J. Frear of 9 May 1872, which is based on the engraving.

When it was in the Baroness Burdett-Coutts collection, the painting was attributed to George Vincent, a landscape painter of the Norwich School who died about 1831. The painting, though, is based on a print of 1849 (fig. 129). Although following the engraving closely, it leaves out a few details: in particular, the man with a cane at the open door on the left, and the three children playing at the door of Shakespeare's house. Presumably the painter found these figures expendable, as they, unlike the others, are oblivious to the building.

The painting shows how the house appeared in the nineteenth century before it was restored by the Shakespeare Birthplace Trust, which acquired the property in 1847. The adjoining building to the right was a public house, the Swan and Maidenhead. It, however, formed part of the original structure owned by Shakespeare's father, though, as shown here, its windows had been modernized and its exterior converted to brick. The double sign over what had been a butcher shop seems to have been put up in 1824, and of course it did not survive the trust's restorations.

The picture, following the format of the print, shows the houses forming a horizontal bracketed by the sky above and the street beneath. The figures and luggage form a gentle V shape that sets off the building. The building itself is depicted as old, even a bit derelict with its crumbling chimney, but its unadorned simplicity makes it appear enduring. It is not so much the sign that identifies this as

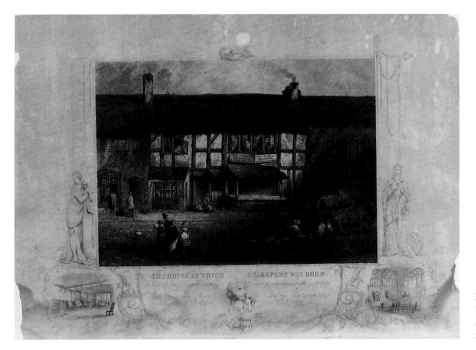

Shakespeare's house as it is the radiant light. Both the print and the painting bring out this sense of a glowing presence to which the people in the street are reacting.

Thomas Nast

Nast, America's first great political cartoonist, was born in Landau, Germany, in 1840. When he was six his family moved to New York, and just nine years later he was already working as an illustrator for *Leslie's Weekly.* In 1860, he traveled to Europe for a year, which included an assignment covering the Italian campaigns of Garibaldi. His productive association with *Harper's Weekly* began in the spring of 1862, and his drawings commenting on the Civil War soon made him a national figure. After the war he achieved enormous influence as a political commentator, and his cartoons were in large part responsible for ending the corrupt reign of New York's "Boss" Tweed of Tammany Hall. By 1880, however, Nast no longer enjoyed a comfortable working relationship with the magazine's editors, and his reputation was in decline. He had built up sizable earnings, but poor investments led to serious financial problems. He devoted his last years to painting, until, in 1902, as a way to pay off his debts, he accepted from President Theodore Roose-

velt the post of consul general to Ecuador. Leaving his family at their home in Morristown, New Jersey, he traveled alone to South America. He died in December 1902, having succumbed to a fever within six months of his arrival.

201 (Plate 34)
Study for THE IMMORTAL LIGHT OF GENIUS
1895
Oil on paper glue-lined to canvas, 14³/₈ × 19¹/₂ in. (36.8 × 49.4 cm.)

Case no. 459

Inscriptions: A small strip of paper has been glued around the edges on all four sides. Pieces of paper with pen-and-ink inscriptions have been glued on top of this strip. At center of top in a penned decorated frame: "APRIL 23TH 1564"; at bottom left: "(SKETCH.)"; at bottom center in a penned decorated frame: "THE IMMORTAL LIGHT OF GENIUS."; at right: "COPYRIGHT 1895 / BY / Th: Nast." ("Th: Nast" is clearly a signature and the printed letters are presumably by the artist as well.)

Provenance: Thomas Nast sale, Anderson Auction Company, 10–13 (10) March 1908, lot 85, $35 plus 10 percent commission, Wright acting as agent

Condition: Along the right edge there are strokes of white paint, apparently applied to even up the edges where the now discolored, attached brown paper was not cut perfectly straight. The paper/fabric support had been originally attached to a wood panel from which it was disengaging. This panel was removed in a restoration of 1988.

Related works: A drawing (ink wash and opaque, 4 × 5½ in.) acquired by Folger in 1906 is also in the FSL (ART Box N269, no. 11). It is very close in its details to the Folger picture and is inscribed at the bottom of its mount, "The Immortal Light of Genius—by Th: Nast. 1895. / For Sir Henry Irving—with complements of the Artist." Paine reproduces a work that is close to this drawing with the caption "Original Study for *The Immortal Light of Genius.*"[1] A photograph (11⅛ × 15⅞ in.) of a framed drawing is also in the collection (ART File S899h1, no. 61). It differs from the painting in that a greater portion of the room is shown at right and at top; the kneeling figure of Tragedy is in armor and has a sword and shield; and the figure of Comedy leans forward in a more pronounced bow and his sword with the wreath on the end is angled downward. This photograph is on the back of a mount for a photograph of General Grant and his staff presented to Nast on 27 March 1895. The Folger picture itself was preparatory to a painting that had been commissioned by Henry Irving, who presented it to the Arthur Winter Memorial Library of the Staten Island Academy. Nast also painted a replica of this picture, which his widow presented in 1903 to the Shakespeare Memorial at Stratford-upon-Avon. The present whereabouts of both pictures are not known.

Engravings: The fact that the sketch bears the phrase "COPYRIGHT 1895" suggests Nast was planning to publish his picture. Jean Miller remembers seeing a prospectus for an engraving, but so far it has not proved possible to relocate.

Thomas Nast received his commission to paint *The Immortal Light of Genius* in 1894 on a trip to Europe in search of work. In London he first received a welcomed commission to paint Lee's surrender to Grant at Appomattox. Paine, the artist's biographer, relates how the second commission came soon after: "One evening, while still in London, he was with Henry Irving at the Beefsteak Club, where Irving entertained his friends after the theatre, and during their talk the great actor, knowing Nast's love of Shakespeare, invited him to make a painting which would convey his devotion to the immortal dramatist."[2] The Civil War picture was one that Nast had wanted to execute, only needing a patron, and the Shakespeare picture sounds as if it fell into the same category. Returning to the States, Nast began work on Lee's surrender, finishing the painting on 9 April 1895, the thirtieth anniversary of the event. After a brief rest, he embarked on his work on Shakespeare, receiving Irving's approval for his conception in a cablegram of 20 July 1895: "Love and greeting, old friend. Shall be delighted (with) what you suggest."[3] Whether Irving gave his approval based on a sketch or only on a description is not known, but it is clear that the idea was fully worked out by the end of the year, since the wash drawing Nast gave Irving of the composition is dated 1895, as is the Folger's finished oil sketch. Irving had an opportunity to see the work at firsthand during his American tour of 1895–96, and a drawing by Nast honoring Irving's visit was given to the actor by the New York Press Club on 11 November 1895. The drawing as reproduced in the *Illustrated American* (fig. 130) shows Uncle Sam presenting Irving with a loving cup. Overhead in the background resides the Stratford Bust flanked by the British lion and the American eagle: for Nast Shakespeare is the glue that bonds these two countries together.

Paine gives 23 April 1896, Shakespeare's birthday, as the day on which Nast completed the picture. On 13 May Irving wrote the artist, saying he had called the day before and had seen the picture and had been delighted with it. In the same letter he mentioned for the first time that he was thinking of presenting the picture to the Arthur Winter Memorial Library on Staten Island.[4] The painting was in place for the dedication of the library at the Staten Island Academy on 15 and 16 June. Irving's choice of recipients obviously was determined by the fact that the president of the academy's board of trustees was William Winter, the drama critic of the *New York Tribune* and author of studies of actors, including a book on Irving published in 1885. Nast, however, was unhappy with the disposition of his painting, feeling Irving should have it rather than the academy.[5] The painting was returned to him almost immediately after the dedication, but

Fig. 130. Thomas Nast, *Uncle Sam Presenting Loving Cup to Sir Henry Irving.* Reproduced in the *Illustrated American,* 16 November 1895.

this point of view. Even the bust on the table, which of course was based on the Stratford Bust, sits in this same spot in other late nineteenth-century depictions of the hallowed room. Only the smallest details have been altered, as, for example, with the door, which was not then divided into panels. To this factual reporting, Nast introduced the figures of Tragedy and Comedy paying homage to the Bard as they offer laurel wreaths to his statue. It is a conception that could easily slip into the ridiculous, but the dramatic lighting helps it bridge the realms of reality and fantasy. An intense yellow light, without a natural source, radiates from the dome of Shakespeare's head, firing the wall behind him and sending a few flickering highlights throughout the darkened room. The head itself, a heroic projection of the rather flaccid features of the original, is so thickly painted that it is almost appropriate to call it sculpted. Even more

Irving must have persuaded his friend to acquiesce. After slight alterations, Nast sent the picture back to the academy in October.[6] Unfortunately, it appears to have been destroyed in a fire.

Nast was a devoted admirer of Shakespeare. Allusions to both the man and his work are frequently encountered in his cartoons. A pilgrimage to Stratford-upon-Avon on a trip to Europe in the summer of 1878 produced an image published in *Harper's Weekly* showing the ghost of the Bard himself haunting the artist's imagination (fig. 131). *The Immortal Light of Genius* is another example of a prosaic reality transformed by the supernatural. The room is the one in which Shakespeare was supposedly born, and Nast's rendering is true to its appearance in the late nineteenth century. Given the perspective and angle that he chose, one suspects that the basis for the design was a photograph or print, of which there were a number, made from

Fig. 131. Thomas Nast, *Ghost of Shakespeare.* Wood engraving in *Harper's Weekly,* 7 December 1878, p. 976.

surprising is that the heavy, projecting lids of the eyes appear to be closed. The viewer, like the statue, witnesses the scene as in a trance. It is in the mind's eye that the action takes place.

1. Albert Bigelow Paine, *Th. Nast: His Period and His Pictures*, New York, 1904, p. 580.
2. Ibid., pp. 545–46.
3. Ibid., p. 547.
4. FSL, Y.c. 485 (71).
5. See Winter's letters to Nast of 17 and 25 June 1896, Y.c. 573 (69 and 70b).
6. See Nast's letter to Winter of 12 September 1896 (FSL, Box 77).

Anonymous

202

SHAKESPEARE'S COAT OF ARMS
Late nineteenth century
Oil on canvas, 24 × 20 in. (61 × 50.8 cm.)

Provenance: Library of J. Parker Norris; Norris sale, American Art Association, 22 November 1922, lot 300 (sold with Shakespeare portrait, see note to no. 156); according to the Folger file card, the painting came to the FSL from Mrs. Folger's house.

Condition: Lined by Finlayson in 1932.

One of the drafts at the College of Arms, dated 20 October 1596, describes the coat of arms granted to the Shakespeares as follows: "Gould. on A Bend Sables. a Speare of the first steeled argent. And for his Creast or Cognizance a falcon. his winges displayed Argent. standing on a wrethe of his Coullors. supporting a Speare Bould. steeled as aforesaid sett uppon a helmet. . . ."[1] All these details (that is, a black diagonal with a silver-pointed gold spear on a gold shield surmounted by a silver falcon grasping another spear and standing on a black-and-gold wreath) are in the painting except for the helmet, which is also not included in the sketch accompanying the College of Arms draft. The coat of arms casts a painted shadow as if it were a three-dimensional object above the surface of the canvas. It is also surrounded by a discrete aureole.

1. Quoted in S. Schoenbaum, *William Shakespeare: A Documentary Life*, New York, 1975, p. 167.

202

Appendix I: Paintings Listed by Text

Shakespeare

All's Well That Ends Well

II, 3 Wheatley, *Helena and Count Bertram before the King of France* (no. 87)

As You Like It

I, 2 Anonymous, *Celia and Rosalind Departing from Orlando* (no. 96)

II, 7 De Wilde, attr., *The Seven Ages of Man* (no. 19)

III, 5 Anonymous, *Eliza Walstein [?] as Rosalind* (no. 129)

Coriolanus

IV, 5 Lawrence, after, *John Philip Kemble as Coriolanus* (no. 114)

V, 3 Westall, attr., *Volumnia Pleading with Coriolanus* (no. 127)

Hamlet

I, 4 Wilson, *William Powell as Hamlet Encountering the Ghost* (no. 128)

III, 2 Hayman, *The Play Scene from "Hamlet"* (no. 36)

III, 3 Christie, *Hamlet Finding the King at Prayer* (no. 14)

III, 4 Herrick, *Hamlet in the Queen's Chamber* (no. 39)

III, 4 Jones, attr., *Hamlet in the Queen's Closet* (no. 43)

IV, 7 Monogrammist T. E., *Ophelia* (no. 21)

V, 1 Lawrence, after, *John Philip Kemble as Hamlet* (no. 115)

V, 1 Liverseege, after, *The Grave-Digger* (no. 46)

I Henry IV

II, 4 Cawse, *Falstaff Boasting to Prince Hal and Poins* (no. 5)

II, 4 Clint, *Falstaff Relating His Valiant Exploits* (no. 15)

II, 4 Hayman, after, *Falstaff's Cowardice Detected* (no. 38)

II, 4 McArdell, attr., *James Quin as Falstaff* (no. 118)

II, 4 Stothard, *Falstaff Describing the Fight at Gadshill* (no. 75)

II, 4 Anonymous, *Falstaff at the Boar's Head Tavern* (no. 98)

II, 4 Anonymous, *Falstaff Impersonating the King* (no. 99)

III, 3 Cawse, *Falstaff Mocking Bardolph's Nose* (no. 6)

III, 3 Cawse, *Falstaff, Prince Hal, and Mistress Quickly* (no. 7)

III, 3 Liverseege, after, *Falstaff and Bardolph* (no. 47)

III, 3 Liverseege, after, *Falstaff and Bardolph* (no. 48)

III, 3 Weekes, *Falstaff and Bardolph* (no. 83)

III, 3 Anonymous, *Falstaff and Bardolph* (no. 100)

IV, 2 Smirke, *Falstaff Instructing Bardolph* (no. 60)

V, 4 Smirke, *Falstaff Struggling with Hotspur's Body* (no. 61)

II Henry IV

II, 1 Dever, *Sir John Falstaff and Mistress Quickly* (no. 18)

II, 4 Stothard, *Falstaff and Doll Tearsheet* (no. 76)

III, 2 Cawse, *Falstaff Choosing His Recruits* (no. 8)

III, 2 Cawse, *Falstaff Choosing His Recruits* (no. 9)

III, 2 Cawse, *Bardolph and Falstaff Putting Wart through the Drill* (no. 10)

III, 2 Hayman, *Falstaff Reviewing His Recruits* (no. 37)

V, 3 Cawse, *Pistol Announcing to Falstaff the Death of the King* (no. 11)

V, 3 Cawse, *Pistol Announcing to Falstaff the Death of the King* (no. 12)

V, 5 Smirke, *Falstaff Rebuked* (no. 57)

II Henry VI

III, 3 Reynolds, studio of, *The Death of Cardinal Beaufort* (no. 51)

Henry VIII

II, 4 Anonymous, *Sarah Siddons as Queen Katharine* (no. 130)

III, 2 Westall, *Wolsey Disgraced* (no. 85)

King Lear

IV, 6 Harrison, *Edwin Forrest as King Lear* (no. 113)

IV, 6 Anonymous, *King Lear* (no. 101)

IV, 7 Smirke, *The Awakening of King Lear* (no. 58)

IV, 7 West, *King Lear and Cordelia* (no. 84)

Love's Labour's Lost

IV, 2 Wheatley, after, *Jaquenetta Approaching Sir Nathaniel with Berowne's Letter* (no. 88)

V, 2 Stothard, manner of, *The Performance of the Nine Worthies* (no. 79)

Macbeth

I, 3 Romney, *John Henderson as Macbeth* (no. 124)

I, 3 Zuccarelli, *Macbeth Meeting the Witches* (no. 95)

I, 5 Anonymous, *Isabella Glyn as Lady Macbeth* (no. 131)

II, 2 Roffe, *Macbeth's Murder of Duncan* (no. 123)

II, 2 Anonymous, *Sarah Siddons as Lady Macbeth* (no. 132)

IV, 1 Abbott, *Macbeth Recoiling from the Apparition of the Crowned Child* (no. 1)

IV, 1 Barker, *Macbeth and the Witches* (no. 3)

IV, 1 Fuseli, *Macbeth Consulting the Vision of the Armed Head* (no. 24)

IV, 1 Romney, *Macbeth and the Witches* (no. 53)

IV, 1 Sully, *Macbeth in the Witches' Cave* (no. 81)

——— Neagle, after, *William C. Macready as Macbeth* (no. 119)

Measure for Measure

II, 2 Hamilton, *Isabella Appealing to Angelo* (no. 32)

The Merchant of Venice

I, 2 Brockmann, *Portia and Nerissa* (no. 4)

III, 2 Stone, Study for *Bassanio Receiving the Letter Announcing Antonio's Losses and Peril* (no. 74)

III, 3 Westall, *Shylock Rebuffing Antonio* (no. 86)

IV, 1 Howard, *Portia Pronouncing Sentence* (no. 42)

IV, 1 Linton, *Portia* (no. 45)

IV, 1 Sully, *Portia and Shylock* (no. 82)

IV, 1 Anonymous, *Shylock* (no. 102)

The Merry Wives of Windsor

I, 1 Dicksee, *Anne Page* (no. 20)

I, 1 Smirke, *Anne Page's Invitation to Slender* (no. 62)

I, 1 Smirke, after, *Anne Page Inviting Slender to Dinner* (no. 72)

II, 2 Jones, G., *Falstaff and Ford at the Garter Inn* (no. 44)

III, 3 Peters, after, *Falstaff Hiding in the Buckbasket* (no. 50)

III, 3 Smirke, *Falstaff Hiding in the Buckbasket* (no. 63)

III, 3 Wright, *Mistress Ford and Falstaff* (no. 89)

A Midsummer Night's Dream

II, 1 Fuseli, *Puck* (no. 25)

II, 1 Romney, Study for *Titania, Puck, and the Changeling* (no. 54)

II, 2 Smirke, *Lysander Declaring His Passion to Helena* (no. 64)

III, 2 Smirke, *Puck's Report to Oberon* (no. 65)

IV, 1 Smirke, *Bottom in the Forest* (no. 66)

IV, 1 Anonymous, *Titania Caressing the Drowsy Bottom* (no. 103)

Othello

III, 3 Green, after, *George Frederick Cooke as Iago* (no. 111)

III, 4 Fradelle, *Othello and Desdemona* (no. 22)

IV, 1 Hook, *Othello's Description of Desdemona* (no. 40)

V, 2 Salter, *Othello's Lamentation* (no. 55)

——— Anonymous, *Actor in the Character of Othello* (no. 133)

Pericles

V, 1 Stothard, *Marina Singing before Pericles* (no. 77)

Richard II

V, 2 Hamilton, *The Duke of York Discovering His Son Aumerle's Treachery* (no. 33)

Richard III

I, 4 Fuseli, *The Two Murderers of the Duke of Clarence* (no. 26)

V, 3 Hamilton, *John Philip Kemble as Richard III* (no. 112)

V, 4 Dance, after, *David Garrick as Richard III* (no. 107)

Romeo and Juliet

II, 2 Dawe, Study for *Miss O'Neill as Juliet* (no. 108)

II, 4 Wright, *Mercutio Bidding Farewell to Juliet's Nurse* (no. 91)

II, 5 Wright, *Juliet and the Nurse* (no. 90)

III, 5 Sohn, after, *Romeo and Juliet* (no. 73)

III, 5 Anonymous, *Romeo and Juliet* (no. 97)

V, 3 Fuseli, *Romeo Stabs Paris at the Bier of Juliet* (no. 27)

V, 3 Peters, *The Death of Juliet* (no. 49)

The Taming of the Shrew

II, 1 Smirke, *Katherina's First Meeting with Petruchio* (no. 67)

IV, 3 Sharp, *Petruchio and the Tailor* (no. 56)

IV, 3 Wright, attr., *Petruchio and the Haberdasher* (no. 92)

IV, 3 Wright, attr., *Petruchio and the Tailor* (no. 93)

V, 2 Smirke, *Katherina's Chastisement of Bianca and the Widow* (no. 68)

The Tempest

I, 2 Abbott, *Prospero Commanding Ariel* (no. 2)

I, 2 Smirke, *Prospero Summoning Ariel* (no. 69)

II, 2 Smirke, *Stephano Confronting the Monster* (no. 59)

II, 2 Anonymous, *Ariel Leading Caliban by a Chain* [?] (no. 104)

III, 1 Smirke, *Ferdinand Proclaiming His Love to Miranda* (no. 70)

IV, 1 Smirke, *Stephano Demanding Trinculo's Gown* (no. 71)

V, 1 Fuseli, *Ariel* (no. 28)

Twelfth Night

I, 5 Frith, *Olivia Unveiling* (no. 23)

II, 3 Hall, *Sir Toby Belch* (no. 30)

II, 3 Hall, *Malvolio Confronting the Revelers* (no. 31)

II, 3 Hamilton, *The Carousing of Sir Toby Belch and Sir Andrew Aguecheek* (no. 34)

III, 1 Stothard, manner of, *Olivia Greeting Cesario in the Garden* (no. 80)

IV, 1 Houghton, *Sir Toby Belch Coming to the Assistance of Sir Andrew Aguecheek* (no. 41)

IV, 3 Hamilton, *Olivia's Proposal* (no. 35)

The Winter's Tale

IV, 4 Cawse, *Autolycus Selling His Wares* (no. 13)

Chaucer, "The Man of Law's Tale"

Rigaud, *Constantia Revealing Herself to Her Father* (no. 52)

Gautier, "Une nuit de Cléopâtre"

Zeigler, *Antony Approaching Cleopatra, Meïamoun Lying Dead at Her Feet* (no. 94)

Homer, *The Iliad*

Cook, *Helen and Priam at the Scæan Gate* (no. 16)

Cook, *Hector Reproving Paris* (no. 17)

Massinger, *A New Way to Pay Old Debts*

Anonymous, *Edmund Kean as Sir Giles Overreach* (no. 134)

Milton, *L'Allegro*

Fuseli, *Faery Mab* (no. 29)

Pastoral Tradition

Stothard, *The Vintage* (no. 78)

Unknown Subject

Anonymous, *Unknown Subject* (no. 105)

Appendix II: List of Family and Donor Portraits and Twentieth-Century Miscellany

A1
P. Mason Carl, HERALDIC LION
After 1974
Acrylic, gold, and silver leaf on masonite, 41½ × 34½ in. (sight)

Juxtaposed with the lion are coats of arms of families in Shakespeare's history plays: Lancaster, Beaufort, Mortimer, and York. The design is based on Robyn Johnson-Ross's black-and-white cover illustration to Donald V. Mehus's pamphlet *Shakespeare's English History Plays: Genealogical Table,* FSL School Series, Charlottesville, Va., 1975.

Gift of the estate of Norman Butler Morgan through P. Mason Carl, executor, 11 August 1982

A2
Gardner Cox, JOHN CLIFFORD FOLGER
Oil on canvas, 40 × 30 in.

Inscribed at lower right in red: "Replica of / Portrait of / J C Folger / Gardner / Cox"

A3
C. B. Currie, FIVE MINIATURES
OF SHAKESPEARE
1928

Inset into a "Cosway Binding" by Riviere & Son of a copy of Boaden 1824 (PR2929 B6 Ex. ill. Copy 2). *Upper left:* After Marshall engraving. *Upper right:* After Janssen Portrait. *Center:* After Droeshout engraving. *Lower left:* After Ozias Humphry's interpretation of Chandos Portrait. *Lower right:* After Ward's engraving of Phillips's painting of Stratford Bust.

A4
Nannette Schweig Hoffman, TITANIA
1972
Oil on canvas mounted on masonite, 40 × 30 in.

Signed at upper right in black: "Nannette"

Gift of Saul C. Hertz in memory of his wife, Miriam Hertz

A5
Everett Raymond Kinstler,
MRS. CHARLES A. DANA
1981
Oil on canvas, 30 × 25 in.

Signed and dated at lower right in red: "Everett Raymond Kinstler / 1 9 8 1"

A6
T. W. Orlando, MR. CHARLES A. DANA
Oil on canvas, 30 × 25 in.

Signed in purple at upper left: "T. W. ORLANDO / AFTER / ERIK G HAUPT"

A7
Frank O. Salisbury, EMILY JORDAN FOLGER
1927
Oil on canvas, 49½ × 39½ in. (sight)

Signed and dated at upper right: "Frank O Salisbury / 1927"

This and no. A8 commissioned from the artist; received in March 1927

A8
Frank O. Salisbury, HENRY CLAY FOLGER
1927
Oil on canvas, 49½ × 39½ in. (sight)

Signed and dated at upper left: "Frank O Salisbury / New York, 1927"

Inscribed on book: "EDWRD+GWYNN"

A9

David Tausky, KATHERINE DULIN FOLGER
Signed at upper right: "Tauozky"
Oil on canvas, 36⅛ × 30³/₁₆ in.

A10

Anonymous, NANCY FOLGER
Nineteenth century
Oil on panel, 29½ × 24½ in. (sight)

Gift of Mrs. James D. Paxton, 23 April 1945

Appendix III: Deaccessioned Paintings

In the early 1960s, Louis B. Wright, the director of the Folger Shakespeare Library, undertook to deaccession paintings in order to make room for more storage space. Three pictures were sold to Amherst College in 1961 and in the following year thirty-eight to Lincoln Kirstein, who was negotiating for the American Shakespeare Festival Theatre and Academy in Stratford, Connecticut (abbreviated in the entries as ASFTA). In these transactions the Library lost a number of fine paintings and sculptures, but the works were sold to institutions that were better able to make them accessible to the public, the Library having limited space for exhibition. The later financial collapse of the American Shakespeare Festival Theatre and the subsequent dispersal of its collection could not then have been foreseen.

In March 1964, at least nineteen more paintings along with numerous other objects were shipped to Parke Bernet Galleries in New York for auction. These works were inferior to the earlier deaccessioned paintings. In fact, only the Buchels were sold by Parke Bernet, the remainder going to Coleman Galleries. The works that were not disposed of there were then passed on again to an antique shop on Third Avenue. The two paintings (nos. D28 and D67) purchased by Prof. Louis Marder of Kent State University in February 1964 were ones that had already been set aside for the Parke Bernet shipment.

A few paintings have unaccountably disappeared from the collection. The majority of these were presumably disposed of soon after the Library's founding, when no records of such transactions were being kept.

The paintings in this section have been given their own series of numbers, beginning with the letter "D" to distinguish them from pictures still in the collection. The entries are also abbreviated, some of the earlier categories having been discarded.

Barney, Joseph (British, 1751–1829)

D1

PROSPERO, MIRANDA, AND FERDINAND
The Tempest I, 2
Signed and dated 1788
Oil on canvas, 39¼ × 51½ in.

Case no. 1649; photograph on file

Provenance: Bought from A. Betts, Esq., London, through Maggs, February 1927, £35 plus 10 percent commission; sold to ASFTA, February 1962; sold Parke Bernet, 15 January 1976, lot 37, repr., $275

Exhibitions: London, Royal Academy of Arts, 1788, no. 207; Amherst, *The Tempest*, 1951

Bell, Hillary (1857–1903)

D2

CHARLES FISHER AS FALSTAFF IN
"THE MERRY WIVES OF WINDSOR"
Signed and dated "86" (depicts performance in Daly's Theatre in 1886)
Oil painting, 35 × 35 in.

Provenance: Augustin Daly sale, Anderson Galleries, 27 November 1912, lot 67, $55 plus 10 percent commission, George D. Smith acting as agent; Parke Bernet shipment, March 1964, Coleman Auction Galleries, 15–16 April 1964, lot 14, $25

Buchel, Charles A. (British, 1872–1950)
(nos. D3–D11)

All of the portraits of actors in character are signed oil paintings. They measure approximately 15½ by 11½ inches, and at least two of them are dated 1904. The two oil sketches from *The Tempest* measure 13½ by 9½ inches. According to Michelmore, all these works were painted for Sir Herbert Beerbohm Tree in 1901 and 1904 to adorn the walls of His Majesty's Theatre during his period as lessee and manager and are reproduced in the *Twelfth Night Souvenir* and *The Tempest as arranged for the Stage by Herbert Beerbohm Tree.*

D3

BASIL GILL AS FERDINAND
The Tempest

Provenance: Sir Herbert Beerbohm Tree sale, Phillips, 13 September 1924, lot 206; bought from Michelmore, October 1921, £200, in a group of three; Parke Bernet shipment, sold Parke Bernet, 21 May 1964, lot 124, $30 for three

D4

LIONEL BROUGH AS TRINCULO
The Tempest

Provenance: Tree sale, Phillips, lot 201; Michelmore catalogue *Shakespeareana Illustrated*, [1923?], no. 27, purchased January 1923, one of seven items for £400; Parke Bernet shipment, March 1964, sold Parke Bernet, 21 May 1964, lot 122, $35 for five

D5

LOUIS CALVERT AS STEPHANO
The Tempest

Provenance: Tree sale, Phillips, lot 208; Michelmore catalogue *Shakespeareana Illustrated*, [1923?], no. 28, purchased January 1923, one of seven items for £400; Parke Bernet shipment, March 1964, sold Parke Bernet, 21 May 1964, lot 122, $35 for five

D6

D. LYN HARDING AS ANTONIO
The Tempest

Provenance: Tree sale, Phillips, lot 203; bought from Michelmore, October 1921, £200, in a group of three; Parke Bernet shipment, March 1964, sold Parke Bernet, 21 May 1964, lot 124, $30 for three

D7

WILLIAM HAVILAND AS PROSPERO
The Tempest

Provenance: Tree sale, Phillips, lot 202; bought from Michelmore, January 1922, £65; Parke Bernet shipment, March 1964, sold Parke Bernet, 21 May 1964, lot 124, $30 for three

D8

PROSPERO'S CAVE (Scene from *The Tempest*)

Provenance: Tree sale, Phillips, lot 199; Michelmore catalogue *Shakespeareana Illustrated*, [1923?], no. 30, purchased May 1923, £22; Parke Bernet shipment, March 1964, sold Parke Bernet, 21 May 1964, lot 122, $35 for five

D9

A WOOD (Scene from *The Tempest*)

Provenance: Tree sale, Phillips, lot 200; Michelmore catalogue *Shakespeareana Illustrated*, [1923?], no. 29, purchased May 1923, £22; Parke Bernet shipment, March 1964, sold Parke Bernet, 21 May 1964, lot 122, $35 for five

D10

NORMAN FORBES AS SIR ANDREW AGUECHEEK
Twelfth Night

Provenance: Tree sale, Phillips, lot 176; bought from Michelmore, October 1921, £200, in a group of three. There is no record of its being part of Parke Bernet shipment, but it is no longer in the collection.

D11

MISS ZEFFIE TILBURY AS MARIA
Twelfth Night

Provenance: Tree sale, Phillips, lot 178; Michelmore catalogue *Shakespeareana Illustrated*, [1923?], no. 26, purchased May 1923, £22; Parke Bernet shipment, March 1964, sold Parke Bernet, 21 May 1964, lot 122, $35 for five

Campbell, Charles William (British, 1855–87)

D12

ELLEN TERRY AS OPHELIA
Hamlet
Oil on canvas, 32 × 16 in.

Provenance: Henry Irving sale, Christie's, 16 December 1905, lot 112, 10 guineas ($75), as by C. C. Campbell; sold to ASFTA, February 1962; sold Sotheby Parke Bernet, 15 January 1976, lot 72, $160

Cawse, John (British, 1779–1862)

D13

FALSTAFF CHOOSING HIS RECRUITS
II Henry IV III, 2
ca. 1818
Oil on canvas, 25¼ × 33¼ in.

Case no. 1750

Provenance: Parsons, January 1928, £40.10.0; sold to ASFTA, February 1962; Yale Center for British Art, 1975

Exhibitions: New Haven, 1981, no. 29, repr.

Chappel, Alonzo (American, 1828–87)

D14

PORTRAIT OF SHAKESPEARE
1858 (Engraved in 1859 as the frontispiece for *The Complete Works of Shakespeare,* Johnson, Fry & Co., New York)
Oil painting, 14 × 15½ in. (as listed in file); oil on paper, 8¾ × 6¾ in. (as listed in 1976 sale catalogue)

Case no. 1311

Provenance: Commissioned by Moncure D. Conway, sold to Folger by his son Eustace Conway through Thomas F. Madigan, October 1923, $175; sold to ASFTA, February 1962; Sotheby Parke Bernet, 15 January 1976, lot 76, as *Shakespeare with His Dog,* $400

Despite the discrepancies in measurements between the Folger file card and the auction catalogue, only one work is presumably involved. One suspects the paper was on a larger mount and it is the mount's measurements that are given on the file card. In the 1859 print, Shakespeare is shown seated, holding a book in his left hand and petting an attentive greyhound with his right.

Clint, George (British, 1770–1854)

D15

EDMUND KEAN AS RICHARD III
Oil painting, 27 × 23 in.

Provenance: Parsons, March 1929, $190. (In 1950 Maurice Block listed this work as not found [no. 30].)

Clint, George, attributed to

D16

A SCENE FROM JOHN HOWARD PAYNE'S "THE MERRY MONARCH"
(Formerly *Madame Vestris and John Philip Kemble in "The Taming of the Shrew,"* IV, 3)
Oil on canvas, 24 × 17½ in.

Case no. 1709; photograph on file

Provenance: Parsons, September 1927, £50; sold to ASFTA, February 1962; sold Sotheby Parke Bernet, 15 January 1976, lot 77, repr., $650; sold Boothbay Theatre Museum Collection, Oliver's Auction Gallery, Kennebunk, Maine, June 22–24 (22) 1990, no. 7 with new identification (also first time the painting was demoted from Clint to attributed to Clint)

Collingwood, William Gersham (British, 1854–1932)

D17

VALLEY OF THE REYKJADATSA [REEKDALE] RIVER FROM DEILDARTUNGA
Oil painting, 10½ × 12½ in.

Provenance: Source unknown; Parke Bernet shipment, March 1964

The scene is of the tragic story of Snarbjorn, the poet associated with the earliest reference to Hamlet. It was presented to Israel Gollancz, the British publisher, on the publication of *Hamlet in Ireland.*

Cruikshank, George (British, 1792–1878)
(nos. D18–19)

D18

THE FIRST APPEARANCE OF WILLIAM
SHAKESPEARE ON THE STAGE OF
THE GLOBE WITH PART OF HIS
DRAMATIC COMPANY IN **1564**
Signed and dated 1864–65
Oil on canvas, 27⅞ × 21⅞ in.

Annotated at lower right: "and this drawing made
by him in 1864-5"

Provenance: Woodin; Parke Bernet, 6–8 January
1942, lot 179; Maggs, cat. 429, $225; sold to ASFTA,
February 1962; Yale Center for British Art, 1975

Exhibitions: New Haven, 1981, no. 39

  This is a copy of an earlier work conceived in
1863.

D19

FALSTAFF AT HERNE'S OAK
The Merry Wives of Windsor V, 5
Signed and dated 1857
Oil painting, 36 × 48 in.

Case no. 1619; photograph on file

Provenance: Purchased from Walter T. Spenser,
London, February 1920, by George D. Smith; acquired by Folger from R. J. C. Lingel, president,
George D. Smith Book Co., December 1926, $1,000;
sold to ASFTA, February 1962; Yale Center for British Art, 1975

Exhibitions: London, British Institution, 1857, no.
446; Amherst, 1952, as *The Wood from "A Midsummer Night's Dream"*; New Haven, 1981, no. 38,
repr.

Darley, Felix O. C. (American, 1822–88)

D20

TOUCHSTONE AND AUDREY
As You Like It III, 3
Signed and dated 1856
Oil on canvas, 27 × 22 in.

Case no. 858

Provenance: Fifth Avenue Auction Room, 13 February 1909, no. 885, $71.50, Smith acting as agent;
sold to ASFTA, February 1962; sold Sotheby Parke
Bernet, 15 January 1976, lot 86, repr., $600

Dicksee, Thomas Francis (British, 1819–95)

D21

OPHELIA
Hamlet III, 1
1875
Oil on canvas, 38 × 25 in.

Provenance: Michelmore catalogue *Shakespeareana Illustrated,* [1923?], repr. in color, $500 (asking
price had been £200; presumably reduced to £125);
sold to Amherst College, February 1961, $300

Exhibitions: Amherst, *Shakespeare,* 1951; traveling
exhibition, *The Grand Tradition: British Art from
Amherst College,* 1988–89, no. 23

Dicksee, Thomas Francis, or Sir Frank
Dicksee (1853–1928) (nos. D22–D23)

D22

OTHELLO AND DESDEMONA
Othello V, 2
Oil on canvas, 44 × 66 in.

Case no. 1927

Provenance: Michelmore, July 1929, £50, as by T. F.
Dicksee; sold to ASFTA, February 1962, as by T. F.
Dicksee; Sotheby Parke Bernet, 15 January 1976, lot
93, as by Frank Dicksee, repr., $1,400

Exhibitions: London, Royal Academy of Arts,
1875?; Liverpool, Walker Art Gallery, *Grand Loan
Exhibition of Pictures,* 1886? (the exhibited picture
was by T. F. Dicksee)

  Although the provenance is given as A. G. Kurtz,
the picture that sold at Sotheby's in 1976 as by Sir
Frank Dicksee, the son of T. F. Dicksee, is presumably the Folger picture. If the Royal Academy label
for the exhibition of 1875 is on the stretcher, as
stated by Michelmore in his letter to Folger of 28

June 1929, then the painting must be by Thomas Francis Dicksee and the 1976 Sotheby catalogue was in error.

D23
JULIET AND THE FRIAR
Romeo and Juliet IV, 1
Signed with initials and dated 1881
Oil on canvas, 31 × 37 in.

Provenance: Maggs, 1926, cat. no. 250, repr. pl. XLIX, as by T. F. Dicksee, £60 (asking price), $270 (payment recorded in Folger file); sold to ASFTA, February 1962, as by T. F. Dicksee; sold Sotheby Parke Bernet, 15 January 1976, lot 92, as by Frank Dicksee, repr., $550

As with the above painting, this picture was first ascribed to T. F. Dicksee and then listed as by Sir Frank Dicksee in the Sotheby sale catalogue. Since it is initialed and has a signed titled label on the stretcher, it is unclear why there should have been any confusion on this point.

Dunbar, Harold (American, b. 1882)

D24
VIOLA ALLEN AS VIOLA IN "TWELFTH NIGHT"
1905
Oil painting, 27½ × 43½ in.

Provenance: Presented by Charles W. Allen, 13 July 1948; Parke Bernet shipment, March 1964; sold Coleman Auction Galleries, 15–16 April 1964, lot 15, $25

Francis, G.(eorge?) (American, fl. late 18th, early 19th centuries)

D25
DAVID GARRICK AS KING LEAR
King Lear III, 5
Signed and dated 1810
Oil on canvas, 17½ × 22 in.

Provenance: Schatzki, January 1945, $180; sold to ASFTA, February 1962; Sotheby Parke Bernet, 15 January 1976, lot 97, repr., $250

Exhibitions: New York, 1964, no. 19, repr.

Francis was an amateur painter who lived in Hartford, Connecticut. His painting is an adaptation of James McArdell's mezzotint reproducing Benjamin Wilson's painting *David Garrick as King Lear.*

Freeman, William Henry (French, fl. 1839–75)

D26a
Recto: SCENE FROM "HAMLET" (I, 4)

D26b
Verso: STUDY OF FALSTAFF
Signed and dated: "W. H. F. 1840"
Oil on cardboard, 12 × 14 in.

Case no. 1388

Provenance: Maggs, 5 February 1925, $145

This painting is recorded as by W. H. Freeman in the card file begun by Mrs. Folger and again in the list compiled by Maurice Block in 1950 (no. 56). It can no longer be located and may have been among the works deaccessioned in 1964. Since the date 1840 does not fit the career of the little-known Baltimore engraver W. H. Freeman (fl. 1815–16) one presumes the artist meant is William Henry Freeman.

Goodwin, Albert (British, 1845–1932)

D27
BEFORE THE CELL OF PROSPERO
The Tempest I, 2
Signed and dated 1908
Gouache and oil, 21 × 30½ in.

Photograph on file

Inscribed on the stool on which the monkey sits: "This is not Caliban! but Miranda's monkey"

Provenance: Michelmore, June 1928, £150 (asking price); sold to ASFTA, February 1962; Sotheby Parke Bernet, 15 January 1976, no. 103, repr., $450

Exhibitions: London, Royal Academy of Arts, 1908; Birmingham, England, City Art Gallery, 1926; Liverpool, Walker Art Gallery, 1927; Southport, Atkinson Art Gallery, 1927; Amherst, *The Tempest*, 1951; New York, 1964, no. 26

Hall, George Henry (American, 1825–1913)

D28
PORTRAIT OF SHAKESPEARE
Oil replica (?) of the painting of 1896 in the Royal Shakespeare Theatre Picture Gallery, Stratford-upon-Avon, 56½ × 47 in. (Stratford-upon-Avon picture measures 50 × 40 in.)

Provenance: Jennie Brownscombe, New York, January 1916, $95 (price included two crayon studies of head of Shakespeare); sold to Louis Marder, Kent State University, February 1964, $200

Hamilton, William (British, 1750/51–1801) (nos. D29–D30; see also D62)

D29
BRABANTIO'S ACCUSATION
AGAINST OTHELLO
Othello I, 3
Oil on panel, 24½ × 19½ in.

Case no. 1838; photograph on file

Provenance: Parsons, September 1928, £45 less 10 percent; sold to ASFTA, February 1962

D30
THE FIRST MEETING OF
ROMEO AND JULIET
Romeo and Juliet I, 5
Oil on canvas, 25 × 30 in.

Photograph on file

Provenance: Parsons, September 1927, 40 guineas; sold to ASFTA, February 1962; Sotheby Parke Bernet, 15 January 1976, lot 108, repr., $600

Hamilton, William, attributed to

D31
HERO AND URSULA WITH BEATRICE
LISTENING IN THE GARDEN
Much Ado about Nothing III, 1
Oil on canvas, 22½ × 16½ in.

Provenance: Maggs, March 1925, £105 for this and no. 50; sold to ASFTA, February 1962; Sotheby Parke Bernet, 15 January 1976, lot 111, $125

This work is a copy of Rev. Matthew William Peters's painting for Boydell's Shakespeare Gallery. Peters's painting was in Boydell's first exhibition of 1789 and was engraved for both the large and small series. Maggs attributed the work to Hamilton, but if it is by the same hand as its companion piece (no. 50), this attribution cannot be sustained.

Harlow, George Henry (British, 1787–1819), after

D32
THE COURT SCENE FOR THE TRIAL
OF QUEEN KATHARINE
Henry VIII II, 4
Oil on canvas, 29 × 38½ in.

Case no. 1852

Provenance: Parsons, October 1928, £42.14.6; sold to ASFTA, February 1962; Sotheby Parke Bernet, 15 January 1976, lot 114, $150

Apparently purchased as Harlow's original canvas of 1802. For a discussion of Harlow's image, see no. 130.

Herrick, William Salter (British, fl. 1852–80) (nos. D33–D34)

D33
OTHELLO TAKING LEAVE OF DESDEMONA
Othello I, 1
Signed and dated 1876
Oil on canvas, 20 × 16 in.

Provenance: Michelmore catalogue *Shakespeareana Illustrated,* [1923?], no. 41, repr. in color; bought by Folger, July 1926, $375; sold to ASFTA, February 1962; sold Sotheby Parke Bernet, 15 January 1976, lot 123, as "Look to Her Moor" (I, 3), repr., $225

According to Michelmore, the picture shows Sir Henry Irving as Othello and Miss Isabella Bateman as Desdemona. The dealer's assertion, however, seems doubtful as Herrick's characterization of the two figures is similar to that in the following picture, which was executed in 1860 before Irving had risen to prominence and before Bateman had made her debut.

D34

"LOOK TO HER MOOR"
Othello I, 3
Signed and dated 1860
Oil on canvas, 41 × 35 in.

Provenance: Michelmore, February 1930, £75; sold to ASFTA, February 1962; sold Sotheby Parke Bernet, 15 January 1976, lot 122, repr., $600

Exhibitions: London, Royal Academy of Arts, 1859, no. 717. (Since the painting is dated 1860, either Herrick retouched the canvas or it was an earlier version that was exhibited at the Royal Academy.)

Hodges, William (British, 1744–97)

D35

JAQUES AND THE WOUNDED STAG
As You Like It II, 1
1790
Oil on canvas, 36¼ × 48½

Provenance: Commissioned by Boydell for £73.10.0; sold by Christie, 17 May 1805, lot 41; bought by Sir Charles Burrell for 75 guineas; acquired by Folger from Parsons, October 1926, £40; sold to ASFTA, February 1962; Yale Center for British Art, 1976

Exhibitions: London, Boydell, 1789, no. 13; London, Boydell, 1802, no. 23; London, Boydell, 1805, no. 137; London, British Institution, 1817, no. 96; British Institution, 1844, no. 116; New Haven, 1981, no. 85, repr.

George Romney helped paint the figures and Sawrey Gilpin may have added the stag.

Kerckhove, Leonard van den. *See* Leonard van der Kerckhove

Lambdin, James Reid (American, 1807–89), after Thomas Sully

D36

GEORGE FREDERICK COOKE AS RICHARD III
Oil painting, 96 × 59 in.

Case no. 200

Provenance: Augustin Daly (on exhibit in Daly's Theatre, New York); Daly sale, Anderson Galleries, 27 November 1912, lot 73, $140 plus 10 percent commission, Smith acting as agent; sold to ASFTA, February 1962

Lawrence, Sir Thomas (British, 1769–1830), after

D37

KEMBLE AS HAMLET
Oil painting, 77 × 44 in.

Case no. 1498

Provenance: James Orrock sale, Christie's, 4–6 June 1904, lot 270; Viscount Leverhulme sale, Anderson Galleries, 17–19 (18) February 1926, lot 156, repr., $1200 plus 10 percent commission, Rosenbach acting as agent; sold to ASFTA, February 1962

Exhibitions: Amherst, *Shakespeare,* 1951

A less-than-life-size version of the Lawrence picture is in the Tate Gallery, London (see no. 115). The Leverhulme picture was sold to Folger as by, rather than after, Lawrence. Dr. Rosenbach wrote Folger on 19 February 1926, "With each of these paintings [this work and D57] goes a certificate of William Roberts, the celebrated English Authority, which should be carefully preserved" (Correspondence File, Rosenbach Museum and Library, FSL).

Leonard van den Kerckhove (also
Kerckhoven) (Belgian, ca. 1828–98)

D38

SHAKESPEARE, OR THE GLORY
OF GREAT BRITAIN
Oil on canvas, 14 ft. 4 in. × 10 ft. 5 in.

Case no. 1875; photograph on file

Provenance: Presented to the Shakespeare Memorial, Stratford-upon-Avon, in 1881 by Capt. E. Birt Lemmon; bought by Folger, December 1928, £140, Sawyer acting as agent; lost by 1950, when Maurice Block compiled his list of paintings in the Folger.

Exhibitions: London, Egyptian Hall, Piccadilly (pamphlet accompanying this exhibition in file); Stratford-upon-Avon, Shakespeare Memorial Exhibition, April, 1881, no. 37

This painting is too large to have been misplaced. Either it never arrived at the library or it was disposed of as being too cumbersome and no record made of its removal. The photograph on file, presumably made before it entered the collection, shows it was not then mounted on a stretcher. A pencil notation in the case lists confirms this was also true when it was stored by Folger: "long roll-unframed / not unrolled." Letters of 29 January 1929 from Sawyer to Tice & Lynch Inc. in New York and to Folger show that the painting was held up by the customs examiner, who curiously questioned the painting's authenticity.

Leslie, Charles Robert (American,
1794–1859)

D39

THE DYING QUEEN KATHARINE'S
INTERVIEW WITH CAPUCIUS
Henry VIII IV, 2
Oil on canvas, 32 × 24 in.

Photograph on file

Provenance: Commissioned by Isumbard Kingdom Brunel, the engineer; sold Christie's, April 1864; James Dugdale of Wroxall Abbey, Warwickshire; bought by Folger from Michelmore, *A Catalogue of*

Shakespeareana, notes and preface by Falconer Madan, [1927], no. 437, £150 (asking price); sold to Amherst College, May 1961, $1000 (for this painting and a bust of Shakespeare by Carrière-Belleuse)

Exhibitions: London, Royal Academy, 1850, no. 136; (the following three exhibitions listed by Madan) International Exhibition, 1862; Royal Academy Exhibition of the Works of the Old Masters, 1870; Manchester, The Royal Jubilee Exhibition, 1887; Amherst, 1950, no. 51; traveling exhibition, *The Grand Tradition: British Art from Amherst College,* 1988–89, no. 22

Long, Edwin (British, 1829–91)
(nos. D40–D41)

D40

SIR HENRY IRVING AS HAMLET
Signed and dated 1880
Oil on canvas, 63 × 44 in.

Provenance: Burdett-Coutts sale, Christie's, 5 May 1922, lot 224, £42 plus 10 percent commission, Rosenbach acting as agent; sold to ASFTA, February 1962; sold Sotheby Parke Bernet, 15 January 1976, lot 129, repr., $2300

Exhibitions: London, Royal Academy of Arts, 1880, no. 416; Amherst, *Shakespeare,* 1951; New York, 1964, no. 39

Philip Rosenbach wrote to Folger on 19 May 1922, "They tell me that the two Irving pictures [D40 and D41] cost the Baroness Coutts 1,000 guineas each."

D41

SIR HENRY IRVING AS RICHARD,
DUKE OF GLOUCESTER
Signed with monogram and dated 1877
Oil on canvas, 57 × 40 in.

Provenance: Burdett-Coutts sale, Christie's, 5 May 1922, lot 225, £33.12.0 plus 10 percent commission, Rosenbach acting as agent; sold to ASFTA, February 1962; sold Sotheby Parke Bernet, 15 January 1976, lot 130, repr., $1500; Bob Jones University, Greenville, S.C.

Exhibitions: London, Royal Academy of Arts, 1878, no. 472; Manchester, Royal Jubilee Exhibition, 1887; New York, 1964, no. 38, repr.; Montgomery, 1985–86, no. 39, repr.

Loutherbourg, Philip James de (1740–1812), attributed to?

D42

FALSTAFF WITH THE BODY OF HOTSPUR
I Henry IV V, 4
ca. 1786
Oil on paper, 12 × 11¼ in.

Photograph on file

Provenance: Michelmore, June 1928, £75 (asking price), bought as by John Opie and entitled *The Young Roscius (Henry West Betty) as Falstaff;* sold to ASFTA, February 1962; Yale Center for British Art, 1975

Exhibitions: Amherst, 1959, as by Opie; New York, 1964, no. 52

Loutherbourg, Philip James de, style of

D43

MACBETH AND THE WITCHES
Macbeth I, 3
Oil on canvas, 17 × 21½ in.

Case no. 1803; photograph on file

Provenance: Parsons, May 1928, £40, as by de Loutherbourg; sold to ASFTA, February 1962; sold Sotheby Parke Bernet, 15 January 1976, lot 132, repr., $175

Exhibitions: Amherst, *Shakespeare,* 1951

Low, Will H. (American, 1853–1932)
(nos. D44–47)

The following four paintings were engraved as illustrations for Dodd Mead's 1900 edition of *As You Like It.* Each is signed and dated 1899, is an oil on canvas, and measures 25½ by 19½ inches.

D44

ROSALIND GIVES ORLANDO
THE NECKLACE
As You Like It I, 2

Provenance: Property of the widow of the artist until her death; presented by Mary B. Danaher, May 1947; sold to ASFTA, February 1962; sold Sotheby Parke Bernet, 15 January 1976, lot 135, repr., $250

D45

ROSALIND, CELIA, AND ORLANDO
As You Like It IV, 1

Provenance: Danaher, 1947; sold to ASFTA, 1962; sold Sotheby Parke Bernet, 15 January 1976, lot 134, $275

D46

JAQUES AND TOUCHSTONE
As You Like It V, 4

Provenance: Danaher, 1947; sold to ASFTA, 1962; sold Sotheby Parke Bernet, 15 January 1976, lot 136, repr., $350

D47

THE MASQUE OF HYMEN
As You Like It V, 4

Provenance: Danaher, 1947; sold to ASFTA, 1962; sold Sotheby Parke Bernet, 15 January 1976, lot 133, $375

Maclise, Daniel. *See* D65

Martin, William (British, 1752–ca. 1831)

D48

IACHIMO IN IMOGEN'S CHAMBER
Cymbeline II, 2
ca. 1784
Oil painting, 57 × 93 in.

Case no. 787; photograph on file

Provenance: Boston Museum Theatre; bought by Folger from Campbell, August 1917, $750 (Campbell catalogue of August 1917, no. 193); sold to ASFTA, February 1962

Exhibitions: London, Royal Academy, 1784, no. 341

Monticelli, Adolphe (French, 1824–66)

D49
LADY MACBETH
Macbeth II, 2
Signed
Oil on panel, 17 × 11½ in.

Case no. 1779

Provenance: Purchased by John Anderson, Jr., from S. P. Avery, Sr.; sold Anderson Galleries, 12 April 1928, lot 122, bought by Folger, Wells acting as agent, $490 plus commission; sold to ASFTA, February 1962; sold Sotheby Parke Bernet, 15 January 1976, no. 147, repr., $750

Exhibitions: Amherst, *Shakespeare,* 1951; New York, 1964, no. 44

Mortimer, John Hamilton (?) (British, 1740–79) (nos. D50–51)

The attribution to Mortimer is highly unlikely. These works were probably after his two prints of Falstaff and Bardolph.

D50
PORTRAIT OF A MAN
(FALSTAFF?) HOLDING STEIN

D51
PORTRAIT OF A SOLDIER
Oil paintings, 13 × 15½ in. each

Provenance: Source unknown, possibly purchased at Evert Jansen Wendell sale, American Art Galleries, 21 October 1919, lot 4861 ("'two oil paintings attributed to Hamilton Mortimer as the originals for his Shakespeare characters,' 15 × 10½ in., in old black frames"); Parke Bernet shipment, March 1964, sold as a pair of portraits of actors, Coleman Auction Galleries, 15–16 April 1964, $7.50

Opie, John. *See* D42

Page, William (American, 1811–85)

D52
SHAKESPEARE READING
Oil painting, 65 × 39 in.

Provenance: On loan by George Page, the artist's son, to the East Liberty Branch of the Carnegie Library, Pittsburgh; presented to FSL by Mrs. Pauline Page Howell, on behalf of her father, George Page, 8 July 1937; sold to ASFTA, February 1962; sold Sotheby Parke Bernet, 15 January 1976, lot 157, $900

Exhibitions: New York, National Academy, 1874, no. 301; Philadelphia, Centennial Exposition, 1876; Chicago Exposition, 1877; National Academy, Exhibition of Page's Pictures, 1877, no. 1

Peters, Rev. Matthew William (1742–1814), attributed to

D53
FALSTAFF IN THE BUCKBASKET
The Merry Wives of Windsor III, 3
Oil on canvas, 28 × 36 in.

Case no. 1874; photograph on file

Provenance: Parsons, January 1929, as by Peters, £51.15.0; sold to ASFTA, February 1962; sold Sotheby Parke Bernet, 15 January 1976, lot 158, repr., $325

This is a very different composition from that for the Boydell Shakespeare Gallery (see no. 50).

Proctor, Charles E. (American)

D54
JOHN MCCULLOUGH AS VIRGINIUS
Signed and dated 1886
Oil on canvas, 54 × 36 in.

Provenance: Augustin Daly (on exhibit in Daly's Theatre, New York); Daly sale, Anderson Galleries, 27 November 1912, lot 72, bought by Folger, Smith acting as agent; Parke Bernet shipment, March 1964

James Sheridan Knowles's play *Virginius* was first performed in 1820.

Robinson, John (British, fl. 1848–85)

D55

ANNE HATHAWAY'S COTTAGE
Oil painting, 12 × 18½ in.

Inscribed: "With compliments from the artist; in memory of a pilgrimage to Stratford-on-Avon and Shottery"

Provenance: From Mrs. Folger's house?; Parke Bernet shipment, March 1964

Rothermel, Peter F. (American, 1817–95)

D56

PORTRAIT OF FRANCES ANNE KEMBLE
Oil painting, 15 × 12 in.

Provenance: De Forest sale, Kesler Art Galleries, New York, 4 May 1922, lot 5; bought by Folger from L. A. D'Aras, April 1929, $200; sold to ASFTA, February 1962; Paul Mellon Collection, Yale Center for British Art, 1975; Mellon sale, Sotheby's, 18 November 1981, lot 142

Shee, Sir Martin Archer (Irish, 1769–1850)

D57

PORTRAIT OF MISS LEE AS OPHELIA
Oil painting, 96 × 57 in.

Provenance: Sold from the collection of the Most Hon. the Marquess Wellesley, April 1852; from the collection of F. W. Cosens, May 1890; from the collection of Asher Wertheimer, March 1923; Viscount Leverhulme sale, Anderson Galleries, 19 February 1926, lot 246, repr., $3,200 plus 10 percent commission, Rosenbach acting as agent; sold to ASFTA, February 1962

Exhibitions: London, Royal Academy of Arts, 1804, no. 80; London, Guildhall, 1904, no. 126

West, Benjamin (American, 1738–1820), attributed to

D58

CORIOLANUS YIELDS TO THE PLEAS OF HIS MOTHER AND SISTER
Coriolanus V, 3
Signed and dated 1792
Oil on canvas, 39 × 52 in.

Provenance: Purchased in London, 1850; Isaac N. Stebbins, Boston; Anderson Galleries, American Art Association sale, 12 April 1928, lot 188, bought by Folger, Wells acting as agent, $500 plus commission; sold to Amherst College, May 1961, $600

Exhibitions: Storrs, William Benton Museum of Art, University of Connecticut, *The Academy of Europe: Rome in the Eighteenth Century,* 1973, no. 44 ("Anthony Clark identified the composition as Masucci's, though the painting itself may be a West studio replica")

While in the Folger collection, the painting was considered to be by West. In 1959 Grose Evans reproduced it with this attribution in his book *Benjamin West and the Taste of His Times* (no. 23). Helmut von Erffa, however, discounted the attribution when he saw the picture at the Folger on 27 December 1960. Prompted by von Erffa, Anthony M. Clark wrote on 21 January 1963 stating his opinion that the picture was a studio replica after Masucci. In *A Summary Catalogue of the Collection at the Mead Art Gallery* (Middleton, Conn., 1978), it is attributed to Benjamin West, and most recently in *British Art,* Mead Art Museum Monographs, vols. 6 and 7, Winter 1985–86, as attributed to West or perhaps from the circle of Agostino Masucci (see pp. 20–22).

Wheatley, Francis (British, 1747–1801)

D59

**THE PRINCESS SHOWING ROSALINE
HER PRESENTS FROM THE KING**
Love's Labour's Lost V, 2
Oil on canvas, 31 × 22 in.

Provenance: Commissioned by Boydell; sold by
Christie, 20 May 1805, lot 13, 9 guineas; bought by
Gladstone, Esq., acquired from Michelmore, June
1928, $312.50; sold to ASFTA, February 1962; sold
Sotheby Parke Bernet, 15 January 1976, lot 187,
repr., $550

Exhibitions: London, Boydell, 1795, no. 7; London,
Boydell, *Small Pictures*, 1796, no. 9; London, Boydell, 1802, no. 99; London, Boydell, 1805, no. 35

Painted for the small series of pictures for the Boydell Shakespeare Gallery. Engraving published on 4
June 1793.

Anonymous (nos. D60–D67)

D60

VANDENHOFF AS CORIOLANUS
Oil on canvas, 35 × 28½ in.

Provenance: Old National Theatre, Boston; bought
by Folger from Libbie, Boston, shortly before 26
June 1905; Parke Bernet shipment, March 1964

D61

PLAY SCENE FROM "HAMLET"
Hamlet III, 2
Oil or tempera painting, 38 × 27 in.

Provenance: Source unknown; Parke Bernet shipment, March 1964

Anonymous (British school,
eighteenth century)

D62

**CORDELIA CHAMPIONED
BY THE EARL OF KENT**
King Lear I, 1
ca. 1770s
Oil painting, 41⅛ × 50½ in.

Case no. 1121; photograph on file

Provenance: Parsons, January 1923, £38, acquired as
by William Hamilton; sold to ASFTA, February
1962; Yale Center for British Art, 1975

Exhibitions: New Haven, 1981, no. 3, repr.

D63

**SCENE FROM "MIDSUMMER
NIGHT'S DREAM" (IV, 1)**

Provenance: Source unknown, $65. (The only information on this painting comes from Block's list of
1950, no. 47. It is unlocated and has presumably left
the collection.)

D64

FALSTAFF
Oil painting, oval, 29 × 24 in.

Case no. 1224

Provenance: Source unknown; Parke Bernet shipment, March 1964; probably the picture sold at
Coleman Auction Galleries, 15–16 April, no. 38,
as "oval picture, man with beard," $22.50.

Anonymous (British school, nineteenth century)

D65
A PROCESSION OF SHAKESPEARE CHARACTERS
ca. 1840
Oil on board, 12¼ × 54¼ in.

Two photographs on file

Provenance: Acquired as by Daniel Maclise from Parsons, December 1927, £47; sold to ASFTA, February 1962; Yale Center for British Art, 1975

Exhibitions: Amherst, 1952, as by Maclise; New Haven, 1981, no. 10

D66
PORTRAIT OF SHAKESPEARE
Oil painting, 33 × 43 in.

Provenance: John Anderson, Jr., January 1910; Parke Bernet shipment, March 1964

This is a copy of the Dexter Portrait (see no. 153).

D67
PORTRAIT OF SHAKESPEARE
Oil on panel, 32 × 39½ in.

Provenance: Anderson sale, 14 February 1921, lot 689, $8.80, bought by Folger; sold to Louis Marder, Kent State University, February 1964

Shakespeare is in the center of the composition, surrounded by portraits of actors, actresses, and relevant dramatic authors.

Abbreviations

Dealers and Auction Houses

American Art Association American Art Association, instituted 1883, Madison Ave., 56th to 57th streets, New York; 6 E. 23rd St. [1911]

American Art Galleries American Art Galleries, affiliated with American Art Association, Madison Square South, New York, and Madison Ave., 56th to 57th streets

Anderson John Anderson, Jr., opened a small auction house under his own name in 1900 at 34 W. 30th St., New York. In 1903 the name was changed to Anderson Auction Company. Anderson, however, soon sold the firm, which continued using his name. "Anderson" in the catalogue refers to the individual, who, as a private dealer, continued to correspond with Folger.

Anderson Auction Company Successor to John Anderson, Jr., and Bangs & Co., W. 29th St., New York [from 1903]; 12 E.t 46th St. [1909–15]

Anderson Galleries Continuation of Anderson Auction Company, Madison Ave. at 40th St., New York [1915]; 489 Park Ave. at 59th St.[1917]; from September 1929 combined with American Art Association

Barnard P. M. Barnard, Antiquarian Bookseller, 10 Dudley Rd., Tunbridge Wells [1918]; Books and Manuscripts, 17 Church Rd., Tunbridge Wells

Betts A. L. Betts, 98 Sutherland Ave., Maida Vale, London W9

Campbell William J. Campbell, Publisher and Bookseller, 1623 Chestnut St., Philadelphia

Christie's Christie, Manson & Woods, Auctioneers, 8 King St., St. James's Square, London

Conway Eustace Conway, attorney, 233 Broadway, New York

D'Aras Louis A. D'Aras, 9 W. 14th St., New York

Dobell P. J. Dobell, 24 Mount Ephraim Rd., Tunbridge Wells

Edwards Francis Edwards, Bookseller, 83A High St., Marylebone, London

Ehrich Galleries "Old Masters," 707 5th Ave., New York

Gregory George Gregory Bookstore, 8 Green St. and 1 Bond St., Bath; Ancient and Modern Bookseller, 5 Argyle St., Bath

Hodgson Hodgson & Co., 115 Chancery Lane, London

Holoway P. W. Holoway, Fine Art Dealer and Specialist Restorer of Prints, Drawings, Etc., 336B King's Rd., Chelsea, London SW3

Kelly Alexander A. Kelly, Restoration of Paintings, 831 Lexington Ave., New York

Libbie C. F. Libbie & Co., Auctioneers and Appraisers, 646 Washington St., Boston

McGirr Newman F. McGirr, Rare Books, Prints, Autographs and Paintings, 10 S. 18th St., Room 211, Philadelphia

Maggs Maggs Bros., Rare Books, Prints and Autographs, 34–35 Conduit St., New Bond St., London

Mayhew A. H. Mayhew, Second-hand and New Bookseller, 56 Charing Cross Rd., London

Meagher Peter Meagher, Appraiser and Bibliographer of Literary Property, 8815 Husson Ave., Hollis, L. I.

Michelmore G. Michelmore & Co., Rare Books, Autographs, Manuscripts, 5 Royal Opera Arcade, Pall Mall, London SW1

Millard Miss Clara Millard, Bookseller, Export and Curio Dealer, Teddington, Middlesex

Montmartre Gallery 39 Wardour St., London W1

Morris Frederick W. Morris, Bookseller, 542 5th Ave., New York

Parsons Edwin Parsons, Fine Art Dealer and Publisher, 5 Amersham Rd., Putney, London SW15 [1927]

Parsons & Sons E. Parsons & Sons, Fine Art Dealers in Books, Prints and Paintings, 45 Brompton Rd., London SW3 [1927]; Fine Art Book and Print Sellers and Picture Dealers [1926 and 1929]; Fine Art Book and Print Sellers and Dealers in Pictures and Original Drawings by the Old Masters [1929]

Pearson J. Pearson & Co., Rare Books and Autographs, 5 Pall Mall Pl., London SW1 (F. Wheeler is the correspondent for firm)

Phillips Phillips, Son & Neale, Auctioneers, 73 New Bond St., London

Puttick and Simpson 47 Leicester Sq., London [1927]

Quaritch Bernard Quaritch, Dealer in Ancient Manuscripts, Rare, Artistic and Scientific Books and Works in Standard Literature, 11 Grafton St., New Bond St., London

Robson Robson & Co. Ltd., Dealers in Rare Books, Autographs, Etc., 7 Hanover St., Regent St., London

Rosenbach Rosenbach Co., Rare Books, Paintings and Prints, Antique Furniture and Objects of Art, 1320 Walnut St., Philadelphia, and 273 Madison Ave., New York

Sabin Frank T. Sabin, Pictures, Drawings, Miniatures, Rare Books, Autographs, Etc., 172 New Bond St., London

Sawyer Charles J. Sawyer Ltd., Booksellers and Fine Art Dealers, 12 and 13 Grafton St., New Bond St., London, and 23 Oxford St., London

Schatzki Walter Schatzki, New York

Scheuer Alwin J. Scheuer, Rare Books, 26 E. 56th St., New York

Sessler Charles Sessler, Importer and Bookseller, 1314 Walnut St., Philadelphia

Smith George D. Smith, Old and Rare Books, Autographs, Prints, Etc., 70 Wall St. and 547 5th Ave., New York

Sotheby Sotheby, Wilkinson & Hodge, Auctioneers, Wellington St., Strand, London [1902]; 34–35 New Bond St., London [1928]

Sotheran Henry Sotheran & Co., Booksellers, Bookbinders, and Publishers, 140 Strand, London

Stonehill C. A. Stonehill, Rare Books and Manuscripts, 45 St. James's Pl., London

Thorp Thomas Thorp, Bookseller, Guilford, England

Union Square Book Shop Dealers in Rare Books, Prints and Autographs, 30 E. 14th St., New York

Walpole Galleries Rare Books, Letters and Manuscripts, 10 E. 49th St., New York

Walters Curtis Walters, Autographs, Rare Books, Prints, 31–33 E. 27th St., New York; Rare and Fine Books, Autographs and Prints, Art Bookbinding, 109–13 W. 57th St., Steinway Hall, New York [1926]

Wells Gabriel Wells, Importer and Dealer, 145 W. 57th St., New York; 489 5th Ave. [1923]

Wright J. O. Wright & Co., Importers of Books and Book-Illustrations, 6 E. 42d St., New York

Exhibitions

Exhibitions held at the Folger Shakespeare Library for which no catalogue was published have not been included.

London, Boydell, 1792 Boydell Shakespeare Gallery, *A Catalogue of the Pictures, &c. in the Shakspeare Gallery, Pall-Mall.*

Dublin, 1793 Irish Shakespeare Gallery, Whistler's Great Room, Exchequer Street.

London, Boydell, 1793 Boydell Shakespeare Gallery, *A Catalogue of the Pictures, &c. in the Shakspeare Gallery, Pall-Mall.*

London, Boydell, 1794 Boydell Shakespeare Gallery, *A Catalogue of the Pictures, &c. in the Shakspeare Gallery, Pall-Mall.*

London, 1794–95 New Shakespeare Gallery, Schomberg House, 88 Pall Mall.

London, Boydell, 1795 Boydell Shakespeare Gallery, *A Catalogue of Small Pictures Painted for the Shakspeare Gallery, Pall-Mall* (bound with the 1794 edition of the catalogue of the large paintings, but the number sequence begins again at "1").

London, Boydell, 1796 Boydell Shakespeare Gallery, *A Catalogue of the Pictures &c. in the Shakspeare Gallery, Pall-Mall.*

London, Boydell, *Small Pictures*, 1796 Boydell Shakespeare Gallery, *A Catalogue of Small Pictures Painted for the Shakspeare Gallery, Pall-Mall,* (bound with the 1796 edition of the catalogue of the large paintings, but the number sequence begins again at "1").

London, Boydell, 1802 Boydell Shakespeare Gallery, *A Catalogue of the Pictures &c. in the Shakspeare Gallery, Pall-Mall* and *A Catalogue of Small Pictures Painted for the Shakspeare Gallery, Pall-Mall* (only one number sequence for both large and small paintings).

London, Boydell, 1805 Boydell Shakespeare Gallery, *The Exhibition of the Shakspeare Galley, Pall-Mall* (last time paintings were shown together; preparatory to their sale).

Stratford-upon-Avon, 1864 Town Hall, *Catalogue of Pictures and Drawings Exhibited at the Town Hall, Stratford-upon-Avon, at the Celebration of the Tercentenary Birthday of William Shakespeare* (the annotated copy referred to in the catalogue is to be found in "Halliwell-Phillips Shakespeareana," FSL W.b.244).

London, 1869 South Kensington Museum, *Catalogue of the Second Special Exhibition of National Portraits Commencing with the Reign of William and Mary and Ending with the Year MDCCC.*

London, 1890 The New Gallery, *Exhibition of the Royal House of Tudor.*

London, 1894 Royal Academy of Arts, *Exhibition of Works by the Old Masters, and by Deceased Masters of the British School; including Special Collections of the Works of Thomas Stothard, R.A., of William Blake, and of John Pettie, R.A.,* Winter Exhibition.

Amherst, 1950 Mead Art Building, Amherst College, *Benjamin West: His Times and His Influence,* 9–30 May 1950 (also see *Art in America* 38 [December 1950]).

Amherst, *Shakespeare*, 1951 Mead Art Building, Amherst College, *Shakespeare, Hamlet, and Macbeth* (no catalogue), 19 February–25 March.

Amherst, *The Tempest*, 1951 Mead Art Building, Amherst College, *The Tempest* (no catalogue), 15 November–5 December.

Amherst, 1952 Mead Art Building, Amherst College, *A Midsummer Night's Dream* (no catalogue), 18 November–20 December.

Amherst, 1959 Mead Art Building, Amherst College, *Henry IV* (no catalogue), February–March.

New York, 1964 M. Knoedler & Co., *William Shakespeare, 1564–1964: An Exhibition of Paintings, Drawings, and Sculptures in the Collection of the American Shakespeare Festival Theatre and Academy,* March.

Washington, 1976–77 Washington, D.C., Federal Reserve Board, *Eighteenth- and Nineteenth-Century English Painting,* 22 November 1976–28 January 1977.

San Francisco, 1979–82 California Academy of Sciences; Kansas City, William Rockhill Nelson Gallery of Art; Pittsburgh, Museum of Art, Carnegie Institute; Dallas Museum of Fine Arts; Atlanta, High Museum of Art; New York, American Museum of Natural History; Washington, D.C., John F. Kennedy Center for the Performing Arts, *Shakespeare: The Globe and the World.*

Buxton, 1980 Buxton Museum and Art Gallery, *Shakespeare's Heroines in the Nineteenth Century,* 22 July–17 August.

New Haven, 1981 Yale Center for British Art, *Shakespeare and British Art.*

Washington, 1985 Washington, D.C., Folger Shakespeare Library, *The Kemble Family: A Theatrical Dynasty,* April–October.

Waterloo, 1985 Waterloo, Canada, Kitchener-Waterloo Art Gallery, *George Romney in Canada.*

Montgomery, 1985–86 Montgomery, Ala., Montgomery Museum of Fine Arts; New York Public Library at Lincoln Center, Library and the Museum of the Performing Arts; Chicago Public Library Cultural Center, *A Brush with Shakespeare: The Bard in Painting, 1780–1910,* December 1985–June 1986.

New Haven, 1987 Yale Center for British Art; London, The Iveagh Bequest, Kenwood, *Francis Hayman.*

References

Altick 1985 Richard D. Altick, *Paintings from Books: Art and Literature, in Britain, 1760–1900*, Columbus, Ohio.

Anglesea 1971 Martyn Anglesea, "David Garrick and the Visual Arts," Master of Letters, University of Edinburgh.

Ashton 1990 Geoffrey Ashton, *The Collector's Shakespeare: His Life and Work in Paintings, Prints, and Photographs*, New York.

Barrell 1940 Charles Wisner Barrell, "Identifying 'Shakespeare,'" *Scientific American*, January 1940, pp. 4–8, 43–45 (reader response published in May 1940 issue, pp. 264, 299, and 300).

Bayne-Powell 1985 Robert Bayne-Powell, *Catalogue of Portrait Miniatures in the Fitzwilliam Museum, Cambridge*, Cambridge.

Biddle and Fielding 1921 Edward Biddle and Mantle Fielding, *The Life and Works of Thomas Sully*, Philadelphia.

Block 1950 Maurice Block, "Report on the Folger Pictures and Art Objects," typescript in FSL by the former curator of the Huntington Art Gallery, San Marino, Calif.

Boaden 1824 James Boaden, *An Inquiry into the Authenticity of Various Pictures and Prints, which, from the Decease of the Poet to our own Times, have been offered to the Public as Portraits of Shakspeare*, London.

Burnim 1984 Kalman A. Burnim, "Looking upon His Like Again: Garrick and the Artist," in Shirley Strum Kenny, ed., *British Theatre and the Other Arts, 1660–1800*, Washington, D.C., pp. 182–218.

Coxhead 1906 A. C. Coxhead, *Thomas Stothard R.A.*, London.

Dotson 1973 Esther Gordon Dotson, "Shakespeare Illustrated, 1770–1820," Ph.D. diss., New York University.

Fink 1959 Frances Sharf Fink, *Heads across the Sea: An Album of Eighteenth-Century English Literary Portraits in America*, Charlottesville, Va.

Friedman 1976 Winifred H. Friedman, "Boydell's Shakespeare Gallery," Ph.D. diss., Harvard University; published by Garland, 1976.

Friswell 1864 J. Hain Friswell, *Life Portraits of William Shakespeare*, London.

Graves 1913 Algernon Graves, *A Century of Loan Exhibitions, 1813–1912*, 5 vols., London.

Graves 1918–21 Algernon Graves, *Art Sales*, 3 vols., London.

Graves and Cronin 1899–1901 Algernon Graves and William Vine Cronin, *A History of the Works of Sir Joshua Reynolds*, 4 vols., London.

Hamilton 1831 Clippings of prints by Normand, *fils*, with their accompanying text in the Witt Library, London, apparently taken from George Hamilton, *The English School*, 2 vols., London.

Hamlyn 1978 Robin Hamlyn, "An Irish Shakespeare Gallery," *Burlington Magazine* 120 (August 1978), pp. 515–29.

Highfill 1973– Philip H. Highfill, Jr., Kalman A. Burnim, and Edward A. Langhans, *A Biographical Dictionary of Actors, Actresses, Musicians, Dancers, Managers and Other Stage Personnel in London, 1660–1800*, Carbondale and Edwardsville, Ill.

Kestner 1986 Joseph Kestner, "Deathless Love," *Opera News* 50 (18 January 1986), pp. 10–15.

Knowles 1831 John Knowles, *The Life and Writings of Henry Fuseli*, 3 vols., London.

Leach 1970 Joseph Leach, *Bright Particular Star: The Life and Times of Charlotte Cushman*, New Haven and London.

Marder 1963 Louis Marder, *His Exits and His Entrances: The Story of Shakespeare's Reputation*, Philadelphia and New York.

Merchant 1959 W. Moelwyn Merchant, *Shakespeare and the Artist*, London and New York.

Norris 1885 J. Parker Norris, *The Portraits of Shakespeare*, Philadelphia.

Odell 1920 George C. D. Odell, *Shakespeare: From Betterton to Irving*, 2 vols.; reprint New York, 1963.

Ogden 1912 William Sharp Ogden, *Shakspere's Portraiture: Painted, Graven, and Medallic*, London; reprinted from *British Numismatic Journal* 7 (1910), pp. 3–58.

Paulson 1982 Ronald Paulson, *Book and Painting: Shakespeare, Milton, and the Bible*, Knoxville, Tenn.

Piper 1962 David Piper, "Notes of Shakespeare Portraits at the Folger Shakespeare Library, Washington, made November 1962," typescript (PR2929/F5).

Piper 1964 *O Sweet Mr. Shakespeare I'll Have His Picture: The Changing Image of Shakespeare's Person, 1600–1800*, exhibition catalogue, National Portrait Gallery, London.

Redgrave 1878 Samuel Redgrave, *A Dictionary of Artists of the English School*, 2d ed., London.

Romney 1830 Rev. John Romney, *Memoirs of the Life and Works of George Romney*, London.

Salaman 1916 Malcolm C. Salaman, *Shakespeare in Pictorial Art*, London.

Schiff 1973 Gert Schiff, *Johann Heinrich Füssli, 1741–1825*, 2 vols., Zurich and Munich.

Schiff and Viotto 1977 Gert Schiff and Paola Viotto, *L'opera completa di Füssli*, Milan.

Schiff and Weinglass (forthcoming) David H. Weinglass's translation from German into English and revised edition of Gert Schiff's *Johann Heinrich Füssli* (1973), to be published by Yale University Press.

Schoenbaum 1970 S. Schoenbaum, *Shakespeare's Lives*, Oxford.

Schoenbaum 1981 S. Schoenbaum, *William Shakespeare: Records and Images*, Oxford.

Spielmann 1906–07 M. H. Spielmann, *The Portraits of Shakespeare*, n.d., reprinted from *Stratford Town Shakespeare*, 1906–07.

Spielmann 1909–10 M. H. Spielmann, "The Janssen, or Somerset, Portrait of Shakespeare," *Connoisseur*, August 1909, pp. 230–27, and February and November 1910, pp. 105–10, 151–58.

Spielmann 1910 M. H. Spielmann, "The Portraits of Shakespeare," in *Encyclopedia Britannica*, 11th ed., vol. 24, pp. 787–93.

Spielmann 1921a M. H. Spielmann, "Shakespeare Portraits: The Burdett-Coutts Collection," *The Times*, 21 September, p. 8.

Spielmann 1921b M. H. Spielmann, "The Burdett-Coutts Shakespeare Portraits," *The Illustrated London News*, 1 October, pp. 428–29.

Spielmann 1922 M. H. Spielmann, "The Miniatures of Shakespeare. I," *Illustrated London News*, 29 April, pp. 624–25.

Spielmann 1924 M. H. Spielmann, *The Title-Page of the First Folio of Shakespeare's Plays*, London.

Spielmann 1935 M. H. Spielmann, "The Shakespeare Festival: Some Little-Known Portraits of the Poet," *Illustrated London News*, 20 April, p. 647.

Sprague 1944 Arthur Colby Sprague, *Shakespeare and the Actors: The Stage Business in His Plays (1660–1905)*, Cambridge, Mass.

Stone and Kahrl 1979 George Winchester Stone, Jr., and George M. Kahrl, *David Garrick: A Critical Biography*, Carbondale and Edwardsville, Ill.

Strong 1969 Roy Strong, *National Portrait Gallery: Tudor and Jacobean Portraits*, 2 vols., London.

Strong 1987 Roy Strong, *Gloriana: The Portraits of Queen Elizabeth I*, London.

Ward and Roberts 1904 Humphry Ward and W. Roberts, *Romney: A Biographical and Critical Essay with a Catalogue Raisonné of his Works*, 2 vols., London.

Waterhouse 1981 Ellis Waterhouse, *The Dictionary of British 18th Century Painters in Oils and Crayons*, Woodbridge, Suffolk.

Wivell 1827 Abraham Wivell, *An Inquiry into the History, Authenticity, and Characteristics of the Shakspeare Portraits*, London.

Wivell 1840 Abraham Wivell, *An Inquiry into the History, Authenticity and Characteristics of the Shakspere Portraits*, London.

Index

Catalogue numbers are in **boldface** type. Page numbers following catalogue numbers refer to references outside the main entry. Page numbers accompanying figure numbers refer to the pages on which the illustrations appear.